John Dewey

The Later Works, 1925–1953

Volume 16: 1949–1952

EDITED BY JO ANN BOYDSTON

TEXTUAL EDITOR,

HARRIET FURST SIMON

ASSISTANT TEXTUAL EDITOR,

RICHARD W. FIELD

With an Introduction by T. Z. Lavine

Southern Illinois University Press

Carbondale and Edwardsville

COMMITTEE ON
SCHOLARLY EDITIONS

AN APPROVED EDITION

MODERN LANGUAGE
ASSOCIATION OF AMERICA

Editorial expenses for this edition have been met in part by grants from
the Editions Program of the National Endowment for the Humanities,
an independent Federal agency, and from the John Dewey Foundation.
Publishing expenses have been met in part by a grant from the John Dewey
Foundation.

Library of Congress Cataloging-in-Publication Data

Dewey, John, 1859–1952.
    The later works, 1925–1953.

    Vol. 16 has introd. by T. Z. Lavine.
    Continues The middle works, 1899–1924.
    Includes bibliographies and indexes.
    CONTENTS: v. 1. 1925.—v. 2. 1925–1927.—[etc.]—v. 16. 1949–1952.
    1. Philosophy—Collected works. I. Boydston, Jo Ann, 1924–. II. Title.
B945.D41 1981   191   80-27285
ISBN 0-8093-1537-8 (v. 16)

Contents

Introduction

By T. Z. Lavine

The new social sciences, obsessed with teleological thought at the turn of the century, also migrated slowly toward bureaucratic ideas. In a witty, opinionated book, *The Process of Government* (1908), Arthur Bentley presented all disciplines with a model of bureaucratic analysis that stripped every vestige of philosophical idealism from the study of fluid group interaction. . . . A revolt in its own right from idealism, pragmatism, like scientific management, carried relatively little traditional baggage. . . . Dewey might have been the great spokesman whom bureaucratic thought so badly needed except for an abiding commitment to the goals of idealism. . . . Throughout his writings ran a limitless faith in the scientific method as the means for freeing people of all ages to learn through exploration and through social experience.

—Robert H. Wiebe
The Search for Order, 1877–1920[1]

I can deeply sympathize with anyone who objects to being tossed into such a floating cosmology. . . . The firm land of 'matter' or even of 'sense' or 'self' is pleasanter, if only it stands firm. To anyone whose tasks can be performed on such ground, I have not the slightest thought of bringing disturbance. But for many of us tasks are pressing, in the course of which our firmest spots of conventional departure themselves dissolve in function. When they have so dissolved, and when we are so involved, there is no hope of finding refuge in

---

1. Wiebe, *The Search for Order, 1877–1920* (New York: Hill and Wang, 1967), pp. 150–52.

some chance island of 'fact' which may appear. The continents go, and the islands.
                                              —Arthur F. Bentley
                                      Behavior, Knowledge, Fact[2]

Social phenomena are not unique in being complexly inter-
woven with [one] another. All existential events, as existential, are in a similar state. But methods of experimentation
and their directive conceptions are now so well established in
the case of physical phenomena that vast bodies of facts seem
to carry their significance with them almost on their face as
soon as they are ascertained. . . . No such state of affairs
exists with reference to social phenomena and facts. . . .
Since scientific methods simply exhibit free intelligence
operating in the best manner available at a given time, the
cultural waste, confusion and distortion that results from the
failure to use these methods, in all fields in connection with
all problems, is incalculable.
                                              —John Dewey
                                      Logic: The Theory of Inquiry[3]

The fateful letter was postmarked Paoli, Indiana, November
15, 1932,[4] and with it came a book. Two and one-half years later
Dewey replies:

                                              New York, May 22, 1935
Dear Mr. Bentley:
    Some time ago I received a copy of your *Linguistic Analy-
sis of Mathematics*. I fear I didn't acknowledge it. . . . Recently I have read it, and am still re-reading it. It has given

2. Bentley, *Behavior, Knowledge, Fact* (Bloomington, Ind.: Principia Press, 1935), p. 183.
3. Dewey, *Logic: The Theory of Inquiry* (New York: Henry Holt and Co., 1938), pp. 511, 512, 535. [*The Later Works of John Dewey, 1925–1953,* ed. Jo Ann Boydston (Carbondale and Edwardsville: Southern Illinois University Press, 1986), 12:504–5, 527.]
4. The correspondence between Dewey and Bentley has been superbly edited, indexed, and introduced. Sidney Ratner and Jules Altman, eds., introduction by Ratner, *John Dewey and Arthur F. Bentley: A Philosophical Correspondence, 1932–1951* (New Brunswick, N.J.: Rutgers University Press, 1964), p. 51. Succeeding references will be to *Correspondence;* all Dewey-Bentley letters are quoted as they appear in the edited *Correspondence.*
    With regard to the significance of the *Correspondence* for Dewey scholarship, Max Fisch notes:

me more enlightenment and intellectual help than any book I
have read for a very long time. I have been engaged during
this year in trying to get my ideas on logical theory into systematic shape for publication,[5] and I cannot put into words
how much your book has meant to me in this process. Besides the great specific help it has given me in attacking the
special theme of the procedure of mathematics, in which I am
rather deplorably ignorant, it has greatly encouraged and
strengthened me in my general position. . . . [Y]our treatment of that subject enabled me to clarify and make more
precise a distinction I had made between control of inquiry
from within and externally, and I have already rewritten
some pages I had set down on that point to the effect that
recent "mathematical logic" as well as the traditional Aristotelian logic assumes control by meanings fixed outside the
operations of inquiry. . . .[6]

By return mail from Paoli came Bentley's exuberant reply:

Paoli, Indiana, May 28, 1935

Dear Mr. Dewey:

It was a very great pleasure indeed to me to know that you
find my book [*Linguistic Analysis of Mathematics*] of use. I
have not exactly been overfertilized with praise, and your

In their nineteen-years-long correspondence, Dewey and Bentley frequently exchanged comments about their respective methods of working,
their critical styles, their views of the relevance and importance of the history of philosophy, and their particular critical and historical essays—each
about the other's as well as his own. This is the chief single source of insight
into Dewey's critical and historical studies. . . . It remains nearly unexplored. ("Dewey's Critical and Historical Studies," in Jo Ann Boydston, ed.,
Guide to the Works of John Dewey [Carbondale and Edwardsville: Southern Illinois University Press, 1970], p. 333.)

5. Dewey is of course referring to his work-in-progress, *Logic: The Theory of
Inquiry,* to be published in 1938 and which would include an acknowledg-
ment of his debt "to the writings of A. F. Bentley" (preface, *Logic,* pp. iv–v
[*Later Works* 12:5]).

6. *Correspondence,* p. 51. Dewey's eventual reading of Bentley's *Linguistic
Analysis of Mathematics* was at the prompting of Ernest Nagel, as Dewey
confesses at a later stage of his developing friendship with Bentley: ". . . One
reason that I have a soft spot about Nagel (as you have too, for what he
might do, but doesn't) is that he directed my attention specifically to your
book on mathematical language after I had had it without reading it for some
time. . . ." Ibid., June 12, 1942, p. 108.

comments, combined with [Karl N.] Llewellyn's somewhat
emphatic endorsement (["The Constitution as an Institution"] in the *Columbia Law Review*) of my earlier work [*The
Process of Government*], make a red-letter week.

   I am especially glad to hear from you at this time, because
I am about to send to the press a book, completed about six
months ago, *Behavior, Knowledge, Fact,* and I have long
wished that I could secure your verification or amendment of
two passages about your work. . . . (*Correspondence,* p. 52.)

Arthur Bentley now enters the "life-career"[7] of John Dewey, in
which he will remain a significant personal and intellectual presence until the correspondence ends nineteen years later with the
last letter from Paoli on December 6, 1951.[8] When the relationship between the two men begins, John Dewey's intellectual pre-
eminence in America had been building incrementally in a series
of philosophic works written over the long teaching years at
Michigan, Chicago, and Columbia and treating of education,
ethics, logic, psychology, epistemology, metaphysics, history of
philosophy, politics, and art.

   Bentley's career, by contrast, is marked externally by hiatuses
and discontinuities. The world of his childhood was the small
town of the prairie, in Freeport, Illinois, and Grand Island, Nebraska, during the Reconstruction period of the nation. He em-
barked upon a college education in 1885–86 at York College,
close to his home in Grand Island,[9] leaving after a year for the
University of Denver, and dropping out again in a few months.

   7. "Life-career," as used by Dewey with reference to the behavior and history of
individual persons, is a persistent topic of disputation with Bentley. *Correspondence,* July 26–November 18, 1935, pp. 53–58, et passim.
   8. Dewey died six months later, on June 1, 1952, in his ninety-third year.
   9. The Stuhr Museum of the Prairie Pioneer, Grand Island, Nebraska, holds
records and correspondence of Charles F. Bentley's bank and of the Bentley
family; the Arthur F. Bentley Collection is held by the Manuscripts Department, Lilly Library, Indiana University, Bloomington; additional Bentley materials are in the John Dewey Papers, Special Collections, Morris Library,
Southern Illinois University at Carbondale.
   For biographical and interpretive materials on Bentley, I have drawn upon
the essay by Sidney Ratner, "Arthur F. Bentley: Behavioral Scientist," in *Correspondence,* pp. 24–36; Sidney Ratner, "A. F. Bentley's Inquiries into the
Behavioral Sciences and the Theory of Scientific Inquiry," in Richard W. Tay-
lor, ed., *Life, Language, Law: Essays in Honor of Arthur F. Bentley* (Yellow
Springs, Ohio: Antioch Press, 1957), pp. 26–57; "The Intellectual Matrix of
Bentley's Social Science," chap. 2 in James F. Ward, *Language, Form, and*

He had experienced one of the many episodes of physical ill health and psychological depression which were to be lifelong recurrences and interruptions. For three years thereafter, Arthur worked in his father's bank in Grand Island before entering the Johns Hopkins University, from which he was graduated in 1892, achieving the distinction of the publication of his undergraduate thesis (1892–93), *The Condition of the Western Farmer as Illustrated by the Economic History of a Nebraska Township*.[10] The collapse of the agrarian land boom which had been triggered by the Homestead Act's promise of cheap land, and the subsequent disastrous effects upon local Nebraska farmers, is examined with a scrupulous methodology based upon data which Arthur gathered with his father. Bentley sees in the resulting situation an interplay of various social forces: the ambitions and naïveté of the farmers with respect to banks and other creditors, land speculators, international grain merchants, market fluctuations, as well as the unpredictable natural conditions of the prairie. With his first venture into the social sciences, there appears what will become the characteristic Bentleyan non-prescriptive, non-reformist view of the social world as a flux of changing forces.[11]

Bentley began graduate work in economics and sociology at Johns Hopkins in 1892–93. He spent the following year in Germany, where he attended the lectures of the economists Adolf Wagner and Gustav Schmoller, as well as those of Georg Simmel and Wilhelm Dilthey. From Dilthey he learned something of the current "revolt against positivism" and the issues involved in the distinctions between the human sciences and the natural sciences. Most important to Bentley were Simmel's seminars in sociology and his teaching on group theory. Returning to Hopkins, Bentley produced a doctoral dissertation, "The Units of Investigation in the Social Sciences," in which he opposed mechanistic

Inquiry: Arthur F. Bentley's Philosophy of Social Science (Amherst: University of Massachusetts Press, 1984), pp. 15–44; "History as Process," chap. 1 in Paul F. Kress, *Social Science and the Idea of Process: The Ambiguous Legacy of Arthur F. Bentley* (Urbana: University of Illinois Press, 1970), pp. 13–42; also upon materials provided by the Stuhr Museum of the Prairie Pioneer and by the Lilly Library, Indiana University.

10. *Johns Hopkins University Studies in Historical and Political Science*, 11th ser., nos. 7–8 (Baltimore: Johns Hopkins University Press, 1893).

11. See Ward, op. cit., pp. 25–26; also Richard Hofstadter, *The Age of Reform* (New York: Vintage Books, 1955), pp. 55–58.

or causal explanations (a view he will maintain and share with Dewey) and presented instead a Diltheyan, "idealist" argument for the centrality of "mind" in social scientific analysis (a view which he and Dewey would later reject).

During his lifetime Bentley's only teaching position[12] was a one-year lectureship in sociology at Chicago for 1895–96, a year of job scarcity in the continuing economic depression. After a few days of Bentley's difficult lectures and monumental reading assignments in French and German sociology, students and teacher agreed to abandon the seminar. Bentley appears to have isolated himself while at Chicago from the galaxy of philosophers and social scientists on the faculty, including George Herbert Mead, Thorstein Veblen, Jacques Loeb, James H. Tufts, Addison W. Moore, James R. Angell, W. I. Thomas, and Albert Michelson.[13]

From this group was to come the formation of the Chicago school of philosophy,[14] under the leadership of Dewey, who had left Michigan for Chicago in 1894–95 (the year before Bentley's arrival as lecturer) to chair the Department of Philosophy, Psychology, and Pedagogy. Under these circumstances, as James Ward observes, Bentley's "natural home would have been at the University of Chicago."[15] Bentley's isolation at Chicago was broken, however, by his crucial encounter with pragmatism and with John Dewey as teacher—he audited (unknown to Dewey) Dewey's seminar in the theory of logic. Like the German philosophers and social theorists with whom he had just studied, Dewey, too, he found, was enlisted in the revolt against positivism and empiricism, countering these views at that time by a Hegelian idealism which could provide, unlike positivism, philosophic significance for meaning and value. In the seminar, Dewey rejected Hegel's Absolute, yet he also rejected the primacy of the individ-

---

12. Aside from a visiting lectureship for 1941–42 in the Columbia philosophy department.
13. Bentley apparently made the acquaintance of W. I. Thomas.
14. See Darnell Rucker, *The Chicago Pragmatists* (Minneapolis: University of Minnesota Press, 1969).
15. Ward, op. cit., p. 44. Ward adds: "Few of Dewey's colleagues and disciples had a first-hand knowledge of currents in European social theory equal to Bentley's. His self-imposed isolation prevented him from contributing these perspectives to the work of the Chicago pragmatists" (ibid.).

ual mind and argued against psychological explanation in the social sciences.[16]

These teachings of Deweyan pragmatism and the revolt against positivism were to become components of Bentley's armament. Fifty years later Dewey and Bentley, no longer strangers, would combine their forces in the revolt against logical positivism and in defense of a pragmatic theory of inquiry. But in the Depression year of 1896, having washed out at Chicago, Bentley could find no academic position. He is finally taken on as a reporter for the *Chicago Times-Herald;* by 1903 he has become an editorial writer for the *Times-Herald* and its successor, the *Chicago Record-Herald.* It is as a Chicago newspaper reporter and editor with a "sense of tremendous social activity taking place,"[17] a feeling that "all the politics of the country, so to speak, was drifting across my desk,"[18] that Bentley wrote *The Process of Government* during the years 1896–1908.

The Process of Government, now regarded as a classic in political science, was virtually ignored until the post–World War II period, when American political scientists discovered Bentley to be a forerunner of current interest-group theory and the realism of pressure politics, as well as a scornful opponent of the idealistic pieties of traditional political science, and of its "legalist" and "institutionalist" perceptions of politics. Bentley was hailed on methodological grounds as an early supporter of the "behavioral revolution" which called for the use of natural scientific methods in the social sciences, and on substantive grounds for offering a group theory of politics.[19]

16. Sidney Ratner has transcribed some of Bentley's notes from the logic seminar: "Dewey urged students to ignore the whole question of subject and object, and to ask instead, 'What is the act of knowing itself?' This for two reasons: first that subject and object are constructions of the primitive acts of knowledge; the second that logical judgment is a form of action, a form of conduct" (*Correspondence,* pp. 27–28).
17. Kress, op. cit., p. 18.
18. Bentley, "Epilogue," in Taylor, *Life, Language, Law,* p. 211.
19. See Ward, op. cit., pp. 45 ff.; Kress, op. cit., pp. 22 ff. The principal figures in the Bentley revival in political science are David B. Truman, *The Governmental Process: Political Interests and Public Opinion* (New York: Alfred A. Knopf, 1951); Bertram M. Gross, *The Legislative Struggle: A Study in Social Combat* (New York: McGraw-Hill Book Co., 1953); Earl Latham, *The Group Basis of Politics: A Study in Basing-Point Legislation* (Ithaca, N.Y.: Cornell University Press, 1952).

The behavioral revolutionists' view of Bentley is now perceived to have been a misreading. How is this to be understood? There was the bold, hard-hitting, "scientific" tone of the one-line preface to *The Process of Government:* "This book is an attempt to fashion a tool." Bentley's behavioral credentials appeared to be attested to by his debunking attacks upon "mentalistic" explanations, upon claims for the causal efficacy of "ideas and ideals," upon the concept of psychological explanation; as well as by his detailed analysis of group theory in relation to interests, values, economics, government, law. Contributing to the misreading was Bentley's writing in the idiom of behavioral political science (with overtones of the Progressivism which he is in process of abandoning). Sidney Ratner catches the affect of Bentley's rhetoric, proclaiming that "the raw materials of government . . . cannot be found in the law books; in the proceedings of constitutional conventions; in the addresses and essays on tyranny or democracy; or in the 'character of the people,' in their specific 'feelings' or 'thoughts,' in their 'hearts' or 'minds.'"

> The raw material can be found only in the actually performed legislating-administrating-adjudicating activities of the nation, and the streams and kinds of activity that gather among the people and rush into these spheres.[20]

Unnoticed by the behavioral political scientists was that part I of *The Process of Government,* having rejected psychological explanation, proceeds to the rejection of the entire category of causal explanation, thus destroying the scientific causal argumentation of the behavioralists themselves, along with common sense explanations of human behavior. Left implicit in Bentley's rejection of causal explanation in *The Process of Government* is his anti-positivism and interpretivism, reflecting the influence of Dilthey, Simmel, and now Dewey. Moreover, under these late Hegelian, Darwinian, and Deweyan influences, Bentley writes as a holistic process theorist in the social sciences: the raw material of these sciences is the group in its meaningful, purposive activity, each group in process, each classifiable by classificatory systems which are themselves in process. "Mental properties" or

---

20. *Correspondence,* introduction, p. 30, quoting from Bentley's *The Process of Government.*

specific types of causes are distorting abstractions from the process of group activity. Mental-physical, inner-outer, individual-social, subjective-objective are not discrete elements segmenting the group; they are dissolved into interactional phases[21] of the process of group activity.

> . . . The activities are interlaced. That, however, is a bad manner of expression. For the interlacing itself is the activity. *We have one great moving process to study, and of this great moving process it is impossible to state any part except as valued in terms of the other parts.*[22]

With this metaphor[23] Bentley perceives the outlines of his process cosmology, in which entities, abstractions, divisions, and separations will be dissolved in their apartness and "interlaced" with other moving parts in ceaseless change.

After the death of his father in 1908 Bentley collapsed into a severe depression which lasted until 1911;[24] that year, following upon the death of his mother, Bentley and his wife moved to Paoli, Indiana. For the rest of his life he would never leave Paoli, except for a few months.[25] He did not resume major writing projects until the 1920s. Prior to the collaboration with Dewey which resulted in *Knowing and the Known* (1949), Bentley produced two important works, *Linguistic Analysis of Mathematics* (1932) and *Behavior, Knowledge, Fact* (1935).[26] These are the works that tie him directly to Dewey.

21. Bentley does not yet use "transactional," which would be appropriate here.
22. *The Process of Government: A Study of Social Pressures* (Chicago: University of Chicago Press, 1908), p. 178 (italics supplied). The Romantic and Hegelian doctrine of internal relations is evident.
23. Bentley, like Dewey, resorts to the expressiveness of the revealing metaphor. Whereas the Deweyan metaphors are religious, unifying, and redemptive, the Bentleyan metaphors are cosmic, destructive, yet daringly liberating. See T. Z. Lavine, "Pragmatism and the Constitution in the Culture of Modernism," *Transactions of the Charles S. Peirce Society*, vol. 20, no. 1 (Winter 1984): 11–12.
24. See letter from Bentley to Joseph Ratner, September 7, 1948, Bentley Collection. Cited by Ward, op. cit., p. 240, n.10.
25. See Ward, op. cit., pp. 18–20, for an interesting parallel between Bentley and Max Weber, linking in each case the depression to the death of the father and to the course of subsequent work.
26. See Ward, op. cit., appendix, for a complete bibliography of Bentley's published and unpublished work, including reading notes.

By the late 1920s Bentley's writing is vigorously responding to the revolution in theoretical physics brought about in relativity theory and to the revolution in the foundations of mathematics brought about by the development of non-Euclidean geometries and the achievement of *Principia Mathematica* in deriving all branches of mathematics from logic. Both developments, as Bentley understands them, carry important implications for scientific inquiry. The success of physics, as evidenced by relativity theory, makes it clear that scientific development requires a clean break with everyday or common sense beliefs and intuitive understandings of the phenomena of the physical world. Inquiry in the social sciences should be guided by this principle, rather than attempting to show continuity with everyday experience by representing social science as second-order or more precise common sense.

As for the revolution in theoretical mathematics, Bentley's *Linguistic Analysis of Mathematics* opposes the claim of Gottlob Frege and Bertrand Russell that mathematics is reducible to logic, which provides its foundation. Bentley problematizes the idea of 'foundations' for mathematics which are provided from outside mathematics itself. Bentley's attack upon mathematical foundationalism takes three forms: He undermines foundational claims by discerning the presence of intuitive judgments, subjectivity, and indeterminateness in the foundational literature. He presents a counter-foundational view of mathematics as itself an empirical, historical area of inquiry, characterized by changing modes of thought with regard to notions within its subjectmatter. Finally, he argues that with the development of a method of postulation ("the most general form of linguistic control which we may establish" in any area of inquiry),[27] contradictions and controversies within mathematics can be overcome. These postulates would constitute a formal structure; they would designate the process by which the structure has been produced; and they would provide from within mathematics itself the "logic" by which it proceeds. Thus the "logical foundations" of mathematics (and, by extension, the inquiry into any subjectmatter) are constituted by rendering explicit, through postulation, the im-

27. *Linguistic Analysis of Mathematics* (Bloomington, Ind.: Principia Press, 1932), pp. 20–22.

plicit practices within the field of mathematics, or of the area in question.[28]

Dewey's intellectual delight[29] in finally reading Bentley's *Linguistic Analysis of Mathematics* is understandable: here was a forceful, informative attack on foundationalism in mathematics which developed and confirmed the principal argument of *Logic: The Theory of Inquiry* that the logical 'foundations' of inquiry are not external to inquiry but in its practices. Having quickly established Bentley's supportive anti-foundationalism in the field of mathematics, Dewey does not appear, at least at this early stage in their relationship, to have picked up any clues which would lead him to question how closely allied were their views. He does not appear to have read *The Process of Government*[30] and to have noted its startling picture of the one great moving process of human activity, knowable by an intersection of multiple, unprioritizable perspectives, which are themselves in process. Nor had Dewey apparently noted Bentley's argument in *Linguistic Analysis of Mathematics*, based upon his understanding of the revolution in physics, that the development of mathematics, like that of every science, requires breaking the connection between common sense and the notions of the discipline. Nor did Dewey perceive that Bentley viewed science as descriptive only, not experimental, and not instrumental to the ends of culture. These Bentleyan views, from which he never departs, undermine Dewey's biologically based naturalism, his principle of continuity between common sense and science, and his conception of the role of science in society.

When Dewey begins to read the page proofs of *Behavior, Knowledge, Fact* at the end of July, 1935, in Hubbards, Nova Scotia, he had already been alerted by Bentley's letter of May 28, 1935, to find in the book a critical evaluation of himself. In *Behavior, Knowledge, Fact* Bentley presents his philosophy of the

---

28. See *Logic: The Theory of Inquiry*, pp. 16 ff.; 404 ff. [*Later Works* 12:23 ff.; 401 ff.].

29. "In personal conversation with [Sidney Ratner] Dewey said that Bentley . . . gave him the final encouragement and push he needed to make the decisive break with formal logic in his *Logic: The Theory of Inquiry*." Ratner, "Bentley's Inquiries," in Taylor, *Life, Language, Law*, p. 41.

30. Dewey makes only two, very brief, references to *The Process of Government* during the years of the correspondence.

behavioral sciences; his focus is first upon contemporary psychological systems and is sharply critical of behaviorism. Although
not behavioristic, Dewey's psychology is disparaged for its unscientific use of "mind-language" but is warmly praised for seeing
that "organism and environment . . . are not before us in sharp
severance from each other. . . . 'Interaction is the primary fact,
and it constitutes a *trans-action*.'"[31] Dewey is praised also for his
definition of psychology as "the behavior of the organism . . .
characterized by changes . . . in an activity that is serial and continuous in reference to changes in an environment that is continuous, while changing in detail."[32]

"What, now," Bentley explodes, "does [psychology] actually
become at his hands? 'Psychology,' he [Dewey] says, . . . 'is concerned with the life-career of individualized activities.' How, one
may ask, can this come about?" Why so constricted a view of
psychology, Bentley asks, in view of Dewey's own construction
of psychology as "immensely wider in its meanings and enormously more significant in its problems"? Why has Dewey fallen
back upon "acts" in a Newtonian language? "We must conclude," says Bentley, "that Dewey's dominant interest in problems of ethics and logic has checked his psychological construction just at the point where it was about to expand into a wider
form than, perhaps, the world has anywhere yet seen. . . ."[33]

By November 14 Dewey responds to Bentley's criticism. He
concedes that he "abstracted" from "the larger temporal-spatial
and social context" in writing about "acts" instead of "modal
patterns of acting." But Dewey argues for the legitimacy of recognizing "an individual organic self or individual" as "a selected
aspect" of the modes of experiencing "that happens to be particularly interesting to me because I have been, in the course of
my own 'life-career,' especially impressed with how damn little
we know about the behavior of *individuals* and consequently

31. *Behavior, Knowledge, Fact,* p. 76.
32. Ibid., p. 78.
33. Ibid., pp. 78, 81. The "wider form" to which Dewey failed to ascend is presumably the cosmically expansive Bentleyan form. "If we want to study this
bit [the writing of this paragraph] of 'what is happening' with any thoroughness at all, we shall have to deal with it elaborately in a frame of wider
happenings across thousands of years and thousands of miles—a frame
wherein it secures a significance vastly greater than that of 'life-career,'
though perhaps not so currently interesting" (ibid., p. 81).

make such a terrible mess of our relations to one another." The letter ends with Dewey's reflective comment that "I feel this particular problem so [deeply] as being basic to all improvement of human relations." [34]

Bentley's response apologizes [35] for his caustic criticism and points to the similarity in the development of their respective theoretical positions. "You, however," he adds, "have a range of practical interests and activities which I forfeit." The moral dimension of Deweyan pragmatism and the melioristic concern for the "life-career" of the individual human being and of the society find no reflection in Bentley's cosmos.

Bentley's "tellurian-sidereal cosmos" has the "great merit," he claims, of being the only world-view we have which "expands 'inwards' and 'outwards' spatially, and 'backwards' and 'forwards' temporally, to house all branches of knowledge." "Against it," Bentley adds, "no construction built up in terms of some pinpoint 'mind of a moment' has any hope whatever for consideration." [36] The "tellurian-sidereal" cosmos is a scientific construct, and, like each of the sciences, is a part of the cosmic process, "a bit of the cosmos inspecting itself." [37] The circularity of the interpretation of the cosmos and the cosmic process which it interprets is characteristic of all modes of knowing which have broken with "Newtonian" traditional epistemology. All sciences are viewed as circular [38] in structure, hence without foundational

---

34. *Correspondence*, p. 57.
35. "I made a snapshot of your action at a bad moment. . . . I needed that snapshot. I am ruthless, irresponsible, willing to seem absurd, where necessary: I probably would not spare my best friend, if his slaughter seemed important for what I was trying to do. In your case, I could not honestly let the matter stand without an indication of the broader position . . ." (ibid., November 18, 1935, pp. 57–58).
36. *Behavior, Knowledge, Fact*, p. 180.
37. Bentley fragment, "Phrasings," 1951–52, Bentley Collection. Cited by Ward, op. cit., p. 232, n.22. See also *Knowing and the Known* (Boston: Beacon Press, 1949), p. 63: "We observe world-being-known-to-man-in-it; we report the observation; we proceed to inquire into it, circularity or no circularity. This is all there is to it. And the circularity is not merely round the circle in one direction: the course is both ways round at once in full mutual function." [This vol., p. 62. Page numbers for succeeding references to *Knowing and the Known* refer to this vol.]
38. "*Circularity*: Its appearance is regarded as a radical defect by non-transactional epistemological inquiries that undertake to organize 'independents' as 'reals.' Normal for inquiry into knowings and knowns in system" ("A Trial Group of Names," *Knowing and the Known*, pp. 260–61).

premises; they are fully postulational and make no references to extra-linguistic reality.

The tellurian-sidereal cosmos is in no sense to be taken as "the hardest of hard Fact" but only Fact as seen from the "local" view of men who have in the course of their history come to 'know' it in this way.[39] Moreover, all knowledge, being local, is in process of change; the future form of the science of physics is unpredictable. This cosmology requires that we pursue our scientific accounts backward across the "few thousand years of social history," and forward to our time, treating all events as phases of one another and all knowledge as local, utilizing cross-sectionally "the ranges of fact, experience, knowledge, and language"— towards an expanding spatial and temporal description of cosmic process.

This is what Bentley describes as his "floating cosmology . . . in the course of which our firmest spots . . . dissolve in function. . . . The continents go, and the islands." Against it Bentley sees the "man in the street" arising with objections to the disappearance of things, persons, causes; to surrendering the primacy of his senses and thoughts as the "beginning and end of all knowledge"; "to the substitution of any 'postulate' in place of his 'real' world"; to the claim that any identifiable object is to be understood as a phase of various scientific inquiries. "His view," Bentley observes, "is that small, prim, assertive, and tenacious view embodied in our practical everyday language. . . ."[40]

But the protestations against the floating cosmology are not confined to the man in the street. Bentley has raised major problems with regard to the cognitive status of objects, human individuals, science, and philosophy itself.[41] These problems and their resolution are pivotal not only in the Dewey-Bentley rela-

39. *Behavior, Knowledge, Fact*, p. 169. Anthropologist Clifford Geertz, in *Local Knowledge* (New York: Basic Books, 1983), makes a similar point with similar ensuing problems.
40. *Behavior, Knowledge, Fact*, p. 172n.
41. Dewey's protestation on behalf of the cognitive legitimacy of the notion of the individual "life-career" was noted above. In a subtle interpretation of Bentley as offering a process philosophy of the social sciences, Paul Kress protests that not only 'particulars' but also individuals are dissolved in the cosmic flux. By rejecting the individual as analytical unit in political science, Bentley fails to be "appropriate to our sense of what political matters are all about."

tionship but in current re-interpretations of Dewey and pragmatism, as well as in a wide range of contemporary philosophic
and methodological contexts.[42]

Bentley's philosophy of social science in *Behavior, Knowledge,
Fact* presents "behavior" as the unit of analysis, defining behavior as "that great type of activity which cannot be held" within
the frames of the sciences of physics or biology "but which requires a directly psychological and social form of research" and
its own "behavioral space-time."[43] But how can social behavior
be scientifically observed? Not by empiricist sensory responses to
stimuli but by "frames of observability that we possess in fixated
or expanding forms."[44] Here Bentley exhibits an affinity with a
later Kuhnian rejection of the distinction between observation
and theory or with a later Schutzian concept of learned social
typifications. His resulting version of "behavior" anticipates in
some respects "action" as used by analytic action theory, or "social action" as used in Weberian interpretive sociology. But his
analysis of "Social Fact" proceeds by means of a cumbersome,
ponderous set of neologisms designed to convey process and
transaction, and rid the language of behavioral science from involvement with metaphysical, mentalistic, or abstracting ele-

---

Kress concludes: "Certainly *Behavior Knowledge Fact* and *Knowing and the
Known* may be read as chronicles of a lost mariner, a man who has thrown
the compass of reason over the side as so much excess ballast." Kress, op. cit.,
pp. 248, 178 (italics supplied).

42. See, among others: Karl-Otto Apel, *Towards a Transformation of Philosophy,* trans. Glyn Adey and David Frisby (London: Routledge and Kegan Paul,
1980); Richard J. Bernstein, *Beyond Objectivism and Relativism* (Phila-
delphia: University of Pennsylvania Press, 1983); Joseph Margolis, *Pragmatism without Foundations: Reconciling Realism and Relativism* (Oxford:
Basil Blackwell, 1986); John J. McDermott, *Streams of Experience: Reflections on the History and Philosophy of American Culture* (Amherst: University of Massachusetts Press, 1986); Richard Rorty, *Consequences of Pragmatism* (Minneapolis: University of Minnesota Press, 1982); Sandra B.
Rosenthal, *Speculative Pragmatism* (Amherst: University of Massachusetts
Press, 1986); R. W. Sleeper, *The Necessity of Pragmatism: John Dewey's
Conception of Philosophy* (New Haven: Yale University Press, 1986); John E.
Smith, *Purpose and Thought: The Meaning of Pragmatism* (Chicago: University of Chicago Press, 1984); H. S. Thayer, *Meaning and Action: A Critical History of Pragmatism* (Indianapolis: Bobbs-Merrill Co., 1968).
43. *Behavior, Knowledge, Fact,* p. 262.
44. Ibid., p. 204.

ments, or with common sense notions of the reality of discrete individuals and objects. These neologisms have the function of "namings" which specify "the range of application for the names we give." Bentley carries his notions of "namings" and "specifications" to *Knowing and the Known*.[45]

Following the first exchange of letters between the two men in 1935, there is a lapse of three years; the correspondence resumes in 1938 after the publication of *Logic: The Theory of Inquiry*, reaching a peak of weekly and daily exchanges as the writing progressed, and tapering off after 1949 with the publication of *Knowing and the Known*.[46]

Each man was fulfilled in certain respects by the other in the relationship. Dewey found someone more sophisticated than himself in logic and mathematics, someone who had already defended a Deweyan position against mathematical foundationalism, who took Dewey's *Logic* seriously, wishing to defend it against its critics, and who had the intellectual capacity and vigor to clarify and strengthen its argumentation in the direction of further development. Moreover, this early admirer-disciple from the Chicago days seemed possessed of a vital, visionary, driving intellectual force which stimulated and fascinated Dewey:

> . . . I *don't* feel a lot of your positions are divergent from mine. I think our different modes of approach complement each other. I hadn't expected at my age (I'm 85 in October)

45. See ibid., pp. 231, 265; *Knowing and the Known*, chaps. 5 and 11.
46. Following are the articles included in *Knowing and the Known*: "A Search for Firm Names," *Journal of Philosophy* 42 (January 4, 1945): 5–6; "On a Certain Vagueness in Logic," ibid. 42 (January 4 and 18, 1945): 6–27, 39–51; "A Terminology for Knowings and Knowns," ibid. 42 (April 26, 1945): 225–47; "Postulations," ibid. 42 (November 22, 1945): 645–62; "Interaction and Transaction," ibid. 43 (September 12, 1946): 505–17; "Transactions as Known and Named," ibid. 43 (September 26, 1946): 533–51, 560; "Specification," ibid. 43 (November 21, 1946): 645–63; "'Definition,'" ibid. 44 (May 22, 1947): 281–306; "Logicians' Underlying Postulations," *Philosophy of Science* 13 (January 1946): 3–19; "The New 'Semiotic,'" *Philosophy and Phenomenological Research* 8 (September 1947): 107–31; "Common Sense and Science: Their Respective Frames of Reference," *Journal of Philosophy* 45 (April 8, 1948): 197–208; "Concerning a Vocabulary for Inquiry into Knowledge," ibid. 44 (July 31, 1947): 421–34; and Reply to "A Letter to Mr. Dewey," ibid. 46 (May 26, 1949): 329–42.

to get a "refresher course" that really refreshed. I feel I've got it through this contact with you. . . .[47]

For his part, Bentley found a renowned public figure, an internationally esteemed philosopher to work with on a specific task utilizing his own logical and mathematical skills to defend and sharpen the arguments of the *Logic* and undertaking the larger intellectual projects of battling, with Dewey, against the threat of logical positivism. Moreover, there was for Bentley the intellectual appeal of moving beyond the issues of political science, mathematics, and psychology which had previously engaged him to the philosophic frame of pragmatism the relationship to Dewey made possible.

As the two men begin their correspondence, they share the spirit of the American cultural revolution of the turn of the nineteenth century and the early years of the twentieth century; there is for both, as for many American intellectuals at that time, a Hegelian deposit in their thought; both hold to a holistic, process philosophy and are accordingly anti-dualistic, anti-foundationalist, anti-abstractionist, anti-formalist; and, in opposition to positivism and empiricism, tend to be interpretivist. Dewey and Bentley shared as well a broadly naturalistic, organism-environment frame; a rejection of traditional metaphysics and epistemology; an opposition to a legislative function on the part of mathematics and logic in relation to inquiry; and a behavioral, in opposition to a mentalistic, approach to the social sciences.

From the start there were differences, as noted above, which the amicable respect with which the two men regard each other cannot conceal. In opposition to the moral dimension of the entirety of Dewey's writings, Bentley deliberately precludes, as unscientific, any moral or political component from his own work; Bentley rejects, as a related issue, Dewey's philosophic consideration of the individual life-career, as an abstraction from social transactional process; Bentley's process cosmology threatens the dissolution of objects and persons, which Dewey resists with

47. *Correspondence*, June 6, 1944, p. 264. Dewey's capacity to be productively stimulated by persons who project creative vitality was life-long. Among earlier instances is his relationship with the journalist-entrepreneur Franklin Ford.

complex and intricate argumentation. Finally, Bentley's conception of science requires discontinuity between ordinary experience and science, whereas for Dewey, intelligent inquiry in the resolution of problematic situations is present throughout human experience. These differences, and the conflicting philosophic ideas they reflect, perseverate through the nineteen years of the correspondence. In 1950 they are still arguing about the "object."[48] Chapter 10, "Common Sense and Science," the only essay signed by Dewey alone in *Knowing and the Known,* and the article *"How, What,* and *What For* in Social Inquiry"[49] continue Dewey's well-established reasoning on this issue.

The question of dominance has understandably been raised about this important intellectual collaboration, especially since it is accessible, not only in the completed product but in the making, through a voluminous correspondence. Paul Kress finds it remarkable that

> the best-known philosopher of his day carried on such an
> exchange with the obscure orchard owner of Paoli . . . when
> both men were in their twilight years; it was remarkable also
> because the obscure Midwesterner dominates the exchange—
> identifying problems, proposing and rejecting solutions,
> tirelessly criticizing, evaluating, and urging. It is the Colum-
> bia professor who expresses gratitude and admiration for his
> friend's insights, and a willingness to entertain challenges to
> positions held over a lifetime.[50]

James Ward cites John McDermott's appraisal as "more balanced" in noting that while

> Bentley, often acidic in style, was mostly on the attack as di-
> rected to their philosophic peers, Dewey was forthright in
> opinion but gentle in manner, ever cutting through Bentley's
> rhetoric to state their shared position with acumen and
> dignity.[51]

48. Ibid., Bentley's letter to Dewey, January 22, 1950, p. 620.
49. This volume, pp. 333–40. Dewey's earlier version, "Means and Consequences—*How, What,* and *What For,*" is printed as part VIII, *Correspondence,* pp. 647–54.
50. Kress, op. cit., pp. 19–20.
51. John J. McDermott, introduction, *The Philosophy of John Dewey,* vol. 1, *The Structure of Experience* (New York: G. P. Putnam's Sons, 1973), p. xxii.

Although Ward proposes that "neither dominates the correspondence," in effect he supports Kress's position. Ward acknowledges that "for the most part it is Bentley who first formulates problems"; that "Bentley was aware that he had done the bulk of the work on the early stages . . . and that the emerging product was 'a specialization of my own type of procedure' rather than . . . philosophy in Dewey's idiom"; and that Dewey was reluctant to sign as co-author, since most of the work was Bentley's.[52]

Finally, on the issue of dominance, Sidney Ratner moves the argument forward by the astute observation[53] that even if it be agreed that Bentley formulates most of the problems, does most of the writing, and that the end product is in Bentley's style, nevertheless it cannot be claimed that Bentley imposes his views on Dewey, since the ideas presented are all to be found in Dewey's work.

In response to Ratner's suggestion it must be said, however, that not all the ideas presented in *Knowing and the Known* are Dewey's, since there are major differences between the two men, as has been noted here. Moreover, Bentley's program is far from being confined to a reflective confirmation of ideas he shares with Dewey. Bentley pursues his own agenda of a process cosmology, and he drives the logic of process, which Dewey shares with him, to its extreme implications, challenging the views that Dewey does not share with him. As the *Correspondence* and *Knowing and the Known* disclose, Deweyan pragmatism, as a type of process philosophy, is not immunized against its own dissolving techniques. Vulnerable thus to the force of Bentley's prodding, Dewey falters as the dissolving operations of his own pragmatism are turned against itself. The end result is a naturalism *in extremis*, the dissolution of the structures that Dewey required for his own long-standing agenda: to reconstruct philosophy and to ameliorate the problems of society by bridging

McDermott provides an astute overview of the relationship and its product and insight into the contrasting styles and the personal significance of the collaboration.
52. Ward, op. cit., pp. 196, 206. See *Correspondence*, August 19–29, 1944, pp. 293–96.
53. Observation made to the writer by Sidney Ratner, June, 1988.

the gap between science and morality. Bentley had, however, already warned of this outcome:

> . . . [O]ur firmest spots of conventional departure themselves dissolve in function. When they have so dissolved . . . there is no hope of finding refuge in some chance island of 'fact' which may appear. (*Behavior, Knowledge, Fact,* p. 183.)

That pragmatism had been emerging as a potential philosophic framework for Bentley was already evident in the developmental line of his thought from *The Process of Government* to *Linguistic Analysis of Mathematics* to *Behavior, Knowledge, Fact,* as his interests focus less on the problems specific to the individual social sciences and mathematics and increasingly upon the issues addressed by the philosophy of the social sciences. Bentley read Mead, Charles S. Peirce, and William James during the 1930s and, as the relationship with Dewey began to flourish, appears to have seen himself as a major figure in the further development of pragmatism and as heir to Peirce's philosophic command of all the fields of knowledge.[54] Pragmatism as Bentley perceived it is a philosophic movement expressive of the tellurian-sidereal cosmic processes which Darwin has disclosed and which Peirce, James, and Dewey had carried forward.

Dewey entered the Peirce-James continuity in the eighteen-nineties, bringing a psychological formulation of stimulus-response in full circuit, rather than in partial "arc," and developing a pragmatism which James saw as offering a "wider panorama" than his own. No one has known better than Peirce . . . how deeply social our knowings are . . . [or] than James in his analysis of the "selves." . . . It was Dewey who broadened the study of knowings into a full cultural form. "Transaction," for Dewey, underlies "action," and the "indeterminate" underlies the "determinate" in a way similar to that in which, for James, the factual datum[55] underlies the purportedly independent subjectives and objectives. In each

54. See Ward, op. cit., pp. 201–2, which draws upon Bentley memoranda of 1939.
55. The reference is to Bentley's article "The Jamesian Datum" (from which this passage is taken), *Journal of Psychology* 16 (July 1943): 35–79, reprinted in Bentley, *Inquiry into Inquiries: Essays in Social Theory,* edited and with an introduction by Sidney Ratner (Boston: Beacon Press, 1954), pp. 230–67 (passage from pp. 260–61). Here Bentley defends James against the segmented misreadings by critics of "The Stream of Thought," chap. IX of

of these cases a view in full system is offered as a vastly richer approach to knowledge than any the dualistically split views have ever yielded . . . [as] where Darwin places nature beneath organism and environment to bring them into system, Peirce by a great vision extrapolates this approach across the full field of knowings. . . . For all four there is a common denominator of formulation—indicated, if not yet advanced in use. . . .

In the currents of this great movement, the next evolvement, which neither Peirce nor Dewey had been able to reach, is the development of a theory of linguistic behavior that would be adequate to pragmatism and the circular systems of behavioral science. This next stage in pragmatism Bentley hoped to achieve through the collaboration with Dewey.

In fact, the intellectual collaboration which eventuated as the twelve chapters of *Knowing and the Known* undertook three distinct but interrelated projects: a critique of formal logicians, in defense of Dewey's *Logic;* a critique of logical positivism, which threatens to usurp the dominance held by pragmatism; as well as the construction of a new language for behavioral inquiry.

The issue with regard to logic was soberly stated by Dewey in the first pages of his introduction to the *Logic.* Contemporary logic exhibits the paradox of there being general agreement with regard to its "proximate subject-matter" but continuous controversy with regard to its "ultimate subject-matter." No one doubts, he says, that the domain of "the relations of propositions to one another" and "the relations expressed by such words as *is, is-not, if-then, only (none but), and, or, some-all,*" demarcates the proximate subjectmatter of logic, as a distinctive field.[56] Logic as ultimate subjectmatter, on the other hand, is located within philosophic theory, and controversy arises with differing views of the ultimate subjectmatter of logic expressing differing ultimate philosophies.

But Dewey proceeds to state the ultimate philosophy which

James's *Principles of Psychology.* Bentley shows that James's thought moved on to view the "stream" as behavioral activity, "the flow of the neutral datum in a natural world of organism-environment." This achievement of James was made possible, on the negative side, by "the final extermination of the ancestral claimant 'consciousness'" (ibid., p. 248).

56. *Logic: The Theory of Inquiry,* p. 1 [*Later Works* 12:9].

the *Logic* is arguing, and to claim that his theory of inquiry "can develop in its own ongoing course the logical standards and forms to which *further* inquiry shall submit." [57]

Dewey is in fact offering not a bold naturalistic replacement of symbolic logic but an ultimate philosophy of naturalism, in which logic is seen to be continuous with all the contexts wherein organism and environment are in transaction. The nerve of the naturalistic argument is to deny (in opposition to contrary philosophies of the ultimate subjectmatter of logic) that logic is to be understood as apart from nature, as in some sense a pure or rational structure which provides an a priori foundation for inquiry.

The issue, then, becomes "apartness." In the chapter "Vagueness in Logic" [58] Bentley takes on the task of defending the *Logic* against formal logicians who separate logic from inquiry. Bentley reviews the treatment of proposition, truth, meaning, language, and fact in the work of Rudolf Carnap, Morris R. Cohen and Ernest Nagel, C. J. Ducasse, C. I. Lewis, Charles W. Morris, and Alfred Tarski, attacking them all (with some exception for Tarski), directing the more devastating criticisms at Cohen and Nagel and at Carnap. [59] The criticism of mathematical founda-

---

57. Ibid., p. 5 [*Later Works* 12:13].
58. Three chapters, chap. 1, "Vagueness in Logic," chap. 8, "Logic in an Age of Science," and chap. 9, "A Confused 'Semiotic,'" are signed by Bentley alone; only chap. 10, "Common Sense and Science," is signed by Dewey alone. All other chapters are jointly signed. As the *Correspondence* makes amply clear, much discussion and rewriting takes place, but, with the exception of chap. 10, the formulation of issues and the actual writing of the chapters is pure Bentley.
59. See, e.g., on Carnap: "It is difficult to tell just where the most vicious center of terminological evil lies in Carnap's procedure. Probably, however, the dubious honor should go to 'concept,' a word that is all things to all sentences" (this vol., p. 27). On Cohen and Nagel: "Literally and with straight-faced attention we are asked by Cohen and Nagel to concern ourselves with propositions that are not physical, not mental, not linguistic, and not even something in process of being expressed or conveyed, . . . but . . . possess truth and falsity on their own account, regardless of all human participation and of any trace of human knowing. All of which is very difficult to accomplish in the Year of Our Lord, 1944. It is even more troublesome factually, since everything we are logically authorized to know about *facts* . . . must be acquired from such 'propositions'" (p. 14). For Bentley's abusive treatment of Nagel, see Ward, op. cit., p. 255, n.10. Nagel's abandoning of his ontological position with regard to logic ("Logic without Ontology," in Y. H. Krikorian, ed., *Naturalism and the Human Spirit* [New York: Columbia University Press, 1944]) is acknowledged in n.10, chap. 1. Nagel is portrayed as advancing to Dewey's "instrumental logic of the nineteen-twenties, which he [Nagel] at that time assailed . . ." (this vol., p. 16).

tionalism Bentley had mounted in *Linguistic Analysis of Mathematics* serves him well here: again he discovers vagueness, slipperiness, intuitive judgments, and terminological confusion. He concludes:

> The "propositions" of Cohen and Nagel, of Ducasse and of Carnap, the "meanings" of Lewis, the "sign vehicles" and "interpretants" of Morris and the "truth" of Tarski all tell the same tale, though in varying degree. What is "man in action" gets distorted when manipulated as if detached; what is "other than man" gets plenty of crude assumption, but no fair factual treatment.[60]

Bentley attempts a final defense of the Dewey-Bentley view of logic when their joint articles begin to be published in the *Journal of Philosophy* in 1945 and are reviewed by Alonzo Church[61] and Arthur F. Smullyan.[62] Both reviewers charge Dewey and Bentley with psychologism, thus reducing logic to psychology. Bentley replies that no reduction was intended; that he and Dewey

> regard knowings and reasonings and mathematical and scientific adventurings even up to their highest abstractions . . . as lying within the general field of behavioral inquiry. . . . None of this involves any interference with the practical differentiations of inquiry as between logic and psychology. . . . Specializations . . . based on methods and on subjectmatters methodologically differentiated remain as valid and usable as ever.[63]

In this reply to the *Journal of Symbolic Logic* reviewers, Bentley makes it clear that his own view of logic is of a formal system meeting criteria of consistency and coherence, neither foundational to inquiry nor "developed" out of ongoing inquiry; logic

---

60. *Knowing and the Known*, p. 45. Dewey and Bentley feared that logical positivism would be perceived as dealing more rigorously with the same problems as pragmatism. See Dewey's letter, April 7, 1939: ". . . My theory about Morris is that . . . he was impressed by the symbolic formalists and decided the weakness of pragmatism was its failure to do justice to the formal-mathematical element . . ." (*Correspondence,* p. 69).

61. *Journal of Symbolic Logic* 10 (December 1945): 132–33.

62. Ibid. 12 (September 1947): 99.

63. *Knowing and the Known,* chap. 12, "Summary of Progress Made," pp. 276–77.

operates with its own postulates from within its own mode of inquiry, as he argued in *Linguistic Analysis of Mathematics*.[64]

Anxious attacks upon logical positivism by Dewey and Bentley appear in the late 1930s and the 1940s in their personal correspondence and in published criticisms of Carnap and Morris in the articles constituting *Knowing and the Known*, as the members of the Vienna Circle, having fled from nazism, begin to publish their views in American journals and to re-establish the unity of science movement. In the summer of 1944, in response to the growing influence of logical positivism, Dewey began working on a series of drafts of a paper on signs, the last draft of which, "What Is It to Be a Linguistic Sign or Name?" he sent to Bentley on May 25, 1945. Dewey was apologetic for diverting his energies from his project with Bentley ("I feel ashamed . . . I had no business switching off for even two days . . ."). But he admits to a compelling "inward pressure" to write an article opposing the positivistically oriented theory of signs which was currently in the philosophic foreground in the form of Charles Morris's *Foundations of the Theory of Signs* (1938). Against "Carnap-Morris" Dewey protests that linguistic sign and referent are not external to one another and separable, as Ogden and Richards [and Carnap and Morris] maintain, but are instead "constituents of one inclusive undivided set of operations" (this volume, p. 304).[65]

While the appeal of logical positivism in America seemed to be

64. See Sleeper, *The Necessity of Pragmatism*, p. 99: ". . . Dewey's conception of logic is not part of logic in the traditional sense, but is rather a conception of intelligent behavior in which traditional logical concepts play a role but are not the whole story. It was Russell's judgment that Dewey's logic of experience belongs to psychology, but it was Dewey's judgment that psychology belongs to the logic of experience. Psychology is part of logic once logic is conceived as a theory of inquiry. But then, so are physics and chemistry, ethics and aesthetics." In the appendix to *Knowing and the Known* (Dewey's letter to Albert G. A. Balz), Dewey writes: "The force of the word 'Logic,' in all probability, has overshadowed for the reader the import of what in my intention was the significant expression, *The Theory of Inquiry*" (this vol., p. 293).
65. Unpublished typescript, sent to Bentley on May 25, 1945 (Bentley Collection, 18 pp.; included in this volume, pp. 297–309). The quotation is from Dewey's letter to Bentley of the same date (Bentley Collection). The reference to "Carnap-Morris" is from Dewey's letter to Bentley, July 12, 1944, *Correspondence*, p. 285. Dewey characteristically omits direct reference to Carnap and Morris in his typescript. Dewey did not complete an article on signs in time for inclusion in *Knowing and the Known*, and this typescript remained unpublished. In recognition of this omission, the preface to *Knowing and the*

its bold empiricism and its logical rigor, the pragmatists' case against logical positivism rested on the thoroughgoing dualism of its empirical and logical components. Dewey and Bentley rejected the foundation in observed atomic facts as the discredited empiricism of subjectivist sense-data; and they rejected the construction of science as a logical system on this foundation as incompatible with the view that the structure of science is not imposed by formal logic, but arises out of scientific practice; they rejected the isolation of observation statements from theoretical statements and also the verifiability test of meaning as further evidence of the strict analytic-synthetic distinction underlying the logical positivists' philosophy of science. However, some points of agreement are conceded: the rejection of metaphysics, and the need for the construction of a language appropriate to scientific inquiry.[66]

But the shadow of logical positivism falls on *Knowing and the Known* and its crucial third project of developing a theory of linguistic behavior adequate to pragmatism and the behavioral sciences. Nature is understood as the ultimate field of inquiry; and a transactional approach in inquiry is held to be required at the present developmental stage of science. Here, *Knowing and the Known* presents its best-known contribution to the philosophy of science: the conception of self-action, interaction, and transaction as three successive and progressive scientific modes of viewing the world. Self-action is the classical mode of viewing

---

Known expresses the hope that "As continuance of our present work . . . the future will see the completion of papers . . . on the significance . . . of the word 'sign'" (pp. 4–5).

Dewey was prompted again in the spring of 1945 to divert his energies from the joint effort by the urge to reply to an article by Emile Benoit-Smullyan, "Value Judgments and the Social Sciences" (*Journal of Philosophy* 42, April 13, 1945, pp. 197–210). Dewey's unpublished response, "Values, Valuations, and Social Facts" (Bentley Collection; included in this volume, pp. 310–17), was sent to Bentley June 20, 1945. Dewey re-affirmed his well-established distinction between valuing and valuation, and his principle of the continuity of inquiry; he argues that judgments concerning values, as well as those concerning the subjectmatter of the social sciences, are appropriately the outcome of the same pattern of inquiry as in all other cognitive subjectmatters.

66. Bentley concludes a ferocious attack on Carnap and other positivists by noting that "with the great objectives of the logical positivists—the expulsion of metaphysics, and the development of a linguistic frame for appraisal and organization—I am in the fullest sympathy" ("The Positive and the Logical," *Inquiry into Inquiries*, p. 112).

things as self-caused by their own essences; interaction is the mode of explanation beginning with mechanistic physics, viewing isolatable units in causal interconnection with other units; the transactional mode views human behavior "without attribution of . . . action to independent self-actors, or to independently inter-acting elements or relations." At present, epistemology, logic, and the social sciences "are still largely on a self-actional basis" with some movement visible toward an interactional procedure.[67] Physics is the model science, having moved from Newtonian interactionalism to the transactionalism of Einsteinian relativity theory and to quantum mechanics. Transaction is that "level" of inquiry "where systems of description and naming are employed to deal with aspects and phases of action, without final attribution to 'elements' or other presumptively detachable or independent 'entities,' 'essences,' or 'realities,' and without isolation of presumptively detachable 'relations' from such detachable 'elements.'"[68]

The Bentleyan cosmic vision of systems of local knowledge ranging across time and space, glimpsed in *Knowing and the Known*'s accounts of transaction, recedes as the project of linguistic reform becomes the central issue. The procedure followed, in accordance with science, is postulational and its outcomes are provisional. The "basic postulate" is that "knowings are observable facts in exactly the same sense as are the subject-matters that are known."[69] As natural events, knowings and knowns are to be "investigated by methods that have been elsewhere successful in the natural sciences," they are to be "taken together as aspects of one event"[70] transactionally observed.

The immediate inquiry is limited to knowings through nam-

67. *Knowing and the Known*, pp. 112, 67, 98.
68. Ibid., pp. 101–2. The continuing influence of *Knowing and the Known* is sustained primarily by the concept of transaction. See, e.g., as a direct influence in literary theory, Louise M. Rosenblatt, *The Reader, the Text, the Poem* (Carbondale and Edwardsville: Southern Illinois University Press, 1978), and in psychology, Hadley Cantril, *Psychology, Humanism, and Scientific Inquiry: Selected Essays*, ed. Albert H. Cantril (New Brunswick, N.J.: Transaction Books, 1988). In cultural anthropology, Clifford Geertz's *The Interpretation of Cultures* (New York: Basic Books, 1973) and in hermeneutics, Hans-Georg Gadamer's *Truth and Method* (New York: Seabury Press, 1975) express a transactional viewpoint.
69. *Knowing and the Known*, p. 48.
70. Ibid., pp. 84, 85.

ings, and the search is continuous through *Knowing and the Known* for a "firm list of names." Namings, like knowings, are to be considered as "directly existential knowings," to be "transactionally studied."[71] Firm names having been scrutinized for vagueness, abstractness, residues of philosophic traditions, self-action or interactionism, and having been transactionally studied, are further submitted to specification. Specification is "the most efficient form of Designation," freeing naming from linguistic barriers by the exclusive "use of widened [scientific] descriptions," in connection with namings. "Specification . . . *is* science, so far as the word 'science' is used for the reporting of the known."[72] And fact is the name designating the "cosmos of knowledge—with nature as known and as in process of being better known—ourselves and our knowings included . . . as factual, as cosmic. . . ."[73]

It may now be seen that the entire conceptual apparatus with which *Knowing and the Known* attempts to construct a theory of language for pragmatism and behavioral science has come from Bentley's *Behavior, Knowledge, Fact*. Postulation, behavior, observation, naming, specification, fact, self-action/interaction/transaction, circularity, the cosmos of knowledge—for all of these, Bentley drew upon his own text. At least in respect to the production of *Knowing and the Known*, Bentley succeeded in his ambition to provide, with the collaboration of Dewey, the next step in the development of pragmatism.

The search for "firm," "leading" names and their specifications led inevitably to the loss of names and relationships which are present in the discourse of Dewey's pragmatism and vulnerable to these strictures of transactional analysis. The list of rejected names includes: reality, experience, naturalism, individual, subject-object, problematic situation, concept, meaning, and knowledge.[74] Dewey registers protestations; arguments ensue; Dewey characteristically concedes. On reality—Bentley: " 'Real.' "

71. Ibid., pp. 258, 273.
72. Ibid., pp. 131, 149, 150. ". . . We have chosen the name 'specification' to designate the most complete and accurate description that the sustained inquiry of an age has been able to achieve based on all the inquiries of earlier ages . . ." (ibid., p. 150).
73. Ibid., p. 58.
74. Sidney Ratner offers a list of "formulations in the *Logic* [which] were taken over without change in *Knowing and the Known*": inquiry, object, connec-

You have had radical trouble with statement here for thirty years or more. . . . You . . . hedge. Hedging has brought no fruit. I am against any more of it."[75] On naming—Bentley: "You propose to strike out . . . that naming is a form of knowing. It is the very heart of our project. . . . Take this out, and we have nothing left." Dewey: "I *don't* want to limit 'knowing' and 'knowledge' to naming instances." Bentley: ". . . We . . . get *Naming* established as well as it can be. . . . After that your interest runs to enriched living. . . . My interest, however, stays on, on the research side."[76] On scientific knowledge—Dewey: ". . . [Y]ou seem to me at times to make the cognitive swallow up everything. I just can't." "My interest has always been in what I would now call the growing points. . . . [U]nless and except for the growing-points, the whole . . . thing would be dead."[77] On experience—Dewey: ". . . I agree with what you say about dropping 'experience,' as not needed. I should like the mode of treatment a little more sympathetic—probably because of my own past struggles."[78] On subject-object—Bentley: ". . . [W]henever a reference to the actively producing *Subject* comes up, you indicate that you have no need . . . for it (. . . ten or twelve such passages in the *Logic*). However, when reference to the *Object* is necessary, you indicate that the object is needed. . . . [Y]ou cannot permit the object to disappear altogether." Dewey: "I doubtless have used the word 'object' in a pre-organism sense."[79]

Ironically, the mission of *Knowing and the Known,* to sharpen the language of the *Logic,* to provide a theory of language for

tion, postulation, reference, relation, situation, and truth. *Correspondence,* introduction, p. 45.

75. *Correspondence,* January 29, 1944, p. 205.
76. Ibid., May 31–June 5, 1944, pp. 260–63.
77. Ibid., January 22, February 2, 1945, pp. 381, 385.
78. Ibid., May 12, 1944, p. 246.
79. Ibid., March 2–9, 1944, pp. 92–94. In an unpublished review of the *Correspondence* made available to me through the kindness of Sidney Ratner, Herbert Schneider wrote: "Bentley teased, lured, drove his friend into revising the basic terminology of his thought, using as an incentive the promise that the resulting theory . . . would be stated in hard and fast, clear and distinct language. . . . The genius of Bentley's strategy [was that] whenever Bentley asked him time and time again what he meant when he wrote so-and-so, and how together they could resolve the apparent contradiction, Dewey replied that the contradiction was real and that he should have said thus-and-so."

pragmatism and the behavioral sciences, to combat the foundationalism of formal logicians and the looming hegemony of logical positivism, is fulfilled in none of these goals. Instead, *Knowing and the Known* emerges as a rigorous scientific transactionalism, mirroring (despite differences) the logical positivism it opposes, offering its own formal language, maintaining the exclusive legitimacy of science as mode of knowledge and as frame of reference, denying cognitive significance to metaphysics and ethics, and denying connection between science and common sense. The scientific transactionalism of *Knowing and the Known* leaves the philosophic constructions of Dewey hopelessly undermined—the great, unifying Darwinian frame of nature, aesthetically experienced in its precariousness and stability, and the linkages of science and morals, of the individual life-career with society, ethics, politics, aesthetics, and science; and the problematic situation, key to the resolution of difficulties. Hopelessly undermined also is the austerely magnificent Bentleyan tellurian-sidereal floating cosmology, spanning millennia in time and space, moving into the future. After the project ended and despite the warmth of the relationship, both appear to be disappointed in its philosophical outcome and its reception. Dewey writes again about the transactional relationship of means and consequences ("*How, What,* and *What For* in Social Inquiry," pp. 333–40) and that of behavioral skills and environmental artefacts ("Importance, Significance, and Meaning," pp. 318–32); and Bentley, perhaps depressed, publishes a forty-year collection of his papers, including "Kennetic Inquiry," a recapitulation of his intellectual career and his contribution to the transactional approach.[80]

It is, however, pragmatism, not logical positivism, that has survived. Pragmatism has become central to current debates concerning foundationalism, in which issues of realism, relativism, transcendentalism, idealism, and the "end of philosophy" are in-

80. Earlier versions of both Dewey essays, previously unpublished, appear in *Correspondence*, pp. 647–68: "Importance, Significance and Meaning," received by Bentley March 31, 1950, and "Means and Consequences—*How, What,* and *What For*," received by Bentley January 5, 1951. "Kennetic Inquiry," published in *Science*, Vol. 112, no. 2922 (December 29, 1950): 775–83, appears as the final essay in Bentley's *Inquiry into Inquiries.*

volved. And it is plausible that "seen through American eyes, the converging themes of the entire movement of contemporary Western philosophy"—phenomenology, Marxism, hermeneutics, deconstruction—"are decidedly pragmatist in cast."[81] In the course of the development of American pragmatism, the richly complex process philosophies of Dewey and Bentley played their major roles. . . . The islands go, the continents linger longer.

81. Margolis, *Pragmatism without Foundations,* p. 201.

Knowing and the Known

Preface

The difficulties attending dependability of communication and mutual intelligibility in connection with problems of knowledge are notoriously great. They are so numerous and acute that disagreement, controversy, and misunderstanding are almost taken to be matters of course. The studies upon which report is made in this volume are the outgrowth of a conviction that a greater degree of dependability, and hence of mutual understanding, and of ability to turn differences to mutual advantage, is as practicable as it is essential. This conviction has gained steadily in force as we have proceeded. We hold that it is practicable to employ in the study of problems of knowing and knowledge the postulational method now generally used in subject-matters scientifically developed. The scientific method neither presupposes nor implies any set, rigid, theoretical position. We are too well aware of the futility of efforts to achieve greater dependability of communication and consequent mutual understanding by methods of imposition. In advancing fields of research, inquirers proceed by doing all they can to make clear to themselves and to others the points of view and the hypotheses by means of which their work is carried on. When those who disagree with one another in their conclusions join in a common demand for such clarification, their difficulties usually turn out to increase command of the subject.

Accordingly we stress that our experiment is one of cooperative research. Our confidence is placed in this method; it is placed in the particular conclusions presented as far as they are found to be results of this method.

Our belief that future advance in knowledge about knowings requires dependability of communication is integrally connected with the transactional point of view and frame of reference we employ. Emphasis upon the transactional grew steadily as our studies proceeded. We believe the tenor of our development will be grasped most readily when the distinction of the transactional from the inter-actional and self-actional points of view is systematically borne in mind. The transactional is in fact that point of view which systematically proceeds upon the ground that knowing is cooperative and as such is integral with communication. By its own processes it is allied with the postulational. It demands that statements be made as descriptions of events in terms of durations in time and areas in space. It excludes assertions of fixity and attempts to impose them. It installs openness and flexibility in the very process of knowing. It treats knowledge as itself inquiry—as a goal *within* inquiry, not as a terminus outside or beyond inquiry. We wish the tests of openness and flexibility to be applied to our work; any attempts to impose fixity would be a denial—a rupture—of the very method we employ. Our requirement of openness in our own work, nevertheless, does not mean we disregard or reject criticisms from absolute points of view. It does, however, require of such criticisms that the particular absolute point of view be itself frankly, explicitly, stated in its bearing upon the views that are presented.

We trust that if these studies initiate a cooperative movement of this sort, the outcome will be progress in firmness and dependability in communication which is an indispensable condition of progress in knowledge of fact.

The inquiry has covered a period of four years and the material has had preliminary publication in one or other of the philosophical journals. We have not undertaken to remove from our pages the overlappings arising out of the protracted inquiry and of the varied manners of presentation. Since new points of approach are involved, along with progress in grasp of the problems, even the repetitions, we may hope, will at times be beneficial. We have taken advantage of this opportunity to make a number of small changes, mostly in phrasings, and in the style and scope of inter-chapter references. Some additional citations from recent discussions have been made. In only one case, we believe, has a substantive change in formulation been made, and that is exhibited in a footnote [see this volume, p. 61].

As continuance of our present work we hope the future will see the completion of papers on the transactional construction of psychology; on the presentation of language as human behavior;

on the application of mathematical symbolism to linguistic namings and to perceivings; and on the significance of the wide range
of employment, both philosophically and in practical life, of the
word "sign" in recent generations.

The reader's attention is called to the Appendix containing a
letter from John Dewey to a philosopher friend. He who fails to
grasp the viewpoint therein expressed may find himself in the
shadow as respects all else we have to say.

We owe our thanks to Joseph Ratner and Jules Altman for
their many suggestions in the course of this study, and to the
latter particularly for his careful work in preparing the Index.

June, 1948

Introduction
A Search for Firm Names

A year or so ago we decided that the time had come to undertake a postponed task: the attempt to fix a set of leading words capable of firm use in the discussion of "knowings" and "existings" in that specialized region of research called the theory of knowledge. The undertaking proved to be of the kind that grows. Firm words for our own use had to be based on well-founded observation. Such observation had to be sound enough, and well enough labeled, to be used with definiteness, not only between ourselves, but also in intercourse with other workers, including even those who might be at far extremes from us in their manner of interpretation and construction. It is clear, we think, that without some such agreement on the simpler fact-names, no progress of the kind the modern world knows as scientific will be probable; and, further, that so long as man, the organism, is viewed naturalistically within the cosmos, research of the scientific type into his "knowings" is a worth-while objective. The results of our inquiry are to be reported in a series of papers, some individually signed, some over our joint names,[1] depending on the extent to which problems set up and investigations undertaken become specialized or consolidated as we proceed. We shall examine such words as fact, existence, event; designation, experience, agency; situation, object, subjectmatter; interaction, transaction; definition, description, specification, characterization; signal, sign, symbol; centering, of course, on those regions of application in which phrasings in the vaguely allusive form of "subject" and "object" conventionally appear.

The opening chapter arose from the accumulation of many

1. Of the papers chosen for incorporation in this book, those forming Chapters 1, 8, and 9 are written by Bentley. That forming Chapter 10 is written by Dewey. The rest were signed jointly. The original titles of some of the papers have been altered for the present use. Places of original publication are noted in an appended comment [see this volume, p. 279].

illustrations, which we first segregated and then advanced to introductory position because we found they yielded a startling diagnosis of linguistic disease not only in the general epistemological field, where everyone would anticipate it, but also in the specialized logical field, which ought to be reasonably immune. This diagnosis furnishes the strongest evidence that there is a need for the type of terminological inquiry we are engaged in, whether it is done at our hands and from our manner of approach, or at the hands and under the differing approach of others. We are in full agreement as to the general development of the chapter and as to the demonstration of the extent of the evil in the logics, its roots and the steps that should be taken to cure it.

One point needs stress at once. In seeking firm names, we do not assume that any name may be wholly right, nor any wholly wrong. We introduce into language no melodrama of villains all black, nor of heroes all white. We take names always as namings: as living behaviors in an evolving world of men and things. Thus taken, the poorest and feeblest name has its place in living and its work to do, whether we can today trace backward or forecast ahead its capabilities; and the best and strongest name gains nowhere over us completed dominance.[2]

It should be plain enough that the discussions in the first chapter, as well as in those that are to follow, are not designed primarily for criticizing individual logicians. In view of the competence of the writers who are discussed, the great variety of the confusions that are found can be attributed only to something defective in the underlying assumptions that influence the writers' approach. The nature of these underlying defects will, we trust, become evident as we proceed; and we hope the specific criticisms we are compelled to make in order to exhibit the difficulty will be taken as concerned solely with the situation of inquiry, and not with personalities.[3]

October, 1944

2. In later development we shall grade the poorer namings as Cues and Characterizations; and the better and best as Specifications.
3. As a preliminary to further appraisal, one may profitably examine Max Wertheimer's discussion of the vague uses of leading terms in the traditional deductive and inductive logics, due to piecemeal dealings with "words" and "things" in blind disregard of structures. *Productive Thinking* (New York, 1945), pp. 204–205.

1.   Vagueness in Logic [1]

I

Logicians largely eschew epistemology. Thereby they save themselves much illogicality. They do not, however, eschew the assumed cosmic pattern within which the standardized epistemologies operate. They accept that pattern practically and work within it. They accept it, indeed, in such simple faith that they neglect to turn their professional skills upon it. They tolerate thereby a basic vagueness in their work. Sometimes they sense such defects in their fellow logicians, but rarely do they look closely at home, or try to locate the source of the defects found in others. Perhaps a tour of inspection by inquirers who use a different approach may indicate the source from which the trouble proceeds and suggest a different and more coherent construction.

The logical texts to which we shall give especial attention are the work of Carnap, Cohen and Nagel, Ducasse, Lewis, Morris, and Tarski. To economize space citations in our text will be made by use of initials of the authors, respectively, *C, CN, D, L, M,* and *T*.[2]

The cosmic pattern to which we have referred is one used by Peirce as an aid to many of his explorations, and commonly accepted as characteristic of him, although it does not at all repre-

---

1. This chapter is written by Bentley.
2. The titles in full of the books or papers specially examined are:
   C: Rudolf Carnap, *Introduction to Semantics,* Cambridge, 1942.
   CN: Morris R. Cohen and Ernest Nagel, *An Introduction to Logic and Scientific Method,* New York, 1934. (References are to the fourth printing, 1937.)
   D: C. J. Ducasse, "Is a Fact a True Proposition?—A Reply," *Journal of Philosophy,* XXXIX (1942), 132–136.
   L: C. I. Lewis, "The Modes of Meaning," *Philosophy and Phenomenological Research,* IV (1943), 236–249.
   M: Charles W. Morris, *Foundations of the Theory of Signs,* Chicago, 1938.

sent his basic envisionment. It introduces for logical purposes three kinds of materials: (1) men; (2) things; (3) an intervening interpretative activity, product, or medium—linguistic, symbolic, mental, rational, logical, or other—such as language, sign, sentence, proposition, meaning, truth, or thought. Its very appearance in so many variations seems of itself to suggest a vagueness in grasp of fundamentals. A crude form of it is well known in Ogden and Richards' triangle (*The Meaning of Meaning*, p. 14) presenting "thought or reference," "symbol," and "referent." Similarly we find Cohen and Nagel remarking (*CN*, p. 16) that "it seems impossible that there should be any confusion between a physical object, our 'idea' or image of it, and the word that denotes it. . . ." Lewis, claiming the authority of Peirce, holds that "the essentials of the meaning-situation are found wherever there is anything which, for some mind, stands as sign of something else" (*L*, p. 236). Carnap sets up "the speaker, the expression uttered, and the designatum of the expression," altering this at once into "the speaker, the expression, and what is referred to" (*C*, pp. 8–9), a change of phrasing which is not in the interest of clarity, more particularly as the "what is referred to" is also spoken of as that to which the speaker "intends" to refer. Morris introduces officially a "triadic relation of semiosis" correlating sign vehicle, designatum and interpreter (*M*, p. 6), sometimes substituting interpretant for interpreter (*M*, p. 3), sometimes using both interpreter and interpretant to yield what is apparently a "quadratic" instead of a "triadic" form, and always tolerating scattered meanings for his leading words.

We view all the above arrangements as varieties of a single cosmic pattern—an ancient patchwork cobbling, at times a crazy quilt. The components shift unconscionably. Anyone who has ever tried to make them lie still long enough for matter-of-fact classification has quickly found this out.

(*International Encyclopedia of Unified Science*, I, No. 2.)

T: Alfred Tarski, "The Semantic Conception of Truth and the Foundations of Semantics," *Philosophy and Phenomenological Research*, IV (1944), 341–376.

Other writings of these logicians will be cited in footnotes. To show the scope of these materials as a basis for judgment, it may be added that the seven logicians examined represent, respectively, The University of Chicago, The College of the City of New York, Columbia University, Brown University, Harvard University, The University of Chicago and The University of California.

We may not take time to show in detail here how radically different all this is from Peirce's basic procedure—our attention will be given to that at another time[3]—but since Peirce is continually quoted, and misquoted, by all parties involved, we shall pause just long enough to illuminate the issue slightly. Such words as Lewis takes from Peirce do *not* mean that minds, signs and things should be established in credal separations sharper than those of levers, fulcrums, and weights; Peirce was probing a linguistic disorder and learning fifty years ago how to avoid the type of chaos Lewis's development shows. Similarly Cohen and Nagel (*CN*, p. 117) quote a sentence from Peirce as if in their own support, when actually they depart not merely from Peirce's intent but from the very wording they quote. In his *Syllabus of Certain Topics of Logic* (1903) Peirce wrote:

> The woof and warp of all thought and all research is symbols, and the life of thought and science is the life inherent in symbols; so that it is wrong to say that a good language is *important* to good thought, merely; for it is of the essence of it.[4]

Peirce here makes flat denial of that separation of word, idea and object which Cohen and Nagel employ, and which they be-

---

3. Peirce experimented with many forms of expression. Anyone can, at will, select one of these forms. We believe the proper understanding is that which is consonant with his life-growth, from the essays of 1868–1869 through his logic of relatives, his pragmatic exposition of 1878, his theory of signs, and his endeavors to secure a functional logic. Recent papers to examine are: John Dewey, "Ethical Subject-Matter and Language," the *Journal of Philosophy*, XLII (1945) and "Peirce's Theory of Linguistic Signs, Thought, and Meaning," *ibid.*, XLIII (1946), 85; Justus Buchler, review of James Feibleman's *An Introduction to Peirce's Philosophy Interpreted as a System, ibid.,* XLIV (1947), 306; Thomas A. Goudge, "The Conflict of Naturalism and Transcendentalism in Peirce," *ibid.,* XLIV (1947), 365. See also Chapter 2, note 5, and Chapter 9, notes 61 and 62 of this volume.

It is of much interest with respect to this issue to note that in a late publication (October, 1944) Otto Neurath, the editor-in-chief of the *International Encyclopedia of Unified Science*, of which Carnap and Morris are associate editors, expressly disavows the threefold position the others have taken and thus makes an opening step towards a different development. "There is always," he writes, "a certain danger of looking at 'speaker,' 'speech,' and 'objects' as three actors . . . who may be separated. . . . I treat them as items of one aggregation. . . . The difference may be essential." (*Foundations of the Social Sciences, International Encyclopedia of Unified Science,* II, No. 1, 11.)

4. *Collected Papers of Charles Sanders Peirce,* ed. by Charles Hartshorne and Paul Weiss (Cambridge, 1931), 2.220. See also footnote 31 in Section IV of this chapter.

lieve "impossible" to confuse. The two world-views are in radical contrast.

Consider again what Peirce, cutting still more deeply, wrote
about the *sign* "lithium" in its scientific use:

> The peculiarity of this definition—or rather this precept
> that is more serviceable than a definition—is that it tells you
> what the word "lithium" denotes by prescribing what you
> are to *do* in order to gain a perceptual acquaintance with the
> object of the word.[5]

Notice the "perceptual"; notice the "object" of the "word."
There is nothing here that implies a pattern of two orders or
realms brought into connection by a third intervening thing or
sign. This is the real Peirce: Peirce on the advance—not bedded
down in the ancient swamp.

The cosmic pattern we shall employ, and by the aid of which
we shall make our tests, differs sharply from the current conventional one and is in line with what Peirce persistently sought. It
will treat the talking and talk-products or effects of man (the
namings, thinkings, arguings, reasonings, etc.) as the men themselves in action, not as some third type of entity to be inserted
between the men and the things they deal with. *To this extent* it
will be not three-realm, but two-realm: men and things. The difference in the treatment of language is radical. Nevertheless it is
not of the type called "theoretical," nor does it transmute the
men from organisms into putative "psyches." It rests in the simplest, most direct, matter-of-fact, everyday, common sense observation. Talking-organisms and things—there they are; if there,
let us study them as they come: the men talking. To make this
observation and retain it in memory while we proceed are the
only requirements we place upon readers of this first chapter.
When, however, we undertake hereafter a changed form of construction, we must strengthen the formulation under this observation, and secure a still broader observation. The revelatory
value of our present report nevertheless remains, whether such
further construction is attempted or not.

In the current logics, probably the commonest third-realm insertion between men and things is "proposition," though among
other insertions "meaning" and "thought" are at times most ac-

5. *Ibid.*, 2.330.

tive rivals for that position. In the first two logics we examine, those of Cohen and Nagel, and of Carnap, we shall give attention primarily to "proposition." Our aim will be to find out what in logic—in these logics, particularly—a proposition *is,* where by "is" we intend just some plain, matter-of-fact characterization such as any man may reasonably well be expected to offer to establish that he *knows what he is talking about* when he names the subjectmatter of his discussion. We shall ask, in other words, what sort of fact a proposition is taken to be.

In the logics, in place of an endeavor to find out whether the propositions in question are facts, we shall find a marked tendency to reverse the procedure and to declare that facts are propositions. Sometimes this is asserted openly and above board; at other times it is covert, or implied. Cohen and Nagel flatly tell us that facts are propositions—"true" propositions, this is to say. Their book (*CN*) is divided between formal logic and scientific method. Under the circumstances we shall feel at liberty to bring together passages from the two portions of the work, and we shall not apologize—formal logic or no formal logic—for a treatment of the issues of fact and proposition in common. Following this we shall examine the manner in which Carnap (*C*), though always seeming to be pushing fact behind him with the flat of his hand, makes his most critical, and possibly his most incoherent, decision—that concerning sentence and proposition—with an eye upon the very "fact" he disguises behind a tangle of meanings and designations.

The issue between proposition and fact is not minor, even though it enters as a detail in logical systematization. It is apparently an incidental manifestation of the determined effort of logicians during the past generation to supply mathematics with "foundations" through which they could dominate it and make further pretense to authority over science and fact as well. (The whole tendency might be shown to be a survival from antiquity, but we shall not go that far afield at this time.) We shall simply stress here that if fact is important to the modern world, and if logic has reached the point where it declares facts to be propositions, then it is high time to reverse the operation, and find out whether *propositions* themselves, as the logicians present them, are facts—and if so, what kind.

II

Cohen and Nagel's *Logic* (*CN*) is outstanding, not only for its pedagogical clarity but for the wide-ranging competence of its authors going far beyond the immediate requirements of a collegiate textbook. The index of their book does not list "fact," *as* "fact," but does list "facts," directing us among other things to a six-page discussion of facts and hypotheses. We are frequently told that a "fact" *is* a "proposition" that is "true." Thus (*CN*, p. 392): "The 'facts' for which every inquiry reaches out are propositions for whose truth there is considerable evidence." Notice that it is their own direct choice of expression, not some inference from it or interpretation of it, that sets our problem. If they had said, as some logicians do, that "fact" is truth, or propositional truth, that might have led us on a different course, but they make "true" the adjective and "proposition" the noun, and thus guide us to our present form of inquiry.

As the case stands, it is very much easier in their work to find out what a "proposition" is *not,* than to find out what it *is.* Propositions are:

> *not* sentences (*CN*, p. 27, No. 1)
> *not* mental acts (*CN*, p. 28, No. 4)
> *not* concrete objects, things, or events (*CN*, p. 28, No. 5).[6]

What, now, are propositions, if they are neither physical, mental, nor linguistic? It takes more ingenuity than we have to make sure; it is a strain even to make the attempt. A form of definition is, indeed, offered thus: "a *proposition* may be defined as anything which can be said to be true or false" (*CN*, p. 27). This is fairly loose language, to start with, and how it operates without involving either the mental or the linguistic is difficult to see. A variant, but not equivalent, phrasing is that a proposition is "something concerning which questions of truth and falsity are significant" (*CN*, p. 28, No. 3). Unfortunately the words "something," "anything," "said" and "significant" in these citations— just dictionary words here, and nothing more—are hard to apply

6. The Cohen-Nagel indexing differs here from the text. It distinguishes propositions from sentences, judgments, resolutions, commands and things. Compare the old "laws of thought" which (*CN*, p. 182) take modernistic dress as laws of propositions.

in the face of all the negations. We are no better off from incidental phrasings such as that a proposition is "information conveyed
by sentences" (*CN*, p. 17), or that it is "objective meaning" (*CN*,
p. 28, No. 4), or that it is what a sentence "signifies" (*CN*, p. 27).
If sentences are actually, as they tell us, just marks or sounds
having a "physical existence" on surfaces or in air waves (*CN*,
p. 27), just how such marks "convey" or "signify" anything
needs elucidation; as for "objective meaning," the words rumble
in the deepest bowels of epistemology. We also note other difficulties when we take their language literally, not impressionistically. While the proposition "must not be confused with the symbols which state it," it cannot be "*expressed* or *conveyed* without
symbols" (*CN*, p. 27); while it is not "object, thing, or event," it
may be "relation," though relations are "objects of our thought,"
and, as such, "elements or aspects of actual, concrete situations"
(*CN*, pp. 28–29); while a proposition is what is "true or false,"
there is no requirement that anyone, living or dead, "*know*
which of these alternatives is the case" (*CN*, p. 29, No. 6).[7]
    Literally and with straight-faced attention we are asked by Co-
hen and Nagel to concern ourselves with propositions that are
not physical, not mental, not linguistic, and not even something
in process of being expressed or conveyed, but that nevertheless
have a tremendous actuality wherein they possess truth and
falsity on their own account, regardless of all human participation and of any trace of human knowing. All of which is very
difficult to accomplish in the Year of Our Lord, 1944. It is even
more troublesome factually, since everything we are logically authorized to know about *facts* (apart from certain "sensations"
and other dubieties residing on the far side of the logical tracks)
must be acquired from such "propositions." Our "knowledge,"
even, the authors tell us, "is *of* propositions" (*CN*, p. 29); and
what a proposition *that* is, unless the "of" by some strange choice
is a synonym of "through" or "by means of."[8]

  7. Note that a proposition is first "not an object," then that it is an "object of
     thought," finally that it is an "aspect of the concrete," and that the first asser-
     tion and its dyadic belying all occur in a single paragraph. What the writers
     "really mean" is much less important logically than what they say (what they
     are able to say under their manner of approach) when they are manifestly
     doing their best to say what they mean.
  8. The word "knowledge," incidentally, is unindexed, but we learn that it "in-
     volves abstraction" (*CN*, p. 371); that it does not cover merely the collecting
     of facts (*CN*, p. 215); that true knowledge cannot be restricted to objects ac-

Supplementing their position that facts are propositions—while propositions are, at the same time, stripped of all the characteristics research workers since Galileo would accept as factual—Cohen and Nagel offer a free account of "facts" (*CN*, pp. 217–218). This, however, clears up nothing. They note "different senses" of "fact" which they proceed at once to render as "distinct things" "denoted" by the word. Apparently they do not intend either four different dictionary meanings of the word, as "senses" would imply, or four distinct "classes of objects," as "denotes" would require (*CN*, p. 31), but something uncertainly between the two. The passage in question reads:

> We must, obviously, distinguish between the different senses of "fact." It denotes at least four distinct things.
> 1 . . . certain discriminated elements in sense perception. . . .
> 2 . . . the propositions which *interpret* what is given to us in sense experience.
> 3 . . . propositions which truly assert an invariable sequence or conjunction of characters. . . .
> 4 . . . those things existing in space or time, together with the relations between them, in virtue of which a proposition is true.

Two of these four do not enter as propositions at all. The other two use the word "propositions" but involve interpretations and technical assertion of types which evidently run far into the "mental" region from which "proposition" is excluded. Whether we have here "senses" or "classes of objects," some kind of organization of the "things" should be offered if the passage is to have any logical relevance whatever. Such organization is conspicuously lacking,[9] and the total effect of the passage is to take advantage of the very confusion that so greatly needs to be cleared away.

---

tually existing (*CN*, p. 21); and that many open questions remain as to immediate knowings (*CN*, p. 5)—nothing of which is significantly treated.

9. Casual comments do not organize. As to the first item, we learn: "All observation appeals ultimately to certain *isolable* elements in sense experience. We search for such elements because concerning them *universal agreement among all people* is obtainable" (italics for "isolable" are theirs, the others ours). Again, a fact in the second or third sense "states" a fact in the fourth. And a fact in the fourth sense is not "true"; it just "is" (*CN*, p. 218). Separately such comments are plausible. Together they scatter like birdshot.

We get no help by going back to the word "meaning," for meaning is as badly off as "proposition" is. Some logicians employ the word heavily—we shall note one of them later—but in the present work, so far as the index indicates, the word merely yields a change of phrasing. The "meaning of a proposition" is something we must know before deciding whether it is "true" (CN, p. 9); no matter how formal our implication, it must not ignore "the entire meaning" (CN, p. 12); universal propositions have meanings that require "at least *possible* matters of fact" (CN, p. 43).

Nor do we get any help when we try the words "true" and "false." No direct discussion of "true" has been observed by us in the book. It enters as the essential "is-ness" of propositions: "if a proposition is true it must always be true" (CN, p. 29). Apparently neither truth nor proposition can survive without an eye on the other, but when emphasis is desired we hear of "true in fact" (as CN, p. 7, p. 76), so that even the axioms must have their truth empirically established (CN, p. 132). This is the only variety of "true" we have noticed, even though we are told that "truths" may be proved out of other "truths." We have the curious situation (1) that facts are propositions; (2) that propositions are truth (or falsity) assertions; (3) that under pressure "true" turns out to be "true in fact"—just like that, no more, no less—and "false," no doubt, the same.

We are about half through with our exhibit, but we shall omit the rest of it. It all comes to the same thing. A word is officially introduced and assigned a task. Turn around once, and when you look back it is doing something else. You do not even need to turn around; just let your direct gaze slip, and the word is off on the bias. Cohen and Nagel believe their logic to be in tune with the infinite, this being a standard convention among logicians. "Its principles," they say, "are inherently applicable because they are concerned with ontological[10] traits of utmost generality"

---

10. More recently, however, Professor Nagel has written a paper, "Logic without Ontology," which will be found in the volume *Naturalism and the Human Spirit* (1944), edited by Y. H. Krikorian. Here he advances to an operational position approximating that of the instrumental logic of the nineteen-twenties, which he at that time assailed in a paper entitled "Can Logic Be Divorced from Ontology?" (*Journal of Philosophy*, XXVI [1929], 705–712), written in confidence that "nature must contain the prototype of the logical" and that "relations are discovered as an integral factor in nature." Also of great inter-

(*CN*, p. v). We, on the contrary, believe their "principles" are inherently defective because they are concerned with verbal traits of the utmost triviality. The practical work of discussing evidence and proof is admirably done in their work. Theoretical construction defaults altogether. But the very deficiencies are valuable—if one will but look at them—as clues to the kind of research that, under our present manner of examination, is most important for the immediate future.

III

When Professor Nagel reviewed Carnap's *Introduction to Semantics* (C) and came to its "propositions," he felt impelled to shake his head sadly at such "hypostatic Platonic entities." [11] Now Carnap's "propositions" may be more *spirituelles* than Cohen-Nagel's—which are hopefully of the earth earthy, even though nothing of the physical, mental, linguistic or communicative is allowed them—but what little difference there is between the two types is one of philosophical convention rather than of character. Nevertheless, such is logic that we are not greatly surprised, while Nagel is grieving over Carnap, to find Carnap placing Cohen-Nagel in the lead among his fellow-travelers, with evidence attached (C, p. 236).

Fact, in Carnap's work, is farther away around the corner than it is in Cohen-Nagel's. It is something logic is supposed never quite to reach, but only to skim past at the edges, with perhaps a little thought-transference on the way. It has a sort of surrogate in "absolute concepts" which are to be recognized as being present when all words agree, and which therefore, somewhat surprisingly, are said to be totally unaffected by language (C, pp. 41–42; p. 89, Convention 17–1). Nevertheless, when Carnap distinguishes proposition from sentence he does it with a hazy eye upon a certain unity of organization which must some way or other, some time or other, be secured between the formal and the factual.

---

est for comparison is his paper "Truth and Knowledge of the Truth" (*Philosophy and Phenomenological Research*, V [1944], 50–68), especially the distinction as it is sharply drawn (p. 68).
11. The *Journal of Philosophy*, XXXIX (1942), 471.

In his thirteen-page terminological appendix which cries "Peace, peace" where there is no peace, Carnap notes two main uses—two "different concepts," he says—for the word "proposition" (C, p. 235). He distills these out of a welter of logical confusions he finds well illustrated in Bertrand Russell. These outstanding uses are first "for certain expressions" and then "for their designata." His elaboration—we cite meticulously, and in full, since this is the only way to make the exhibit plain—runs:

> 'Proposition.' The term is used for two different concepts, namely for certain expressions (I) and for their designata (II).
>
> I: As 'declarative sentence.' Other terms: 'sentence,'* 'statement' (Quine), 'formula' (Bernays).
>
> II*: As "that which is expressed (significd, formulated, represented, designated) by a (declarative) sentence" (§§ 6 and 18). Other terms: 'Satz an sich' (Bolzano), 'Objectiv' (A. Meinong), 'state of affairs' (Wittgenstein), 'condition.'

The asterisks are used by Carnap to mark the terminology he himself adopts. In I, he states he will use the word "sentence" for what others might call declarative sentence, statement, or formula. In II*, he adopts the word "proposition" for whatever it is he there sets forth. 'Sentence' (I) and 'Proposition' (II) together make up what the man in the street would call a sentence: roughly, this is to say, an expression of meaning in words. A reader who merely wants a whiff of characterization while the semantic march proceeds may be satisfied with the passage as we have cited it. It offers, however, serious difficulty to the man who wants to grasp what is involved before he goes farther. We propose to take this passage apart and find out what is in it; for nothing of the semantic construction is safe if this is defective. Since Carnap offers us "pure" semantics—free from all outer influence, practical or other—*we shall give it "pure" linguistic analysis, staying right among its sentences,* and dragging nothing in from the outside. He is meticulous about his definitions, his theorems and his conventions; we shall be meticulous about the verbal materials out of which he builds them. This will take much space, but no other course is possible. One great hindrance is the way he slips one word into the place of another, presumably in synonymic substitution, but usually with so much wavering of allusion that delivery becomes uncertain. Such shifting verbal sands make progress slow. For our immediate purposes, we shall employ *italics* to display precisely the wordings we quote as we dissect them.

The word "proposition," if used without quotation marks, would be an "expression (sign, word)." Supplied with single quotation marks—thus '*Proposition*'—it becomes "a name for that expression . . . in the metalanguage for that language" (*C*, p. 237). Having written down '*Proposition*,' he then proceeds: *The term is used for.* . . . Here "term" is an evasive word, unindexed, unspecified and undiscussed in his text. (It, together with certain other evasive words, will be given separate attention later.) In the present passage it represents either "proposition" or '*proposition*' or possibly a mixture of both. Look at it, and it should represent the latter. Read it, and you will think it represents the former. We shall risk no opinion, more particularly because of the vagueness of what follows.[12] Taking the *is used for,* however, we may venture to guess we have here a substitute for "names" (as the word "names" is used in *C*, p. 237), with an implication of variety in namings, and this evasively with respect to "current" uses on the one side, and names as they "ought to be" used on the other. Our criticism here may look finical, but it is not. When the word "term" is used in a vital passage in a logic, we have a right to know exactly how it is being used.

If we add the next three words, the declaration thus far seems to be to the effect that the name of the expression, or perhaps the

12. A competent critic, well acquainted with Carnap, and wholly unsympathetic to our procedure, attacks the above interpretation as follows: Since Carnap (*C*, p. 230, line 16) writes "Concept. The word is. . . . ," it is evident that to Carnap '*concept*' is here a word, not a name for a word; it is evident further that under even a half-way cooperative approach the reader should be able to carry this treatment forward five pages to the case of '*proposition*,' accepting this latter frankly as "word" not "term," and ceasing to bother. Unfortunately for our critic this course would make Carnap's treatment in both instances violate his prescription and thus strengthen our case. All we have done is to exhibit an instance of vagueness, drawing no inference here, and leaving further discussion to follow. To consider and adjust are (1) proposition-as-fact; (2) "proposition" as a current logical word; (3) 'proposition' in the metalanguage; (I) Carnap's prescription for 'sentence'; (II) Carnap's prescription for 'proposition'; (*a*) factual adequacy for 'sentence'; (*b*) factual adequacy for 'proposition'; (*c*) general coherence of the textual development within the full syntactic-semantic-pragmatic construction. It is this last with which we are now concerned. Partial or impressionistically opinionative analyses are not likely to be pertinent.

expression itself, names variously, for various people, *two different concepts.*

The word "concept" dominates this sentence and produces its
flight from simplicity and its distortion. What follows is worse.
We face something undecipherable and without clue. Balanced
against "concept" in some unknown form of organization we
find *certain expressions (I) and . . . their designata (II).* Here
concept introduces (presents? represents? applies to? names?
designates? includes? covers?) certain expressions *and* their (certain) designata. If he had said in simple words that "proposition"
is currently used in two ways, one of which he proposes to call
'sentence,' and the other, 'proposition,' the reader's attention
might have been directed to certain features of his account, in
which something factually defective would have been noted.[13]
What concerns us, however, is not this defect but his elaborate
apparatus of terminological obscurity, and to this we shall restrict ourselves. Holding for the moment to the three words
"concept," "expression" and "designatum," and noting that the
"certain" designata here in question are "propositions," we turn
to his introductory table (C, p. 18) in which he offers his "terminology of designata." Applying our attention to this we are led to
report that for Carnap:

    1. concepts are one variety of designata, the other varieties
being individuals and propositions;

    2. designata enter as entities, with which, so far as we are
told, they coincide in extension;

    3. expressions (signs, terms), in the functions they perform
in the *Semantics,* are not entities, but are balanced theoretically over against entities; they live their lives in a separate
column of the table, the whole distinction between syntactics
and semantics resting in this separation of the columns;

    4. propositions, though entities, are most emphatically not

13. Carnap reports his distinctions I and II as appearing in the literature along
with mixed cases (C, p. 235). His illustrations of his II, and of the mixed
cases, fit fairly well. However, the wordings of Baldwin, Lalande, Eisler,
Bosanquet, etc., cited for I, though they have some superficial verbal similarity, would not come out as at all "the same," if expanded in their full expressive settings, *viz.:* American, French, German and British. Certainly none
would come out "the same as" Carnap's completely meaningless "expression" which, nevertheless, expresses all that men take it to express.

a variety of concept; they are collateral to the whole group of concepts;

5. despite (3) and (4) the important terminological passage before us (from *C*, p. 235) reads: *for . . . concepts, namely, for certain expressions . . . and*[14] *for their designata . . . ;*

6. there is a curious shift of phrasing between the paragraphs of our citation (*C*, p. 235), where "the term" is the expressed or implied subject for each sentence: in the introductory statement it is used "for" concepts, in I "as" an expression, and in II "as" a designatum; in loose colloquial phrasing such shifts are familiar, but where the whole technique of a logic is at stake they make one wonder what is being done.[15]

There is a marked difference in allusion and in verbal "feel" between "entity" and "designatum" in the above procedure, so that a report on the extension and intension of these two words would be helpful. Such a report, however, would require adjust-

14. Carnap, if memory is correct, once displayed five varieties of "and," to which Bühler added two more. One wonders whether this "and" is one of them. Another illustration, an unforgettable one, of his libertine way with little connectives is his impressive advance from "not" to "especially not" in setting up the status of "formal" definition (*International Encyclopedia of Unified Science*, I, No. 3, 16).

15. Again, the welcome comment of a critic unsympathetic to our procedure is of interest. As to (3) he asserts that since expressions consist of sign-events and sign-designs, the former being individuals and the latter properties, and since both individuals and properties are entities, therefore expressions are themselves entities. We have no breath of objection to such a treatment; only if this *is* the view of the *Semantics*, why does the classification (p. 18) conflict? Or, alternatively, if the great technical advance rests on separating expressions from entities, what does it mean when we are told in answer to a first simple question that, *of course*, expressions *are* entities too? As to (4) and (5) our critic in a similar vein asserts that for Carnap propositions are properties of expressions, that properties are concepts, and hence that propositions *are* concepts. Here again, one asks: If so, why does Carnap classify them differently in his table? Dissecting our critic's development of his thesis we find it to contain the following assertions:

1. *Being a proposition* is a property of entities.
2. *Being a proposition* is therefore a concept.
3. The *property* (being a proposition) is named 'proposition.'
4. The *property* (being a proposition) is not a proposition.
From which we can hardly avoid concluding:
5. That which is named 'proposition' is not a proposition.
We leave these to the reader's private consideration, our own attention being occupied with the one central question of whether double-talk, rather than straight-talk, is sanitary in logic.

ments to the word "object," which is one of the vaguest in Carnap's text—an adjustment that we may well believe would be wholly impracticable for him under his present methods. It would be helpful also, as we shall see, if we could distinguish the cases in which a concept enters as an "entity" from those in which it is used as a sign or expression. In the present instance we have already found much room for suspicion that it is used, in part, "as" a sign and not "for" a designatum.[16] It seems to have never occurred to him that the "concept" that runs trippingly throughout the text requires terminological stability with respect to the "concept" that enters among the materials, objects or objectives, of his inquiry.

The case being as it is, our report on the nineteen-word sentence comprising the first paragraph of the citation must be that it tells us that a certain expression, or its name, is used to name concepts which in their turn either are or name certain expressions *and* their designata, although neither the expressions nor their designata are officially concepts.

Having thus made his approach to "proposition" in a characteristic mixture of allusions, he now turns to the distinctions he himself intends to display. Earlier (*C,* p. 14), and as a legitimate labor-saving device, he had said that the word "sentence" was to stand for "declarative sentence" throughout his treatise. His desire and aim is to study the coherence of certain types of connective signs (calculus) in such declarative sentences in separation from the substance of the declaration (semantics). To do this he splits the common or vulgar "sentence" of the man in the street into two separate "things." This sort of "thing-production" is, of course, the outstanding feature of his entire logical attitude. The coherence-aspect now presents itself as the first "thing" (I), even though under his preliminary tabulation (as we have already seen) it is not listed among the "entities." The "meaning" portion, or substance of the declaration (II), is no longer to be called "sentence" under any circumstance whatever,[17] but is to be named

16. Our phraseology in the text above is appalling to us, but since we here are reflecting Carnap it seems irremedial. The indicated reform would be to abandon the radical split between sign-user and sign with respect to object, as we shall do in our further development.

17. However, before he concludes his terminological treatment he introduces (*C,* p. 236) certain sentences that he says are "in our terminology sentences in semantics, not in syntax." This is not so much a contradictory usage as it is an illustration of the come-easy, go-easy dealing with words.

'proposition.' These names, it is to be understood, themselves belong in the metalanguage as it applies to the object language. As before, we shall not argue about the merits of the position he takes but confine ourselves to the question: how well, how coherently, does he develop it?

Since the sentence in question is a declarative sentence, one might reasonably expect that any "proposition" carved out of it would be described as "that which is declared." It is not so described. Carnap shifts from the word "declare" to the word "express," and characterizes 'proposition' as *that which is expressed.* "Expressions" (inclusive of "sentences") had previously, however, been separated from meaningfulness, when "meaning" was closely identified as "proposition." (We shall later display this in connection with "language" and with "meaning.") Despite this, the verb "expressed" is now used to establish that very meaningfulness of which the noun "expression" has been denied the benefit. Thus the word "express" openly indulges in double-talk between its noun and verb forms.[18] For any logic such a procedure would rate as incoherent. Yet before we recover from it, whether to make outcry or to forgive, we find ourselves in worse. We at once face four synonymic (or are they?) substitutes for *expressed,* namely: *signified, formulated, represented, designated.* Each of these words breathes a different atmosphere. "Signified" has an internally mentalistic feel, sucking up the "signs," so to speak, into the "significance"; "formulated" wavers between linguistic embodiment and rationalistic authority; "designated" has its origins, at least, among physical things, no matter how it wanders; "represented" holds up its face for any passing bee to kiss that is not satisfied with the other pretty word-flowers in the bouquet.[19]

18. The source of tolerance for such contradictions is well enough known to us. It lies in the reference of the "meanings" to a mental actor behind the scenes. This is apart, however, from the immediate purpose of discussion at the present stage. Consider "adequacy" as intention (C, p. 53); also "sign" as involving intent (*International Encyclopedia of Unified Science,* I, No. 3, p. 4; and similarly C, p. 8).

19. Alonzo Church, referring to this passage in its original magazine appearance, holds that the charge of inconsistency against Carnap's switch from "designation" to "expression" fails because the various alternatives Carnap suggests for "expression" refer, partially at least, to the views of others. This, at any rate, is the way we understand him. Church's words are: "The charge of inconsistency to Carnap because he says 'officially' that a sentence *designates* a proposition but on page 235 writes of sentences as *expressing* propositions

At this point we should probably pause for a discussion of "designation." Designation is not a chance visitor, but a prominent inmate of the system. As such it certainly ought not to be tossed around as one among several casual words. Neither it nor any of its derivatives, however, has gained place in the terminological appendix. Full discussion would take much time and space. We shall here confine ourselves to a few hints. At its original entrance (C, p. 9) the status of designatum is so low that it is merely "what is referred to," possibly something outside the logic altogether. We have seen it gain the status of "what is expressed" in substitution for "what is declared" in a fast company of "meanings" that run far beyond the range of the usual official identification of meaning with designatum. Designation is sometimes a "relation" of a type that can "apply" (C, p. 49) to expressions; again "having a certain designatum" may be "a semantical property of an expression";[20] still again it tells what the speaker *intends* to refer to (C, p. 8); and there are times when Carnap inspects an open question as to whether the designata of sen-

---

(along with a list of alternatives to the verb 'express') fails, because it is obvious that in the latter passage Carnap is describing the varied views of others as well as his own" (The *Journal of Symbolic Logic*, X [1945], p. 132). The situation here seems to be about as follows: (1) Carnap's "designate" and "express" do not separate into an earlier official and a later casual or descriptive use, but both appear in a single passage of eight lines (C, p. 235) which is as "official" as anything in his text, and which we have already cited in full. (2) The pseudosynonyms for "express" are not attributed to other writers, but are run in without comment apparently as current usages. (3) In the succeeding page and a half of discussion he gives to other writers only one of these words, namely "represent," enters as employed by a specific other writer—in this case by Bosanquet (compare note 13 above). (4) The alternatives for "express" do not appear in the portion of the passage dealing with 'sentence,' but strangely enough in that portion dealing with 'proposition,' that is to say with "that which is expressed by a sentence." (5) Even if Church were correct in identifying here "the varied views of others," the point would be irrelevant for use as keystone in a charge of default in proof; our passage in question might be called irrelevant or flippant, but certainly never a determining factor. (6) The charge in our text is one of abundant chaos in Carnap's linguistic foundations, and never of a particular inconsistency. We strongly recommend the careful examination of the texts of Carnap and Church alongside our own in this particular disagreement, and equally of the other positions Church attributes to us in comparison with the positions we actually take in our examination. Only through hard, close work in this field can the full extent of the linguistic chaos involved become evident.
20. Rudolf Carnap, *Formalization of Logic* (Cambridge, 1943), pp. 3–4.

tences may not be "possible facts . . . or rather thoughts" (C, p. 53). *Officially* he decides that the designatum of a sentence (I) is a proposition (II*), much as the designatum of an object-name is an object (C, p. 45; p. 50 Des-Prop; p. 54; p. 99). Suppose the proposition is the designatum of the sentence; suppose the proposition (as we shall note later) may be called "true" as well as the sentence (which latter is officially what is "true" or "false") (C, p. 26, p. 90, p. 240); and suppose that "true" is built up around designation. It would then appear that the proposition which "is" the designatum of its own sentence must have somewhere beyond it certain sub-designata which it sub-designates directly instead of by way of its master (or is it servant?) sentence. This is far too intricately imaginative for any probing here. It looks plausible, but whether it makes sense or not we would not know.

The three-realm pattern of organization Carnap uses includes speakers (I), expressions (II) and designata (III). It is now in desperate state. We are not here arguing its falsity—we shall take care of that in another place—but only showing the *incoherence it itself achieves.* Expressions (II) are meaningful or not, but on any show-down they presumptively take speakers (I) to operate them. The meaning of an expression (II) is a designatum (III), but soon it becomes in a special case an expression-meaning that has not moved out of realm II. This designatum (as object) in II is presumptively given justification by comparison with an object in III, although the object in III is so void of status of its own in the logic (other than "intuitively" nominal) that it itself might do better by seeking its own justification through comparison with the proposition-object in II.

The soil in which such vegetation grows is "language" as Carnap sees it. Here he seems to have become progressively vaguer in recent years.[21] We found Cohen-Nagel asserting flatly that language consists of physical things called "signs." Carnap proceeds to similar intent part of the time, but differently the rest of the time, and always avoids plain statement. Consider the first sentence of his first chapter (C, p. 3):

21. However, to his credit, he seems to have largely dropped or smoothed over the older jargon of physical language, physical thing-language, and observable thing-predicates (as in *International Encyclopedia of Unified Science,* I, No. 1, 52).

> A *language,* as it is usually understood, is a system of
> sounds, or rather of the habits of producing them by
> the speaking organs, for the purpose of communicating with
> other persons, i.e., of influencing their actions, decisions,
> thoughts, etc.

Does "usually" give *his* understanding? If the sounds are physical, in what sense are they in system? Can physics set up and discuss such a "system"? How do "habits" [22] of producing differ
from "producing," especially when "speaking organs" are specified as the producers? Does the "i.e." mean that "communicating" is always an "influencing"? What range have the words
"purpose," "actions," "decisions," "thoughts"? Sounds are perhaps physical, habits physiological, communications and influencings broadly behavioral, and the other items narrowly "psychical." May not, perhaps, any one of these words—or, indeed,
still more dangerously, the word "person" under some specialized stress its user gives it—destroy the presumable import of
many of the others?

Even if we accept the cited sentence as a permissible opening,
surely better development should at once follow. Instead we find
nothing but wavering words. We are told (C, pp. 4–5) that utterances may be analyzed into "smaller and smaller parts," that "ultimate units" of expressions are called "signs," that expressions
are finite sequences of signs and that expressions may be "meaningful or not." We are not told whether signs are strictly physical
sounds or marks, or whether they are products, habits or purposes. Later on (C, p. 18) we find sign, term and expression used
as equivalents. We suspect as the work proceeds that the word
"sign" is used mostly where physical implications are desired,
and the word "term" mostly for the logical, while the word "expression" is waveringly intermediate—the precision-status being
more that of campaign oratory than of careful inquiry. When the
accent mark on a French *é* is viewed as a separate sign from the *e*
without the accent (C, p. 5), "sign" seems clearly physical. When
expression is "any finite sequence of signs," "sign" is certainly

22. In an earlier paper (*ibid.,* I, No. 3, 3) such "habits" were called "dispositions," and we were told both that language is a system of dispositions and
   that its elements are sounds or written marks. Whether Carnap regards dispositions as sounds, or sounds as dispositions, he does not make clear.

physical if the word "physical" means anything at all. Still, an expression may be a name, a compound or a sentence (C, p. 25, p. 50). And when an expression expresses a proposition, what are we to say? Again the issue is evaded. We get no answer, and surely we are not unreasonable in wanting to find out before we get too far along. Not knowing, not being able to find out—this is why we have here to search into the text so painfully.

All in all, the best that we are able to report of Carnap's procedure is that 'proposition' or proposition appears as or names an entity, this entity being the certain meaning or designatum that is meant or designated by a non-designating and meaningless, though nevertheless declarative, sentence, representing, whether internally or externally, certain other designata besides itself, and manipulated through a terminology of "concepts" under which it at times is, and at times is not, itself a concept.

It is difficult to tell just where the most vicious center of terminological evil lies in Carnap's procedure. Probably, however, the dubious honor should go to "concept," a word that is all things to all sentences. We shall exhibit a few samples of his dealings with this word, and then quote what he once said in a moment when he stopped to think about it—which is not the case in the book in hand. The word, as he uses it, derives, of course, from Begriff, which among its addicts on its native soil can without fatigue insert itself a dozen times on a page for any number of pages. In the present book (C) "concept" is employed in thirteen of the thirty headings of the constructive sections lying between the introductory chapter and the appendix, without in any case having determinable significance. The appendix (C, p. 230) lists three types of current uses for the word "concept": (1) psychological; (2) logical; (3) "as term or expression." The first and last of these uses he rejects. Among variations in the logical use he accepts the "widest," using asterisks (see C, p. 229 n.) to make the word "concept" cover properties, relations, functions, all three.

One could show without difficulty that Carnap's own practical use of "concept" is heavily infected with the psychological quality, despite his disavowal of this use; one can likewise show that he frequently uses the word for "term" or "expression," and this perhaps as often as he uses it for some form of "entity." We find him (C, p. 41) treating concepts as being "applicable" to certain attributes in almost precisely the same way that in another passage (*C*, p. 88) he makes terms "apply."²³ On pages 88 and 89 all semantical concepts are based on relations; some concepts are relations, and some are attributed to expressions only, not to designata. We get glimpses of such things as "intuitive concepts" (*C*, p. 119) and heavy use of "absolute concepts" of which a word later. Endless illustrations of incoherent use could be given, but no instance in which he has made any attempt to orient this word-of-all-work either to language, to thing, or to mind.

The passage in which he once stopped for an instant to think about the word may be found in his paper "Logical Foundations of the Unity of Science,"²⁴ published a few years before the present book. He wrote:

> Instead of the word 'term' the word 'concept' could be taken, which is more frequently used by logicians. But the word 'term' is more clear, since it shows that we mean signs, e.g., words, expressions consisting of words, artificial symbols, etc., of course with the meaning they have in the language in question.

The vagueness of his position could hardly be more vividly revealed. It is as if a microscopist could not tell his slide from the section he mounted on it, and went through a lot of abracadabra about metaslides to hide his confusion. Not until the words "concept" and "term" are clarified will a metalanguage be able to yield clear results.

"Term" runs "concept" a close second. One finds an interesting illustration (*C*, p. 89) where Carnap finds it convenient to use "the same term" for a certain "semantical concept" and for its corresponding "absolute concept." He goes on to remark, though without correcting his text, that what he really meant was "the same word," not "the same term," but in Convention 17−1 he

23. An interesting case of comparable confusion (superficial, however, rather than malignant) appears in the word "function," which is listed (*C*, p. 18) among the "entities," although "expressional function" and "sentential function" (both non-entitative) appear in the accompanying text. Terminological discussion (*C*, pp. 232−233) strongly favors the entitative use but still fails to star it as Carnap's own. The starring gives endorsement to the expressive uses cited above. In place of expression and entity consider, for comparison's sake, inorganic and organic. Then in place of a function among entities we might take a rooster among organisms. Carnap's "expressional function" can now be compared to something like "inorganic rooster."

24. *International Encyclopedia of Unified Science*, I, No. 1 (1938), 49.

goes back to "term" again. Thus a single "term" is authorized by convention to designate (if "designate" is the proper word) two meanings (if "meanings" is the proper word) at a critical stage of inquiry. Carnap considers the ambiguity harmless. Indeed he says "there is no ambiguity." The use of an admittedly wrong word in his convention was apparently the lesser of two evils he was facing, since if one takes the trouble to insert what he says is the right word (*viz.*, word) for what he says is the wrong word (*viz.*, term) in the convention and then skeletonizes the assertion, one will somewhat surprisingly find oneself told that "a word . . . will be applied . . . without reference to a language system."[25] Similarly a term may apply both to attributes and to predicates that designate attributes, i.e., both to designata and to expressions (C, p. 42).

For a mixture of terms and concepts his defense of his "multiple use" of term (C, p. 238) is worth study. A "radical term" may "designate" relations between propositions or relations between attributes (both cases being of "absolute concepts"), or between sentences or between predicates (these cases being "semantical"). In other words every possible opening is left for evasive manipulation.

"Definition" gets into trouble along with "term" and "concept." It enters, not by positive assertion, but by suggestion, as a matter of abbreviations, equalities and equivalences (C, p. 17). However, we find concepts that are entities being defined as liberally as terms that are expressions (C, p. 33). The absolute concepts are heavily favored in this way (C, p. 41, p. 90). One may even seek definitions to be in agreement with intuitive concepts for which only vague explanations have been given (C, p. 119).

---

25. Carnap has, as is well known, a standing alibi in all such cases as this. It is that he is not talking about an actual language, but about an abstract system of signs with meanings. In the present case there would seem to be all the less excuse for vacillating between word and term. If the distinctions are valid, and are intended to be adhered to, exact statement should not be difficult. It is, of course, understood that the general problem of the use of "word" and "term" is not being raised by us here; no more is the general problem of the entry of "fact," whether by "convention" or not, into a logic. For further comparison, and to avoid misinterpretation, the text of Convention 17–1 follows: "A term used for a radical semantical property of expressions will be applied in an absolute way (i.e. without reference to a language system) to an entity u if and only if every expression $\mathfrak{A}$, which designates u in any semantical system S has that semantical property in S. Analogously with a semantical relation between two or more expressions."

So many experiences has definition had *en route* that, when the calculus is reached, the assurance (C, p. 157) that definition may be employed there also seems almost apologetic.[26]

An excellent illustration of the status of many of the confusions we have been noting—involving also the mystery of "object" in the logic—is found in the case of Function (C, pp. 232–233) a brief notice of which is given in footnote 23 on page 43. Here a certain designatum is referred to as "strictly speaking, the entity determined by the expression." The word "determined" interests us, but is difficult to trace back to its den. The "entity" is what gets determined. Surely the "expression," taken *physically* as a sign, cannot be the determiner, nor can it, as a word of record, label, or tag, have initiative assigned it. Designation appears frequently as a "relation" between entity and expression, but we are told nothing to indicate that the expression is the active, and the entity the passive, member of the "relation." Back in its hide-out a "determiner" doubtless lurks, as soul, or intellect, or mind, or will—it can make little difference which, so long as something can be summoned for the task. Our objection at the moment is not to such a soul—that issue lying beyond our immediate range—but to the bad job it does; for if the *expression,* with or without such a proxy, determines the *entity,* it gives the lie to the whole third-realm scheme of relational construction for expression, sentence, proposition and designatum.

We have written at length about expression and concept, and briefly about term, designation, definition and object. The word "relation" (presumptively entitative) is found in suspicious circumstances, similar to those of concept and the others. Thus (C, p. 49) you can "apply" a relation to a system. The word "meaning" deserves further mention as it is involved with all the rest. Most frequently "meaning" stands for designatum (C, p. 245); wherever a "sentence," as in the calculus, appears as meaningless, it is because designation (as "meaning") is there excluded from consideration. However, if one examines the passages in which meaning is casually spoken of, and those in which sense or meaning is brought into contact with truth-conditions (C, p. 10, p. 22, p. 232), the case is not so simple. In *Formalization of Logic* (p. 6) it occurs to Carnap that he might let pure semantics

26. Again, we are not assailing Carnap's actual research into linguistic connectivities. The point is the importance of talking coherently about them.

abstract from "the meaning of descriptive signs" and then let syntax abstract from "the meaning of all signs, including the logical ones." This manner of observation could be carried much farther, and with profit, since one of the first practical observations one makes on his work is that six or eight layers of "meaning" could be peeled apart in his materials, and that he is highly arbitrary in establishing the two or three sharp lines he does.

We have said nothing about "true" in Carnap's procedure, for there is almost nothing that can be said dependably. He introduces it for "sentences" (and for classes of sentences), but takes the privilege at times of talking of the truth of "propositions," despite the sharp distinctions he has drawn between the two on the lines we have so elaborately examined (C, p. 26, p. 90; and compare p. 240 on "deliberate ambiguity"). He has C-true, L-true, F-true, and 'true,' distinguished (and legitimately so, if consistently organized and presented); he might have many more.

The situation may be fairly appraised in connection with "interpretation," an important word in the treatise. Leaving pragmatics for others, Carnap considers syntax and semantics as separate, with an additional "indispensable" distinction between factual and logical truth *inside* the latter (C, p. vii). A semantical system is a system of rules; it is an interpreted system ("interpreted by rules," p. 22); and it may be an interpretation of a calculus (p. 202). It also turns out, though, that interpretation is not a semantical system but a "relation" between semantical systems and calculi, belonging "neither to semantics nor to syntax" (C, p. 202, p. 240).

Fact does not enter by name until the work is more than half finished (C, p. 140), except for slight references to "factual knowledge" (C, p. 33, p. 81) and possibly for a few rare cases of presumptively positive use of "object" such as we have already mentioned (C, p. 54). However, it has a vociferous surrogate in "absolute concepts," the ones that are "not dependent upon language" and merely require "certain conditions with respect to truth-values" (C, p. 35)—"conveniences" (C, p. 90)—which are able to be *much less important* than the L- and C-concepts and, at the same time, to serve chiefly as *a basis* for them (C, p. 35).

We repeat once more that the significance we stress in our inquiry lies entirely in the interior incoherence of current logical statement it exhibits. While (as we have intimated) we believe the source of such incoherence is visible behind its smoke-screens, the weight of our argument does not rest upon our opinion in this respect.

We find it further only fair to say of Carnap that in many respects he is becoming less assertive and more open to the influence of observation than he has been in the past. He recognizes now, for example (C, p. 18), something "not quite satisfactory" in his namings for his designata. He is aware that his basic distinction between logical and descriptive signs (C, p. vii, p. 56, p. 59, p. 87) needs further inquiry. He sees an *open* problem as to extensional and intensional language systems (C, p. 101, p. 118). He notes the "obviously rather vague" entry of his L-terms (C, p. 62). At one point he remarks that his whole structure (and with it all his terminology) may have to change (C, p. 229). More significant still, he has a moment when he notes that "even the nature of propositions" is still controversial (C, p. 101).

If he should come to question similarly his entitative concentrations he might have a better outlook, but in his latest publication he still feels assured that certain critical semantical terms can be "exactly defined on the basis of the concept of entities satisfying a sentential function," and that "having a certain designatum is a semantical property of an expression," [27] though just how he would build those two remarks together into a coherent whole we do not know. His confidence that his own semantics is "the fulfillment of the old search for a logic of meaning which had not been fulfilled before in any precise and satisfactory way" (C, p. 249) needs modification, it would thus appear, under the various qualifications we have considered.

IV

Let us next glance at three specialized treatments of proposition, meaning and designation: those of Morris, Ducasse and Lewis.[28]

27. *Formalization of Logic*, p. xi, p. 3.
28. Procedure should be like that of entomologists, who gather specimen bugs by the thousands to make sure of their results. It should also be like that of engineers getting the "bugs" (another kind, it is true) out of machinery. Space considerations permit the exhibit of only a few specimens. But we believe these specimens are significant. We trust they may stimulate other "naturalists" to do field work of their own. Compare the comment of Karl Menger

Morris attaches himself to Carnap. His contribution (apart from the verbal chaos of his semiotic) lies in the "pragmatics" he has added to the earlier "semantics" and "syntactics" (M, p. 6, p. 8) to yield the three "irreducibles," the "equally legitimates" (M, p. 53) that form his rotund trinity. Carnap gratefully accepts this offering with qualifications (C, p. 9). It enables him to toss all such uncomfortable issues as "gaining and communicating knowledge" to the garbage bucket of pragmatics, while himself pursuing unhampered his "logical analysis" (C, p. 250) in the ivory tower of syntactics and in the straggling mud huts of semantics scattered around its base. Neither Carnap nor Morris seems to be aware—or, if aware, neither of them is bothered by the fact— that pragmatism, in every forward step that has been taken in the central line from Peirce,[29] has concentrated on "meanings"—in other words, on the very field of semantics from which Carnap and Morris now exclude it. To tear semantics and pragmatics thus apart is to leap from Peirce back towards the medieval.[30]

As for the "semiotic" which he offers as a "science among the sciences" (M, p. 2), as underlying syntactics, semantics and pragmatics, and as being designed to "supply a language . . . to improve the language of science" (M, p. 3), we need give only a few illustrations of the extent to which its own language falls below the most ordinary standards of everyday coherence. He employs

---

when in a somewhat similar difficulty over what the "intuitionists" stood for in mathematics. "Naturally," he wrote, "a sober critic can do nothing but stick to their external communications." "The New Logic," *Philosophy of Science*, IV (1937), 320. Compare also our further comment on this phase of inquiry in Chapter 3, note 48.

29. In "How to Make Our Ideas Clear" (1878) where "practical" bearings and effects are introduced, and where it is asserted that "our conception of these effects is the whole of our conception of the object" (*Collected Papers*, 5.402).

30. That even Morris himself has now become troubled appears from a later discussion in which—under the stimulus of a marvelously succulent, syllabic synthesis applied to "linguistic signs," namely, that they are "transsituationally intersubjective"—he votes in favor of a "wider use of 'semantics'" and a "narrower use of 'pragmatics'" hereafter (*Philosophy of Science*, X [1943], 248–249). Indeed, Morris' whole tone in this new paper is apologetic, though falling far short of hinting at a much-needed thorough-going house-cleaning. No effect of this suggested change in viewpoint is, however, manifested in his subsequent book, *Signs, Language, and Behavior* (New York, 1946), nor is his paper of 1943 as much as listed in the bibliography therein provided.

a "triadic relation" possessing "three correlates": sign vehicle, designatum and interpreter (M, p. 6). These, however, had entered three pages earlier as "three (or four) factors" where "interpretant" was listed with the parenthetic comment that "interpreter" may be a fourth. Concerning each of these three (or four) factors in his "triadic relations," he writes so many varying sentences it is safe to say that in simple addition all would cancel out and nothing be left.

Consider the dramatic case of the birth of an interpretant.[31] You take a certain "that which" that *acts* as a sign and make it produce an *effect* (called interpretant) on an interpreter, *in virtue of which* the "that which" becomes, or "is," a sign (M, p. 3, lines 23–25). Four pages later the sign may *express* its interpreter. The words are incoherent when checked one against another. As for the signs themselves, they are "simply the objects" (M, p. 2); they are "things or properties . . . in their function" (M, p. 2); they are something "denoting the objects" (M, p. 2); they are something to be determined for certain cases by "semantical rule" (M, pp. 23–24); they are something of which (for other cases) one can say that "the sign vehicle is only that aspect of the apparent sign vehicle in virtue of which semiosis takes place" (M, p. 49) etc., etc. Some signs designate without denoting (M, p. 5);[32] others indicate without designating (M, p. 29). Some objects exist without semiosis (M, p. 5), and sometimes the designatum of a sign need not be an "actual existent object" (M, p. 5). Comparably a man may "point without pointing to anything" (M, p. 5), which is as neat a survival of medieval mentality in the modern age as one would wish to see.[33]

In Morris' procedure language is one thing, and "using it" is

31. Where Morris allots a possible four components to his "triadic relation" he employs the evasive phrase-device "commonly regarded as," itself as common in logic as outside. (Cf. Carnap's "language as it is usually understood," which we have discussed previously.) The word "interpretant" is of course lifted verbally, though not meaningfully, from Peirce, who used it for the operational outcome of sets of ordered signs (*Collected Papers*, 2.92 to 2.94, and cf. also 2.646). The effect (outcome or consequences) of which Peirce speaks is definitely *not* an effect upon an interpreter. There is no ground in Peirce's writings for identifying "interpretant" with "interpreter."

32. A demonstration of the meaninglessness of Morris' treatment of denotation and designation—of objects, classes and entities—has been published by George V. Gentry since this paper was prepared (the *Journal of Philosophy*, XLI [1944], 376–384).

33. For Morris' later development of "sign" (1946) see Chapter 9.

another. He may talk behaviorally about it for a paragraph or two, but his boldest advance in that direction would be to develop its "relation" to the "interpreter" ("dog" or "person") who uses it. Sometimes, for him, science *is* a language; at other times science *has* a language, although semiotic has a better one. A "dual control of linguistic structure" is set up (*M*, pp. 12–13) requiring both events and behaviors, but independently physical signs and objects that are not actual find their way in. Similarly, in the more expansive generalizations, at one time we find (as *M*, p. 29) that syntactic or semantic rules are only verbal formulations within semiotic, while at other times (as *M*, p. 33) we learn that syntactics must be established before we can relate signs to interpreters or to things. The net result is such a complete blank that we find it almost exciting when such a venturesome conclusion is reached as marked an earlier paper by Morris: that "signs which constitute scientific treatises have, to some extent at least, a correlation with objects." [34]

V

Ducasse has labored industriously to discover what a proposition actually "is," if it is the sort of thing he and Cohen-Nagel believe it to be. We do not need to follow him through his long studies since, fortunately, he has recently provided a compact statement. Rearranging somewhat his recipe for the hunting of his snark (*D*, p. 134), though taking pains to preserve its purity, we get:

> Catch an assertion (such as "the dog is red"). Note it is "the verbal symbol of an opinion." Pin it securely on the operating table.
> Peel off all that is "verbal" and throw away. Peel off all "epistemic attitude" (here "belief") and throw away also.
> The remainder will be a *proposition*.
> Dissect carefully. The proposition will be found to have two components, both "physical entities": the first, a "physical object"; the second, a "physical property."
> Distill away from these components all traces of conscious

34. *International Encyclopedia of Unified Science*, I, No. 1 (1938), p. 69.

process—in especial, as to "object," all that is perceptual; as to "property," all that is conceptual.

When this has been skilfully done you will have remaining the pure components of the pure proposition, with all that is verbal or mental removed.

Further contemplation of the pure proposition will reveal that it has the following peculiarities: (*a*) if its two components cleave together in intimate union, the first "possessing" the second, then the proposition is "true," and the "true proposition" is "fact"; (*b*) if the second component vanishes, then what remains (despite the lack of one of its two essential components) is still a proposition, but this time a "false proposition," and a false proposition is "not a fact," or perhaps more accurately, since it is still an important something, it might be called a "not-fact."

This is no comfortable outcome. The only way it can "make" sense, so far as one can see is by continuous implied orientation towards a concealed mental operator, for whom one would have more respect if he came out in front and did business in his own name.[35]

VI

Lewis illustrates what happens when words as physical facts are sharply severed from meanings as psychical facts, with

---

35. A later attempt by Ducasse is found in a paper, "Propositions, Truth, and the Ultimate Criterion of Truth" (*Philosophy and Phenomenological Research,* IV [1944], 317–340), which became available after the above was written. In it the confusion heightens. For Ducasse, now, no proposition has either a subject or a predicate (p. 321). Many varieties of "things" or "somethings" are introduced, and there is complete absence of information as to what we are to understand by "thing" or "something." Thus: "the sort of thing, and the only sort of thing, which either is true or is false is a proposition" (p. 318); it is to be sharply discriminated from "other sorts of things called respectively statements, opinions, and judgments . . ." (p. 318); "the ultimate . . . constituents of a proposition are some *ubi* and some *quid*—some *locus* and some *quale*" (p. 323); "a fact is not something to which true propositions 'correspond' in some sense . . . a fact *is* a true proposition" (p. 320). Incidentally a proposition is also the *content* of an opinion (p. 320) from which we may infer that a fact, being a true proposition, is likewise the content of an opinion. It is very discouraging.

the former employed by a superior agency—a "mind"—to "convey" the latter (*L*, p. 236). He makes so sharp a split between ink-marks and meanings that he at once faces a "which comes first?" puzzler of the "chicken or egg" type, his sympathies giving priority to the meanings over the wordings.

He tells us (*L*, p. 237) that "a linguistic expression is constituted by the association of a verbal symbol and a fixed meaning." Here the original ink-spot-verbal is allotted symbolic quality (surely it must be "psychic") while the meaning is allegedly "fixed" (which sounds very "physical"). Our bigamist is thus unfaithful in both houses. He is doubly and triply unfaithful, at that, for the last part of the cited sentence reads: "but the linguistic expression cannot be identified with the symbol alone nor with the meaning alone." First we had physical words and mental meanings; then we had verbal symbols and fixed meanings; now we have symbol alone and meaning alone, neither of them being expressive. He uses, it is true, a purportedly vitalizing word—or, rather, a word that might vitalize if it had any vitality left in it. This word is "association," outcast of both philosophy and psychology, a thorough ne'er-do-well, that at best points a dirty finger at a region in which research is required.

So slippery are the above phrasings that no matter how sternly one pursues them they cannot be held fast. The signs are physical, but they become verbal symbols. A verbal symbol is a pattern of marks; it is a "recognizable pattern"; it becomes a pattern even when apart from its "instances"; it winds up as an "abstract entity" (all in *L*, pp. 236–237). Expression goes the same route from ink-spots on up (or down), so that finally, when the symbol becomes an abstract entity, the expression (originally a physical "thing") becomes a "correlative abstraction" (*L*, p. 237).

A term is an expression that "names or applies to" (one would like to clear up the difference or the identity here) "a thing or things, of some kind, actual or thought of" (again plenty of room for clarification); it changes into something that is "capable" of naming, where naming is at times used as a synonym for "speaking of" (*L*, p. 237); in the case of the "abstract term," however, the term "names what it signifies" (*L*, p. 239). One would like to understand the status of proposition as "assertable content" (*L*, p. 242); of a "sense-meaning" that is "intension in the mode of a criterion in mind" (*L*, p. 247); of signification as "comprehensive essential character" (*L*, p. 239). One could even endure a little information about the way in which "denote" is to be maintained as different from "denotation," and how one can avoid "the awkward consequences" of this difference by adopting the word "designation" (apparently from Carnap and Morris, and apparently in a sense different from either of theirs)—an effort which Lewis himself does not find it worth his while to make (*L*, p. 237). Finally, if "meaning" and "physical sign" cannot be better held apart than Lewis succeeds in doing, one would like to know why he tries so elaborately.[36]

VII

We shall discuss Bertrand Russell's logical setting in Chapter 8. His terminology, as previously noted, appears confused, even to Carnap, who finds Russell's explanations of his various uses of the word "proposition" very "difficult to understand" (*C*, pp. 235–236). The voluminous interchanges Russell has had with others result in ever renewed complaints by him that he is not properly understood. Despite his great initiative in symbolic formulation in the border regions between logic and mathematics, and despite the many specializations of inquiry he has carried through, no progress in basic organization has resulted from his work. This seems to be the main lesson from logical inquiry in general as it has thus far been carried on. We may stress this highly unsatisfactory status by quoting a few other remarks by logicians on the work of their fellows.

Carnap, in his latest volume,[37] regrets that most logicians still leave "the understanding and use of [semantical] terms . . . to common-sense and instinct," and feels that the work of Hilbert and Bernays would be clearer "if the distinction between expressions and their designata were observed more strictly"—and this despite his own chaos in that respect.

36. Professor Baylis finds some of the same difficulties we have found in Lewis' procedure, and several more, and regards portions of it as "cagey" (*Philosophy and Phenomenological Research*, V [1944], 80–88). He does not, however, draw the conclusion we draw as to the radical deficiency in the whole scheme of terminology. Professor Lewis, replying to Professor Baylis (*ibid.*, 94–96), finds as much uncertainty in the latter as the latter finds in him.
37. *Formalization of Logic*, pp. xii, xiii.

Cohen and Nagel in their preface pay their compliments to their fellows thus:

Florence Nightingale transformed modern hospital practice by the motto: Whatever hospitals do, they should not spread disease. Similarly, logic should not infect students with fallacies and confusions as to the fundamental nature of valid or scientific reasoning.

Tarski, whose procedure is the next and last we shall examine, writes (*T*, p. 345):

It is perhaps worth while saying that semantics as it is conceived in this paper (and in former papers of the author) is a sober and modest discipline which has no pretensions of being a universal patent medicine for all the ills and diseases of mankind whether imaginary or real. You will not find in semantics any remedy for decayed teeth or illusions of grandeur or class conflicts. Nor is semantics a device for establishing that every one except the speaker and his friends is speaking nonsense.

VIII

Tarski's work is indeed like a breath of fresh air after the murky atmosphere we have been in. It is not that he has undertaken positive construction or given concentrated attention to the old abuses of terminology, but he is on the way—shaking himself, one might say, to get free. His procedure is simple, unpretentious, and cleared of many of the ancient verbal unintelligibilities. He does not formally abandon the three-realm background and he occasionally, though not often, lapses into using it—speaking of "terms," for example, as "indispensable means for conveying human thoughts" [38]—but he seems free from that persistent, malignant orientation towards the kind of fictive mental operator which the preceding logicians examined in this chapter have implicitly or explicitly relied upon. He sets "sen-

38. Alfred Tarski, *Introduction to Logic and to the Methodology of Deductive Sciences* (New York, 1941), p. 18. Compare also his remark about "innate or acquired capacity," *ibid.*, p. 134.

tences" (as expressions) over against "objects referred to" (*T*, p. 345) in a matter-of-fact way, and goes to work. He employs a metalanguage to control object-languages, not as an esoteric, facultative mystery, but as a simple technical device, such as any good research man might seek in a form appropriate to his field, to fixate the materials under his examination.[39]

In his latest appraisal of "true" under the title "The Semantic Conception of Truth," Tarski concludes that for a given object-language and for such other formalized languages as are now known (*T*, p. 371, n. 14)—and he believes he can generalize for a comprehensive class of object-languages (*T*, p. 355)—"a sentence is true if it is satisfied by all objects, and false otherwise" (*T*, p. 353). The development, as we appraise it, informs us that if we assume (*a*) isolable things (here we make explicit his implicit assumption of the "thing") and (*b*) human assertions about them, then this use can be consistently maintained. In his demonstration Tarski discards "propositions," beloved of Cohen-Nagel, Carnap and Ducasse, saying they are too often "ideal entities" of which the "meaning . . . seems never to have been made quite clear and unambiguous" (*T*, p. 342). He establishes "sentences" with the characteristics of "assertions," and then considers such a sentence on the one hand as in active assertion, and on the other hand as designated or named, and thus identified, so that it can be more accurately handled and dealt with by the inquirer. After establishing certain "equivalences of the form (*T*)" which assure us that the sentence is well-named (*x* is true if, and only if, *p*) (*T*, p. 344), he sharpens an earlier formulation for "adequacy," the requirement now becoming that "all equivalences of the form (*T*) can be asserted" (*T*, p. 344). (For all of this we are, of course, employing our own free phrasing, which we are able to do because his work, unlike the others, is substantial enough to tolerate it.) "A definition of truth is 'adequate' if all these

39. In the preface to the original (Polish) edition of his *Logic* he had held that "the concepts of logic permeate the whole of mathematics," considering the specifically mathematical concepts "special cases," and had gone so far as to assert that "logical laws are constantly applied—be it consciously or unconsciously—in mathematical reasonings" (*ibid.*, pp. xvii–xviii). In his new preface (*ibid.*, p. xi, p. xiii) he reduces this to the assurance that logic "seeks to create . . . apparatus" and that it "analyzes the meaning" and "establishes the general laws." Even more significantly he remarks (*ibid.*, p. 140) that "meta-logic and meta-mathematics" means about the same as "the science of logic and mathematics." (Compare also *ibid.*, p. 134.)

equivalences follow from it." Given such adequacy we have a "semantic" conception of truth, although the expression (*T*) itself is not yet a definition.

To demonstrate his conclusion Tarski identifies as primarily semantic: (1) designation (denoting), (2) satisfaction (for conditions), (3) definition (unique determining); he calls them "relations" between "sentences" and "objects." "True," however, he says, is not such a "relation"; instead it expresses a property (or denotes a class) of sentences (*T*, p. 345). Nevertheless it is to be called "semantic" because the best way of defining it is by aid of the semantic relations (*T*, p. 345). His outcome, he thinks, is "formally correct" and "materially adequate," the conditions for material adequacy being such as to determine uniquely the extension of the term "true" (*T*, p. 353). *What he has done is to make plain to himself at the start what he believes truth to be in everyday use, after which by prolonged study he advances from a poorer and less reliable to a richer and more reliable formulation of it.* We do not say this in deprecation, but rather as high praise of the extent of progress in his standpoint. We may quote his saying that his aim is "to catch hold of the actual meaning of an old notion" (*T*, p. 341; compare also p. 360, bottom paragraph), where, if one strikes out any remaining sentimentality from the word "actual" and treats it rigorously, the sense becomes close to what we have expressed.

We must nevertheless, to make his status clear, list some of the flaws. He does not tell us clearly what he intends by the words "concept," "word," "term," "meaning" and "object." His applications of them are frequently mixed.[40] "Word" shades into "term," and "term" into "concept," and "concept" retains much of its traditional vagueness. Designation and satisfaction, as "relations," enter as running between expression and thing (the "semantic" requirement), but definition, also a relation, runs largely between expressions (a very different matter).[41] "True," while

---

40. Thus *Logic*, p. 18, p. 139. For "object" see *T*, p. 374, n. 35. He recognizes the vagueness in the word "concept" (*T*, p. 370, n. 4) but continues to use it. His employment of it on page 108 of the *Logic* and his phrasing about "laws . . . concerning concepts" are of interest. His abuses of this word, however, are so slight compared with the naïve specimens we have previously examined that complaint is not severe.

41. For "definition," consider the stipulating convention (*Logic*, p. 33) and the equivalence (p. 150) and compare these with the use of "relation" (*T*, p. 345) and with the comments (*T*, p. 374, n. 35). It is not the use of the single word

not offered as a "relation," is at one stage said to "denote," although denoting has been presented as a relating. The word "meaning" remains two-faced throughout, sometimes running from word (expression) to word, and sometimes from word to thing.[42] Lacking still is all endeavor to organize men's talkings to men's perceivings and manipulatings in the cultural world of their evolution. The ancient non-cultural verbal implications block the path.

IX

        Along with proposition, truth, meaning and language, "fact" has been in difficulties in all the logics we have examined. We displayed this in Section II through the development of a curious contrast as to whether a fact is a proposition or a proposition a fact. The answer seemed to be "Neither." In various other ways the puzzle has appeared on the sidelines of the logics throughout.

Now, "fact" is not in trouble with the logics alone; the philosophies and epistemologies are equally chary of looking at it straight. Since direct construction in this field will occupy us later on, we shall here exhibit the character of this philosophical confusion by a few simple illustrations from the philosophical dictionaries and from current periodical essays.[43] Consider first what the dictionaries report.

The recently published *Dictionary of Philosophy*[44] limits itself to three lines as follows:

_____

"definition" for different processes that is objectionable, but the confusion in the uses.

42. Thus *Logic*, p. 133; one can discard first of all "independent meanings," and then the customary meanings of "logical concepts," and finally, apparently, "the meanings of all expressions encountered in the given discipline . . . without exception." The word "meaning" is, of course, one of the most unreliable in the dictionary, but that is no reason for playing fast and loose with it in logic.

43. The only considerable discussion of fact we have noted is the volume *Studies in the Nature of Facts* (University of California Publications in Philosophy, XIV [1932]), a series of eight lectures by men of different specializations. An examination of the points of view represented will reward anyone interested in further development of this field.

44. D. D. Runes, editor (New York, 1942).

Fact (Lat. factus, p.p. of facio, do): Actual individual occurrence. An indubitable truth of actuality. A brute event.
Synonymous with actual event.

Any high-school condensation of a dictionary should do better
than that. This is supplemented, however, by another entry, allotted three times the space, and entitled "Fact: in Husserl"
(whatever that may literally mean). Here unblinking use is made
of such locutions as "categorical-syntactical structure," "simply
is" and "regardless of value."

Baldwin's definition of a generation ago is well known. Fact is
"objective datum of experience," by which is to be understood
"datum of experience considered as abstracted from the experience of which it is a datum." This, of course, was well enough
among specialists of its day, but the words it uses are hardly
information-giving in our time.

Eisler's *Wörterbuch* (1930 edition) makes *Tatsache* out to be
whatever we are convinced has objective or real *Bestand*—whatever is firmly established through thought as content of experience, as *Bestandteil* of the ordering under law of things and
events. These again are words but are not helps.

Lalande's *Vocabulaire* (1928 edition) does better. It discusses
fact to the extent of two pages, settling upon the wording of Seig-
nobos and Langlois that "La notion de *fait*, quand on la précise,
se ramène à un jugement d'affirmation sur la réalité extérieure."
This at least sounds clear, and will satisfy anyone who accepts its
neat psychology and overlooks the difficulties that lie in *jugement*, as we have just been surveying them.

Turning to current discussions in the journals for further illustration we select three specimens, all appearing during the past
year (1944). Where mere illustration is involved and all are alike
in the dark, there is no need to be invidious, and we therefore
omit names and references, all the better to attend to the astonishing things we are told.

1. "Fact: a situation having reality in its own right independent of cognition." Here the word "situation" evidently enters
because of its indefiniteness; "reality in its own right" follows
with assertion of the most tremendous possible definiteness; and
"independent of cognition," if it means anything, means "about
which we know nothing at all." The whole statement is that fact

is something very vague, yet most tremendously certain, about which we know nothing.

2. "There is something ultimately unprovable in a fact." Here a rapturous intellectualism entertains itself, forgetting that there has been something eventually uncertain about every "truth" man has thus far uncovered, and discrediting fact before trying to identify it.

3. "A fact can be an item of knowledge only because the *factual* is a character of reality. . . . Factual knowledge means the awareness of the occurrence of events felt, believed, or known to be independent of the volitional self. . . . The sense of fact is the sense of the self confronting the not-self." The outcome of this set of warring assertions is a four-fold universe, containing: (*a*) reality; (*b*) truth; (*c*) a sort of factuality that is quasi-real; (*d*) another sort of factuality that is quasi-true. Poor "fact" is slaughtered from all four quarters of the heavens at once.

The citations above have been given not because they are exceptional, but because they are standard. You find this sort of thing wherever you go. No stronger challenge could be given for research than the continuance of such a state of affairs in this scientific era.

X

Enough evidence of linguistic chaos has been presented in this paper to justify an overhauling of the entire background of recent logical construction. This chaos is due to logicians' accepting ancient popular phrasings about life and conduct as if such phrasings were valid, apart from inquiry into their factual status within modern knowledge. As a result, not only is logic disreputable from the point of view of fact, but the status of "fact" is wretched within the logics. The involvement both of logic and fact with language is manifest. Some logics, as anyone can quickly discover, look upon language only to deny it. Some allot it incidental attention. Even where it is more formally introduced, it is in the main merely tacked on to the older logical materials, without entering into them in full function.

Our understanding thus far has been gained by refusing to accept the words man utters as independent beings—logicians' playthings akin to magicians' vipers or children's fairies—and by insisting that language is veritably man himself in action, and thus observable. The "propositions" of Cohen and Nagel, of Ducasse and of Carnap, the "meanings" of Lewis, the "sign vehicles" and "interpretants" of Morris and the "truth" of Tarski all tell the same tale, though in varying degree. What is "man in action" gets distorted when manipulated as if detached; what is "other than man" gets plenty of crude assumption, but no fair factual treatment.

We said at the start that in closing we would indicate a still wider observation that must be made if better construction is to be achieved. The locus of such widened observation is where "object," "entity," "thing" or "designatum" is introduced. "Things" appear and are named, or they appear as named, or they appear through namings. Logics of the types we have been examining flutter and evade, but never attack directly the problem of sorting out and organizing words to things, and things to words, for their needs of research. They proceed as though some sort of oracle could be issued to settle all puzzles at once, with logicians as the priests presiding over the mysteries.

This problem, we believe, should be faced naturalistically. Passage should be made from the older half-light to such fuller light as modern science offers. In this fuller light the man who talks and thinks and knows belongs to the world in which he has been evolved in all his talkings, thinkings and knowings; while at the same time this world in which he has been evolved is the world of his knowing. Not even in his latest and most complex activities is it well to survey this natural man as magically "emergent" into something new and strange. Logic, we believe, must learn to accept him simply and naturally, if it is to begin the progress the future demands.

2. The Terminological Problem

Science uses its technical names efficiently. Such names serve to mark off certain portions of the scientific subjectmatter as provisionally acceptable, thereby freeing the worker's attention for closer consideration of other portions that remain problematic. The efficiency lies in the ability given the worker to hold such names steady—to know what he properly names with them—first at different stages of his own procedure and then in interchange with his associates.

Theories of knowledge provide their investigators with no such dependable aids. The traditional namings they employ have primitive cultural origins and the supplemental "terms" they evolve have frequently no ascertainable application as names at all.

We have asserted that the time has come when a few leading names for knowings and knowns can be established and put to use. We hold further that this undertaking should be placed upon a scientific basis; where by "scientific" we understand very simply a form of "factual" inquiry, in which the knowing man is accepted as a factual component of the factual cosmos, as he is elsewhere in modern research. We know of no other basis on which to anticipate dependable results—more particularly since the past history of "epistemology" is filled with danger-signs.

What we advocate is in very simple statement a passage from loose to firm namings. Some purported names do little more than indicate fields of inquiry—some, even, do hardly that. Others specify with a high degree of firmness. The word "knowledge," as a name, is a loose name. We do not employ it in the titles of our chapters and shall not use it in any significant way as we proceed. It is often a convenience, and it is probably not objectionable—at least it may be kept from being dangerous—where there is no stress upon its accurate application and no great probability that a reader will assume there is; at any rate we shall thus occasionally risk it. We shall rate it as No. 1 on a list of "vague words"[1] to which we shall call attention and add from time to time in footnotes. Only through prolonged factual inquiry, of which little has been undertaken as yet, can the word "knowledge" be given determinable status with respect to such questions as: (1) the range of its application to human or animal behaviors; (2) the types of its distribution between knowers, knowns, and presumptive intermediaries; (3) the possible localizations implied for knowledges as present in space and time. In place of examining such a vague generality as the word "knowledge" offers, we shall speak of and concern ourselves directly with knowings and knowns—and, moreover, in each instance, with those particular forms of knowings and knowns in respect to which we may hope for reasonably definite identifications.

I

The conditions that the sort of namings we seek must satisfy, positively and negatively, include the following:

1. The names are to be based on such observations as are accessible to and attainable by everybody. This condition excludes, as being negligible to knowledge, any report of purported observation which the reporter avows to be radically and exclusively private.

2. The status of observation and the use of reports upon it are to be tentative, postulational, hypothetical.[2] This condition excludes all purported materials and all alleged fixed principles that are offered as providing original and necessary "foundations" for either the knowings or the knowns.

3. The aim of the observation and naming adopted is to pro-

1. Even the words "vague," "firm" and "loose," as we at this stage are able to use them, are loosely used. We undertake development definitely and deliberately within an atmosphere (one might perhaps better call it a swamp) of vague language. We reject the alternative—the initial dependence on some schematism of verbal impactions—and propose to destroy the authoritarian claims of such impactions by means of distinctions to be introduced later, including particularly that between specification and definition.
2. The postulations we are using, their origin and status, will be discussed in a following chapter. See also Dewey, *Logic: The Theory of Inquiry* (New York, 1938), Chap. 1, and Bentley, "Postulation for Behavioral Inquiry" (the *Journal of Philosophy*, XXXVI [1939], 405–413).

mote further observation and naming which in turn will advance and improve. This condition excludes all namings that are asserted to give, or that claim to be, finished reports on "reality."

The above conditions amount to saying that the names we need have to do with knowings and knowns in and by means of continuous operation and test in work, where any knowing or known establishes itself or fails to establish itself through continued search and research solely, never on the ground of any alleged outside "foundation," "premise," "axiom" or *ipse dixit*. In line with this attitude we do not assert that the conditions stated above are "true"; we are not even arguing in their behalf. We advance them as the conditions which, we hold, should be satisfied by the kind of names that are needed by us here and now if we are to advance knowledge of knowledge. Our procedure, then, does not stand in the way of inquiry into knowledge by other workers on the basis either of established creeds or tenets, or of alternative hypotheses; we but state the ground upon which we ourselves wish to work, in the belief that others are prepared to cooperate. The postulates and methods we wish to use are, we believe, akin to those of the sciences which have so greatly advanced knowledge in other fields.

The difficulties in our way are serious, but we believe these difficulties have their chief source in the control exercised over men by traditional phrasings originating when observation was relatively primitive and lacked the many important materials that are now easily available. Cultural conditions (such as ethnological research reveals) favored in earlier days the introduction of factors that have now been shown to be irrelevant to the operations of inquiry and to stand in the way of the formation of a straightforward theory of knowledge—straightforward in the sense of setting forth conclusions reached through inquiry into knowings as themselves facts.

The basic postulate of our procedure is that knowings are observable facts in exactly the same sense as are the subjectmatters that are known. A glance at any collection of books and periodicals discloses the immense number of subjectmatters that have been studied and the various grades of their establishment in the outcome. No great argument is required to warrant the statement that this wide field of knowledge (possessed of varying depths in its different portions) can be studied not only in terms of things[3] known, but also in terms of the knowings.

In the previous chapter we pointed out instances, in the works of prominent contemporary logicians, of an extraordinary confusion arising from an uncritical use in logic, as theory of knowledge, of forms of primitive observation; sometimes to the utter neglect of the fuller and keener observation now available, and in other cases producing such a mixture of two incompatible types of observation as inevitably wrecks achievement. It was affirmed in that chapter that further advance will require complete abandonment of the customary isolation of the word from the man speaking, and likewise of the word from the thing spoken of or named. In effect, and often overtly, words are dealt with in the logics as if they were a new and third kind of fact lying between man as speaker and things as spoken of. The net result is to erect a new barrier in human behavior between the things that are involved and the operating organisms. While the logical writers in question have professedly departed from the earlier epistemological theories framed in terms of a mind basic as subject and an external world as object, competent analysis shows that the surviving separation their writings exhibit is the ghost of the seventeenth-century epistemological separation of knowing subject and object known, as that in turn was the ghost of the medieval separation of the "spiritual" essence from the "material" nature and body, often with an intervening "soul" of mixed or alternating activities.

Sometimes the intervening realm of names as a new and third kind of fact lying between man as speaker and things as spoken of takes the strange appearance of a denial not only of language as essential in logic, but even of names as essential in language. Thus Quine in a recent discussion of the issue of "universals" as "entities" tells us that "names generally . . . are inessential to language" and that his "suppression of names is a superficial re-

3. "Thing" is another vague word. It is in good standing, however, where general reference is intended, and it is safer in such cases than words like "entity" which carry too great a variety of philosophical and epistemological implications. We shall use it freely in this way, but for more determinate uses shall substitute "object" when we later have given this latter word sufficient definiteness.

vision of language." The world in which he operates would thus seem comparable with that of Whitehead in which "language" (including apparently that which he himself is using) is "always ambiguous," and in which "spoken language is merely a series of squeaks."[4] One may admire the skill with which Quine uses his method of abstraction to secure a unified field for symbolic logic in which "all names are abstract," and in which the bound variables of quantification become "the sole vehicle of direct objective reference," and still feel that the more he detaches his symbolic construction from the language he is referring to through the agency of the language he is using, the more he assimilates his construction to the other instances of "intervening" language, however less subtly these latter are deployed.

The importance we allot to the introduction of firm names is very quickly felt when one begins to make observation of knowledge as a going fact of behavioral activity. Observation not only separates but also brings together in combination in a single sweep matters which at other times have been treated as isolated and hence as requiring to be forced into organization ("synthesized" is the traditional word) by some outside agency. To see language, with all its speakings and writings, as man-himself-in-action-dealing-with-things is observation of the combining type. Meaningful conveyance is, of course, included, as itself of the very texture of language. The full event is before us thus in durational spread. The observation is no longer made in terms of "isolates" requiring to be "synthesized." Such procedure is common enough in all science. The extension as observation in our case is that we make it cover the speaker or knower along with the spoken of or known as being one common durational event. Here primary speaking is as observable as is a bird in flight. The inclusion of books and periodicals as a case of observable man-in-action is no different in kind from the observation of the steel girders of a bridge connecting the mining and smelting of ores with the operations of a steel mill, and with the building of bridges, in turn, out of the products. For that matter, it is no dif-

4. Alfred North Whitehead, *Process and Reality* (New York, 1929), p. 403; W. V. Quine, "On Universals," the *Journal of Symbolic Logic*, XII (1947), p. 74. Compare also W. V. Quine, *Mathematical Logic*, Second Printing (Cambridge, 1947), pp. 149–152 *et al.*

ferent from observation extended far enough to take in not just a bird while in flight but bird nest-building, egg-laying and hatching. Observation of this general type sees man-in-action, not as something radically set over against an environing world, nor yet as something merely acting "in" a world, but as action *of* and *in* the world in which the man belongs as an integral constituent.

To see an event filling a certain duration of time as a description across a full duration, rather than as composed of an addition or other kind of combination of separate, instantaneous, or short-span events is another aspect of such observation. Procedure of this type was continuously used by Peirce, though he had no favorable opportunity for developing it, and it was basic to him from the time when in one of his earliest papers he stressed that all thought is in signs and requires a time.[5] The "immediate"

---

5. "The only cases of thought which we can find are of thought in signs" (*Collected Papers*, 5.251); "To say that thought cannot happen in an instant but requires a time is but another way of saying that every thought must be interpreted in another, or that all thought is in signs" (*ibid.*, 5.253). See also comment in our preceding chapter, pp. 8–11. For a survey of Peirce's development (the citations being to his *Collected Papers*) see "Questions Concerning Certain Faculties Claimed for Man" (1868), 5.213 to 5.263, "How to Make Our Ideas Clear" (1878), 5.388 to 5.410, "A Pragmatic Interpretation of the Logical Subject" (1902), 2.328 to 2.331, and "The Ethics of Terminology" (1903), 2.219 to 2.226. On his use of leading principles, see 3.154 to 3.171 and 5.365 to 5.369; on the open field of inquiry, 5.376n; on truth, 5.407, 5.565; on the social status of logic and knowledge, 2.220, 2.654, 5.311, 5.316, 5.331, 5.354, 5.421, 5.444, 6.610; on the duplex nature of "experience," 1.321, 5.51, 5.284, 5.613. For William James's development, see his essays in *Mind, a Quarterly Review of Psychology and Philosophy* in the early eighteen-eighties, Chapter X on "Self" in *The Principles of Psychology* (New York, 1890), the epilogue to the *Briefer Course* (New York, 1893) and *Essays in Radical Empiricism* (New York, 1912). For Dewey, see *Studies in Logical Theory* (Chicago, 1903), *How We Think* (Boston, 1910, revised 1933), *Essays in Experimental Logic* (Chicago, 1916), *Experience and Nature* (Chicago, 1925), *Logic: The Theory of Inquiry,* and three psychological papers reprinted in *Philosophy and Civilization* (New York, 1931) as follows: "The Reflex Arc Concept in Psychology" (1896, reprinted as "The Unit of Behavior"), "The Naturalistic Theory of Perception by the Senses" (1925) and "Conduct and Experience" (1930). See also *Context and Thought* (University of California Publications in Philosophy, XII [1931], 203–224), "How Is Mind to Be Known?" (the *Journal of Philosophy,* XXXIX [1942], 29–35) and "By Nature and by Art" (*ibid.,* XLI [1944], 281–292). For Bentley, see *The Process of Government* (Chicago, 1908), *Relativity in Man and Society* (New York, 1926), *Linguistic Analysis of Mathematics* (Bloomington, Indiana, 1932), *Behavior, Knowledge, Fact* (Bloomington, Indiana, 1935),

or "neutral" experience of William James was definitely an effort at such a form of direct observation in the field of knowings. Dewey's development in use of interaction and transaction, and in presentation of experience as neither subjective nor objective but as a method or system of organization, is strongly of this form; his psychological studies have made special contributions in this line, and in his *Logic: The Theory of Inquiry* (1938), following upon his logical essays of 1903 and 1916, he has developed the processes of inquiry in a situational setting. Bentley's *Process of Government* in 1908 developed political description in a manner approaching what we would here call "transactional," and his later analysis of mathematics as language, his situational treatment of behavior and his factual development of behavioral space-time belong in this line of research.

If there should be difficulty in understanding this use of the word "observation," the difficulty illustrates the point earlier made as to the influence of materials introduced from inadequate sources. The current philosophical notion of observation is derived from a psychology of "consciousness" (or some version of the "mental" as an isolate), and it endeavors to reduce what is observed either to some single sensory quality or to some other "content" of such short time-span as to have no connections— except what may be provided through inference as an operation outside of observation. As against such a method of obtaining a description of observation, the procedure we adopt reports and describes observation on the same basis the worker in knowledge—astronomer, physicist, psychologist, etc.—employs when he makes use of a test observation in arriving at conclusions to be accepted as known. We proceed upon the postulate that *knowings* are always and everywhere inseparable from *the knowns*— that the two are twin aspects of common fact.

---

three papers on situational treatment of behavior (the *Journal of Philosophy*, XXXVI [1939], 169–181, 309–323, 405–413), "The Factual Space and Time of Behavior" (*ibid.*, XXXVIII [1941], 477–485), "The Human Skin: Philosophy's Last Line of Defense" (*Philosophy of Science*, VIII [1941], 1–19), "Observable Behaviors" (*Psychological Review*, XLVII [1940], 230–253), "The Behavioral Superfice" (*ibid.*, XLVIII [1941], 39–59) and "The Jamesian Datum" (the *Journal of Psychology*, XVI [1943], 35–79).

II

"Fact" is a name of central position in the material we propose to use in forming a terminology. If there are such things as facts, and if they are of such importance that they have a vital status in questions of knowledge, then in any theory of knowings and knowns we should be able to characterize fact—we should be able to say, that is, that we know what we are talking *about* "in fact" when we apply the word "fact" to the fact of Fact.[6] The primary consideration in fulfilling the desired condition with respect to Fact is that the activity by which it is identified and the *what* that is identified are both required, and are required in such a way that each is taken along with the other, and in no sense as separable. Our terminology is involved in fact, and equally "fact" is involved in our terminology. This repeats in effect the statement that knowledge requires and includes both knowings and knowns. Anything named "fact" is such both with respect to the knowing operation and with respect to what is known.[7] We establish for our use, with respect to both fact and knowledge, that we have no "something known" and no "something identified" apart from its know*ing* and identify*ing,* and that we have no know*ing* and identify*ing* apart from the somewhats and somethings that are being known and identified. Again we do not put forth this statement as a truth about "reality," but as the only position we find it possible to take on the ground of that reference to the observed which we regard as an essential condition of our inquiry. The statement is one about ourselves observed in action in the world. From the standpoint of what is observable, it is of the same straightforward kind as is the statement that when chopping occurs something is chopped and that when seeing takes place something is seen. We select the name "fact" because we believe that it carries and suggests this "double-barrelled" sense (to borrow a word from William James), while such words

6. The wretched status of the word "fact" with respect to its "knowing" and its "known" (and in other respects as well) was illustrated in Chapter 1, Section IX.
7. It may be well to repeat here what has already been said. In making the above statement we are not attempting to legislate concerning the proper use of a word, but are stating the procedure we are adopting.

as "object" and "entity" have acquired from traditional philosophical use the signification of something set over against the doing or acting. That Fact is literally or etymologically *something done or made* has also the advantage of suggesting that the knowing and identifying, as ways of acting, are as much ways of doing, of making (just as much "behaviors," we may say), as are chopping wood, singing songs, seeing sights or making hay.

In what follows we shall continue the devices we have in a manner employed in the preceding paragraph, namely the use of quotation marks, italics, and capitalized initials as aids to presentation, the two former holding close to common usage, while the third has a more specialized application. We shall also freely employ hyphenization in a specialized way, and this perhaps even more frequently than the others. Thus the use of the word "fact" without quotation marks will be in a general or even casual manner. With quotation marks "fact" will indicate the verbal aspect, the word, sometimes impartially, and sometimes as held off at arm's length where the responsibility for its application is not the writer's. With initial capitalization Fact may be taken to stand for the full word-and-thing subjectmatter into which we are inquiring. Italicising in either form, whether as "*fact*" or as Fact will indicate stress of attention. Hyphenization will indicate attention directed to the importance which the components of the word hyphenized have for the present consideration. The words *inter-action* and *trans-action* will enter shortly in this way, and will receive a considerable amount of hyphenizing for emphasis throughout. No use of single quotation marks will be made to distinguish the name of a thing from the thing, for the evident reason that expectantly rigid fixations of this type are just what we most need to avoid. All the devices mentioned are conveniences in their way, but only safe if used cautiously. Thus in the third preceding sentence (as in several others) its most stressed words, there inspected as words, should have quotation marks, but to use such marks would in this case destroy the intended assertion. Rather than being rigorous our own use will be casually variable. This last is best at our present stage of inquiry.

For the purpose of facilitating further inquiry what has been said will be restated in negative terms. We shall *not* proceed as if we were concerned with "existent things" or "objects" entirely apart from men, nor with men entirely apart from things. Accordingly, we do not have on our hands the problem of forcing them into some kind of organization or connection. We shall proceed by taking for granted human organisms developed, living, carrying on, of and in the cosmos. They are there in such system that their operations and transactions can be viewed directly—including those that constitute knowings. When they are so viewed, knowings and knowns come before us differentiated within the factual cosmos, not as if they were there provided in advance so that out of them cosmos—system—fact—knowledge—have to be produced. Fact, language, knowledge have on this procedure cosmic status; they are not taken as if they existed originally in irreconcilably hostile camps. This, again, is but to say that we shall inquire into knowings, both as to materials and workmanship, in the sense of ordinary science.[8]

The reader will note (that is, observe, give heed to) the superiority of our position with respect to observation over that of the older epistemological constructions. Who would assert he can properly and in a worth-while manner *observe* a "mind" *in addition to* the organism that is engaged in the transactions pertinent to it in an observable world? An attempt to answer this question in the affirmative results in regarding observation as private introspection—and this is sufficient evidence of departure from procedures having scientific standing.[9] Likewise, the assertion or belief that things considered as "objects" outside of and apart from human operations are observed, or are observable, is equally absurd when carefully guarded statement is demanded of it. Observation is operation; it is human operation. If attributed to a "mind" it itself becomes unobservable. If surveyed in an observ-

8. It is practically impossible to guard against every form of misapprehension arising from prevalent dominance of language-attitudes holding over from a relatively pre-scientific period. There are probably readers who will translate what has been said about knowings-knowns into terms of epistemological idealism. Such a translation misses the main point—namely, that man and his doings and transactions have to be viewed as facts within the natural cosmos.

9. "Conceptions derived from . . . anything that is so occult as not to be open to public inspection and verification (such as the purely psychical, for example) are excluded" (Dewey, *Logic*, p. 19 [*Later Works* 12:26]).

able world—in what we call cosmos or nature—the object observed is as much a part of the operation as is the observing organism.

This statement about observation, in name and fact, is necessary to avoid misinterpretation. It is not "observation," however, to which we are here giving inquiry; we shall not even attempt to make the word "firm" at a later stage. In the range in which we shall work—the seeking of sound names for processes involving naming—observation is always involved and such observation in this range is in fusion with name-application, so that neither takes place except in and through the other, whatever further applications of the word "observation" (comparable to applications of "naming" and of "knowing") may in widened inquiries be required.

If we have succeeded in making clear our position with respect to the type of name for which we are in search, it will be clear also that this type of name comes in clusters. "Fact" will for us be a central name with other names clustering around it. If "observation" should be taken as central, it in its turn could be made firm only in orientation to its companionate cluster. In any case much serious cooperative inquiry is involved. In no case can we hope to succeed by first setting up separated names and then putting them in pigeonholes or bundling them together with wire provided from without. Names are, indeed, to be differentiated from one another, but the differentiation takes place with respect to other names in clusters; and the same thing holds for clusters that are differentiated from one another. This procedure has its well-established precedents in scientific procedure. The genera and species of botany and zoology are excellent examples—provided they are taken as determinations in process and not as taxonomic rigidities.[10]

10. Other defects in the language we must use, in addition to the tendency towards prematurely stiffened namings, offer continuous interference with communication such as we must attempt. Our language is not at present grammatically adapted to the statements we have to make. Especially is this true with respect to the prepositions which *in toto* we must list among the "vague words" against which we have given warning. Mention of special dangers will be made as occasion arises. We do the best we can, and discussion, we hope, should never turn on some particular man's personal rendering of some particular preposition in some particular passage. The "Cimmerian" effect that appears when one attempts to use conventional linguistic equipment to secure direct statement in this region will be readily recalled.

III

In certain important respects we have placed limitations on the range of our inquiry and on the methods we use. The purpose is to increase the efficiency of what we do. These decisions have been made only after much experimentation in manners of organization and presentation. The main points should be kept steadily in mind as we now stress them.

As already said, we do not propose to issue any flat decrees as to the names others should adopt. Moreover, at the start we shall in some cases not even declare our permanent choices, but instead will deliberately introduce provisional "second-string" names. For this we have two sound reasons. First, our task requires us to locate the regions (some now very largely ignored) that are most in need of firm observation. Second, we must draw upon a dictionary stock of words that have multiple, and often confusedly tangled, applications. We run the risk that the name first introduced may, on these accounts, become involved in misapprehensions on the reader's part, sufficient to ruin it for the future. Hence the value of attempting to establish the regions to be named by provisional namings, in the hope we shall secure stepping stones to better concentration of procedure at the end.

We do not propose in this inquiry to cover the entire range of "knowledge"; that is, the entire range of life and behavior to which the word "knowledge," at one time or another and in one way or another can be applied. We have already listed "knowledge" as a vague word and said we shall specify "knowings" and "knowns" for our attention. Throughout our entire treatment, "knowledge" will remain a word referring roughly to the general field within which we select subjectmatters for closer examination. Even for the words "knowings" and "knowns" the range of common application runs all the way from infusoria approaching food to mathematicians operating with their most recondite dimensions. We shall confine ourselves to a central region: that of identifications under namings, of knowing-by-naming—of "specified existence," if one will. Time will take care of the passage of inquiry across the border regions from naming-knowing to the simpler and to the more complex forms.

We shall regard these naming-knowings directly as a form of knowings. *Take this statement literally as it is written.* It means we do not regard namings as primarily instrumental or specifically ancillary to something else called knowings (or knowledge) except as any behavior may enter as ancillary to any other. We do not split a corporeal naming from a presumptively noncorporeal or "mental" knowing, nor do we permit a mentaloid "brain" to make pretense of being a substitute for a "mind" thus maintaining a split between knowings and namings. This is postulation on our part; but surely the exhibits we secured in the preceding chapter of what happens in the logics under the separation of spoken word from speaking man should be enough to justify any postulate that offers hope of relief. The acceptance of this postulate, even strictly during working hours, may be difficult. We do not expect assent at the start, and we do not here argue the case. We expect to display the value in further action.

IV

Thus far we have been discussing the conditions under which a search for firm names for knowings and knowns must be carried on. In summary our procedure is to be as follows: Working under hypothesis we concentrate upon a special region of knowings and knowns; we seek to spotlight aspects of that region that today are but dimly observed; we suggest tentative namings; through the development of these names in a cluster we hope advance can be made towards construction under dependable naming in the future.

1. *Fact, Event, Designation.* We start with the cosmos of knowledge—with nature as known and as in process of being better known—ourselves and our knowings included. We establish this cosmos as *fact*, and name it "fact" with all its knowings and its knowns included. We do *not* introduce, either by hypothesis or by dogma, knowers and knowns as prerequisites to fact. Instead we observe both knowers and knowns as factual, as cosmic; and never—either of them—as extra-cosmic accessories.

We specialize our studies in the region of naming-knowings, of knowings through namings, wherein we identify two great *factual aspects* to be examined. We name these *event* and *designation.* The application of the word "fact" may perhaps in the end need to be extended beyond the behavioral processes of event-designation. Fact, in other words, as it may be presumed to be present for animal life prior to (or below) linguistic and proto-linguistic behaviors, or as it may be presumed to be attainable by mathematical behaviors developed later than (or above) the ranges of the language behavior that names, is no affair of ours at this immediate time and place. We note the locus of such contingent extensions, leave the way open for the future, and proceed to cultivate the garden of our choice, namely, the characteristic Fact we have before us.

Upon these namings the following comments will, for the present, suffice:

(*a*) In Fact-Event-Designation we do not have a three-fold organization, or a two-fold; we have instead one system.

(*b*) Given the language and knowledge we now possess, the use of the word "fact" imposes upon its users the necessity of selection and acceptance. This manifest status is recognized terminologically by our adoption of the name "designation."

(*c*) The word "aspect" as used here is not stressed as information-giving. It must be taken to register—register, and nothing more—the duplex, aspectual observation and report that are required if we are to characterize Fact at all. The word "phase" may be expected to become available for comparable application when, under the development of the word "aspect," we are sufficiently advanced to consider time-alternations and rhythms of event and of designation in knowledge process.[11]

(*d*) "Event" involves in normal use the extensional and the durational. "Designation" for our purposes must likewise be so taken. The Designation we postulate and discuss is not of the nature of *a* sound or *a* mark applied *as* a name *to* an event. Instead of this it is the entire activity—the behavioral action and activity—of naming through which Event appears in our knowing as Fact.

(*e*) We expect the word "fact" to be able to maintain itself for terminological purposes, and we shall give reasons for this in a succeeding chapter, though still retaining freedom to alter it. As for the words "event" and "designation," their use here is provisional and replacement more probable. Should we, for example,

---

11. "Aspect" and "phase" may stand, therefore, as somewhat superior to the "vague words" against which we give warning, though not as yet presenting positive information in our field.

adopt such words as "existence" and "name," both words (as the case stands at this stage) would carry with them to most readers many implications false to our intentions—the latter even more than the former; understanding of our procedure would then become distorted and ineffective.

(*f*) "Fact," in our use, is to be taken with a range of reference as extensive as is allotted to any other name for cosmos, universe or nature, where the context shows that knowledge, not poesy, is concerned. It is to be taken with its pasts and its futures, its growings-out-of and its growings-into; its transitions of report from poorer to richer, and from less to more. It is to be taken with as much solidity and substantiality as nature, universe or world, by any name whatsoever. It is to be taken, however, with the understanding that instead of inserting gratuitously an unknown something as foundation for the factually known, we are taking the knowledge in full—the knowings-knowns as they come: namely, both in one—without appeal to cosmic tortoise to hold up cosmic elephant to hold up cosmic pillar to hold up the factual cosmos we are considering.

(*g*) In a myopic and short-time view Event and Designation appear to be separates. The appearance does no harm if it is held where it belongs within narrow ranges of inquiry. For a general account of knowings and knowns the wider envisionment in system is proposed.

(*h*) Overlapping Fact, as we are postulating it within the range of *namings,* are, on one side, perceptions, manipulations, habituations and other adaptations; on the other side, symbolic-knowledge procedures such as those of mathematics. We shall be taking these into account as events-designated, even though for the present we are not inquiring into them with respect to possible designatory, quasi-designatory or otherwise fact-presenting functions of their own along the evolutionary line. Our terminology will in no way be such as to restrict consideration of them, but rather to further it, when such consideration becomes practicable.

(*i*) If Designations, as we postulate them for our inquiry, are factually durational-extensional, then these Designations, as designat*ings, are* themselves Events. Similarly, the Events as events are designational. The two phases, designating and designated, lie within a full process of designation. It is not the subjectmatter before us, but the available language forms, that make this latter statement difficult.[12]

(*j*) Most generally, Fact, in our terminology, is not limited to what any one man knows, nor to what is known to any one human grouping, nor to any one span of time such as our own day and age. On the designatory side in our project of research it has the full range and spread that, as we said above, it has on the event side, with all the futures and the pasts, the betters and the poorers, comprised as they come. In our belief the Newtonian era has settled the status of fact definitely in this way, for our generation of research at least. First, Newtonian mechanics rose to credal strength in the shelter of its glorified absolutes. Then at the hands of Faraday, Clerk Maxwell and Einstein, it lost its absolutes, lost its credal claims, and emerged chastened and improved. It thus gained the high rating of a magnificent approximation as compared with its earlier trivial self-rating of eternal certainty. The coming years—fifty, or a thousand, whatever it takes—remain quite free for change. Any intelligent voice will say this; the trouble is to get ears to hear. Our new assurance is better than the old assurance. *Knowing and the known, event and designation—the full knowledge—go forward together.* Eventuation is observed. Accept this in principle, not merely as a casual comment on an accidental happening:—you then have before you what our terminology recognizes when it places Fact-

12. This paragraph replaces one noted in the Preface as deleted. As first written it read, after the opening sentence, as follows: "Similarly, the Events as designational, *are* Designations. It is not the subject-matter before us, but the available language forms that make this latter statement difficult. The two uses of 'are' in the sentences 'Events are Designations' and 'Designations are Events' differ greatly, each 'are' representing one of the aspects within the broader presentation of Fact. To recognize events as designated while refusing to call them designations in the activity sense, would be a limitation that would maintain a radical split between naming and named at the very time that their connective framework was being acknowledged. Our position is emphatic upon this point. It is clear enough that in the older sense events are not designations; it should be equally clear and definite that in our procedure and terminology they are designational—designation—or (with due caution in pluralizing) Designations. To control the two uses of the word 'are' in the two forms of statement, and to maintain the observation and report that 'Designations are Events,' while also 'Events are Designations'—this is the main strain our procedure will place upon the reader. Proceeding under hypothesis (and without habituation to hypothesis there will be no advance at all) this should not be too severe a requirement for one who recognizes the complexity of the situation and has an active interest in clearing it up."

in-growth as a sound enough base for research with no need to bother over minuscular mentals or crepuscular reals alleged to be responsible for it.

2. *Circularity.* When we said above that designations are events and events designations, we adopted *circularity*—procedure in a circle—openly, explicitly, emphatically. Several ways of pretending to avoid such circularity are well known. Perhaps at one end everything is made tweedledum, and perhaps at the other everything is made tweedledee, or perhaps in between little tweedledums and little tweedledees, companionable but infertile, essential to each other but untouchable by each other, are reported all along the line. We have nothing to apologize for in the circularity we choose in preference to the old talk-ways. We observe world-being-known-to-man-in-it; we report the observation; we proceed to inquire into it, circularity or no circularity. This is all there is to it. And the circularity is not merely round the circle in one direction: the course is both ways round at once in full mutual function.

3. *The Differentiations That Follow.* Given fact, observed aspectually as Event and as Designation, our next indicated task is to develop further terminological organization for the two aspects separately. We shall undertake this shortly and leave the matter there so far as the present preliminary outline is concerned. To aid us, though, we shall require firm statement about certain tools to be used in the process. We must, that is, be able to name certain procedures so definitely that they will not be confounded with current procedures on a different basis. Events will be differentiated with respect to a certain range of plasticity that is comparable in a general way to the physical differentiations of gaseous, liquid and solid. For these we shall use the names Situation, Occurrence and Object. As for Designation, we shall organize it in an evolutionary scheme of behavioral sign processes of which it is one form, the names we apply being Sign, Signal, Name and Symbol. The preliminary steps we find it necessary to take before presenting these differentiations are: first, steady maintenance of a distinction among the various branches of scientific inquiry in terms of selected subjectmatters of research, rather than in terms of materials assumed to be waiting for research in advance; second, a firm use of the word "specification" to designate the type of naming to be employed as contrasted with the myriad verbal processes that go by the name of

"definition"; third, the establishment of our right to selective observational control of specific situations within subjectmatters by a competent distinction of *trans*-actions from *inter*-actions.

4. *Sciences as Subjectmatters.* The broad division of regions of scientific research commonly recognized today is that into the physical, the biological and the psychological. However mathematics, where inquiry attains maximum precision, lacks any generally accepted form of organization with these sciences; and sociology, where maximum imprecision is found, also fails of a distinctive manner of incorporation.[13] Fortunately this scheme of division is gradually losing its rigidities. A generation or two ago physics stood aloof from chemistry; today it has constructively incorporated it. In the biological range today, the most vivid and distinctive member is physiology, yet the name "biology" covers many gross adaptational studies not employing the physiological techniques; in addition, the name "biology" assuredly covers everything that is psychological, unless perchance some "psyche" is involved that is "non-" or "ultra-" human. The word "psychological" itself is a hold-over from an earlier era, in which such a material series as "*the* physical," "*the* vital" and "*the* psychic" was still believed in and taken to offer three different realms of substance presented as raw material by Nature or by God for our perpetual puzzlement. If we are to establish knowings and knowns in a single system of Fact, we certainly must be free from addiction to a presumptive universe compounded out of three basically different kinds of materials. Better said, however, it is our present freedom from such material enthrallment, attained for us by the general advance of scientific research, that at long last has made us able to see all knowings and knowns, by hypothesis, as in one system.

Within Fact we shall recognize the distinctions of the scientific field as being those of subjectmatters, not those of materials,[14] unless one speaks of materials only in the sense that their differences

13. We shall deal with the very important subject of mathematics elsewhere. Sociological inquiries, with the exception of anthropology, are hardly far enough advanced to justify any use of them as subjectmatters in our present inquiry.

14. An extended consideration of many phases of this issue and approaches to its treatment is given by Coleman R. Griffith in his *Principles of Systematic Psychology* (Urbana, Illinois, 1943). Compare the section on "The Scientific Use of Participles and Nouns" (pp. 489–497) and various passages indexed under "Science."

themselves arise in and are vouched for strictly by the technological procedures that are available in the given stages of inquiry. Terminologically, we shall distinguish *physical, physiological* and *behavioral*[15] regions of science. We shall accept the word "biological" under our postulation as covering unquestionably both physiological and behavioral inquiries, but we find the range of its current applications much too broad to be safe for the purposes of the present distinctive terminology. The technical differentiation, in research, of physiological procedures from behavioral is of the greatest import in the state of inquiry today, and this would be pushed down out of sight by any heavy stress on the word "biological," which, as we have said, we emphatically believe *must* cover them both. We wish to stress most strongly that physical, physiological and behavioral inquiries in the present state of knowledge represent three great distinctive lines of technique; while any one of them may be brought to the aid of any other, *direct* positive extension of statement from the firm technical formulations of one into the information-stating requirements of another cannot be significantly made as knowledge today stands. Physical formulation does not directly yield heredity, nor does physiological formulation directly yield word-meanings, sentences and mathematical formulas. To complete the circle, behavioral process, while producing physical science, cannot directly in its own procedure yield report on the embodied physical event. This circularity, once again, is in the knowledge—in the knowings and the knowns—not in any easy-going choice we are free and competent to make in the hope we can cleave to it, evidence or no evidence.

15. Our use of the word "behavioral" has no "behavioristic" implications. We are no more behavioristic than mentalistic, disavowing as we do, under hypothesis, "isms" and "istics" of all types. The word "behavior" is in frequent use by astronomers, physicists, physiologists and ecologists, as well as by psychologists and sociologists. Applied in the earlier days of its history to human conduct, it has drifted along to other uses, pausing for a time among animal-students, and having had much hopeful abuse by mechanistic enthusiasts. We believe it rightfully belongs, however, where we are placing it. Such a word as "conduct" has many more specialized implications than has "behavior" and would not serve at all well for the name for a great division of research. We shall be open to the adoption of any substitutes as our work proceeds, but thus far have failed to find a more efficient or safer word to use. In such a matter as this, long-term considerations are much more important than the verbal fashions of a decade or two.

5. *Specification.* The word "definition," as currently used, covers exact symbolic statements in mathematics; it covers procedures under Aristotelian logic; it covers all the collections of word-uses, old and new, that the dictionaries assemble, and many still more casual linguistic procedures. The word "definition" must manifestly be straightened out, if any sound presentation of knowings and knowns is to be secured.[16] We have fair reason to believe that most of the difficulty in what is called the "logic of mathematics" is due to an endeavor to force consolidation of two types of human behavior, both labeled "definition," (though one stresses heavily, while the other diverges from, the use of namings) without preliminary inquiry into the simpler facts of the life linguistic. In our terminology we shall assign the word "definition" to the region of mathematical and syntactical consistency, while for the lesser specimens of "dictionary definition" we shall employ the name "characterization." In our own work in this book we shall attempt no *definition* whatever in the formal sense we shall assign the word. We shall at times not succeed in getting beyond preliminary characterization. Our aim in the project, however, is to advance towards such an accuracy in naming as science ever increasingly achieves. Such accuracy in naming we shall call "specification." Consider what the word "heat" stood for in physics before Rumford and Joule, and what it tells us in physical specification today. Consider the changes the word "atom" has undergone in the past generation. Modern chemical terminology is a highly specialized form of specification of operations undertaken. However, the best illustration for our purposes is probably the terminology of genera and species. In the days when animals were theological specialities of creation, the naming level was that of characterization. After demonstration had been given that species had natural origins, scientific specification, as we understand it, developed. We still find it, of course, straining at times towards taxonomic rigidities, but over against this we find it forever rejuvenating itself by free inquiry up even

16. The task of straightening out proved to be more complex, even, than we had estimated. It led us to drop the word "definition" altogether from technical terminology, thus reducing it for the time being to the status of a colloquialism. We nevertheless permit our text in this passage to appear unrevised, since we are more interested in the continuity of inquiry than we are in positive determinations of word-usage at this stage. *See* the introductory remarks to Chapter 7, and the summary in Chapter 11.

to the risk of its own obliteration. Abandonment of the older magic of name-to-reality correspondence is one of the marks of specification. Another will be observed when specification has been clearly differentiated from symbolic definition. In both its aspects of Event and Designation we find Fact spread in "spectrumlike" form. We use "specification" to mark this scientific characteristic of efficient naming. Peirce's stress on the "precept that is more serviceable than a definition" [17] involves the attitude we are here indicating. Specification operates everywhere in that field of inquiry covered by affirmation and assertion, proposition and judgment, in Dewey's logical program. The defects of the traditional logics exhibited in Chapter 1 were connected with their lack of attention to the accurate specification of their own subjectmatters; at no point in our examination did we make our criticisms rest on consistency in definition in the sense of the word "consistency" which we shall develop as we proceed through the differentiation of symbol from name and of symbolic behavior from naming behavior.

6. *Transaction.* We have established Fact as involving both Designation and designated Event. We have inspected inquiry into Fact in terms of subjectmatters that are determinable under the techniques of inquiry, not in terms of materials presented from without. [18] Both treatments make selection under hypothesis a dominant phase of procedure. Selection under hypothesis, however, affects all observation. We shall take this into account terminologically by contrasting events reported in interactions with events reported as transactions. Later chapters will follow dealing with this central issue in our procedure: the right, namely, to open our eyes to see. Here we can only touch broadly upon it. Pre-scientific procedure largely regarded "things" as possessing powers of their own, under or in which they acted. Galileo is the scientist whose name is most strongly identified with the change to modern procedure. We may take the word "*action*" as a most general characterization for events where their durational process is being stressed. Where the older approach had most commonly seen *self-action* in "the facts," the newer approach took form under Newton as a system of interaction, marked especially

17. See Chapter 1, Section I.
18. Again, a very vaguely used word.

by the third "law of motion"—that action and reaction are equal and opposite. The classical mechanics is such a system of interaction involving particles, boundaries, and laws of effects. Before it was developed—before, apparently, it could develop—observation of a new type differing from the pre-Galilean was made in a manner essentially transactional. This enters in Galileo's report on inertia, appearing in the Newtonian formulation as the first "law of motion," namely, that any motion uninterfered with will continue in a straight line. This set up a motion, directly, factually, as event.[19] The field of knowings and knowns in which we are working requires transactional observation, and this is what we are giving it and what our terminology is designed to deal with. The epistemologies, logics, psychologies and sociologies today are still largely on a self-actional basis. In psychology a number of tentative efforts are being made towards an *interactional* presentation, with balanced components. Our position is that the traditional language currently used about knowings and knowns (and most other language about behaviors, as well) shatters the subjectmatter into fragments in advance of inquiry and thus destroys instead of furthering comprehensive observation for it. We hold that observation must be set free; and that, to advance this aim, a postulatory appraisal of the main historical patterns of observation should be made, and identifying namings should be provided. Our own procedure is the *transactional*, in which is asserted the right to see together, extensionally and durationally, much that is talked about conventionally as if it were composed of irreconcilable separates. We do not present this procedure as being more real or generally valid than any other, but as being the one now needed in the field where we work. In the same spirit in which physicists perforce use both particle and wave presentations we here employ both interactional and transactional observation.[20] Important specialized studies belong in

19. In the psychological range the comparable fundamental laboratory experiments of import for our purposes are those of Max Wertheimer upon the direct visual observability of motions. See "Experimentelle Studien über das Sehen von Bewegung" (*Zeitschrift für Psychologie*, LXI [1912], 161–265). In a much weakened form his results are used in the type of psychology known as "Gestalt," but in principle they still await constructive development.
20. The word "field" is a strong candidate for use in the transactional region. However, it has not been fully clarified as yet for physics, and the way it has been employed in psychological and social studies has been impressionistic

this field in which the organism is made central to attention. This is always legitimate in all forms of inquiry within a transactional setting, so long as it is deliberately undertaken, not confusedly or with "self-actional" implications. As place-holders in this region of nomenclature we shall provisionally set down *behavior-agent* and *behavior-object*. They represent specialized interactional treatments within the wider transactional presentation, with organisms or persons or actors named uncertainly on the one hand and with environments named in variegated forms on the other.

7. *Situation, Occurrence, Object.* We may now proceed to distinguish Situation, Occurrence and Object as forms of Event. Event is durational-extensional; it is what "takes place," what is inspected as "*a* taking place." These names do not provide a "classification," unless classification is understood as a focusing of attention within subjectmatters rather than as an arrangement of materials. The word "situation" is used with increasing frequency today, but so waveringly that the more it is used the worse its own status seems to become. We insist that in simple honesty it should stand *either* for the environment of an object (interactionally), *or* for the full situation including whatever object may be selectively specified within it (transactionally), and that there be no wavering. We shall establish our own use for the word *situation* in this latter form. When an event is of the type that is readily observable in transition within the ordinary spans of human discrimination of temporal and spatial changes, we shall call it *occurrence*. The ordinary use of "event" in daily life is close to this, and if we generalize the application of the word, as we have provisionally done, to cover situation and object as well as occurrence, then we require a substitute in the more limited place. Occurrence fairly fills the vacancy. *Object*[21] is chosen as the clearly indicated name for stabilized, enduring situations,

---

and often unscrupulous. "Field" must remain, therefore, on our list of vague words, candidates for improvement. When the physical status of the word is settled—and Einstein and his immediate associates have long concentrated on this problem—then if the terminology can be transferred to behavioral inquiry we shall know how to make the transfer with integrity. See Chapter 5, note 17.

21. "The name *objects* will be reserved for subject-matter so far as it has been produced and ordered in settled form by means of inquiry; proleptically, objects are the *objectives* of inquiry" (*Logic: The Theory of Inquiry*, p. 119 [*Later Works* 12:122]). For "situation" see *ibid.*, pp. 66 ff. [*LW* 12:72 ff.]. The word "occurrence" is, as has been indicated, provisionally placed.

for occurrences that need so long a span of time, or perhaps so minute a space-change, that the space and time changes are not themselves within the scope of ordinary, everyday perceptual attention. Thus any one of the three words Situation, Occurrence and Object may, if focusing of attention shifts, spread over the range of the others, all being equally held as Event. We have here a fair illustration of what we have previously called a word-cluster. The Parthenon is an object to a visitor, and has so been for all the centuries since its construction. It is nevertheless an occurrence across some thousands of years. While for certain purposes of inquiry it may be marked off as object-in-environment, for thoroughgoing investigation it must be seized as situation, of which the object-specification is at best one phase or feature. There is here no issue of reality, no absolute yes or no to assert, but only free determination under inquiry.

8. *Sign, Signal, Name, Symbol.* When we turn to Designation, our immediate problem is not that of distinguishing the variety of *its* forms. Specification, the form most immediately concerning us, has already been noted. What we have to do instead is to place designation itself among behavioral events. Circularity is again here strikingly involved. Our treatment must be in terms of Event as much as in terms of Designation, with full convertibility of the two. The event is behavioral. Designation (a behavioral event) can be viewed as one stage in the range of behavioral evolution from the sensitive reactions of protozoa to the most complex symbolic procedures of mathematics. In this phase of the inquiry we shall alter the naming. Viewing the behavioral event, we shall name it directly Name instead of replacing "name" by "designation" as seemed necessary for provisional practical reasons on the obverse side of the inquiry. At a later stage we shall undertake to establish the characteristic behavioral process as *sign*, a process not found in either physical or physiological techniques of inquiry. We shall thus understand the name "sign" to be used so as to cover the entire range of behavioral activity. There are many stages or levels of behaviors, but for the greater part of our needs a three-level differentiation will furnish gross guidance. The lower level, including perceptions, manipulations, habituations, adaptations, etc., we shall name *signal* (adapting the word from Pavlov's frequent usage). Where organized language is employed as sign, we shall speak of *name*. In mathematical regions (for reasons to be discussed fully later) we shall speak

of *symbol*. Signal, Name and Symbol will be the three differentiations of Sign, where "sign" indicates most broadly the "knowl-
edge-like" processes of behavior in a long ascending series. Vital
to this construction, even though no development for the moment may be offered, is the following statement: The name "Sign"
and the names adjusted to it *shall all be understood transactionally,* which in this particular case is to say that they do not name
items or characteristics of organisms alone, nor do they name
items or characteristics of environments alone; in every case, they
name the *activity* that occurs *of both together.*

V

By the use of Sign-Signal-Name-Symbol we indicate the
locus for the knowing-naming process and for other behavioral
processes within cosmos. By the use of Fact-Event-Designation
we specify the process of event-determination through which
cosmos is presented as itself a locus for such loci. The two types
of terminology set forth different phases of a common process.
They can be so held, if we insist upon freedom for transactional
observation in cases in which ancient word-forms have fractured
fact and if we lose fear of circularity. It is our task in later chapters
to develop this terminology and to test it in situations that arise.
  For the present our terminological guide-posts, provisionally
laid out, are as follows:

SUGGESTED EXPERIMENTAL NAMING

Fact: Our cosmos as it is before us progressingly in
                   knowings through namings.
Event:[22]   "Fact" named as taking place.
Designation: Naming as taking place in "fact."
Physical,   Differentiations of the techniques of inquiry,
Physiological,   marking off subjectmatters as sciences un-
Behavioral: der development, and not constricted to con-
                   formity with primitive pre-views of "mate-
                   rials" of "reality."

---

22. The word "existence" was later substituted for "event" in this position. See
    Chapter 11.

Characterization: Linguistic procedure preliminary to developed specification, including much "dictionary-definition."

Specification: Accuracy of designation along the free lines through which modern sciences have developed.

Definition:[23] Symbolic procedure linguistically evolved, not directly employing designatory tests.

Action (Activity): Event stressed with respect to durational transition.

Self-Action: Pre-scientific presentation in terms of presumptively independent "actors," "souls," "minds," "selves," "powers" or "forces," taken as activating events.

Interaction: Presentation of particles or other objects organized as operating upon one another.

Transaction:[24] Functional observation of full system, actively necessary to inquiry at some stages, held in reserve at other stages, frequently requiring the breaking down of older verbal impactions of naming.

Behavior-Agent: Behavioral organic action, interactionally inspected within transaction; agent in the sense of *re*-agent rather than of act*or*.

Behavior-Object: Environmental specialization of object with respect to agent within behavioral transaction.

Situation: Event as subjectmatter of inquiry, always transactionally viewed as the full subjectmatter; never to be taken as detachable "environment" over against object.

Occurrence:[25] Event designated as in process under transitions such as are most readily identifiable in everyday human-size contacts.

23. The word "definition" later dropped from technical terminological use, so far as our present development goes.
24. For introductory uses of the word see John Dewey, "Conduct and Experience," in *Psychologies of 1930* (Worcester, Massachusetts). Compare also his *Logic: The Theory of Inquiry*, p. 458 [*LW* 12:452], where stress is placed on the *single continuous event*.
25. The word "event" was later substituted for "occurrence" in this usage. See Chapter 11.

Object:	Event in its more firmly stabilized forms— never, however, as in final fixations—always available as subjectmatter under transfer to situational inspection, should need arise as inquiry progresses.
Sign:	Characteristic adaptational behavior of organism-environment; the "cognitive" in its broadest reaches when viewed transactionally as process (not in organic or environmental specialization).
Signal:	Transactional sign in the perceptive-manipulative ranges.
Name:	Specialized development of sign among hominidae; apparently not reaching the full designational stage (excepting, perhaps, on blocked evolutionary lines) until *homo sapiens.*
Symbol:	A later linguistic development of sign, forfeiting specific designatory applications to gain heightened efficiency in other ways.

The above terminology is offered as provisional only. Especially is further discussion needed in the cases of Event, Occurrence, and Definition. Later decisions, after further examination, are reported in Chapter 11, with several footnotes along the route serving as markers for progress being made.

We regard the following as common sense observation upon the manner of discourse about knowledge that we find current around us.

The knowledge of knowledge itself that we possess today is weak knowledge—perhaps as weak as any we have; it stands greatly in need of de-sentimentalized research.

Fact is notoriously two-faced. It is cosmos as noted by a speck of cosmos. Competent appraisal takes this into account.

What is beyond Fact—beyond the knowing and the known— is not worth bothering about in any inquiry undertaken into knowings and knowns.

Science as *inquiry* thrives within limits such as these, and science offers sound guidance. Scientific specification thrives in, and requires, such limits; why, then, should not also inquiry and specification for knowings and the known?

Knowings are behaviors. Neither inquiry into knowings nor inquiry into behaviors can expect satisfactory results unless the other goes with it hand in hand.[26]

26. Attention is called in summary to the "vague words" one is at times compelled to use. "Knowledge," "thing," "field," "within" and "without" have been so characterized in text or footnotes; also all prepositions and the use of "quotes" to distinguish names from the named; even the words "vague" and "firm" as we find them in use today. "Aspect" and "phase" have been indicated as vague for our purposes today, but as having definite possibilities of development as we proceed. It will be noticed that the word "experience" has not been used in the present text. No matter what efforts have heretofore been made to apply it definitely, it has been given conflicting renderings by readers who among them, one may almost say, have persisted in forcing vagueness upon it. We shall discuss it along with other abused words at a later place.

3. Postulations

I

In the search to secure firm names for knowings and knowns, we have held, first, that man, inclusive of all his knowings, should be investigated as "natural" within a natural world;[1] and, secondly, that investigation can, and must, employ sustained observation akin in its standards—though not, of course, in all its techniques—to the direct observation through which science advances.

Scientific observation does not report by fiat; it is checked and rechecked by many observers upon their own work and the work of others until its report is assured. This is its great characteristic. From its simplest to its most far-reaching activities it holds itself open to revision in a degree made strikingly clear by what happened to the Newtonian account of gravitation after its quarter millennium of established "certainty." The more scientific and accurate observation becomes, the less does it claim ultimacy for the specific assertions it achieves.

Where observation remains open to revision, there is always a certain "if" about it. Its report is thus conditional, and the surrounding conditions, under careful formulation, become the postulation under which it holds place. In the case of problems of

---

1. By "natural world" with man "natural" within it, the reader should understand that background of inquiry which since Darwin's time has become standard for perhaps all fields of serious scientific enterprise with the single exception of inquiry into knowings and knowns. We shall not employ the words "naturalism" or "naturalistic." We avoid them primarily because our concern is with free research, where the word "nature" specifies nothing beyond what men can learn about it; and, secondly, because various current metaphysical or "substantial" implications of what is called "naturalism" are so alien to us that any entanglement with them would produce serious distortion of our intentions.

limited range, where conditions are familiar to the workers (as, for example, in a physical laboratory, for a particular experiment under way), an unqualified report of the verified results as "fact" is customary and meets no objection. Where, however, assertions that run far afield are involved, the postulational background must be kept steadily in view, and must be stated as conditional to the report itself; otherwise serious distortions may result.

This is emphatically required for a search such as ours in the case of knowings and knowns. Our procedure must rest on observation and must report under postulation. Simply and directly we say that the sciences work in nature, and that any inquiry into knowings and knowns must work in the same nature the sciences work in and, as far as possible, along the same general lines. We say observation is the great scientific stronghold. We say that all[2] observations belong in system, and that where their connections are not now known it is, by postulation, permissible to approach them as if connection could be established. We totally reject that ancient hindrance put upon inquiry such as ours by those who proclaim that the "knower" must be in some way superior to the nature he knows; and equally by those who give superiority to that which they call "the known." We recognize that as observers we are human organisms, limited to the positions on the globe from which we make our observations, and we accept this not as being a hindrance, but instead as a situation from which great gain may be secured. We let our postulations rise out of the observations, and we then use the postulations to increase efficiency of observation, never to restrain it. It is in this sense of circularity that we employ those very postulations of nature, of observation and of postulation itself, that our opening paragraphs have set down.[3]

The dictionaries allot to the word "postulate" two types of ap-

2. The word "all" is, of course, one more vague word. Heretofore we have avoided it altogether—or hope we have. An adequate technical language for our purposes would have one word for the "all" of scientific specification, and another for the "all" of symbolic definition. As we have previously said, our discussions limit themselves strictly to the former use.
3. Compare the three conditions of a search for names set down at the start of Chapter 2, Section I, and accompanied by the three negations: that no purely private report, no "foundations" beyond the range of hypothesis, and no final declaration secure from the need of further inquiry can safely be accepted or employed.

plication. One presents something "taken for granted as the true basis for reasoning or belief"; the other, "a condition required for further operations." Our approach is manifestly of this second type.[4] We shall mark this by speaking of postulations rather than of postulates, so far as our own procedures are concerned. This phrasing is more reliable, even though at times it will seem a bit clumsy.

What we have said is equivalent to holding that postulations arise out of the field of inquiry, and maintain themselves strictly subject to the needs of that field.[5] They are always open to reexamination. The one thing they most emphatically *never* are is unexaminable.

To this must be added a further comment that postulation is double-fronted.[6] It must give as thorough a consideration to attitudes of approach in inquiry as it does to the subjectmatter examined, and to each always in conjunction with the other.[7]

It is very frequently said that no matter what form of inquiry one undertakes into life and mind one involves himself always in metaphysics and can never escape it. In contrast with this hoary adage, our position is that if one seeks with enough earnestness to identify his attitude of workmanship and the directions of his orientation, he can by-pass the metaphysics by the simple act of keeping observation and postulation hand-in-hand; the varied "ultimates" of metaphysics become chips that lie where they fall. Our postulations, accordingly, gain their rating, not by any pecu-

4. Max Wertheimer, *Productive Thinking* (New York, 1945), p. 179 reports a conversation with Einstein concerning the latter's early approaches to relativity. In answer to a direct question Einstein said: "There is no . . . difference . . . between reasonable and arbitrary axioms. The only virtue of axioms is to furnish fundamental propositions from which one can derive conclusions that fit the facts."
5. Dewey, *Logic: The Theory of Inquiry* (New York, 1938), pp. 16–19 [*Later Works* 12:23–26].
6. Bentley, *Behavior, Knowledge, Fact* (Bloomington, Indiana, 1935), Chap. XXX. It is in the behavioral field particularly that this characteristic must never for a moment be neglected.
7. One further comment on the word "postulation" is needed. We are not here attempting to determine its final terminological status, but merely specifying the use we are now making of it. In the end it may well be that it should be assigned to the region of Symbol (Chapter 2, Section IV, #8) and a different word employed in such territory as we are now exploring. We are choosing "postulation" instead of "hypothesis" for the immediate task because of its greater breadth of coverage in ordinary use. Freedom, as always, is reserved (Chapter 2, Section III, and Chapter 11) to make improvements in our provisional terminology when the proper time comes.

liarity or priority they possess, but by the plainness and openness of their statement of the conditions under which work is, and will be, done. If this statement at times takes categorical verbal form, this is by way of endeavor at sharpness of expression, not through any desire to impose guidance on the work of others.

In the course of our preliminary studies for this series of reports we assembled a score or two of groups of postulations. These experiments taught us the complexity of the problem and the need for a steady eye upon all phases of inquiry. Instead of obtaining a single overall postulation, as we might have anticipated, we found that the more thorough the work became, the more it required specializations of postulations, and these in forms that are complementary. We shall display certain of these postulations, primarily as aids to our further discussion, but partly because of the interest such exhibits may have for workers in collateral fields. We further hope the display may stimulate cooperation leading to better formulation from other experimenters with similar manners of inquiry.

In approaching the examination let the reader recall, first, that we have previously selected namings as the species of knowings most directly open to observation, and thus as our best entry to inquiry;[8] and, secondly, that we have taken the named and the namings (being instances of the known and the knowings) as forming together one event for inquiry[9]—one transaction[10]— since, in any full observation, if one vanishes, the other vanishes also. These things we observe; we observe them under and through the attitudes expressed in our opening paragraphs; as such observations they form the core of the postulatory expansion to follow.[11]

8. Chapter 2, Section IV and Chapter 1, Section I.
9. Chapter 2, Section III.
10. Chapter 2, Section IV and Chapters 4 and 5.
11. One of the authors of this volume (J. D.) wishes to make specific correction of certain statements in his *Logic: The Theory of Inquiry* about *observation*. As far as those statements limit the word to cases of what are called "sense-perception"—or, in less dubious language, to cases of observation under conditions approaching those of laboratory control—they should be altered. For the distinction made in that text between "observation" and "ideation" he would now substitute a distinction between two phases of observation, depending on comparative temporal-spatial range or scope of subjectmatter. What is called observation in that text is only such observations as are limited to the narrower ranges of subjectmatter; which, however, hold a distinctive and critical place in the testing of observations of the more extensive type.

II

In order to make plain the background against which our postulations can be appraised, we start by exhibiting certain frequently occurring programs for behavioral inquiry,[12] which are to be rated as postu*lates* rather than as postu*lations* under the differentiation we have drawn between the two words. Characteristic of them is that they evade, ignore, or strive to rid themselves of that "circularity"[13] in knowledge which we, in contrast, frankly accept as we find it. Characteristic, further, is that their proponents take them for granted so unhesitatingly in the form of "truths" that they rarely bring them out into clear expression. It is because of this latter characteristic that we cannot readily find well-organized specimens to cite but are compelled to construct them as best we can out of the scattered materials we find in works on epistemology, logic, and psychology. Because their type is so different from the postulations we shall develop for our own use, we label them with the letters *X, Y,* and *Z* in a series kept separate at the far end of the alphabet.

X. Epistemological Irreconcilables

1. "Reals" exist and become known.
2. "Minds" exist and do the knowing.
3. "Reals" and "minds" inhabit irreconcilable "realms."[14]
4. Epistemological magic[15] is required to reveal how the one irreconcilable achieves its knowing and the other its being known.

Y. Logical Go-Betweens

1. "Reals" exist ("objects," "entities," "substances," etc.).
2. "Minds" exist ("thoughts," "meanings," "judgments," etc.).
3. "Thirds" exist to intervene ("words," "terms," "sentences," "propositions," etc.).

12. For the word "behavior," see Chapter 2, n. 15.
13. Chapter 2, Section IV, #2.
14. With variations of "more or less" (though still "irreconcilable"), and with special limiting cases on one side or the other in which winner takes all.
15. "Magic" (dictionary definition): "Any supposed supernatural art."

4. Logical exploration of "thirds"[16] will reconcile the irreconcilables.

Z. Physiologic-psychologic Straitjackets

1. "Reals" exist as matter, tactually or otherwise sensibly vouched for.
2. "Minds" exist as mentaloid manifestations of organically specialized "reals."[17]
3. Study of organically "real" matter (muscular, neural, or cortical) yields knowledge of matter, including the organic, the mentaloid, and the knowledges themselves.
4. The "certainty" of matter in some way survives all the "uncertainties" of growing knowledge about it.

These three groups of postulates all include non-observables; that is, through the retention of primitive namings surviving from early cultures they adopt or purport to adopt certain materials of inquiry that cannot be identified as "objects" under any of the forms of observation modern research employs.[18] X is in notorious disrepute except among limited groups of epistemological specialists. Y works hopefully with linguistic devices that our preceding examination has shown to be radically deficient.[19] Z is serviceable for simple problems at the level of what used to be called "the senses," and at times for preliminary orderings of more complex subjectmatters, but it quickly shows itself unable to provide the all-essential direct descriptions these latter require. All three default not only in observability, but also in the

16. Though always with the risk of other thirds "to bite 'em; And so proceed *ad infinitum.*"
17. Watson's early "behaviorism" (far remote, of course, from the factual behavior of our inquiry) included an identification of linguistic procedure as physiological process of vocal organs—an identification that lacked not merely the transactional view we employ, but even an interactional consideration of the environment. An excellent recent illustration of much more refined treatment is that of Roy Wood Sellars, the *Journal of Philosophy,* XLI (1944), who writes (p. 688): "I think we can locate the psychical as a *natural isolate* in the functioning organism and study its context and conditions." The issue could hardly be more neatly drawn between the "process" we are to investigate and the purported "things" the X, Y, and Z postulates offer for examination.
18. Cf. postulations B5 and B6, below. For "objects," see Chapter 2, Section IV.
19. Chapter 1, Section X.

characteristics of that manner of approach which we have here called "natural" (though Z has aspirations in this latter direction).[20] Beyond this, as already indicated, all three are employed rather as articles of faith than as postulations proper.

III

In contrast with the approaches X, Y, and Z, we shall now write down in simple introductory statement what we regard as the main features of the postulations which, inspired by and in sympathy with the progress modern sciences have made, are most broadly needed as guides to inquiry into behaviors as natural events in the world.

A. POSTULATIONS FOR BEHAVIORAL RESEARCH

1. The cosmos: as system or field of factual inquiry.[21]
2. Organisms: as cosmic components.
3. Men: as organisms.
4. Behavings of men: as organic-environmental events.
5. Knowings (including the knowings of the cosmos and its postulation): as such organic-environmental behavings.

The above postulations are to be taken literally and to be scrupulously so maintained in inquiry.

So important is the italicized sentence, and so common and vicious that manner of lip-service to which hands and eyes pay no attention, that we might well give this sentence place as a sixth postulation.

Entry No. 1 accepts positively the cosmos of science as the locus of behavioral inquiry. This acceptance is full and unqualified, though free, of course, from the expansive applications speculative scientists so often indulge in. No. 2 and No. 3 are

20. One of our earlier experimental formulations may be mentioned: (*a*) existing epistemologies are trivial or worse; (*b*) the source of the trouble lies in primitive speech conventions; (*c*) in particular, the presentation of a "mind" as an individual "isolate," whether in "psychical" or in "physiological" manifestation, is destructive.
21. The system is named Fact (Chapter 2, Section IV, #1).

perhaps everywhere accepted, *except for inquiry into knowings and knowns.* No. 4 differs sharply from the common view in which the organism is taken as the locus of "the behavior" and as proceeding under its own powers in detachment from a comparably detachable environment, rather than as a phase of the full organic-environmental event.[22] No. 5, so far as we know, is not yet in explicit use in detailed research of the sort we are undertaking, and its introduction is here held to be required if firm names for knowings and knowns are to be achieved.

Following postulations *A* for behavioral events, as subjectmatters, we now set forth postulations *B* for inquiry into such behavioral subjectmatters. The type of inquiry we have before us is that which proceeds through Designation. Long ago we chose naming-events as the particular variety of knowings upon which to concentrate study.[23] Now we are selecting Designation[24] as the specialized method of inquiry we are to employ. Before proceeding to more detail with postulations *A*, we complement them with postulations *B*, as if we set a right hand over against a left somewhat in the manner we have already spoken of as "doublefronted." *A* and *B* together offer us instances of that "circularity" we find wherever we go, which by us is not merely recognized, but put to work—not deplored but seized upon as a key to observation, description, and controlled inquiry.[25] The procedure looks complex but we cannot help it any more than the physicists of three generations ago could "help it" when electricity (to say nothing of electromagnetic waves) refused to stay in locations or submit to a mathematics that had sufficed, until that time, for the mechanics of particles.

Given complementary postulations *A* and *B*, one may expect to find the components of one postulation reappearing in the other, but differently stressed, and under different development. Thus postulation *A*1 views Fact in the aspect of Event, whereas *B*1 views it in the aspect of inquiry under or through Designation

22. For legitimate procedures in provisional detachments, see postulations *D*8 and *G*3.
23. Chapter 2, Sections II and III.
24. Chapter 2, Section IV, #1. For the distinction provisionally employed between the word "naming" and "designation," see Chapter 2, Section IV, #8.
25. No priority is assumed for *A* over *B* or *vice versa.* Postulations *A* enter first into our immediate treatment as the needed offset to the current fracturings and pseudo-realistic strivings of *X*, *Y*, and *Z*.

("event" being here understood with the range given in Chapter 11 to the word "existence"). Similar cases appear frequently; they are typical and necessary.

B. Postulations for Inquiry into Subjectmatters under Designation [26]

1. A single system of subjectmatters is postulated, to be called cosmos or nature.

2. Distribution of subjectmatters of inquiry into departments varies [27] from era to era in accordance with variation in the technical stage of inquiry.

3. Postulations for each of the most commonly recognized present departments (physical, physiological, and behavioral) are separately practicable, free from the dictatorship of any one over another, yet holding all in system. [28]

4. The range of the knowings is coextensive with the range of the subjectmatters known.

5. Observation, such as modern technique of experiment has achieved, or fresh technique may achieve, is postulated for whatever is, or is to be, subjectmatter. Nothing enters inquiry as inherently non-observable nor as requiring an independent type of observation of its own. What is observed is linked with what is not then and there observed.

26. Not to be overlooked is the express statement in the text that these postulations *B* are for research through namings, and are *not* set up for all types of search and formulation whatsoever. We cultivate our present gardens, leaving plenty of room for other gardens for future workers.

27. "Varies . . . in accordance with" might be profitably replaced by "is in function with," if we could be sure that the word "function" would be understood as indicating a *kind* of problem, and not as having some positive explanatory value for the particular case. Unfortunately too many of the uses of "function" in psychological and sociological inquiry are of the pontifical type. The problem is to indicate the aspectual status, despite the poverty of available language (Introduction, and Chapter 2, n. 1). For discussion of the content of postulation *B2*, see Chapter 2, Section IV, #4, and compare also the postulation of continuity, *Logic: The Theory of Inquiry*, p. 19 [*Later Works* 12:26], *et al.*

28. Postulations *A* have this characteristic in contrast with postulations *Z*. The free development of subjectmatters in *B2* and *B3* coincides in effect with the express rejection of "reals" in *B9*, *C7*, and *H1*. It also removes the incentive to the romantic types of "emergence" which often enter when "substantive reals" depart.

6. The subjectmatters of observation are durational and extensional.

7. Technical treatments of extensions and durations developed in one department of subjectmatter are to be accepted as aids for other subjectmatters, but never as controls beyond their direct value in operation.[29]

8. "Objects" in practical everyday identifications and namings prior to organized inquiry hold no permanent priority in such inquiry.[30] Inquiry is free and all "objects" are subject to examination whether as they thus practically come or with respect to components they may be found to contain, or under widened observation as transactional—in all cases retaining their extensional and durational status.[31]

9. Durationally and extensionally observable events suffice for inquiry. Nothing "more real" than the observable is secured by using the word "real," or by peering for something behind or beyond the observable to which to apply the name.[32]

Having focussed postulations B upon the aspect of inquiry, we now return to the aspect of event in A.[33] Our declared purpose

29. Bentley, "The Factual Space and Time of Behavior," the *Journal of Philosophy,* XXXVIII (1941), pp. 477–485. No interference is intended with the practical pre-scientific attitudes towards space and time so far as their everyday practical expression is concerned. Although long since deprived of dominance in the physical sciences, these attitudes remain dominant in psychological and sociological inquiry, and it is this dominance in this region that is rejected under our present postulation. See also the footnote to D3, postulation H4, and comment in the text following postulations D.
30. Chapter 2, Section IV, #7. Bentley, "The Human Skin: Philosophy's Last Line of Defense," *Philosophy of Science,* VIII (1941), 1–19.
31. Chapter 2, Section IV, #6. Compare postulation A4.
32. B9 restates what results if B2 is accepted and put to work thoroughly—"the addition of the adjective 'real' to the substantive 'facts' being only for rhetorical emphasis" (Dewey, *Context and Thought,* University of California Publications in Philosophy, XII [1931], 203–224). Compare also the statement by Stephen C. Pepper, the *Journal of Philosophy,* XLII (1945), 102: "There is no criterion for the reliability of evidence . . . but evidence of that reliability—that is, corroboration." Professor Pepper's discussion of what happens under "the attitude of expecting an unquestionable criterion of truth and factuality to be at hand" runs strongly along our present line.
33. Both "focus" and "aspect" are double-barrelled words, in William James's sense. One cannot focus without something to focus with (such as a lens in or out of his eye) or without something to focus on. As for the word "aspect" (see also Chapter 2, n. 11), this word originally stressed the viewing; an ar-

is to examine naming behaviors as knowings, and to hold the naming behaviors as events in contact with the signaling behaviors on one side and with the symboling behaviors on the other.[34] In expansion from A as events we shall therefore next present postulations C for knowings and D for namings, and shall follow these with indications of what will later be necessary as E for signalings and F for symbolings.

Postulations C are looser than the others, as will be evident at once by our permitting the vague word "knowledge" to creep in. There is sound reason for this. We secure an introductory background in the rough along the lines of ordinary discussion, against which to study namings as knowings. From future study of namings a better postulation for knowings should develop. A comment on the possible outcomes for C will follow.

C. POSTULATIONS FOR KNOWINGS AND KNOWNS AS BEHAVIORAL EVENTS[35]

1. Knowings and knowns (knowledge, knowledges, instances of knowledge) are natural events. A knowing is to be regarded as the same kind of an event *with respect to its being known* (i.e., just as much "extant") as an eclipse, a fossil, an earthquake, or any other subjectmatter of research.

2. Knowings and knowns are to be investigated by methods that have been elsewhere successful in the natural sciences.

3. Sufficient approach has already been made to knowledge about knowledge through cultural, psychological, and physio-

---

chaic meaning was a gaze, glance, or look, and a transitive verb still is usable, "to aspect." In more recent English "aspect" has been transferred in large measure to "object," but there are many mixed uses, even some that introduce locations and directions of action as between observer and observed. In any case the word applies to the "object," not absolutely but with reference to an observer, present or remote.

34. Chapter 2, Section IV, #8.

35. Two of our earlier experimental formulations may be helpful in their variation of phrasing. Thus: (a) knowings are natural events; (b) they are known by standard methods; (c) enough is known about knowings and knowns to make the use of such methods practicable. Again: (a) knowers are in the cosmos along with what is known and to be known; (b) knowings are there too, and are to be studied (observed) in the same way as are other subjectmatters.

logical investigations to make it practicable to begin today to use this program.[36]

4. As natural events, knowings and knowns are observable; as observable, they are enduring and extensive within enduring and extensive situations.[37]

5. Knowings and knowns are to be taken together as aspects of one event.[38] The outstanding need for inquiry into knowledge in its present stage is that the knowings and knowns be thus given transactional (as contrasted with interactional) observations.

6. The observable extensions of knowings and knowns run across the inhabited surface of the earth; the observable durations run across cultures,[39] backward into pre-history, forward into futures—all as subjectmatters of inquiry. Persistence (permanence and impermanence) characterize the knowings and the knowns alike.[40]

7. All actualities dealt with by knowledge have aspects of the knowing as well as of the known, with the knowings themselves among such actualities known.

Inspection of postulations C shows that the first two of the group provide for the development of A in accord with B2, while the third serves to make emphatic—against the denial everywhere prevalent—our assertion that inquiry *can* proceed on these lines. The fourth is in accord with B5, B6, and B7 as to observation, while the fifth states the type, and the sixth the range, of the observation needed. The seventh, in accord with B9, keeps in place the ever-needed bulwark against the traditional totalitarian hypostatizations.

36. Dewey, "How Is Mind to Be Known?" the *Journal of Philosophy*, XXXIX (1942), pp. 29–35.
37. Chapter 2, Section I.
38. Chapter 2, Section I: "We proceed upon the postulate that *knowings* are always and everywhere inseparable from *the knowns*—that the two are twin aspects of common fact."
39. The word "social" is not used, primarily because of its confused status. It is sometimes opposed to "individual," sometimes built up out of "individuals," and, as it stands, it fails to hint at the transactional approach we express. "Culture" is comparatively non-committal, and can be understood much more closely as "behavioral," in the sense we have specified for that word.
40. In contrast to the usual program of concentrating the impermanence (or the fear of it) in the knowing, and assigning the permanence, in measure exceeding that of its being known, to the knowns.

D. Postulations for Namings and the Named as Specimens of Knowings and Knowns[41]

1. Namings may be segregated for special investigation within knowings much as any special region within scientific subject-matter may be segregated for special consideration.

2. The namings thus segregated are taken as themselves the knowings to be investigated.[42]

3. The namings are directly observable in full behavioral durations and extensions.[43]

4. No instances of naming are observed that are not themselves directly knowings; and no instances of knowings within the range of naming-behaviors (we are not here postulating for signal or symbol behaviors) that are not themselves namings.[44]

5. The namings and the named are one transaction. No instance of either is observable without the other.[45]

6. Namings and named develop and decline together, even though to myopic or close-up observation certain instances of ei-

---

41. An earlier formulation, combining something of both the present postulations D and E, and perhaps of interest for that reason, ran as follows: (a) knowledge is a sign system; (b) names are a kind of naturally developed sign; (c) naming and "specifying existence" are one process. These statements, however, must all be taken transactionally, if they are to represent our approach properly.

42. Chapter 2, Section III. In other words, under our postulation names do not enter as physical objects, nor as tools or instruments used by a psychical being or object, nor as being constructively separate from behavior in some such form as "products," nor as any other manner of externalization dependent on some supersubtle internalization. Under our postulation all such dismemberments are rejected as superfluous. The procedure, therefore, includes no such nostalgic plaint as that of the legendary egg to the hen: "Now that you have laid me, do you still love me?"

43. Full duration and extension is not represented adequately and exclusively by such specialized devices as clock-ticks and foot-rules (see $B7$). Though these have developed into magnificent approximations for physics, they lack necessary pasts and futures across continents such as are involved in histories, purposes, and plans. They are therefore inadequate for inquiry into knowings, namings, and other behaviors.

44. Compare the requirements set up in our appraisal of the logics (Chapter 1, Sections I and X) that talkings be treated as "the men themselves in action."

45. Cf. Chapter 1, Section X; Chapter 2, Section IV. A full behavioral space-time form must be employed, comprising (but not limited by) physical and physiological spaces and times. The application of physical and physiological techniques is of course highly desirable, so far as they reach. Objectionable only are claims to dominate beyond the regions where they apply.

ther may appear to be established apart from the participation of the other.[46]

7. Warranted assertion, both in growth and in decline, both as to the warranty and the warranted, exhibits itself as a phase of situations in all degrees of development from indeterminate to determinate. The strongest warranted assertion is the hardest of hard fact, but with neither the determinacy, nor the warranty, nor the hardness, nor even the factuality itself ranging beyond the reach of inquiry—for what is "hard fact" at "one" time is not assuredly "hard" for "all" time.

8. The study of either naming or named in provisional severance as a phase of *the transaction* under the control of postulations $D4$ and $D5$, is always legitimate and useful—often an outstanding need. Apart from such controls it falsifies.[47]

9. The study of written texts (or their spoken equivalents) in provisional severance from the particular organisms engaged, but nevertheless as durational and extensional behaviors under cultural description, is legitimate and valuable.[48] The examina-

46. Our own experience in the present inquiry is evidence of this, although the postulation ought to be acceptable at sight throughout its whole range of application. Starting out to find careful namings for phases of the subjectmatter discussed in the literature, we were quickly drawn into much closer attention to the named; this phase of the inquiry in turn depended for success on improvement in the namings. The two phases of the inquiry must proceed together. Rigidity of fixation for the one leads to wreckage for the other.

47. An illustration that casts light on the status of naming and named with respect to each other may be taken from the earlier economics, which tried to hold consumption and production apart but failed miserably. Again, one may study the schemes of debtors and the protective devices of creditors, but unless this is done in a full transactional presentation of credit-activity one gains little more than melodrama or moralizing—equally worthless for understanding.

48. This procedure was followed, so far as was practicable, in our examination of the logics, where the intention was never criticism of individuals, but always exhibition of the characteristics of the logical-linguistic mechanisms at work at present in America. As a technique of inquiry this is in sharp contrast with the ordinary practice. Through it we secured various exhibits of subjectmatters admitted—indeed even boasted—by their investigators to be neither fish, nor flesh, nor good red herring—neither physical, nor mental, nor linguistic; aliens in the land of science, denizens of never-never land; and likewise of various procedures in the name of consistency, tolerating the abandonment of the simplest standards of accuracy in naming at every other step. Unfortunately, specimens being few, we cannot carry on discussion under the anonymity which an entomologist can grant his bugs when he handles them by the tens and hundreds of thousands. To refer to a writer by name is much the same *sort* of thing as to mention a date, or as to name a periodical with its

tion is comparable to that of species in life, of a slide under a microscope, or of a cadaver on the dissection table—directed strictly at what is present to observation, and not in search for non-observables presumed to underlie observation, though always in search for more observables ahead and beyond.[49]

10. Behavioral investigation of namings is to be correlated with the physiology of organism-in-environment rather than with the intra-dermal formulations which physiologists initially employed in reporting their earlier inquiries.[50]

Inspection of postulations *D* shows that the first four present definite subjectmatters for inquiry within the mistily presented regions of *C*. The fifth, sixth and seventh give further specifications to *C*5 and *C*6. The eighth provides for legitimate interac-

----

volume and page numbers. So far as inquiry into "knowledge" is concerned, the "you" and the "I" have their ethical and juridical valuations but offer little definiteness as to the activity under way; and this is certainly as true of the epistemologist's variety of "subject," as it is of any other. Recall the famous observation of William James, which has thus far been everywhere neglected actually in psychological and sociological research, that "the word 'I' . . . is primarily a noun of position like 'this' and 'here.'" (*A Pluralistic Universe*, New York, 1909, p. 380; *Essays in Radical Empiricism*, New York, 1912, p. 170.)

49. The classical illustration of the sanctification of the reduplicative non-observable as an explanation of the observable is, of course, to be found in the third interlude Molière provided for *Le Malade imaginaire*, in which the candidate for a medical degree explains the effect of opium as due to its *virtus dormitiva*. Its words should be graven on the breastbone of every investigator into knowledge. The candidate's answer was:

> Mihi a docto Doctore
> Domandatur causam et rationem quare
> Opium facit dormire.
> A quoi respondeo,
> Quia est in eo
> Virtus dormitiva,
> Cujus est natura
> Sensus assoupire.

Pierce, in quoting this (5.534), remarks that at least the learned doctor noticed that there was *some* peculiarity about the opium which, he implies, is better than not noticing anything at all.

50. As one stage in dealing with environments physiologists found it necessary to take account of "internal" environments, as in Claude Bernard's "milieu." Since then they have passed to direct consideration of transdermal processes, which is to say: their adequate complete statements could not be held *within* the skin but required descriptions and interpretations running *across* it in physiological analogue of what behaviorally we style "transactional."

tional inquiry within the transactional presentation, in sharp contrast with disruption of system, pseudo-interactions of mind-matter, and the total default in results offered by the older procedures for which *X, Y,* and *Z* stand as types. The ninth and tenth present supplementary techniques of practical importance.

IV

It is evident from these comments, as well as from the comments on postulations *C,* that although we are doing our best to phrase each separate postulation as definitely as the language available to us will permit, we are nevertheless allowing the selection and arrangement of the postulations within each group to proceed informally, since forced formality would be an artifice of little worth.

Two further comments are of special interest.

The first is that while we felt a strong need in our earlier assemblage of *B* and of *C* for the protective postulations *B*9 and *C*7, and while we shall later find it desirable to re-enforce this protection with postulation *H*1, the program of inquiry into namings as knowings represented by postulations *D,* in accord with *B*2, has already positively occupied the field, to fill which in older days the "reals" were conjured from the depths.

The second comment is that the greatest requirement for progressive observation in this field is freedom from the limitations of the Newtonian space and time grille, and the development of the more complete behavioral space and time frame, for which indications have been given in *B*7 and *D*3 and in the accompanying footnotes, and upon which stress will be placed again in *H*4.

V

In the case of signalings and symbolings which, along with namings, make up the broadest differentiation of behaviors, both as evolutionary stages and as contemporary levels,[51] it would be a waste of time to attempt postulatory elaboration un-

51. Chapter 2, Sections IV and V.

til much further preliminary description had been given. This will be developed elsewhere. For the present the following indications of the need must suffice.

E. INDICATED POSTULATION FOR SIGNALING BEHAVIORS

1. Signaling behaviors—the regions of perception-manipulation,[52] ranging from the earliest indirect cues for food-ingestion among protozoa and all the varied conditionings of animal life, to the most delicate human perceptional activities—require transactional observation.

2. The settings for such words as "stimulus," "reaction," and "response," furnished under postulations of the types X, Y, and Z, have resulted in such chaos as to show that this or some other alternative development is urgently required.

F. INDICATED POSTULATION FOR SYMBOLING BEHAVIORS

1. Symboling behaviors—the regions of mathematical and syntactical consistency—require transactional observation.

2. In current inquiries "foundations" are sought for mathematics by the aid of logic which—if "foundations" are what is needed—is itself notoriously foundation-less.[53]

3. Differentiation of the naming procedures from the symboling procedures as to status (function), methods, and type of results secured—and always under progressive observation—is the indicated step.[54]

We have now postulations C and D and preparatory comments E and F focussed upon behaviors in their aspect as Event in expansion from postulations A. Over against all of these, but in accord with them, we have postulations B focussed upon the

---

52. The word "manipulation" is used in its standard widened application and not in limitation to the "manual."

53. Theorists such as Russell and other logicists are found who in their prideful panoply demand (at least when occasion seems ripe) that no science be recognized as such until it has been dubbed Sir Science and thus legitimatized by Logic.

54. For introductory considerations, see Bentley, *Linguistic Analysis of Mathematics* (Bloomington, Indiana, 1932).

aspect of inquiry through designation—the region in which science develops. Postulations *C*, as has already been said, are of lower grade than *D*, as is marked by their employment of the vague word "knowledge," their purpose having been to furnish a rough background for the attempt in *D*, to present namings as knowings direct. Postulations *C* are in further danger of being misinterpreted by some, perhaps many, readers in the sense rather of *B* than of *A*, of designation rather than of event, of the knowing rather than of the known. With postulations *C* thus insecurely seated, what may we say of their probable future?

Of the three types of vagueness in the word "knowledge,"[55] those of localization,[56] distribution, and range of application, the first two have been dealt with in preceding postulations. As for the third, the word bundles together such broadly different (or differently appearing) activities as "knowing how to say" and "knowing how to do"; and, further, from these as a centre, has spreading applications or implications running as far down the scale as protozoan sign-behavior, and as far up as the most abstruse mathematical construction. Should future inquiry find it best to hold the word "knowledge" to a central range correlated with, or identified as, language-behaviors, then postulations *C* would merge with *D*. Should it be found preferable to extend the word, accompanied perhaps by the word "sign," over the entire behavioral range, then postulations *C* would return into *A* to find their home. We have no interest in sharp classification under rigid names—observable nature is not found yielding profitable results in that particular form. We do not expect to offer any prescription as to how the word "knowledge" should be used, being quite willing to have it either rehabilitate itself or, as the case may be, fall back into storage among the tattered blanket-wordings of the past. Whatever the future determination, narrow, wide, or medium, for the word "knowledge," postulations *C* keep the action provisionally open.

In the opening paragraphs of this chapter we held that man's knowings should be treated as natural, and should be studied through observation, under express recognition of the postulatory

55. Chapter 2, Section I.
56. The old plan of dumping "knowledge" into a "mind" as its peculiar variety of "nature" and thus evading the labor of research, has long since ceased to be attractive to us.

status of observation itself in the transitions of both observations and postulations out of pasts and into futures. We believe that we have not failed throughout in proceeding in accordance therewith. These opening attitudes might perhaps have been themselves set forth as general postulations for the whole inquiry. The objection to this procedure is that the three main words, "nature," "observation," and "postulation," have such varied possible readings that, put together, they make a kite to which too many tails can be attached. From them, however, may be extracted certain statements concerning procedure with namings and things-named which may be offered in postulational form. They present—still from the designational approach as in postulations B—the cosmos as in action, the inquirers within it as themselves in action, and the whole process as advancing through time and across space. They are applicable to physical and physiological subjectmatters as well as to behavioral. Whether the aspect of inquiry B, as well as that of events D, E and F, will permit broadening in the future is a question that may be left for future discussion.

G. POSTULATIONAL ORIENTATION[57]

1. Subjectmatters of inquiry are to be taken in full durational spread as present through durations of time, comparable to that direct extensional observation they receive across extensions of space.[58]

57. This particular orientation does not preclude recognition of differences between namings that designate subjectmatters across indefinitely extended durations and expanses and those designating subjectmatters definitely limited in these respects. It is suggested, though not here postulated, that such differences may present the grounds for the rigid separations alleged in various traditional theories of knowledge to exist between theoretical and practical, and between rational and empirical, components; likewise for those alleged as between subjectmatters of sense-perception and of scientific knowledge, in ways that constitute radical obstacles to interpretation.

58. Impressionistically one could say that duration is of the "very nature" of the event, of its "essence," of its "body and texture," though these are types of phrasing to avoid in formal statement, no matter how helpful they may seem for the moment. To illustrate: consider the "texture" of the "situations" in Dewey's *Logic: The Theory of Inquiry* as compared with the usual discussions of his viewpoint. These "situations," both "indeterminate" and "deter-

2. Namings of subjectmatters are to be taken as durational, both as names and with respect to all that they name. Neither instantaneities nor infinitesimalities, if taken as lacking durational or extensional spread, are to be set forth as within the range of named Fact.

3. Secondary namings falling short of these requirements are imperfections, often useful, but to be employed safely only under express recognition at all critical stages of report that they do not designate subjectmatters in full factuality.[59]

Still lacking in our development and not to be secured until we have gained further knowledge of Signal and Symbol is an efficient postulational organization of Symbol with Designation within modern research. Under Symbol the region of linguistic "consistency" is to be presented. Under Designation we consider, as repeatedly stressed, not some "real existence" in a corruptly ultrahuman extension of the words "real" and "exist," but instead an "existency" under thoroughgoing behavioral formulation. It is, we hope, not forcing words too far for the impressionistic statement of the moment if we say that this may be in a "persistency" of durations and extensions such as postulations G require.

It is practicable to postulate rejections as well as acceptances. Under postulations G we have in effect rejected all non-extensionals, non-durationals, and non-observables of whatever types, including all purported ultimate "isolates." To emphasize this for the present issues of inquiry into knowledge, we now set down the following cases as among the most harmful. Let it be understood that these rejections, like all the other postulations, are offered, not as matters of belief or disbelief, but for the aid they may give research.

---

minate," are cultural. Any report, discussion, or criticism that does not recognize this is waste effort, so far as the issues involved are concerned.

59. Non-durational applications of such words as "sensation" and "faculty" in psychology have resulted in making these words useless to advanced systematic inquiry. Current words requiring continual watchfulness in this respect are such as "concept," "relation," "abstract," "percept," "individual," "social." In contrast our use of Fact, Event, and Designation is designed for full durational form, however faulty some of the phrasings in provisional report may remain.

H. POSTULATIONAL REJECTS

1. All "reals" beyond knowledge.
2. All "minds" as bearers of knowledge.
3. All assignments of behaviors to locations "within" an organism in disregard of the transactional phases of "outside" participation (and, of course, all similar assignments to "outsides" in similar disruption of transactional event).
4. All forcible applications of Newtonian space and time forms (or of the practical forms underlying the Newtonian) to behavioral events as frameworks or grilles of the checkerboard type, which are either (1) insisted upon as adequate for behavioral description, or (2) considered as so repugnant that behavior is divorced from them and expelled into some separate "realm" or "realms" of its own.

VI

One faces often the temptation to exhibit certain of the postulations as derived from others. We would advise against it, even when the durational postulation is used as source. We are impressed with the needlessness, under our approach, of "deriving" anything from anything else (except, of course, as may be convenient in propaedeutic display, where such a procedure perhaps properly belongs). The postulations present different stresses and offer different types of mutual aid, but no authoritarianism such as logics of ancient ancestry demand, including even (and sometimes peculiarly) those which strive to make their logicism look most positive. Many lines of ordering will suggest themselves as one works. If behaviors are durational, and knowings are behaviors, then the knowings become observable. If knowings and knowns are taken as in system, then one quickly arrives at a durational postulation in trying to report what one has observed; and from the durational one passes to the transactional. On the other hand, from this last, if arrived at first, one passes to the durational. This is, indeed, but a final reiteration of what was stressed in the opening paragraphs. Observation and postulation go hand in hand. The postulations hang together, not by grace of any one, or any two, or any three of them, but by organization in respect to the direction of approach, the points of entry, and the status of the audience—the status, that is, of the group of interested workers at the given time and place in history, and of that whole society-in-cosmos of which they themselves are components.

4.   Interaction and Transaction

I

Our preliminary sketch of the requirements for a firm terminology for knowings and knowns placed special stress on two procedures of knowledge[1] called Transaction and Specification. Specification was distinguished from Definition and the immediate development of Transaction was connected with Specification rather than with Definition.

We propose in succeeding chapters to discuss Transaction and Specification at some length, each on its own account, and to show how important it is for any theory of knowledge that their characteristics as natural processes of knowing-men and things-known should be fully understood. Before undertaking this, however, it will be well to display in the present chapter, the extent to which the transactional presentation of objects, and the determination of objects as themselves transactional, has been entering recent physical research. In so doing, the transactional presentation will be brought into contrast with the antique view of self-actions and with the presentation of classical mechanics in terms of interactions. The discussion will not be widened, however, beyond what is needed for the immediate report.

The reader will recall that in our general procedure of inquiry no radical separation is made between that which is observed and the observer in the way which is common in the epistemologies and in standard psychologies and psychological constructions. Instead, observer and observed are held in close organization. Nor is there any radical separation between that which is named and the naming. Comparably knowings and knowns,

---

1. The word "knowledge" has the value here of a rough preliminary description, loosely indicating the field to be examined, and little more.

as inclusive of namings and observings, and of much else as well, are themselves taken in a common system of inquiry, and not as if they were the precarious products of a struggle between severed realms of "being." It is this common system of the knowing and the known which we call "natural," without either preference or prejudice with respect to "nature," such as now often attends the use of that word. Our position is simply that since man as an organism has evolved among other organisms in an evolution called "natural," we are willing under hypothesis to treat all of his behavings, including his most advanced knowings, as activities not of himself alone, nor even as primarily his, but as processes of the full situation of organism-environment; and to take this full situation as one which is before us within the knowings, as well as being the situation in which the knowings themselves arise.[2]

What we call "transaction," and what we wish to show as appearing more and more prominently in the recent growth of physics, is, therefore, in technical expression, neither to be understood as if it "existed" apart from any observation, nor as if it were a manner of observing "existing in a man's head" in presumed independence of what is observed. The "transaction," as an object among and along with other objects, is to be understood as unfractured observation—just as it stands, at this era of the world's history, with respect to the observer, the observing, and the observed—and as it is affected by whatever merits or defects it may prove to have when it is judged, as it surely will be in later times, by later manners.

II

When Comte cast a sweeping eye over the growth of knowledge as far as he could appraise it, he suggested three stages or levels which he called the theological, the metaphysical, and the positive. One would not want to accept these stages today, any more than one would want to adopt Comte's premature scheme for the organization of the sciences. Nevertheless, his

2. For formal recognition and adoption of the "circularity" involved in the statement in the text, see Chapter 2, Section IV, #2.

general sketch has entered substantially into everyone's comprehension. Roughly speaking, the animistic personifications and personalizations of the world and its phenomena were prevalent in the early days; hypostatizations such as physical "forces" and "substances" followed them; only in recent centuries have we been gaining slowly and often painfully, that manner of statement called positive,[3] objective, or scientific. How the future may view even our best present opinions is still far from clear.

Let us consider a set of opposed tendencies which, for the moment, in everyday English we may call the narrowing and widening of the scope of scientific observation with respect to whatever problem is on hand. By way of introduction, we may trace such an alternation of viewpoints for the most general problems of physics from Newton to Maxwell.

For many generations, beginning with Galileo after his break with the Aristotelian tradition, and continuing until past the days of Comte, the stress in physical inquiry lay upon locating units or elements of action, and determining their interactions. Newton firmly established the system under which particles could be chosen and arrayed for inquiry with respect to motion, and so brought under definite report. But not all discovery resulted in the establishment or use of new particles. In the case of heat, for example, it did not come to pass that heat-particles were identified. "The progress of science," say Einstein and Infeld, "has destroyed the older concept of heat as a substance."[4]

3. Comte's "positive" retained something from his "metaphysics," just as his "metaphysics" retained something from his "theological." He substitutes "laws" for "forces," but gives them no extensive factual construction. "Logical positivism" has anachronistically accepted this Comtean type of law, emptied it of what factuality it had, and further formalized it. Such a "positive" does not get beyond short-span, relatively isolated, temporal sequences and spatial coexistences. Its background of expression, combined with a confused notion of the part mathematics plays in inquiry, is what often leads scientists to regard "laws" as the essential constituents of science, instead of stressing directly the factual constructions of science in space-time.

4. Albert Einstein and Leopold Infeld, *The Evolution of Physics* (New York, 1938), p. 51. We shall use the Einstein-Infeld book for repeated citation, not at all for confirmation of our views or for support of our development, but in order to have before the reader's eyes in the plainest English, authoritative statements of certain features of physics which everyone ought to know, but which in the fields of knowledge-theory are put to use by few. Since we shall have a good deal to do (although little expressly to say) with the way in which rigidly established views block needed progress—a point to which

Particles of a definitely Newtonian type were, it is true, retained in the work of Rumford and Joule, and later of Gibbs; and energy was advocated for a long time as a new substance with heat as one of its forms. But the particle fell upon statistical days (evil, indeed, from the point of view of its older assuredness), and what heat became in the end was a configuration in molecular ranges rather than a particulate presence. Faraday's brilliant observation found that all which happened electrically could not be held within the condenser box nor confined to the conducting wire. Clerk Maxwell took Faraday's observations and produced the mathematical formulation through which they could be expressed.[5] Maxwell's work furnished the structure for the developments of Roentgen, Lorentz, Planck, and Einstein, and their compeers, and for the more recent intra-atomic exploration. His posthumous book, *Matter and Motion*, has a lucidity which makes it a treasure to preserve and a model that all inquirers, especially those in newly opening fields, can well afford to study. The following is from the Preface to this book, dated 1877, and included in the British edition of 1920, edited by Sir Joseph Larmor:

> Physical science, which up to the end of the eighteenth century had been fully occupied in forming a conception of natural phenomena as the result of forces acting between one body and another, has now fairly entered on the next stage of progress—that in which the energy of a material system is conceived as determined by the configuration and motion of that system, and in which the ideas of configuration, motion, and force are generalised to the utmost extent warranted by their physical definitions.

Although Maxwell himself appreciated what was taking place, almost two generations were needed before physicists generally

---

Max Wertheimer, whom we shall later quote, has recently given vivid illustration—a further comment by Einstein and Infeld is significant: "It is a strange coincidence that nearly all the fundamental work concerned with the nature of heat was done by non-professional physicists who regarded physics merely as their great hobby" (*ibid.*, p. 51).

5. "The most important event in physics since Newton's time," say Einstein and Infeld of Maxwell's equations, "not only because of their wealth of content, but also because they form a pattern for a new type of law" (*ibid.*, p. 148).

began to admit it: *teste,* their long hunting for that greatest of all victims of the Snark that was Boojum, the ether: the process of re-envisionment is far from completed in physics even yet. The very word "transaction," which we are to stress, was, indeed, used by Maxwell himself in describing physical events; he even speaks of "aspects" of physical transactions in much the sense that we shall employ that word.[6] Thus:

> If we confine our attention to one of the portions of matter, we see, as it were, only one side of the *transaction*—namely, that which affects the portion of matter under our consideration—and we call this aspect of the phenomenon, with reference to its effect, an External Force acting on that portion of matter, and with reference to its cause we call it the Action of the other portion of matter. The opposite aspect of the stress is called the Reaction on the other portion of matter.

Here we see the envisionment that Maxwell had gained in the electromagnetic field actually remodeling his manner of statement for mechanical systems generally. Maxwell was opening up new vistas from a footing in the firmest organization of inquiry the world had ever possessed—that of the Newtonian mechanics. Though our own position is one in which the best we can hope for is to be able to introduce a small degree of order into an existing chaos, we can use his work, and the results that came from it, in our support, believing as we do that, as progress is made, the full system of human inquiry may be studied as if substantially one.

III

With this much of introductory display let us now set down in broad outlines three levels of the organization and presentation of inquiry in the order of their historical appearance, understanding, however, as is the way with evolutions generally, that something of the old, and often much of it, survives within or alongside the new. We name these three levels, those of Self-Action, Interaction, and Transaction. These levels are all human

6. *Matter and Motion,* Article XXXVIII. The italics for the word "transaction" are supplied by us.

INTERACTION AND TRANSACTION   101

behaviors in and with respect to the world, and they are all presentations of the world itself as men report it. We shall permit ourselves as a temporary convenience the irregular use of hyphenization in these names as a means of emphasizing the issues involved in their various applications. This is comparable to a free use of capitalization or of quotation marks, and to the ordinary use of italics for stress. It has the particular value that it enables us to stress the inner confusions in the names as currently used.[7]

Self-action: where things are viewed as acting under their own powers.

Inter-action: where thing is balanced against thing in causal interconnection.

Trans-action:[8] where systems of description and naming are employed to deal with aspects and phases of action, without final

7. Our problem here is to systematize the three manners of naming and knowing, named and known. Self-action can hardly be written, as writing and reading proceed today, without its hyphen. Transaction, we shall in the end argue, should be established in such a way that hyphenization would be intolerable for it except, perhaps, in purely grammatical or etymological examination. Inter-action, in contrast, within the range of our present specialized field of study, will appear to be the verbal thief-of-the-world in its commoner uses, stealing away "men's minds," mutilating their judgments and corrupting the very operation of their eyesight. The word "thing" as used in the characterizations in the text is deliberately chosen because it retains its idiomatic uses, and is almost wholly free from the more serious of the philosophers' distortions which commonly go with the whole flock of words of the tribe of "entity." For our future use, where a definite *outcome* of inquiry in its full behavioral setting is involved, the word "object" will be employed.

8. "Transaction," in ordinary description, is used for the consideration as detached of a "deal" that has been "put across" by two or more actors. Such a verbal shortcut is rarely objectionable from the practical point of view, but that is about all that can be said for it. For use in research adequate report of the full event is necessary, and for this again adequate behavioral description must be secured. Dewey's early employment of the word "transaction" was to stress system more emphatically than could be done by "interaction." (See his paper "Conduct and Experience" in *Psychologies of 1930* [Worcester, Mass.]. Compare also his use of "integration" in *Logic: The Theory of Inquiry.*) The beginnings of this attitude may be found in his paper "The Reflex Arc Concept in Psychology" (1896). Bentley's treatment of political events was of the transactional type in his *The Process of Government* (Chicago, 1908), though, of course, without the use of that name. John R. Commons has used the word comparably in his *Legal Foundations of Capitalism* (New York, 1924) to describe that type of economic inquiry in which attention centres on the working rules of association rather than on material goods or human feelings. George H. Mead's "situational" is often set forth in transactional form, though his development is more frequently interactional rather than transactional.

attribution to "elements" or other presumptively detachable or independent "entities," "essences," or "realities," and without isolation of presumptively detachable "relations"[9] from such detachable "elements."

These provisional characterizations will be followed in a later chapter by alternatives showing the variety of points of view from which the issues that are involved must be approached. The reader will note that, while names are given as if for the events observed, the characterizations are in terms of selective observation, under the use of phrasings such as "are viewed," "is balanced against," and "are employed." These are the two aspects of the naming-named transaction, for which a running exhibit is thus given, pending clarification as the discussion advances.

The character of the primitive stage of Self-action can be established easily and clearly by a thousand illustrations, past and present—all confident in themselves as factual report in their times, without suspicion of the way in which later generations would reduce them to the status of naïve and simple-minded guesswork.

For Trans-action at the latest end of the development we can show a clean status, not as assertion of its existence, but as a growing manner of observation of high efficiency at the proper time and place, now rapidly advancing to prominence in the growth of knowledge.

As for Inter-action, it furnished the dominant pattern of scientific procedure up to the beginning of the last generation. However, as a natural result of its successes, there grew up alongside it a large crop of imitations and debasements—weeds now ripe

9. It should be fairly well evident that when "things" are too sharply crystallized as "elements," then certain leftovers, namely, the "relations," present themselves as additional "things," and from that pass on to becoming a variety of "elements" themselves, as in many current logics. This phase of the general problem we do not intend here to discuss, but we may stop long enough to quote the very instructive comment Max Wertheimer recently made on this sort of thing. He had made a careful study of the way in which a girl who was secretary to the manager of an office described to him the character of her office setup, and he devoted a chapter to her in his book *Productive Thinking* (New York, 1945). His analysis of her account showed it defective in that it "was blind to the structure of the situation" (p. 137), and he was led to the further comment that her procedure was "quite similar to the way a logistician would write a list of relations in a relational network" (p. 138). Compare also Wertheimer's paper "On Truth," *Social Research* (1934), 135–146.

for the hoe. To avoid very possible misunderstandings, it is desirable to give a sub-classification of the main types of procedure that may from time to time present themselves as, or be appraised as, interactions. We find:

(*a*) Independently formulated systems working efficiently, such as Newtonian mechanics.

(*b*) Provisionally separated segments of inquiry given an interactional form for convenience of study, though with underlying recognition that their results are subject to reinterpretation in wider systems of description; such, for example, as the investigation of certain inter-actions of tissues and organs within the skin of an organism, while remembering, nevertheless, that the "organism-as-a-whole" transactionally viewed (with perhaps also along with it a still wider transactional observation of the "organism-in-environment-as-a-whole") must come into account before final reports are reached.

(*c*) Abuses of (*a*) such as often occurred when, before the Einstein development, efforts were made to force all knowledge under the mechanistic control of the Newtonian system.[10]

(*d*) Grosser abuses much too common today, in which mixtures of self-actional "entities" and inter-actional "particles" are used to produce inter-actional explanations and interpretations *ad lib.*: as when selves are said to inter-act with each other or with environmental objects; when small portions of organisms are said to inter-act with environmental objects as in the traditional theories of sensation; when minds and portions of matter in separate realms are brought by the epistemologies into pseudo-

---

10. The positions we shall take are in several important respects close to those taken by Richard C. Tolman in his address prepared for the symposium in commemoration of the 300th anniversary of Newton's birth ("Physical Science and Philosophy," the *Scientific Monthly*, LVII [1943], 166–174). Professor Tolman uses a vocabulary of a different type from that which we employ—one relying on such words as "subjective," "objective," "abstraction," "conceptual" etc.—but these wordings are not the significant matter we have in mind. The essential points are that he treats distinctions between the sciences as resting in the techniques of inquiry that are available (pp. 171–172), and that he strongly opposes as a "fallacious assumption" the view that "phenomena at one level of abstraction can necessarily be completely treated at a lower level of abstraction" (p. 174). (Compare our procedure, in Chapter 2, Section IV, #4.) We insert this note not to involve Professor Tolman in our construction, but to provide an alternative form of expression for views comparable in these respects to our own that may better suit the needs of persons who find our own manner unfamiliar or undesirable.

interactional forms; or, probably worst of all, when a word's meaning is severed from the word's actual presence in man's behavior, like a sort of word-soul from a word-body.

IV

Returning now to physics for a further examination of its increasing use of transaction, we may preface discussion with a few general words on self-action. We need not go far back into cultural history to find the era of its dominance. It took Jupiter Pluvius to produce a rainstorm for the early Romans, whereas modern science takes its *pluvius* free from Jupiter. The *Lares* and *Penates* which "did" all that happened in the household multiplied so excessively in Rome that in time they became jokes to their own alleged beneficiaries. The Druid had, no doubt, much tree lore useful for his times, but to handle it he wanted a spirit in his tree. Most magic has this type of background. It took Robin Goodfellow, or one of his kind, a Brownie perhaps, to make cream turn sour. In modern times we have flocks of words of respectable appearance that spring from this source: such words as "substance," "entity," "essence," "reality," "actor," "creator," or "cause," and thus, indeed, the major part of the vocabulary of metaphysics.[11]

Aristotle's physics was a great achievement in its time, but it was built around "substances." Down to Galileo men of learning almost universally held, following Aristotle, that there exist things which completely, inherently, and hence necessarily, possess Being; that these continue eternally in action (movement) under their own power—continue, indeed, in some particular ac-

11. The distinction between ancient rigidities of naming and scientific names of the firm (but not rigid) type, such as we desire to attain in our own inquiry, stands out clearly here. The ancient substances needed rigidity, fixation of names to things in final one-to-one correspondence. Pre-Darwinian classification of living forms showed the rigid trend as opposed to modern freedom of development. We have surviving today in obscure corners numerologies and other superstitions under which things are controlled by the use of the right names. We even find remnants of the ancient view in many of our modern logics which seek domination by verbal development. Bertrand Russell's logical atomism with its never-ceasing striving after minutely named "realities" may be mentioned in this connection.

tion essential to them in which they are engaged. The fixed stars, under this view, with their eternal circular movements, were instances. What did not, under the older pattern, thus act through its inherent power, was looked upon as defective Being, and the gradations ran down to "matter" on its lowest level, passive and inert.

Galileo's work is generally recognized as marking the overthrow of Self-action in physical doctrine, and it was just this feature which aroused so much hatred among the men of the ancient tradition. An excellent account—probably the best yet given—will be found in Max Wertheimer's book *Productive Thinking*.[12] Departing from the Aristotelian view that eternal force had to be applied to any inert body to put it in motion and to keep it in motion, Galileo made use of an inclined plane in substitution for a falling weight, as a direct aid to observation. Here he identified acceleration as the most significant feature for his purposes. He then considered the opposed case of a weight tossed upwards, using similarly an ascending inclined plane for his guide, and identified negative acceleration. Together, these yielded him the limiting case of the horizontal plane constructively lying between the descending and the ascending planes. He thus identified the fact (more pretentiously spoken of as a "principle" or "law") of inertia in its modern form: a mass once in motion continues in motion in a straight line, if not interfered with by other moving masses. Its motion, in other words, is no longer supposed to be dependent on the continued push applied to it by an "actor." This discovery was the needed foundation for the interactional development to come. Moreover, the new view itself was transactional with respect to the situation of its appearance: what, namely, had been an incident or result of some-

12. Quotations of pertinent phrases from both Aristotle and Galileo are given by Einstein and Infeld in the opening chapter of their book previously cited. Wertheimer concentrates attention on the "structure" or "Gestalt" which governed Galileo's search. Seen as a stage of development in understanding and presentation in the cultural setting in which it was produced, this is in the line of our treatment. Seen, however, as Wertheimer has continued to see it, as a mental activity of self-actional parentage applied to an outer world of objects, it falls far short of the manner of statement which we believe to be necessary. The "mind" Wertheimer relies on is far too reminiscent of the older days in which the "physical" opposed to it was an all-too-solid fixture. Wertheimer, in his last book, has nevertheless dropped much of the traditional mentalistic phraseology; and this with no loss to his presentation.

thing else was now taken up into direct report as event.[13] Hobbes quickly anticipated what Newton was later to establish, and Descartes made it his prime law of nature. For Newton it became the first law of motion, leading, through a second law concerning direction and proportionality of force, to the third law, namely, that action and reaction are equal and opposed—in other words, to the establishment of the full inter-actional system of mechanics.

The Newtonian construction—unexcelled for its efficiency within its sphere—viewed the world as a process of "simple forces between unalterable particles."[14] Given a closed system of this kind the inter-actional presentation had now been perfected. This, however, had been achieved at the cost of certain great omissions. Space and time were treated as the absolute, fixed, or formal framework within which the mechanics proceeded—in other words, they were omitted from the process itself. The failure to inquire into the unalterability of the particle was similarly an "omission," though one could freely select whatever "unalterables" one wished for experimental introduction as different problems arose. One immediate effect of Newton's success *within* his accepted restrictions was to hold him to the corpuscular theory of light and make him hostile to the competing wave theory of Huygens.

Einstein's treatment, arising from new observations and new problems, brought space and time into the investigation as among the events investigated. It did more than that: it prepared the scene for the particle itself to go the way of space and time.[15] These steps were all definitely in the line of the transactional approach: the seeing together, when research requires it, of what before had been seen in separations and held severally apart. They provide what is necessary at times and places to break

13. In his early study of perception Max Wertheimer made the comparable demonstration that motion could be *directly* perceived. "Experimentelle Studien über das Sehen von Bewegung," *Zeitschrift für Psychologie*, LXI (1912), 161–265.

14. Einstein and Infeld, *op. cit.*, pp. 58, 255.

15. "Insofar as wave mechanics has recognized two words that used to be associated with electrons—*position* and *momentum*—and has provided mathematical expressions as sort of tombstones to correspond to these words, it has done so with the least invocation of trouble to itself," W. F. G. Swann, "The Relation of Theory to Experiment in Physics," *Reviews of Modern Physics*, XIII (1941), 193.

down the old rigidities: what is necessary when the time has come for new systems.

The new foundation that has been given physics on a transactional basis, replacing the old inter-actional extremism, has not yet been made complete. Rival treatments and interpretations have their special places, and what the outcome will be is not wholly clear. Einstein himself devotes his efforts to securing a general field theory, but singularities remain in the field, with which he has not as yet been able successfully to deal. Whether "field" *in physics* is to represent the full situation, or whether it is to be used for an environment to other components is not *our* problem, and is not essential to a general consideration of the transactional phase of inquiry. Our assertion is the right to see in union what it becomes important to see in union; together with the right to see in separation what it is important to see in separation—each in its own time and place; and it is this right, when we judge that we require it for our own needs, for which we find strong support in the recent history of physics. The physicist can readily find illustrations of the two-fold need in his daily work. The changes in stress across the generations, from force as a centre to the *vis viva* of Leibnitz, and then on to energy as a special kind of thing in addition to material things, and to the development of the de Broglie equation connecting mass and energy, are in point. Energy now enters more and more in the guise of a described situation rather than in that of an asserted "thing." Long ago some significance, apart from mere puzzlement, was found in the facts that an electric current was not present without a circuit and that all that happened was not "inside" the wire. Twenty years ago physicists began to ask whether light could "start" from a light source, near or distant, if it did not have its place of arrival waiting for it. Today, as indicative of the status of physics, we get discussions strewn with sentences such as the following: "'The path of a light ray,' without including the environment of the light ray in the description, is an incomplete expression and has no operational meaning"; "The term 'path of a particle' has no more operational meaning than 'path of a photon' in ordinary optics"; "Speaking exactly, a particle by itself without the description of the whole experimental setup is not a physical reality"; "We cannot describe the state of a photon on its way from the sun"; "The law [of causality] in its whole generality cannot be stated exactly if the state variables by which the world is described are not mentioned specifically." [16]

Our aim in this examination of the transformation of viewpoints in physics has been solely to make clear how largely the manner of approach we propose to employ for our own inquiry into knowings and knowns has been already developed by the most potent of all existing sciences. We may supplement what has been said, for the benefit of any still reluctant philosophical, epistemological, or logical reader, by a few citations from the Einstein and Infeld work previously quoted. "The earth and the sun, though so far apart," were, under Newton's laws, "both actors in the play of forces. . . . In Maxwell's theory there are no material actors" (p. 152); "We remember the [mechanical] picture of the particle changing its position with time. . . . But we can picture the same motion in a different way. . . . Now the motion is represented as something which *is,* which exists . . . and not as something which changes . . ." (pp. 216–217); "Science did not succeed in carrying out the mechanical program convincingly, and today no physicist believes in the possibility of its fulfillment" (p. 125); "The concepts of substances, so essential to the mechanical point of view, were more and more suppressed" (p. 148); "The properties of the field alone appear to be essential for the description of phenomena; the differences in source do not matter" (p. 138); "The electromagnetic field is, in Maxwell's theory, something real" (p. 151).

So far as the question of what is called "physical reality" arises in this connection, a reference to a well-known discussion between Einstein and Niels Bohr about ten years ago is pertinent. In contrast with his transactional (i.e., free and open) treatment of *physical* phenomena, Einstein has remained strongly self-actional (i.e., traditionally constrained) in his attitude towards man's activity in scientific enterprise. His position is that "physical concepts are free creations of the human mind" (*op. cit.,* p. 33), and that "the concepts of the pure numbers . . . are creations of the thinking mind which describe the reality of our

16. These phrasings are all from Philipp Frank's excellent monograph, *Foundations of Physics,* the most recent publication of the *International Encyclopedia of Unified Science* (I, No. 7 [1946], 39, 45, 48, 53).

world" (*ibid.*, p. 311).[17] Bohr, in contrast, appears to have a much freer view of a world that has man as an active component within it, rather than one with man by fixed dogma set over against it. In the discussion in question, which involved the issues of momentum in wave theory, Einstein and his associates, Podolsky and Rosen, chose a criterion of reality based upon prediction to the effect that "if" (without disturbance) "one can predict with certainty the value of a physical quantity," then "there exists an element of physical reality corresponding to this physical quantity." In order to have a complete theory (and not merely a "correct" one), they held that "every element of the physical reality must have a counterpart in the physical theory"; and further they offered their proof that either "the quantum-mechanical description of reality given by the wave function is not complete," or "when the operators corresponding to two physical quantities do not commute, the two quantities cannot have simultaneous reality." In reply Bohr, employing his "notion of complementarity," held that the Einstein-Podolsky-Rosen "criteria of physical reality" contained "an essential ambiguity" when applied to quantum phenomena. He asserted further that while relativity had brought about "a modification of all ideas regarding the absolute character of physical phenomena," the still newer features of physics will require "a radical revision of our attitude as regards physical reality."[18] What is involved here is an underlying, though not explicitly developed, conflict as to the manner in which mathematics (as symbolic) applies to physics (as fact-seeking). This in turn involves the organization of symbol with respect to name among the linguistic behaviors of men.

17. Various significant comments on Einstein's attitude in this respect, which Wertheimer largely shares, will be found scattered through the latter's book, *Productive Thinking,* previously cited.
18. "Can Quantum-Mechanical Description of Physical Reality Be Considered Complete?" A. Einstein, B. Podolsky, and N. Rosen, *Physical Review,* XLVII (1935); Niels Bohr, *ibid.,* XLVIII (1935).

5. Transactions as Known and Named

I

Following an exhibit in the preceding chapter of the extent to which the manner of observing we call "transactional" is being employed in recent physics, we wish now to show something of its entry into physiology. On this basis we shall discuss its importance for behavioral inquiry and we shall especially stress the outstanding need for its employment in inquiries into knowings and knowns as human behaviors, if such inquiries are to achieve success.

A brief reminder of the terminology provisionally employed is desirable. In a natural factual cosmos in course of knowing by men who are themselves among its constituents, naming processes are examined as the most readily observable and the most easily and practicably studied of all processes of knowing.[1] The name "Fact" is applied to such a cosmos with respect both to its naming-knowing and its named-known aspects. The naming aspect of Fact is styled Designation; the named aspect is styled Event. The problem as to whether knowings-knowns of other forms[2] than namings-nameds should be brought into such inquiry prior to its development is postponed on about the same basis that a biologist proceeds with inquiry into either plant or animal life prior to securing a sharp differentiation between the two or a sharp separation of both of them together from physical event. In general, it is to be observed that the range of the known which we have thus far been developing under the name "event"

1. See Chapter 2, Section III; Chapter 3, Sections I and III.
2. These other forms include not only the full range of the perceptive-manipulative (Signal), but also those of non-naming linguistic processes such as mathematics (Symbol). For the words "event" and "existence" see Chapter 2, note 22, and the characterizations given the words in Chapter 11.

is, later in this book, to be presented as the full range which the word "existence" can cover in coherent application.

The name "Object" is applied to Event well established as the outcome of inquiry. The name "Specification" is applied to that most efficient form of Designation which has developed in the growth of modern science.[3] Transaction is, then, that form of object-presentation in improved Specification, which is becoming more and more importantly employed in the most advanced scientific inquiry, though still grossly disregarded in backward enterprises, and which is wholly neglected in present-day inquiries into knowledge as the knowing-known procedures of men. Transaction will be discussed in the present chapter and Specification in the next.

To reduce the occasion for some of the ordinary forms of misunderstanding, and to avoid frequent reminder of them in the text, attention is now called to certain positions common in whole or in large degree to current epistemologies, psychologies, and sociologies. These are positions which are *not* shared by us, and which may *in no case* be read into our work whether pro or con by persons who wish properly to appraise it.

1. We employ no basic differentiation of subject *vs.* object, any more than of soul *vs.* body, of mind *vs.* matter, or of self *vs.* not-self.

2. We introduce no knower to confront what is known as if in a different, or superior, realm of being or action; nor any known or knowable as of a different realm to stand over against the knower.

3. We tolerate no "entities" or "realities" of any kind, intruding as if from behind or beyond the knowing-known events, with power to interfere, whether to distort or to correct.

4. We introduce no "faculties" or other operators (however disguised) of an organism's behaviors, but require for all investigation direct observation and usable reports of events, without which, or without the effort to obtain which, all proposed procedure is to be rejected as profitless for the type of enterprise we here undertake.

5. In especial we recognize no names that pretend to be expres-

3. The word "science" in our use stands for free experimental observation and naming, with the understanding that the advanced branches of scientific inquiry are necessary aids to the backward branches, but never their dictators.

sions of "inner" thoughts, any more than we recognize names that pretend to be compulsions exercised upon us by "outer" objects.

6. We reject the "no man's land" of words imagined to lie between the organism and its environmental objects in the fashion of most current logics, and require, instead, definite locations for all naming behaviors as organic-environmental transactions under observation.

7. We tolerate no finalities of meaning parading as "ultimate" truth or "absolute" knowledge, and give such purported finalities no recognition whatever under our postulate of natural system for man in the world.

8. To sum up: Since we are concerned with what is inquired into and is in process of knowing as cosmic event, we have no interest in any form of hypostatized underpinning. Any statement that is or can be made about a knower, self, mind, or subject—or about a known thing, an object, or a cosmos—must, so far as we are concerned, be made on the basis, and in terms, of aspects of event which inquiry, as itself a cosmic event, finds taking place.

II

It was said of Transaction in Chapter 4 that it represents that late level in inquiry in which observation and presentation could be carried on without attribution of the aspects and phases of action to independent self-actors, or to independently interacting elements or relations. We may now offer several additional characterizations[4] correlated with the preliminary one and indicating the wide range of considerations involved. We may take the ancient, indeed, largely archaic, stages of self-action for granted on the basis of what has already been said of them and

4. The reader will recall that in the present treatment we do not hope to get beyond characterization, but must leave the greater accuracy of specification for future development, when additional phases of the issue have been examined. The use of hyphenization as a device for emphasizing interior confusions in words continues now and then in the text. The following from the British weekly *Notes and Queries* a hundred years ago may be profitably examined by the muddled victims of unhyphenized "interaction" today: "A neglect of mental hyphenization often leads to mistake as to an author's meaning, particularly in this age of morbid implication."

subject to the illustrations that will be given hereafter, and we may economize space by confining immediate attention to a comparison of transaction with interaction.

Consider the distinction between the two as drawn in terms of description. If inter-action is inquiry of a type into which events enter under the presumption that they have been adequately described prior to the formulation of inquiry into their connections, then—

Transaction is inquiry of a type in which existing descriptions of events are accepted only as tentative and preliminary, so that new descriptions of the aspects and phases of events, whether in widened or narrowed form, may freely be made at any and all stages of the inquiry.

Or consider the distinction in terms of names and naming. If inter-action is found where the various objects inquired into enter as if adequately named and known prior to the start of inquiry, so that further procedure concerns what results from the action and reaction of the given objects upon one another, rather than from the reorganization of the status of the presumptive objects themselves, then—

Transaction is inquiry which ranges under primary observation across all subjectmatters that present themselves, and proceeds with freedom toward the re-determination and re-naming of the objects comprised in the system.

Or in terms of Fact. If inter-action is procedure such that its inter-acting constituents are set up in inquiry as separate "facts," each in independence of the presence of the others, then—

Transaction is Fact such that no one of its constituents can be *adequately* specified as fact apart from the specification of other constituents of the full subjectmatter.

Or with respect to Elements. If inter-action develops the particularizing phase of modern knowledge, then—

Transaction develops the widening phases of knowledge, the broadening of system within the limits of observation and report.

Or in terms of Activity. If inter-action views things as primarily static, and studies the phenomena under their attribution to such static "things" taken as bases underlying them, then—

Transaction regards extension in time to be as indispensable as is extension in space (if observation is to be properly made), so that "thing" is in action, and "action" is observable as thing, while all the distinctions between things and actions are taken as marking provisional stages of subjectmatter to be established through further inquiry.

Or with special attention to the case of organism and environment. If inter-action assumes the organism and its environmental objects to be present as substantially separate existences or forms of existence, prior to their entry into joint investigation, then—

Transaction assumes no pre-knowledge of either organism or environment alone as adequate, not even as respects the basic nature of the current conventional distinctions between them, but requires their primary acceptance in common system, with full freedom reserved for their developing examination.[5]

Or more particularly with specialized attention to knowings and knowns. If, in replacement of the older self-action by a knower in person, inter-action assumes little "reals" interacting with or upon portions of the flesh of an organism to produce all knowings up to and including both the most mechanistic and the most unmechanistic theories of knowledge,[6] then—

Transaction is the procedure which observes men talking and writing, with their word-behaviors and other representational activities connected with their thing-perceivings and manipulations, and which permits a full treatment, descriptive and functional, of the whole process, inclusive of all its "contents," whether called "inners" or "outers," in whatever way the advancing techniques of inquiry require.

And finally, with respect to inquiry in general. Wherever interactional presentation, on the basis of its special successes in spe-

---

5. How much need there is for precision in these respects is well indicated by a paragraph in a recent book on the general characteristics of evolution by one of America's most distinguished biologists. His phrasings were first that "the organism develops . . . structures and functions," next that "the organism becomes adapted to . . . conditions," and finally that "evolution produces . . . etc." First the organism is actor, next the environment is actor, and lastly "evolution" is hypostatized to do the work. And all in a single paragraph. Such phrasings indicate, of course, inattention to the main issues involved.

6. Descartes, in his discussion of vision in the first five or six chapters of his *Dioptrique*, gives a fascinating account of sensation as mechanistically produced. It should be specially valuable to modern laboratory workers in the field since it lacks the ordinary protective jargon of professional life, and gets down to the verbal bone of the matter. Descartes was far from liking it in its full application, but in the case of vision, he did not see how he could avoid its apparatus of tubes, rods, and animal spirits.

cial fields, asserts itself dogmatically, or insists on establishing its procedure as authoritative to the overthrow of all rivals, then—

Transactional Observation is the fruit of an insistence upon the right to proceed in freedom to select and view all subjectmatters in whatever way seems desirable under reasonable hypothesis, and regardless of ancient claims on behalf of either minds or material mechanisms, or any of the surrogates of either.[7]

Thoroughly legitimate interactional procedures, it will be recalled from our previous discussion,[8] are all those which, like classical mechanics, are held adequately within their frameworks of hypothesis; and also those others which represent provisional partial selections of subjectmatters with recognition of the need for later statement in wider system. Abuses of interactional procedure are found, on the other hand, in the endeavors now happily fast disappearing, to force classical mechanistic control upon other enterprises of inquiry; and in the many quasi-interactional mixtures of diluted self-actors and pseudo-particles which remain largely in control of inquiry in the psychologies, sociologies, and epistemologies.

III

If we turn now to consideration of the biological fields of inquiry we find that much, but not all, of the old-fashioned self-actional has been discarded. The "vital principle" is an outstanding illustration. Employed until recent decades to mark the dis-

7. The reader of philosophical specialization may be interested in comparing Kant's substance, causation, and reciprocity. Cassirer's substance and function has interest so far as he develops it. The words "analysis" and "synthesis" suggest themselves, but a cursory survey of discussions in that form has shown little of interest. More suggestive, perhaps, for the philosophical specialist, is the now almost wholly discarded "objective idealism" of men like Green, Bradley, and Caird. The basic terminology of this group of men, using "absolute mind" as a starting point, may be stripped off so as to open the way to see more clearly what they were practically seeking. They show us a full system of activity, a dislike for crude dualisms, and a desire to get rid of such breakages as those the epistemologies capitalize. Along with this went a tolerance for, and even an interest in, the growth, and in that sense the "life," of the system itself. Our own development, of course, in contrast, is of the earth earthy, representing strictly an interest in improved methods of research, for whatever they are worth here and now.

8. Chapter 4, Section II.

tinction of "life" from "mechanism," it proved in the end to amount to nothing more than a sort of honorific naming. What is left of it, when it is not a mere appendage to some irrelevant creed, is mostly found lurking in obscure corners, or entering by way of incidental implication. Today the marvelous descriptions we possess of living processes provide adequate differentiation from the very different, even if themselves equally marvelous, descriptions of physical processes. The orthogenesis of Henry Fairfield Osborn sought to read "direction" into evolutionary lines with the implication of "control," but more and more today, despite his elaborate exhibits, biologists hold that developed description by itself is a far more useful "interpretation" than any appeal to "directives."[9]

Today we find transactional as well as interactional procedures used in the *details* of physiological and biological inquiry; but for *general* formulations we find little more than preliminary approaches to the transactional. This is seen on the large scale in the heavily theoretical separation that is maintained between the organism and the environment and the attribution of many activities to the former as if in independence.[10] As over against the vitalisms the "cell theory" in its radical form stands as a representative of interactional treatment. Views of the type called "organismic," "organismal," etc., except where they contain reminiscences of the old *self*-actional forms, stand for the trans-

9. Osborn's use of the word "interaction" is characteristically in contrast with ours. In developing his "energy" theory in his book *The Origin and Evolution of Life* (London, 1917) he considered action and reaction as usually taking place simultaneously between the parts of the organism, and then added interaction as an additional something connecting non-simultaneous actions and reactions. Interactions therefore appeared as a new product controlling the others, illustrated by such forms as instincts, functions of coordination, balance, compensation, cooperation, retardations, accelerations, etc. The "directing power of heredity" was thus set forth as "an elaboration of the principle of interaction" (pp. 4–6, 15–16).
10. A prevailing type of logical reflection of this older attitude towards the organism will be found in Carnap's assertion that "It is obvious that the distinction between these two branches [physics and biology] has to be based on the distinction between *two kinds of things* which we find in nature: organisms and nonorganisms. Let us take this latter distinction as granted" ("Logical Foundations of the Unity of Science," *International Encyclopedia of Unified Science*, I, No. 1, 45; italics not in the original). As against this rigidified manner of approach, compare the discussion of the organism and behavior in John Dewey's *Logic: The Theory of Inquiry* (New York, 1938), pp. 31–34 [*Later Works* 12:37–40].

actional approach intra-dermally. Such special names as "organismic" were felt to be needed largely because the word "organic," which could serve as an adjective either for "organism" or for "organ," had been too strongly stressed in the latter usage. Transactional treatment, if dominant, would certainly desire to allot the leading adjective rather to the full living procedure of the organism than to minor specialized processes within it; and if ancillary adjectives were needed as practical conveniences, then it would adapt them to the ancillary inquiries in interactional form.[11] The anticipated future development of transdermally transactional treatment has, of course, been forecast by the descriptive spade-work of the ecologies, which have already gone far enough to speak freely of the evolution of the habitat of an organism as well as of the evolution of the organism itself.

The history of the cell in physiology is of great significance for our purposes. For almost a hundred years after Schleiden and Schwann had systematized the earlier scattered discoveries,[12] the cell was hailed as the basic life unit. Today there are only limited regions of physiological report in which the cell retains any such status. What the physiologist sees in it is not what it is, or is supposed to be "in itself," but what it is within its actual environment of tissues. Some types of inquiry are readily carried on in the form of interactions between one cell and other cells. So far

11. For the intra-organic transactional observation, with occasional still wider envisionments, see the works of J. v. Uexküll, W. E. Ritter, and Kurt Goldstein. Lawrence J. Henderson's book *The Fitness of the Environment* (New York, 1913) should also be examined. Ritter lists among the most forceful of the earlier American advocates of the "organismal theory" as against the extreme forms of the "cell theory" C. O. Whitman, E. B. Wilson, and F. R. Lillie. Goldstein refers in biology to Child, Coghill, Herrick, and Lashley; in psychiatry to Adolf Meyer and Trigant Burrow; in psychology to the *Gestalt* school; and adds references in philosophy to Dilthey, Bergson, Whitehead, and Dewey. Henderson, with reference to Darwin's "fitness," says that it is a "mutual or reciprocal relationship between the organism and the environment," and again that "the fitness of the environment is both real and unique" (*op. cit.*, p. v, pp. 267–271). To rate as more fundamental than any of these is the discussion by J. H. Woodger in his *Biological Principles* (London, 1929), a book which is far from having received the attention it deserves. Especially to examine are Chapters VI on the theory of biological explanation, VII on structure-function, and VIII on the antithesis between organism and environment.
12. For the slow process of identifying the cell as distinctive structure, see the discussion by E. B. Wilson in *The Cell in Development and Heredity*, 3d ed. (New York, 1937), pp. 2–4.

as this type of treatment proves adequate for the work that is in hand, well and good. But other types of inquiry require attention in which the interactional presentation is not adequate, and in which broader statements must be obtained in full transactional form in order to secure that wider conveyance of information which is required. One can, in other words, work with cells independently, or with cells as components of tissues and organs; one can put organs into interaction, or one can study the organs as phases of organisms. Biographical treatment of the "organism as a whole" may or may not be profitable. If it is not, this is usually not so much because it fails to go deeply enough into cellular and organic details, as because it fails to broaden sufficiently the organic-environmental setting and system of report. Its defect is precisely that it centres much too crudely in the "individual" so that whether from the more minute or from the more extended viewpoint, the "individual" is precariously placed in knowledge, except as some reminiscence of an ancient self-actional status is slipped in to fortify it for those who accept that kind of fortification.

The gene, when it was first identified by name and given experimental study "on suspicion," seemed almost as if it held the "secret of life" packed into its recesses. Laboratory routine in genetics has become stylized, and is today easy to carry on in standard forms. The routine experimenter who emerges from its interesting specialties and lifts his voice as a radio pundit is apt to tell us all in a single breath, unabashed, that many a gene lives a thousand generations unchanged, and that each new-born organism has precisely two genes of each and every kind in each and every cell, one from each parent. One wonders and hunts his textbooks on grammar and arithmetic. But under wider observation and broader viewpoints we find little of that sort of thing. With gene-position and gene-complex steadily gaining increased importance for interpretative statement, the gene, like many a predecessor that has been a claimant for the rank of element or particle in the universe, recedes from its claims to independence *per se,* and becomes configurational within its setting. The genetic facts develop, but the status of self-actor attributed to the gene at the start proves to be a "fifth-wheel" characteristic: the physiological wagon runs just as well without the little genetic selves—indeed, all the better for being freed from their needless encumbrance.[13] In much the way that in the preceding chapter we employed a recent interpretive book in the physical range, for the significance of its wordings rather than for fixation of authority, we may here cite from Julian Huxley's *Evolution, the Modern Synthesis* (New York, 1942). We are told: "Genes, all or many of them, have somewhat different actions according to what neighbours they possess" (p. 48); "The effect produced by any gene depends on other genes with which it happens to be co-operating." . . . "The environment of the gene must include many, perhaps all other genes, in all the chromosomes" (p. 65); "The discreteness of the genes may prove to be nothing more than the presence of predetermined zones of breakage at small and more or less regular distances along the chromosomes" (pp. 48–49); "Dominance and recessiveness must be regarded as modifiable characters, not as unalterable inherent properties of genes" (p. 83); "To say that rose-comb is inherited as a dominant, even if we know that we mean the genetic factor for rose-comb, is likely to lead to what I may call the one-to-one or billiard-ball view of genetics." . . . "This crude particulate view . . . of unanalysed but inevitable correspondence . . . is a mere restatement of the preformation theory of development" (p. 19). We have here a clear illustration of the newer feeling and newer expression for physiology comparable to that of other advanced sciences.[14]

Organisms do not live without air and water, nor without food ingestion and radiation. They live, that is, as much in processes across and "through" skins as in processes "within" skins. One might as well study an organism in complete detachment

13. Such an entitative superfluity exemplifies the position we are taking throughout our entire discussion: Why retain for the purpose of general interpretation "entities" (i.e., supposititious things-named) that no longer figure in actual inquiry, nor in adequate formulation of its results? Why not get rid of such items when worn out and dying, instead of retaining their sepulchral odor till the passing generations cause even the latter to die away? The split of "nature" into two "realms"—two superfluities—is the instance of such entitative survival to which we elsewhere find it necessary to give ever-renewed consideration.

14. The results secured by R. Goldschmidt and Sewall Wright should also be compared. For the former, see his *Physiological Genetics* (New York, 1938). For the latter see "The Physiology of the Gene," *Physiological Reviews*, XXI (1941). T. Dobzhansky and M. F. Ashley Montagu write (*Science*, CV, June 6, 1947, p. 588): "It is well known that heredity determines in its possessor not the presence or absence of certain traits, but, rather, the responses of the organism to its environments."

from its environment as try to study an electric clock on the wall in disregard of the wire leading to it. Reproduction, in the course of human history, has been viewed in large measure self-actionally (as fiction still views it) and then interactionally. Knowledge of asexual reproduction was an influence leading to re-interpretation on a fully racial basis, and recent dairy practices for insemination make the transdermally transactional appearance almost the simple, natural one.

Ecology is full of illustrations of the interactional (where the observer views the organism and the environmental objects as if in struggle with each other); and it is still fuller of illustrations of the transactional (where the observer lessens the stress on separated participants, and sees more sympathetically the full system of growth or change). The issue is not baldly that of one *or* the other approach. It is not even an issue as to which shall be the basic underlying construction—since foundations in general in such questions are much less secure than the structures built upon them.[15] It is, in view of the past dominance of the interactional procedure in most scientific enterprise, rather an issue of securing freedom for wider envisionment.

The development of taxonomy since Linnaeus throws much light on the lines of change. He brought system and order among presumed separates. The schematism of taxonomy has at times sought rigidity, and even today still shows such tendencies among certain diminishing types of specialists. The very wording of Darwin's title, *The Origin of Species,* was a challenge, however, to the entire procedure of inquiry as it had been carried on for untold years. Its acceptance produced a radical change in taxonomic understanding—a method which rendered imperative observation across extended spatio-temporal ranges of events previously ignored. Taxonomy now tends to flexibility on the basis of the widened and enriched descriptions of advancing knowledge.[16]

15. Georg Simmel, *Soziologie: Untersuchungen über die Formen der Vergesellschaftung,* Zweite Auflage (Leipzig, 1922), p. 13.
16. E. Mayr, *Systematics and the Origin of Species* (New York, 1942). The author (pp. 113–122) offers a highly informative account of the learning and naming issues in biological nomenclature, ranging from the "practical devices" of the systematist to the "dynamic concepts" of the evolutionist, and compares a variety of treatments including the morphological, the genetic, the biological-species, and the criterion of sterility. His discussion moves back and forth between the natural processes of naming and the facts-in-nature to

The distinction of transactional treatment from interactional—the latter often with surviving traces of the self-actional—may be seen in the way the word "emergence" is often used. At a stage at which an inquirer wants to keep "life," let us say, within "nature," at the same time not "degrading" it to what he fears some other workers may think of "nature"—or perhaps similarly, if he wants to treat "mind" within organic life—he may say that life or mind "emerges," calling it thereby "natural" in origin, yet still holding that it is all that it was held to be in its earlier "non-natural" envisionment. The transactional view of emergence, in contrast, will not expect merely to report the advent out of the womb of nature of something that still retains an old non-natural independence and isolation. It will be positively interested in fresh direct study in the new form. It will seek enriched descriptions of primary life processes in their environments and of the more complex behavioral processes in theirs. It is, indeed, already on the way to gain them. The advances in the transactional direction that we can note in biological inquiries, while, of course, not as yet so striking as those in physical sciences, are nevertheless already extensive and important.[17]

IV

We have considered physiological inquiry in transactional forms and we have mentioned, in passing, other biological inquiries such as those concerning trends of evolution, adaptations, and ecologies. We turn now to the wide ranges of adaptive

---

be named. When we come later to discuss characterization, description, and specification, it will be evident (1) that the account can be given from the point of view of either aspect, and (2) that the recognition of this very complementarity is basic to our whole procedure. The twenty-two essays in the volume *The New Systematics* (Oxford, 1940) edited by Julian Huxley also furnish much material for profitable examination in this connection.

17. For a discussion of the entry of the fundamental field theory of physics into biology, see "A Biophysics Symposium" (papers by R. E. Zirkle, H. S. Burr and Henry Margenau), the *Scientific Monthly*, LXIV (1947), 213–231. In contrast, for typical instances of the abuse of field and other mathematical terminology in psychology, see Ivan D. London, "Psychologists' Misuse of the Auxiliary Concepts of Physics and Mathematics," the *Psychological Review*, LI (1944), pp. 266–291.

living called behaviors, including thereunder everything psychological and everything sociological in human beings, and embracing particularly all of their knowings and all of their knowns. If physiology cannot successfully limit itself to the interactions between one component of living process within the skin and other components within it, but must first take a transactional view within the skin, following this with further allowance for transdermal process, then very much more strongly may behavioral inquiries be expected to show themselves as transdermally transactional.[18] Manifestly[19] the subjectmatter of behavioral inquiries involves organism and environmental objects jointly at every instant of their occurrence, and in every portion of space they occupy. The physiological setting of these subjectmatters, though itself always transactionally organic-environmental, submits itself to frequent specialized investigations which, for the time being, lay aside the transactional statement. The behavioral inquiries, in contrast, fall into difficulties the very moment they depart from the transactional, except for the most limited minor purposes; their traditional unsolved puzzles are indeed the outcome of their rejecting the transactional view whenever it has suggested itself, and of their almost complete failure to allow for it in any of their wider constructions. The ancient custom, of course, was to regard all behaviors as initiated within the organism, and at that not by the organism itself, but rather by an actor or resident of some sort—some "mind," or "psyche," or "person" attached to it—or more recently at times by some "neural centre" imitative of the older residents in character. The onesided inadequacy of this view is what, so often, has called out an equally one-sided opposed view, according to which the organism is wholly passive, and is gradually moulded into shapes

18. See Bentley, "The Human Skin: Philosophy's Last Line of Defense," *Philosophy of Science*, VIII (1941), 1–19. Compare J. R. Firth, *The Tongues of Men* (London, 1937), pp. 19–20. "The air we talk and hear by, the air we breathe, is not to be regarded as simply outside air. It is inside air as well. We do not just live within a bag of skin, but in a certain amount of space which may be called living space which we continue to disturb with some success. And the living space of man is pretty wide nowadays. Moreover we never live in the present." "In dealing with the voice of man we must not fall into the prevalent habit of separating it from the whole bodily behaviour of man and regarding it merely as a sort of outer symbol of inward private thoughts."
19. This is "manifest," of course, only where observation has begun to be free. It is far from manifest where ancient categories and other standardized forms of naming control both the observation and the report.

adapted to living by independent environmental conditions, mechanistically treated. Both of these views, one as much as the other, are alien to us.

Summing up positions previously taken, we regard behaviors as biological in the broad sense of that word just as much as are any other events which biologists more immediately study. We nevertheless make a technical,—indeed almost a technological— distinction between physiological and behavioral inquiries comparable to the technological distinction between physical and physiological. This is simply to stress the difference in the procedures one must use in the respective inquiries, and to note that the technical physiological statement, no matter how far it is developed, does not directly achieve a technical behavioral statement. One may, in other words, take into account all known physical procedures about the moon, and likewise all known physiological procedures of the human body, and yet not arrive, through any combination or manipulation whatsoever, at the formulation, "rustic, all agape, sees man in moon." This last needs another type of research, still "natural," but very different in its immediate procedures. The distinction is never one of "inherent materials," nor one of "intellectual powers," but always one of subjectmatter at the given stage of inquiry.[20]

As for the self-actional treatment of behaviors (much of which still remains as a heritage of the past in the laboratories) it is probably safe to say that after physicists knocked the animism out of physical reports, the effect was not to produce a comparable trend in organic and behavioral fields, but just the reverse. All the spooks, fairies, essences, and entities that once had inhabited portions of matter now took flight to new homes, mostly in or at the human body, and particularly the human brain. It has

20. Chapter 2, Section IV, #4 to #8. We do not undertake to make a comparable distinction between psychological and sociological inquiries. This latter distinction is standard among "self-actional" treatments, where the "individual" enters in the traditional exaggeration customary in most interactional treatments. Transactionally viewed, a widening or narrowing of attention is about all that remains indicated by such words as "social" and "individual." As we have elsewhere said, if one insists on considering individual and social as different in character, then a derivation of the former from the latter would, in our judgment, be much simpler and more natural than an attempt to produce a social by joining or otherwise organizing presumptive individuals. In fact most of the talk about the "individual" is the very finest kind of an illustration of isolation from every form of connection carried to an extreme of absurdity that renders inquiry and intelligent statement impossible.

always been a bit of a mystery as to just how the commonplace "soul" of the Middle Ages, which possessed many of the Aristotelian virtues as well as defects, came to blossom out into the overstrained, tense, and morbid "psyche" of the last century or two. To Descartes, whether rightly or wrongly, has fallen much of the blame. The "mind" as "actor," still in use in present-day psychologies and sociologies, is the old self-acting "soul" with its immortality stripped off, grown desiccated and crotchety. "Mind" or "mental," as a preliminary word in casual phrasing, is a sound word to indicate a region or at least a general locality in need of investigation; as such it is unobjectionable. "Mind," "faculty," "I. Q.," or what not as an actor in charge of behavior is a charlatan, and "brain" as a substitute for such a "mind" is worse. Such words insert a name in place of a problem, and let it go at that; they pull out no plums, and only say, "What a big boy am I!" The old "immortal soul" in its time and in its cultural background roused dispute as to its "immortality" not as to its status as "soul." [21] Its modern derivative, the "mind," is wholly redundant. The living, behaving, knowing organism is present. To add a "mind" to him is to try to double him up. It is double-talk; and double-talk doubles no facts.

Interactional replacements for self-actional views have had minor successes, but have produced no generally usable constructions. This is true regardless of whether they have presented the organic inter-actors, which they set over against physical objects, in the form of minds, brains, ideas, impressions, glands, or images themselves created in the image of Newtonian particles. Despite all the fine physiological work that has been done, *behavioral* discussions of vision in terms of images of one kind or another are in about as primitive a state as they were a hundred years ago. [22] The interactional treatment, as everyone is aware, entered psychological inquiry just about the time it was being re-

21. The historical differentiations between spirit, soul, and body throw interesting light on the subject. Any large dictionary will furnish the material.
22. For example, Edwin G. Boring in *A History of Experimental Psychology* (New York, 1929), p. 100, speaking of the work of Johannes Müller, writes: "In general, Müller remains good doctrine to-day, although we know that perceived size is neither entirely relative nor entirely proportional to visual angle." This despite the fact that he had ascribed to Müller the view that "It is the retina that the sensorium perceives directly," and added that "it is plain that, for Müller, the theory of vision is merely the theory of the excitation of the retina by the optical image." This is perhaps mainly carelessness in statement, but what a carelessness!

moved from basic position by the physical sciences from which it was copied.[23]

The transactional point of view for behaviors, difficult as it may be to acquire at the start, gains freedom from the old duplicities and confusions as soon as it is put to firm use. Consider ordinary everyday behaviors, and consider them without subjection to either private mentalities or particulate mechanisms. Consider closely and carefully the reports we make upon them when we get rid of the conversational and other conventional by-passes and short-cuts of expression.

If we watch a hunter with his gun go into a field where he sees a small animal already known to him by name as a rabbit, then, within the framework of half an hour and an acre of land, it is easy—and for immediate purposes satisfactory enough—to report the shooting that follows in an interactional form in which rabbit and hunter and gun enter as separates and come together by way of cause and effect. If, however, we take enough of the earth and enough thousands of years, and watch the identification of rabbit gradually taking place, arising first in the sub-naming processes of gesture, cry, and attentive movement, wherein both rabbit and hunter participate, and continuing on various levels of description and naming, we shall soon see the transactional account as the one that best covers the ground. This will hold not only for the naming of hunter, but also for accounts of his history back into the pre-human and for his appliances and techniques. No one would be able successfully to speak of the hunter and the hunted as isolated with respect to hunting. Yet it is just as absurd to set up hunting as an event in isolation from the spatio-temporal connection of all the components.

A somewhat different type of illustration will be found in the

23. The recent work of Egon Brunswik goes as far, perhaps, on the transactional line as any. He recently ("Organismic Achievement and Environmental Probability," *Psychological Review*, L [1943], 259n) suggested coupling "psychological ecology" with "ecological psychology" in what seemed a functional manner from both sides. In contrast Kurt Lewin, speaking at the same meeting, suggested the name "ecological psychology" but rather for the purpose of getting rid of factors undesirable in his mentalistically fashioned "life space" than for improvement of system. Clark Hull, also on the same program, holds that organic need and organic environment must be "somehow jointly and simultaneously brought to bear" upon organic movement (the phrasing from his book *Principles of Behavior* [New York, 1943], p. 18, where he italicizes it) and he bridges across the gap by a series of intervening variables of a fictional, pseudo-logical character.

comparison of a billiard game with a loan of money, both taken as events. If we confine ourselves to the problem of the balls on the billiard table, they can be profitably presented and studied interactionally. But a cultural account of the game in its full spread of social growth and human adaptations is already transactional. And if one player loses money to another we cannot even find words in which to organize a fully interactional account by assembling together primarily separate items. Borrower cannot borrow without lender to lend, nor lender lend without borrower to borrow, the loan being a transaction that is identifiable only in the wider transaction of the full legal-commercial system in which it is present as occurrence.

In ordinary everyday behavior, in what sense can we examine a talking unless we bring a hearing along with it into account? Or a writing without a reading? Or a buying without a selling? Or a supply without a demand? How can we have a principal without an agent or an agent without a principal? We can, of course, detach any portion of a transaction that we wish, and secure provisional descriptions and partial reports. But all this must be subject to the wider observation of the full process. Even if sounds on the moon, assuming the necessary physical and physiological waves, match Yankee Doodle in intensity, pitch, and timbre, they are not Yankee Doodle by "intrinsic nature," in the twentieth century, whatever they might have been thought to be in the Dark Ages, or may perhaps be thought to be today by echoistic survivals of those days;[24] they need action if they are to yankeedoodle at all.

When communicative processes are involved, we find in them something very different from physiological process; the transactional inspection must be made to display what takes place, and neither the particles of physics nor those of physiology will serve. Many a flint chip fools the amateur archaeologist into thinking it is a flint tool; but even the tool in the museum is not a tool in fact except through users of such tools, or with such tool-users brought into the reckoning. It is so also with the writing, the buying, the supplying. What one can investigate a thing *as,* that is what it *is,* in Knowledge and in Fact.

24. Echolatry might be a good name to apply to the attitudes of our most solemn and persevering remembrancers of things past—and done with. "Echoist," by the way, is a good word in the dictionaries, and should not be wholly lost from sight.

V

When we come to the consideration of the knowings-knowns as behaviors, we find Self-action as the stage of inquiry which establishes a knower "in person," residing in, at, or near the organism to do (i.e., to perform, or have, or be—it is all very vague) the knowing. Given such a "knower," he must have something to know; but *he* is cut off from it by being made to appear as a superior power, and *it* is cut off from *him* by being made to appear just as "real" as he is, but of another "realm."

Interaction, in the interpretation of knowings, is a somewhat later stage which assumes actual "real" things like marbles which impinge on certain organic regions such as nerve endings or perhaps even brain segments. Here we still have two kinds of "reals" even though superficially they are brought somewhat closer together in physical-physiological organization. The type of connection is superficial in this case because it still requires a mysticism similar to that used for self-actions to bridge across from the little real "thing" to the little "real" sensation as organic, psychic, or psychologic—where by the word "mysticism" is meant nothing "mystic" itself, but merely some treatment that does not yield to description, and quite often does not want to.

The transactional presentation is that, we believe, which appears when actual description of the knowledge process is undertaken on a modern basis. At any rate it is the kind of presentation which has resulted from our own attempts at direct observation, description, and naming; it is for aid in appraising our results that we have, in this present chapter and the one immediately preceding it, examined comparable procedures in other scientific fields and upon other scientific subjectmatters. The steps we have taken, it will be recalled, are to say that we cannot efficiently name and describe except through observation; that the word "knowledge" is too broadly and vaguely used to provide a single subjectmatter for introductory inquiry; that we can select as a compact subjectmatter within "knowledges" generally the region of knowings-through-namings; that here observation at once reports that we find no naming apart from a named, and no named apart from a naming in such separation that it can be used as direct subject of *behavioral* inquiry—whatever physical or physiological observations we can incidentally make on the namings and the named in provisional separations; that such observations in fused systems *must* be steadily maintained if we are to attain complete behavioral report; and that, if this procedure requires an envisionment for behavioral purposes of space and time that is more extensive and comprehensive than the earlier physical and physiological reports required, such envisionment is then what we must achieve and learn to employ.

The outcome of self-actional and interactional procedures, so far as any competent theory of knowledge is concerned, has been and still is chaos, and nothing more. One can easily "think of" a world without a knower, or perhaps even of a knower without a world to belong to, and to know. But all that "think of" means in such a statement is "to mention in crude language," or "to speak crudely." The hypostatizing fringes of language are what make this "easy." While "easy," it is nevertheless not "possible," if "possible" covers carrying through to a finish, and if "think" means sustained consideration that faces all difficulties, holds to coherent expression, and discards manifestly faulty experimental formulations wherever and whenever it finds them—in short, if the "thinking" strives to be "scientifically" careful. A "real world" that has no knower to know it, has, so far as human inquiry is concerned (and this is all that concerns us), just about the same "reality" that has the palace that in Xanadu Kubla Khan decreed. (That, indeed, has had its reality, but it was not a reality beyond poetry, but in and of it.) A knower without anything to know has perhaps even less claim to reality than that. This does not deny the geologic and cosmic world prior to the evolution of man within it. It accepts such a world as known to us, as within knowledge, and as with all the conditionings of knowledge; but it does not accept it as something superior to all the knowledge there is of it. The attribute of superiority is one that is, no doubt, "natural" enough in its proper time and place, but it too is "of and in" knowledge, not "out of" or "beyond."[25] In other words, even these knowings are transactions of knowing and known jointly; they themselves as knowings occupy stretches of time and space as much as do the knowns of their report; and they include the knower as himself developed and known within the known cosmos of his knowledge.

25. Many a man is confident in saying that he knows for certain (and often with a very peculiar certainty) what is behind and beyond his personal knowings. We are well aware of this. Nevertheless, we do not regard it as good practice in inquiry when dependable results are sought.

How does it come to pass, one may ask, if the naming-named transaction as a single total event is basic as we say it is, that historically our language has not long since developed adequate special naming for just this basic process itself? The answer lies partially in the fact that, so far as ordinary conversational customs are concerned, it frequently happens that the most matter-of-fact and commonplace things are taken for granted and not expressly written down. For the rest of the answer, the part that concerns the professional terminology of knowledge and of epistemology, the sad truth is that it has long been the habit of the professionals to take words of the common vocabulary, stiffen them up somewhat by purported definition, and then hypostatize "entities" to fit. Once given the "entities" and their "proper names," all factual contact, including carefully managed observation, defaults. The names ride the range (in the west) and rule the roost (in the east). All too often the bad names get crowned while the good names get thumbs down. The regions in which this happens are largely those in which procedure is governed by the grammatical split between the subject and the object of the sentence rather than by observation of living men in living linguistic action. In such theoretical interpretations an unobservable somewhat has been shoved beneath behavioral naming, so that "naming as such" is personified into a ready-made faculty-at-large simply waiting for entities to come along for it to name; though most regrettably without that supernatural prescience in attaching the right name to the right animal which Adam showed in the Garden of Eden. The absurdity is thus standardized; after which not merely epistemology but linguistics, psychology, sociology, and philosophy proceed to walk on artificial legs, and wobbly-creaky legs at that. Turn the subject and object of the sentence into disconnected and unobservable kinds of entities, and this is what happens.

The organism, of course, seems in everyday life and language to stand out strongly apart from the transactions in which it is engaged. This is superficial observation. One reason for it is that the organism is engaged in so many transactions. The higher the organism is in the evolutionary scale, the more complicated are the transactions in which it is involved. Man especially is complex. Suppose a man engaged in but one transaction and that with but one other man, and this all his life long. Would he be viewed in distinction from that transaction or from that other man? Hardly. Much analysis, if an analyzer existed, would at least be necessary to separate him out as a constituent of what went on. A "business man" would not be called a business man at all if he never did any business; yet the very variety of his other transactions is what makes it easy to detach him and specialize him as a "business man." Consider the great variety of his other transactions, and it becomes still easier to make "a man" out of him in the sense of an "essence" or "substance," or "soul" or "mind," after the pattern demanded by the general noun. He comes thus, in the end, to be considered as if he could still be a man without being in *any* transaction. It is precisely modern science which reverses this process by driving through its examinations more thoroughly. When actions were regarded as separate from the actor, with the actor regarded as separate from his actions, the outcome, individually and collectively, was to bring "essence" into authority. The procedures of Galileo, Newton, and Darwin, steadily, bit by bit, have destroyed this manner of observation; and the procedures which must follow hereafter will complete it for the most complex human behavioral activities. They will reverse the old processes and bring the transactions into more complete descriptive organization without the use of either self-actional powers, or interactional "unalterable particles" behind them.[26]

26. A discussion of "The Aim and Progress of Psychology" by Professor J. R. Kantor (*American Scientist,* XXXIV [1946], 251–263) published after the present paper was written, may be examined with profit. It stresses the modern "integrated-field stage" of science, with special reference to psychology, in contrast with the earlier "substance-property" and "statistical-correlation" stages.

6. Specification

I

Having discussed at length the status of those events of the known and named world which we have styled "transactions," we proceed now to examine that linguistic activity through which Transaction is established: namely, Specification.[1]

Specification, in our provisional terminology, is the most efficient form of Designation, and Designation is that behavioral procedure of naming which comprises the great bulk of linguistic activities, and which, in the line of evolution, lies intermediate between the earlier perceptional activities of Signaling and the later and more intricately specialized activities of Symboling.

It will be recalled that we have inspected Fact most generally as involving and covering at once and together the naming process and the "that" which the naming is about. The choice of the word "fact" to name the most general transaction of "knowledge," was made because in practically all of its many varied uses this word conveys implications of the *being known* along with those of the *what* that is known; moreover, Fact applies to that particular region of the many regions covered by the vague word "knowledge" in which namings are the prominent feature. It is in this region that "knowledge" is most generally considered to be "knowledge of existence" in perhaps the only sense of the word "existence" having practical utility—that, namely, in which the existence is being affirmed with a considerable measure of security as to its details.[2]

---

1. We shall continue, as heretofore, to capitalize some of our main terms where stress on them seems needed, and particularly where what is in view is neither the "word" by itself nor the "object" by itself, but the general presentation of the named-as-in-naming. We shall continue also the occasional use of hyphenization as a device for emphasis.
2. For naming and knowing see Chapter 2, Section III. For comment on "existence" see Chapter 11.

Taking Fact as inclusive of both the naming and the named in common process, we adopted Designation for the naming phase of the transaction, and Event for the phase of the named. Events (or "existences," if one is prepared to use the latter word very generally and without specialized partisan stress) were distinguished as Situations, Occurrences, and Objects; and Objects were then examined in their presentations as Self-actions, Interactions, and Trans-actions—all of this, of course, not as formal classification, but as preliminary descriptive assemblage of varieties. The "self," "inter," and "trans" characteristics appear in Situations and Occurrences as well as in Objects, but it is in the more determinate form of Objects that the examination can most closely be made.

When we now turn to the examination of the processes of Designation we must on the one hand place designation definitely within the evolutionary range of behaviors; on the other hand we must examine the stages of its own development, leading up to Specification as its most efficient and advanced stage. The first of these tasks is necessary because a disjunction without a conjunction is usually more of a deception than of a contribution; but the pages we give to it furnish no more than a sketch of background, the further and more detailed treatment being reserved for a different connection.[3] In the second of these tasks we shall differentiate Cue, Characterization, and Specification as the three stages of Designation, and shall give an account of Specification freed from the hampering limitations of the symbolic procedures of Definition.[4]

3. Of psychology today one can sharply say (1) if its field is behavior, and (2) if human behavior includes language, then (3) this behavioral language is factor in all psychology's presentations of assured or suspected fact, and (4) psychological construction today shows little or no sign of taking this linguistic factor into account in its double capacity of being itself psychologic fact and at the same time presenter of psychologic fact. The problem here is, then, the terminological readjustment of psychological presentation to provide for this joint coverage of the naming and the named in one inquiry.
4. The word "definition" is used throughout the present chapter, as in preceding chapters, to stand for procedures of symboling as distinct from those of designating. This choice was made mainly because recent developments of technique, such as those of Tarski, Carnap, and symbolic logicians generally, have either adopted or stressed the word in this sense. After the present chapter, however, we shall abandon this use. In preparing our succeeding chapter, to appear under the title "Definition," we have found such complex confusions that misunderstanding and misinterpretations seem to be inevitable, no matter how definition is itself "defined." The effect of this change will be to

II

Designation, as we have said, covers naming. "Naming" would itself be an adequate name for the processes to be considered under Designation—and it would be our preferred name—if the name "name" itself were not so tangled and confused in ordinary usage that different groups of readers would understand it differently, with the result that our own report would be largely *mis*-understood. For that reason, before going further, we shall insert here a few paragraphs about the common understandings as to "name," and as to their difference from the specialized treatment we introduce as Designation. Some of these positions have been discussed before, and others will be enlarged upon later.

Naming we take as behavior, where behavior is process of organism-in-environment. The naming type of behavior, by general understanding so far as present information goes, is one which is characteristic of *genus homo* in which almost alone it is found. Except as behavior—as living behavioral action—we recognize no name or naming whatever. Commonly, however, in current discussions, name is treated as a third type of "thing" separate both from organism and from environment, and intermediate between them. In colloquial use this makes little difference. But in the logics and epistemologies, a severed realm of phenomena, whether explicit or implicitly introduced, matters a great deal. Such an intervening status for "name," we, by hypothesis, reject.

Name, as a "thing," is commonly spoken of as a tool which man or his "mind" uses for his aid. This split of a "thing" from its function is rejected. Naming is before us not as a tool (however it may be so described from limited viewpoints), but as behavioral process itself in action, with the understanding, nevertheless, that many forms of behavior, and perhaps all, operate as instrumental to other behavioral processes which, in turn, are instrumental to them.

---

reduce the word "definition" from the status of a "specification" to that of a "characterization" as this distinction is now to be developed. Progress towards specification in the use of the word "definition" is, of course, what is sought, no matter how unattainable it may seem in the existing logical literature.

Treatments of name as thing or tool accompany (or are accompanied by; the point is not here important) the splitting of "word" from "meaning"—"word," whether crudely or obscurely, being taken as "physical," with "meaning" as "mental." The split of a sign-vehicle from a sign, stressed as one of maximum theoretical importance in certain recent efforts at construction in this general field, is merely the old rejected split in a new guise. Under the present approach such a treatment of name, or of any other word, is regarded as deficient and inefficient, and is therefore banished.[5]

Under the above approach naming is seen as itself directly a form of knowing, where knowing is itself directly a form of behavior; it is the naming type of knowing behavior (if one wishes to widen the scope of the word "knowledge"), or it is the distinctive central process of knowledge (if one prefers to narrow the scope of the word "knowledge" thus far). Our hypothesis is that by treating naming as itself directly knowing, we can make better progress than in the older manners.

Naming does things. It states. To state, it must both conjoin and disjoin, identify as distinct and identify as connected. If the animal drinks, there must be liquid to drink. To name the drinking without providing for the drinker and the liquid drunk is unprofitable except as a tentative preliminary stage in search. Naming selects, discriminates, identifies, locates, orders, arranges, systematizes. Such activities as these are attributed to "thought" by older forms of expression, but they are much more properly attributed to language when language is seen as the living behavior of men.[6] The talking, the naming, is here oriented to the full organic (currently "organismic" or "organismal") process rather than to some specialized wording for self, mind, or thinker, at or near, or perhaps even *as*, a brain.

5. The issue here is not one of personal "belief," whether pro or con. It is one of attitude, selection, decision, and broader theoretical formulation. Its test is coherence of achievement. *Practical* differentiations of specialized investigation upon half a dozen lines with respect to word, or along half a dozen other lines with respect to word-meaning, are always legitimate, and often of great practical importance. For some account of the abuses of sign and sign-vehicle see Chapter 11.

6. However, if language is not regarded as life-process by the reader, or if thought is regarded as something other and higher than life-process, then the comparison in the text will not be acceptable to him.

All namings are positive. "Not-cow" is as much positive naming as is "cow"—whatever the cow itself might think about that. The cow's local point of view does not govern all theoretical construction. If the negatives and the positives alike stand for something, this something is as thoroughly "existential" in the one case as in the other.

Written names are behavioral process as much as spoken names are. Man's diminishment of the time-period, say, to the span of his day or of his life, does not govern decision as to what is behavioral or what is not.

The "what" that is named is no fiction. "Hercules" was a name in its time for something existently cosmic or cultural—not as "reality at large," but always as "specified existence." "Sea-serpents" and "ghosts" have played their parts, however inactive they may be as existential namings today. Trilobites are inactive, but they nevertheless made animal history.

These viewpoints that we have set down are not separates fortuitously brought together. They are transactional. They form, for this particular region of inquiry, the substance of what is meant by "transaction" in our use. That they will not "make sense" from the inter-actional point of view, or from the self-actional point of view, is only what is to be expected. They make sufficient sense as fact to be usable by us in hypothesis, and the test of their value will be in the outcome of such use.

III

If we are to examine Designations as behaviors, we must first establish the characteristics of behavior as we see it. That the name "behavior," however elsewhere used, can, in biological studies, be applied without misunderstanding to certain adjustmental types of animal activities, will hardly be disputed. That a behavioral statement in this sense is not itself directly a physiological statement, nor a physiological statement itself directly a behavioral one, will likewise hardly be disputed, as matters stand today, however much one may hope or expect the two forms of statement to coalesce some time in the future, or however valuable and indeed indispensable the primary understanding of the physiological may be for any understanding of the behavioral.

Extend either form of statement as far as you wish, holding it closely within its own vocabulary; it will, nevertheless, not directly convert itself into the other. Moreover attempts to limit the application of the word "behavior" to the overt muscular and glandular activities of an organism in the manner of a generation ago have not proved satisfactory. Too much development in terms of the participation of the "whole organism"—or, better said, of "the rest of the organism" has of late been made; and recent attempts to revive the older narrow construction for the interpretation of knowledge have had misfortunes enough to serve as ample warnings against such programs.

We shall take the word "behavior" to cover all of the adjustmental activities of organism-environment, without limiting the word, as is sometimes done, to overt outcomes of physical or physiological processes. This latter treatment involves too crude a disregard of those factual processes which in older days were hypostatized as "mental," and which still fall far short of acquiring "natural" description and reports. In the older psychologies (and in many still with us), whether under "mental" or "physiological" forms of statement, the distinction of the typically human behaviors from non-human and also of behaviors generally from the non-behavioral, was made largely in terms of "faculties" or "capacities" assumed to be inherent in the organism or its running mate, the "mind" or "soul." Thus we find "purposiveness" stressed as the typically "animal" characteristic; or accumulations of complexly-interrelated habits, or certain emotional, or even moral, capacities. In our case, proceeding transactionally, nothing, so far as we know, of this "capacitative" manner of statement remains in stressed use at critical points of research. Regarding behaviors as events of organism-environment in action, we shall find the differentiation of behavioral processes (including the purposive) from physical or physiological to rest upon types of action that are observable directly and easily in the full organic-environmental locus.

Sign: Developing behaviors show indirections of action of types that are not found in physical or physiological processes. This is their characteristic. The word "indirection" may, no doubt, be applicable to many physiological processes as compared with physical, but it is not the word by itself that is important. The particular type of indirection that is to be found in behaviors we shall call *Sign,* and we shall so use the word "sign" that where sign is found we have behavior, and where behavior occurs sign-process is involved. This is an extremely broad usage, but we believe that, if we can make a sound report on the factual case, we are justified in applying the word as we do.[7]

At a point far down in the life-scale Jennings identified sign as a characteristic behavioral process forty years ago. He was studying the sea-urchin, and remarked that while it tends to remain in dark places and light is apparently injurious to it, "yet it responds to a sudden shadow falling upon it by pointing its spines in the direction from which the shadow comes." "This action," Jennings continues, "is defensive, serving to protect it from enemies that in approaching may have cast the shadow. The reaction is produced by the shadow, but it *refers,* in its biological value, to something behind the shadow."[8]

This characteristic of Sign is such that when we have followed it back in protozoan life as far as we can find traces of it, we have reached a level at which we can pass over to the physiological statement proper and find it reasonably adequate for what we observe as happening. This makes the entry of the "indirection" which we call "sign" a fair border-line marker between the physiological and the behavioral. The sign-process characterizes perceptions all the way up the path of behavioral evolution; it serves directly for the expanded discussion of differentiated linguistic representation; it deals competently with the "properties" and the "qualities" that have for so long a time at once fascinated and annoyed philosophers and epistemologists; it can offer inter-

---

7. The *Oxford Dictionary* has twelve main dictionary definitions of sign, and a number of subdivisions. The *Century* has eleven. In modern discussion the uses are rapidly increasing, but no one usage is yet fixed for the field we are at work in. Usages range from saying that sign is a form of energy acting as a stimulus, followed by the application of the word for almost any purpose that turns up, to presenting it as a product of mind-proper. No one use can claim the field till it has been tried out against others; and certainly no candidate should even enter itself until it has been tried out in its own backyard and found capable of reasonably coherent usage.

8. H. S. Jennings, *Behavior of the Lower Organisms* (New York, 1906), p. 297. Jennings has himself never made a development in terms of sign, despite the highly definite description he so early gave it. Karl Bühler, who was one of the first men to attempt a broad use of a sign-process for construction, quoted this passage from Jennings in his *Die Krise der Psychologie* (Jena, 1927), p. 80, at about the time it began to attract attention among psychologists in the United States.

pretation across all varieties of expressive utterance up to even their most subtle forms. All these phases of behavior it can hold together simply and directly.

Having adopted an interchangeability of application for sign and behavior, our position will be as follows: If we fall away from it, that fact will be evidence of defect in our development; if we fall seriously away that will be indication of an insecurity in our basic hypotheses themselves; if we can maintain it throughout—not as *tour de force* but as reasonably adequate factual statement—this will furnish a considerable measure of evidence that the manner of construction is itself sound.

We have indicated that behavior is envisaged transactionally and that sign itself is a transaction. This means that in no event is sign in our development to be regarded as consisting of an "outer" or detached "physical" thing or property; and that in no event is it to be regarded as the kind of an ear-mark that has no ear belonging to it, namely, as a detached "mental thing." Sign, as we see it, will not fit into a self-actional interpretation at all; nor will it fit into an interactional interpretation.

If this is the case an important question—perhaps the most important we have to face—is the exact location of sign. Precisely *where* is the event that is named when the name "sign" is applied? Sign is process that takes place only when organism and environment are in behavioral transaction. Its locus is the organism and the environment, inclusive of connecting air, electrical and light-wave processes, taken all together. It is these in the duration that is required for the event, and not in any fictive isolation apart from space, or from time, or from both. A physiologist studying breathing requires air in lungs. He can, however, temporarily take for granted the presence of air, and so concentrate his own attention on the "lungs"—on what *they* do—and then make his statement in that form. He can, that is, for the time being, profitably treat the transaction as interactional when the occasion makes this advantageous. The student of the processes of knowings and knowns lacks this convenience. He cannot *successfully* make such a separation at any time. Epistemologies that isolate two components, that set them up separately and then endeavor to put them together again, fail; at least such is our report on the status of inquiry, and such our reason for proceeding transactionally as we do.

It is evident that time in the form of clock-ticks and space in the form of foot-rules yield but a poor description of such events as we report signs to be. Treat the events as split into fragments answering to such tests as clocks and rules may give, and you have a surface account, it is true, but one that is poor and inadequate for the full transaction. Even physics has not been able to make the advances it needs on any such basis. The spatial habits of the electrons are bizarre enough, but they are only the prologue. When physicists find it practicable to look upon 92 protons and 142 neutrons as packed into a single nucleus in such a way that the position of each is "spread out" over the entire nuclear region, certainly it should be permissible for an inquirer into man's behavioral sign-processes to employ such pertinent space-forms with pasts and futures functioning in presents, as research plainly shows to be necessary if observation is to be competent at all. At any rate any one who objects to freedom of inquiry in this respect may properly return to his own muttons, for subsequent proceedings will not interest him at all.

Taking Sign, now, as the observable mark of all behavioral process, and maintaining steadily transactional observation in replacement of the antique fixations and rigidities, we shall treat Signal, Designation, and Symbol as genera of signs, and so of behaviors. Similarly within the genus Designation, we may consider Cue, Characterization, and Specification as species. In this we shall use "genus" and "species" not metaphorically, but definitely as natural aids to identification.

Signal: All the earlier stages of sign up to the entry of language we group together under the name "signal." Signal thus covers the full sensori-manipulative-perceptive ranges of behavior, so far as these are unmodified by linguistic behaviors. (Complex problems of linguistic influencings will surely have to be faced at later stages of inquiry, but these need not affect our terminology in its preliminary presentation.) Signals like all signs are transactional. If a dog catches sight of the ear of a rabbit and starts the chase, signal behavior is involved. The signal is not the rabbit's ear for itself, nor is it the identification mechanism in the dog; it is the particular "fitness" of environment and organism— to use Henderson's word; it is the actual fitting in the performance. Pavlov's conditioned reflex, as distinguished from simple reflexes that can tell their stories directly in terms of physical-physiological excitations and reactions, is typical signaling, and Pavlov's own use of the word "signal" in this connection is the main reason for our adoption of it here.[9] The Pavlov process must, however, be understood, not as an impact from without nor as a production from within, but as a behavioral event in a sense much closer to his own descriptions than to those of many comparable American laboratory inquiries. It must be a feature of the full stimulus-response situation of dog and environmental objects together. If we take bird and berry in place of dog and rabbit, berry is as much a phase of signal as bird is. Divorce the two components—disregard their common system—and there *is* no signal. Described in divorcement the whole picture is distorted. Signaling is always action; it is event; it occurs; and only as occurrence does it enter inquiry as subjectmatter. It is not only transactional as between dog and rabbit and between bird and berry, but each instance of it is involved in the far wider connections of the animal's behaviors. No such fact is ever to be taken as an isolate any more than one animal body is to be taken as an isolate from its genus, species, race, and family. If one takes either the sensory, the motor, or the perceptional as an isolate, one again distorts the picture. Each case of signal, like every other case of sign, is a specific instance of the continued durational sign-activity of life in the organic-environmental locus. The motor phase has its perceptive-habitual aspect, and the perceptive phase has its motor aspect, with training and habit involved.

IV

Designation: Designation develops from a basis in Signaling. Signaling is organic-environmental process that is transactional. Designation in its turn is transactional organic-

9. Allowing for a difference in the forms of expression shown by the use of such a word as "relation," Bartley and Chute in *Fatigue and Impairment in Man* (New York, 1947) plan to differentiate the word "signal" along very much the lines of our text. They write (p. 343): "Neither items in the physical world nor perceived items are themselves signals. A signal merely expresses the relation between the two, as determined by the functional outcome." They, however, still retain the word "stimulus" separately for the "physical items from which the signals arise."

environmental process, but with further differentiation both with respect to the organism and with respect to the environment. With respect to the organism the "naming" differentiates; with respect to the environment the "named" differentiates. On neither side do we consider detachment as factual. The organism is not taken as a "capacity" apart from its environmental situation. The environment is not taken as "existing" in detachment from the organism. What is "the named" is, in other words, not detached or detachable environmental existence, but environment-as-presented-in-signaling-behavior. In other words, signalings are the "named," even though the namer in naming develops a language-form presumptively presenting an "outer" as detachable. Neither "naming" nor "named" under our procedure is taken as either "inner" or "outer," whether in connections or separations. The process of designation becomes enormously more complex as it proceeds; in it environmental determinations and namings unfold together. We make our approach, however, not in terms of the late complex specializations, but instead in terms of the growth in its early stages. The *what* that is assumed in the earliest instances is, then, not a *thing* in detachment from men (as most logicians would have us believe); much less is it some "ultimate reality," "provisional reality," "subsistence," or metaphysical "existence" (whatever such "things" may be taken to be). What is "cued" in the earliest forms of naming is some action-requirement within the sign-process, that is, within behavior. When one of a pair of birds gives a warning cry to his mate, or when a man says "woof" to another man as sign of bear-trail or bear-presence, it is behavior that is brought in as named; it is transactionally brought in, and is transaction itself as it comes. One can go so far back along the evolutionary line that the bird-call or the "woof" or some more primitive predecessor of these has, under such observation and report as we can make, not yet reached so much as the simplest differentiating stage with respect to "naming and named." But when the differentiating stage *is* reached, then the "named" that differentiates within the behavior is an impending behavioral event—an event in process—the environing situation included, of course, along with the organism in it. Both bird-call and woof indicate something doing, and something to be done about it.

The transactional locus of a designation in one of its earliest forms is very narrow—just the range of the creatures in communication, and of the sensori-manipulative-perceptive events directly presented in the communication. When and as the designation-event develops more complexity, the locus widens. Intermediate stages of namings intervene. Some of them push themselves temporarily into the foreground of attention, but even so are in fact members of a total inclusive transaction, and are given isolation and independence only in theories that depart from or distort observation. One may name a law, say the price-control act, without ever putting one's "finger" on it. In fact our experts in jurisprudence talk indefinitely about a statutory or other law without being able to specify what any law *is*, in a way equivalent to a direct "fingering." And while, in this talking and writing about the law, limiting intervening namings become temporarily the focus of direct attention, the *what* that is named is the law in its entire reach.

It is in this transition to more and more complex designations that the descriptive accounts are most likely to go astray. The cry "Wolf" is quickly brought to rest through actions that yield a "yes" or "no." The cry "Atomic Bomb" is evidently on a different level. It is in the cases of highly developed designations that it is most necessary to take our clue from the simpler cases so as to be firmly and solidly aware that name cannot be identified as a process in an organism's head or "mind," and that the named cannot be identified with an object taken as "an entity on its own account"; that the naming-transaction has locus across and through the organisms-environments concerned in all their phases; and that it is subject to continued development of indefinite scope so that it is always in transit, never a fixture.

We shall give attention to the two less complex stages of designation, namely, Cue and Characterization, merely far enough to lead up to the presentation of Specification as the perfected (and ever-perfecting) stage of naming, and so as to provide the ground for its differentiation from symbol and definition. So far as the terminology used is concerned, it may seem strange to group the thing-name, Cue, with the action-names, Characterization and Specification, as we are doing. But since all designations are designations in and of behavioral activities, the preliminary noun-form used does not greatly matter. We might, perhaps, set up

Cue, Common Noun, Term[10] as one series of names to range the field; or, as an alternative, we might use Ejaculation, Characterization, and Specification. Provided the behavioral transactions are taken as names with respect to developing action, the selection of terminology may well be left open for the present.

Cue: By Cue is to be understood the most primitive language-behavior. Wherever transactional sign on the signal level begins to show differentiation such that out of it will grow a verbal representation of any signal process, we have the beginnings of Cue. It is not of prime importance whether we assert this as first arising on the sub-human animal level, and say that language comes into being there, or whether we place the first appearance of true language among men. The general view is that the regions of cue, in contrast with those of signal, are characteristically communicative, but this issue, again, is not one of prime importance. Such questions lie in the marginal regions which modern science (in distinction from older manners of inquiry) does not feel it necessary to keep in the forefront of attention. Life is life, whether we can put a finger on the line that marks the boundary between it and the non-living, or whether a distinction here is far beyond our immediate powers; and much energy will be saved if we postpone such questions till we have the facts. Biology learned about its marginal problems from the viruses and could have got along just as well or better without the oceans of opinionative disputation over the "vital principle" in older days.

The illustrations of designation above were mainly from the lower levels and will serve for cue. Cue, as primitive naming, is so close to the situation of its origin that at times it enters almost as if a signal itself. Face-to-face perceptive situations are characteristic of its type of locus. It may include cry, expletive, or other single-word sentences, or any onomatopoeic utterance; and in fully developed language it may appear as an interjection, exclamation, abbreviated utterance, or other casually practical communicative convenience. Though primarily name grown out of signal, it may at times have the guise of more complex name reverted to more primitive uses. We may perhaps say that cue is

---

10. Decision as to the use of the word "term" is one of the most difficult to make for the purposes of a safe terminology. Mathematics uses the word definitely, but not importantly. Logics, as a rule, use it very loosely, and with much concealed implication.

signal with focal localization shifted from organism-object to organism-organism, but with object still plain in reach.

The transition from signal to cue may be indicated in a highly artificial and wholly unromantic way through a scheme which, fortunately, is devoid of all pretense to authority as natural history. On the branches of a tree live three snakes protectively colored to the bark, and enjoying vocal chords producing squeaks. Transients at the tree are squeaking birds: among them, A-birds with A-squeaks that are edible by snakes, and B-birds with B-squeaks that pester snakes. Bird-squeaks heard by snakes enter as signals, not as bird-squeaks alone, nor as snake-heard sounds alone, but strictly as events in and of the full situation of snake-bird-tree activity. Snake-squeaks, onomatopoeically patterned, are cues between snakes—primitive verbalisms we may call them, or pre-verbalisms. The evolutionary transition from bird-squeaks warning snakes, to snake-squeaks warning snakes is not one from external signs to internal signs, nor from the automatic to the mental, but just *a slight shift in the stresses of the situation.* When cue appears, we have a changed manner of action. When cue is studied transactionally, we change our stress on these subjectmatters of inquiry. Our change is slight, and one of growth in understanding, elastic to the full development of inquiry. It is not a breakage such as a self-actional account produces, nor even a set of minor breakages such as interactional treatment involves. The change to transactional treatment permits descriptions such as those on which perfected namings are built up.

The cue-stage of designation was not mentioned in our sketch of terminology in Chapter 2, our arrangement there being designed to give preliminary stress to the distinction of definition from specification. Signal was chosen as a name for the perceptive-manipulative stage of sign process largely on the basis of Pavlov's use of it. Cue was chosen for its place because all "dictionary definitions" (except one or two that lack the sign character altogether) make it verbal in nature. It may be, however, especially in view of Egon Brunswik's recent studies,[11] that

11. Egon Brunswik, "Organismic Achievement and Environmental Probability," *Psychological Review,* L (1943), 255. See also Tolman and Brunswik, "The Organism and the Causal Texture of the Environment," *Psychological Review,* XLII (1935), 43. Both cue and signal overlap in ordinary conversational

the words "cue" and "signal" could better be made to shift places. Our purpose here is solely to establish at once the manners of disjunction and of conjunction of cue and signal, and an interchange of names would not be objectionable.

Characterization: Out of cue there develops through clustering of cues—i.e., through the growth of language—that type of naming which makes up almost all of our daily conversation. It is the region of evolving description, which answers well enough for current practical needs, but is limited by them in scope. The wider the claims it makes, the less value it has. It is the region where whale in general is a fish because it lives in the water like any "proper" fish. Words cease to be of the type of "this," or "that," or "look," or "jump quick," and come to offer a considerable degree of connection among and across environmental situations, occurrences, and objects. The cues overlap and a central cue develops into a representative of a variety of cues. The interconnections are practical in the colloquial sense of everyday life. Horse is named with respect to the way one does things with and about horses, and with respect to the way horse does things with and about us. The noun enters as an extension of the pronoun, which is a radically different treatment from that of ordinary grammar. The characterizations move forward beyond the "immediately present" of the cues as they widen their connections, but for the most part they are satisfied with those modes of linguistic solvency which meet the requirements set by an immediately present "practical" communicative situation.

The first great attempt to straighten out the characterizations and bring them under control was perhaps made by the Greek sophists, and this led the way to Aristotle's logic. The logics that have followed Aristotle, even those of today that take pride in calling themselves non-Aristotelian, are still attempting to bring characterizations under the control of rules and definitions—to get logical control of common namings. All theories of linguistics, at least with a rare exception or two, make their developments along these lines. In the region of characterization the view arises

use, a fact of interest here. George H. Mead occasionally used "signal" in much the region where we use "cue." Mead's treatment of the animal-man border regions will be of interest (*Mind, Self and Society* [Chicago, 1934], pp. 61–68, 81, *et al.*).

that if naming occurs there must exist a "some one" to do the naming; that such a "some one" must be a distinctive kind of creature, far superior to the observed world—a creature such as a "mind" or personified "actor"; and that for such a "some one" to give a name to "anything," a "real" thing or "essence" [12] must exist somewhere apart and separate from the naming procedure so as to get itself named. (The word "must" in the preceding sentences merely reports that where such practical characterizations are established they think so well of themselves that they allege that every form of knowledge "must" adapt itself to them.) Alien as this is from modern scientific practice, it is, nevertheless, the present basis of most linguistic and logical theory and of what is called "the philosophy of science." [13] It is in this stage that namings and the named get detachable existences assigned to them by reflecting or theorizing agents, their immediate users being, as a rule, protected against this abuse by the controls exercised in conversational exchange by the operative situation directly present to those who participate in the oral transaction. Indeed, one may go so far as to doubt whether the distorted theory would have arisen if it had not been for the development of written documents with their increasing remoteness from determination by a directly observed situation. Given the influence of written, as distinct from spoken, language, it is dubious whether theoretical or philosophical formulations could have taken any form other than the one they now have, until a high degree of the development of the methods of inquiry now in use in advanced subjects had provided the pattern for statement in the form we term specification as complementary with transaction.

Description: Before passing to specification it will be well to attend to the status of names and naming with respect to descriptions. Phrasings develop around namings, and namings arise within phrasings. A name is in effect a truncated description. Somewhat similarly, if we look statically at a stable situation after a name has become well established, a description may be called an expanding naming. The name, in a sense which is

12. The recent revival of the word "essence" in epistemological discussion, as in Santayana's writings, is of itself convincing evidence of this statement.
13. The difficulties in which the logics find themselves are examined in Chapters 1 and 8.

useful if one is careful to hold the phrasing under control, may be said to name the description, and this even more properly at times than it is said to name the object. For naming the object does not legitimately, under our approach, name an object unknown to the naming system; what it names is the object-named (with due allowance for the other forms of knowing on the sensori-manipulative-perceptive level of signal); and the object-named is far more fully set forth in description than by the abbreviated single word that stands for the description. Beebe[14] mentions a case in which a single word, Orthoptera, in the Linnaean scheme precisely covered 112 words which Moufet had required for his description a hundred years earlier. The process of description begins early and is continuous while naming proceeds in its own line of growth, whatever arbitrary substitutes for it may at times be sought. Take two yellow cats and one black cat. Some little while afterwards, culturally speaking (a few tens of thousands of years, perhaps) primitive man will mark the color distinction, not as color for itself, but as color in contrast with other color. Put his color-naming in system with cat-naming, and you have the beginnings of description. "Cat" begins now to stand not merely for anti-scratch reaction, or for cat-stew, but for an organization of words into description. Bertrand Russell and several of his contemporaries have had a great deal of trouble with what they call "descriptions" as compared with what Russell, for instance, calls "logical proper names." Fundamentally Russell's "proper names" are analogues of the cue— reminiscent of primeval yelps and of the essences and entities that descend from them, to which it is that Russell wishes to reduce all knowledge. At the far extreme from his form of statement stands specification as developed out of characterization by expanding descriptions which in the end have attained scientific caliber. It is to Specification rather than to survivals of primitive catch-words that our own procedure directs itself in connection with progress in knowledge. Our most advanced contemporary cases of scientific identification should certainly not be compelled to comply with a demand that they handcuff themselves "logically" to a primitive type of observation and naming, now scientifically discarded.

14. William Beebe, editor, *The Book of Naturalists* (New York, 1944), p. 9.

V

Specification: Specification is the type of naming that develops when inquiry gets down to close hard work, concentrates experimentally on its own subjectmatters, and acquires the combination of firmness and flexibility in naming that consolidates the advances of the past and opens the way to the advances of the future. It is the passage from conversational and other "practical" namings to namings that are likewise practical—indeed, very much more practical—for research. The whale ceases to be a fish on the old ground that it lives in water and swims, and becomes established instead as a mammal because of characterizations which are pertinent to inquiries covering wide ranges of other animals along with the whale, bringing earlier "knowns" into better system, and giving direction to new inquiries. "Fish," as a name, is displaced for whale, not because it fails to conform to "reality," but because in this particular application it had been limited to local knowings which proved in time to be obstructive to the further advance of inquiry in wider ranges. Scientific classificatory naming, as it escapes from the bonds of rigidity, illustrates the point in biology. In physics it is illustrated by the atom which ceases to be a little hard, round, or cubical "object" that no one can make any smaller, harder, or rounder, and has become instead a descriptive name as a kind of expert's shorthand for a region of carefully analyzed events. Incidentally this procedure of specification is marked by notable inattention to the authority so often claimed for ancient syllogistic reasoning carried on in patterns fixed in advance.[15] The surmounting of the formal or absolute space and time of Newton, and the bringing of space and time together under direct physical description, is the outstanding illustration of the work of specification in recent physics, and our account in a preceding chapter[16] of the advance of

15. The issues, of course, are of the type so long debated under the various forms of contrast between what is called empiricism and what is called rationalism, these names merely marking the condition surrounding their entry into specialized modern prominence. Such issues are, however, held down by us to what we believe we are able to report under direct observation of the connections between language and event in current scientific enterprise in active operation.

16. Chapter 4. For a complete account, of course, a full appraisal of the participation of mathematics would be necessary; that is, of the system of organization of symbol with name.

transactional presentation of physical phenomena might in large part have been developed as a report upon specification. The developmental process in "science" is still far from complete. In biological work, organism and object still often present themselves in the rough as characterizations without specification, even though much specification has occurred in the case of physiological inquiry. In psychological and societal subjectmatters procedures are even more backward. It is astonishing how many workers in these latter fields relegate all such issues to "metaphysics" and even boast that they are "scientific" when they close their eyes to the directly present (though unfortunately most difficult) phases of their inquiry.

In our preliminary account of naming we have said that it states and connects. Cue states and characterization connects. Specification goes much further. It opens and ranges. By the use of widened descriptions it breaks down old barriers, and it is prepared to break down whatever shows itself as barrier, no matter how strongly the old characterizations insist on retention. What it opens up it retains for permanent range from the furthest past to the best anticipated futures. Also it retains it as open. It looks back on the ancient namings as at least having been designational procedure, no matter how poor that procedure was from man's twentieth-century point of view. It looks upon further specifications as opening a richer and wider world of knowledge. In short it sees the world of knowledge as in growth from its most primitive forms to its most perfected forms. It does not insert any kind of a "still more real" world behind or beneath its world of knowledge and fact.[17] It suspects that any such "real" world it could pretend to insert behind the known world would be a very foolish sort of a guessed-at world; and it is quite content to let full knowledge come in the future under growth in-

17. Philipp Frank, *Between Physics and Philosophy* (Cambridge, 1941), using a terminology and a psychological base very different from ours, writes: "Our modern theoretical physics, which admits progress in all parts of the symbol system, is skeptical only when viewed from the standpoint of school philosophy" (p. 102); "There are no boundaries between science and philosophy" (p. 103); "Even in questions such as those concerning space, time and causality, there is scientific progress, along with the progress in our observations" (p. 102); "The uniqueness of the symbol system can be established within the group of experiences itself without having recourse to an objective reality situated outside, just as the convergence of a sequence can be established without the need of discussing the limit itself" (p. 84).

stead of being leaped at in this particular instant. It welcomes hypotheses provided they are taken for what they are. Theories which sum up and organize facts in ways which both retain the conclusions of past inquiries and give direction to future research are themselves indispensable specifications of fact.

The word "specification" will be found making occasional appearances in the logics though not, so far as we have observed, with definitely sustained use. A typical showing of contrasted use appears in Quine's *Mathematical Logic,* where a "principle of application or specification" is embodied in Metatheorem *231. The name "specification" itself hardly appears again in his book, but the principle so named—or, rather, its symbolic embodiment—once it has entered, is steadily active thereafter. Nonsymbolically expressed, this principle "leads from a general law, a universal quantification, to each special case falling under the general law." In other words, whereas we have chosen the name "specification" to designate the most complete and accurate description that the sustained inquiry of an age has been able to achieve based on all the inquiries of earlier ages, this alternative use by Quine employs it for the downward swoop of a symbolically general law to fixate a substitute for the name of the thing-named. This is manifestly one more illustration of the extremes between which uses of words in logical discussion may oscillate.

Specification, as we thus present it, *is* science, so far as the word "science" is used for the reporting of the known. This does not mean that out of the word "science" we draw "meanings" for the word "specification," but quite the contrary. Out of a full analysis of the process of specification we give a closer meaning to the word "science" as we find it used in the present era. Scientists when confronting an indeterminacy alien to classical mechanics, may seem as agitated as if on a hot griddle for a month or a year or so; but they adapt themselves quickly and proceed about their business. The old characterizations did not permit this; the new specifications do; this is what is typical of them. There is a sense in which specification yields the veritable object itself that is present to science; specification, that is to say, as one aspect of the process in which the object appears in knowledge, while, at the same time, the object, as event, yields the specification. It is not "we" who are putting them together in this form;

this is the way we find them coming. The only object we get is the object that is the result of inquiry, whether that inquiry is of the most primitive animal-hesitation type, or of the most advanced research type. John Dewey has examined this process of inquiry at length on its upper levels—those known as "logic"—and has exhibited the object in the form of that for which warranted assertion is secured.[18]

The scientific object, in this broad sense, is that which *exists*. It reaches as far into existence as the men of today with their most powerful techniques can reach. In our preliminary suggestions for terminology we placed event in contrast with designation as the existential aspect of fact. We should greatly prefer to place the word "existence" where we now provisionally place event, and shall probably do so when we are ready to write down the determinations at which we aim. Exist, the word, is derivative of the Latin *sto* in its emphatic form, *sisto*, and names that which stands forth. What stands forth requires temporal and also spatial spread. Down through the ages the word "existence" has become corrupted from its behavioral uses, and under speculative philosophy has been made to stand for something which is present as "reality" and on the basis of which that which is "known" is rendered as "phenomenon" or otherwise to the knower. Common usage, so far as the dictionaries inform us, leans heavily towards the etymological and common-sense side, though, of course, the philosophical conventions get their mention. The common man, not in his practical use, but if asked to speculate about what he means, would probably offer his dogmatic assurance that the very "real" is what exists. *Solvitur ambulando* is a very good practical solution of a practical question, but *solvitur* in the form of a dogmatic assertion of reality is something very different. Dr. Johnson (if it was Dr. Johnson) may kick the rock (if it was a rock), but what he demonstrates is kicked-rock, not rock-reality, and this only within the linguistic form then open to him. We believe we have ample justification for placing existence where we now place event in our terminological scheme—only delaying until we can employ the word without too much risk of misinterpretation by hearer or reader.

18. John Dewey, *Logic: The Theory of Inquiry* (New York, 1938), p. 119 [*Later Works* 12:122].

If, however, we do this, then specification and existence are coupled in one process, and with them science; though again it must be added, not science in a purely "physical" or other narrow rendering of the word, but science as it may hope to be when the best techniques of observation and research advance into the waiting fields.

VI

The passage from characterization to specification is not marked by any critical boundary. Nor is the passage from everyday knowledge to scientific knowledge, nor that from everyday language to scientific language. Our attention is focused on lines of development and growth, not on the so-called "nature" of the subjectmatter of inquiry. If we are wrong about observing events in growth, then the very inquiry that we undertake in that form should demonstrate that we are wrong. Such a demonstration will be more valuable than mere say-so in advance that one should, or should not, make such an attempt. The regions of vagueness remain in specification, but they decrease. They are Bridgman's "hazes." Their main implication is, however, transformed. The earlier vagueness appeared as defect of human capacity, since this latter did not seem to succeed in reaching the infinite or the absolute as it thought it ought to. The newer vagueness, under the operation of specification, is a source of pride. It shows that work to date is well done, and carries with it the assurance of betterment in the future.

It is common for those who favor what is called "naturalism" to accept, with qualifications, many phases of the development above. We are wholly uninterested in the phases of the "ism," and solely concerned with techniques of inquiry. For inquiry into the theory of knowledge, to avoid wastage and make substantial progress, we believe the attitude indicated must be put to work one hundred per cent, and without qualification either as to fields of application or ranges of use. We have, however, not yet discussed the manner in which symbol and definition, which we do not permit to interfere with designation, may be put to work in the service of the latter. Nor have we shown the intimate connection between the techniques of specification and the establishment of transaction as permissible immediate subjectmatter and report. These problems are among those remaining for a further inquiry which, we trust, will be continued along the lines we have thus far followed.

7. The Case of Definition

I

It is now time to give close attention to the status of the word "definition" in present-day discussions of knowings and knowns, and especially in the regions called "logic." We began by accepting the word as having soundly determinable specialized application for mathematics and formal logic, but by rejecting it for use with the procedures of naming.[1] Naming procedures were styled "designations," and their most advanced forms, notable especially in modern science, were styled "specifications." Thereby definition and specification were held in terminological contrast for the uses of future inquiry.

Throughout our inquiry we have reserved the privilege of altering our terminological recommendations whenever advancing examination made it seem advisable. This privilege we now exercise in the case of the word "definition." For the purposes of the present discussion we shall return the word to its ordinary loose usage, and permit it to range the wide fields of logic in its current great variety of ways. This step was forced upon us by the extreme difficulty we found in undertaking to examine all that has to be examined under "definition," while we ourselves stood committed to the employment of a specialized use of the word. It is much better to abandon our suggested preference than to let it stand where there is any chance that it may distort the wider inquiry.

Our present treatment in effect deprives the word "definition" of the status we had planned to allot it as a "specification" for procedures in the mathematical and formal logical fields. Since

1. See especially Chapter 2, Section IV, #5.

we had previously rejected it as a specification for namings, it will now as a name, for the time being at least, be itself reduced to the status of a characterization.[2]

Regardless of any earlier comments,[3] we shall for the present hold in abeyance any decision as to the best permanent employment of the word. The confusions that we are to show and the difficulties of probing deep enough to eliminate them would seem sufficient justification for rejecting the word permanently from any list of firm names. On the other hand the development of its specialized use in formal logic along the line from Frege and Hilbert down to recent "syntactics" (as this last is taken in severance from its associated "semantics") would perhaps indicate the possibility of a permanent place for it, such as we originally felt should be allotted it.

If we begin by examining the ordinary English dictionaries, the *Oxford, Century, Standard,* and *Webster's,* for the definitions they provide for definition itself, we shall find them vague and often a bit shifty in setting forth the nature of their own peculiar type of "definition," about which they might readily be expected to be the most definite: namely, the traditional uses of words. Instead, they are strongly inclined to take over some of the authority of the philosophies and the logics, in an attempt to make the wordings of these latter more intelligible to the general reader. Two directions of attention are manifest, sharply phrased in the earlier editions, and still present, though a bit more vaguely, in the later. First, there is a distinction between definition as an "act" (the presence of an "actor" here being implied) and definition as the "product" of an act (that is, as a statement in verbal form); and then there is a distinction between the defining of a word and the defining of a "thing," with the "thing," apparently, entering the definition just as it stands, as a component directly of its own right, as a word would enter. Moreover, what is striking here is the strong effort to *separate* "act" and "product" as different *kinds* of "meanings" under differently numbered entries, while at the same time *consolidating* "word" and "thing" in close *phrasal union,* not only inside the definition of "act" but

2. For this terminology, see Chapter 6, Section IV.
3. See Chapter 2, Section IV, #5; Chapter 6, note 4; see also Chapter 11.

also inside that of "product." In the *Oxford Dictionary* (1897)[4] entry No. 3 is for the "act" and entry No. 4 is for the statement *produced* by the act. The "act," we are told, concerns "what a thing is, or what a word means," while the "product" provides in a single breath both for "the essential nature of a thing," and for the "form of words by which anything is defined." Act and product are thus severed from each other although their own "definitions" are so similar they can hardly be told apart. So also with the *Century* (1897), in which act and product are presented separately in definitions that cover for each not only "word or phrase," but also what is "essential" of or to a "thing." The *Standard* has offered continuously for fifty years as conjoined illustrations of definition: "a *definition* of the word 'war'; a *definition* of an apple." The latest edition of *Webster* (revision 1947) makes "essential nature" now "archaic"; runs acts and processes of explaining and distinguishing together, with formulations of meaning such as "dictionary definitions" added to them for good measure; and then secures a snapshot organization for Logic by a scheme under which "traditional logic" deals with the "kinds of thing" in terms of species, genera, and specific differences, while "later schools of logic" deal with statements "either of equivalences of connotation, or intension, or of the reciprocal implications of terms."

Now, a distinction between words and things other than words along conventional lines is easy to make. So is one between an "act" and the products of acts, especially when an "actor," traditionally hypostatized for the purpose, is at hand ready for use. In the present case of the dictionaries, what apparently happens is that if an actor is once obtained and set to work as a "definer," then all his "definings" are taken to be one *kind* of act, whether concerned with words or with things: whereupon their products are taken as equally of one *kind*, although *as* products they belong to a realm of "being" different from that to which actors as actors belong. In the present inquiry we shall have a continuous eye on the dealings logical definition has with words and things, and on the manner in which these dealings rest on its separation of product from acts. We shall not, however,

---

4. We omit, of course, entries irrelevant to the problem of knowings and knowns.

concern ourselves directly with the underlying issues as to the status of acts and products with respect to each other.[5] As to this it is here only to be remarked that in general any such distinction of product from act is bad form in modern research of the better sort. Fire, as an "actor," expired with phlogiston, and the presence of individually and personally existing "heat" is no longer needed to make things hot.

These remarks on what the ordinary dictionaries accomplish should keep our eyes close to the ground—close to the primary facts of observation—as we advance in our further examinations. Whether a dictionary attempts patternings after technical logical expressions, whether it tries simplified wordings, or whether it turns towards evasiveness, its troubles, under direct attention, are in fairly plain view. Elsewhere the thick undergrowth of verbiage often subserves a concealment.

II

This inclusion of *what a thing is* with *what a word says* goes back to Aristotle. Aristotle was an observer and searcher in the era of the birth of science. With him, as with his contemporaries, all knowledge, to be sound, or, as we should say today, to be "scientific," had to win through to the completely fixed, permanent, and unchangeable: to the "essence" of things, to "Being." Knowledge was present in definition, and *as* definition.[6] Word and thing, in this way, came before him conjoined. The search for essences came to be known classically as "clarification."[7] Clarification required search in two directions at once.

5. For some illustrations of the separation of "acts" and "products" in the logics, under a variety of formulations, see Chapter 1, particularly Sections I and X. In Chapter 9 product follows product and by-product follows by-product; here Sections I and IV exhibit the range of wordings employed. In Chapter 8 five of the six logicians examined make use of separable products under one form or another as basic to their constructions.
6. "Opinion" was allowed for as dealing with uncertainties, but on a lower level. It was *not* science; it was *not* definition.
7. Felix Kaufmann is one of the comparatively few workers in this field who make deliberate and sustained—and in his case, powerful—efforts to develop "clarification" in the classical sense (*Methodology of the Social Sciences* [New York, 1944]). He expressly affirms this approach (*Philosophy and Phenomenological Research,* V, 1945, p. 351) in the sense of *Meno,* 74 ff., and *Theaetetus,* 202 ff.

Definition must express the essences; it must also be the process of finding them. Species were delimited through the "forms" that make them *what* they are. It was in the form of Speech (*Logos*) that logic and ontology must come into perfect agreement.

Aristotle thus held together the subjectmatters which came together. He did not first split apart, only to find himself later forced to try to fit together again what had thus been split. The further history is well known to all workers in this field. The Middle Ages retained the demand for permanence, but developed in the end a sharp split between the name and thing, with an outcome in "isms." On one side were the nominalists (word-dizzy, the irreverent might say), and on the other side the realists (comparably speaking, thing-dizzy). Between them came to stand the conceptualists, who, through an artificial device which even today still seems plausible to most logicians, inserted a fictitious locus—the "concept"—in which to assemble the various issues of word and thing. The age of Galileo broke down the requirements of immutability, and substituted uniformities or "laws" for the old "essences" in the field of inquiry. Looking back upon that age, one might think that the effect of this change on logic would have been immediate and profound. Not so. Even today the transformation is incomplete in many respects, and even the need for it is often not yet brought into the clear. John Stuart Mill made a voyage of discovery, and developed much practical procedure, as in the cases of naming and induction, but his logic held to dealings with "laws" as separate space-time connections presented to knowledge, and was essentially pre-Darwinian in its scientific setting, so that many of the procedures it stresses are now antiquated.[8]

The Aristotelian approaches were, however, sufficiently jarred to permit the introduction in recent times of "non-Aristotelian" devices. These were forecast by a new logic of relations. These "relations," though not at all "things" of the ancient types, nevertheless struggled from the start (and still struggle) to appear as new variations of the old, instead of as disruptive departures

8. Mill managed to see adjectives as names (*Logic*, I, Chapter II, Section 2) but not adverbs. By way of illustration drawn from our immediate range of subjectmatters, consider how much sharper and clearer the adverb "definitely" is in its practical applications than is an adjectival assertion of definite*ness*, or a purported "nounal" determination of what "definition" substantively *is*.

from it. Logical symbols were introduced profusely after the pattern of the older mathematical symbols, but more as usable notations than as the recognition of a new outlook for logic.

In addition to the greatly changed appearance since Greek
days of the "objects" presented as "known," as the so-called
"contents" of knowledge,[9] there are certain marked differentiations in techniques of presentation (in the organization of
"words" and "sentences" to "facts") which are of high significance for the logic of the future. For one thing, there is the difference between what "naming" has come to be in science since
Darwin, and what it was before his time; for another, there is the
difference between what a mathematical symbol is in mathematics today and what it was when it was still regarded as a type of
naming.[10] Neither of these changes has yet been taken up into
logical understanding to any great extent, however widely discussion in the ancient forms of expression has been carried on.
The common attempt is to reduce logical, mathematical, and scientific procedures to a joint organization (usually in terms of
some sort of single mental activity presumed at work behind
them) in such a way as to secure a corresponding forced organization of the presumptive "things," logical, mathematical, and
scientific, they are supposed to deal with.

One may illustrate by such a procedure as that of Bertrand
Russell's "logical atomism," in which neither Russell nor any of
his readers can at any time—so far as the "text" goes—be quite
sure whether the "atoms" he proposes are minimal "terms" or
minimal "reals." Comparably, in those logical systems which use

9. Consider, for example, astronomy, with respect to which Greek science
found itself inspecting a fixed solar system moving about the fixed earth,
with sun and moon moving backward and forward, and the firmament of
fixed stars rotating above. Its physics offered four fixed elements, different in
essence, with earth movements downward toward their proper "end"; fire
movements upwards into the heavens; air and gas movements upwards as far
as the clouds or moon; and water movements, and those of all liquids, back
and forth. Its biology had fixed animal and plant species, which remained
fixed until Darwin.

10. The problem in this respect began as far back as the first uses of zero or
minus-one, and has only disappeared with the heavy present employment of
the wave in mathematical formulation. Professor Nagel has lately given such
fine illustrations of this status that, with his permission, we should like to recommend to the reader the examination of his pages as if directly incorporated
at this point as a part of our text (the *Journal of Philosophy*, XLII, 1945,
pp. 625–627).

"syntactics" and "semantics," as soon as these distinctions have been made, an attempt follows to bring them together again by "interpretations." But the best of these "interpretations" are little more than impressionistic manifestations of wishfulness, gathering within themselves all the confusions and uncertainties which professedly have been expelled from the primary components. Although the "definitions" in such treatments are established primarily with reference to "syntactics" they spawn various sub-varieties or queer imitations on the side of "semantics." We seem to have here exhibits of the conventional isolations of form from content, along with a companionate isolation of things from minds, of a type that "transactional"[11] observation and report overcome.

In summary we find word and thing in Aristotle surveyed together but focused on permanence. In the later Middle Ages they came to be split apart, still with an eye on permanence, but with nothing by way of working organization except the tricky device of the "concept" as a third and separate item. Today logic presents, in this historical setting, many varieties of conflicting accounts of definition, side-slipping across one another, compromising and apologizing, with little coherence, and few signs of so much as a beginning of firm treatment. We shall proceed to show this as of the present. What we may hope for in the future is to have the gap between name and object done away with by the aid of a modern behavioral construction which is Aristotelian in the sense that it is freed from the post-Aristotelian dismemberment of man's naming activities from his named world, but which at the same time frees itself from Aristotle's classical demand for permanence in knowledge, and adapts itself to the modern view of science as in continuing growth.[12] Act and product belong broadly together, with product, as proceeds, always in action, and with action always process. Word and thing belong broadly together, with their provisional severance of high practical importance in its properly limited range, but never as full description nor as adequate theoretical presentation, and always *in* action.

11. See Chapter 5.
12. Compare the development in John Dewey, *Logic: The Theory of Inquiry*, Chap. XXI, on "Scientific Method: Induction and Deduction," especially pages 419, 423, 424 [*Later Works* 12:415, 418–20].

III

Since, as we have said, we are attempting to deal with this situation on the ground level, and in the simplest wordings we can find, it may be well to preface it with a brief account of an inquiry into definition carried on throughout in highly sophisticated professional terminology, which exhibits the confusions in fact, though without denouncing them at their roots. Walter Dubislav's *Die Definition*[13] is the outstanding work in this field. In discussing Kant and Fries he remarks that they do not seem to observe that the names they employ bring together into close relations things that by rights should be most carefully held apart; and in another connection he suggests that one of the important things the logician can do is to warn against confounding definitions with verbal explications of the meaning of words. His analysis yields five types (*Arten*) of definitions, the third of which, he is inclined to think, is merely a special case of the first. These are: (1) Special rules of substitution within a calculus; (2) Rules for the application of the formulas of a calculus to appropriate situations of factual inquiry; (3) Concept-constructions; (4) Historical and juristic clarifications of words in use; (5) Fact-clarifications, in the sense of the determination of the essentials (*Inbegriff*) of things (*Gebilde*), these to be arrived at under strictly logical-mathematical procedure out of basic presuppositions and perceptual determinations, within a frame of theory; and from which in a similar way and under similar conditions all further assertions can be deduced, but with the understanding (so far as Dubislav himself is concerned) that things-in-themselves are excluded as chimerical.[14] A comparison of the complexly terminological composition of No. 5 with the simple statements of Nos.

13. Third edition (Leipzig, 1931), 160 pages (*Beihefte der "Erkenntnis,"* 1). Citations from pages 17, 131. Historically Dubislav finds four main "theories" of definition: the Aristotelian essence and its successors to date (*Wesensbestimmung*); the determination of concepts (*Begriffsbestimmung*); the fixation of meanings, historical and juristic (*Feststellung der Bedeutung . . . bzw., der Verwendung*); and the establishment of new signs (*Festsetzung über die Bedeutung . . . bzw., der Verwendung*).
14. The characterization of type No. 5 in the text above is assembled from two paragraphs of Dubislav's text (pp. 147, 148) which are apparently similar, but still not alike in content. Dubislav's own view as to what should be regarded as definition makes use of type No. 1 along lines of development from Frege to Hilbert (with a backward glance at Pascal), and in the expectation that its "formal" can be made "useful" through definitions of type No. 2.

1, 2, and 4, or even with the specialized appearance of simplicity in No. 3, gives a fair idea of the difficulties of even talking about definition from the older viewpoints.

IV

Definition may be—and often is—talked about as an incidental, or even a minor, phase of logical inquiry. This is the case both when logic is seen as a process of "mind" and when the logician's interest in it is primarily technological. In contrast with this view, the processes of definition may be seen as the throbbing heart—both as pump and as circulation—of the whole knowledge system. We shall take this latter view at least to the extent that when we exhibit the confusions in the current treatments of definition, we believe that we are not exhibiting a minor defect but a vital disease. We believe, further, that here lies the very region where inquiry into naming and the named is the primary need, if dependable organization is to be attained. The field for terminological reform in logic generally is much wider, it is true, than the range of the word "definition" alone, and a brief reminder of these wider needs may be in order. In logic a definition may enter as a proposition, or as a linguistic or mental procedure different from a proposition; while, alternatively, perhaps all propositions may be viewed as definitions. A proposition itself may be almost anything;[15] it consists commonly of "terms," but terms, even while being the "insides" of propositions, may be either words or non-verbal "things." The words, if words enter, may either be meanings, or have meanings. The meanings may be the things "themselves" or other words. Concepts may appear either as "entities" inserted between words and things, or as themselves words, or as themselves things. Properties and qualities are perhaps the worst performers of all. They may be anything or everything, providing it is not too definite.

The following exhibits, some of confusion, others of efforts at clarification, are offered much as they have happened to turn up in current reading, though supplemented by a few earlier memoranda and recollections. We shall display the confusions directly on the body of the texts, but intend thereby nothing invidious to

15. For illustrations and references as to propositions, see Chapter 8, Section V.

the particular writers. These writers themselves are simply "the facts of the case," and the case itself is one, at this stage, for observation, not for argumentation or debate.

For philosophers' views we may consult the philosophical dictionaries of Baldwin (1901), Eisler (German, 1927), Lalande (French, 1928), and Runes (1942). If definition "clarifies," then the philosophical definitions of definition are far from being themselves definitions. Ancient terminologies are at work, sometimes with a slight modernization, but without much sign of attention to the actual life-processes of living men, as modern sciences tell us about them. Robert Adamson, in Baldwin, proceeds most firmly, but also most closely under the older pattern.[16] Both acts and resultant products are, for him, definitions, but the tops and bottoms of the process—the individual objects, and the *summa genera*—are "indefinables."[17] Nominal definitions concern word-meanings, and real definitions concern the natures of things defined; analytic definitions start with notions as given, and synthetic definitions put the notions together; rational definitions are determined by thought, and empirical definitions by selective processes. This is all very fine in its way, but effectively it says little of present-day interest.

Lalande first identifies "definition" in a "general logic" dealing with the action of *l'esprit;* and then two types in "formal" logic, one assembling known terms to define the concept, the other enunciating equivalences. He also notes the frequent extension of the word "definition" to include all propositions whatsoever. Eisler adds to *Nominaldefinition* and *Realdefinition*, a *Verbaldefinition,* in which one word is merely replaced by others. Besides this main division he reports minor divisions into analytic, synthetic, and implicit, the last representing Hilbert's definition of fundamental geometrical terms.

Alonzo Church, in Runes's dictionary, stands closer to con-

16. Adamson, who was one of the most impartial observers and keenest appraisers of logical theory, himself remarked in *A Short History of Logic* (Edinburgh and London, 1911), p. 20, that "looking to the chaotic state of logical text-books . . . one would be inclined to say that there does not exist anywhere a recognised, currently received body of speculations to which the title logic can be unambiguously assigned."

17. The introduction of such an "indefinable," of which we shall later find various examples, is, in effect, to make proclamation of ultimate impotence precisely at the spot in logical inquiry where sound practical guidance is the outstanding need.

temporary practice, but shows still no interest in what in ordinary modern inquiry would be considered "the facts of the case," namely, actual uses. He mixes a partial report on contemporary practices with a condensed essay on the proprieties to such an extent that it is difficult to know what is happening.[18] For a first grouping of definitions, he offers (a) (in logistic systems proper) nominal or syntactical definitions which, as conventional abbreviations or substitutions, are merely a sort of minor convenience for the logician, though nevertheless, it would seem, they furnish him one hundred per cent of his assurance; and (b) (in "interpreted logistic systems") semantical definitions which introduce new symbols, assign "meanings" to them, and cannot appear in *formal* development, although they may be "carried" implicitly by nominal definitions, and are candidates for accomplishing almost anything that may be wished, under a properly adapted type of "intent." As a second grouping of definitions he offers the "so-called real" definitions which are not conventions as are syntactical and semantical definitions, but instead are "propositions of equivalence" (material, formal, etc.) between "abstract entities"; which require that the "essential nature" of the definiendum be "embodied in" the definiens; and which sometimes, from other points of approach, are taken to convey assertions of "existence," or at least of "possibility." He notes an evident "vagueness" in "essential nature" as this controls "real" definition, but apparently sees no source of confusion or any other difficulty arising from the use of the single word "definition" for all these various purposes within an inquiry, nor in the various shadings or mixtures of them, nor in the entry of definienda and definientia, sometimes in "nominal" and sometimes in "real" forms, nor in livening up the whole procedure, wherever it seems desirable, with doses of "interpretative" intent.[19]

18. It is proper to recall that the contributors to Runes's dictionary had much fault to find with the way their copy was edited, and that, therefore, the dictionary text may not fully represent Professor Church's intention. The difficulty to be stressed is, however, not peculiar to his report. A similar confused mixture of what is "historical" with what is "factual" is general. The Runes classification, as we find it, is in this respect vague at almost every point of differentiation. More broadly for all four philosophical dictionaries, the manifestly unclarified phrasings seem to outnumber the attempted clarifications a dozen to one.
19. How curiously this sort of thing works out can be seen in the opening pages of Church's *Introduction to Mathematical Logic*, Part I (Princeton, 1944), in

Here are other specimens, old and new, of what is said about definition. Carnap expressly and without qualification declares that a definition "means" that a definiendum "is to be an abbreviation for" a definiens, but in the same inquiry introduces definitions that are not explicit but recursive, and provides for definition rules as well as for definition sentences. Elsewhere he employs two "kinds" of definition, those defining respectively logical and empirical "concepts," and makes use of various reduction processes to such an extent that he is spoken of at times as using "conditioned" definitions.[20] Tarski makes definition a stipulation of meaning which "uniquely determines," differentiating it thus from "designation" and "satisfaction."[21] An often quoted definition of definition by W. L. Davidson is that "It is the object of Definition to determine the nature or meaning or signification of a thing: in other words definition is the formal attempt to answer the question 'What is it?'"[22] H. W. B. Joseph writes: "The definition of anything is the statement of its essence: what makes it that, and not something else."[23] J. H. Woodger limits the word for axiom-systems to "one quite definite sense," the "explicit"—understanding thereby substitutability; however differently the word might elsewhere be used.[24] Henry Margenau

---

which he writes (p. 1): "In the formal development we eschew attributing any meanings to the symbols of the Propositional Calculus"; and (p. 2): "We shall be guided implicitly by the interpretation we eventually intend to give it." Repeated examinations which several interested inquirers have made into Church's words, "meanings," "natural," "necessary," "language," "implicit," and "interpretation," as he has used them in the context of the sentences just quoted, have given no aid towards reducing the fracture in his constructional bone. As pertinent to the issue it may be recalled that Kurt Gödel, in analyzing Russell's procedure, came to the conclusion that Russell's formalism could not "explain away" the view that "logic and mathematics (just as physics) are built up on axioms with a real content" (*The Philosophy of Bertrand Russell*, P. A. Schilpp, editor [Chicago, 1944], p. 142). Again, Hermann Weyl in the *American Mathematical Monthly* (1946), p. 12, remarks of Hilbert that "he is guided by an at least vaguely preconceived plan for such a proof."

20. Carnap, R., *Introduction to Semantics* (Cambridge, 1942), pp. 17, 31, 158. "Testability and Meaning," *Philosophy of Science*, III (1936), pp. 419–471, especially pp. 431, 439, 448; IV (1937), pp. 1–40.

21. *Introduction to Logic* (New York, 1941), pp. 33–36, pp. 118 ff. "The Semantic Conception of Truth," *Philosophy and Phenomenological Research*, IV (1944), p. 345, and notes 20 and 35.

22. *The Logic of Definition* (London, 1885), p. 32.

23. *An Introduction to Logic* (Oxford, 1916), p. 72.

24. *The Axiomatic Method in Biology* (Cambridge, England, 1937), p. 4.

distinguishes between constitutive and operational.[25] A. J. Ayer
has "explicit" or "synonymous" definition in contrast with philosophical "definition in use."[26] Morris Weitz employs the names
"real" and "contextual."[27] A. W. Burks proposes to develop a
theory of ostensive definition which describes "definition in terms
of presented instances, rather than in terms of already defined
concepts," and says that counter-instances as well as instances
must be pointed at; such definition is thereupon declared to be
classification.[28] W. E. Johnson decides that "every definition must
end with the indefinable," where the indefinable is "that whose
meaning is so directly and universally understood, that it would
be mere intellectual dishonesty to ask for further definition";
he also thinks, interestingly enough, that it would "seem legitimate . . . to define a proper name as a name which *means* the
same as what it *factually indicates*."[29] G. E. Moore insists on a
sharp separation between defining a word and defining a concept, but leaves the reader wholly uncertain as to what the distinction between word and concept itself might be in his system,
or how it might be defined to others.[30] What current philosophizing can accomplish under the aegis of the loose and vagrant use
of "definition" by the logics is illustrated by Charles Hartshorne
in a definition of "reality" which ideal knowledge is said to "provide" or "give" us by the aid of a preliminary definition of "perfect knowledge." This "definition" of "reality" is: "The real is
whatever is content of knowledge ideally clear and certain,"[31]

25. "On the Frequency Theory of Probability," *Philosophy and Phenomenologi-
    cal Research*, VI (1945), p. 17.
26. *Language, Truth and Logic* (New York, 1936), pp. 66–69. A comparison of
    the respective uses of the word "explicit" by Carnap, Woodger, and Ayer
    might be instructive.
27. "Analysis and the Unity of Russell's Philosophy," in *The Philosophy of
    Bertrand Russell* (P. A. Schilpp, editor) (Chicago, 1944), pp. 120–121. The
    following pronouncement (p. 121) on the subject would seem worthy of pro-
    found pondering: "The value or purpose of real and contextual definitions is
    that they reduce the vagueness of certain complexes by calling attention to
    their various components."
28. "Empiricism and Vagueness," the *Journal of Philosophy*, XLIII (1946),
    p. 478.
29. *Logic* (Cambridge, England, 1921), Part I, pp. 105–106; pp. 93–94.
30. "A Reply to My Critics," in *The Philosophy of G. E. Moore* (P. A. Schilpp,
    editor) (Chicago, 1942), pp. 663–666.
31. "Ideal Knowledge Defines Reality: What Was True in 'Idealism,'" the *Journal
    of Philosophy*, XLIII (1946), p. 573.

and in it, however innocent and simple the individual words may look separately, there is not a single word that, in its immediate context, is itself clear or certain.

The above specimens look a good deal like extracts from a literature of escape, and some might rate well in a literature of humor. No wonder that Professor Nagel says of Bertrand Russell (who may be regarded as one of the ablest and most active investigators of our day in such matters) that "it is often most puzzling to know just what he is doing when he says that he is 'defining' the various concepts of mathematics"; [32] and that Professor Skinner, discussing the problems of operational definition with some of his psychological colleagues, tells them that while definition is used as a "key term," it itself is not "rigorously defined," and that "modern logic . . . can scarcely be appealed to by the psychologist who recognizes his own responsibility." [33]

V

Turn next to recent reports of research into the question. A paper by H. H. Dubs, "Definition and Its Problems," [34] gives an excellent view of the difficulties logicians face when they strive to hold these many processes together as one. Present theories of definition are recognized by him as confused, and the time is said to have arrived when it has become necessary to "think through" the whole subject afresh. Throwing dictionary definition [35] aside as irrelevant, "scientific definitions" are studied as alone of logical import, with logic and mathematics included among the sciences. Science itself is described as a linkage of concepts, and the general decision is reached for definition that it must tell us what the "concepts" are which are to be associated

32. In his contribution to *The Philosophy of Bertrand Russell*, edited by P. A. Schilpp, p. 326.
33. "Symposium on Operationism," *Psychological Review*, LII (1945), pp. 270–271.
34. *Philosophical Review*, LII (1943), pp. 566 ff.
35. It is interesting to note that one of his requirements for a dictionary definition is that it "must be capable of being written down." This is not demanded for the "scientific definition" for which there are "two and only two" specific requirements: it must be commensurate with what it defines, and it must define a term only in terms that have been previously defined.

with a "term or word" so as to determine when, "in immediate experience or thought," there is present the "entity or event" denoted by that term or word.

Definitions, in Dubs' development, are classified as conceptual or non-conceptual. The former is, he says, what others often call "nominal" and occurs where term is linked only with term. The latter are inevitable and occur where the linkage runs back to "logical ultimates" or "indefinables." Cutting across this classification appears another into "essential" and "nominal" (sometimes styled "real" and "accidental") depending on whether we can or cannot so define a term as to denote "all" the properties of the object or other characteristic defined. Practically, he reports, scientific definition consists almost entirely of the conceptual and the nominal, even though "scientific" has been adopted as the name of *all* definition pertinent to logic.

If we examine the non-conceptual indefinables in this presentation, we find that they consist of (*a*) causal operations (necessarily "wordless"), (*b*) direct pointings or denotings (that "cannot be placed in books"), and (*c*) intermediate hermaphroditic specimens, half pointings and half verbalizings. Dubs is not at all pleased to find his scheme of definition falling back upon the "indefinable," but his worry is mainly in the sense that he would prefer to reach "ultimates." He solaces himself slightly by hoping that it is just an affair of nomenclature. Nevertheless, since in certain cases, such as those of logic and mathematics, indefinables are seen entering which, he feels sure, are *not* ultimates, he feels compelled to keep the "indefinable" as an outstanding component of definition (or, shall we say, of the "definable"?) without permitting this peculiarity to detract from the hope that he has secured a new "practical and consistent" theory.

Especially to note is that while his leading statement about definition depends upon the use of such words as "concept," "term or word," "immediate experience," "thought," and "entity or event," no definition or explanation of any sort for these underlying words is given. They rate thus, perhaps, as the indefinables of the definition of definition itself, presumably being taken as so well known in their mental contexts that no question about them will be raised. We have already seen the indefinable mentioned by Adamson and Johnson (and the related "ostensive" by Burks), and we shall see more of the peculiar problem they raise as we go along.

Consider another type of examination such as that offered by John R. Reid under the title: "What Are Definitions?"[36] Here the effort is to solve the problem of definition not by classifying, but by the building up, or "integration," of a "system of ideas" into an "articulated unity." Taking for consideration what he calls a "definitional situation," he distinguishes within it the following "factors" or "components": a "definitional relation," a "definitional operation," and a "definitional rule." While distinct, these factors are not to be taken as "isolated." The "rule" seemingly is given top status, being itself three-dimensional, and thus involving sets of symbols, sets of cognitive interpretants, and particular cases to which the rule can apply. He holds that we cannot *think* at all without this definitional equipment, and stresses at the same time that the symbols, as part of the equipment, would not exist at all except in mental activity. This makes "mental activity" both cause and product, and apparently much the same is true for "symbol." The above points are elaborately developed, but all that is offered us in the way of information about definition itself is a recognition, in currently conventional form, that definitions may be either "syntactical" or "semantical," and that the word "definition" remains ambiguous unless it has an accompanying adjective thus to qualify it. This difference is assumed, but the differentiation is not studied; nor, apparently, is it considered to be of much significance in theory.

Not by pronouncement, but in their actual procedures, both Dubs and Reid bring definition under examination as a facultative activity in the man who does the defining and who is the "definer," and as having, despite its many varieties, a single "essential" type of output. Where Dubs undertakes through cross-classifications to make the flagrant conflicts in the output appear harmonious, Reid strives to establish unity through a multiplication of "entities," arriving thus only at a point at which the reader, according to his likings, will decide either that far too many entities are present, or nowhere near enough.[37]

36. *Philosophy of Science*, XIII (1946), pp. 170–175.
37. Reid's asserted background for his inquiry into definition may be illustrated by the further citations: "A . . . relation is the symbolic product of an . . . operation . . . according to . . . rule." "These distinctions are . . . not only 'real' . . . but . . . fundamental for . . . understanding." We must not deny "the irreducible complexity of the relevant facts." "Definitions . . . are . . . not assertable statements." Reid is here frank and plain about what ought to be in the open, but which in most discussions of definition is left tacit.

VI

Let us turn next to the deliberation of a group of six scientists and logicians in a recent symposium from which we have already quoted one speaker's pungent comment.[38] On the list of questions offered by the American Psychological Association for especial examination was one (No. 10), which asked: "What is a definition, operational or otherwise?" Two of the contributors, so far as they used the word "definition" at all, used it in conventional ways, and gave no direct attention to its problems, so we can pass them by. Two others, Feigl and Boring, used stylized phrasings, one in a slightly sophisticated, the other in a currently glib form, and have interest here merely to note the kind of tunes that can be played.

Feigl regards definition as useful in minor ways in helping to specify meanings for terms or symbols. Since it deals with terms or symbols it is always "nominal," and the "so-called real" definitions rate as mere descriptions or identifications. Nevertheless, although all definition is "nominal," it always terminates in something "not nominal," namely, observation. This might leave the reader uncertain whether a definition is still a definition after it has got beyond the nominal stage, but Feigl gets rid of this difficulty by calling it "a mere question of terminology." Boring defines definition as a "statement of equivalence," and says it can apply between a term and other terms or between a term and "events"—blandly inattentive to the question as to just in what sense a "term" can be *equivalent* to an "event." He further distinguishes definitions as either operational or non-operational, without, apparently, any curiosity as to the nature of the difference between the operational and the non-operational, nor as to what might happen to an assured equivalence on the operation table with or without benefit of anesthetic.

This leaves two contributors to the symposium, Bridgman, the physicist, and Skinner, the psychologist, to give useful practical attention to the business in hand, operational and definitional.[39]

38. "Symposium on Operationism," *Psychological Review*, LII (1945), pp. 241–294. Introduction by the editor, Herbert S. Langfeld. Contributions by Edwin G. Boring, P. W. Bridgman, Herbert Feigl, Harold E. Israel, Carroll C. Pratt, and B. F. Skinner.
39. Bridgman, however, is still deeply concerned with his old query as to the "public" *vs.* the "private" in knowledge; and the other contributors were so

Bridgman, standing on the firm practical ground he has long held with respect to physical procedure, treats definitions as statements applying to terms. Such definitions, he says, presuppose checking or verifying operations, and are thus not only operational, but so completely so that to call them "operational" is a tautology. Skinner, making the same kind of hard, direct operational analysis of the psychological terms that Bridgman made twenty years ago for physical terms, tosses out by the handful the current evasive and slippery phrasings wherever he finds them, and lays the difficulties, both in the appraisals of operation and in the appraisals of definition, to the fact that underlying observation and report upon human behaviors are still far too incomplete to give dependable results. He rejects dualisms of word and meaning, and then settles down to the application of plain, practical, common sense to the terminology in use—to the problem, namely, of what words can properly stand for in observation and experimentation in progress, and to the tentative generalizations that can be made from the facts so established. Skinner agrees with Bridgman that operational analysis applies to all definitions. For him a good answer to the question "What is a definition?" would require, first of all, "a satisfactory formulation of the effective verbal behavior of the scientist." His own undertaking is to contribute to the answer "by example." The others in this symposium might well be asked to become definite as to the status of whatever it is they mean when they say "*non*-operational."

The examinations, both by Bridgman and by Skinner, are held to the regions we ourselves have styled "specification" in distinction from those of "symbolization." For us they lead the way from the antiquated manners of approach used by the other workers we have just examined to three papers, published in the *Journal of Philosophy* in 1945 and 1946, in which much definite progress has been made. They are by Abraham Kaplan, Ernest Nagel, and Stephen C. Pepper. We shall note the advances made and the openings they indicate for future work. We regret it if other equally advanced investigations have failed to attract our attention.

---

bemused by it that in the seventeen pages of "rejoinders and second thoughts" following the primary papers, one-third of all the paragraphs directly, and possibly another third indirectly, had to do with this wholly fictitious, time-wasting issue.

VII

Kaplan's paper is styled "Definition and Specification of Meaning."[40] In it he examines "specification of meaning" as a process for improving the applicability of terms, and as thus leading the way towards definition in the older logical sense of a "logical equivalence between the term defined and an expression whose meaning has already been specified." He sets up the connection between specification and equivalence of meaning as a goal, but does not undertake to deal with its problems, limiting himself here instead to an examination of some of the matters to take account of in such a theory. He acutely observes that much of the best work of science is done with "concepts" such as that of species for which all the long efforts of the biologists have failed to secure any "definition" whatever, and proceeds to ask how this can be possible if definition is so potent and so essential as logicians make it out to be. Treating "specification of meaning" as "hypothetical throughout," he leads up to the question: How does such a development of meaning come to approximate, and in the end to attain, the character of logical definition in which the meanings are no longer held within the limits of hypothesis (though, nevertheless, under the reservation that in the end, definition may possibly come to appear as "only a special form of specification")?

A great field of inquiry is thus opened, but certain difficulties at once demand attention. Kaplan employs, as if well understood, certain key-words in connection with which he gives no hint of specification on their own account. These include such words as "concept," "term," and "meaning." In what sense, for example, in his own development, does "specification of meaning" tell more than "specification" alone? What additional "meaning" is added by the word "meaning"? Is this "meaning" in any way present apart from or in addition to its "specification"? If "meaning" adds anything, should its particular contribution not be made clear at an early point in the treatment—a point earlier, indeed, than Kaplan's present discussion? What is the difference between "meaning" by itself and "meaning of a term"—a phrase often alternatively used? If "term" has to have a "meaning" and its

40. The *Journal of Philosophy*, XLIII (1946), pp. 281–288.

"meaning" has to be separately "specified," is the inquiry not being carried on at a stage twice removed—and unnecessarily removed at that—from direct observation? If three stages of "fact" are thus employed, should not their differentiation be clearly established, or their manner of entry at least be indicated? These questions are asked, not to discourage, but as encouragement for, the further examination which Kaplan proposes, if the relations of equivalence and specification are to be understood.

VIII

Nagel, in his paper "Some Reflections on the Use of Language in the Natural Sciences,"[41] understands by "definition" very much what Kaplan understands by specification. He does not, for the immediate purposes of his discussion of language, generalize the problem as Kaplan does, but he shows brilliantly the continuous revision and reconstruction of uses which an active process of definition involves. We have already cited, in passing, his valuable pages on the growing abandonment by mathematicians of their older expectations that their symbols should have efficient status as names. He provides an illuminating illustration of the underlying situation in the case of "constant instantial velocity" which by its very manner of phrasing makes it operationally the "name" of nothing at all, while nevertheless it steadily maintains its utility as a phrase.[42] He eliminates the claims of those types of expression which, applied in a variety of meanings through a variety of contexts, manage to fascinate or hypnotize the men who use them into believing that, as expressions, they possess "a generic meaning common to all" their varieties of applications. He could even have used his own word "definition" as an excellent example of such a form of expression. In the background of his vividly developed naturalistic appraisal of the processes of knowledge, all of these steps have high significance for further progress.

41. The *Journal of Philosophy*, XLII (1945), pp. 617–630.
42. His statement, of course, is not in terms of "naming." As he puts it, such expressions "are *prima facie inapplicable* to anything on land or sea"; they "*apparently* have no pertinent use in connection with empirical subject-matter," as "no overtly identifiable motions of bodies can be characterized" by them. *Ibid.*, pp. 622–623.

IX

Pepper's account of "The Descriptive Definition"[43] undertakes a form of construction in the very region which Kaplan indicates as locus of the great problem. His "descriptive definition" is so close to what we ourselves have described as "specification" that, so far as his introductory characterization goes, we could gladly accept his account of it, perhaps free from any reservation, as meeting our needs. It offers at the least a fair alternative report to that which we seek. His framework of interpretation is, however, another matter, and his "descriptive definition," as he sees it, is so intricately built into that framework that it must be appraised as it there comes.

Like Kaplan, with his specification of meaning, Pepper envisions the old logical definition as basic to the display and justification of a descriptive definition. He notes that "in empirical enquiry observers desire expressions which ascribe meanings to symbols with the definite proviso that these meanings shall be as nearly true to fact as the available evidence makes possible." To this end the reference of description is "practically never" to be taken as "unalterable." He does not offer a fully positive statement, but at least, as he puts it in one phrasing, the "reference" of the symbol under the description is "intended" to be altered whenever "the description can be made more nearly true." The descriptive definition thus becomes "a convenient tool constantly responsible to the facts," rather than "prescriptive in empirical enquiry."[44]

So far so good. Men are shown seeking knowledge of fact, elaborating descriptions, and changing names to fit improved descriptions. But Pepper finds himself facing the query whether this is "definition" at all? Perhaps, he reflects, the nominal and the

43. The *Journal of Philosophy*, XLIII (1946), pp. 29–36.
44. Merely as a curiosity, showing the way in which words used in logic can shift back and forth, Peirce once undertook (2.330) to suggest much the same thing as Pepper now develops. Pepper's language is that "a nominal definition is by definition prescriptive." Peirce's wording was: "this definition—or rather this precept that is more serviceable than a definition." Precept and prescription are not the same etymologically, but their uses are close. Peirce's "precepts" would be a close companion for Pepper's descriptive definition; while Pepper's "prescription," in its none too complimentary use, matches closely what Peirce felt compelled to understand by definition.

real definitions of logical theory, the equations, the substitutions, and the ostensive definitions have exclusive rights to the field and will reject "descriptive" definitions as intruders? At any rate he feels it necessary to organize descriptive definition with respect to these others, and with a continuing eye on the question whether he can get from or through them authority for what he wishes to accomplish. Though still committing himself to the wearing of a coat of many definitional colors, the organization he seeks is in a much more modern spirit than the classifications of Dubs or the "articulated unity" of Reid.

He begins by making descriptive definition one of two great branches of definition. Against it he sets nominal definition. The former is known by its being "responsible to facts meant by the symbol." The latter is not thus responsible, but either assumes or ignores facts, or else is irrelevant to them. Nominal definition in turn has two species: the equational and the ostensive.

The equational species is said to be strictly and solely a matter of the substitution of symbols. Whether this is an adequate expression for all that goes on in the equational processes of mathematics and in the development of equivalences, and whether it is really adequate for his own needs, Pepper does not discuss. What he is doing is to adopt a manner of treatment that is conventional among logicians who deal with logical "products" displayed on logical shelves instead of with the logical activity of living men, even though his own procedure is, culturally speaking, much further advanced than is theirs. For our present purposes we need to note that in *his* program equational definition is substitution—it is *this, and nothing more.*

The ostensive species of definition is (or "involves" or "refers to") a non-symbolic meaning or source of meaning for a symbol. It is primarily and typically a "pointing at." Pepper here examines the "facts" before him with excellent results. He suggests the interpretation of such "pointing" as "indication," and then of "indication" as "operation." The indicative "operation" at which he arrives in place of ostensive definition along the older lines is, however, still allotted status as itself a "definition." In this, there is a survival of influences of the "word and thing" mixture, even at the very moment when important steps are being taken to get rid of such conventional congealment. Old-timers could talk readily of "ostensive *definition*" because they lived reasonably misty lives and avoided analysis in uncomfortable quarters. Pepper makes a pertinent analysis, and we are at once startled into asking: Why and how can such an ostensive or indicative operation be itself called a "definition" in any careful use of either of the words, "ostensive" or "definition"? Is there something logically in common between finger-pointing without name-using, and name-using without finger or other pointing action? If so, just *what* is it? And above all, just *where* does it "existentially" have specific location?

Pepper's problem, now, is to organize the descriptive to the ostensive and to the equational. The problem is of such great importance, and every fresh exploration of it is of such great interest, that we shall take the space to show what is apt to happen when "substitution" in the guise of "equation" is employed as organizer for a presumptively less dependable "description." We are given three diagrams, and these with their accompanying texts should be carefully studied. The diagram for equational definition shows that the symbol, "*S*," is "equated with" and is "*equationally* defined by" other "symbols." The diagram for ostensive definition shows that such an "*S*" "indicates" and is "*ostensively* defined by" an "empirical fact," "*O*." The diagram for descriptive definition expands to triadic form. "*S*" is symbol as before. "*O*" is advanced from "fact" to "field," while remaining empirical. "*D*" is added to stand for description. Further distinctive of this diagram is the entry into its formulations of the words "tentative," "hypothetical," and "verifies," along with "describes." The scheme of the diagram then develops in two parallel manners of expression, or formulations:

FORMULATION A	FORMULATION B
1. (*D-O*): *D* hypothetically describes	(or) is verified by .... *O*.
2. (*S-D*): *S* is tentatively equated with	(or) is descriptively defined by *D*.
3. (*S-O*): *S* tentatively indicates	(or) is ostensively defined by *O*.[45]

45. Certain features of the diagram should be mentioned in connection with the above transcription. There is a bare possibility, so far as diagrammatic position goes, that the "tentatively indicates" and the "ostensively defined" on the *S-O* line should change places; our choice was made to hold the "tenta-

Under Formulation A, it would seem easy or "natural" to condense the statements to read that, given a hypothetical description of "something," we can take a word to stand tentatively for that description, and this word will then also serve as a tentative indication of the "something." Under Formulation B, we might similarly say (though various other renderings are possible) that, given a verified description of something, that description descriptively defines a word which in turn is (or is taken as) ostensively defined by the something; or we might perhaps more readily think of an ostensive hint leading through naming and description to verification or imagined verification followed by a thumping return to "ostensive *definition*." (In a discussion in another place Pepper, to some extent, simplifies his report by saying of the descriptive definition that "strictly speaking, it is an arbitrary determination of the meaning of a symbol in terms of a symbol group, subject, however, to the verifiability of the symbol group in terms of certain indicated facts.")[46] But would it not be still more informative if one said that what substantially this all comes to is a report that men possess language in which they describe events (facts, fields)—that they can substitute single words for groups of words—that the groups of words may be called descriptive definitions—and that the words so substituted serve to indicate the facts described, and, when regarded as "verified," are linked with "indicative operations" styled "ostensive"?

Thus simplified (if he will permit it) Pepper's development may be regarded as an excellent piece of work towards the obliteration of ancient logical pretenses, and it might well be made required reading in preliminary academic study for every budding logician for years to come. Our only question is as to the effec-

---

tives" and "hypothetical" together in one set. The *S-D* and *S-O* statements under Formulation A (the latter transformed to read "is . . . taken to indicate") are noted as "at the same time," which possibly indicates orders of succession elsewhere which we have overlooked. (We are far from wishing to force any such successions into the treatment.) The shiftings from active to passive verb forms may have some significance which we overlook, and the specific subject indicated for the passive verbs would be interesting to know. These difficulties are slight, and we trust none of them has interfered with a proper rendering by us of Professor Pepper's position.
46. *The Basis of Criticism in the Arts* (Cambridge, 1945), p. 31. The structural diagram in the book for the *D-O* of Formulation A uses the word "describes," and has not yet made the limitation "hypothetically describes."

tiveness of his procedure, for he carries it on as if it were compelled to subject itself to the antique tests supplied by the traditional logical scheme. We may ask: if equation is substitution or
substitutability—precisely this, and nothing else—why not call
it substitution in place of equation? Would not such an unequivo-
cal naming rid us of a bit of verbal trumpery, and greatly heighten
definiteness of understanding? If equation runs pure and true
from symbol to symbol, what possibly can "tentative" equating
be as a type of equating itself, and not merely as a preliminary
stage in learning? If one turns the phrase "is equated with" into
the active form "equals," how pleasing is it to find oneself saying
that "S tentatively equals D"? Or, if we are told, as in one passage, that the description is "not flatly equated" with the symbol,
but only equated "to the best of our abilities," does this add clarity? Descriptions are meant to be altered, but equations not;
again, the question arises, how is it that descriptive definitions
can be equated? How can "verifies" become an alternative phrasing for "hypothetically describes"? Should not the alternative
form in the diagram be perhaps, "hypothetically verifies," but
then what difference would there be between it and "description" itself? In introducing the "ostensive," Pepper views it in the
older manner as dealing with "facts of immediacy," despite his
own later reduction of it to indicative operation, and his retention of it as definition.[47] But just what could a tentative immediacy be?

The main question, further, remains: Why employ one single
name, even under the differentiations of genus and species, for
such varied situations in human behavior? If we take "e" for
equationally, "o" for ostensively, and "d" for descriptively, Pepper's varieties of definition may be set down as follows:

> *e-defined* is where a word S is substitutable for other
> words.
> *o-defined* is where a word is used operationally to indicate
> an object, O.
> *d-defined* is where a word tentatively indicates an O, by
> being tentatively substitutable for a description, D, which

47. *Ibid.*, pp. 27 ff.

latter hypothetically describes the O; or alternatively (and perhaps at some different phase of inquiry), d-defined is where a word is o-defined *via,* or in connection with, the "verification" of the D by the O.

In preliminary, conventional forms of statement, the report would seem to be that the e-definition, *as he offers it* (though we do not mean to commit ourselves to such a view), seems to be primarily a matter of language-organization; the o-definition seems to lie in a region commonly, though very loosely, called "experience"; and the d-definition, so far as any one can yet see, does not seem to lie comfortably anywhere as a species of a common genus.

X

We have seen many conflicting renderings of the word "definition" offered us by acute investigators who are currently engaged in a common enterprise in a common field. Recalling these conflicts, may one not properly say that this display by itself, and just as it stands, provides sufficient reason for a thorough terminological overhaul; and that, without such an overhaul and reorganization, the normal practical needs for intercommunication in research will fail to be properly met? The one word "definition" is expected to cover acts and products, words and things, accurate descriptions and tentative descriptions, mathematical equivalences and exact formulations, ostensive definitions, sensations and perceptions in logical report, "ultimates," and finally even "indefinables." [48] No one word, anywhere in careful technical research, should be required to handle so many tasks. Where, outside of logic—except, perhaps, in ancient theology or modern stump-speaking—would such an assertion be tolerated as that of the logicians when, among the "definables" of definition, they push "indefinables" boldly to the front? Here seems to

48. As we have already indicated, this confusion of a great variety of things under a single name is most probably maintained under some primitive form of reference of them all to a purportedly common source in a single human "capacity," "action," or "act," derivative of the medieval soul.

be a witches' dance, albeit of pachydermally clumsy logical will-o'-the-wisps. What more propriety is there in making definition cover such diversities than there would be in letting some school-boy, poring perversely over the pages of a dictionary, report that the Bengal tiger, the tiger-lily, the tiger on the box, and the tiger that one on occasion bucks, are all species of one common genus: *Tiger?*

The types of definition we have inspected appear to fall roughly into three groups: namely, equivalence as in mathematics, specification as in science, and a traditionally derived mixed logical form which hopes and maneuvers to establish specifications ultimately under a perfected logical pattern of equivalences. The worst of the affair is that present-day logic not only accepts these different activities and all their varieties as evident phases of a common process, but actually sees the great goal of all its labors to lie in their fusion into a single process, or unit in the logical system. The outcome is just the chaos we have seen.

The problem here to be solved is not one for a debating society, nor is it one for a formal calculating machine. It requires to be faced in its full historical linguistic-cultural setting. The great phases of this setting to consider are: the *logos* and the Aristotelian essences; the late medieval fracture of namings from the named as separate "things" in the exaggerated forms of "nominals" and "reals"; the artificially devised "concept" inserted to organize them; the survival into modern times of this procedure by conceptual proxy under a common, though nowhere clarified, substitution of "word" (or "sentence") for "concept"; the resultant confusedly "independent" or "semi-independent" status of "words," "terms," and "propositions" as components of subjectmatter; and finally the unending logical discussion of the connections of science and mathematics carried on in the inherited terminology, or in slight modifications of it, with no adequate factual examination at any stage, of the modern developments of scientific designation and mathematical symbolization in their own rights.

In this setting, and in the illustrations we have given, one feature appears that has great significance for our present consideration as showing the excesses to which the existing terminological pretenses may lead. This is the entry, of which we have repeatedly taken note,[49] and which will now receive a little closer attention, of the "ultimates" and "indefinables" as components at once of "definition" and of "reality." What we have called "specifications" and "symbolizations" can surely rate as current coin of the logical fields, no matter who does the investigating, and no matter how thorough or how precarious today's understanding of them is. The "indefinables" and the "ultimates," in contrast, are counterfeit. In them, as they enter logical discussion, we have neither good working names, nor intelligible equivalences, nor verifiable factual references, but instead pretenses of being, or of having more or less the values of, all three at once. They enter through "ostensive" definitions, or through some verbal alternative for the ostensive, but in such a way that we are unable to tell whether the "definition" itself is "about" something, or "is" the something which it is "about," or how such phrasings as "is" and "is about" are used, or just what meanings they convey. John Stuart Mill remarked a hundred years ago that, however "unambiguously" one can make known who the particular man is to whom a name belongs "by pointing to him," such pointing "has not been esteemed one of the modes of definition."[50] "Pointing" on the basis of previous mutual understanding is one thing, but the kind of understanding (or definition) that might be developed from pointing alone in a communicational vacuum, offers a very different sort of problem. Nevertheless, regardless of all such absurdities the ostensive definition, since Mill's time, has gained very considerable repute, and is, indeed, a sort of benchmark for much modern logic, to which, apparently, the possession of such a name as "ostensive definition" is guarantee enough that somewhere in the cosmos there must exist a good, hard fact to go with the name. The ostensives, and

49. In the preceding reports we have had mention of indefinables by Adamson, Johnson, and Dubs. Ostensive definition has been variously treated by Pepper and Burks. Feigl also considers the ostensive definition, saying that it is "rather fashionable nowadays." He believes there should be no trouble with it, as it is either "a designation rule formulated in a semantical metalanguage" or "a piece of practical drill in the learning of the 'right use' of words." Dubs, for his part, finds it "not quite clear" enough to use.

50. Op. cit., Book I, Chapter VIII, Section 2. For a discussion in a wider background than the present of the whole problem of "demonstratives" including both the "pointings" and the "objects" pointed-at, see J. Dewey, Logic: The Theory of Inquiry, pages 53–54, 124, and 241–242 [Later Works 12:59–60, 127, 240–41].

their indefinables and ultimates, seem, indeed, to be a type of outcome that is unavoidable when logic is developed as a manipulation of old terminologies using "definers," "realities," and "names" as separate components, instead of being undertaken as an inquiry into a highly specialized form of the behaviors of men in the world around them. Ostensive behavior can be found. Definitional behavior can be found. But the mere use of the words "ostensive definition" is not enough to solve the problem of their organization.

If we try, we may take these procedures of defining the indefinables apart so as to see, in a preliminary way at least, what they are made of and how they work. What are these indefinables and ultimates assumed to be (or, verbally, to stand for) as they enter definition? Are they regarded as either "physical" or "mental"? Usually not. Instead they are spoken of as "logical" entities or existences, a manner of phrasing as to which the less it is inquired into, the better for it. Certainly there are words involved, because, without its linguistic presentation as "ostensive," there is no way, apparently, in which such definition would be before our attention at all. Certainly, also, there are "things" involved—"things" in the sense of whatever it is which is beyond the finger in the direction the finger points. Certainly also there is a great background of habit and orientation, of behavior and environment, involved in every such pointing. More than this, in any community using language—and it is a bit difficult to see how definition in any form would be under close scrutiny except in a language-using community—a large part of the background of such pointing is linguistic. Suppose we consider as sample exhibits in the general region of pointings a masterless wild dog alert and tense with nose turned towards scent of game; a trained pointer in field with hunting master, the master pointing with hand for benefit of comrade towards sign of motion in brush; a savage hunter pointing or following with his eye another hunter's pointing; a tropic savage as guest in arctic watching Eskimo's finger pointed towards never-before-seen snow, and finally, the traditional Patagonian getting first sight of locomotive as Londoner points it out. Traditionally the Patagonian sees nothing of what a locomotive "is," and certainly it would be stretching matters to assume that the immediate case of "pointing" *defined* the locomotive to him.[51] Hardly anywhere would a theorist speak of the wild dog as engaged in definition. In the intervening cases there are various gradations of information established or imparted *via* sign. Where does distinctive "definition" begin, and why? Where does it cease, and why? These questions concern varieties of events happening, and names needed in their study.

It is our most emphatically expressed belief that such a jumble of references as the word "definition" in the logics has today to carry cannot be brought into order until a fair construction of human behaviors across the field is set up, nor until within that construction a general theory of language on a full behavioral basis has been secured.[52] We have sketched tentatively in preceding chapters some of the characteristics which we believe such construction will have. Identifying behavior in general with organic-environmental sign-process, transactionally viewed, we have noted the perceptive-manipulative activities at one end of the range, and then three stages of the designatory use of language, followed by another type of use in symbolization. Given such a map of the behavioral territory, the various sorts of human procedure insistently lumped together under the name of "definition" could be allocated their proper operating regions. Among them the "ostensive," now so absurdly present, should be able, under a much needed transmutation, to find a proper home.

51. Cf. the discussion of "demonstratives" in Dewey's *Logic: The Theory of Inquiry,* pp. 125–127 [*Later Works* 12 : 128–30].
52. We have already cited Skinner's view that without a developed behavioral base modern logic is undependable, and we repeat it because such a view so rarely reaches logicians' ears. Their common custom is to discard into the "pragmatic" all uncomfortable questions about logic as living process, forgetting that the "pragmatic" of Peirce and James, and of historical status, is quite the opposite, since it interprets meanings, concepts, and ideas in life. Skinner's conclusion is that eventually the verbal behavior of the scientists themselves must be interpreted, and that if it turns out that this "invalidates our scientific structure from the point of view of logic and truth-value, then so much the worse for logic, which will also have been embraced by our analysis."

8. Logic in an Age of Science[1]

I

Among the subjectmatters which logicians like at times to investigate are the forms of postulation that other branches of inquiry employ. Rarely, however, do they examine the postulates under which they themselves proceed.[2] They were long contented to offer something they called a "definition" for logic, and let it go at that. They might announce that logic dealt with the "laws of thought," or with "judgment," or that it was "the general science of order." More recently they are apt to connect it in one or another obscure way with linguistic ordering.

We may best characterize the situation by saying that while logicians have spent much time discussing how to apply their logic *to* the world, they have given almost no examination to their own position, as logicians, *within* the world which modern science has opened. We may take Darwin's great demonstration of the "natural" origin of organisms as marking the start of the new era in which man himself is treated as a natural member of a universe under discovery rather than as a superior being endowed with "faculties" from above and beyond, which enable him to "oversee" it. If we do this, we find that almost all logical enterprises are still carried on in pre-Darwinian patterns. The present writer is, indeed, aware of only two systems (and one of these a suggested project rather than a developed construction) which definitely undertake an approach in a modern manner. The

---

1. This chapter is written by Bentley.
2. Sub-postulations within a wider, tacitly accepted (i.e., unanalysed) postulatory background are common enough. The present viewpoint is that of Morris R. Cohen when he writes: "The philosophic significance of the new logic, the character of its presuppositions, and the directions of its possible application are problems which have attracted relatively little reflective thought." *A Preface to Logic* (New York, 1944), p. ix.

rest are almost wholly operated under the blessing, if not formally in the name, of "thinkers," "selves," or superior realms of "meanings." The present memorandum will sketch the new form of approach and contrast it with typical specimens of the old.

Two great lines of distinction between pre-Darwinian and post-Darwinian types of program and goals for logic may readily be set down.

While the former are found to center their attention basically upon *decisions* made by individual human beings (as "minds," "deciders," or otherwise "actors"), the latter describe broadly, and appraise directly, the presence and growth of knowings in the world, with "decisions" entering as passing phases of process, but not as *the* critical acts.

While enterprises of pre-Darwinian types require certainties, and require these to be achieved with perfection, absoluteness, or finality, the post-Darwinian logic is content to hold its results within present human reach, and not strive to grasp too far beyond.

Examined under these tests the recent logics of the non-Aristotelian, multivalued, and probability types all still remain in the pre-Darwinian or "non-natural" group, however they may dilute their wordings with respect to the certainties. A century ago Boole undertook to improve logic by mathematical aid, and there was great promise in that; but Russell, following the mind-steeped Frege, and himself already thoroughly indoctrinated to understanding and interpretation by way of "thought" or "judgment," reversed this, and has steadily led the fight to make logic master and guardian[3] in the ancient manner, with never a moment's attention to the underlying problem: *Quis custodiet ipsos custodes?*

The lines of distinction we have mentioned above might, perhaps, be made the basis for two contrasting sets of postulations. In some respects such postulations could be developed as sharply as those which geometers set up with respect to parallels. But such a course would be practicable only on the condition that the key words employed in them could be held to sharply established meanings. However, as logic and its surrounding disciplines now

3. In his very latest publication Bertrand Russell still writes: "From Frege's work it followed that arithmetic, and pure mathematics generally, is nothing but a prolongation of deductive logic," *A History of Western Philosophy* (New York, 1945), p. 830.

186   KNOWING AND THE KNOWN

stand, this necessary linguistic precision cannot be attained. A single man might allege it, but his fellows would not agree, and at his first steps into the linguistic market-place he would find each logician he approached demanding the right to vary the word-meanings, and to shape them, here subtly, there crudely, out of all semblance to the proposed postulational use.[4]

Since such a course will not avail, we may try another. We may hunt down in several logics the most specific statements each of them has made in regard to the issues in question. We may then assemble these as best we can. We shall not in this way obtain postulations[5] in the sense in which more securely established inquiries can obtain them, but we may at times secure fair approximations. Where we cannot get even this far forward, we can at least present skeletons of the construction of logical systems, such that they contain the materials out of which postulations may perhaps be derived if in the end the logicians involved will ever attend closely enough to what they are doing. If careful appraisals are to be secured, work of this kind is essential, even though it as yet falls far below the standards we could wish.

We shall consider six logical procedures, half of them in books published in 1944 and 1945, and all now under active discussion. We shall take them in three groups: first the "natural"[6] construc-

4. Samples of logicians' linguistic libertinism can be found anywhere, anytime, in current periodicals. Thus, for instance, in a paper just now at hand, we find "principles" of deduction referred to "intuition" for their justification, and this along with the suggestion that intuition should be "reinforced by such considerations as . . . ingenuity may suggest." A few paragraphs later a set of "principles" containing wholly naïve uses of the word "true" are declared to be "intuitively obvious." Lack of humor here goes hand in hand with inattention to the simpler responsibilities of speech; Max Black, "A New Method of Presentation of the Theory of the Syllogism," the *Journal of Philosophy*, XLII (1945), 450–51.
5. Compare Chapter 3 where groups of postulations are presented looking towards a natural theory of knowings and knowns.
6. In characterizing these logics as "natural," it is to be understood that the word "natural," as here used, is not to be taken as implying something specifically "material" as contrasted with something specifically "mental." It stands for a single system of inquiry for all knowledge with logic as free to develop in accordance with its own needs as is physics or physiology, and to develop in system with either or both of these as freely as they develop in system with each other. Many logicians rated by us as non-natural would label themselves "naturalistic." Thus Russell declares that he "regards knowledge as a natural fact like any other" (*Sceptical Essays* [New York, 1928], page 72), though our examination of his materials and procedures will give him quite the contrary rating.

tions of John Dewey and J. R. Kantor;[7] next, the sustained efforts of Morris R. Cohen and Felix Kaufmann to adapt old mentalistic-individualistic forms of control to modern uses; finally the desperate struggles of two outstanding logician-philosophers, Bertrand Russell and G. E. Moore, to secure victory with their ancient banners still waving. Our purpose is not so much to debate the rights and wrongs of these procedures, as it is to exhibit the differences in materials and workmanship, and to indicate the types of results thus far offered.

II

John Dewey's wide professional and public following derives more from his philosophical, educational, and social studies than from his logic. Nevertheless for over forty years he has made logic the backbone of his inquiry. His preliminary essays on the subject go back, indeed, to the early nineties. The *Studies in Logical Theory* appeared in 1903, the *Essays in Experimental Logic* in 1916, and *Logic: The Theory of Inquiry* in 1938, all in a single steadily maintained line of growth which stresses inquiry directly as the great subjectmatter of logic along a line of development foreseen and tentatively employed by Charles Sanders Peirce.[8] With Dewey the method and outcome of inquiry becomes warranted assertion. "Proof," which the older logics endeavored to establish under validities of its own for the control of knowledge, is here to be developed within, and as a phase of, inquiry; all certainty becomes subject to inquiry including the certainties of these very canons of logic which older logics had treated as the powerful possessors of certainty in their

---

7. If Otto Neurath had lived to develop his position further than he did, we could doubtless list him also on the "natural" side. He was from the beginning much further advanced in this respect than others of his more active associates in the projected *International Encyclopedia of Unified Science,* of which he was editor-in-chief. His most recent publication is *Foundations of the Social Sciences,* a monograph contributed to the Encyclopedia.

8. "As far as I am aware, he (Peirce) was the first writer on logic to make inquiry and its methods the primary and ultimate source of logical subject-matter," John Dewey, *Logic: The Theory of Inquiry* (New York, 1938), p. 9n [*Later Works* 12:17n]. The fourth of the postulates for Dewey in the text is frequently called "the postulate of continuity," and perhaps offers the straightest and widest route from Darwin through Peirce to Dewey.

own right. Man is thus seen to advance in his logical action as well as in all his other affairs *within* his cosmos, so that the dicta and ultimacies of the older *super*-natural rationalities, presumptively possessed by men, fall forfeit. The basic attitudes adopted in Dewey's *Logic,* the makings of a postulation for it, will be found in his first chapter. We list six section headings from this chapter and supplement them with two other characteristic attitudes. These are numbered 1 to 8, and are followed by a dozen more specialized determinations, here numbered 9 to 20.

DEWEY[9]

1. "Logic is a progressive discipline" (p. 14[21]);
2. "The subject-matter of logic is determined operationally" (p. 14[22]);
3. "Logical forms are postulational" (p. 16[23]);
4. "Logic is a naturalistic theory; . . . rational operations *grow out of* organic activities" (pp. 18–19[26]);
5. "Logic is a social discipline" (p. 19[26]);
6. "Logic is autonomous; . . . inquiry into inquiry . . . does not depend upon anything extraneous to inquiry" (p. 20[28]);
7. "Every special case of knowledge is constituted as the outcome of some special inquiry" (p. 8[16]);
8. "Logical theory is the systematic formulation of controlled inquiry" (p. 22[29]) with "the word 'controlled' . . . standing for the methods of inquiry that are developed and perfected in the processes of continuous inquiry" (p. 11[19]).
9. Inquiry, through linguistic development of terms and propositions, arrives in judgment at warranted assertions upon existence (Chapter VII);
10. Propositions and propositional reasonings are intermediate and instrumental in inquiry (pp. 113, 166, 181,

9. All page references are to *Logic: The Theory of Inquiry* [bracketed numbers refer to corresponding pages in *Later Works* 12]. Professor Dewey has made further development since the *Logic* was published, particularly with respect to the organization of language, logical forms, and mathematics. Such advances are intimated, but not expressly set forth, in the numbered paragraphs of the text, since it is desirable, for all logics discussed, to hold the presentation to what can be directly verified by the reader in the pages of the works cited.

310[116–17, 167–68, 182, 309], *et al.*); propositions
are not found in independence or as isolates, but only
as members of sets or series (p. 311[310]);

11. Terms enter as constituents of propositions and as conditioned by them, never in independence or as isolates
(p. 328[327–28]);

12. Singular and generic propositions are conjugates, the former specifying "kinds," the latter organizations of "kinds"
(pp. 358–9[355–57]);

13. The development of propositions in "generic derivation
or descent where differentiation into kinds is conjoined
with differentiation of environing conditions" is an
equivalent in logic to the biological advance which
established the origin of species (pp. 295–6[295]);

14. Singular propositions (and with them "particulars") appear as incomplete or imperfect, rather than as "simple,"
"atomic," or otherwise primordial (p. 336n[335n],
p. 342[340]);[10]

15. The propositions called "universal" are intermediate
stages of inquiry like all others, and are to be examined
on various levels of instrumental differentiation (Chapters XIV, XV, XX);

16. The adequate development of the theory of inquiry must
await the development of a general theory of language
in which form and matter are not separated (p. iv[4]);

17. Mathematical forms, and logical forms generally, are
properly to be studied in severance from their subjectmatters only when it is recognized that the severance is
provisional, and that their full setting in determinate human action is to be taken into account in the final construction (Chapter XVII);

18. The canons of the old logic (including non-contradiction),
now entering as forms attained in and with respect to
inquiry, lose all their older pretenses to authority as
inherent controls or as intuitively evident (pp. 345–
6[343–45]), and, when detached from their place in "the
progressive conduct of inquiry," show themselves as
"mechanical and arbitrary" survivals (p. 195[195]).

10. The radical nature of the advance in postulate 14 over older treatments will
be plain when the postulations for Russell are considered. For the equally radical postulate 19 see postulate B-8, and its context, in Chapter 3, Section III.

19. "Objects" as determined through inquiry are not determined as existences antecedent to all inquiry, nor as
detached products; instead they enter knowledge as
conditioned by the processes of their determination
(p. 119[122]);

20. No judgments are to be held as *super*-human or as final;
organisms and environments alike are known to us in
process of transformation; so also are the outcomes in
judgment of the logical activities they develop (Chapters I
to V; p. 345n[343n]).

The other natural approach to logic to be considered is that of
J. R. Kantor in his book *Psychology and Logic* (Bloomington,
Indiana, 1945). He makes his development upon the basis of his
interbehavioral psychology which rates as one of the most important advances in psychological construction since William
James. The "natural" characteristic of this psychology is that it
undertakes not merely to bring organism and environmental object into juxtaposition, but to investigate their behavioral activities under a form of functional interpretation throughout.
Applying his approach to the field of logic Kantor offers eight postulates for a "specificity logic." These follow in his own wordings,
and in the main from the first chapter of his book. Two ancillary
statements, 2.1 and 4.1, and a few other phrasings, have been
supplied from other chapters to compensate compactly for the
detachment of the leading postulates from their full contextual
exposition.

KANTOR[11]

1. "Logic constitutes primarily a series of operations."
2. "Logical theory is continuous with practice"; the "theory . . . constitutes . . . the *study* of operations"; the
"practice . . . consists of those *operations* themselves."
2.1 "Interbehavioral psychology assumes that organisms

11. All wordings are those of the section-headings of the postulates or of the immediately following text, except as follows: The sentence in 2.1 is from page
140, lines 11–12; the second sentence in 4 is from page 168, lines 13–14; the
sentences in 4.1 are from page 294, lines 9–10, and page 7, lines 3–4; the
sentence in 5 is from page xiii, lines 2–3; the second sentence in 7 is from
page xiii, line 6.

and objects exist before they become the subject matter of the various natural sciences."

3. "Logical operations constitute interbehavioral fields." "The materials must be regarded as . . . performing operations coordinate with those of the logician."

4. "Logical operations have evolved as techniques for achieving systems as products." "No other generalization is presupposed than that system building goes on."

4.1 "Not only can the work be separated from the product, but each can be given its proper emphasis." "We may interbehave with . . . the objects of our own creation."

5. "Logic is essentially concerned with specific events."

6. "Since logic consists of actual interbehavior it sustains unique relations with the human situations in which it occurs." "As a human enterprise logic cannot escape certain cultural influences."

7. "Logic is inseverably interrelated with psychology." "Logic . . . entails a psychological dimension."

8. "Logic is distinct from language." It "is not . . . primarily concerned with . . . linguistic things." "Contrary to logical tradition, for the most part, symbols, sentences, or statements are only means for referring to . . . or for recording . . ."

The two procedures so outlined resemble each other in their insistence upon finding their subjectmatter in *concretely* observable instances of logical behavior; in their stress upon *operational* treatment of their subjectmatter; in their establishment of *natural* and *cultural* settings for the inquiry; and in their insistence that organism and environment be viewed together as *one system*. Kantor's 1, 2, 4, 5 and 6 follow in close correspondence with Dewey's 2, 8, 4, 7 and 5, while Dewey's 1 and 3 should easily be acceptable to him. Within so similar a framework, however, marked differences of treatment appear. This, of course, is as it should be when a live field of fresh research is being developed. Dewey's 6 and Kantor's 3 and 7 might perhaps raise problems of interpretation in their respective contexts. The marked difference, however, is to be found in Kantor's 2.1 and 4.1 as compared with Dewey's 19, and in Kantor's 8 as compared with Dewey's 9 and 16. Kantor treats the system of organism and environment "interactionally," while Dewey makes the "transactional" approach basic. Kantor introduces "pre-logical materials" as requisite for logical activity, distinguishes logical activity sharply from linguistic activity, and offers as outcomes logical products akin in pattern to physical products and serving as stimulants to men in the same manner these latter do. Dewey, in contrast, exhibits inquiry as advancing from indeterminate to determinate situations in full activity throughout, and requires the "objects" determined by inquiry to be held within its system, future as well as past. Where Kantor holds himself to what can be accomplished from a start in which human organisms and environmental objects are presented to logic ready-formed as the base of its research, Dewey brings within his inquiry those very processes of knowledge under which organisms and objects are themselves identified and differentiated in ordinary life and in specific research as components of such a natural world.[12] We have thus within a very similar "natural" background two contrasting routes already indicated for further development.

III

The four other logics which we shall consider retain as presumptively basic various materials and activities derived from the vocabularies and beliefs of pre-Darwinian days. Such items of construction include, among many others, "sense-data," "concepts," "propositions," "intuitions," "apprehensions," "meanings," and a variety of "rationals" and "empiricals" taken either as individually separable "mental existences," as directly present "objects of mind," or as philosophical offspring of terminologi-

12. This difference is well brought out by a remark of Bridgman's which Kantor quotes in order to sharpen his statement of his own position. Bridgman holds that "from the operational point of view it is meaningless to attempt to separate 'Nature' from 'knowledge of nature.'" Kantor finds Bridgman's view a departure from correct operational procedure. Dewey, on the contrary, would be in full agreement with Bridgman in this particular respect. P. W. Bridgman, *The Logic of Modern Physics* (New York, 1927), p. 62; Kantor, "The Operational Principle in the Physical and Psychological Sciences," the *Psychological Record*, II (1938), p. 6. For an appraisal of Kantor's work under a point of view sharply contrasted with that taken in the present text see the review by Ernest Nagel, the *Journal of Philosophy*, XLII (1945), 578–80.

cal interbreeding between them. The question which concerns us is as to how such materials enter into construction and how they behave.[13] In the work of Cohen and Kaufmann we shall find earnest endeavor to smooth them into place in a modern world of knowledge. Thereupon in the light of what these men give us— or, rather, of what they have failed to give us thus far—we shall be able to get a clearer view of the violent struggles of Russell, and the intricate word-searchings of Moore, as they strive to establish and organize logical controls under their ancient forms of presentation.[14]

Professor Cohen's desire to strengthen logical construction had stimulation from Peirce on one side and from the later blos-

13. Typical confusions of logical discussion have been examined from a different point of view in Chapter 1. Certain characteristics of the work of Carnap, Cohen and Nagel, Ducasse, Lewis, Morris, and Tarski are there displayed. A thorough overhauling has long been needed of the procedures of Carnap and other logical positivists, both with respect to their logic and their positiveness, and this is now promised us by C. W. Churchman and T. A. Cowan (*Philosophy of Science*, XII [1945], 219). One device many logicians employ to justify them in maintaining the antiquated materials is their insistence that logic and psychology are so sharply different that they must leave each other alone—in other words, that while psychology may be allowed to "go natural," logic may not be so allowed. This argument of the logicians may be all very well as against an overly narrowed psychology of the non-natural type; but by the same token an overly narrowed logic results. The problem is one of full human behavior—how human beings have evolved with all their behaviors—no matter how convenient it has been found in the popular speech of the past to scatter the behaviors among separate departments of inquiry.

14. For an extreme "mentalistic" and hopefully "solipsistic" base for logic, the procedures of C. I. Lewis may be brought into comparison by anyone sufficiently interested. Lewis is represented by the following "postulates," which, from any "natural" point of view, rate as disintegrating and unworkable traditions: (1) Knowledge involves three components, the activity of thought, the concepts which are produced by thought, and the sensuously given; (2) The pure concept and the content of the given are mutually independent; neither limits the other; (3) The concept gives rise to the *a priori* which is definitive or explicative of concepts; (4) Empirical knowledge arises through conceptual interpretation. See *Mind and the World-Order* (New York, 1929), pp. 36 ff.; *The Pragmatic Element in Knowledge,* Univ. of California Publications in Philosophy, VI (1926); *A Survey of Symbolic Logic* (Berkeley, Calif., 1918). A characteristic determination arising in such a background is that if "analytic facts" can "function propositionally," then "they are called propositions"; so that "the proposition 'Men exist' is literally one and the same with the fact that men might exist." (Lewis and Langford, *Symbolic Logic* [New York, 1932], p. 472.) For other illustrations of what happens to ordinary integrity of expression under such a construction see my notes on Lewis' vocabulary, the *Journal of Philosophy* (1941), pp. 634–5. See also Chapter 1, Section VI.

soming of symbolic logic on the other. He has not, however, taken a path which permits him to find Dewey's manner of construction adequate in the direct line from Peirce.[15] The citations we assemble are taken verbatim from his latest book. While they have been removed from their immediate contexts and rearranged, it is hoped that no one of them has been warped from its accurate significance in his construction.

COHEN[16]

1. "Symbols . . . represent . . . only . . . general properties" (p. 8, line 6);
2. "Science studies the . . . determinate properties of things" (p. 17, line 18). Physics, e.g., "starts with material assumptions, i.e., assumptions true only of certain objects, namely entities occupying time and space" (p. 16, line 3);
3. In the manipulation of symbols . . . "the meaning of our final result follows from our initial assumptions" (p. 8, line 13);
4. "The assumption that the objects of physics . . . must conform to logic is necessary in the sense that without it no science at all can be constructed" (p. 16, lines 15–16);
5. "The rules according to which . . . symbols can be combined are by hypothesis precisely those according to which the entities they denote can be combined" (p. 8, lines 8–10);
6. "Logically . . . existence and validity are strictly correlative" (p. 15, line 26).

This reads smoothly enough but it makes science, and apparently logic also, depend for foundations upon a "necessary assumption"—where "necessary" is what we cannot avoid, and "assumption" what we have to guess at. It separates two great

15. See his discussion of Dewey's *Experimental Logic* (1916) reprinted as an appendix to his book *A Preface to Logic* (New York, 1944).
16. All citations in the text are from *A Preface to Logic*. Compare the following from Cohen's essay, "The Faith of a Logician," in *Contemporary American Philosophy* (New York, 1930), p. 228: "Logical laws are thus neither physical nor mental, but the laws of all possible significant being."

ranges of human attention, one called that of "symbols," the other that of the "determinate properties of things." However modernized their garb, these are little other than the ancient "reason" and "sense." Their organization is by *fiat*, by the flat assertion that they *must* be correlated. Such *fiat* is employed precisely because "system" has *not* been established. If the "entities occupying time and space" make up "nature," then the "symbols" remain "non-natural" in the sense in which we have employed the word, so long as they are not brought within a common system of interpretation, but enter merely by decree.

Professor Kaufmann, as we shall report him, works under a similar severance of certain of man's activities from the environing "nature" upon, within, or with respect to which, these activities are carried on. He develops a far-reaching, intricate, and in his own way powerful, analysis to establish organization for them conjointly. He accepts and admires Dewey's "theory of inquiry" as an outstanding contribution to knowledge but not by itself as an adequate logic. He holds that the theory of deduction must be grounded in intuitional meanings, and that with it must be correlated a theory for the empirical procedures of science in terms of the scientists' *decisions*. Far from regarding himself as severing the logical process and its canons from nature, he holds that what he is doing is to "define inquiry in terms of the canons."[17] This, however, still leaves the contrast with Dewey striking since the latter's undertaking has been to describe the canons along with all other logical activity as inquiry going on, rather than to use canons as criteria of its definition. The following are Professor Kaufmann's "tenets":

KAUFMANN[18]

1. The work of the logic of science is to clarify the rules of scientific procedure.

17. From private correspondence.
18. The book here characterized is Felix Kaufmann's *Methodology of the Social Sciences* (New York, 1944). Page references are not given as the presentation in the text has Professor Kaufmann's endorsement as it stands with the proviso that "he does not maintain that scientists always consciously apply the rules in their inquiries" but that "he does maintain the reference to the rules is

2. The corpus of science consists of propositions that have been accepted in accordance with such rules.

3. Changes in the corpus of a science, either by acceptance of a proposition into it, or by the elimination of a proposition from it, are called scientific decisions.

4. Scientific decisions are distinguished as correct or incorrect in terms of rules of procedure called *basic*. (Other rules called *preference* rules concern appropriateness of approach.) Basic rules as well as preference rules may be changed. Standards for the correctness of such changes are called rules of the second (or higher) order.

5. Principles governing the scientific acceptance or elimination of propositions, and placing limitation upon the changes of basic rules, are the reversibility of all decisions, the recognition of observational tests, the exclu-

---

logically implied when the correctness of scientific decisions or the appropriateness of the methods applied is judged." "Formulations of such judgments which do not contain reference to the rules," he regards as "elliptical." The following citations, which Professor Kaufmann quite properly insists should be understood in the full context of the book, are assembled by the present writer who, properly also, he hopes, believes they are essential to show the manner in which expression under this procedure develops: "The contrast between deductive reasoning (in the strict sense) and empirical procedure . . . will be the guiding principle of our analysis and . . . the key to the solution of . . . problems" (*op. cit.*, p. 3); "The most general characterization of scientific thinking" is "that it is *a process of classifying and reclassifying propositions by placing them into either one of two disjunctive classes in accordance with presupposed rules*" (p. 40); "The distinction between the logical order of meanings and the temporal order of inquiry" is "all important" (p. 39); The "temporal aspect of inquiry does not enter into the timeless logical relations among propositions" (p. 30); "The fundamental properties of the system of rules are invariable" (p. 232); The "genuine logical theory of empirical procedure" is "*a theory of correct scientific decisions in given scientific situations*" (p. 65); Language requires "a system of rules that gives to particular acoustical phenomena the function of symbols for particular thoughts" (p. 17); "Lack of distinction in language is, in most cases, the consequence of unclear thought" (p. 27); "Concepts and propositions *are* meanings" (p. 18); In "problems of empirical science" and "logical analysis" . . . "we have to presuppose (elementary) meanings" (p. 19). Kaufmann reiterates and emphasizes his difference from Dewey in a late paper (*Philosophy and Phenomenological Research,* VI [1945], 63n.) when he states that he cannot follow Dewey when the latter dismisses "intuitive knowledge of meanings" along with "intuitive knowledge of sense data."

sion of contradictions, and the decidability in principle of all propositions.

6. The two last mentioned principles are called procedural correlates of the principles of contradiction and of excluded middle respectively. The former states that the basic rules of procedure must be such as to foreclose the emergence of contradiction in science. The latter states that the basic rules must be such as not to foreclose the verifiability of any given statement.

7. The correctness of scientific decisions in terms of basic rules depends solely on the knowledge established at the time, i.e., on previously accepted propositions which now serve as *grounds* for the acceptance of new ones.

8. Identifiable propositional meanings are presupposed in scientific decisions.

9. The presupposition of identifiable propositional meanings implies that we take it for granted that for any two given propositions it is determined whether or not one is entailed in the other, and whether or not one contradicts the other.

10. Entailment and contradiction are recognizable either directly in immediate apprehension of meanings or indirectly by deductive process.

11. Deductive processes are autonomous within scientific inquiry and can be described without reference to verification or invalidation.

In his construction Professor Kaufmann rejects the demand for the logical determination of ontological certainty in its older and more brazen form.[19] He is, indeed, unfriendly in many respects to its newer and more insidious forms. However, although he can content himself without the ontological specialized search, he cannot content himself without the ontological searcher. He retains the non-natural "mental"—the "ego," "person," "decider," or basic "knower"—if not as existential possessor, then

19. See the two typical marks of distinction between pre-Darwinian and post-Darwinian programs and goals suggested in the opening paragraphs of this chapter. Kaufmann's tenets #5 and #7 mark steps of his advance.

at least as subsistential vehicle or conveyor, of meanings. He sees science as composed of propositions, the propositions as being meanings (i.e., generally as "thoughts," or "concepts"), and the meanings as enjoying some sort of logically superordinate[20] existence over, above, or beyond, their physical, physiological, or behavioral occurrence. He requires decisions to get the propositions, rules to get the decisions, and higher rules to get changes in the lower rules; behind all of which he puts a backlog of invariant (i.e., unchangeable) properties which the rules possess. Underlying all logical procedure he requires the presupposed meanings and the invariant properties; and underlying these he requires the intuition or immediate apprehension which operates them. Deduction is intuition indirectly at work. We are in effect asked to adopt a sort of indirectly immediate apprehension. It feels uncomfortable.

If we compare this with Dewey's "natural" procedure,[21] we find Dewey offering us science, not as a corpus of "propositions" embalmed in "decisions" made in accordance with prescribed "rules," but as the actual observable ongoing process of human inquiry in the cosmos in which it takes place. "Propositions," for him, are instruments, not exhibits. What happens, happens, and no need is found to insert "intuition" behind it to *make* it happen, or to be the happening. Meaningful utterance is taken as it comes, and not as separated from life and language. "Decision" is the long process of appraisal, often requiring cultural description; it is never some intermediate act-under-rule. The outcome in judgment is not a "conception" nor even a "pronouncement," but the full activity that rounds out inquiry. Finally the canons

20. The word "superordinate" is here employed by me as an evasive compromise. Kaufmann would say that "the meanings" are "presupposed in," "essential to," "logically implied by," or "necessary for the definition of" the "inquiry." I would say that what his development actually accomplishes is to retain them as "prior to," "superior to," "independent of," or "in a realm apart from" the "inquiry." He fully satisfies me that my wording is not what he intends, but without affecting my view that I am nevertheless describing what he in effect does.

21. Direct comparison of particular phrases is not simple, because the whole method of expression—the "linguistic atmosphere"—varies so greatly. However, K2 may be compared with D10 and D15; K4 with D5; K7 with D19; and K10 with D18. In addition the citations about language in footnote 18, taken from Kaufmann's pages 17 and 27 are at the extreme opposite pole, so far as present issues go, from D16.

are to Dewey outgrowths of inquiry, not its presuppositions; their high value, when in active inquiry is fully recognized, but when set off by themselves they are found mechanical, arbitrary, and often grievously deceptive. This difference is not one of creed or opinion—Dewey's work is not to be taken on any such basis as that; it is a difference of practical workmanship, with the "credal" aspects trailing behind, and with the report we here give furnishing merely the clues to the practice.

IV

We come now to the struggle of Russell and the subtleties of Moore in their efforts to secure a logic under these ancient patterns of speech—logical, ontological, psychological, and metaphysical—in which sensings and conceivings, world and man, body and mind, empiricals and rationals, enter in opposing camps. Russell offers rich complexes of such materials, and their kaleidoscopic shiftings are so rapid that it is most of the time difficult to center one's eye on the spot where the issues are clearest. His great and everywhere recognized early achievements in symbolic logic and in planning its organization with mathematics have ended with his efforts in the last half of his life to find out what actually he has been dealing with. His view today seems as strong as in his earlier years—perhaps even stronger—that unless a man adopts some metaphysics and puts it to work, he cannot even make a common statement in everyday language.[22]

To represent Russell we shall establish a base in his Logical Atomism of 1918–1919 and 1924, and supplement this, where it seems desirable, by citations from earlier and later papers. The clumsiness of our report is regrettable, but it is due to overlapping and ever-shifting applications by Russell of such words as "simple," "particular," "entity," and "symbol," which make plain, direct citation often risky, and at times altogether impracticable.[23]

22. Or at least this seems to be the purport of such a conclusion as that "the goal of all our discussions" is "that complete metaphysical agnosticism is not compatible with the maintenance of linguistic propositions" (*An Inquiry into Meaning and Truth* [New York, 1940], p. 437).
23. A specimen of Russell's conflicting phrasings from his book *What I Believe*, is quoted by Cassius J. Keyser in *Scripta Mathematica*, III (1935), 29, as follows: (page 1) "Man is a part of Nature, not something contrasted with Na-

RUSSELL[24]

1. "Ultimate simples," (in theory if not in practical research) are entities "out of which the world is built" (M, 1919, 365). They "have a kind of reality not belonging to anything else" (M, 1919, 365). "Simple" objects are "those objects which it is impossible to symbolize otherwise than by simple symbols" (M, 515).
2. Propositions and facts are complexes. "I do not believe that there are complexes . . . in the same sense in which there are simples" (LA, 374).
3. Complexes are to be dealt with through their component simple entities or simple symbols. "It seems obvious to me that what is complex must be composed of simples" (LA, 375). "Components of a proposition are the symbols . . . ; components of the fact . . . are the meanings[25] of the symbols" (M, 518).
4. Simple symbols are those "not having any parts that are symbols, or any significant structure" (LA, 375. Cf. M, 515).
5. Knowledge is attained through the fixation of the right simples by the right logical proper names, i.e., symbols (the argument of M and LA throughout).

---

ture"; (p. 16) "We are ourselves the ultimate and irrefutable arbiters of value, and in the world of value Nature is only a part. Thus in this world we are greater than Nature."
24. The sources of the citations from Russell are indicated as follows:
   M. "The Philosophy of Logical Atomism," *Monist* (1918), 495–527; (1919), 32–63, 190–222, 345–380. Page references are to the 1918 volume unless otherwise indicated.
   LA. "Logical Atomism," *Contemporary British Philosophy*, New York, First Series, 1924, pp. 359–383.
   RC. "Reply to Criticisms," *The Philosophy of Bertrand Russell*, P. A. Schilpp, editor (Chicago, 1944), pp. 681–741.
   I. *An Inquiry into Meaning and Truth.*
25. What Russell intends by meaning is, in general, very difficult to determine. It is not that no light is thrown on the question but entirely too many kinds of light from too many points of view, without sifting. Most profitable is an examination of all the passages, a dozen or more, indexed in the *Inquiry*. See also M, 506–8; LA, 369; and Bertrand Russell, *Mysticism and Logic* (New York, 1918), pp. 223–4.

"An atomic proposition is one which does . . . actually name . . . actual particulars" (M, 523).[26]

6. As a controlling principle: "Wherever possible, substitute constructions out of known entities for in-
ferences to unknown entities" (LA, 363).[27]

7. Among the simples consider the particulars (M, 497).[28]
These are "the *terms* of the relation" in atomic facts
(M, 522). Proper names properly apply to them and to
them alone (M, 508, 523, 524). "Particulars have this
peculiarity . . . in an inventory of the world, that each
of them stands entirely alone and is completely self-
subsistent" (M, 525).

8a. Particulars are known by direct acquaintance. "A name
. . . can only be applied to a particular with which the
speaker is acquainted" (M, 524).[29] "The word 'red' is a
simple symbol . . . and can only be understood through
acquaintance with the object" (M, 517).

8b. "Simples" are not "experienced as such"; they are

26. For a discussion in terms of "basic propositions" see I, p. 172, p. 362, p. 414.
Here the contrast between Russell and Dewey is so sharp (see Dewey, No. 14,
preceding) that the extensive discussions between the two men could be reduced to a one-sentence affirmation on this point and a one-page exhibit of
the context of discussion, historical and contemporary.

27. An alternative form will be found in a paper in *Scientia*, 1914, reprinted in
Mysticism and Logic, p. 155: "Wherever possible, logical constructions are
to be substituted for inferred entities."

28. These are variously called logical atoms, ultimate constituents, simple entities, etc. "Such ultimate simples I call 'particulars,'" *The Analysis of Mind*
(New York, 1921), p. 193. They are the hardest of hard facts, and the most
resistant to "the solvent influence of critical reflection." They may be sense-
data, or entities called "events" (LA, 381) or sometimes point-instants or
event-particles. Mathematical-physical expressions sometimes join them
among the ultra-safe. If Russell would establish definite usage for at least one
or two of these words, his reader might have an easier time doing justice to
him. It is particularly disconcerting to find the particulars turning out to be
themselves just words, as where (I, 21) he speaks of "egocentric particulars,
i.e., words such as 'this,' 'I,' 'now,' which have a meaning relative to the
speaker." If "terms" are "words" for Russell (I would not presume to say)
then the second sentence in point #7 in the text also makes particulars out to
be symbols rather than entities. For indication of Russell's logical atoms and
proper names as of the nature of "cues" and similar primitive behaviors, see
Chapter 4, note 11, Chapter 6, Section IV and Chapter 7, Section II.

29. Compare *Problems of Philosophy* (New York, 1912), p. 91; "On the Nature
of Acquaintance," *Monist* (1914).

"known only inferentially as the limit of analysis" (LA, 375).[30]

9. For success in attaining knowledge it becomes necessary to sort propositions into types. "The doctrine of types leads . . . to a more complete and radical atomism than any that I conceived to be possible twenty years ago" (LA, 371).

10. In "The Type's Progress," the stages thus far (1945) have been:

a) The *entities*[31] exist in a variety of types;

b) "The theory of types is really a theory of *symbols, not of things*" (M, 1919, 362);

c) Words (symbols) are all of the *same* type (LA, 369);

d) The meanings of the symbols may be of *any* type (I, 44; *see also* LA, 369);

e) (when the going seems hard) "Difference of type means difference of syntactical function" (RC, 692);[32]

f) (when the going seems easy) "There is not one relation of meaning between words and what they stand for, but as many relations of meaning, each of a different logical type, as there are logical types among the objects for which there are words" (LA, 370);

30. If there has been any systematic progress in Russell's work as the years pass by with respect to attitudes 8a and 8b, I have failed to detect it. The difference seems rather one of stress at different stages of argumentation. If the clash as here reported seems incredible, I suggest an examination of a particularly illuminating passage in Professor Nagel's contribution to *The Philosophy of Bertrand Russell*, p. 341, in which, though without directly mentioning the incoherence, he notes (a) that Russell holds that some particulars are perceived, and at least some of their qualities and relations are immediately apprehended; (b) that Russell believes his particulars are simples; and (c) that Russell admits that simples are not directly perceived, but are known only inferentially as the limit of analysis. Further light on the situation may be gained from Nagel's penetrating analysis of *An Inquiry into Meaning and Truth*. The *Journal of Philosophy*, XXXVIII (1941), 253–270.

31. RC, 691; *Principles of Mathematics* (Cambridge, England, 1903); *Introduction to Mathematical Philosophy* (New York, 1919); also, off and on, at any stage of his writings. Note the similar difficulty for "particulars," point #7 and footnote 28.

32. I, p. 438: "Partly by means of the study of syntax, we can arrive at considerable knowledge concerning the structure of the world."

g) (and at any rate) "Some sort of hierarchy is necessary. I hope that in time, some theory will be developed which will be simple and adequate, and at the
same time be satisfactory from the point of view
of what might be called logical common sense"
(RC, 692).[33]

Probably the sharpest criticism to be made of Russell's workmanship is to point out his continual confounding of "symbol"
and "entity." We have had illustrations of this in the cases, both
of the "particular" and of the "type." Fusion of "symbol" and
"entity" is what Russell demands, and confusion is what he gets.
With an exhibit as prominent as this in the world, it is no wonder
that Korzybski has felt it necessary to devote so much of his writings to the insistent declaration that the word is *not* the thing.[34]
His continued insistence upon this point will remain a useful
public service until, at length, the day comes when a thorough
theory of the organization of behavioral word and cosmic fact
has been constructed.

Turning now to Moore, we find him using much the same line
of materials as does Russell, but he concentrates on the ultimate
accuracies of expression in dealing with them. Whether primarily classified as a logician or not, he outlogics the logics in his
standards of logical perfection. Where Russell proposes to force
the ultimate simples of the world to reveal themselves, Moore
takes a frank and open base in the most common-sense, matter-
of-fact, personal experiences he can locate, accepting them in the
form of "simplest" propositions. He then takes account of sense-
data, linguistic expressions, the conceptual and propositional
meaningfulness of these latter, man's belief in them, his feelings
of certainty about his beliefs, and his assertions of known truth;
plus, of course, the presumptive "realities" he takes to be in-

33. For the latest illustration of Russell's confusion of statement, pages 829–834
of his *A History of Western Philosophy* (New York, 1945) may profitably be
examined. A passing glance will not suffice since the main characteristic of
philosophical language is to make a good appearance. A cold eye, close dissection, and often much hard work is necessary to find out what kind of a
skeleton is beneath the outer clothing.
34. Alfred Korzybski, *Science and Sanity: An Introduction to Non-Aristotelian
Systems and General Semantics* (New York, 1933).

volved. Where Russell finds himself compelled continually to assert that his critics fail to understand him, Moore is frank in his avowal that he is never quite sure that he understands himself.[35] He is as willing to reverse himself as he is to overthrow others. His virtues of acuity and integrity applied to his presuppositions have yielded the following development:

MOORE[36]

1. Start with common sense statements, such as "this is my body," "it was born," "it has grown," "this is a chair," "I am sitting in this chair," "here is my hand," "here is another hand." Examine these as propositions, and in all cases under reduction to the simplest expression that can be reached—such, that is to say, as is most secure of ordinary acceptance, and is least liable to arouse conflict (CS, 193–195).[37]

2. Accept these common-sense propositions as "wholly true" (CS, 197); as what "I know with certainty to be true" (CS, 195).[38]

3. In such a proposition, if it is thus held true, "there is always some *sense-datum* about which the proposition

35. Russell remarked to Professor Schilpp, the editor of the volume *The Philosophy of Bertrand Russell,* that "his greatest surprise, in the reading of the twenty-one contributed essays, had come from the discovery that 'over half of their authors had *not* understood' him (i.e., Russell)" (*op. cit.,* p. xiii). For Moore see No. 9 and No. 10 of the skeleton construction of his logical procedure, which follows.

36. The sources of the citations from Moore are indicated as follows:
    CS. "A Defence of Common Sense," *Contemporary British Philosophy,* Second Series (New York and London, 1925), pp. 193–223;
    RC. "A Reply to My Critics," *The Philosophy of G. E. Moore,* P. A. Schilpp, editor (Chicago, 1942), pp. 535–677.

37. See also "Proof of an External World," *Proceedings of the British Academy,* XXV (1939), pp. 273–300. Professor Nagel's comment in his review of *The Philosophy of G. E. Moore* in *Mind* (1944), 60–75, will be found of interest.

38. Included are physical objects, perceptive experiences taken as mental, remembered things, and other men's bodies and experiencings. "I think I have nothing better to say than that it seems to me that I *do* know them, with certainty. It is, indeed, obvious that, in the case of most of them, I do not know them *directly*" . . . , but . . . "In the past I have known to be true *other* propositions which were evidence for them" (CS, 206).

in question is a proposition," i.e., its "subject" is always a sense-datum (CS, 217). Moreover such a proposition is "unambiguous," so that "we understand its
meaning" in a way not to be challenged, whether we
do or do not "know what it means" in the sense of
being able "*to give a correct analysis* of its meaning"
(CS, 198).[39]

4. On the basis of such simplified common sense propositions having sense-data for subjects, very many[40] other
   instances of knowledge in propositional form can be
   tested and appraised through Analysis.

5. In Analysis a "concept, or idea, or proposition" is
   dealt with, "and *not* a verbal expression" (RC, 663,
   664). The word "means" should not be used since that
   implies a "verbal expression," and therefore gives a
   "false impression" (RC, 664; this passage is seventeen
   years later than that in #3 above, where the word
   "means" is still employed).

6. To "give an analysis" of a concept you must come
   across (or, at least, you "must mention") another
   concept which, like the first, "applies to" an object
   (though it neither "means" nor "expresses" it) under
   circumstances such that (a) "nobody can know" that
   the first concept "applies" without "knowing" that the
   second applies; (b) "nobody can verify" that the first
   applies without "verifying" that the second applies;
   and (c) "any expression which expresses" the first
   "must be synonymous with any expression which
   expresses" the second (RC, 663).[41]

7. Otherwise put, a "correct" analysis in the case of concepts is one which results in showing that two con-

39. "I think I have always both used, and intended to use, 'sense-datum' in such a
    sense that the mere fact that an object is *directly apprehended* is a *sufficient*
    condition for saying that it is a sense-datum" (RC, 639). A remarkable illus-
    tration of his careful expression may be found in the passage on page 181 of
    his paper, "The Nature of Sensible Appearances," *Aristotelian Society*, Sup-
    plementary Vol. VI (1926).
40. "Very many" is to be understood in the sense in which Moore uses the words
    (CS, 195), with a trend towards, but not immediate assertion of, "all."
41. Note the confidently reiterated "nobody can" and the "must."

cepts expressed by different expressions "must, in some sense" be the same concept (RC, 666).[42]

8. To establish itself in firm status for the future, Analysis has two primary tasks, (a) it must make a successful analysis of sense-data (CS, 216–222); (b) it must make a successful analysis of Analysis itself (compare RC, 660–667).

9. Analysis of sense-data has thus far been unsatisfactory. Its present status is best exhibited in a particular case of analysis. Take, for example, "the back of my hand" as "something seen," and seek to establish what, precisely, *is* the sense-datum that enters as subject of the "common sense" and "wholly true" proposition: "This is the back of my hand." In 1925 Moore reported that "no philosopher has hitherto suggested an answer that comes anywhere near to being *certainly* true" (CS, 219). In 1942 his report was "The most fundamental puzzle about the relation of sense-data to physical objects is that there does seem to be some reason to assert . . . paradoxes" (RC, 637).[43]

10. Analysis of Analysis itself also arrives at paradox, so that in the outcome it may be said: "I do not know, at all clearly, *what* I mean by saying that '*x* is a brother' is identical with '*x* is a male sibling,' and that '*x* is a cube'

---

42. In the typical case, however, one concept is opposed to two or more concepts, these latter being accompanied in their consideration by explicit mention of their method of combination (RC, 666).

43. Moore has written: "I define the term (sense-datum) in such a way that it is an open question whether the sense-datum which I now see in looking at my hand and which is a sense-datum of my hand is or is not identical with that part of its surface which I am now actually seeing" (CS, 218). In simplified report his analysis in the case of "the back of my hand" discriminates "a physical object," "a physical surface," and a certain "directly seen" (such as one has in the case of an after-image or double-image). Moore's analysis with respect to the second and third of these has results which indicate to him that at the very time at which he not only feels sure but *knows* that he is seeing the second, he is in a state of doubt whether the third, which also he is seeing (and that *directly* in the indicated sense), is identical with the second or not; recognizing that it may be identical, in which case he is in a position of both "feeling sure of and doubting the very same proposition at the same time" (paradox I); or "so far as I can see," at any rate, "I don't *know* that I'm not" (paradox II). It is to the second form of the paradox that the comment cited in the text above refers (RC, 627–653, and particularly 636–637, also CS, 217–219).

is *not identical* with '*x* is a cube with twelve edges'"
(RC, 667).[44]

It may be suggested on the basis of the above display of Moore's techniques and results that his Analysis could reasonably be carried still further. Analysis of "concept" and of "proposition," of "expression" and of "meaning," and of "datum" as well as of "sense," might lead towards solutions. This, however, would involve untrammelled inquiry into "man's analyzing procedures" for whatever such procedures might show themselves operationally to be, in a full naturalistic setting. And this, again, would require throwing off the limitations imposed by the old vocabularies that place "man the analyzer" outside of, or over against the world of his analysis.[45] The differences in spatial and temporal location are huge between what is "sense-datum" and what is "wholly true." The range of the one is a bit of an organism's living in a bit of environment. The range the other seems to claim is all, or even more than all, of space and time. Analysis will surely need to be super-jet, if it is to make this transit, fueled as it is proposed it be by "concept, idea, and proposition," and these alone.

V

The reader who wishes to appraise for himself the situations we have exhibited—and especially the reader who has been accustomed to the use of his hands and eyes on materials such as enter any of the natural sciences—may be interested in an experiment. Let him look on logicians' writings as events taking place

44. The analysis of Analysis which Moore offers (RC, 664–665) declares equivalence as to concepts between expressions of the form: this "concept" is "identical" with that, this "propositional function" is "identical" with that, and "to say this" is "the same thing" as "to say that." But if we proceed to another form which also we feel we must accept, such as "to be this" is "the same thing" as "to be that," we have, we are told, reached a paradox, which, as between expressions and concepts, remains unresolved.

45. It is significant in this connection that Moore tells us that it is always "things which other philosophers have said" that suggest philosophical problems to him. "I do not think," he remarks, "that the world or the sciences would ever have suggested to me any philosophical problems." *The Philosophy of G. E. Moore,* p. 14.

in the world. Let him pick out some phase of these events for study. Let him be willing to examine it at least as carefully as he might the markings of a butterfly's wings, remembering also that the present level of inquiry into logic is not much further advanced than that into butterflies was when they were still just museum curiosities, and modern physiology undreamt of. This will mean clearing his work bench of all superfluous terminologies, and "getting down to cases," with the cases under examination, whatever they are, pinned down on the bench and not allowed to squirm themselves out of all decent recognition. Suppose such an inquirer has noticed the word "proposition" frequently present in the text. On the assumption, however rash, that logical terms are supposed to denote, name, designate, point at, or refer to something factually determinate, let him then select the presumptive fact "proposition" for his examination. By way of preliminary orientation, if he should examine the six logicians we have considered he would find that for Dewey a proposition is an instrumental use of language (D9, D10, D15, D16); for Kantor it is a "product" of logical interbehavior;[46] for Cohen "propositions are linguistic forms with meanings that are objective relations between such forms and certain states of fact";[47] for Kaufmann a proposition is a "meaning" developed from a base in intuition, fundamentally presupposed as such by logic, and not therein to be investigated.[48] For Russell it may be a class of sentences, or the meaning or significance of a sentence, or even at times something he doubts the existence of;[49] for Moore, it is a dweller in a land of thoughts, companion of concepts and of ideas, and to be found midway (or perhaps some other way) between

46. J. R. Kantor, *Psychology and Logic,* p. 223, pp. 282–3; also "An Interbehavioral Analysis of Propositions," *Psychological Record,* 5 (1943), p. 328.
47. M. R. Cohen, *A Preface to Logic,* p. 30. Also: "Acts of judgment, however, are involved in the apprehension of those relations that are called meanings." See also M. R. Cohen and E. Nagel, *An Introduction to Logic and Scientific Method* (New York, 1934), pp. 27, 28, 392, where facts are made of propositions, and propositions are specifically declared to be neither physical, mental, linguistic, nor communication, and to be identifiable by the sole characteristic that whatever else they are they are "true or false."
48. Felix Kaufmann, *Methodology of the Social Sciences,* pp. 18, 19.
49. B. Russell, *An Inquiry into Meaning and Truth,* pp. 208, 210, 217, 237 *et al.; Proceedings of the Aristotelian Society,* XI (1911), 117; *Mysticism and Logic,* p. 219; *Monist* (1918), p. 504.

words and objects.[50] Here is surely not merely "food for thought" but much incentive to matter-of-fact research. A few further trails for searchers to follow are mentioned in the footnote.[51]

In the preceding examination I have done my best to be accurate and fair. I hope I have at least in part succeeded. Certainly I have squandered time and effort triple and quadruple what I would have agreed to at the start. I find myself unwilling to close without expressing my personal opinion more definitely than I have heretofore. The procedures of Russell and Moore seem so simple-minded it is remarkable they have survived at all in a modern world. Those of Cohen and Kaufmann are heroic efforts to escape from the old confusions, yet futile because they fail to pick up the adequate weapons. In what may grow from the two other enterprises I have, of course, great hopes.

50. See phrasings in Moore, #1, #3, #5 et al. To Moore all such items are as familiar as the tongues of angels, and it is difficult, perhaps even impossible to find a direct cite.
51. Kaplan and Copilowish, Mind (1939), 478–484; Lewis and Langford, Symbolic Logic, p. 472; A. P. Ushenko, The Problems of Logic (1941), pp. 171, 175, 219; Roy W. Sellars in Philosophy and Phenomenological Research, V (1944), 99–100; G. Ryle, Proceedings of the Aristotelian Society, Supplementary Vol. IX (1929), pp. 80–96. An excellent start, and perhaps even a despairing finish, may be made with the Oxford Dictionary, or some other larger dictionary.

9.   A Confused "Semiotic"[1]

I

Charles Morris, in *Signs, Language, and Behavior* (New York, 1946) declares himself a semiotician (p. 354) operating in harmony with "behavioristicians" (pp. 182, 250). "Semiotic," he tells us, is "the science of signs," and "semiosis" is that sign-process which semioticians investigate (p. 353). If he is to "lay the foundation for a comprehensive and fruitful science of signs," his task is, he says, "to develop a language in which to talk about signs" (pp. v, 4, 17, 19), and for this, he believes, "the basic terms . . . are stable in terms drawn from the biological and physical sciences" (p. 19). It is possible in this way, he believes, to "suggest connections between signs and the behavior of animals and men in which they occur" (p. 2).

Here is a most laudable enterprise. I wish to examine carefully the technical language Professor Morris develops, find out whether it contains the makings of dependable expression such as we commonly call "scientific," and appraise his own opinion that the terms he adopts are "more precise, interpersonal, and unambiguous" than those favored by previous workers in this field (p. 28). The numerous special features of this book, often of high interest and value, I shall leave to others to discuss.[2]

1. This chapter is written by Bentley.
2. A discussion by Max Black under the title "The Limitations of a Behavioristic Semiotic" in the *Philosophical Review*, LVI (1947), 258–272, confirms the attitude of the present examination towards several of Morris' most emphasized names such as "preparatory," "disposition" and "signification." Its discussion is, however, on the conventional lines of yes, no, and maybe so, and does not trace back the difficulty into traditional linguistic fixations as is here attempted. See also reviews by A. F. Smullyan in the *Journal of Symbolic Logic*, XII (1947), 49–51; by Daniel J. Bronstein in *Philosophy and Phenomenological Research*, VII (1947), 643–649; and by George Gentry and Virgil C. Aldrich in the *Journal of Philosophy*, XLIV (1947), 318–329.

We are greatly aided in our task by the glossary the author furnishes us. In it he "defines"[3] or otherwise characterizes the main "terms" of semiotic, and stars those which he deems "most important" as "the basis" for the rest. We shall center our attention on a central group of these starred terms, and upon the linguistic material out of which they are constructed. The reader is asked to keep in mind that the problem here is not whether, impressionistically, we can secure a fair idea as to what Professor Morris is talking about and as to what his opinions are, but rather whether his own assertion that he is building a scientific language, and thus creating a science, can be sustained through a close study of his own formulations. The issue will be found to be one of maximum importance for all future research and appraisal of knowings and knowns. Our conclusion will be that his attempt is a failure.

We are somewhat hampered by the fact that, although he builds throughout with respect to behavior, he does not "define" the terms he takes over from "general behavior theory," but says that these "really operate as undefined terms in this system" (p. 345). It is evident that this manner of being "undefined" is not at all the same as the manner we find in a geometrician's postulated "elements." Instead of freeing us from irrelevant questions, it burdens us at almost every step with serious problems as to just how we are to understand the writer's words.

There are other difficulties such as those that arise when we find a term heavily stressed with respect to what it presents, but with no correlated name or names to make clear just what it excludes. The very important term "preparatory-stimulus" is a case in point; the set of variations on the word "disposition," later listed, is another. The difficulty here is that in such instances one is compelled to interpolate other names to make the pattern a bit clearer to oneself, and this always invokes a risk of injustice which one would wish to avoid.

From this point on I shall use the word semiotic to name, and to name only, the contents of the book before us. I shall use the word semiosis to name, and to name only, those ranges of

3. I shall permit myself in this chapter to use the words "define" and "term" casually and loosely as the author does. This is not as a rule, safe practice, but in the present case it eliminates much incidental qualification of statement, and is, I believe, fairer than would be a continual quibbling as to the rating of his assertions in this respect.

sign-process[4] which semiotic identifies and portrays. It is evident that, so proceeding, the word "semiotician" will name Professor Morris in his characteristic activity in person, and nothing else.

Four none too sharply maintained characteristics of the point of view that underlies semiotical procedure may now be set down for the reader's preliminary guidance:

1. Semiotic "officially"[5] declares the word "behavior" as in use to name, and to name only, the muscular and glandular actions of organisms in goal-seeking (i.e., "purposive") process.[6]

2. Semiosis is expressly envisaged, and semiotic is expressly constructed, with reference to behavior as thus purposive in the muscular-glandular sense. If there exists anywhere any sign-process not immediately thus oriented, it is *technically* excluded from the semiotic which we have before us. (One form of behavioral process which most psychologists regard as involving sign, but which Morris' formulation excludes, is noted in footnote 48 following.) The assurance the semiotician gives us that semiotic provides us with a universal sign-theory does not alter this basic determination; neither does the weft of "sign-signify-significatum" and "sign-denote-denotatum" woven upon this muscular-purposive warp to make a total web.[7]

3. The two other main "factors" of semiotical inquiry—namely, stimulus and disposition to respond—are *not* behavior in the strict sense of the term in semiotic (even though now and then referred to nontechnically as behavioristic or behavioral).

4. With a very few, wholly incidental, exceptions all "official" reports in semiotic are made through the use of such key words as "produce," "direct," "control," "cause," "initiate," "motivate," "seek," and "determine."[8] Semiotic works thus in terms of

4. "Sign-process" is used by Morris in a very general and very loose sense. See Assertion No. 25 following.
5. I shall use the word "official" occasionally to indicate the express affirmations of the glossary as to terminology; this in the main only where contrasts suggest themselves between the "official" use and other scattered uses.
6. The word "behavioristics" is used loosely for wider ranges of inquiry. The compound "sign-behavior" is sometimes loosely, sometimes narrowly used, so far as the component "behavior" is concerned.
7. This statement applies to semiotic as it is now before us and to the range it covers. Professor Morris leaves the way open for other "phenomena" to be entered as "signs" in the future (p. 154, *et passim*). These passages refer in the main, however, to minor, marginal, increments of report, and do not seem to allow for possible variations disruptive of his behavioral construction.
8. A longer list of such words with illustration of their application will be given later in this chapter.

putative "actors" rather than through direct description and report upon occurrences. This characteristic is so pronounced as to definitely establish the status of the book with respect to the general level of scientific inquiry.

Recall of the above characteristics will be desirable to avoid occasional misunderstandings.

Our primary materials of inquiry are, as has been said, to be found in a central group of the terms that are starred as basic. In fabricating them, the semiotician uses many other words not starred in the glossary, and behind and beyond these certain other words, critical for understanding, though neither starred nor listed. Among the starred terms that we shall examine as most important for our purposes are *sign, *preparatory-stimulus, *response-sequence, *response-disposition, and *significatum. Among unstarred words conveying key materials are behavior, response, stimulus and stimulus-object. Among key words neither starred nor listed are 'reaction,' 'cause,' 'occasion,' 'produce,' 'source,' and 'motivate.' It is interesting to note that *preparatory-stimulus is starred, but stimulus and stimulus-object are not (while "object" is neither indexed nor discussed in any pertinent sense); that *behavior-family is starred but behavior is not; that *response-disposition and *response-sequence are starred but response is not; that *sign and *sign-family are starred but sign-behavior is not. We have thus the "basic" terms deliberately presented in nonbasic settings.

II

Before taking up the terminological organization of semiotic, it will be well to consider two illustrations of the types of statement and interpretation that frequently appear. They serve to illuminate the problems that confront us and the reasons that make necessary the minuteness of our further examination.

Consider the following: "For something to be a sign to an organism . . . does not require that the organism signify that the something in question is a sign, for a sign can exist without there being a sign that it is a sign. There can, of course, be signs that something is a sign, and it is possible to signify by some signs what another sign signifies" (p. 16).

The general purport of this statement is easy to gather and

some addicts of Gertrude Stein would feel at home with it, but precision of expression is a different matter. The word "sign" is used in semiotic in the main to indicate either a "stimulus" or an "object,"[9] but if we try to substitute either of these in the statement we find difficulty in understanding and may lose comprehension altogether. Moreover, the verb "signify," closely bound with "sign" and vital in all semiotical construction, is found strangely entering with three types of subjects: an "organism" can signify; a "sign" can signify; and indefinitely "it is possible" to signify.

Try, next, what happens in the development of the following short sentence: "Signs in the different modes of signifying signify differently, have different significata" (p. 64).

We have here a single bit of linguistic expression (centering in the word "sign") differentiated with respect to participations as subject, verb, or object, and with the three phases or aspects, or whatever they are, put back together again into a sentence. What we have before us looks a bit like a quasi-mathematical organization of sign, signify, and significatum, the handling of which would require the firm maintenance of high standards; or else like a pseudophysical construction of the general form of "Heat is what makes something hot." We shall not concern ourself with the possible difficulties under these respective interpretations, but solely with what happens to the words in the text.

The sentence in question opens a passage dealing with criteria for differentiating modes of signifying (pp. 64–67). I have analyzed the elusive phrasings of its development half a dozen times, and offer my results for what they may be worth as a mere matter of report on the text, but with no great assurance that I have reached the linguistic bottom of the matter. It appears that the semiotician starts out prepared to group the "modes of signifying" into four types: those answering respectively to queries about "where," "what," "why," and "how" (p. 65, lines 9, 10, 11; p. 72, lines 6–7 from bottom of page). To establish this grouping semiotically, he employs an extensive process of phrase-alternation. He first gives us a rough sketch of a dog seeking food, thereby to "provide us with denotata of the signs which we

9. A variety of other ranges of use for the word will be noted later: see Assertions No. 1, 2, 3, 19, 29, and 32; also footnote 31.

wish to introduce" (p. 65). Here he lists four types of "stimuli," presents them as "signs," and calls them identifiors, designators, appraisors, and prescriptors. He tells us (p. 65, bottom) that these stimuli "influence" behaviors, "and so" dispositions (although, in his official definition for sign,[10] behaviors do not influence dispositions but instead these latter must be built up independently prior to the behaviors). Next he shifts his phrasings in successive paragraphs from disposition to interpretant, and then from interpretant to significatum, saying what appears to be the same thing over again, but each time under a different name. Finally he revamps his phrasing again into a form in which it is not the stimulus that "disposes" but the interpreter who "is disposed."[11] He then suggests that a new set of names be introduced for four major kinds of significata: namely, *locatum, discriminatum, valuatum,* and *obligatum.* Since there is no official difference between significatum and signification (p. 354) he now has acquired names indicative of the four "modes of signifying" which is what was desiderated.

If the reader will now take these two sets of names and seek to discover what progress in inquiry they achieve, he will at once find himself involved in what I believe to be a typical semiotic uncertainty. This is the problem of verbal and nonverbal signs, their analysis and organization.[12] Taking the case of identifior

10. See Assertion No. 19 later in this paper, and the accompanying comment.
11. Such a shift as this from an assertion that the stimulus (or sign or denotatum) "disposes the dog" to do something to the assertion that "the interpreter (i.e., the dog) is disposed" to do it, is common in semiotic. The trouble is that the "is disposed to" does not enter as a proper passive form of the verb "disposes," but is used practically (even if not categorically) to assert power in an actor; and this produces a radical shift in the gravamen of construction and expression. As a personal opinion, perhaps prematurely expressed, I find shifts of this type to be a major fault in semiotic. They can be successfully put over, I believe, only with verbs carefully selected *ad hoc,* and their employment amounts to something very much like semiotical (or, perhaps more broadly, philosophical) punning.
12. The words sign, signify, and significatum are employed, often indiscriminately for both language and nonlanguage events. Available typographical marks for differentiation are often omitted, as with the cited matter in the text. Distinction of interpretation in terms of interpreters and their powers to "produce" seems here wholly irrelevant. This situation is high-lighted by almost any page in the Glossary. The glossary entries are at times technically offered as "definitions," at times not, and they are frequently uncertain in this respect. The reports on these entries may begin "A sign . . ."; "A term . . ."; or "A possible term. . . ." But also they may begin: "An object . . ."; "An or-

and *locatum* as developed on pages 64–69, (I am following here the typographical pattern of the text) one finds that both of these words enter without addition of the single quotation marks which are added when it is the word, as a *word,* that is under examination. Now in the case of identifior the lack of single quotation marks corresponds with the use of the word in the text where certain nonverbal facts of life, such as dog, thirst, water, and pond, are introduced. In the case of *locatum,* however, the word enters directly as sign, with indirect reference to it as a term. The italics here are apparently used to stress the status of locatum and its three italicised companions as "special terms for the special kinds of significata involved in signs in the various modes of signifying" (p. 66). The textual introduction of *locatum* in extension from identifior is as follows: "We will use *locatum, discriminatum, valuatum,* and *obligatum* as signs signifying the significata of identifiors, designators, appraisors, and prescriptors" (p. 67). Under this treatment semiotic yields the following exhibits:

a) The identifior has for its significatum location in space and time.[13]

b) *Locatum* is a sign signifying the significatum of identifior.

c) *Locatum* therefore has for its significatum a location in space and time.

d) The significatum of *locatum* thus differentiates one of the great "modes of signifying" which are the subject of investigation—the one, namely, concerning locations.

Here we have an army of words that march up the hill, and then march down again. What is the difference between "loca-

ganism . . ."; "A significatum . . ."; or "The time and place. . . ." Thus the entry for *locatum* reads: "Locatum. . . . A significatum of an identifior." To correspond with the treatment in the text, this should perhaps have been put: Locatum. . . . A sign (word?, name?, term?) for the significatum of an identifior. This form of differentiation is usually unimportant in nontechnical cases, and I do not want to be understood as recommending it or adopting it in any case; it is only for the comprehension of semiotic that it here is mentioned. My report on the cases of identifior and *locatum* as first presented in magazine publication was defective in phrasing in this respect. Reexamination has shown this blind spot in semiotic to be much more serious than I had originally made it out to be.

13. Elsewhere expressed: "Identifiors *may be said* to signify location in space and time" (p. 66, italics supplied).

tion" at the beginning and "location" at the end? How great is the net advance? This can perhaps best be appraised by simplifying the wording. If we drop the word 'significatum' as unproductively reduplicative with respect to 'sign' and 'signify,' we get something as follows:

a) That which a sign of location signifies is location.

b) *Locatum* is a sign used to signify that which a sign of location signifies.

c) *Locatum* thus signifies location.

d) *Locatum* now becomes a special term to name this particular "mode of signifying."

A second approximation to understanding may be gained by substituting the word 'indicate' for 'signify,' under a promise that no loss of precision will thereby be involved. We get:

a) Signs of location indicate locations (and now my story's begun).

b) *Locatum*, the word, is "used" to indicate what signs of location indicate.

c) *Locatum* thus indicates location.

d) Location, thus indicated by *locatum*, enables the isolation behaviorally (p. 69) of that "mode of signifying" in which signs of location are found to indicate location (and now my story is done).

In other words the progress made in the development from terms in *or* to terms in *um* is next to nothing.

The semiotician seems himself to have doubts about his terms in "um," for he assures us that he is not "peopling the world with questionable 'entities'" and that the "um" terms "refer only to the properties something must have to be denoted by a sign" (p. 67). But "'property' is a very general term used to embrace . . . the denotata of signs" (p. 81), and the locatum and its compeers have been before us as significata, not denotata; and signifying and denoting are strikingly different procedures in semiosis, if semiotic is to be believed (pp. 347, 354).[14] The degree of salva-

<hr>

14. The status of denotation with respect to signification is throughout obscure in semiotic. The practical as distinguished from the theoretical procedure is expressed by the following sentence from p. 18: "Usually we start with signs which denote and then attempt to formulate the significatum of a sign by observing the properties of denotata." Unfortunately before we are finished "properties" will not only have appeared as the source of signs but also as the

tion thus achieved for the terms in "um" does not seem adequate.

These and other similar illustrations of semiotical procedure put us on our guard as to wordings. The second of them is important, not only because it provides the foundation for an elaborate descriptive classification of significations which is one of the main developments of semiotic,[15] but further, because it displays the attitude prominent throughout semiotic whereunder subjects, verbs, and objects are arbitrarily severed and made into distinct "things" after which their mechanistic manipulation over against one another is undertaken as the solution of the semiotical problem.

III

With this much of a glimpse at the intricacy of the terminological inquiry ahead of us, we may proceed to examine the semiotician's basic construction line upon line. We shall take his main terminological fixations, dissect their words (roughly "lansigns" in semiotic, p. 350),[16] and see if, after what microscopic attention we can give them, they will feel able to nest down comfortably together again. We shall consider thirty-three such assertions, numbering them consecutively for ease of reference. Only a few of them will be complete as given, but all of them, we hope, will be true-to-assertion, so far as they go, whether they remain in the original wordings or are paraphrased. Paraphrases are employed only where the phrasings of the text involve so much correlated terminology that they are not clear directly and immediately as they stand.

Where first introduced, or where specially stressed, typographi-

---

last refuge of some of the significata. As concerns Morris' "where," "what," "why," and "how" modes of "signifying," comparison with J. S. Mill's five groups (existence, place, time, causation, and resemblance), *A System of Logic* (I, Chap. VI, Sec. 1) may have interest, as also the more elaborate classification by Ogden and Richards in connection with their treatment of definition (*The Meaning of Meaning* [New York, 1923], pp. 217ff.).

15. Not examined in the present chapter, which is confined to the problem of underlying coherence. See footnote 53.

16. However, "the term 'word' . . . corresponds to no single semiotical term" (p. 222).

cal variations will be employed to indicate to the reader whether the term in question is stressed as basic by the semiotician in person, or is selected for special attention by his present student. Stars and italics are used for the basic starred word of the glossary; italics without stars are used for words which the glossary lists unstarred; single quotes are used for unlisted words which semiotic apparently takes for granted as commonly well enough understood for its purposes. Where no page reference is given, the citation or paraphrase will be from the glossary definition for the term in question. Practical use in this way of italics, asterisks, and single quotation marks has already been made in the last paragraph of Section I of this chapter.

We first consider the materials for prospective scientific precision that are offered by the general linguistic approach to the word "sign."

1. Sign (preliminary formulation): "Something" that "controls behavior towards a goal" (p. 7).

2. Sign (roughly): "Something [17] that directs behavior with respect to something that is not at the moment a stimulus" (p. 354).

3. *Sign (officially): A kind of "stimulus." [18]

4. *Stimulus:* [19] A "physical energy."

5. *Stimulus-object:* "The 'source' of a stimulus."

6. 'Stimulus-properties': "The 'properties' of the 'object' that produce stimuli" (p. 355).

We have here the presentation of sign on one side as an object or property, and on the other side as an energy or stimulus. We have the unexplained use of such possibly critical words as "source of," "produce," "direct," "control." We are given no definite information as to what organization the words of this latter group have in terms of one another, and so far as one can discover the problems of their organization are of no concern to semiotic. The way is prepared for the semiotician to use the word "sign" for either object or stimulus, when and as convenient, and if and as equivalent.

A second group of words involved in the presentation of the

---

17. For the use of "thing" in "something" compare: "The buzzer is the sign" (p. 17); "The words spoken are signs" (p. 18).
18. For type of stimulus and conditions see Assertion No. 19 following and compare Nos. 29 and 32.
19. "*Stimulus:* Any physical energy that acts upon a receptor of a living organism" (p. 355).

basic "preparatory-stimulus" has to do with impacts upon the organism.

7. 'Reaction': Something that "a stimulus 'causes' . . . in an organism" (p. 355).

8. *Response:* "Any action of a muscle or gland."

9. **Preparatory-stimulus:* "A stimulus that 'influences' a response to some other stimulus." It "necessarily 'causes' . . . a reaction . . . but this reaction need not be a response."[20]

10. Evocative Stimulus (at a guess)[21]: a presumptively primary or standard form of stimulus which is *not* "preparatory," i.e., which, although a stimulus, is not in the semiotic sense a "sign."

To its primarily established "object" or "stimulus" semiotic has now added the effect that the object or stimulus has—that which it (or energy, or property) causes (or produces, or is the source of)—namely, the reaction. One form of reaction it declares to be "any action of a muscle or gland," and it names this form response. Another form (or kind, or variant, or differentiation) of stimulus is one which "influences" some other response by necessarily causing a reaction which is not a response; this form is called "preparatory."

It is important to know what is happening here.[22] Names widely used, but thus far not established in firm dependable construction by the psychologies, are being taken over "as is," with

20. "If something is a preparatory-stimulus of the kind specified in our . . . formulation it is a sign" (p. 17).

21. "In a sign-process something becomes an evocative stimulus only because of the existence of something else as a preparatory-stimulus" (p. 308). This name does not appear, so far as I have noted, except in this one passage. I insert it here because something of the kind seems necessary to keep open the question as to whether, or in what sense, psychological stimuli are found (as distinct from physiological excitations) which are *not* signs. I do not want to take issue here on either the factual or terminological phases of the question, but merely to keep it from being overlooked. (See p. 252, note D.) The words quoted may, of course, be variously read. They might, perhaps, be intended to indicate, not a kind of stimulus genetically prior to or more general than "preparatory-stimulus," but instead a kind that did not come into "existence" at all except following, and as the "product" of, preparatory stimulation.

22. A little attention to such reports as that of the committee of the British Association for the Advancement of Science which spent seven years considering the possibility of "quantitative estimates of sensory events" would be of value to all free adaptors of psychological experiment and terminology. See S. S. Stevens, "On the Theory of Scales of Measurement," *Science,* CIII (1946), 677–80.

no offer of evidence as to their fitness for semiotical use.[23] "Stimulus" is, of course, the characteristic word of this type. The word "response," although it is much more definitely presented as presumptively a form of reaction, is almost always (I could perhaps venture to say, always) called "action" rather than "reaction"—an attitude which has the effect of pushing it off to a distance and presenting it rather "on its own" than as a phase of semiosical process.[24]

We shall next see that the part of reaction which is *not* response (or, at least, some part of that part) is made into a kind of independent or semi-independent factor or component, viz., disposition; and that a part of that part which *is* response is made into another such factor, viz., behavior. Dispositions and behaviors are thus set over against each other as well as over against stimuli; and the attempt is made to organize all three through various unidentified types of causation without any apparent inquiry into the processes involved.

11. *Response-disposition:*[25] "The state of an organism at a given time such that" (under certain additional conditions) "a given response takes place." "Every preparatory-stimulus causes a disposition to respond" but "there may be dispositions to respond which are not caused by preparatory-stimuli" (p. 9).

12. 'Disposition': Apparently itself a "state of an organism." Described as like being "angry" before "behaving angrily"; or like having typhoid fever before showing the grosser symptoms (p. 15).[26]

13. 'State of an organism': Illustrated by a 'need' (p. 352) or by a brain wave (p. 13). It is a something that can be 'removed' by a goal-object (p. 349), and something "such that" in certain

---

23. See, however, Morris' appendices No. 6 and 7, and remarks on his relation to Tolman toward the end of the present chapter.

24. John Dewey's "Reflex Arc" paper of 1896 should have ended this sort of thing forever for persons engaged in the broader tasks of construction. The point of view of recent physiology seems already well in advance of that of semiotic in this respect.

25. The same as *disposition to respond* (pp. 348, 353). The "additional conditions" are "conditions of need" and "of supporting stimulus-objects" (p. 11). "*Need*" is itself an 'organic state' (p. 352), but no attempt to "probe" it is made (p. 250).

26. I have noticed nothing more definite in the way of observation or description. Discussion of dispositions and needs (and of producers and interpreters) with respect to expression, emotion, and usage, will be found on pp. 67–69.

circumstances" "a response takes place" (p. 348). (Semiotic rests heavily upon it, but as with 'disposition' there is little it tells us about it.)

14. *Interpretant:* "The disposition in an interpreter to respond because of a sign." "A readiness to act" (p. 304). Perhaps "synonymous" with "idea" (pp. 30, 49).[27]

15. *Interpreter:* "An organism for which something is a sign."

We now have needs, states of the organism, and dispositions, all brought loosely into the formulation. Beyond this some dispositions are response-dispositions, and some response-dispositions are caused by signs. Also as we shall next find (No. 16) some sign-caused responses are purposive, and under the general scheme there must certainly be a special group of sign-caused, purposive dispositions to mediate the procedure, though I have not succeeded in putting a finger clearly upon it. What for the moment is to be observed is that the sign-caused, purposive-or-not, response-disposition gets rebaptized as "interpretant." Now a sharp name-changing *may* be an excellent aid to clarity, but this one needs its clarity examined. Along with being an interpretant, it demands an "interpreter," not professedly in place of the "organism," but still with a considerable air of being promoted to a higher class. While dispositions are mostly "caused," interpretants tend to be "produced" by interpreters and, indeed, the radical differentiation between signals and symbols (Nos. 20 and 21) turns on just this difference. Dispositions have not been listed as "ideas," but interpretants are inclined to be "synonymous" with ideas, while still remaining dispositions. There is also a complex matter of "signification" which runs along plausibly, as we shall later see, in terms of interpretants, but is far from being at home among dispositions directly arising out of stimulant energy. These are matters, not of complaint at the moment, but merely to be kept in mind.

Having developed this much of semiotic—the disposition factor—so as to show, at least partially, its troublesome unclarity, we may now take a look at "response" in semiosis as distinct

27. Semiotic, while not using "mentalist" terms at present, retains mentalist facts and suggests the possibility that "all mentalist terms" may be "incorporable" within semiotic at some later time (p. 30).

from stimulus and from disposition; in other words, at behavior, remembering always that the problem that concerns us is one of precision of terminology and of hoped-for accuracy of statement.

16. *Behavior:* "Sequences of . . . actions of muscles and glands" (i.e., of "responses") "by which an organism seeks goal-objects." "Behavior is therefore 'purposive.'"

17. *Behavior-family:* A set of such sequences similar in initiation and termination with respect to objects and needs.[28]

18. *Sign-behavior:* "Behavior in which signs occur." Behavior "in which signs exercise control" (p. 7).

Here we have behavior as strictly muscle-gland action to put alongside of sign as stimulus-energy and of interpretant as non-muscular, nonglandular reaction. Despite this distinctive status of behavior, it appears that sign-behavior is a kind of behavior that has signs occurring *in* it, or, alternatively, a kind *in which* signs exercise control. In such a rendering sign-behavior becomes approximately equivalent to the very loosely used "sign-process" (No. 25, q.v.).[29] This is no trifling lapse but is a confusion of expression lying at the very heart of the semiotical treatment of semiosical process.

We know fairly well where to look, not only when we want to find physical "objects" in the environment, but also when we seek the "muscles and glands" that make up "behavior," being in this respect much better off than when comparably we seek to find a locus for a disposition or an interpretant. Nevertheless a variety of problems arise concerning the technical status of behavior which may be left to the reader to answer for himself, reminding him only that precision of statement is what is at stake. Such problems are whether (1) muscle-gland action, set off independently or semi-independently for itself is intelligibly to be considered as itself "purposive"; (2) what muscle-gland action

---

28. This is a very useful verbal device, but not one, so far as I have observed, of any significance in the construction, though it is listed (pp. 8–11) as one of the four prominent "concepts" in semiotic along with stimulus, disposition and response. What it accomplishes is to save much complicated phrasing with respect to similarities absent and present. The typically pleonastic phrasing of the "definition" is as follows: "Any set of response-sequences which are initiated by similar stimulus-objects and which terminate in these objects as similar goal-objects for similar needs."

29. For loose uses of "sign-behavior" see pp. 15 and 19.

would be as theoretically "purposive," apart from stimulation; and (3) what part the "glands" play in this purposive semiotical construction. Probably only after the semiotical plan of locations for stimuli, signs, and purposes in terms of receptors, muscles, and glands has been worked out, can one face the further problem as to what locations are left over for dispositions and interpretants. On this last point the semiotician is especially cagey.[30]

We are now, perhaps, in a position to consider more precisely what a sign may be in semiotic:

19. *Sign* (officially)[31]: a preparatory-stimulus which,

(*a*) in the absence of certain evocative stimulation,[32]

(*b*) secures a reinvocation of, or replacement for, it, by

(*c*) "causing" in the organism a response-disposition,[33] which is

(*d*) capable of achieving[34] a response-sequence such as the evocative stimulus would have 'caused.'

All this takes place under a general construction that semiosis has its outcomes in purposive behavior, where the words "pur-

---

30. Professor George V. Gentry, in a paper "Some Comments on Morris's 'Class' Conception of the Designatum," the *Journal of Philosophy*, XLI (1944), 383–384, examined the possible status of the interpretant and concluded that a neurocortical locus was indicated, and that Morris did not so much reject this view as show himself to be unaware that any problem was involved. This discussion concerned an earlier monograph by Morris (*Foundations of the Theory of Signs, International Encyclopedia of Unified Science*, I, 2, 1938) and is well worth examining both for the points it makes and for the manner in which Morris has disregarded these points in his later development.

31. Many other manners of using the word "sign" appear besides those in Assertions No. 1, 2, 3, 29, and 32. A sign may be an activity or product (p. 35). It may be "any feature of any stimulus-object" (p. 15). "An action or state of the interpreter itself becomes (or produces) a sign" (p. 25). "Actions and states and products of the organism . . . may operate as signs" (p. 27). Strictly "a sign is not always a means-object" (p. 305). Thus despite the definitions, formal and informal alike, a sign may be an action, an act, a thing, a feature, a function, an energy, a property, a quality, or a situation; and this whether it is produced by an object (as in the opening statements) or is produced by an organism in its quality as interpreter (as in much later development).

32. Officially: "in the absence of stimulus-objects initiating response-sequences of a certain behavior-family."

33. "Causes in some organism a disposition to respond by response-sequences of this behavior-family."

34. I have found no verb used at this point, or at least do not recall any and so introduce the word "achieve" just by way of carrying on. A form of "delayed causation" is implied but not definitely expressed.

posive" and "behavioral" are co-applicable, and where behavior proper in the semiotic sense is an affair of muscles and glands.[35]

It should now be sufficiently well established on the basis of the body of the text that a sign in semiotic is officially a kind of stimulus, produced by an object, which "causes" a disposition (perhaps one named "George") to appear, and which then proceeds to "let George do it," the "it" in question being behavior, that is, muscle-gland action of the "purposive" type. Under this *official formulation,* thunder, apparently, would not semiotically be a sign of storm unless it "caused" a disposition to put muscles and glands into purposive action.[36] Sign, as stimulus, belongs strictly under the first of the three basic, major, operative, relatively independent or semi-independent (as they are variously described) factors: stimulus, disposition, and overt body-action. Not until this is plainly understood will one get the full force and effect of the dominant division of signs in semiotical construction, viz., that signs are divided officially into two groups: those produced by interpreters and all others.

20. *Symbol:* "A sign that is produced by its interpreter and that acts as a substitute for some other sign with which it is synonymous."

21. *Signal:* "A sign that is not a symbol."

22. *Use of a Sign:* "A sign is used . . . if it is produced by an interpreter as a means. . . ."[37] "A sign that is used is thus a means-object."

Certain questions force themselves upon our attention.

If a sign is by official definition a "stimulus" produced by a "property" of an "object" which is its "source," in what sense

35. For this background of construction see the nondefinitional statement for 'behavior' in the glossary, as this is factually (though not by explicit naming) carried over into the formal definition of *Behavior-family.*
36. If a discussion of this arrangement were undertaken, it would need to be stressed that the causation found in semiotic is of the close-up, short-term type, such as is commonly called mechanistic. No provision seems to be made for long-term, intricate interconnection. See also footnote 49 following.
37. The omitted words in the definition for "use of a sign" cited above are "with respect to some goal." Insert them and the definition seems plausible; remove them and it is not. But they add nothing whatever to the import of the definition, since sign itself by the top definition of all exists only with respect to some goal.

can the leading branch of signs be said to be produced by "interpreters," rather than by "properties of objects"?

Assuming factual distinctions along the general line indicated
by signal and symbol, and especially when such distinctions are
presented as of maximum importance, ought not semiotic, as a
science stressing the need of terminological strength, be able to
give these distinctions plain and clear statement? [38]

What sense, precisely, has the word "use" in semiotic when
one compares the definition for "symbol" with that for "use"? [39]

Three other definitions, two of them of starred terms, next
need a glance:

23. *Sign-vehicle:* "A particular event or object . . . that functions as a sign." "A particular physical event—such as a given
sound or mark or movement—which *is* a sign will be *called* a
sign-vehicle" (p. 20; italics for "is" and "called" not used in
Morris' text).

24. *Sign-family:* "A set of similar sign-vehicles that for a
given interpreter have the same signification."

25. 'Sign-process': "The status of being a sign, the interpretant, the fact of denoting, the significatum" (p. 19).[40]

The peculiarities of expression are great. How is an object that
"functions" as a sign different from another object that "stimu-
lates" us as a sign or from one that "is" a sign? Is the word "particular" which modifies "event" the most important feature of
the definition, and what is its sense? We are told (p. 20) that the
distinction of sign-vehicle and sign-family is often not relevant,
but nevertheless is of theoretical importance. Just what can this
mean? We hear talk (p. 21) of sign-vehicles that have "significata"; but is not signification the most important characteristic

38. The section on signal and symbol (Chapter I, Sec. 8) has impressed me as one
of the most obscure in the book, quite comparable in this respect with the
section on modes of significance used earlier for illustration.
39. The probable explanation of the separation of use from mode can be found
by examining the first pages of Chapter IV. *Cf.* also pp. 92, 96, 97, 104, 125.
40. The text rejects the word "meaning" as signifying "any and all phases of
sign-process" and specifies for "sign-processes" by the wording above. Apparently the ground for rejection of "meaning" would also apply to "sign-
process." "Sign-behavior" (No. 18 above) is often used as loosely as is "sign-
process." The phrasing cited above is extremely interesting for its implicit
differentiation of "status" and "fact" in the cases of sign and denotatum from
what would appear by comparison to be an implied actuality for interpretant
and significatum.

of sign itself rather than of vehicle? If sign is energy is there some sense in which its vehicle is *not* energetic?

On the whole we are left with the impression that the distinction between "sign" and "sign-vehicle," so far as linguistic signs go, is nothing more than the ancient difference between "meaning" and "word," rechristened but still before us in all its ancient unexplored crudity. What this distinction may amount to with respect to non-linguistic signs remains still more in need of clarification.[41]

Our attention has thus far been largely concerned with the semiosis of goal-seeking animals by way of the semiotical vocabulary of object, stimulus, disposition, need, muscle, and gland. We are now to see how there is embroidered upon it the phraseology of the epistemological logics of the past in a hoped-for crystallization of structure for the future.

26. *Signify:* "To act as a sign." "To have signification." "To have a significatum." (The three statements are said to be "synonymous.")

27. 'Signification': "No attempt has been made to differentiate 'signification' and 'significatum'" (p. 354).

28. *Significatum:* "The conditions" for "a denotatum."[42]

29. Sign (on suspicion): The "x" in "x *signifies its significatum.*"[43]

---

41. By way of showing the extreme looseness of expression the following phrasings of types not included in the preceding text may be cited. Although signs are not interpretants or behaviors but stimuli, they "involve behavior, for a sign must have an interpretant" (p. 187), they are "identified within goal-seeking behavior" (p. 7), they are "described and differentiated in terms of dispositions . . ." (p. v). Interpretants, although dispositions, are "sign-produced behavior" (pp. 95, 104) or even "sign-behavior" (p. 166). A fair climax is reached in the blurb on the cover of the book (it is a good blurb in showing, as many others do, which way the book-wind blows), where all the ingredients are mixed together again in a common kettle by the assertion that this "theory of signs" (incidentally here known as semantics rather than as semiotic) "defines signs in terms of 'dispositions to respond'—that is, in terms of behavior." Along with these one may recall one phrasing already cited in which signs were spoken of as influencing behaviors first and dispositions later on in the process.

42. Significatum: "The conditions such that whatever meets these conditions is a denotatum of a given sign" (p. 354).

43. "A sign is said to signify its significatum" (p. 354). "Signs in the different modes of signifying signify differently" (p. 64). "Signs signifying the significata of . . ." (p. 67).

30. *Denote:* "A sign that has a denotatum . . . is said to denote its denotatum."

31. *Denotatum:* "Anything that would permit the completion of the response-sequences to which an interpreter is disposed because of a sign." "Food in the place sought . . . is a denotatum" (p. 18). "A poet . . . is a denotatum of 'poet'" (p. 106).

32. Sign (on suspicion): The "y" in "y *denotes its denotatum.*"

33. *Goal-object:* "An object that partially or completely removes the state of an organism (the need) which motivates response-sequences."

The above is obviously a set of skeletons of assertions, but skeletonization or some other form of simplification is necessary if any trail is to be blazed through this region of semiotic. If we could be sure whether denotata and goal-objects were, or were not, "the same thing" for semiotic we might have an easier time deciphering the organization.[44] The characterizations of the two are verbally fairly close: "anything" for denotata is much like "an object" for goal-objects; "permitting completion" is much the same as "removing the need"; "is disposed" is akin to "motivates." But I have nowhere come across a definite statement of the status of the two with respect to each other, though, of course, I may have easily overlooked it. The first semiotical requirement for a denotatum is that it be "actual," or "existent" (pp. 17–20, 23, 107, 168; disregarding, perhaps, the case [p. 106] in which the denotatum of a certain ascriptor is "simply a situation such that . . ."). As "actual" the denotatum is that which the significatum is "conditions for." The significatum may remain "conditions" in the form of an "um" component of semiotic even if no denotatum "actually" exists,[45] so that the goal-object would then apparently be neither "actual" nor "existent" (except, perhaps, as present in "the mind of the interpreter" or in some terminological representative of such a "mind"). If goal-object and denotatum could be organized in a common form we

44. There is also a very interesting question as to means-objects: whether they enter as sign-produced denotata or as directly acting objects which are not denotata at all. But we must pass this one over entirely. Compare Assertion No. 22, and footnote 36.

45. "All signs signify, but not all signs denote." "A sign is said to signify (but not denote) its significatum, that is, the conditions under which it denotes" (pp. 347, 354).

might, perhaps, be able to deal more definitely with them. We are in even worse shape when we find, as we do occasionally, that significata may be "properties" as is the case with "formators" (pp. 157–158), or in their coverage of "utilitanda properties" (p. 304; see also p. 67); and that "property" itself is "a very general term used to embrace the denotata (*sic*) of signs . . ." (p. 81). Perhaps all that we can say descriptively as the case stands is that "denotatum" and "goal-object" are two different ways of talking about a situation not very well clarified with respect to either.

IV

I have endeavored to limit myself thus far to an attempt to give what may be called "the facts of the text." I hope the comments that I have interspersed between the numbered assertions have not gone much beyond what has been needed for primary report. In what follows I shall call attention to some of the issues involved, but even now not so much to debate them as to show their presence, their complexities, and the lack of attention given them.

In our preliminary statement of the leading characteristics of semiotic it was noted that the interpretation was largely in terms of causation and control. What this type of statement and of terminology does to the subjectmatter at the hands of the semiotician may be interestingly seen if we focus attention upon the verbs made use of in the official accounts of "sign." What we are informed is (1) that if we are provided with a "stimulus-object" possessing "properties," then (2) these properties *produce* a kind of stimulus which (3) *influences* by (4) *causing* a disposition to appear, so that if (5) a state of the organism (a need) *motivates,* and if (6) the right means-objects are in place, then (7) it will come to pass that that which was produced at stage No. 4 proves to *be such that* (8) a response-sequence *takes place* wherein or whereby (9) the stimulus object of stage No. 1 or some other object is *responded* to as a goal-object which (10) in its turn *removes* the state of the organism (the need) that was present in stage No. 5.

What these shifting verbs accomplish is clear enough. Whichever one fits most smoothly, and thus most inconspicuously, into a sentence is the one that is most apt to be used. A certain fluency is gained, but no precision. I have not attempted to make a full list of such wordings but have a few memoranda. "Produce," for example, can be used either for what the organism does, for what a property does, for what an interpreter does, or for what a sign does (pp. 25, 34, 38, 353, 355). It may be voluntary or involuntary (p. 27), though non-humans[46] are said seldom to produce (p. 198). In the use of a comparable verb, "to signify," either organisms or signs may be the actors (p. 16). Among other specimens of such linguistic insecurity are 'because of' (p. 252), 'occasion' (pp. 13, 155), 'substitute for' (p. 34), 'act as' (p. 354), 'determine' (p. 67), 'determine by decision' (p. 18), 'function as' (p. 354), 'be disposed to' (p. 66), 'connects with' (p. 18), 'answers to' (p. 18), 'initiates' (p. 346), 'affects in some way' (p. 9), 'affects or causes' (p. 8), 'controls' (p. 7), 'directs' (p. 354), 'becomes or produces' (p. 25), 'seeks' (p. 346), and 'uses' (p. 356). One can find sentences (as on p. 25) which actually seem to tell us that interpreters produce signs as substitutes for other signs which are synonymous with them and which originally made the interpreter do what they indicated, such that the substitutes which the interpreter himself has produced now make him do what the signs from without originally made him do.[47] The "fact" in question is one of familiar everyday knowledge. Not this fact, but rather the peculiarities of statement introduced by semiotical terminology are what here cause our concern.

V

Though vital to any thorough effort at research and construction, two great problems are left untouched by semiotic. These problems are, first, the factual organization of what men

---

46. Another interesting remark about animals, considering that semiotic is universal sign-theory, is that "even at the level of animal behavior organisms tend to follow the lead of more reliable signs" (p. 121).

47. No wonder that a bit later when the semiotician asks, "Are such words, however, substitutes for other synonymous signs?" he finds himself answering, "This is a complicated issue which would involve a study of the genesis of the signs produced" (p. 34). The "such words" in question are the kind that "are symbols to both communicator and communicatee at least with respect to the criterion of producibility."

commonly call "stimulus" with that which they commonly call "object"; and, secondly, the corresponding organization of what the semiotician calls "interpreter" with what he calls "interpretant," or, more generally, of the factual status with respect to each other of "actor" and "action." The interpreter-interpretant problem is manifestly a special case of the ancient grammatical-historical program of separating a do-er from his things-done, on the assumption that the do-er is theoretically independent of his things-done, and that the things-done have status in some fairy realm of perfected being in independence of the doing-do. The case of stimulus-object on close inspection involves a quite similar issue. In semiotic the interior organization of disposition, interpretant, and significatum offers a special complexity. We can best show the status of these problems by appraising some of the remarks which the semiotician himself makes about the stepping stones he finds himself using as he passes through the swamps of his inquiry. No systematic treatment will be attempted since the material we have before us simply will not permit it without an enormous amount of complicated linguistic dissection far greater than the present occasion will tolerate.

Semiotic stresses for its development three main components: sign, disposition, and behavior; the first as what comes in; the second as a sort of intervening storage warehouse; the third as what goes out. For none of these, however, despite the semiotician's confidence that he is providing us "with words that are sharpened arrows" (p. 19), can their semiotical operations be definitely set down. Sign, as we have seen, is officially stimulus, practically for the most part object or property, and in the end a glisteningly transmogrified denoter or signifier. Behavior parades itself like a simple fellow, just muscles and glands in action; but while it is evidently a compartment of the organism it doesn't fit in as a compartment of the more highly specialized interpreter, although this interpreter is declared to be the very organism itself in sign action, no more, no less; moreover, behavior is purposive in its own right, though what purposive muscles and glands all on their own may be is difficult to decipher. As for disposition (or rather response-disposition, since this is the particular case of disposition with which semiotic deals), it is, I shall at least allege, a monstrosity in the form of Siamese triplets, joined at the butts, hard to carve apart, and still harder to keep alive in union. One of these triplets is disposition physiologically speaking, which is just common habit or readiness to act. Another is interpretant which is disposition-in-signing (though why such double naming is needed is not clearly made evident). The third member of the triplet family is significatum, a fellow who rarely refers to his low-life sib but who, since he is not himself either incoming stimulus or outgoing muscle or gland action, has nowhere else to be at home other than as a member of the disposition-triplets—unless, indeed, as suspicion sometimes suggests, he hopes to float forever, aura-like or soul-like, around and above the other two.

The semiotician offers us several phrasings for his tripartite organization of "factors," (of which the central core is, as we have just seen, itself tripartite). "The factors operative in sign-processes are all either stimulus-objects or organic dispositions or actual responses" (p. 19). "Analysis," we are told, yields "the stimulus, response, and organic state terminology of behavioristics" (p. 251). The "three major factors" correspond to the "nature" of the environment, its "relevance" for needs, and the "ways in which the organism must act" (p. 62). The "relative independence of environment, need, and response" is mentioned (pp. 63–64).

Despite this stressed threeness in its various forms, the practical operation of semiotic involves five factors, even if the "disposition-triplets" are seen as fused into one. The two needed additions are object as differentiated from stimulus at one end, and interpreter (or personified organism) as differentiated from interpretant at the other. (This does not mean that the present narrator wishes to introduce such items. He does not. It merely means that he finds them present and at work in the text, however furbished.) Object and stimulus we have seen all along popping in and out alternatively. "Interpreter" enters in place of interpretant whenever the semiotician wishes to stress the organism as itself the performer, producer, or begetter of what goes on. What this means is that, at both ends, the vital problems of human adaptational living in environments are entirely ignored—the problems, namely, of stimulus-object[48] and of actor-action.

48. A few references occur in semiotic to modern work on perception (pp. 34, 191, 252, 274), but without showing any significant influence. The phenomenal constancy studies of Katz, Gelb, Bühler, Brunswik, and others on foundations running back to Helmholtz would, if given attention, make a great dif-

What evidence does the semiotician offer for the presence of a disposition? He feels the need of evidence and makes some suggestions as to how it may be found (pp. 13–15). Each of his remarks exhibits an event of sign-process such that, if one *already believes* in dispositions as particulate existences, then, where sign-process is under way, it will be quite the thing to call a disposition in to help out. None of his exhibits, however, serves to make clear the factual presence of a disposition, whether for itself or as interpretant or as significatum, in any respect whatever as a separate factor located between the stimulation and the action. The only manifest "need" that the introduction of such a disposition seems to satisfy is the need of conforming to verbal tradition.

The issue here is not whether organisms have habits, but whether it is proper semiotically (or any other way) to set up a habit as a thing caused by some other thing and in turn causing a third thing, and use it as a basic factor in construction. Three passages of semiotic let the cat neatly out of the bag. The first says that even though a preparatory stimulus is the 'cause' of a disposition, "logically . . . 'disposition to respond' is the more basic notion" (p. 9). The second tells us that sign-processes "within the general class of processes involving mediation" are "those in which the factor of mediation is an interpretant" (p. 288). The third citation is possibly even more revealing, for we are told that "the merit of this formulation" (i.e., the use of a conventional, naïvely interpolated "disposition") "is that it does not require that the dog or the driver respond to the sign itself"

---

ference in the probable construction. (For a simple statement in a form directly applicable to the present issues see V. J. McGill, "Subjective and Objective Methods in Philosophy," the *Journal of Philosophy,* XLI [1944], 424–427.) There is little evidence that the developments of Gestalt studies even in the simpler matters of figure and ground have influenced the treatment. The great question is whether "property," as semiotic introduces it, is not itself sign, to start out with. Semiotic holds, for example, that sign-process has nothing to do with a man reaching for a glass of water to drink, unless the glass of water is a sign of something else. The reaching is "simply acting in a certain way to an object which is a source of stimulation," (p. 252) from which it would appear that in semiotic no "response-disposition" is involved in getting water to drink—a position which seems strange enough to that manner of envisionment known as common sense, but which nevertheless will not be objected to in principle by the present writer in the present chapter, if consistently maintained and successfully developed.

(p. 10);[49] this being very close to saying that the merit of semiotic is that it can evade the study of facts and operate with puppet inserts.

There is another very interesting employment of disposition which should not be overlooked even though it can barely be mentioned here. Semiotic employs a highly specialized sign about signs called a "formator." The signs corresponding to the "modes of signification," at which we took an illustrative glance early in this chapter, are called "lexicators." The formator, however, is not a lexicator. Nevertheless it has to be a "sign," in order to fill out the construction; while to be a sign it has to have a "disposition" (interpretant). This, in the ordinary procedure, it could not attain in ordinary form. It is therefore allotted a "second-order disposition" (p. 157); and this,—since "interpretant" *via* "interpreter" represents the ancient "mind" in semiotic,—is about equivalent to introducing a two-story "mind" for the new "science" to operate with.

As concerns disposition-to-respond and interpretant in joint inspection, all that needs to be said is that if interpretant is simply one species of disposition and can so be dealt with, there is no objection whatever to naming it as a particular species. But, as we have seen in repeated instances, disposition shows itself primarily as a thing seemingly 'caused' from 'without,' while interpretant is very apt to be a thing, or property, or characteristic 'produced' from 'within.' Evading the words 'within' and 'without,' and switching names around does not seem to yield sufficient "science" to cope with this problem.

Consider next the significatum in its status in respect to the interpretant. Remarks upon this topic are rare, except in such a casual form as "a significatum . . . always involves an interpretant (a disposition . . .)" (pp. 64–65). At only one point that I have noted is there a definite attempt at explication. We are told (p. 18) that "the relation between interpretant and significatum is worth noting." Here we find the significatum as a sort of inter-

49. The probable reason why the semiotician is so fearful of getting objects and organisms into direct contact (and he repeatedly touches on it) is that his view of "causation" is of the billiard-ball type, under the rule "once happen, always happen." His "intervening third" is a sort of safety valve for the cases in which his rule does not work. Which is again to say that he makes no direct observation of or report upon behavioral process itself.

pretant turned inside out. The situation will be well remembered by many past sufferers from the ambiguity of the word "meaning." In effect, if the interpretant is a disposition with a certain amount of more or less high-grade "meaning" injected into it, then a significatum is this meaning more or less referable to the environment rather than to the interpreter. "The interpretant," we are told, "*answers to* the behavioral side of the behavior-environment complex"; as against this, "the significatum . . . *connects with* the environmental side of the complex" (p. 18, italics supplied). Here the interpretant enters "as a disposition," and the significatum enters "as a set of terminal[50] conditions under which the response-sequence can be completed," i.e., under which the "disposition" can make good. What this whole phase of semiotic most needs is the application to itself of some of its specialized ascriptors with designators dominant.

As for the organization of significatum with denotatum, and of both with ordinary muscle action and goal objects, there seems little that can be said beyond the few problems of fact that were raised following Assertions No. 26 to 33 in the text above. These comments had to be held to a minimum because the interior organization lies somewhere behind a blank wall. To be noted is that while to be "actual" or "existent" is the great duty imposed on the denotatum, the significatum is allotted its own type of actuality[51] and thingness, which is manifestly not of the denotatum type, but yet is never clearly differentiated from the other. Here is one of the greatest issues of semiotic—one which may be put in the form of the question "how comes that conditions are *ums?*" The semiotician could well afford to keep this question written on his every cuff.[52] The other great question as to the significata is, of course: How does it come about that the sign (stimulus) of

50. "Terminal" in this use seems much more suggestive of goal-object or denotatum than it is of significatum.

51. See also the paper by Professor Gentry, previously mentioned, which very competently (and from the philosophical point of view far more broadly than is attempted here) discusses this and various other deficiencies in Morris' sign theory.

52. Semiotic offers, however, a set of working rules under which it believes difficulties such as those of the theory of types can be readily solved (p. 279). These are: that a sign as sign-vehicle can denote itself; that a sign cannot denote its own significatum; that a sign can neither denote nor signify its interpretant (pp. 19, 220, 279). Herein lies an excellent opening for further inquiries into the fixations of "um."

No. 19 in any of its crude forms, "object," "property," "thing," or "energy," mushrooms into the stratosphere of "the good," "the beautiful," and "the true," with or without the occasional accompanying "denotation" of a few actual goodies, pretties, or verities?

VI

At the start of this chapter it was said that our examination would be expressly limited to an appraisal of the efficiency of the technical terminology which semiotic announced it was establishing as the basis for a future science; we left to others the discussion of the many interesting and valuable contributions which might be offered along specialized lines. The range of our inquiry has thus been approximately that which Professor Morris in a summary and appraisal of his own work (p. 185) styles "the behavioral analysis of signs." The specialized developments which he there further reports as "basic to his argument" are the "modes" of signifying, the "uses" of signs, and the "mode-use" classification of types of discourse, with these all together leading the way to a treatment of logic and mathematics as discourse in the "formative mode" and the "informative use" (pp. 169ff., 178ff.).[53] Reminder is made of these specialized developments at this point in order to maintain a proper sense of proportion as to what has here been undertaken. It is, of course, practicable for a reader primarily interested in mode, use, and type to confine himself to these subjects, without concern over the behavioral analysis underlying their treatment.

With respect to the materials which semiotical terminology identifies, we may now summarize. The organism's activities with respect to environments are divided into stimulations, dis-

---

53. Something of the manner in which "modes of signifying" were identified was presented in an illustrative way in the earlier part of the present paper. The distinction, and at the same time close relation, of uses and modes is discussed in the book (pp. 96–97). The combination of use and mode for the classification of types of discourse is displayed in tabular form on p. 125. As for "everything else" in the book, Morris composedly writes (p. 185) that "our contention has been merely that it is possible to deal with all sign phenomena in terms of the basic terminology of semiotic, and hence to define any other term signifying sign phenomena in these terms."

positions, and responses. Sign-processes are similarly divided: a certain manner of indirect stimulation is called sign; the sign produces, not a response in muscle-gland action, but a kind of disposition called interpretant; the interpretant, in turn, under proper conditions, produces a particular kind of muscle-gland action—the "purposive" kind—which is called behavior.[54] Sign must always be a stimulus; disposition (so far as sign-process is concerned) always the result of a sign;[55] and behavior always a purposive muscular or glandular action; if semiotic is to achieve its dependable terminological goal.[56]

With respect to the actualization of this program, we quickly discover that semiotic presents a leading class of signs (symbols) which are *not* stimuli in the declared sense, but instead are "produced by interpreters" (all other signs being signals). We learn also that many interpretants are commonly produced by interpreters (by way of symbols) although they are themselves dispositions, and dispositions (so far as sign-process goes) are caused by properties of objects. We discover that significata have been introduced into the system without any developed connection with the terminology of goal-objects, purposive behaviors, dispositions, interpretants, or even with that of sign, save as the word "sign" enters into the declaration that "signs signify significata." We find also certain interstitial semiotical appellations called denotata and identified only in the sense of the declaration that "signs" (sometimes) "denote denotata." We have the "use" of a sign made distinct from its behavioral presence; we have denotata declared to be actual existences in contrast with significata which are "the conditions" for them; we then have significata gaining a form of actuality while denotata shrink back at times

54. The fact that some of these names are starred as basic and others not, and that those not starred are the underlying behavioral names, was noted earlier in this chapter. The attempt is thus made to treat sign authoritatively without establishing preliminary definiteness about the behavior of which sign is a component. It should now, perhaps, be clear that the confusion of terminology is the direct outgrowth of this procedure, as is also the continual uncertainty the reader feels as to what precisely it is that he is being told.

55. "There may be dispositions to respond which are not caused by preparatory-stimuli" (p. 9).

56. It is to be understood, of course, that semiotic presents itself as open to future growth. The open question is whether the present terminology will permit such a future growth by further refinement, or whether the primary condition for growth is the eradication of the terminology from the ground up.

into something "situational." As a special case of such terminological confusion we have significata showing themselves up
in an emergency as "properties," although "property" is in general the producer of a stimulus (p. 355) and although it is in particular described as "a very general term used to embrace . . .
denotata" (p. 81); so that the full life-history of the process
property-sign-signify-significatum-denote-denotatum-property
ought to be well worth inquiry as an approach to a theory of
sign-behavior.[57]

A glance at some of the avowed sources of semiotic may throw
some light on the way in which its confusions arise. Its use of the
word "interpretant" is taken from Charles Sanders Peirce,[58] and
its treatment in terms of "purposive" response is from what Professor Morris calls "behavioristics," more particularly from the
work of Edward C. Tolman.[59] The difficulty in semiotic may be
fairly well covered by saying that these two sources have been
brought into a verbal combination, with Tolman providing the
basement and ground floor while Peirce provides the penthouse
and the attics, but with the intervening stories nowhere built up
through factual inquiry and organization.

Peirce very early in life[60] came to the conclusion that all thought
was in signs and required a time. He was under the influence of
the then fresh Darwinian discoveries and was striving to see the
intellectual processes of men as taking place in this new natural
field. His pragmaticism, his theory of signs, and his search for a

57. The position of the writer of this report is that defects such as we have shown
are not to be regarded, in the usual case, as due to the incompetence of the
workman, but that they are inherent in the manner of observation and nomenclature employed. Generations of endeavor seem to him to reveal that
such components when split apart as "factors" will not remain split. The
only way to exhibit the defects of the old approach is upon the actual work of
the actual workman. If Professor Morris or any one else can make good upon
the lines he is following, the credit to him will be all the greater.
58. See Morris, *op. cit.*, p. v, and Appendix 2. On page 27 of his text, his analysis
of semiotic is "characterized as an attempt to carry out resolutely the insight
of Charles Peirce that a sign gives rise to an interpretant and that an interpretant is in the last analysis a 'modification of a person's tendencies toward
action.'"
59. In addition to a citation in the opening paragraph of this chapter, see *op. cit.*,
p. 2: "A science of signs can be most profitably developed on a biological
basis and specifically within the framework of the science of behavior." For
Tolman see Appendix 6.
60. "Questions Concerning Certain Faculties Claimed for Man," *Journal of
Speculative Philosophy*, II (1868); *Collected Papers*, 5.253.

functional logic all lay in this one line of growth. Peirce introduced the word "interpretant," not in order to maintain the old
mentalistic view of thought, but for quite the opposite purpose,
as a device, in organization with other terminological devices, to
show how "thoughts" or "ideas" as subjects of inquiry were not
to be viewed as psychic substances or as psychically substantial,
but were actually processes under way in human living. In contrast with this, semiotic uses Peirce's term in accordance with its
own notions as an aid to bring back *sub rosa*,[61] the very thing
that Peirce—and James and Dewey as well—spent a good part of
their lives trying to get rid of.[62]

Tolman has done his work in a specialized field of recognized
importance. Along with other psychologists of similar bent he
took animals with highly developed yet restricted ranges of behavior, and channelized them as to stock, environment, and activities. He then, after many years, developed a terminology to
cover what he had observed. I keep his work close to my table
though I may not use it, perhaps, as often as I should. The fact
that the results which Tolman and his fellow workers have secured may be usefully reported in terms of stimulus, need, and

61. This assertion is made categorically despite Morris's sentence (p. 289) in
which he assures us that "The present treatment follows Peirce's emphasis
upon behavior rather than his more mentalistic formulations." A typical expression by Peirce (2.666, *circa* 1910) is "I really know no other way of defining a habit than by describing the kind of behavior in which the habit
becomes actualized." Dewey's comment (in correspondence) is that it is a
complete inversion of Peirce to identify an interpretant with an interpreter.
Excellent illustrations of the creation of fictitious "existences" in Morris' manner have recently been displayed by Ernest Nagel (the *Journal of Philosophy*,
XLII [1945], 628–630) and by Stephen C. Pepper (*ibid.*, XLIII [1946], 36).
62. John Dewey in a recent paper "Peirce's Theory of Linguistic Signs, Thought,
and Meaning" (the *Journal of Philosophy*, XLIII [1946], 85–95) analysed
this and other of Morris' terminological adaptations of Peirce, including especially the issues of pragmatism, and suggested that "'users' of Peirce's writings should either stick to his basic pattern or leave him alone." In a short
reply Morris evaded the issue and again Dewey stressed that Morris' treatment of Peirce offered a "radically new version of the subject-matter, intent,
and method of pragmatic doctrine," for which Peirce should not be called a
forerunner. Again replying, Morris again evaded the issue (*ibid.*, pp. 196,
280, 363). Thus, so far as this discussion is concerned, the issue as to the
propriety of Morris' statement that he offers "an attempt to carry out resolutely the insight of Charles Peirce" remains still unresolved. In still another
way Morris differs radically from Dewey. This is in regarding his development of semiotic as made "in a way compatible with the framework of
Dewey's thought." (*Signs, Language, and Behavior*, p. 273.)

response does not, however, suggest to me that this report can be straightway adopted as a basic formulation for all procedures of human knowledge. When Tolman, for example, recognizes "utilitanda" one can know very definitely what he intends; but when Morris takes up Tolman's "utilitanda properties" and includes them, "when signified, under the term 'significatum'" (p. 304) just as they stand, intelligibility drops to a much lower level.

Semiotic thus takes goal-seeking psychology at the rat level, sets it up with little change, and then attempts to spread the cobwebs of the older logics and philosophies across it. The failure of Morris' attempt does not mean, of course, that future extensions of positive research may not bring the two points of approach together.

Broadening the above orientation from immediate sources to the wider trends in the development of modern knowledge, we may report that much of the difficulty which semiotic has with its terminology lies in its endeavor to conciliate two warring points of view. One point of view represents the ancient lineage of selves as actors, in the series souls, minds, persons, brains. The other derives from Newtonian mechanics in which particles are seen as in causal interaction. The former is today so much under suspicion that it makes its entries largely under camouflage. The latter is no longer dominant even in the physics of its greatest successes. Harnessing together these two survivors from the past does not seem to yield a live system which enables sound descriptions of observations in the manner that modern sciences strive always to attain.

VII

So great are the possibilities of misinterpretation in such an analysis as the above that I summarize anew as to its objectives. I have aimed to make plain the "factors" (as purported "facts") which Professor Morris' "terms" introduce, but to reject neither his "factors" nor his "terms" because of my own personal views. I admit them both freely *under hypothesis* which is as far as I care to go with any alternatives which I myself propose. This, manifestly, is not easy to achieve with this subject and in this day, but one may at least do his best at trying. Under this approach his "terms" are required to make good both as between themselves and with respect to the "facts" for which they are introduced to stand. To test their success I take the body of his text for my material and endeavor to ascertain how well his terms achieve their appointed tasks. What standards we adopt and how high we place them depends on the importance of the theory and on the claims made for it. When in his preface Professor Morris names an associate as having done "the editing of the various rewritings," although in the immediately preceding paragraph this same associate had been listed among advisers none of whom "saw the final text," we recognize a very trifling slip. When slips of this kind in which one statement belies another appear in the body of a work in such an intricate field as the present one, we recognize them as unfortunate but as something our poor flesh is heir to. But when such defects are scattered everywhere—in every chapter and almost on every page of a book purported to establish a new science to serve as a guide to many sciences, and when they affect each and every one of the leading terms the book declares "basic" for its construction, then it is time to cry a sharp halt and to ask for a redeployment of the terminological forces. This is the state of the new "semiotic" and the reason for our analysis. Only the radical importance of the inquiry for many branches of knowledge can justify the amount of space and effort that have been expended.

10.   Common Sense and Science[1]

The discussion that follows is appropriately introduced by saying that both common sense and science are to be treated as transactions.[2] The use of this name has negative and positive implications. It indicates, negatively, that neither common sense nor science is regarded as an entity—as something set apart, complete and self-enclosed; this implication rules out two ways of viewing them that have been more or less current. One of these ways treats them as names for mental faculties or processes, while the other way regards them as "realistic" in the epistemological sense in which that word is employed to designate subjects alleged to be knowable entirely apart from human participation. Positively, it points to the fact that both are treated as being marked by the traits and properties which are found in whatever is recognized to be a transaction:—a trade, or commercial transaction, for example. This transaction determines one participant to be a buyer and the other a seller. No one exists as buyer or seller save *in and because of* a transaction in which each is engaged. Nor is that all; specific things *become* goods or commodities because they are engaged in the transaction. There is no commercial transaction without things which only are goods, utilities, commodities, in and because of a transaction. Moreover, because of the exchange or transfer, both *parties* (the idiomatic name for *participants*) undergo change; and the goods undergo at the very least a change of *locus* by which they gain and lose certain connective relations or "capacities" previously possessed.

Furthermore, no given transaction of trade stands alone. It is enmeshed in a body of activities in which are included those of

1. This chapter is written by Dewey.
2. See Chapters 4 and 5 of this volume.

production, whether in farming, mining, fishing, or manufacture. And this body of transactions (which may be called industrial) is itself enmeshed in transactions that are neither industrial, commercial, nor financial; to which the name "intangible" is often given, but which can be more safely named by means of specifying rules and regulations that proceed from the system of customs in which other transactions exist and operate.

These remarks are introductory. A trade is cited as a transaction in order to call attention to the traits to be found in common sense and science *as* transactions, extending to the fact that human life itself, both severally and collectively, consists of transactions in which human beings partake together with non-human things of the milieu along with other human beings, so that without this togetherness of human and non-human partakers we could not even stay alive, to say nothing of accomplishing anything. From birth to death every human being is a *Party,* so that neither he nor anything done or suffered can possibly be understood when it is separated from the fact of participation in an extensive body of transactions—to which a given human being may contribute and which he modifies, but only in virtue of being a partaker in them.[3]

Considering the dependence of life in even its physical and physiological aspects upon being parties in transactions in which other human beings and "things" are also parties, and considering the dependence of intellectual and moral growth upon being a party in transactions in which cultural conditions partake—of which language is a sufficient instance—, the surprising thing is that any other idea has ever been entertained. But, aside from the matters noted in the last footnote (as in the part played by religion as a cultural institution in formation and spread of the view that soul, mind, consciousness are isolated independent entities), there is the fact that what is necessarily involved in that process of living gets passed over without special attention on account of its familiarity. As we do not notice the air in the physiological transaction of breathing till some obstruction occurs, so with the

3. No better illustration of this fact can be found than the fact that it was a pretty extensive set of religious, economic, and political transactions which led (in the movement named individualism) to the psychological and philosophical theories that set up human beings as "individuals" doing business on their own account.

multitude of cultural and non-human factors that take part in all we do, say, and think, even in soliloquies and dreams. What is called *environment* is that in which the conditions called physical are enmeshed in cultural conditions and thereby are more than "physical" in its technical sense. "Environment" is not something around and about human activities in an external sense; it is their *medium,* or *milieu,* in the sense in which a *medium* is *inter*mediate in the execution or carrying *out* of human activities, as well as being the channel *through* which they move and the vehicle *by* which they go on. Narrowing of the medium is the direct source of all unnecessary impoverishment in human living; the only sense in which "social" is an honorific term is that in which the medium in which human living goes on is one by which human life is enriched.

I

I come now to consideration of the bearing of the previous remarks upon the special theme of this paper, beginning with common sense. Only by direct active participation in the transactions of living does anyone become *familiarly acquainted* with other human beings and with "things" which make up the world. While "common sense" includes more than knowledge, this acquaintance knowledge is its distinguishing trait; it demarcates the frame of reference of common sense by identifying it with the life actually carried on as it is enjoyed or suffered. I shall then first state why the expression "common sense" is a usable and useful name for a body of facts that are so basic that without systematic attention to them "science" cannot exist, while philosophy is idly speculative apart from them because it is then deprived of footing to stand on as well as a field of application.

Turning to the dictionary we find that the expression "common sense" is used as a name for "the general sense, feeling, judgement, of mankind or of a community." It is highly doubtful whether anything but matters with which actual living is directly concerned could command the attention, and control the speech usage of "mankind," or of an entire community. And we may also be reasonably sure that some features of life are so exigent that they impinge upon the feeling and wit of all mankind—such as need for food and means of acquiring it, the capacity of fire to give warmth and to burn, of weapons for hunting or war, and the need for common customs and rules if a group is to be kept in existence against threats from within and without. As for a community, what can it be but a number of persons having certain beliefs in common and moved by widely shared habits of feeling and judgment? So we need not be surprised to find in the dictionary under the caption "common sense" the following: "Good sound practical sense . . . in dealing with every-day affairs." Put these two usages together and we have an expression that admirably fits the case.[4]

The everyday affairs of a community constitute the *life* characteristic of that community, and only these common life-activities can engage the general or common wits and feelings of its members. And as for the word "sense" joined to "common," we note that the dictionary gives as one usage of that word "intelligence in its bearing on action." This account of sense differs pretty radically from the accounts of "sensation" usually given in books on psychology but nevertheless it tells how colors, sounds, contacts actually function in giving direction to the course of human activity. We may summarize the matters which fall within the common sense frame of reference as those of the uses and enjoyments common to mankind, or to a given community. How, for example, should the *water* of direct and familiar acquaintance (as distinct from H_2O of the scientific frame) be described save as that which quenches thirst, cleanses the body and soiled articles, in which one swims, which may drown us, which supports boats, which as rain furthers growth of crops, which in contemporary community life runs machinery, including locomotives, etc., etc.? One has only to take account of the water of common use and enjoyment to note the absurdity of reducing water to an assemblage of "sensations," even if motor-muscular elements are admitted. Both sensory qualities and motor responses are without place and significance save as they are enmeshed in uses and enjoyments. And it is *the latter* (whether in terms of water or any

4. Both passages are quoted from the *Oxford Dictionary*. The first and more general one dates in the illustrative passage cited over one hundred years earlier than the more limited personal usage of the second use. Together they cover what are sometimes spoken of as "objective" and "subjective" uses, thus anticipating in a way the point to be made next.

substance) which is a *thing* for common sense. We have only to pay attention to cases of which this case of water is representative, to learn respect for the way in which children uniformly describe things,—"It's what you do so-and-so with." The dictionary statement in which a thing is specified as "*that* with which one is occupied, engaged, concerned, busied," replaces a particular "*so-and-so*" by the generalized "*that,*" and a particular *you* by the generalized *one.* But it retains of necessity the children's union of self-and-thing.

II

The words "occupied, engaged, concerned, busied," etc., repay consideration in connection with the distinctive subjectmatter of common sense. *Matter* is one of the and-so-forth expressions. Here is what the dictionary says of it:—"A thing, affair, concern, corresponding to the Latin *res,* which it is often used to render." A further statement about the word brings out most definitely the point made about children's way of telling about anything as something in which a human being and environmental conditions cooperate:—"An event, circumstance, state or course of things which is the object of consideration or of practical concern." I do not see how anything could be more inclusive on the side of what philosophers have regarded as "outer or external" than the words found in the first part of the statement quoted; while "consideration and practical concern" are equally inclusive on the side of the "inner" and "private" component of philosophical dualisms.[5]

Since "subject, affair, business" are mentioned as synonyms of matter, we may turn to them to see what the dictionary says, noting particularly the identification of a "*subject*" with "*object of consideration.*" *Concern* passed from an earlier usage (in which it was virtually a synonym of *dis-cern*) over into an object of care, solicitude, even anxiety; and then into that "with which one is busied, occupied," and *about* which one is called upon to act. And in view of the present tendency to restrict *business* to

5. This case, reinforced by others to follow, is perhaps a sufficient indication of the need philosophy has to pay heed to words that focus attention upon human activities as transactions in living.

financial concern, it is worth while to note that its original sense
or force was *care, trouble. Care* is highly suggestive in the usage.
It ranges from solicitude, through caring *for* in the sense of
fondness, and through being deeply stirred, over to caring *for* in
the sense of *taking* care, looking after, paying attention systematically, or *minding. Affair* is derived from the French *à faire.* Its
usage has developed through love-intrigues and through business
affairs into "what one has to do or has ado with"; a statement
which is peculiarly significant in that *ado* has changed from its
original sense of that which is *a doing* over into a doing "that is
forced on one, a difficulty, trouble." *Do* and *ado* taken together
pretty well cover the conjoint under*takings* and under*goings*
which constitute that "state and course of things which is the object of consideration or practical concern." Finally we come to
thing. It is so far from being the metaphysical substance or logical entity of philosophy that is external and presumably physical,
that it is "that with which one is concerned in action, speech, or
thought":—three words whose scope not only places *things* in
the setting of transactions having human beings as partners, but
which so cover the whole range of human activity that we may
leave matters here for the present.[6] I cannot refrain, however,
from adding that the words dealt with convey in idiomatic terms
of common sense all that is intended to be conveyed by the technical term *Gestalt,* without the rigid fixity of the latter and with
the important addition of emphasis on the human partner.

It does not seem as if comment by way of interpretation were
needed to enforce the significance of what has been pointed out. I
invite, however, specific attention to two points, both of which
have been mentioned in passing. The words "concern," "affair,"
"care," "matter," "thing," etc., fuse in indissoluble unity senses
which when discriminated are called *emotional, intellectual,
practical,* the first two being moreover marked traits of the last
named. Apart from a given context, it is not even possible to tell
which one is uppermost; and when a context of use is present, it
is always a question of emphasis, never of separation. The supremacy of subjectmatters of concern, etc., over distinctions usually made in psychology and philosophy, cannot be denied by
anyone who attends to the facts. The other consideration is even

6. All passages in quotation marks are from the *Oxford Dictionary.*

more significant. What has been completely divided in philosophical discourse into man *and* the world, inner *and* outer, self
and not-self, subject *and* object, individual *and* social, private
and public, etc., are in actuality parties in life-transactions. The
philosophical "problem" of how to get them together is artificial.
On the basis of fact, it needs to be replaced by consideration of
the conditions under which they occur as *distinctions,* and of the
special uses served by the distinctions.[7]

Distinctions are more than legitimate *in their place.* The trouble
is not with making distinctions; life-behavior develops by making
two distinctions grow where one—or rather none—grew before.
Their place lies in cases of uncertainty with respect to *what* is to
be done and *how* to do it. The prevalence of "wishful thinking,"
of the danger of allowing the emotional to determine what is
taken to be a cognitive reference, suffices to prove the need for
distinction-making in this respect. And when uncertainty acts to
inhibit (suspend) immediate activity so that what otherwise
would be *overt* action is converted into an *examination* in which
motor energy is channeled through muscles connected with
organs of looking, handling, etc., a distinction of the factors
which are obstacles from those that are available as resources is
decidedly in place. For when the obstacles and the resources are
referred, on the one hand, to the self as a factor and, on the
other hand, to conditions of the medium-of-action as factors,
a distinction between "inner" and "outer," "self" and "world"
with respect to cases of this kind finds a legitimate place within
"the state and course" of life-concerns. Petrifaction of distinctions of this kind, that are pertinent and recurrent in specific conditions of action, into inherent (and hence absolute) separations
is the "vicious" affair.

7. The list given can be much extended. It includes "pursuit, report, issue, involvement, complication, entanglement, embarrassment; enterprise, undertaking, undergoing," and "experience" as a double-barreled word. As a general thing it would be well to use such words as *concern, affairs,* etc., where
now the word *experience* is used. They are specific where the latter word is
general in the sense of vague. Also they are free from the ambiguity that attends
experience on account of the controversies that have gathered about it. However, when a name is wanted to emphasize the inter-connectedness of all concerns, affairs, pursuits, etc., and it is made clear that *experience* is used in that
way, it may serve the purpose better than any word that is as yet available.

Philosophical discourse is the chief wrong-doer in this matter. Either directly or through psychology as an ally it has torn the intellectual, the emotional, and the practical asunder, erecting each into an entity, and thereby creating the artificial problem of getting them back into working terms with one another. Especially has this taken place in philosophy since the scientific revolution of a few centuries ago. For the assumption that it constituted natural science an entity complete in and of itself necessarily set man and the world, mind and nature as mindless, subject and object, inner and outer, the moral and the physical, fact and value, over against one another as inherent, essential, and therefore *absolute* separations. Thereby, with supreme irony, it renders the very existence of extensive and ever-growing knowledge the source of the "problem" of how knowledge is possible anyway.

This splitting up of things that exist together has brought with it, among other matters, the dissevering of philosophy from human life, relieving it from concern with administration of its affairs and of responsibility for dealing with its troubles. It may seem incredible that human beings as *living* creatures should so deny themselves as alive. In and of itself it is incredible; it has to be accounted for in terms of historic-cultural conditions that made heaven, not the earth; eternity, not the temporal; the supernatural, not the natural, the ultimate worthy concern of mankind.

It is for such reasons as these that what has been said about the affairs and concerns of common sense is a significant matter (in itself as well as in the matter of connections with science to be discussed later) of concern. The attention that has been given to idiomatic, even colloquial, speech accordingly has a bearing upon philosophy. For such speech is closest to the affairs of everyday life; that is, of common (or shared) living. The intellectual enterprise which turns its back upon the matters of common sense, in the connection of the latter with the concerns of living, does so at its peril. It is fatal for an intellectual enterprise to despise the issues reflected in this speech; the more ambitious or pretentious its claims, the *more* fatal the outcome. It is, I submit, the growing tendency of "philosophy" to get so far away from vital issues which render its problems not only technical (to some extent a necessity) but such that the more they are discussed the more controversial are they and the further apart are philosophers among themselves:—a pretty sure sign that somewhere on the route a compass has been lost and a chart thrown away.

III

I come now to consideration of the frame of reference that demarcates the method and subjectmatter of science from that of common sense; and to the questions which issue from this difference. I begin by saying that however the case stands, they are *not* to be distinguished from one another on the ground that science is *not* a human concern, affair, occupation. For that is what it decidedly is. The issue to be discussed is that of the *kind* of concern or care that marks off scientific activity from those forms of human behavior that fall within the scope of common sense; a part of the problem involved (an important part) being how it happened that the scientific revolution which began a few short centuries ago has had as one outcome a general failure to recognize science as itself an important human concern, so that, as already remarked, it is often treated as a peculiar sort of entity on its own account—a fact that has played a central role in determining the course taken by epistemology in setting the themes of distinctively *modern* philosophy.

This fact renders it pertinent, virtually necessary in fact, to go to the otherwise useless pains of calling attention to the various features that identify and demarcate science as a concern. In the first place, it is a *work* and a work carried on by a distinct group or set of human beings constituting a profession having a special vocation, exactly as is the case with those engaged in law or medicine, although its distinction from the latter is becoming more and more shadowy as an increasing number of physicians engage in researches of practically the same kind as those engaged in by the men who rank as scientists; and as the latter increasingly derive their special problems from circumstances brought to the fore in issues arising in connection with the source and treatment of disease. Moreover, scientific inquiry as a particular kind of work is engaged in by a group of persons who have undergone a highly specialized training to fit them for doing that particular kind of work—"job" it would be called were it not for the peculiar aura that clings to pursuits labeled "intellectual." Moreover, the work is done in a special kind of workshop, specifically known as *labor*-atories and observatories, fitted out with a particular kind of apparatus for the carrying on of a special kind of occupation—which from the standpoint of the amount of monetary capital invested in it (although not from the side of its distinctive returns) is a business. Just here is a fitting place, probably *the* fitting place to note that not merely the physical equipment of scientific workshops is the net outcome of long centuries of prior *cultural* transformation of physiological processes (themselves developed throughout no one knows how many millions of years), but that the *intellectual* resources with which the work is done, indeed the very problems involved, are but an aspect of a continuing cultural activity: an aspect which, if one wishes to call attention to it *emphatically,* may be called a *passing* phase in view of what the work done *there and then* amounts to in its intimate and indispensable connection with all that has gone before and that is to go on afterwards. For what is done on a given date in a given observatory, laboratory, study (say of a mathematician) is after all but a re-survey of what *has* been going on for a long time and which *will* be incorporated, absorbed, along with it into an activity that will continue as long as the earth harbors man.

The work done could no more be carried out without its special equipment of apparatus and technical operations than could the production of glass or electricity or any one of the great number of industrial enterprises that have taken over as integral parts of *their* especial work processes originating in the laboratory. Lag of popular opinion and repute behind actual practice is perhaps nowhere greater than in the current ignoring of—too often ignorance of—the facts adduced; one of which is the supposition that scientific knowing is something done by the "mind," when in fact science as practiced today began only when the work done (i.e., life activities) by sense and movement was refined and extended by adoption of material devices and technological operations.

I may have overdone the task of indicating how and why "science" is a concern, a care, and an occupation, not a self-enclosed entity. Even if such is the case, what has been said leads directly up to the question:—What is the distinctive concern of science as a concern and occupation by which it is marked off from those of common sense that grow directly out of the conduct of living? In principle the answer is simple. Doing and knowing are both involved in common sense and science—involved so intimately as to be necessary conditions of their existence. Nor does the difference between common sense and science consist in the fact that knowing is the *important* consideration in science but not in common sense. It consists of the position occupied by each member in relation to the other. In the concerns of common sense knowing is as necessary, as important, as in those of science. But knowing there is for the sake of *agenda,* the *what* and the *how* of which have to be studied and to be learned—in short, *known* in order that the necessary affairs of everyday life be carried on. The relation is reversed in science as a concern. As already emphasized, doing and making are as necessarily involved as in any industrial technology. But they are carried on for the sake of advancing the system of knowings and knowns. In each case doing remains doing and knowing continues to be knowing. But the concern or care that is distinctively characteristic of common sense concern and of scientific concern, with respect to *what* is done and known, and *why* it is done and known, renders the subjectmatters that are proper, necessary, in the doings and knowings of the two concerns as different as is H_2O from the water we drink and wash with.

Nevertheless, the first named is *about* the last named, although what one consists of is sharply different from what the other consists *of.* The fact that what science is *of* is *about* what common sense subjectmatter is *of,* is disguised from ready recognition when science becomes so highly developed that the *immediate* subject of inquiry consists of what has *previously* been found out. But careful examination promptly discloses that unless the materials involved can be traced back to the material of common sense concerns there is nothing whatever for scientific concern to be concerned with. What is pertinent here is that science is the example, *par excellence,* of the liberative effect of abstraction. Science is *about* in the sense in which "about" is *away* from; and is *of* in the sense in which "of" is *off* from:—how far off is shown in the case repeatedly used, water as H_2O where use and enjoyment are sweepingly different from the uses and enjoyments which attend laboratory inquiry into the makeup of water. The liberative outcome of the abstraction that is supremely manifested in scientific activity is the transformation of the affairs of common sense concern which has come about through the vast return wave of the methods and conclusions of scientific concern into the uses and enjoyments (and sufferings) of everyday affairs; together with an accompanying transformation of judgment and of the emotional affections, preferences, and aversions of everyday human beings.

The concern of common sense knowing is "practical," that of scientific doing is "theoretical." But *practical* in the first case is not limited to the "utilitarian" in the sense in which that word is disparagingly used. It includes all matters of direct enjoyment that occur in the course of living because of transformation wrought by the fine arts, by friendship, by recreation, by civic affairs, etc. And "theoretical" in the second instance is far away from the *theoria* of pure contemplation of the Aristotelian tradition, and from any sense of the word that excludes elaborate and extensive doings and makings. Scientific knowing is that particular form of *practical* human activity which is concerned with the advancement of *knowing* apart from concern with *other* practical affairs. The adjective often affixed to knowing of this kind is "pure." The adjective is understandable on historic grounds, since it demanded a struggle—often called *warfare*—to free natural inquiry from subordination to institutional concerns that were irrelevant and indeed hostile to the business of inquiry. But the idea that exemption from subjection to considerations extraneous and alien to inquiry as such is inherent in the essence or nature of science *as an entity* is sheer hypostatization. The exemption has itself a *practical* ground. The actual course of scientific inquiry has shown that the best interests of human living in general, as well as those of scientific inquiry in particular, are best served by keeping such inquiry "pure," that is free, from interests that would bend the conduct of inquiry to serve concerns alien (and practically sure to be hostile) to the conduct of knowing as its own end and proper terminus. This end may be called the *ideal* of scientific knowing in the *moral* sense of that word—

a guide in conduct. Like other directive moral aims, it is far as yet from having attained complete supremacy:—any more than its present degree of "purity" was attained without a hard struggle against adverse institutional interests which tried to control the methods used and conclusions reached in which was asserted to be science:—as in the well-known instance when an ecclesiastical institution dictated to "science" in the name of particular religious and moral customs. In any case, it is harmful as well as stupid to refuse to note that "purity" of inquiry is something to be striven for and to be sustained by the scrupulous attention that depends upon noting that scientific knowing is one human concern growing out of and returning into other more primary human concerns. For though the existing state of science is *one* of the interests and cares that determine the selection of things to be investigated, it is not the only one. Problems are not self-selecting, and the *direction* taken by inquiry is determined by the human factors of dominant interest and concern that affect the choice of the matters to be specifically inquired into.

The position here taken, namely that science is a matter of concern for the conduct of inquiry *as inquiry* sharply counters such statements as that "science is the means of obtaining practical mastery over nature through understanding it," especially when this view is expressly placed in contrast with the view that the business of scientific knowing is to find out, to *know* in short. There can be no doubt that an important, a very important *consequence* of science is to obtain human mastery over nature. That fact is identical with the "return wave" that is emphasized. The trouble is that the view back of the quotation ignores entirely the kind of human *uses* to which "mastery" is put. It needs little discernment to see that this ignoring is in the interest of a preconceived dogma—in this particular case a Marxist one—of what genuine mastery consists of. What "*understanding*" nature means is dogmatically assumed to be already known, while in fact anything that legitimately can be termed *understanding* nature is the outcome of scientific inquiry, not something established independent of inquiry and determining the course of "science." That science is itself a form of doing, of practice, and that it inevitably has reflex consequences upon other forms of practices, is fully recognized in the account here given. But this fact is the very rea-

COMMON SENSE AND SCIENCE   255

son why scientific knowing should be conducted without pre-determination of the practical consequences that are to ensue from it. That is a question to be considered on its *own* account.

There is, then, a problem of high importance in this matter of the relation of the concerns of science and common sense with each other. It is not that which was taken up by historic epistemologies in attempting to determine which of the two is the "truer" representative of "reality." While a study of the various human interests, religious, economic, political-military, which have at times determined the direction pursued by scientific inquiry, contributes to clear vision of the problem, that study is itself historical rather than philosophical. The problem of concern may be introduced (as I see it) by pointing out that a reference to the *return* of scientific method and conclusions into the concerns of daily life is purely factual, descriptive. It contains no implication of anything honorific or *intrinsically* desirable. There is plenty of evidence that the outcome of the return (which is now going on at an ever-increasing speed and in ever-extending range) is a mixture of things approvable and to be condemned; of the desirable and the undesirable. The *problem,* then, concerns the possibility of giving direction to this return-wave so as to minimize evil consequences and to intensify and extend good consequences, and, if it is possible, to find out how such return is to be accomplished.

Whether the problem is called that of philosophy or not is in some respects a matter of names. But the problem is *here* whatever name be given. And for the future of philosophy the matter of names may prove vital. If philosophy surrenders concern with pursuit of Reality (which it does not seem to be successful in catching), it is hard to see what concern it can take for its distinctive care and occupation save that of an attempt to meet the need just indicated. Meantime, it is in line with the material of the present paper to recur to a suggestion already made: namely, that perhaps the simplest way of getting rid of the isolations, splits, divisions, that now trouble human living, is to take seriously the concerns, cares, affairs, etc., of common sense, as far as they are transactions which (i) are constituted by the indissoluble active union of human and non-human factors; in which (ii) traits and features called intellectual and emotional are so far from being independent of and isolated from practical concerns, things done and to be done, *facta* and *facienda,* that they belong to and are possessed by the one final practical affair—the state and course of life as a body of transactions.[8]

8. In the course of consulting the *Oxford Dictionary* (s.v. Organism) I found the following passage (cited from Tucker, 1705–1774): "When an artist has finished a fiddle to give all the notes in the gamut, but not without a hand to play upon it, this is an organism." Were the word *organism* widely understood as an organization in which a living body and environing conditions cooperate as fiddle and player work together, it would not have been necessary to repeat so often the expression "organic-environmental." The passage may also stand as a typical reminder of what a transaction is. The words "not without" are golden words, whether they are applied to the human or to the environmental partners in a transaction.

II.   A Trial Group of Names

Undertaking to find a few firm names for use in connection with the theory of knowledge—hoping thereby to promote cooperation among inquirers and lessen their frequent misinterpretations of one another—we at once found it essential to safeguard ourselves by presenting in explicit postulation the main characteristics of our procedure.[1]

The first aspect of this postulatory procedure to stress is that the firm namings sought are of that type of firmness attained by modern science when it aims at ever-increasing accuracy of specification rather than at exactness (q.v.) of formulation, thus rejecting the old verbal rigidities and leaving the paths of inquiry freely open to progress.

An observation which, we believe, any one can make when the actual procedures of knowledge theorists are examined is that these procedures deal with knowings in terms of knowns, and with knowns in terms of knowings, and with neither in itself alone. The epistemologist often comments casually on this fact, and sometimes discusses it at length, but rarely makes any deliberate effort to act upon it. No attempt at all, so far as we are aware, has been made to concentrate upon it as a dependable base for operations. We accept this observation and report as a sound basis for an inquiry under which the attainment of firm names may be anticipated, and we adopt it as our guiding postulation.

Such a postulation, wherever the inquiry is not limited to some particular activity of the passing moment but is viewed broadly in its full scope, will at once bring into the knowing and the known as joint subjectmatter all of their positings of "existence," inclusive of whatever under contrasting manners of approach

1. See Chapter 3.

might be presumed to be "reality" of action or of "being" under-lying them. Taking this subjectmatter of inquiry as one single system, the factual support for any theory of knowings is then found to lie within the spatial and temporal operations and con-clusions of accredited science. The alternative to this—and the sole alternative—is to make decision as to what is and what is not knowledge rest on dicta taken to be available independent of and prior to these scientific subjectmatters, but such a course is not for us.

Under this postulation we limit our immediate inquiry to knowings through namings, with the further postulation that the namings (as active behaviors of men) are themselves before us as the very knowings under examination. *If* the namings alone are *flatus vocis,* the named alone and apart from naming is *ens fatuum.*

The vague word "knowledge" (q.v.) in its scattered uses covers in an unorganized way much territory besides that of naming-knowing.[2] Especially to remark are the regions of perception-manipulation on the one hand, and the regions of mathematically symbolic knowledge on the other. These remain as recognized fields of specialized study for all inquiry into knowledge. Whether or not the word "knowledge" is to be retained for all of these fields as well as for namings-knowings is not a question of much impor-tance at the present imperfect stage of observation and report.

Some of the words here appraised may be taken as key-names for the postulation employed, and hence as touchstones for the other names. *Fact* is thus used for knowings-knowns in system in that particular range of knowings-knowns, namely, the namings-nameds, which is studied. *Designation* is used as a most general name for the naming phases of the process, and *Existence* as a most general name for the named phases. Attention is called to the distinction between *inter* and *trans* (the former the verbal locus of much serious contemporary confusion), and to the increasingly

2. How much territory the word "knowledge" is made to cover may be seen from what is reported of it in Runes' *The Dictionary of Philosophy* (1942). Knowledge appears as: "Relations known. Apprehended truth. Opposite of opinion. Certain knowledge is more than opinion, less than truth. Theory of knowledge, or epistemology (q.v.), is the systematic investigation and exposi-tion of the principles of the possibility of knowledge. In epistemology: the relation between object and subject."

firm employment of the words "aspect" and "phase" within the transactional framework of inspection.

Certain changes are made from our earlier recommendations.[3] "Existence" replaces "event," since we have come to hope that it may now be safely used. "Event," then, replaces "occurrence." "Definition" has been demoted from its preliminary assignment, since continued studies of its uses in the present literature show it so confused as to rate no higher than a crude characterization. "Symbolization" has been given the duty of covering the territory which, it was earlier hoped, "definition" could cover. "Exact" for symbolization has been substituted for "precise," in correlation with "accurate" for specification. The names "behavior-object" and "behavior-agent" have been dropped, as not needed at the present stage of inquiry, where object and organism suffice.

The reader will understand that what is sought here is clarification rather than insistent recommendation of particular names; that even the most essential postulatory namings serve the purpose of "openers," rather than of "determiners"; that if the distinctions herein made prove to be sound, then the names best to be used to mark them may be expected to adjust themselves in the course of time under attrition of the older verbal abuses; and that every division of subjectmatters through disjunction of names must be taken in terms of the underlying conjunctions that alone make the disjunctions soundly practicable by providing safety against absolutist applications.

Accurate: When specification is held separate from symbolization (q.v.), then separate adjectives are desirable to characterize degrees of achievement in the separate ranges. Accurate is recommended in the case of specification. See *Exact.*

Action, Activity: These words are used by us in characterizations of durational-extensional subjectmatters only. Where a stressed substantive use of them is made, careful specification should be given; otherwise they retain and promote vagueness.

Actor: A confused and confusing word; offering a primitive and usually deceptive organization for the complex behavioral transactions the organism is engaged in. Under present postula-

---

3. Compare especially the tentative list of words suggested at the close of Chapter 2.

tion Actor should always be taken as postulationally transactional, and thus as a Trans-actor.

Application: The application of a name to an object may often be spoken of advantageously where other phrasings mislead. See *Reference.*

Aspect: The components of a full transactional situation, being not independents, are aspects. The word is etymologically correct; the verb "aspect" is "to look out." See *Phase.*

Behavior: A behavior is always to be taken transactionally: i.e., never as *of* the organism alone, any more than *of* the environment alone, but always as of the organic-environmental situation, with organisms and environmental objects taken as equally its aspects. Studies of these aspects in provisional separation are essential at many stages of inquiry, and are always legitimate when carried on under the transactional framework, and through an inquiry which is itself recognized as transactional. Transactionally employed, the word "behavior" should do the work that "experience" has sought to do in the past, and should do it free from the shifting, vague, and confused applications which have in the end come to make the latter word so often unserviceable. The phrase "human behavior" would then be short for "behavior with the understanding that is human."

Behavioral: Behavioral inquiry is that level of biological inquiry in which the processes examined are not currently explorable by physical or physiological (q.v.) techniques. To be understood in freedom equally from behavioristic and from mentalistic allusions. Covers equally the ranges called "social" and those called "individual."

Biological: Inquiry in which organic life is the subjectmatter, and in which the processes examined are not currently explorable by physical (q.v.) techniques; covers both physiological and behavioral inquiry.

Characterization: The intermediate stage of designation in the evolutionary scale, with cue (q.v.) preceding, and specification (q.v.) following; includes the greater part of the everyday use of words; reasonably adequate for the commoner practical purposes.

Circularity: Its appearance is regarded as a radical defect by non-transactional epistemological inquiries that undertake to organize "independents" as "reals." Normal for inquiry into knowings and knowns in system.

Coherence: Suggests itself for connection (q.v.) as established under specification, in distinction from consistency attained in symbolic process.

Concept, Conception: Conception has two opposed uses: on one side as a "mentalistic entity"; on the other as a current phrasing for subjectmatters designed to be held under steady inspection in inquiry. Only the latter is legitimate under our form of postulation. In any event the hypostatization set up by the word "concept" is to be avoided; and this applies to its appearance in formal logic even more than elsewhere.

Connection: To apply between objects under naming. See *Reference* and *Relation*.

Consciousness: The word has disappeared from nearly all research, but survives under various disguises in knowledge theory. Where substantively used as something other than a synonym of a comparable word, "awareness," we can find under our postulation no value whatever in it, or in its disguises, or in the attitudes of inquiry it implies.

Consistency: To be used exclusively in symbolic ranges. See *Coherence.*

Context: A common word in recent decades carrying many suggestions of transactional treatment. However, where it obscures the issues of naming and the named, i.e., when it swings obscurely between verbal and physical environments, it is more apt to do harm than good.

Cosmos: Commonly presents "universe as system." If the speaking-knowing organism is included in the cosmos, and if inquiry proceeds on that basis, cosmos appears as an alternative name for Fact (q.v.).

Cue: The earliest stage of designation in the evolutionary scale. Some recent psychological construction employs cue where the present study employs signal. Firm expression is needed in some agreed form. If a settled psychologist's use develops, then it, undoubtedly, should govern.

Definition: Most commonly employed for specification (q.v.), though with varied accompanying suggestions of dictionary, syllogistic, or mathematical adaptation. These latter, taken in a group, provide a startling exhibit of epistemological chaos. In recent years a specialized technical application has been under development for the word in formal logic. Establishment in this last use seems desirable, but the confusion is now so great that it is here deemed essential to deprive the word of all terminological status above that of a characterization (q.v.) until a sufficiently large number of experts in the fields of its technical employment can establish and maintain a specific use.[4]

Designation: The knowing-naming phase of fact. To be viewed always transactionally as behavior. The word "name" (q.v.) as a naming may advantageously be substituted wherever one can safely expect to hold it to behavioral understanding. Extends over three levels: cue, characterization, and specification.

Description: Cues organizing characterizations; characterizations developing into specifications. Not to be narrowed as is done when brought too sharply into contrast with narration as temporal. A name is, in effect, a truncated description. Somewhat similarly, with respect to an established name, a description may be called an expanded naming.

Entity: Assumed or implied physical, mental, or logical independence or semi-independence (the "semi" always vague or evasive) in some part of a subjectmatter under inquiry; thus, a tricky word, even when not positively harmful, which should be rejected in all serious inquiry. See *Thing* that, in its idiomatic use, is free from the misleading pretentiousness of entity.

Environment: Situations, events, or objects in connection (q.v.) with organism as object. Subject to inquiry physically, physiologically, and, in full transactional treatment, behaviorally.

Epistemological: As far as this word directly or indirectly assumes separate knowers and knowns (inclusive of to-be-knowns) all epistemological words are ruled out under transactional procedure.

Event: That range of differentiation of the named which is better specified than situation, but less well specified than object. Most commonly employed with respect to durational transition. (In earlier sketches employed where we now employ Existence.)

Exact: The requirement for symbolic procedure as distinguished from the requirement of accuracy (q.v.) for specification.

Excitation: A word suggested for specific use where *physio-*

4. Chapter 2, notes 16 and 23; Chapter 6, note 4; and Chapter 7, Section I.

logical process of environment and organism is concerned and where distinction from behavioral stimulus (q.v.) in the latter's specific use is required.

Existence: The known-named phase of fact, transactionally inspected. Established through designation under an ever-increasing requirement of accuracy in specification. Hence for a given era in man's advance, it covers the established objects in the evolving knowing of that era. Not permitted entry as if at the same time both a "something known" and a "something else" supporting the known. Physical, physiological, and behavioral subjectmatters are here taken as equally existential, however different the technical levels of their treatment in inquiry at a given time may be. Both etymologically and in practical daily uses this application of the word is far better justified than is an extra-behavioral or absolutist rendering (whether physicalist or mentalist) under some form of speculative linguistic manipulation.

Experience: This word has two radically opposed uses in current discussion. These overlap and shift so as to cause continual confusion and unintentional misrepresentation. One stands for short extensive-durational process, an extreme form of which is identification of an isolated sensory event or "sensation" as an ultimate unit of inquiry. The other covers the entire spatially extensive, temporally durational application; and here it is a counterpart for the word "cosmos." The word "experience" should be dropped entirely from discussion unless held strictly to a single definite use: that, namely, of calling attention to the fact that *Existence* has organism and environment as its aspects, and cannot be identified with either as an independent isolate.

Fact: The cosmos in course of being known through naming by organisms, themselves among its phases. It is knowings-knowns, durationally and extensionally spread; not what is known to and named by any one organism in any passing moment, nor to any one organism in its lifetime. Fact is under way among organisms advancing in a cosmos, itself under advance as known. The word "fact," etymologically from *factum,* something done, with its temporal implications, is much better fitted for the broad use here suggested than for either of its extreme and less common, though more pretentious applications: on the one hand for an independent "real"; on the other for a "mentally" endorsed report. Whether the word may properly apply to the cosmic pre-

sentation of inferior non-communicating animals, or to that of a
superior realm of non-naming symbols, is for others to develop
at other times and places. *See* Chapter 2, Section IV.

Field: On physical analogies this word should have important
application in behavioral inquiry. The physicist's uses, however,
are still undergoing reconstructions, and the definite correspondence needed for behavioral application cannot be established.
Too many current projects for the use of the word have been
parasitic. Thorough transactional studies of behaviors on their
own account are needed to establish behavioral field in its own
right.

Firm: As applied to a proposed terminology for knowings and
knowns this word indicates the need of accuracy (q.v.) of specification, never that of exactness of symbolization. For the most
firm, one is to take that which is least vague, and which at the
same time is most free from assumed finality—where professed
finality itself, perhaps, is the last word in vagueness.

Idea, Ideal: Underlying differences of employment are so many
and wide that, where these words are used, it should be made
clear whether they are used behaviorally or as names of presumed existences taken to be strictly mental.

Individual: Abandonment of this word and of all substitutes
for it seems essential wherever a positive *general theory* is undertaken or planned. Minor specialized studies in individualized
phrasing should expressly name the limits of the application of
the word, and beyond that should hold themselves firmly within
such limits. The word "behavior" (q.v.) as presented in this vocabulary covers both individual and social (q.v.) on a transactional basis in which the distinction between them is aspectual.

Inquiry: A strictly transactional name. It is an equivalent of
knowing, but preferable as a name because of its freedom from
"mentalistic" associations.

Inter: This prefix has two sets of applications (see *Oxford
Dictionary*). One is for "between," "in-between," or "between
the parts of." The other is for "mutually," "reciprocally." The result of this shifting use as it enters philosophy, logic, and psychology, no matter how inadvertent, is ambiguity and undepen-
dability. The habit easily establishes itself of mingling without
clarification the two sets of implications. It is here proposed to
eliminate ambiguity by confining the prefix *inter* to cases in

which "in between" is dominant, and to employ the prefix *trans* where the mutual and reciprocal are intended.

Interaction: This word, because of its prefix, is undoubtedly the source of much of the more serious difficulty in discussion at the present time. Legitimate and illegitimate uses in various branches of inquiry have been discussed in chapters 4 and 5. When transactional and interactional treatments come to be explicitly distinguished,[5] progress in construction should be more easily made. For the general theory of knowings and knowns, the interactional approach is entirely rejected under our procedure.

Knowledge: In current employment this word is too wide and vague to be a *name* of anything in particular. The butterfly "knows" how to mate, presumably without learning; the dog "knows" its master through learning; man "knows" through learning how to do an immense number of things in the way of arts or abilities; he also "knows" physics, and "knows" mathematics; he knows *that, what,* and *how.* It should require only a moderate acquaintance with philosophical literature to observe that the vagueness and ambiguity of the word "knowledge" accounts for a large number of the traditional "problems" called *the problem of knowledge.* The issues that must be faced before firm use is gained are: Does the word "knowledge" indicate something the organism possesses or produces? Or does it indicate something the organism confronts or with which it comes into contact? Can either of these viewpoints be coherently maintained? If not, what change in preliminary description must be sought?

Knowings: Organic phases of transactionally observed behaviors. Here considered in the familiar central range of namings-knowings. The correlated organic aspects of signalings and symbolings are in need of transactional systematization with respect to namings-knowings.

Knowns: Environmental phases of transactionally observed behaviors. In the case of namings-knowings the range of the knowns is that of existence within fact or cosmos, not in a limitation to the recognized affirmations of the moment, but in process of advance in long durations.

---

5. Transactions: doings, proceedings, dealings. Interaction: reciprocal action or influence of persons or things on each other (*Oxford Dictionary*).

Language: To be taken as behavior of men (with extensions such as the progress of factual inquiry may show to be advisable into the behaviors of other organisms). Not to be viewed as composed of word-bodies apart from word-meanings, nor as word-meanings apart from word-embodiment. As behavior, it is a region of knowings. Its terminological status with respect to symbolings or other expressive behaviors of men is open for future determination.

Manipulation: See *Perception-Manipulation.*

Matter, Material: See *Physical* and *Nature.* If the word "mental" is dropped, the word "material" (in the sense of matter as opposed to mind) falls out also. In every-day use, both "mental" and "material" rate at the best as characterizations. In philosophy and psychology the words are often degraded to "cues."

Mathematics: A behavior developing out of earlier naming activities, which, as it advances, more and more gains independence of namings and specializes on symboling. See *Symbol.*

Meaning: A word so confused that it is best never used at all. More direct expressions can always be found. (Try for example, speaking in terms of "is," or "involves.") The transactional approach does away with that split between disembodied meanings and meaningless bodies for meanings which still enters flagrantly into much discussion.

Mental: This word not used by us. Usually indicates an hypostatization arising from a primitively imperfect view of behavior, and not safe until the splitting of existence into two independent isolates has been generally abandoned. Even in this latter case the word should be limited to service as emphasizing an aspect of existence. See *Behavior* and *Transaction.*

Name, Naming, Named: Language behavior in its central ranges. Itself a form of knowing. Here, at times, temporarily and technically replaced by the word "designation," because of the many traditional, speculatively evolved, applications of the word "name," closely corresponding to the difficulties with the word "concept" (q.v.), many of them still redolent of ancient magic. The word "name" will be preferred to the word "designation," as soon as its use can be assumed in fully transactional form and free from conventional distortions.

Nature: See *Cosmos* and *Fact.* Here used to represent a single system of subjectmatters of inquiry, without implication of predetermined authoritative value such as is usually intended when the word "natural*ism*" is used.

Object: Within fact, and within its existential phase, object is that which acquires firmest specification, and is thus distinguished from situation and event. This holds to the determination of Dewey (*Logic,* p. 119; also pp. 129, 520, *et al.* [*Later Works* 12:122, 132, 513]) that in inquiry object "emerges as a definite constituent of a resolved situation, and is confirmed in the continuity of inquiry," and is "subject-matter, so far as it has been produced and ordered in settled form."

Objective: A crude characterization which seems easily enough intelligible until one observes that in the behavioral sciences almost every investigator calls his own program objective, regardless of its differences from the many self-styled objective offerings that have gone before. As often employed the word has merely the import of impartial, which might advantageously replace it. Objective is used so frequently to characterize aspects of "subject" rather than of "object," that its own status with respect both to subject and to object should be carefully established before use.

Observation: To be taken as durationally and extensionally transactional, and thus neither separately in terms of the observing, nor separately in terms of the observed. Always to be viewed in the concrete instance but never as substantively stressed "act," nor in any other way as isolated or independent. Always to be postulationally guarded in current technical employment, and always to remain tentative with respect to future observing and knowing. See *Experience.*

Operational: The word "operation" as applied to behavior in recent methodological discussions should be thoroughly overhauled and given the full transactional status that such words as "process" and "activity" (q.v.) require. The military use of the word is suggestive of the way to deal with it.

Organism: Taken as transactionally existent in cosmos. Presentations of it in detachment or quasi-detachment are to be viewed as tentative or partial.

Organization: See *System.*

Percept: To be taken transactionally as phase of signaling behavior. Never to be hypostatized as if itself independently "existing."

Perception-Manipulation: Taken jointly and inseparably as the range of signal behaviors. Differences between perception and manipulation seemed striking in the earlier stages of the development of psychology, but today's specialization of inquiry should not lose sight of their common behavioral status.

Phase: Aspect of fact in sufficiently developed statement to exhibit definite spatial and temporal localizations.

Phenomenon: A word that still has possibilities of convenient use, if deprived of all of those implications commonly called subjective, and used for provisional identifications of situation with no presumptive "phenomenine" behind it for further reference.

Physical: One of the three, at present, outstanding divisions of the subjectmatters of inquiry. Identifiable through technical methods of investigation and report, not through purported differences in material or other forms of purported substance.

Physiological: That portion of biological inquiry which forms the second outstanding division of the subjectmatter of all inquiry as at present in process; differentiated from the physical by the techniques of inquiry employed more significantly than by mention of its specialized organic locus. See *Behavioral.*

Pragmatic: This word is included here (but no other of its kind except epistemological) solely to permit a warning against its current degradation in making it stand for what is practical to a single organism in limited durational spread—this being a use remote from that of its origin.

Process: To be used aspectually or phasally. See *Activity.*

Proposition: Closely allied to proposal both etymologically and in practical daily use. Widely divorced from this, and greatly confused in its current appearances in the logics. Many efforts in the last two decades to distinguish it clearly from assertion, statement, sentence, and other words of this type upon the basis of the older self-oriented logics, have only served to increase the difficulties. Sufficient light is thrown upon its status by its demand, concealed or open, that its component terms be independent fixities while at the same time it hypostatizes itself into an ultimate fixity. Treated in Dewey's *Logic: The Theory of Inquiry* under radically different construction as an intermediate and instrumental stage in inquiry.

Reaction: To be coupled with excitation in *physiological* reference (q.v.).

Real: Its use to be completely avoided when not as a recognized synonym for genuine as opposed to sham or counterfeit.

Reality: As commonly used, it may rank as the most metaphysical of all words in the most obnoxious sense of metaphysics, since it is supposed to name something which lies underneath and behind all knowing, and yet, as Reality, something incapable of being known in fact and as fact.

Reference: Behavioral application of naming to named. See *Connection* and *Relation*.

Relation: Various current uses, ranging from casual to ostentatious; rarely with any sustained effort at localization of the "named," as is shown by ever-recurrent discussions (and, what is worse, evasions) as to whether relation (assumed to have a certain existence somewhere as itself factual) is "internal" or "external." Suggested by us to name system among words, in correlation with reference and connection (q.v.).[6]

Response: To be coupled with stimulus in the signal range of behavior.

Science, Scientific: Our use of this word is to designate the most advanced stage of specification of our times—the "best knowledge" by the tests of employment and indicated growth.

Self: Open to aspectual examination under transactional construction. Where substantively stressed as itself an object, self should not be permitted also an aura of transactional values, tacitly, and apart from express development.[7]

Self-Action: Used to indicate various primitive treatments of the known, prior in historical development to interactional and transactional treatments. Rarely found today except in philosophical, logical, epistemological, and a few limited psychological regions of inquiry.

Sentence: No basic distinction of sentence from word nor of meaning of sentence from verbal embodiment of sentence remains when language is viewed as transactionally behavioral.

6. See Dewey, *Logic: The Theory of Inquiry* (New York, 1938), p. 55 [*Later Works* 12:61], for such a presentation.
7. In illustration: Mead's wide-ranging transactional inquiries are still taken by most of his followers in the sense of interesting comments on an object, namely the "self," in independence.

Sign: This name applied transactionally to organic-environmental behavior. To be understood always as sign-process; never with localization of sign either in organism or in environment separately taken. Hence never as if signs were of two kinds: the natural and the artificial. Coterminous with behavioral process, and thus technically characteristic of all behaviors viewed in their knowing-known aspects. Distinctive as technical mark of separation of behavioral from physiological process, with the disjointure of research in the present day on this borderline more marked than that on the borderline between physics and physiology, where biophysics is making strong advance. Evolutionary stages and contemporary levels differentiated into signal, name, and symbol.

Sign-Process: Synonym for *Sign.*

Signal: The perceptive-manipulative level and stage of sign in transactional presentation. Border-regions between signaling and naming still imperfectly explored, and concise characterizations not yet available.

Situation: The more general, and less clearly specified, range of the named phase of fact. In our transactional development, the word is not used in the sense of environment; if so used, it should not be allowed to introduce transactional implications tacitly.

Social: The word in its current uses is defective for all *general* inquiry and theory. See *Individual.*

Space-Time: Space and time alike to be taken transactionally and behaviorally—never as fixed or given frames (formal, absolute, or Newtonian) nor exclusively as physical specializations of the types known since relativity.[8]

Specification: The most highly perfected naming behavior. Best exhibited in modern science. Requires freedom from the defectively realistic application of the form of syllogism commonly known as Aristotelian.

Stimulus: An unclarified word, even for most of its key-word uses in psychology. The possibility of an adequate transactional specification for it will be a critical test of transactional construc-

8. See Bentley, "The Factual Space and Time of Behavior," the *Journal of Philosophy,* XXXVIII (1941), 477–485.

tion. The indicated method of procedure will be through the thorough-going substitution of nouns of action such as "stimulation" in place of substantive nouns such as "stimulus" is usually taken to be.

Subject: This word can profitably be dropped, so long as subjects are presented as in themselves objects. Subject was object in Greece and remains unclarified today. Might be properly used, perhaps, in the sense of "topic" as "subjectmatter undergoing inquiry," in differentiation from "object" as "subjectmatter determined by inquiry."

Subjective: Even less dependable as a word than objective (q.v.).

Subjectmatter: Whatever is before inquiry where inquiry has the range of namings-named. The main divisions in present-day research are into physical, physiological, and behavioral.

Substance: No word of this type has place in the present system of formulation. See *Entity*.

Symbol: A non-naming component of symboling behavior. To be taken transactionally, and not in hypostatization. Thus comparable with name and signal.

Symboling, Symbolization: An advance of sign beyond naming, accompanied by disappearance of specific reference (q.v.) such as naming develops.

System: Perhaps a usable word where transactional inquiry is under way. Thus distinguished from organization which would represent interaction. "Full system" has occasionally been used to direct attention to deliberately comprehensive transactional procedure.

Term: This word has today accurate use as a name only in mathematical formulation where, even permitting it several different applications, no confusion results. The phrase "in terms of" is often convenient and, simply used, is harmless. In the older syllogism term long retained a surface appearance of exactness (q.v.) which it lost when the language-existence issues involved became too prominent. For the most part in current writing it seems to be used loosely for "word carefully employed." It is, however, frequently entangled in the difficulties of concept. Given sufficient agreement among workers, term could perhaps be safely used for the range of specification, and this without complications arising from its mathematical uses. It might, then, be characterized as follows: Term: a firm name as established through inquiry; particularly, a name for the group of all those names that name whatever has acquired technically assured standing as object.

Thing: Most generally used for anything named. This very generality gives it frequent advantage over its pretentious substitutes, Entity and Substance, and more particularly over Object in the common case in which the type of objectivity involved is not specified. Though sometimes facilitating epistemological or logical evasion, its very looseness of application is safer than the insufficiently analyzed rigidities of the other words mentioned. *See* Chapter 2, note 3, Chapter 4, note 7, and Chapter 10, Section II.

Time: See *Space-Time.*

Trans: This prefix has, in older usage, the sense of beyond, but in much recent development it stands for across, from side to side, etc. To be stressed is the radical importance at the present time of a clear differentiation between trans and inter (q.v.).

Transaction: The knowing-known taken as one process in cases in which in older discussions the knowings and knowns are separated and viewed as in interaction. The knowns and the named in their turn taken as phases of a common process in cases in which otherwise they have been viewed as separated components, allotted irregular degrees of independence, and examined in the form of interactions. See *Interaction.*

Transactor: See *Actor.*

True, Truth: These words lack accuracy in modern professedly technical uses, in that the closer they are examined, it frequently happens, the more inaccurate they appear. "Warranted assertion" (Dewey) is one form of replacement. Confinement to "semantic" instances is helpful, so far as "semantic" itself gains accuracy of use. A subjectmatter now in great need of empirical inquiry, with such inquiry apparently wholly futile under traditional approaches.

Vague: This word is itself vaguely used, and this as well in our preceding inquiries as elsewhere. It should be replaced by names specifying the kind and degree of inaccuracy or inexactness implied.

Word: To be used without presumptive separation of its "meaning" as "mental" from its "embodiment" (air-waves, marks on paper, vocal utterances, etc.) as "physical"; in other words, to be taken always as behavioral transaction, and thus as a subject-matter examined whole as it comes, rather than in clumsily fractured bits.

Some of the above words enter our trial group of names as representative of the postulation we have adopted. The remainder fall into two sub-groups: words, namely, that may probably be clarified and salvaged, and others that show themselves so confused and debased that we unqualifiedly urge their rejection from all technical discourse at the present time. This is as far as we have been able to proceed in terminological systematization under the chaotic state of current discussion.

With respect to our central postulations: first, that knowings-knowns are to be transactionally studied, and secondly, that namings, when transactionally studied, show themselves as directly existential knowings, we renew our repeated reminder and caution. We are all aware that knowings, as behaviors, lie within, or among, wider ranges of behaviors. We are also all aware that the word "knowing" is itself variously applied to phenomena at perhaps every scattered stage of behavior from the earliest and simplest organic orientations to the most complex displays of putatively extrapolated supra-organic pseudocertainties. The range of our own inquiry—the central range of technically transactional fact-determination—will be declared by some readers to demand its own "interpretation" on the basis of behavioral activities taken as antecedent and "causal" to it. By others all inquiry in our range will be declared to be under the control of powers detached from, and presumptively "higher" than, any such behavioral activity. Our own assertion is that, no matter how dogmatically either of these declarations may be made, the passage of time will more and more require an ever broadening and deepening inquiry into the characteristic processes of organization and system they involve. It is our hope that the more naïve fiats will some day cease to be satisfactory even to their most ardent pronouncers. Progress from stylized cue or loose characterization to careful specification becomes thus a compelling need, and it is with the possibilities of such progress under postulation that we have here experimented. Detachable empiricals and detachable rationals are alike rejected.

Finally, both with regard to postulation and to terminology, we are *seeking* the firm (q.v.) and not trying to decree it.

12. Summary of Progress Made

The research upon which we have made report has exhibited itself in three main phases: at the beginning, an endeavor to secure dependable namings in the chosen field; next, a display of the current linguistic insecurity in activities in those fields; thirdly, an initial development of the transactional approach which becomes necessary, in our view, if reliable namings are to be secured. The first of these phases is presented in Chapters 2, 3, and 11, and has been allowed to rest with such terminological suggestions as the last of these chapters offers. The second, seen in Chapters 1, 7, 8, and 9, was expanded far beyond preliminary expectation, as it became clear to us that, without increased recognition of the extent of the underlying linguistic incoherence, little attention would be paid to the need for reform. The third was sketched in Chapters 4, 5, 6, and 10; its further development remains for later presentation in psychological, linguistic, and mathematical ranges corresponding to the levels of Signal, Designation, and Symbol within Behavior.

In most general statement our chosen postulatory approach presents the human organism as a phase of cosmic process along with all of his activities including his knowings and even his own inquiries into his knowings as themselves knowns. The knowings are examined within the ranges of the known, and the knowns within the ranges of the knowing; the word "ranges" being here understood, not as limiting the research in any way, but as vouching for its full freedom and openness. This approach does not imply an absorption of knowing activities into a physical cosmos, any more than it implies an absorption of the physical cosmos into a structure of knowings. It implies neither. This must be most emphatically asserted. Emphasis is all the more necessary because the position of the present writers, whether in their separate inquiries or in the present joint undertaking, is so frequently mis-stated. In illustration, two recent notices of our procedure in the technical journal that we regard as standing closest to our field of inquiry [1] have described us as neglecting a difference, radical in nature, taken to exist between psychological and logical facts: a difference which, they appear to hold, ought to be known to everyone as crucial for all inquiries in this field. One reviewer goes even further, in disregard of our most explicit expression at other points, when from a detached preliminary phrase he infers that we reject "abstraction" from both mathematical and logical operations. This latter opinion will, we feel sure, be dissipated upon even the most hasty survey of our texts. The former is likewise a misunderstanding that cannot maintain itself under study. We may assure all such critics that from early youth we have been aware of an *academic* and *pedagogical* distinction of logical from psychological. We certainly make no attempt to deny it, and we do not disregard it. Quite the contrary. Facing this distinction in the presence of the actual life processes and behaviors of human beings, we deny any rigid *factual* difference such as the academic treatment implies. Moreover, it has been our sustained effort throughout all our inquiry to show the practicability of theoretical construction upon a new basis by offering the beginnings of its development. We have as strong an objection to the assumption of a science of psychology severed from a logic and yet held basic to that logic, as we have to a logic severed from a psychology and proclaimed as if it existed in a realm of its own where it regards itself as basic to the psychology. We regard knowings and reasonings and mathematical and scientific adventurings even up to their highest abstractions, as activities of men—as veritably men's behaviors—and we regard the study of these particular knowing behaviors as lying within the general field of behavioral inquiry; while at the same time we regard psychological inquiry itself and all its facts and conclusions as being presented to us under the limitations and qualifications of their being known. None of this involves any interference with the practical differentiations of inquiry as between logic and psychology, any more than it interferes with

1. Alonzo Church, Review of four papers by John Dewey and Arthur F. Bentley, the *Journal of Symbolic Logic*, X (1945), pp. 132–133; Arthur Francis Smullyan, Review of the paper, "'Definition,'" by John Dewey and Arthur F. Bentley, *ibid.*, XII (1947), p. 99.

differentiations within either of these fields taken separately. Specializations of attention and effort based on methods and on subjectmatters methodologically differentiated remain as valid and usable as ever.

The difficulty in mutual understanding in such cases as the above lies, we believe, in the various conventionally frozen sets of implications which many of the crucial words that are employed carry over from the past, and which have not yet been resolved under factual examination. They are like the different focussings of different linguistic spectacles which yield strangely different pictures of presumptive fact. It is this deficiency in communication that calls for the extended examination we have given several of the leading current texts. It is this deficiency also that explains the often clumsy and labored expression we have permitted ourselves to retain in the endeavor to keep the right emphasis upon the intended subjects of our statements. Striking illustration of the dangers of ordinary rhetorical formulation have been provided several times in the course of preliminary publication through the effects that have followed some of the kindly efforts of proofreaders, copyeditors or other good friends to improve our diction by the use of conventional phrasings.

It is often claimed that work in our field of research should be confined to specific problems in limited regions, and that in this way alone can be found safety and escape from metaphysical traps. However we cannot accept this claim. For any reader who regards our procedures and postulations as more general than the present state of inquiry justifies, we suggest consideration of the closing words of Clerk Maxwell in his treatise, *Matter and Motion*, from which we have made earlier citations.[2] Maxwell was discussing the development of material systems, while we are interested in the development of knowledge systems. We cite him strictly upon an issue as to *methods of inquiry* useful in their proper times and places to man, the irrepressible inquirer, and without any implication whatever of preference for material systems over knowledge systems, or *vice versa*. His attention became concentrated upon the use of hypothesis in "molecular science," and he declared that the degree of success in its use "de-

---

2. J. Clerk Maxwell, *Matter and Motion* (London, 1891), Articles CXLVIII and CXLIX.

pends on the generality of the hypothesis we begin with." Given the widest generality, then we may safely apply the results we hypothetically secure. But if we frame our hypothesis too specifically and too narrowly then, even if we get resulting constructs agreeable to the phenomena, our chosen hypothesis may still be wrong, unless we can prove that no other hypothesis would account for the phenomena. And finally:

> It is therefore of the greatest importance in all physical inquiries that we should be thoroughly acquainted with the most general properties of material systems, and it is for this reason that in this book I have rather dwelt on these general properties than entered on the more varied and interesting field of the special properties of particular forms of matter.

With the word "behavioral" inserted for the words "physical" and "material," this well expresses our attitude towards our own inquiry. Since it was the mathematics of Clerk Maxwell, dealing with the unparalleled observations of Faraday, that led in the end to the Einsteinian transformation of Newtonian physics, upon one of the highest levels of the use of hypothesis that the world has known, there is much justification for citing Maxwell authoritatively upon this issue. The citation, of course, is not in any way used to give support to our own form of generalization. It applies, instead, to whatever wide-ranging treatment in this field may in the course of time succeed in establishing itself, whosesoever it may be. For the moment the argument is used solely against men of epistemological despair.

We stress once more what has been our theme throughout: namely, that Specification and Transaction, the one on the side of the knowings, the other on the side of the knowns, make common advance. Once under way, once free of the negations and suppressions of ancient verbal lineage, they will be able to make ever more rapidly their joint advances. They make possible at once full spatial-temporal localization, and reference within it to the concrete and specific instance.

Since we have repeatedly said that the recognition of underlying problems and the opening of paths for further construction seems more important to us than the pronouncement of conclusions, we add a memorandum of the places of original publication of our reports for the possible use of anyone desirous of appraising the changes of procedure that came about in the course of the development. The original of Chapter 8 appeared in *Philosophy of Science*, XIII (1946); that of Chapter 9 in *Philosophy and Phenomenological Research*, VIII (1947). The publication of the material of the other chapters was in the *Journal of Philosophy*, XLII, XLIII, XLIV, XLV (1945, 1946, 1947, 1948) and, except for that of Chapter 10, in the order in which the chapters appear in this volume. The preface and the summary in Chapter 12 were later added. The present Introduction accompanied Chapter 1 in the original publication.

Appendix
Dewey's Reply to Albert G. A. Balz

The following letter was written by John Dewey to a philosopher friend after the chapters of this volume were in type. The friend's questionings that elicited this reply will be found in the *Journal of Philosophy,* XLVI (1949), pp. 313–329 [see this volume, Appendix 1].

I

Discovery Bay,
Jamaica

My dear A——:

In sending you this letter I cannot do otherwise than begin with expressing my appreciation of the spirit in which you have written. I also wish to express my gratitude to you for affording me this opportunity to restate the position which, as you suggest, has occasioned difficulties to others as well as to yourself.

When, however, I began to write to you in reply, I found myself in a quandary; in fact, on the horns of a dilemma. On the one hand it seemed obligatory for me to take up each one of your difficulties one by one, and do what I could to clarify each point. The more, however, I contemplated that course, the more I became doubtful of its success in attaining the desired end of clarification. If, I thought, I had not been able to make my position clear in the course of several hundred pages, how can I expect to accomplish that end in the course of a small number of pages devoted to a variety of themes? The other horn of the dilemma was that failure to take up all your points might seem to show a disrespect for your queries and criticism which I am very far from feeling. While I was pondering this matter, I received a letter from a younger fellow student of philosophy. In this letter, written naturally in ignorance of our proposed discussion, he quoted some words written by me some thirty years or more ago. The passage reads: "As philosophers, our disagreements with one another as to conclusions are trivial in comparison with our disagreements as to problems; to see the problem another sees, in the same perspective and at the same angle—that amounts to something. Agreement as to conclusions is in comparison perfunctory."

When I read this sentence it was as if a light dawned. It then occurred to me that I should proceed by trying to show that what is said by me in the book which is the source of your intellectual difficulties, is set forth in a context which is determined, entirely and exclusively, by problems that arise in connection with a development of a Theory of Inquiry; that is, in the context of problems that arise in undertaking an inquiry into the facts of inquiry. Accordingly, I concluded that I might best accede to your request for clarification of the difficulties you have experienced by means of a fresh statement of some of the fundamentals of my position. Since your difficulties and questions hang together, I am sure you will find no disrespect in my treating them as a systematic whole instead of as if they were scattered, independent, and fragmentary. There is also no disrespect in the belief that their systematic nature is due to the fact that you read what was actually written in the context of connection with the conduct of *inquiry* as if it were written in an *ontological* context—especially as this latter context is classic, in comparison with which that set forth in my *Theory of Inquiry* is an upstart.

I hope, accordingly, dear A——, that you will understand why what is here said delays in coming to a direct answer to specific questions you raise. In order to make my position clear as a whole I have to begin at the beginning, which in the present case lies far back of your questions. I think, for example, that the importance in my writings of what is designated by the words "situation" and "problematic" must have escaped you. Whether this be so or not, we have right here at hand what seems to be an excellent example of their meaning. "Situation" stands for something inclusive of a large number of diverse elements existing across wide areas of space and long periods of time, but which, nevertheless, have their own unity. This discussion which we are here and now carrying on is precisely part of a situation. Your letter to me and what I am writing in response are evidently parts of that to which I have given the name "situation"; while these items are conspicuous features of the situation they are far from being the only or even the chief ones. In each case there is prolonged prior study: into this study have entered teachers, books, articles, and all the contacts which have shaped the views that now find themselves in disagreement with each other. It is this complex of fact that determines also the applicability of "problematic" to the present situation. That word stands for the existence of something questionable, and hence provocative of investigation, examination, discussion—in short, inquiry. However, the word "problematic" covers such a great variety of occasions for inquiry that it may be helpful to specify a number of them. It covers the features that are designated by such adjectives as confusing, perplexing, disturbed, unsettled, indecisive; and by such nouns as jars, hitches, breaks, blocks—in short, all incidents occasioning an interruption of the smooth, straightforward course of behavior and that deflect it into the kind of behavior constituting inquiry.

The foregoing, as I quite recognize, my dear friend, is an indirect approach to the questions you raise. Perhaps I can render it somewhat more direct by calling attention to the fact that the unsettled, indecisive character of the situation with which inquiry is compelled to deal affects all of the subjectmatters that enter into all inquiry. It affects, on the one hand, the observed existing facts that are taken to locate and delimit the problem; on the other side, it affects all of the suggestions, surmises, ideas that are entertained as possible solutions of the problem. There is, of course, nothing at all sacred in employing the words "potentiality" and "possibility" to designate the subjectmatters in inquiry that stand for progress made in determining, respectively, the problem and its solution. What is important, and from the standpoint of my position, all important, is that the tentative, on-trial nature of the subjectmatters involved in each case be recognized; while that recognition can hardly be attained unless some names are given. The indecisive and tentative nature of the subjectmatters involved might have been expressed by using either the word "potentiality" or the word "possibility" for the subjectmatters of both the problem and solution. But in that case, it would have been at once necessary to find sub-terms to designate the distinctive places held and the specific offices or functions performed by subjectmatters constituting what is taken during the conduct of inquiry, as on the one hand the problem to be dealt with and on the other hand the solution suggested: both of them, let it be recalled, being tentative on-trial since both are equally implicated in doubt and inquiry.

From the standpoint of conduct of inquiry it directly follows that the nature of the problem as well as of the solution to be reached is *under* inquiry; failure in solution is sure to result if the problem has not been properly located and described. While this fact is not offered as a justification of the use of the particular words "potentiality" and "possibility," given the standpoint of connection with inquiry, it does imperatively demand the use of two different words as *names* and as names for two disparate but complementary uses.

In any case, dear friend, what has been said has a much wider application than simply to the meaning to be assigned to these two words. For it indicates how and why meaning assigned to *any* phase or aspect of my position which puts what is said in an ontological context instead of that of inquiry is sure to go amiss in respect to understanding. And when I say this, I say it in full recognition of the fact that exclusion of the need of ontological backing and reference of any kind may quite readily convert your difficulty and doubt into outright rejection. But, after all, rejection based upon understanding is better than apparent agreement based on misunderstanding. I should be happy indeed, dear A——, to obtain your assent to my view, but failing that, I shall be quite content if I can obtain an understanding of what it is that my theory of inquiry is trying to do if and when it is taken to be, wholly and exclusively, a theory of knowledge.

II

I hardly need remind you that there is nothing new in recognizing that both observed facts and ideas, theories, rational principles, have entered in fundamental ways into historic discussion of philosophical theories of knowledge. There is nothing new to be found in the fact that I have made them the subject-matter of a problem. Whatever relative novelty may be found in my position consists in regarding the *problem* as belonging in the context of the conduct of inquiry and not in either the traditional ontological or the traditional epistemological context. I shall, accordingly, in the interest of elucidation attempt another line of approach: one in terms of familiar historical materials.

One outstanding problem of modern philosophy of knowledge is found in its long preoccupation with the controversy between empiricism and rationalism. Even today, when the controversy has receded at least temporarily into the background, it cannot be denied by one who surveys the course of the historical discussion that important statements were made with respect both to what was called experience and what was called reason, and this in spite of the fact that the controversy never reached the satisfactory conclusion constituted by the two parties arriving at agreement. It is not a mere biographical fact, accordingly, if I call attention to the fact that I am in no way an inventor of the problem in a theory of knowledge of the relation to each other of observed factual material on one side and ideational or theoretical material on the other side. The failure of the controversy to arrive at solution through agreement is an important ground of the idea that it is worth while to take these constituents of controversy out of an ontological context, and note how they look when they are placed in the context of the use they perform and the service they render in the context of *inquiry*. The net product of this way of viewing the two factors in the old controversy is expressed in the phrase "The Autonomy of Inquiry." That phrase does more than merely occur in the book that is the source of the discussion in which we are now engaged, since its use there was intended to serve as a key to understanding its contents. The elimination of ontological reference that at first sight may seem portentous actually amounts to the simple matter of saying that whatever claims to be or to convey knowledge has to be found in the context of inquiry; and that this thesis applies to *every* statement which is put forth in the theory of knowledge, whether the latter deals with its origin, its nature, or its possibility.

III

In approaching the special topic of mathematical subject-matter and mathematical inquiry, I find it necessary, as well as advisable, to begin with the topic of Abstraction. According to the standpoint taken in *The Theory of Inquiry,* something of the nature of abstraction is found in the case of *all* ideas and of all theories. Abstraction from assured and certain existential reference belongs to *every* suggestion of a possible solution; otherwise inquiry comes to an end and positive assertion takes its place. But subjectmatters constituting during the course of inquiry what is taken to be the *problem* are also held in suspense. If they are not so maintained, then, to repeat, inquiry comes automatically to an end. It *terminates* even though the termination is not, with respect to inquiry, a *conclusion.* A flight away from what there and then exists does not of itself accomplish anything. It may take the form of day-dreaming or building castles in the air. But when the flight lands upon what for the purpose of inquiry is an idea, it at once becomes the point of departure for instigating and directing new observations serving to bring to light facts the use of which will develop further use and which thereby develop awareness of the problem to be dealt with, and consequently serve to indicate an improved mode of solution; which in turn instigates and directs new observation of existential material, and so on and on till both problem and solution take on a determinate form. In short, unless it is clearly recognized that in *every* case of obstructed ongoing behavior *"ideas"* are temporary deviations and escapes, what I have called their functional and operational standing will not be understood. Every *idea* is an *escape,* but escapes are saved from being *evasions* so far as they are put to use in evoking and directing observations of further factual material.

I am reasonably confident, dear A——, that in this one point at least we shall find ourselves in agreement. I do not believe that either of us is in sympathy with the wholesale attacks upon abstractions that are now being made in some quarters. Theories as they are used in scientific inquiry are themselves matters of systematic abstraction. Like ideas, they get away from what may be called the immediately given facts in order to be applicable to a much fuller range of relevant facts. A scientific theory differs from the ideas which, as we say, "pop into our heads," only in its vast and systematic range of applicability. The peculiarity of *scientific* abstraction lies in the degree of its freedom from *particular* existential adhesions.

It follows as a matter of course that abstraction is carried on indefinitely further in scientific inquiry than there is occasion for carrying it on in connection with the affairs of everyday life. For, in the latter case, an abstraction loses its serviceability if it is carried beyond applicability to the *specific* difficulty then and there encountered. In the case of scientific inquiry, theory is carried to a point of abstraction which renders it available in dealing with a maximum variety of possible uses. What we call *comprehensiveness* in the case of a theory is not a matter of its own content, but of the serviceability in range of application of that content. It is perhaps worth while to notice that the Newtonian theory was, for a long time, believed to be completely comprehensive in respect to all astronomical subjectmatter; not merely that which had already been observed but to all that ever could possibly be observed. Finally, there occurred what in the case of an everyday affair of life would be called a *hitch* or *block*. Instead of the discrepancy being accepted as a finality it was, however, at once *put to use* in suggesting further development upon the side of theory as abstraction. The outcome constitutes what is known as "The Relativity Theory." Newton had carried *his* abstraction to a point which was shocking to many of his contemporaries. They felt that it took away the reality which gave point and zest to the affairs of life, moral and esthetic as well as practical in a utilitarian sense. In so doing they made the same mistake that professional philosophers made after them. They treated a use, function, and service rendered in conduct of inquiry as if it had ontological reference apart from inquiry.

When viewed from the standpoint of its position in the conduct of inquiry, the relativity theory rendered space and time themselves subjectmatters of inquiry instead of its fixed limits. In the Newtonian theory they had been treated as an *Ultima Thule* beyond which scientific inquiry could not possibly go. These considerations may be used, dear A——, as an example of how submitting inquiry to ontological reference obstructs it. But here they are mentioned on account of their bearing on the question of mathematical subjectmatter. No matter how far physical theory carries its abstractions, it would contradict the very intent of the latter if they went beyond possibility of application to every kind of *observable* existential materials. The privilege of *that* use and office is reserved for mathematical inquiry. The story of the development of mathematical inquiry shows that its advances have usually been occasioned by something which struck some inquirer as a hitch or block in the previous state of its subject-matter. But in the course of the last one or two generations, mathematicians have arrived at the point at which they see that the heart of the work they are engaged in is the method of free postulation. It is hardly necessary to note how the constructions in which the interior angles of a triangle are, as the case may be, either less or more than two right angles, have removed the ontological obstructions that inhered in Euclidean geometry. While in most respects I am compelled to admit that important features of my position are incompatible with philosophical theories that have received authoritative and, so to say, official formulations, in this matter of mathematics, I believe, dear A——, that I am "on the side of the angels." At all events, I did not invent the position that I have taken in the foregoing statements. I took it over almost bodily from what the mathematicians have said who have brought about the recent immense advances in that subject. It is the progress of mathematical inquiry *as* mathematical which has profoundly shaken the ontological rigidity once belonging to the circle and the triangle as their own immutable "essences." I cannot, accordingly, refrain from mentioning the role that considerations similar to those just mentioned have played in inducing me to undertake an attempt to convert all the *ontological,* as prior to inquiry, into the *logical* as occupied wholly and solely with what takes place in the conduct of inquiry as an ever-going concern.

IV

In the hope that it may further a clarified understanding of my position, I shall now take up another outstanding problem of modern epistemological philosophy. It is a familiar fact that the historical systems of epistemological philosophy did their best to make ontological conclusions depend upon prior investigation of the conditions and nature of knowledge. A fact which is not so familiar, which indeed is often ignored, is that this attempt was itself based upon an ontological assumption of literally tremendous import; for it was assumed that whatever else knowledge is or is not, it is dependent upon the independent existence of a *knower* and of something *to be known;* occurring, that is, between mind and the world; between self and not-self; or, in words made familiar by use, between subject and object. The assumption consisted in holding that the subjectmatters designated by these antithetical terms are separate and independent; hence the problem of problems was to determine some method of harmonizing the status of one with the status of the other with respect to the possibility and nature of knowledge. Controversy on this topic, as is the case with the other historic problem already mentioned, has now receded into the background. It cannot be affirmed, however, that the problem is settled by means of reaching an agreed-upon solution. It is rather as if it had been discovered that the competing theories of the various kinds of realism, idealism, and dualism had finally so covered the ground that nothing more could be found to say.

In this matter also it accordingly occurred to me that it might be a good idea to try the experiment of placing in the context of inquiry whatever matters were of moment and weight in what was urged by the various parties to the controversy. For observed and observable facts of inquiry are readily available: there is a mass of fact extending throughout the whole recorded intellectual history of man, in which are manifest for study and investigation both failures and successes—much as is the case in the story of any important human art. In this transfer of matters at issue from their prior ontological setting into a context that is set *wholly and only* by conditions of the conduct of inquiry, what had been taken to be inherent ontological demands were seen to be but arbitrary assumptions from their own standpoint, but important distinctions of use and office in the progressive carrying on of inquiry.

In pursuing this line of inquiry, it proved to be a natural affair to take as a point of departure the physiological connection and distinction of organism and environment as the *most readily observable* instance of the *principle* involved in the matter of the connection and distinction of "subject and object." Consideration of the simpler physiological activities which significantly enough already bore the name "functions" served to indicate that a life-activity is not anything going on *between* one thing, the organism, and another thing, the environment, but that, *as* life-activity, it is a simple event over and across that distinction (not to say separation). Anything that can be entitled to either of these names has first to be located and identified as it is incorporated, engrossed, in life-activity. Hence there was presented in an acute form the following problem: Under what conditions of life-activity and to what consequences in the latter is the distinction relevant?

The issue involved in this question coalesced, almost of itself, with the point of view independently reached in regard to knowing as inquiry with respect to its origin in the event of a hitch, blockage, or break, in the ongoing of an active situation. The coalescence worked both ways. With respect to the distinction within the course of physiological life-activity, the obvious suggestion was that the subjectmatters to which the names "organism" and "environment," respectively, apply are distinguished when some function, say digestion, is disturbed, unsettled, and it is necessary, *in order to do something about it* which will restore the normal activity (in which organs and foods work together in a single unified process) to *locate* the source of the trouble. Is there something wrong inside? Or is the source of the disturbance located in water or in food that has been taken into the system? When such a distinction is once clearly made there are those who devote themselves especially to inquiry into the structures and processes that can be *referred* distinctively to the organism (although they could not take place and be capable of such reference without continuous partnership in a single transaction), while others study the relations of air, climate, foods, water, etc., to the maintenance of health—that is, of unified functionings.

What happens when distinctions which are indispensable to form and use in an efficient conduct of inquiry—that is to say, one which meets its own conditions *as* inquiry—are converted into something ontological, that is to say, into something taken to exist on its own account prior to inquiry and to which inquiry must conform, is exhibited, I submit, my dear questioner, in the epistemological phase of modern philosophy; and yet the new science could not have accomplished its revolution in astronomy, physics, and physiology if it had not *in the course of its own development* of method been able, by means of such distinctions as those to which theory gave the names "subject" and "object,"

"mind" and "the world," etc., to slough off the vast mass of irrelevant pre-conceptions which kept ancient and medieval cosmology from attaining scientific standing.

It is not implied, however, that what has just been said covers
the whole scope of the problem. There remains the question of
why at a particular time the distinction between knower and the
subjectmatter to be known became so conspicuous and so central as to be for two centuries or more one of *the* outstanding
philosophical issues. No such problem was urgent in either ancient or medieval philosophy. The idea that most directly suggests itself as an indication of a solution of this problem is
that the rather sudden and certainly striking emergence of the
"subject-object" problem is intimately connected with the cultural conditions that mark the transition of the medieval period
into that age that is called *modern*. This view of the matter is, I
believe, an interesting and even important hypothesis; it is one
which in another connection might be followed out with advantage. It is introduced here, however, solely for whatever service it
may render in understanding a position which, like that set forth
in *The Theory of Inquiry,* transfers what had been taken to be
ontological separations into distinctions that serve a useful, indeed necessary, function in conduct of inquiry.

Before leaving this endeavor to clarify my position through
reference to well-known events in the history of philosophy, I
shall mention a third matter which, unlike the two already mentioned, is still more or less actively pursued in contemporary
philosophical discussion. I refer here to the extraordinary contrast that exists beyond peradventure between the subjectmatters
that are known in science and those known in the course of our
everyday and common living—common not only in the sense of
the usual but of that which is shared by large numbers of human
beings in the conduct of the affairs of their life. To avoid misunderstanding it should be observed that the word "practical"
has a much fuller meaning when used to designate these affairs
than it has when it is used in a narrow utilitarian way, since it
includes the moral, the political, and the artistic. A simple but
fairly typical example of the undeniable contrast between the
subjectmatters of this common life and the knowings that are appropriate to it, and the subjectmatter and method of scientific
knowing, is found in the radical unlikeness of the water we

drink, wash with, sail boats upon, use to extinguish fires, etc., etc., and the H_2O of scientific subjectmatter.

It would appear dogmatic were I to say that the problem involved in this radical unlikeness of subjectmatters is insoluble if its terms are placed in an ontological context. But the differences between, say, a spiritualistic and a materialistic ontological solution remind us how far away we are from any agreed-upon solution. It hardly seems unreasonable to suggest that parties to the controversy are lined up on the basis of preferences which are external to the terms of the issue rather than on grounds which are logically related to it. When the issue pertaining to and derived from this contrast is placed and treated in the context of different types of *problems* demanding different methods of treatment and different types of subjectmatter, the problem involved assumes a very different shape from that which it has when it is taken to concern the ontological "reality." It would be irrelevant to the present issue were I to attempt to tell just what form the problem and its solution assume when they are seen and treated in the context of inquiry. It is relevant, however, to the understanding of the point of view to say that it demands statement on the ground of types of problems so different that they are capable of solution only in terms of types of subjectmatter as unlike one another as are those exemplified in the case of "*water.*" I may, however, at least point out that a thirsty man seeking water to drink in a dry land would hardly be furthered in the emergency in which he finds himself by calling upon H_2O as his subjectmatter; while, on the other hand, the physicist engaged in his type of problem and inquiry would soon be brought to a halt if he could not treat water as H_2O. For it is on account of *that* mode of treatment that water is taken out of isolation as a subject of knowledge and brought into vital and intimate connection with an indefinitely extensive range of other matters qualitatively and immediately of radically different kinds from water and from one another.

It seems pertinent at this point, my dear A——, to refer to that aspect of my theory of knowledge to which I gave the name "instrumentalism." For it was intended to deal with the problem just mentioned on the basis of the idea or hypothesis that scientific subjectmatter grows out of and returns into the subjectmatter of the everyday kind;—the kind of subjectmatter to which *on the basis of ontological interpretation* it is totally and un-qualifiedly opposed. Upon the basis of this view the metaphysical problem which so divided Berkeley from Sir Isaac Newton, and which has occupied such a prominent place in philosophy ever since the rise of new physical science, is not so much resolved as dissolved. Moreover, new construction accrues to the subject-matter of physical science just because of its extreme unlikeness to the subjectmatters which for the sake of brevity may be called those of common sense. There is presented in this unlikeness a striking example of the view of the function of thoroughgoing abstraction mentioned shortly ago. The extreme remoteness of the subjectmatter of physical science from the subjectmatter of everyday living is precisely that which renders the former appli-cable to an immense variety of the occasions that present them-selves in the course of everyday living. Today there is probably no case of everyday living in which physical conditions hold a place that is beyond the reach of being effectively dealt with on the ground of available *scientific* subjectmatter. A similar statement is now coming to hold regarding matters which are specifically physiological: note, in evidence, the revolution that is taking place in matters relating to illness and health. Negative illustra-tion, if not confirmation, may be supplied by the backward state of both knowledge and practice in matters that are distinctively human and moral. The latter in my best judgment will continue to be matter of customs and of conflict of customs until inquiry has found a method of abstraction which, because of its degree of remoteness from established customs, will bring them into a light in which their nature will be indefinitely more clearly seen than is now the case.

As I see the matter, what marks the scientific movement that began a few centuries ago and that has accomplished a veritable revolution in the methods and the conclusions of natural science are its *experimental* conduct and the fact that even the best estab-lished theories retain *hypothetical* status. Moreover, these two traits hang together. Theories as hypotheses are developed and tested through being put to use in the conducting of experimental activities which bring to the light of observation new areas of fact. Before the scientific revolution some theories were taken to be inherently settled beyond question because they dealt with Being that was eternal and immutable. During that period the word "hypothesis" meant that which *was placed under* subject-matters so firmly as to be beyond the possibility of doubt or question. I do not know how I could better exemplify what I mean to be understood by the functional and operational character of ideational subjectmatter than by the radical change that in the development of scientific inquiry has taken place in the working position now attached to hypothesis, and to *theory* as hypothetical.

Let me say, my friend, that I have engaged in this fairly long, even if condensed, historical exposition solely for the sake of promoting understanding of my position. As I have already indicated, I did not originate the main figures that play their parts in my theory of knowing. I tried the experiment of transferring the old well-known figures from the stage of ontology to the stage of inquiry. As a consequence of this transfer, the scene as it presented itself to me was not only more coherent but indefinitely more instructive and humanly dramatic.

In any event the various factors, ancient and modern, of historical discussion and controversy were precipitated in the book whose subjectmatter is the occasion of this present exchange of views. I am aware that I have not made the kind of reply which in all probability you felt you had a right to anticipate. At the same time, while I have taken advantage of considerations that have occurred to me since the text in question was written, I do not believe that I have departed from its substantial intent and spirit. Yet I am bound to acknowledge that the occasion of precipitating historical materials into the treatise under discussion was the great variety of works on logical theory that appeared during the nineteenth century. As I look back I am led to the conclusion that the attempt conscientiously to do my full duty by these treatises is accountable for a certain cloudiness which obscures clear vision of what the book was trying to do. The force of the word "Logic," in all probability, has overshadowed for the reader the import of what in my intention was the significant expression, *The Theory of Inquiry*. For that source of misapprehension I accept full responsibility. I am, accordingly, the more grateful to you, my dear friendly critic, for affording me this opportunity for restatement, which, I venture to hope, is free from some of the encumbrances that load down the text. I shall be content if I have succeeded in this response to your request for clarification in conveying a better understanding of the *problem* that occupied me. As I reflect upon the historical course of philosophy I am unable to find its course marked by notable successes in the matter of conclusions attained. I yield to none, however, in admiring appreciation of the liberating work it has accomplished in opening new perspectives of vision through its sensitivity to problems it has laid hold of in ways which, over and over again, have loosened the hold upon us exerted by predispositions that owe their strength to conformities which became so habitual as not to be questioned, and which in all probability would still be unquestioned were it not for the debt we owe to philosophers.

Very sincerely yours,

JOHN DEWEY

Typescripts

What Is It to Be a Linguistic Sign or Name?

It is not news that the subject designated by the caption of this article is now the centre of much current discussion. To one who analyzes with care the material which is appearing on this topic it will not be news that in spite of the seeming eclipse of the epistemological problem, much of this material has for its unstated premise the traditional subject-object dualism. In consequence signs, of the linguistic order, are presented as go-betweens, neither flesh, fish, nor fowl.[1] By way of a different approach without getting directly involved in the old controversies I begin by pointing out that while being a sign is a case of representation or standing for, the latter names are applied to affairs that are not usually called signs. Congressmen, vicars, spokesmen, legal agents, deputies, etc., etc., are representatives:—a fact which makes it appropriate to quote the following from C. S. Peirce. "To stand for, that is to be in such relation to another that for certain purposes it is treated . . . as if it were that other."[2] Now, whatever else signs are or are not they fall within the scope of representations as thus defined, and, as just suggested, approach from this point of view has the advantage of getting completely around, or completely dropping out the usual epistemological, subject-object, person-things, associations. Thus approached it is hardly necessary to point out the all but revolu-

1. See the articles by A. F. Bentley, "On a Certain Vagueness in Logic," the *Journal of Philosophy,* Vol. XLII, Nos. 1 and 2, Jan. 4 and 18, 1945 [see this volume, pp. 8–45].
2. *Collected Papers,* Vol. II, p. 155, most of the examples given being taken directly from this same passage of Peirce's. (The text of the latter appeared first in Baldwin's *Dictionary of Philosophy and Psychology,* Vol. II, p. 464.)

[From unpublished typescript in the Arthur F. Bentley Collection, Manuscripts Department, Lilly Library, Indiana University, Bloomington, 18 pp., dated 25 May 1945. For Dewey's new start for this paper, see this volume, pp. 472–74, "Note on 'What Is It to Be a Linguistic Sign or Name?'"]

tionary change in biological development wrought by the appearance of language. As means of enabling us human beings to treat certain things as if for certain purposes they were the things they stand for, nothing compares in range, particularity, and flexibility with words.

And when the function of words as representatives is under discussion, it is advisable to turn Peirce's statement the other end around. The advantage that accrues from having and being able to employ things in the capacity of "standing for" or representatives is not with reference to *them;* it is with reference to what is stood for. This is obvious enough in the case of, say, specified colors on a litmus paper standing for the presence of an acid or an alkali. There is not merely the immediate great saving of time and energy, but there is the indefinitely extensive mediating advantage of linking up the fact of being acid or alkali with a vast system of other facts. As a matter of precaution, not as announcing anything new, I point out the immense advantage of linguistic things, sounds and marks, over other things in their function as representatives. The *words* acid and alkali are under much more ready command than is a piece of litmus paper and enter more readily and into an indefinitely more extensive range of combinations than does the thing tested by application of litmus paper.

These commonplaces obtain significance when they are put in direct connection with that phrase of the passage from Peirce which mentions ability to *treat* that which serves as a representative as if it were something else. As an illustrative, we may take the case of a man who acquires the status of being a Congressman. There are, doubtless, advantages, emoluments, powers, accruing to him in consequence. But these things are not the purpose nor significance of the institution of political representation. In the degree they tend to be such we have the fact significantly called "corruption," perversion. Legitimately such representation is the device that has been worked out historically to get certain things of wide concern accomplished and to prevent certain other things occurring. It is in this respect that the word "*treat*" is of supreme importance in the passage quoted. The matter of being representative, and of being a sign (linguistic) as a special case, is a strictly behavioral matter and can be intelligently discussed only in a behavioral context. This fact so stands out in the case of deputies, authorized attorneys, vicars, etc., as to render them the best cases to start discussion with. It holds equally of certain other examples cited by Peirce in the passage of which a part has been quoted;—viz., Symptom, counter, description, diagram; and in fact, words generally.[3] In this connection it is worth citing another passage from Peirce. Speaking of "lithium"—the word—after saying that "if you search among minerals that are vitreous, translucent, grey or white, very hard, brittle and insoluble for one which imparts a crimson tinge to an unluminous flame . . . [the material being submitted to a number of specified tests], that material is a specimen of lithium," he adds: "The peculiarity of this definition, or *rather of this precept*, more useful than a definition, is that it tells you what the word lithium denotes by prescribing what you *are to do* in order to get a perceptual acquaintance with the object of that word."[4]

It is a question, worth consideration, why such seemingly obvious considerations are persistently neglected even to the point of perversion of Peirce's plain meaning by those claiming to follow him. The epistemological atmosphere accounts for this fact in part. But I think that reading current literature on the topic will show that it is reinforced by another consideration. For in that literature the reader continually finds that the illustrative material is the following sort. Discussion of words as representatives or signs is constantly discussed by employing, as if they were appropriate illustrative material, such words as *cat, stone, water*. So usual is this practice that it is safe to say the first reaction of many readers of this last sentence will be in effect, "Well why not? What better example would any one want to have?"

In reply to that question, I make the downright answer that such a course begs every important issue involved. What the writer is doing entirely and exclusively is to tell about social usage under the guise of telling something of logical—or at least

3. As is indicated in the articles of Bentley previously referred to, current "semanticists" who believe they are following Peirce get the discussion into a fictitious and thoroughly misty realm because they drop out just this behavioral context. Another effort more absurd than the attempt to view fundamental logical features as characteristics of things called signs in and of themselves, i.e., as matters of "pure form," has never happened even in the most devious chapters of philosophical history. Yet this is characteristic of most of contemporary effort in "logistics."
4. Vol. II, p. 189. (Italics not in original.) Obviously "stands for," "represents," "is a sign of" can be substituted for "denotes" with no change of sense.

logistic-semantical—significance about what it is to be a sign. The questions at issue are begged because the use of familiar, (socially) well-established cases systematically passes over in silence all the behavioral operations by means of which the words in question become signs. There are few human beings of such a low grade that they do not know what the spoken sound "cat" stands for, and, provided they can read, what the written or printed word stands for.

The point of these remarks will probably become clearer if one substitutes for instances drawn from established, readily understood social usage, cases which are still scientifically unsettled, say, what the word "cancer" stands for, or cases that are still in process of scientific determination involving great modification of previous status as to *what* they stand for, e.g., *atom, gravitation;* or finally take into consideration the way in which the *scientific* meaning of even such words as water, cat, iron, has developed out of their ordinary every day application or denotative reference.

Any one who employs this manner of approach will, I believe, have no difficulty in saying that even the popular, more or less standardized reference, or standing-for, or signness, of the words stone, cat, water, (i) expresses the net *result* of behavioral operations performed across wide areas of space and long durations of time, and (ii) serves as *direction* for performance of specifiable operations in the present and future. From sheer familiarity we tend to take these considerations for granted in cases that are familiar from sheer force of usage;—hence the advantage of taking "scientific" cases for illustrative material.

II

If it is questioned whether or not current use of words of socially standardized, previously determined, social usage is guilty of the charge brought, I suggest examination of the current literature in which the word "referent" figures largely. It is still worth while, because of its enduring influence, to begin with Ogden-Richards's *Meaning of Meaning.* The "epistemological" influence is explicitly evident in their triangular scheme, the three corners of which are, quoting, "Word or Symbol, Object, that to which the symbol refers, and called the Referent, and Meaning or Thought."[5] Even more explicit is the following passage: "There are three factors involved when any statement is made or interpreted. 1. Mental processes. 2. The symbol. 3. The referent," while even more significant is the sentence which immediately follows: "The *theoretical problem* of Symbolism is *How are these three Related?*"[6] I have italicized this passage because it indicates so clearly that the constituents of the only significant and genuine problem are taken as if the problem they constitute had already been solved so that "the theoretical problem" which is then left is factitious. The case is noteworthy as a striking instance of the begging of the issue already mentioned, while in addition it brings out clearly that the net effect is to substitute a problem so artificial that it is bound, if taken seriously, to generate controversies that cannot possibly be settled. Instead of inquiring how it is that a certain thing acquires its function as a representation, cases are taken in which social usage has given a thing that capacity; instead of asking how it is that just *this* thing and not some other becomes that which is stood for, or designated, it is assumed that the object is already there waiting to be referred to. Instead of a discussion of how and to what end being a sign or representation and being a referent are determined, we have at the very most merely a discussion of how this particular thing, *already* determined to be a *sign* comes to refer to or stand for that particular thing *already* determined to be an *object*.

The case of Ogden-Richards is especially instructive because in addition to the epistemological groundwork already mentioned the "solution" they proffer of the problem stated in their own terms makes evident that what they are investigating is a matter of common social usage. For their solution of "the theoretical problem" of how three things, namely something already settled upon as a sign, something already somehow known to be a "thought" and something else already known to be an object and a certain kind of object, are "related" falls back entirely upon social usage. It is what they call "causal theory" or one of "external contexts," employing their own words. The external

5. Op. cit., p. 11.
6. Op. cit., p. 243.

contexts in question are recurrent clumps, or sets, of events which because of the frequency of their occurrence or repeated association make such an impression on the nervous system that certain sounds and (eventually if one learns to read) certain marks become firmly associated with certain "external objects." [7] That the "solution" that is given takes for granted the existence of the sign-function on one side and of "objects" waiting to be designated on the other side will be evident to a careful reader of the "causal theory." It will also be evident that it takes for granted that human beings (called minds or thoughts by the authors) inhabit a social medium in which they hear certain sounds so frequently associated with certain things that the association is firmly impressed on them (i.e., on their "thoughts" or "mental processes") through their nervous systems. This, I submit is what the solution of Ogden-Richards comes to. If it accounts for anything it is simply how, the sign function being taken for granted, a given sound comes, under given social conditions, to stand for a certain *given* "object." It might be taken, leaving out the "thoughts," as an account of how it comes about that in an English-speaking community a certain sound stands for, say, bread while in a French community another sound has the ability and function of standing for it: a rather minor outcome for the elaborate apparatus involved in writing it.

I conclude this section by saying that a number of influences have conspired to effect the dropping out of explicit reference to the "thought" corner of the triangle. In consequence the triangle has tended to be reduced to a line with a sign at one end and an object at the other as its "referent." But the fact they are both taken ready-made, so to speak, speaks eloquently of the fact that a ghostly relic of thought hovers over the discussion, perhaps as "person," perhaps as organism, perhaps as a nervous system, perhaps as just speaker or the namer who *uses* signs,[8] but in any case as something outside of and behind the sign-functioning system.

One gets the impression from the more recent writings dealing

7. Op. cit., pp. 81–86, passim.
8. See the articles of Bentley already mentioned, and the summary references p. 229 and p. 230 of the article by Dewey and Bentley, "A Terminology for Knowings and Knowns," *Journal of Philosophy,* Vol. XLII, No. 9, April 26, 1945 [see this volume, pp. 51–53, notes 5 and 6].

with the general subject that authors write as if they felt that since this speaker as a separate entity is common to all special cases, it may be taken for granted in every particular case and accordingly cancels out. In so far an advance is made, forwarded no doubt by the general fatigue resulting from the failure of prolonged epistemological controversies to arrive at any settlement. But no significant constructions have resulted; rather a transfer of controversial issues to a new field, new at least as far as language is concerned.

III

I now leave it to the reader's own inspection of recent literature concerning signs to pass upon the justice of what has been said, and turn to presentation of considerations upon the positive or "constructive" side. The fundamental or underlying postulate is that one and the same set of behavioral operations determine something to be a sign and something else to be its "referent" in strict conjunction. That is, the very same set of operations which constitute something as a sign and as a sign of just the thing which it is used at the time and place as a sign of, are the operations that establish the specifically named or designated which is its "referent."[9] This general statement is so broad in scope that it may not be especially intelligible in the present state of discussion unless it is broken up into a bill of particulars.

I begin by bringing forward facts having to do with the distinction between the sign-capacity of designation found in pre-scientific and non-scientific idiomatic speech and names that have been established as to their reference or representative capacity by those specialized systematic inquiries that have the name or title of "scientific." The topic has been previously mentioned, as for example in the "popular" and scientific reference of "water"; or, on a somewhat higher level, say, in the matter of the distinctive meanings of "atom" in Greek natural philosophy

9. Otherwise stated, a transaction, to which the name *Reference* applies, is the one undivided and primary fact, and *Sign* and *Referent* are its inseparable co-partners, just as buyer-seller are the constituents of a commercial transaction and speaker-hearer of a linguistic transaction. For the name "transaction," see the last article mentioned above, pp. 242–3 [see this volume, pp. 66–68].

and in present-day physics. The point that concerns us here is that the difference in question is one exclusively of the kinds of operations that are determining and decisive in the two cases. Stated briefly, leaving it to the reader to pass upon the cogency of what is said, in the "popular" type of case (previously identified as that of current social usage) the operations are of a relatively gross nature and are only incidentally concerned with the advancement of knowing or inquiry, being mainly concerned with uses and enjoyments in the direct course of every day life:—with results of the kind usually denominated "practical."[10]

The chief point on this kind is that what is called social or popular linguistic usages are themselves an integral part of social usages that are capable of being viewed as non-linguistic: Namely, habits, customs, institution of behaviors which involve, physiologically, a good deal more than the vocal-organs and ear; and which involve, beyond the skin of each one who acts, materials and tools (utensils, etc.), and other human beings in cooperative and competitive actions. What "water" is the sign of or stands for, for example, is that which is currently and overtly used to drink, to wash with, to swim in, to sail or row on, to get drowned in, etc., depending upon the range of behaviors engaged in by a given group at a given stage of culture.

I do not see how anyone who takes more than a very casual and superficial view of the facts can doubt, first, that specifiable behavioral operations, *doings and makings* which involve the body, things and other human beings, determine certain things, like gestures, sounds, etc., to be signs, and, secondly, that they do so because the same operations, drinking, washing, etc., determine at one and the same time that subjectmatter which is the "referent" of the sign. In short, the "object" as that meant or stood for is determined conjointly, literally and strictly, with the enactment or determination of other things as signs for them. Sign and thing designated are constituents of one inclusive undivided set of operations; any distinction drawn between them is

10. In my *Logic: The Theory of Inquiry,* the expression "Common Sense" is used to name the kind of knowings and knowns that has to be marked off from the knowings-knowns that claim the name "Science." See *Common Sense* in Index. The appropriateness of the word may of course be questioned; the existence of a distinctive subjectmatter of the kind specified cannot be intelligently brought into question.

the result of *post* or reflective operations.[11] Aside from vitiation through the influence of epistemological assumptions, the "causal" theory of Ogden-Richards is aside from the mark because it postulates factors that are wholly and explicitly "external" to one another and hence can be related only through "associations" à la Hume. If one starts from and with the facts of "social" behavior, with the customary and traditional activities one observes going on all around him and in some of which he directly partakes, he should have no difficulty in seeing that gesturing and speech in which some things enter as signs and other things enter as that designated are directly inclusive of both "signs" and "objects as referents." That utensils, tools, apparatus, are things made and are things used, and that making and the using are transactions of the sort to which the word "social" is usually, if loosely, applied, are I suppose, fairly evident facts. It is absurd to suppose that we make water, stones, grass, by any such direct operations as are involved in the case of "artificial" objects. But I do not suppose that any one would deny that, say, wheat, beefsteak, etc., etc., have that meaning determined and evoked by the name *food* because of certain things being involved, in the most literal sense of taking active part, in certain habitual ways of behavior by means of which the things in question serve certain life functions. Any one who will seriously observe the changes that take place in words *as* signs in conjunction with changes in socio-cultural activities will be bound, I believe, to conclude that "meaning" is no more inherent in things as "objects" in independence of human ways of behaving than it is inherent in the sounds and marks that are upon occasion surrogates for things in human behavior when the things are not directly present.

After this somewhat prolonged discussion, the topic of "scientific" knowings-knowns may be dealt with briefly. The following considerations are reasonably obvious without extensive argument. (1) The departure as respects subjectmatter are the things stood for or designated by names in current popular usage: The water we drink, the iron we heat and hammer into shape, the air we breathe, the plants we cultivate, etc. Scientific procedures in

11. That later treatment of them as distinctive is itself a constituent of a total transaction, which takes place subsequently, and is of course involved in the position taken, though the point will not be developed here.

the course of their development produce things, subjectmatters, and cases not previously known. But there is nothing unique in this fact. The same sort of event took place in times when behavior was, say, the production predominantly, if not exclusively, of alloys like bronze. Of perhaps even greater importance is the fact that the physical processes employed by inquiries falling within the scientific phase were at the outset of development of modern methods taken over quite directly from the "practical" arts and, no longer in stage of development, however technically specialized, they have been no more than refinements and extensions through combination of these earlier processes. The same thing holds of the apparatus, the instrumentalities characteristic of scientific research. In so far, science itself in its instruments, processes and materials presents itself *as* systematic refinement, elaboration and extension of behavior of the "practical" or "common sense" sort.

In discussions of a more specialized sort I have repeatedly pointed out that such facts as those just cited prove that the much-mooted problem of the relation of scientific "objects" to "objects" of (sense) perception is, *as ordinarily stated and discussed,* a thoroughly artificial one resting upon arbitrary postulates. The obvious facts of the case show, however, that the distinction of what is designated in popular usage by *water* and what is designated to a physicist by H_2O is not intrinsically counterfeit. And this fact brings me to the next point.

(2) The distinction, *with respect to subjectmatter,* is primarily one of span of duration temporally speaking and range of extent spatially speaking. The subjectmatter designated by *water* in popular every day usage is *from the standpoint of what is designated by H_2O* some thing arbitrarily isolated, cut off from its connections. This statement is not, however, to be perverted into the statement that the cutting off is arbitrary from its own or the "practical" standpoint. The wisest physicist on earth drinks the temporally-spatially localized water that he sees and touches through immediate use of bodily organs of sight, touch, temperature. The difference is still there, nevertheless. To the one who is *a*-scientific, as far as use of the procedural method of the latter is concerned, that designated, or stood for, by *water* is unique by virtue of immediate qualities which shut it off from systematic connection with qualitatively unlike things. To one of scientific habit the immediately present (i.e., the short-span, local extent,

subjectmatter) is a phase, a specifiable emphasis, of subject-matter which is indefinitely extensive spatially and enduring temporally.

(3) The fact running through both of the points just made is that while scientific knowings-knowns employ behavioral operations [12] of the same general sort, or "type," of that of "practical" everyday knowings-knowns (usually termed in philosophical writings, because of psychology with onesided emphasis, "perceptual"), the direction, the sense, is markedly different. There is of course a knowing-known operation-product involved in every case of seeing and using water, iron, wood, the soil, etc., etc. But it is subordinated to what I have called use-enjoyment. In scientific namings, that is, in the system of signs deserving the name and title of scientific inquiry, advancement of knowledge and the place occupied and work done by any given inquiry within specified expansions in spatial-range of the knowledge-corpus at hand becomes the controlling phase. This does not signify that use-enjoyment is excluded. On the contrary, it signifies that it is transformed. Accomplishment of knowings-knowns becomes that which is primarily and predominatingly enjoyed, and the result of the performance is put to use in bringing about further extensions of the system in which it belongs.

IV

The foregoing discussion may be briefly summarized. 1. Being a name or *linguistic* sign is a matter of the performance of

---

12. Continued repetition of the adjective "behavioral" may seem indulgence in superfluity. But "operationalism" is frequently criticized—and sometimes stated—in a way that distorts its postulates and conclusions because of failure of attention to what "behavioral" stands for, is a sign of—or, as simply as possible, names. In this connection I call attention to the article of Frank E. Hartung in *Philosophy of Science*, Vol. 9, No. 4, Oct. 1942, entitled "Operationalism: Idealism or Realism?" and of the same author in the issue of Oct. 1944, Vol. 11, No. 4, entitled "Operationism as a Cultural Survival." Irrespective of the force of the criticism with respect to the special subjectmatter criticized, the careful reader will note the reduction of perception to "sensory" elements with complete exclusion of manipulative behavior, the socalled "motor" factor, which is not only an ingredient of all perception but which determines the presence and function of the socalled "sensational" elements:—"manipulative" being here used to apply to modes of behavior not involving the hand as well as including the latter.

behavioral operations.[13] 2. To be name, or de-signation, a sign, is to have taken on the function, capacity or ability, of reference to a *specified,* a discriminated and identified, subjectmatter. 3. One and the same set of behavioral operations determines, in strict conjunction or conjugation, *sign* and *referent*. For they are aspects of one and the same transaction, which may, perhaps, be suitably designated by the name "Reference" or Referential Function, which is a matter of behavioral *application*.[14]

(4) When due precautions are taken, it is possible to distinguish three aspects of Naming—being Named in such a way as to render each capable of specialized treatment. The result is (a) study of things established as signs, whether popularly or scientifically, apart from what they name—apart, that is, from what they are *as* signs. The whole range of linguistics, in all its many aspects, belongs here, that which makes the material studied as linguistic being taken for granted and hence ignored. When, however, the ignoring is systematic and becomes denial, the result is found in those volumes, chapters and lines of contemporary logistics in which *logical* considerations are treated as inherently separated from subjectmatter and hence from conclusions of inquiry.

(b) It is obviously possible to study what is designated or "signi*fied,*" apart from specific study of signs as such. When this selective emphasis is converted into systematic (or "philosophic") discussion it results in theories which imply that "Objects" are one independent matter, something else—thoughts, or speakers or whatever—another, and names a third intervening thing. (c) Processes of *application* involved in the inclusive behavioral

13. The adjective *linguistic* is prefixed, in italics, to indicate what is not expressly discussed here:—Names do not exhaust the Sign-Field. They are developments out of signs of a physiological order, to which the Dewey-Bentley article previously mentioned gives the name "signals" to differentiate them from words as signs—the latter being in turn differentiated from the subjectmatter of mathematics, called *symbolic,* where symbols are not *names.* See pp. 244–45 of "A Terminology for Knowings and Knowns" [pp. 69–70].

14. "Reference" is the word suggested to name the inclusive function in my *Logic: The Theory of Inquiry.* See pp. 54–56 [*Later Works* 12:60–62]. Unfortunately, the indicated usage is not uniformly adhered to. A more serious matter is failure to note, explicitly, and to develop the fact that the behavioral operations to which the name is given enact at one and the same time and place the refer*ring* that in one aspect of the total function constitutes being a sign and in another aspect of the same function an "object" as referent. The matter, I hope, is partly safeguarded by the account given of "object" as name. See, for example, p. 119 [*Later Works* 12:122].

operations may also be selected for special study. Then we get as legitimate outcome that aspect of language study called syntax the illegitimate expression being the doctrine of complete separation of what is called form from anything and everything called, variously, factual, existential, and often called *ontological* because of its alleged supreme and "normative" nature as applying to every possible form of Being (always in Capitals), whether actual or capable of space-time actuality or not, a "Realm" which is now a favored playground for irresponsible revelling.

(5) Scientific naming is a development out of "practical" naming in which names progressively part with their earlier narrowly restricted applications because of behavioral operations tending to enactment, as *designated* subjectmatter, of subjectmatter indefinitely extended in duration and spatial extent. There can be little doubt that the word "science" is now frequently given a kind of superstitious status. Historically, because of contrast with beliefs currently established prior to developments coming to a head in the sixteenth and seventeenth centuries and because of the severe conflicts scientific men had to undergo in their method socially acknowledge, this fact is easy to account for. An attitude which is often tinged with idolatry is replaced by one of legitimate and wholesome respect, expressed in transformation of belief-forming attitudes, when it is seen that the heart and life-blood of scientific method and scientific names is that in them subjectmatters and problems are taken of a narrow and limited space-time context, easily converted into sheer isolationism, into a context which is indefinitely expanding in range and application. The next great socio-cultural change waits upon development of scientific methods in application to socio-cultural subjectmatter. Any one who has a grasp on what scientific method is and does will abstain from objections based upon the notion that such development and application reduces this subjectmatter to physical or physiological subjectmatter. He will see that it marks an enlargement of the never-ending process of taking events, facts, out of a narrow setting into an ever more extensive one. He will see that the result instead of being one of reduction to "lower" (that is narrower) terms is one of ever growing understanding of what takes place with increased clarity and firmness in those transactions of communication which tend toward understanding in the sense of coming to working agreement.

Values, Valuations, and Social Facts

In his recent paper, "Value Judgments and the Social Sciences,"[1] Mr. Benoit-Smullyan remarks that the debate whether social sciences can reach evaluative conclusions now seems *vieux jeu*. It hardly seems probable that such an important issue as that of the possibility that sciences of social events may afford guidance in dealing with future social events will ever be *vieux jeu,* however desirable it may be that some of the terms in which it has been discussed be discarded. But I can easily imagine that further discussion on my part of the distinction between valuing as direct behavior and valuation as critical examination of cases of that sort of behavior may seem to be idle repetition. Nevertheless, I am venturing to take Mr. Benoit-Smullyan's article as the text upon which to hang further remarks on this topic. As the purpose of my article results in its being mainly adversely critical, I preface it with saying that I am in full agreement with the strictures he passes upon the positivist school as represented by Lévy-Bruhl on one side and by the "purists" on the other side; and that I find myself in hearty agreement with the tenor of the practical conclusions he reaches in the closing section of his paper. But the theoretical position which is taken to support these conclusions seems to me seriously defective.

I

I begin with repeating what I have said on previous occasions: *Valuing* is a dangerously ambiguous word. As used in

1. *Journal of Philosophy,* Vol. XLII, pp. 197–210.

[From unpublished typescript in the Arthur F. Bentley Collection, Manuscripts Department, Lilly Library, Indiana University, Bloomington, 9 pp., dated 20 June 1945.]

ordinary speech, it is a name for both acts of prizing, holding dear, being attached, loyal, treating with affectionate care, and for what are technically called e-valuations. The latter are of the order of judgments. For they subject to deliberate and presumably systematic examination cases of direct prizing that have occurred or that are proposed to occur. In the course of ordinary speech, the context generally makes it clear in which sense the word is used, and no serious harm results. I do not believe the same thing can be said of philosophical discussions regarding Values and Valuations, the latter in the sense of judgments. Too often it seems as if the discussion were vitiated by failure of the writer to present a contextual situation either to himself or to the reader. In consequence, traits of prizing, of *esteeming,* are transferred to judgments—and contrariwise traits of judgments as appraisals and estimations are carried over into acts in which there is no weighing of habits and acts of holding precious so as to discover their respective grounds and claims, or, as it may be put, the value of given valuing.[2]

Before coming to specific discussion of cases of confused identification of two quite different sorts of things, I prefix a remark which would be quite unnecessary if contextual situations were habitually borne in mind. In the case of valuing as clinging to, being actively devoted to, searching for and holding on to, anything in the wide world of persons and things may be prized. Because of the prizing it becomes a "value." But it is not values which are then "valued." In the case of valuation as *judgment* it is however precisely some instance of a value—in the sense of something that has been prized—which is its subjectmatter. Is this friend of mine worthy of the affection I have lavished upon him? Does that object of devoted search merit the time and energy spent upon it? The distinction here drawn is commonplace outside of theoretical discussion. One attitude is proverbially warm; the other cool and cooling. It is also a commonplace of moral exhortations. It is the source of the negative admonition against being carried away by appetite and passion; it is the

2. To avoid misunderstanding, I add that the distinction made in the above text does not imply that there is no cognitive or "intellectual" aspect in cases of prizing behavior. But that aspect is not concerned with investigation of the prizing itself. Evaluation or "judgment," on the other hand, depends specifically upon the fact that some instance, or some class of instances, of prizing-behavior has become questionable so that it is felt it cannot be engaged in until it has been subjected to inquiry.

ground of appeal to "reason." It is expressed in the maxim *Respice Finem*—think of consequences before acting.

II

After prefatory remarks, I come to consideration of their bearing upon the paper of Mr. Benoit-Smullyan. The following passage from his article furnishes an excellent point of departure. "Value judgments always and necessarily have an emotional component. . . . In the second place, value judgments seem also to involve a volitional element. The person judging appears to be making some sort of a choice, a choice which commits him to a certain loyalty in the future and possibly to a given line of action. He is incurring an obligation to defend and support the thing judged good, and to act in such a way as to preserve its existence."[3]

It is hardly needful to dwell upon the likeness of traits here imputed to judgment and the traits belonging to valuing as prizing, holding dear. If we use psychological language, the latter is as marked an instance of emotional-volitional behavior as can be found. It is, one may say, emotional-volitional conduct *par excellence,* awareness of an *object,* the "intellectual" factor involved being absorbed into and, so to speak, enswathed in a set of affections-aversions that are commitments to specifiable courses of action. It is also pretty evident that attribution of these features to value-judgment automatically institutes a gulf between judgments of value and all other kinds of judgments. In consequence, it institutes, equally automatically, a difference between the logic of inquiry in the case of social subjectmatter and all other subjectmatters of science.

It seems reasonable to suppose, however, that the transfer from the attitudes and habits of loyalty, concern, attachment which are so important aspects and constituents of social facts over to the judgments which are the outcomes of scientific inquiry is not so flagrant an affair as it appears on the surface. There is good reason for holding that it is mediated by some change which actually takes place because of judgment. What the author is talking about is neither the original behavioral-prizings nor yet the

3. Op. cit., p. 202.

judgment proper, but the change in commitments and affections (and "values") which results as a consequence of having taken, through the medium of inquiry, an attitude of better understanding behaviors previously engaged in more blindly or more casually, less thoughtfully. That such is the case seems to be pretty substantiated by the overt shift from judgment over to the human being engaged in judging that is found in the following passage: "The person judging appears to be making a choice . . . incurring an obligation," etc. In any case, while I cannot see that it makes any sense at all to attribute emotional-volitional constituents to judgment, it makes good sense to point out that since the judgment is *about* subjectmatter of this kind (as other judgments are about potatoes, or fossils, or whatever), the *outcome* of the judgment may well be to prepare the way for a different "emotional-volitional" attitude. In fact it is hard to see what other ground than such a possibility can be reasonably offered for taking thought in matters of behavior instead of plunging blindly ahead.

I have mentioned that ascription of emotional-volitional attitudes to judgment qua judgment at once marks off value-judgments from every other sort of judgment. This is admitted, or perhaps one should say claimed by the author, although under the cover of a distinction between value-judgments and something called "existential" judgments. In spite of the fact that this division is almost canonical at the present time with a certain school of writers, I cannot see that it amounts to anything save denial that socalled "value-judgments" are judgments at all, since they fail to satisfy the conditions which have to be met in all subjectmatters of recognized scientific standing if a statement is to be called *judgment*. But of course the fact that the logical distinction which is supposed to be drawn rests upon denial, by assumption, that values and valuations are themselves factual or "existential" is the fundamentally important matter. The assumption that value-judgments are about something that doesn't *exist* is extraordinary enough in itself. When we add to that remarkable fact the further fact that, *prima facie,* the presence of valuings and valuations is just that which distinguishes social events as facts or existences from the subjectmatter, say, of physical science, the extraordinariness involved seems to amount to incredibility.

III

I suggest accordingly that we substitute for the distinction made by Mr. Benoit-Smullyan (along with many other writers) between two kinds of *judgment*, the distinction between relatively *direct* behavioral prizings, loyalties, etc., and relatively indirect behavioral operations in which these prizings are subjected to critical inspection. We start from and with what can hardly be denied to be fact:—Namely, that we are constantly and perforce, because of the very conditions of living, engaged in affections, admirations, aversions, preferences, and also in "judgments" about them. All movements, causes, all affairs of widespread concern are expressions of behavioral attitudes of the direct kind. Evaluations are employed to defend, to support and buttress, the movements, causes, policies in question. Because of pressure of social facts (not because, that is, of private whim) certain of the more primary human attitudes become suspect;— clash of group-values and valuations being perhaps the most outstanding source of their being subjected to doubt, question, and more systematic "rational" consideration.[4]

The difference between behavioral attitudes called primary (in a comparative sense) and those called secondary and derived, or, specifically, between valuings and valuations in the senses previously specified, is then a difference of phase or emphasis. In principle there is no difference between this case and that, say, of drinking and enjoying water on one hand and investigating the chemistry of water on the other hand. There is some "knowledge" involved, some "cognitive" aspect, in the more direct

4. The presence of quotation marks about "rational" is not to be taken as implying that the rationality involved *must* be "rationalizing" in its psychoanalytic sense. The extent to which such is the case at present only poses the problem of *how* discussions on such matters are to be brought more definitely into line with procedures which are practically standard in subject-matters which have achieved, after long struggle, scientific standing. This problem certainly requires the intensification and extension of a certain affection and certain practical habit, usually given the name of scrupulous regard or esteem for truth and the reduction of certain other affections and modes of esteem. But that which is intensified and extended in range is not a component of judgment but a condition favorable to the occurrence of judgment as an event in human behavior while the "emotional-volitional" attitudes excluded are so far from being "components" that their strength in preventing the occurrence of judgment-events is just the ground for the effort to reduce their efficacy.

cases. But the *subjectmatter* of investigation is not what it is in the comparatively indirect or reflective case. A human being is concerned in each of the indirect cases, and he has not parted with preferences—with biases if you please. But in those cases to which the name *Judgment* is applicable the nature of preference has changed. It is now a preference for finding out, for learning, to which other preferences and prizings are, temporarily at least, subordinated. There is no logical or theoretical point of view or line of approach from which judgments about "values," about cases of valuing in the sense specified, can be differentiated from any other type of judgment *qua* judgment. But the very fact that we are dealing with *judgment* signifies that differences in *subjectmatter* must be fully and firmly acknowledged; it is as much refusal to meet the conditions set by a given problem of judgment to try to reduce prizings as subjectmatter to the terms of, say, molecular subjectmatter as it would be to insist that because they swim in the sea whales must be fish and can be judged only in piscian terms.

IV

I shall now state briefly the respect in which the "practical" conclusion to be drawn from the foregoing account is in general agreement with that expressed by Mr. Benoit-Smullyan as far as the social sciences are concerned. For our author in spite of his own dualism of value- and existential-judgments emphasizes the harm that has been done by a certain *interpretation* of this dualism: an interpretation which as he says has exerted "a profoundly unfortunate influence upon the development of the social sciences," having led to the doctrine that "value judgments are *un*scientific and must be excluded from the *life* of the *scientist*." [5] The policy often called that of "neutrality" and which our author terms passivity, is one of being "imbued with contempt for and distrust of value judgments and with a deep-seated unwillingness to become at all involved in problems of social policy."

In conclusion I propose to state briefly how a conclusion of the

5. Op. cit., p. 204. The fact that the italics are in the original text seems particularly significant in view of the shift from the logical to the "personal" which has been pointed out.

same general nature, with respect to inquiries into sociological subjectmatter, follows, directly or without ambiguity and switching from one point of view to another, from the account already given in this article.

1. There is nothing peculiarly "personal" about the prizings, loyalties, ties which are subjectmatter of those inquiries that result in "evaluations." Their *locus* may be said to be "personal" if one so choose. But this fact no more determines the character and features of the events in question than the fact that the central geographical locus of an earthquake in say northern Japan overrides the fact of its being an earthquake. Policies, institutions, customs are the seat of "valuings"; they are in this sense *sociological* phenomena or manifestations *par excellence.*

2. In what has preceded emphasis has fallen chiefly upon the relative places and operations of valuings and valuations in behavior as a *temporal* spread. This emphasis needs to be supplemented—and corrected as to its one-sidedness—by express noting of spatial spread. For since both valuings and valuations are currently embodied in customs, institutions, etc., they extend over a considerable range of territory. In short, although sociological events as subjectmatter of study have their own characteristic and specifying features, *they are temporal-spatial,* and hence in line with all subjectmatters of scientific inquiry. "Individualized" locus of date and place of occurrence is not a case of immaculate birth which takes them out of the possibility of "scientific" approach and attack.

3. The history of astronomy and physics as sciences, as well as biology, shows what a struggle these subjects had to undergo in order to arrive at that kind and degree of "neutrality" which would permit events of an effective-inquiry sort to take place. It is obvious without argument that sociological events are intimately and still more deeply enswathed with biases, prejudices, preferences, etc., that are hostile to the effective rise of that special kind of preference and loyalty which evokes and directs competent impartial inquiry—that which now is conventionally called "objective." And just as in astronomy and physics this and that scientific inquirer became emancipated from the conditions which had earlier obstructed inquiry in the degree in which the vocation of inquiry became socially established and confirmed, so one may say, with considerable assurance, will it be in the case

of investigation and report of sociological events with respect to their valuing-and-valuation aspects. Because inquiries and judgments of the kind called scientific are themselves social events, developing in the medium of other social events and finding their place upon them, there is no peculiar logical or theoretical problem about their capacity to exert "practical" influence. There are problems aplenty. But they are all aspects of the associated "practical" problem of how the behavioral attitudes called scientific shall become more widely naturalized in the actual conditions of living.

Importance, Significance, and Meaning

This essay marks an attempt to develop a number of considerations which are reasonably fundamental in the theory of knowing and of what it is to be known, which form the substance of a recently published collection of articles by A. F. Bentley and the present writer.[1] The articles that are gathered together in this volume had been prepared for by a series of prior publications. Omitting periodical publications, reference may be made here to the following works by Bentley: *Process of Government* (1908, reprinted 1935, 1949); *Relativity in Man and Society* (1926); and *Behavior, Knowledge, Fact* (1935); while Dewey had followed *How We Think* (1910) by his *Essays in Experimental Logic* (1916); and a more systematic treatise, *Logic: The Theory of Inquiry* (1938). It is pertinent to note that the positions set forth in the recent joint volume had been in process of independent maturing for some forty years; the book thus represents a view which, whatever else be said about it, is not casual nor improvised but is the outcome of studies carried on over a long period and taking critical account, between them of a large number of traditional and contemporary movements. Moreover it has seemed to the writers that the convergence in conclusions of inquiries having different backgrounds and traversing different areas of subjectmatter is a valid source of increased confidence in the community positions that took shape as a conse-

---

1. *Knowing and the Known*, Beacon Press, Boston (1949).

[Introductory section from unpublished June 1950 typescript in the Arthur F. Bentley Collection, Manuscripts Department, Lilly Library, Indiana University, Bloomington, 3 pp. Remainder of essay from typescripts in the John Dewey Papers, Box 58, folder 9, Special Collections, Morris Library, Southern Illinois University at Carbondale, and Bentley Collection, 23 pp. each, dated 30 and 31 March 1950; published in *John Dewey and Arthur F. Bentley: A Philosophical Correspondence, 1932–1951,* ed. Sidney Ratner and Jules Altman (New Brunswick, N.J.: Rutgers University Press, 1964), pp. 658–68.]

quence. It is relevant to the present essay (since it is by but one of the authors of the joint volume) to say that the unlikeness in original interest and background and in subjectmatter consists, speaking in general terms, in the fact that Bentley's approach was distinctly from the side of science especially as contemporary developments in physical and biological science bear upon the problem of bringing into existence a competent scientific and effective method of inquiry into human relationships as they now exist; a work which involves a critical study of traditional and current psychological and societal theories with respect to their ineptness in providing intellectual instrumentalities that are competent to initiate and develop scientific study of the human relationships that constitute the modern or contemporary world.

The concern of the present writer on the other hand had been with the subjectmatter constituting the issues, problems and conclusions of the chief doctrinal systems of philosophy, reaching the conclusion that thoroughgoing reconstruction is necessary if they are to give direction to human activity in a time when scientific, industrial, and political revolutions have profoundly disturbed, in fact largely disintegrated, the conditions of life in which these systems were generated and to which they were applicable as far as they had any directive function. The critical study of philosophical conclusions disclosed that their inefficacy to life-activities and their problems as of the twentieth century centre in the virtually complete irrelevance of the method of knowing (conventionally known as Logic) framed in pre-scientific, pre-industrialized and pre-nationalistic periods to guide in a fruitful way the inquiries that would give that understanding of present human conditions which is the prerequisite of formation of intelligent policies. The appeal of the discussions to be found in *Knowing and the Known* is chiefly directed to those who on one side (doubtless much the larger number) appreciate the need of development of a scientific method with respect to the facts of human relationships as they exist in the present age; and, on the other side, to those whose concern with philosophy is of the order of Socrates, faithful to his conviction that philosophy is love of wisdom and that wisdom, while based on the best science obtainable, has to do with policies which put that science to use in the guidance of our common human life.

The pertinence of this otherwise overlong introduction to the present essay lies in the fact that while intended to carry on that convergence of studies with respect to the theme of method undertaken on the one hand from the definitely scientific point of view and on the other hand from that of historical doctrines, the restatement of the main postulates of the *Knowing and the Known* volume is here made in terms which while with respect to language employed are not technically philosophical are undoubtedly influenced by their author's long concern with philosophical issues. They are perhaps especially applicable because it is only towards the close that there is explicit reference to Importance, Significance, and Meaning as naming the subjects which in their connection with one another are taken by the author to delimit the subjectmatter that traditionally goes by the name of Logic.

I

The immediate occasion of any instance of knowing as inquiry, according to the view to be presented in what follows, is (i) the occurrence of an event in the ongoing course of life-activity which interferes in one way or another with the ongoing course of the behavior that has been proceeding smoothly and which in consequence (ii) deflects it in the case of *human* knowings into what may properly be termed a *reflective* channel, provided "reflective" be taken literally as standing for deliberate *going-over of the conditions* of direct straightaway behavior (iii) preparatory to its resumption. In terms of more specific and also more general application to inquiry behavior, animal or human, investigating, looking into, is both intermediate and mediating in the course of life behavior, which, as such, is always sequential, consecutive, in its continuity. Beginning because of an interruption, a disturbance, an unsettlement of the life-behavior going on, its work is to discover how its ongoing course may be restored by means of (a) finding out what the matter is, and of (b) finding how the immediately sequential activity may overcome or get around the obstacle that is the occasion of the "hitch" in the specific way of behavior that is in process.

It is not possible for the writer, in the present state of theory, to ignore the fact that what has been said will seem to many persons to be altogether too common and coarse, indeed degrading a view of such an undertaking as knowing. The case of higher and finer, more complex instances of human knowing will be dealt with later; but it is pertinent to say here that when knowing is treated as inquiry, and then inquiry is treated as one way of life-behavior among other ways, it is obligatory to set out with a statement of as wide, or general, application as possible. No one who has watched pre-human animals will, I suppose, deny that animals investigate their surroundings as to conditions of how to proceed. They are watchful, wary, in the presence of danger; they are ingeniously adaptive in protecting themselves and also in conducting themselves so as to catch their prey unawares. Be it remembered that what is here said is concerned with observable behavior, not with respect to some unobserved suppositious factor, mental or whatever, and it will hardly be denied that the sniffings, the cocking of ears, the poising of the body and head, the turnings and fixations of the eyes that are present in the case of wild animals with which one is familiar are temporary deflections of ongoing behavior into an intermediate route of examination of conditions about them in their bearing upon *what* to do: that is, *how* to proceed in subsequent behavior. There is nothing covert in these statements; they are not made to conceal something to be sprung later upon an unsuspecting reader, but to direct attention to facts which (from the *standpoint* and *view* to be presented in this article) constitute the comprehensive pattern of knowing as inquiry even though they be systematically ignored in many traditional theories.

II

Express consideration of human inquiry as behavior may then well begin with a highly rudimentary case. Take the case of a motorist who, arriving at a crossroads and not knowing which direction to take, pauses to look at a signboard which he has espied. The existence of two roads, only one of which takes him where he has planned to go, constitutes the interruption, interference, "hitch" that occasions deflection of immediate *straight-*

away proceeding on his journey into the channel or route of *inquiry.* Seeing that the hand pointing say in the righthand direction has attached to it the name of the town to which he is going, he turns and proceeds in that direction. In this simple case of knowing (and of a-known as its consequence) I can hardly imagine that anyone will deny that the looking-seeing activity is as much an integral part of the journey as is the conduct of the motorist in steering his car, nor yet that while it is a constituent of the journey it is a temporary deflection of ongoing behavior into what was termed an *intermediate* and *mediating* way or route of behavior. There was a "hitch"; an uncertainty; a question; questioning; the answer to the latter is manifested in and is constituted by resumption of straightaway activity.

From the standpoint of a theory that regards this as an exemplary—although extremely simple—case of inquiry, it follows (i) that pausing to look served, and was undertaken so as to serve, as a *means to a consequence,* the latter consisting of obtaining direction as to how to proceed; while (ii) the instruction, information resulting from the looking *as* inquiry, was had by *using* what is seen as a *sign:* a point that may seem trivial to the point of tautology in the case of looking at a *signboard,* but which is fundamental and indispensable from the standpoint of the incident in reference to the theory of inquiry as knowing. To *perceive* in the sense of *observing* is identical, positively and negatively, with observing in the sense of paying heed to what is observed as *directive or sign* in further actions. When things seen, heard, touched, smelled and tasted are *observed,* noted, heeded, they are treated as serving a specific function or office. The office in question is that serving an end-in-*view,* or purpose which is entertained; hence it involves a need to be *tested* by its meeting or failing to fulfill the end for the sake of which it was used as a *sign;* in consequence, a fact which involves concern for additional observation, namely, the consequences actually occurring as distinct from those wanted and held in view. In the case of a signboard at a crossroads, it would be decidedly extraordinary if its dependability *as* sign had to be tested by observing what took place in consequence of employing it as a directive in behavior. But as will appear later, while that fact affects the *adequacy* or *completeness* of it as an exemplary or typical instance with respect to theory, it does not affect it as far as it goes.

III

　　Before concluding then from what has been said that the heart and the life-blood of human knowing is that inquiry as an intermediate and mediating way of behavior is constituted by determination of subjectmatters as on one hand means to consequences, and on the other hand of things as *consequences* of means used (as would be the case if our motorist had to be constantly on the look-out so as to note the results of having turned in a given direction), another more complex instance will be introduced. The instance selected is that of a physician called in to deal with a patient. It is safe to say that the physician *perceives* many things as he comes into the sick-room that he regards as unimportant in signifying, telling the directive use to be made of them in treating the patient. But as a matter of theory it holds that he has no *sure* ground for deciding in advance just which of the things that offer themselves to sight and hearing are signs and which are not. Some of them like the furnishings of the room are heeded only as directives to his locomotion; yet it *may* turn out that the position of the bed with respect to the light and air reaching it from a window has in the given case to be treated as significant with respect to the way of treatment of the patient. But what is outstanding in this case is (1) that observations undertaken in order to find out what is the trouble, the "matter," or just what sort of a "hitch" has to be dealt with are indefinitely more numerous, varied and continuous than in the case of the suppositious motorist. It is as if the motorist in order to find out the direction in which to move had to study the board for hours, use various instruments to make out just what the board said or was a sign of with respect to how to proceed; and at that, had not only to call upon a store of facts previously learned and *to be* learned by consulting books, periodicals, etc., to find out what the seen fact indicated or told as a sign, and also had to come back day after day to study it, particularly with reference to noting changes that have taken place with respect to *their* signifying capacity.

　　(2) This, however, is only half the story and with respect to theory—although not with respect to practice—the less important half. By the very terms of the case as described the motorist does not have to investigate his destination; that is settled in ad-

vance, and his only question is *how* to get there. It may be asserted that the case is the same in the matter of the physician's inquiry; his goal is also settled in advance, being the restoration of the health of his patient. The specious nature of the assumption of identity is evident, however, when it is noted that the end of restoration is the same in the case of every physician in treatment of every patient; accordingly it provides no directive whatever to inquiry in any particular case. As ultimate destination it is as settled in advance as is destination in the case of the motorist. Hence in one case, as in the other, it does not enter in any way into *inquiry;* in one case as in the other the *what,* the subjectmatter, of inquiry is to find out *how* to arrive at the destination settled upon. When it is accomplished, restoration of health is an *end* inquiry; it is its close, its limit; its termination. Naturally every inquiry aims at arriving where it will no longer be needed in that particular case. The end in and for *inquiry* in the case of the physician, as in every other inquiry of any degree of complexity, is that of discovery of the process of restoring health; making out this, a specific way of proceeding; a *how* to act. *Practically* speaking when the inquiry is over the end is the end and that suffices; *during* the inquiry its end is to discover what the trouble is with a view to find out how to deal with it. Assumption that a *limit* of inquiry is identical with the end-in-view *during* inquiry is a flagrant absurdity. It assumes the work inquiry has to accomplish has already been done. *What* to do in the case of inquiries under way is all one with *how* to proceed under given conditions, in which the first, the primary office of inquiry, is to ascertain what the conditions are at a specific time and place since the latter are indispensable conditions of finding out what to do as the *sine qua non* or as in attainment of the goal or destination as a settled and ended matter.

From the standpoint of facts observed or observable what has been said is a laboring of the obvious; not so from the standpoint of traditional and still rife theories. A mechanic doing his job knows (as does the physician engaged in his special activity) that consequences which are actually reached depend upon the means employed so that the goal or destination to be reached operates as a factor in the work that he is doing only if, when, and as it is translated into an end *held in view* as *means* (i) of selecting conditions to serve as signs, indications, of what the trouble is to be dealt with; which is itself often an exceedingly long-continued process first of making and then of revising observations (as in the case of the diagnosis of a physician); while consequences as ends-in-view are also used as means in determining what to do. Consequences are also *in process* of development or are changing as long as inquiry continues, change being as proper in their case as being final and settled is proper to an end as a destination to be reached. Observation of conditions as they are at the beginning of an inquiry and as they are at various stages of inquiry-behavior as it proceeds is a matter of determination of events in their office, use, function of *means to consequences*. This fact is so evident in the case of the physician's diagnosis that it will not be dwelt upon in that case. It must, however, be expressly acknowledged as an indispensable part of observed facts in their theoretical bearing. For they prove that treating things as means to consequences and treating proposed ends-in-view as also means to a final consequence is, as was said, the life-blood of intelligent behavior in general and of inquiry as a particular phase of intelligent behavior. As a matter of record rather than as an additional matter, it is here noted that as long as inquiry proceeds, conditions observed as signs of the matter to be dealt with as a problem which is to be solved by inquiry, and ends-in-view used as means of directing activity so as to solve the problem as it is made out, are tentative, on trial; inquiry being competent in the degree in which observations made are such as to provide *improved* means with which to operate. Whatever else is to be said or left unsaid about dogmatisms and dogmas, with respect to *inquiry,* to knowing *in process,* they are fatal. To be *bound* to a given conclusion is the exact opposite of being *required* to inquire so as to find out the means of reaching a conclusion as a decision that warrants resumption of decisive behavior.

We thus return to the thesis of knowing as intermediate and mediate in life behavior and, in the case of dog chasing rabbit, as they poise tense bodies, cock ears, turn head and eyes, sniff the air as successive integral phases of directing an inclusive ongoing process of living. The pattern of inquiry-behavior as intermediate and mediate is the same in all these cases. In each one of them inquiry as knowing maintains the transactional qualification that is so manifest when an animal, whether dog or man, partakes of food. Because of the greater simplicity of pre-human animal behavior it is easier to take account of lookings and seeings, listenings and hearings, as integral constituents of continually ongoing life-activity in their case. Another advantage in paying at least passing heed to the latter is that it exhibits so definitely the intrinsic absurdity of sensationalistic empiricism with its isolation first of the sensory from the motor—to which as sensory it is subordinate—and then of the motor from the ongoing course of the particular ongoing life-activity within which it takes place and operates. The facts of the case, in reference to sensation, are so outstandingly obvious in the case of dog and rabbit, hen, chick, hawk, etc., etc., that it does not seem possible that they would have escaped attention in theory had not some wholly extraneous non-natural factor have got so lodged in the view taken of human activities and affairs as to blind vision.

However, this recognition of unity of pattern with reference to inquiry as intermediate and mediating form of transactional behavior is not the end of the story. On the contrary, it renders the more urgent and acute the question of determining how the differences within the unity of pattern arise and function. The issue involved is so involved with a variety of highly complicated controversial issues, that it is fortunate that the intention of this paper is to obtain understanding of a certain theoretical point of view rather than to obtain its acceptance. The latter would demand surrender of cherished traditional doctrines; those which have recourse on one side to spirit, soul, reason, intellect, mind, consciousness, as a ready-made independent self-active entity; and/or on the other side have recourse to reduction, via say special cerebral organs, or "the organism as a whole," to terms that have been found to work with a high measure of success in physical or mayhap physiological inquiries.[2] The influence of one or other of these two doctrines is still so great that it probably would be over-optimistic to anticipate widespread agreement; but a certain measure of understanding may, perhaps, be hoped for.

Observed and observable facts make it evident that all distinctively human intelligent behavior is attended with use of artefacts, appliances, implements, tools, weapons, head- and foot-

2. To one having even a rudimentary sense of irony and who is willing to indulge it, the fact that "spiritualistic" and "materialistic" interpretations and explanations are cut from the same cloth by use of one and the same logical pattern should prove amusing.

gears, etc., and with use of *arts,* which (as words used as names indicate) are akin to artefacts; and which are acquired, learned under and because of tuition of others who in turn have derived their aptitudes from parents, instructors, etc., in a succession of events going back to the first appearance of man on earth; skills, which be it noted, would *not* exist, and would be idle if they did exist, were it not for those specific artefacts which constitute language as a human concern.

That animals communicate with one another and that their communications give *de facto* direction to subsequent behavior is too obvious to need being dwelt upon. There is no evidence, however, that the activities through which pre-humans communicate differ in kind from their acts say in getting and eating food. That is to say, although in some animals they are marvelously developed (e.g., the chimpanzee) there is no reason to infer they are either more or less *native,* "natural," *raw,* in the sense of being independent of intentional use of artefacts.

The facts to which attention is here called are so much a matter of course, and observation of them is so inevitable and recurrent, that it is laboring the obvious to note them just as facts. Noting them, however, in their bearing on the *theory* of human action in general and human inquiry in particular lies at the other pole. To go into detail would be to engage in writing a history of civilization. It is not only physically impossible to enter upon that task here, but if there were set forth even an extensive record of only three artefacts, the wheel, fire, and conversion of "natural" seeds into articles of cultivation, there is no way in which readers can be forced into considering the facts cited in their status of evidence for a given theory. The most that can be done is to *invite* the cooperation of others; and if doctrinal precommitments are too strong the invitation will be declined— without thanks. Nevertheless, it is an indispensable part of the invitation to note that the arts—and all activities akin to arts in being intentionally undertaken and involving use of *means* (including both skills and appliances)—are what they are because both *environing* and organic partakers in behavioral transactions have undergone marked transformation from their native or natural estate. It may sound strange to say that all appliances, implements, *works* of art, from a hoe to a thermometer, from a polished flint to the radar, would be wholly useless, and would *not* be instruments of action, if sounds of the human voice and marks made on paper by human beings had not also undergone transformation into names which stand for things. But the oddity, if such there seems to be, is due to the fact that the two are so actually, existentially, intimately unified in every human intelligent act that the feeling of oddity is due to the attempt to view them in separation even in imagination. The role of magic in certain stages of human culture is evidence of how names as themselves were used as effective appliances in dealing with environing conditions in lack of the material appliances by which to obtain desired consequences.

Instead then of accumulating cultural facts as evidence for the view that artful transformation of environing and organic conditions in their mutually complementary partnerships suffices to explain what is distinctive of human behavior, I shall point out how that is so, from the side of theory. Take the case of as simple an appliance as the hoe and an art as simple as that of the rudest gardener who has skill in using the hoe as means-to-consequences in cultivation of plants for food. To one who has never seen or heard of the use to which the hoe is put, the end it serves, and of the consequences following upon its use as means to consequent events, a hoe may be *perceived* as a curiously shaped thing—just as many adults have *perceived* polished stones without having had a sense of the part they have played in some age of culture. If curiosity is aroused and is satisfied as to why the thing seen or touched has the peculiar conformation it presents to view, then perception becomes *observation;* mere noticing becomes *noting.* An event in the way of specifically human behavior has come into existence. It is not just something to which pre-human animals are indifferent but that attention, heeding, involves, brings with it, an end as a consequence *in-view.* Its being itself held in view, or heeded, as *means* for bringing something wanted into existence is all one with having the latter in view as a directive in subsequent proceedings. *De facto* processes become intentional proceedings as *de facto* successions and subsequents are held in view. The hoe is a sign, an index, of what is still future in fact but which *as* held *in view operates* in the present to bring future events, which would not otherwise take place, into existence.

It may not accord with customary linguistic usage to say that whatever is observed as a means-to-consequence tells something;

conveys information; gives advice; operates as a warning as much as if a human stood on guard to keep others out of threatening danger. Of course the art of speech makes possible a vast extension of what the hoe has to say for itself. But this extension, say into the habits and traditions of remote early stages of culture, could not take place were it not first for a physical grasp of a hoe as a tool in attaining an end in view, and when so used were it not followed by that apprehension which is capable of indefinitely expanded grasp, and hence of things future and past, far beyond the reach of sense-perception.

For foresight has developed, no one knows how slowly or in what round-about ways, into that systematic intentional foresight that bears the name planning; and *planned* appliances and skills indefinitely extended the range or scope of schemes of activity that look ahead into the future, and that can be carried into effect only by means of reorganization of past events. Wisdom as prudence could hardly have come into existence without a store of things to care for which is itself as *store* a tie of the past to present and future. Only in recent periods of human history have there been in existence means for planning human arrangements on a large scale; that is, with respect to consequences distant in space and remote in time. Even so, we have as yet acquired so little wisdom with respect to use of the terrifically powerful new skills and new mechanical appliances suddenly and without preparation put at our disposal, that the events which result, with *physical* inevitability, from the machinery are sub-sequential, not *con*sequential; of a physical rather than of a human order. Human beings *operate,* run, the machines but they do not *use* them. The difference between operating and using is no merely verbal matter of the kind with which what is now boomed as semantics is occupied. It involves nothing less than a problem of change in personal and institutional behavior so basic and comprehensive that it may include even the future physical existence of mankind. To operate is possible on the ground of existent habits and traditions—personal and institutional. To *use* is possible—as the entire previous discussion indicates—only on the basis of direction by ends-*in-view* systematically arrived at and framed by means of consideration of means available.

There have been periods in human history when operation of available resources on the ground of habit and precedent was reasonably pertinent. That time is no more. For the habits and precedents which now operate were developed and justified under conditions that have little in common with those which now determine what follows; what is physically sub-sequent but which one can hardly be pessimistic enough to believe are consequences of deliberate and matured intention.

The intrinsic difficulties in the way of framing ends-in-view which would work in the direction of *use* of the mechanical appliances and skills that have developed in a state of historical absentmindedness are enormous. But they are artificially reinforced and exacerbated by systematic propagation of the docrine that "nature" suffices to do what should be done. That doctrine was outgrown ever since the day when men with adequate wit took account of how increasingly dependent is man upon works of art and the skilled workings of art which transform nature for human use and enjoyment. With the advent of world-wide operation of mechanical appliances and skills for *use* of which men were virtually completely unprepared, and the *sub*sequential events of which penetrate every remotest nook and corner of life, it is not possible to find an adjective that does justice to the enormity of the assumption that is. There is, however, no intimation in what is said that development of ends-in-view and of the kind of planning that may ensure use as distinct from operation is an easy or simple problem. It is rather credible that it will take centuries to accomplish its solution; and that it will be the main preoccupation of mankind for long and difficult ages to come. But it is at least relevant to note that systematic acknowledgment in philosophy of the role of artefacts and arts in specifically human activity, with corresponding elimination of all the unrealities that have been depended upon to do the work that they actually accomplish, may be the means by which philosophy would recover a position of esteem and respect.

IV

It is time, perhaps more than time, to be explicit with respect to what the words name that are used in the title of this article. It should not, however, come as a surprise to one who has followed the course of the foregoing discussion to be told that, according to the view herein presented, the distinguishing and identifying mark of distinctively human activity in every one of its many varieties, knowing included, is the demand made in it and upon it, with respect to its measure as *intelligently* managed, to consider, weigh, estimate, judge or pass upon the *importance* of what is presented, suggested, in any way entertained and held in view with how to proceed when difficulties and obstacles are incurred. According to this view, importance is the generic term; significance and meaning are the specific ways in which the issue of importance has to be dealt with; there being species because all behavior is transactional so that importance as a concern of knowing is twofold. It has to be determined with respect to both the *environing* and the *organic* ways of responsive, adaptive, behavior that enter into every mode of behavior.

Both of the partaking constituents of behavior have *de facto* importance; they *bear* decisively upon the activity that follows and is subsequent. Quite literally they import the following activity; that which succeeds in the sense of being successive in time whether or not it succeeds when viewed as a mode of life-behavior. Because of the foresight and intention, that are made possible through artful products and artfully acquired skills, human beings anticipate what is to come; the *sub*sequent then becomes a consequence *to be* achieved, reached, and as such is an end-*in-view*. As a further result, importance of environing conditions and organic ways of treating them are inquired into, investigated, examined, weighed, judged in advance of being put to actual overt use in bringing about events which in any case *follow* activity engaged in. Until things are seen to have a bearing upon the consequences of activities engaged in, they may be *perceived;* they are seen, touched or heard. It is impossible for human living creatures to avoid seeing, hearing, touching a great variety of matters to which they are indifferent until they have a reason for whether they may not be either helpful or harmful in respect to what is done. A theoretical statement has *also* to note that importance is of two distinguishable but inseparable co-working and reciprocally complementary ways because life-behavior is transactional. When a transaction is intelligently conducted, and is intentional and deliberate, environing conditions and organic modes of responsive treatment have each of them to be weighed with respect to their importance; that is with respect to the consequences which are [# # #] to end as termination quite as much as environing conditions that are employed *as* means.

Since, as previous discussion should have made clear, environing conditions are weighed and estimated as *signs,* indices, of how to proceed, *significance* is beyond peradventure a fit or suitable word to name their distinctive mode of importance—though of course there is nothing of pre-established harmony in its use. The suitability of *meaning* as name for the importance of the contribution made by the organic partner—especially with respect to words as names—is from the standpoint of current philosophical terminology a highly questionable matter. By setting up the logical as a kind of existence which is neither physical nor mental nor yet a functional service of behavior as inquiry, a "domain" or realm of "essences" has been created; *meaning* has in philosophical usage become neither fowl, flesh nor good red herring. Only one who has familiarity with the literature of the subject can even begin to be aware of how confusing, obfuscating, and boring in its multiplicity of elaborations the word "meaning" has become. But when one has recourse to the idiomatic usage of meaning *to mean* is to intend, the suitability of *meaning* to name way or mode of artfully skilled ways of organized action is as evident of *significance* as name for the complementary way of being important.

How, What, and *What For* in Social Inquiry

I

The basic postulation in the following discussion is that the heart and life blood of *intelligent* behavior consists of continued and deliberate attention to the relation of things which are viewed and treated as *means* to those which are viewed and treated as consequences, it being understood that the connection in question is thoroughly *reciprocal:* that is, consequences have to be determined on the ground of what is selected and handled as means in exactly the same sense in which the converse holds and demands constant attention if activities are to be intelligently conducted, instead of in a routine or a spasmodic way.

The expression "postulation" is deliberately used instead of "postulate" in order to emphasize that postulation is itself a case of behavioral activity and hence is an integral component of the entire behavioral process; while "postulate" is often, perhaps usually, employed in another sense, namely, that of a principle laid down in advance and consequently exercising some authoritative control over the behavior that ensues.

I do not argue the case here because this entire article is an exposition of the position just set forth. But it is fitting to point out that the distinction just made is of basic not merely casual import. For what is at stake or issue is nothing less than the ques-

[From revised January 1951 typescript, 13 pp., and signed, holograph addition, pp. 14–18, in the John Dewey Papers, Box 59, folder 13, Special Collections, Morris Library, Southern Illinois University at Carbondale. For same paper edited by Joseph Ratner, see Appendix 3. Earlier version, "Means and Consequences— *How, What,* and *What For,*" published in *John Dewey and Arthur F. Bentley: A Philosophical Correspondence, 1932–1951,* ed. Sidney Ratner and Jules Altman (New Brunswick, N.J.: Rutgers University Press, 1964), pp. 649–54.]

tion of whether behavior is to be viewed and treated as basic instead of derived and hence as controlling and as authoritative with respect to the entire scope of activities which, being *intelligent,* are specifically *human,* or whether the properties that render it intelligent are introduced from a source extraneous to human behavior—whether this outside factor is called *soul, mind, subject, intellect,* or *brain* making little difference. It makes little difference since it is taken to be extraneous instead of a name for properties that belong intrinsically in and to behavior as far as the latter is specifically human.

The bearing or import of the position just stated is probably most immediate and direct in application to that centrally important way or mode of intelligent behavior which is designated *knowing,* and the outcome of which is institution of the subject-matters that are said to be the *knowns* whether of everyday "practical" behavior, or of that theoretical way of behavior termed "science."

Postponing for the present consideration of the import of this position upon what is designated *knowns,* I begin with the bearing of the position upon the process and operations constituting *knowing* when that is systematically looked upon as a mode of behavior.

Probably the most obvious consideration is the *negative,* namely, the complete ruling out of any need to introduce or refer to considerations of terms either ontological or epistemological or that mixture of the two which has flourished so abundantly in the post-medieval systems commonly called "modern" but which in fact are heavily loaded with a heritage from Greek-medieval systems in which *Being* as synonymous with the immutable or unchanging is the all-determining authoritative fact.

The simplest way to present the significance of the statement just made is to call attention to the place occupied and the office performed in "modern" philosophy (so-called) by matters designated by the names subject, object, mind-world (no matter whether mind is viewed in terms of sense or of "rational" intellect, nous). In anticipation of later discussion, it may be noted at this point that it was theoretically possible ("conceivable") to view the subjectmatters involved as discriminated from and connected with one another on the basis of the function respectively and reciprocally *performed* (the *service* rendered) by each in the effective promotion of cognitive, intellectual behavior—that is, *knowing*. But what took place actually and historically is that the previous bias in favor of the *immutable* was so projected into the distinction and the relation of the matters termed subject and object, mind and world, that they were viewed as themselves of two contrary immutable ontological kinds. There are few systems and/or doctrines of the post-fifteenth century no matter whether sensationalistically empirical or rationally noetic, whether idealistic ("spiritualistic") or "materialistic-mechanistic," that can be understood without steady attention to the fact that they are operating in terms of the mental and the material, the psychical and the physical, or more generally the inherently subjective and inherently objective, as two independently given immutable kinds of existence: the fact that as existences they were endowed with spatial-temporal qualifications being of immense technical importance in contrast with the prior *supra*-temporal-spatial value accorded to "Being" but being negligible in import with respect to consequences entailed in making it imperative to treat "knowing" as an action-reaction taking place between two independent and opposed kinds of entitative existences—the fatal heritage of Greek-medieval ontology with respect to a theory of knowing professing to be independently "epistemological" but in fact determined in every aspect and phase by the heritage introduced by the older identification of true Being with the unchanging—the "essentially" and "by nature" immutable.

II

I come now to the specific subjects constituting the title of this article, the mode of treatment consisting, as already indicated, in regarding the *how*, the *what* (or subjectmatter), and the *why* or what for as interconnected transactional distinctions which it is urgently important to institute and to observe in the conduct of behavior that is intelligent in general and that in particular constitutes the way of behaving that is knowing.

It is hardly necessary to engage in elaborate argument in behalf of the proposition that there is no intelligent human behavior which does not depend on *foresight of consequences* that are likely to ensue from the course of behavior entered upon. Without going into the matter in detail it is pertinent to refer here to a previous article of mine on "Common Sense and Science"* (as synonymous with practically and theoretically instituted knowings) in which the distinction between them is based (inclusively and exclusively) upon the *range of consequences* intentionally or designedly involved. A man crossing a street in which there is two-way traffic has to note, observe, heed what is going on with respect to the consequences of the *particular* act in which he is engaged. Installation of a system of red and green lights to direct the course of traffic generally is a technological device that could not exist apart from the much more extensive purview or survey provided by knowledge of the way or form constituting scientific knowing.

What is important for the purpose of the present discussion is that while anticipated, foreseen consequences constitute, or are, the *what* of that which is done, of the behavior enacted, the way in which foresight of consequences (as the what of a given behavior) serviceably operates is by means of directing deliberate search for the specific conditions by active use of which as means the consequences that are foreseen will be attained, preferably in the most economical and effectual way, a qualification which emphasizes the point already made about the comprehensive, the inclusive, foresight that distinguishes the *scientific* way of knowing. Since the more generic the foresight the less likely is the kind of action which will be obstructive and troublesome in forming as well as executing future plans which will satisfy the conditions to be met in such conduct as is intelligent rather than merely routine on one side and/or casually and hastily improvised on the other side.

The *theoretical* implications of the facts just adduced may need explicit statement. In brief, they amount to the impossibility of setting up any separation or conflict within *intelligent* behavior between its *what* and its *how*. With respect to knowing, foreseen consequences as forming its *what* are an integral component of the *how*, that is, the procedure, or method, of knowing. If this were not the case, if foresight did not accomplish a distinctive use, service, office, function of this sort, there would be no differ-

* See this volume, pp. 242–56.

ence between it and the idle daydreaming in which consequences are anticipated on the ground of their immediate agreeableness. Separation of the *what* of a course of activity from its *how*, in the sense of the continuing sequence, consecutiveness, which is the mark of any intelligent activity, results inevitably in those absurdities which bear respectively the names of *ends-in-themselves* and *means-in-themselves*—a striking instance of giving way to the ever-present philosophical fallacy of reifying, hypostatizing that which in fact is functional. A volume could be written upon the harm that has resulted in moral-political theory by treating things, *res,* subjectmatters which function as means and consequences, as if they were such "by nature" or in their "essential" being—the inevitable outcome, logically, is setting up some things as ends-in-themselves and other things as inherently, necessarily, means-in-themselves. Look, for instance, at the sharp division that is currently accepted as gospel truth between *moral* subjectmatters and *economic* subjectmatters. The separation is now so thoroughly established as to be regarded as virtually "self-evident." In consequence it is not noted that inquiry, knowing, in both cases is tied down in advance. Instead of being free to follow where the subjectmatters involved (that is, in question) may lead, it is *pre*-committed to reaching certain conclusions. If certain matters are in and of themselves means and only means, and other things are of necessity, by nature or essence, ends and only ends, all that remains is a dialectical development of matters already asserted to be so fixedly given "by nature" or in essence as to be completely immune to investigation. They are in effect if not in name sacred, protected by a taboo that is not to be brought into question under any circumstances. At the very time when the moral (i.e., the human) consequences of industrial and financial arrangements are most in need of systematic critical scrutiny they are brought under the cover of being necessary because of the essence of the matter, while on the other side the human, or moral, principles and standards which were fixed in situations radically other than those which now prevail are given a thoroughly factitious, artificial authoritative prestige.[1]

1. The fact previously emphasized that immutability as the inherent necessary property of any and all subjectmatters which are "scientific" was carried over and projected into the physical and the psychological objective-subjective domains of existence, is of course of direct and controlling import in this matter.

III

Discussion now takes up the *what for* or *why* in its connection with the means-consequence function. It is possible, though not of course certain, that the presence of "what" in any expression has a certain "what for" import not to be found in the expression "why." At all events, the fact of its presence may be used to suggest that in its reference and bearings it is a refined amplification of the *what* as *foreseen consequences* and it is not consequential or of moment with respect to behavior unless it is a matter of affection, in the sense of care, concern, deliberate consideration of the "why," the purpose.

Determination of *what* is required to complete apprehension of the *function* served by the *what*. Like the *what,* the *why* is subject to reification; and all so-called "normative" theory is the result of treating the "what" or "why" as something absolute, or as "in itself," instead of in the use to which it is actually put. Whatever may be said about certain subjectmatters as subjects of mere description as over against those which are said to be normative, when one fastens attention upon *method* it is clear that accurate and comprehensive knowledge—that kind of knowledge termed "scientific"—has coincided with elimination of reference to essences, inherent natures, and the substitution for the latter of deliberate respect for the body of spatial-temporal factualities that are involved. Until the "normative" subjects take to heart the lesson of the history of scientific inquiry, there is no hope of making any assured advance. It would be difficult to hit upon a fact for investigation that would prove more fertile or more rewarding with respect to the theory of knowings-knowns than study of the history of astronomy, physics, physiology, geology, with regard to the role played in these fields by fixed standards, principles, as determinative and hence as authoritative.

The theory involved in the historical material is not far to seek.

The "revolution" actually effected in "modern" science consisted in the substitution of two immutables for the one ontological, rational immutability of Greek-medieval science. In consequence, the significance of the scientific revolution for the theory of knowings-knowns is still the central issue in contemporary philosophical thought.

Every such procedure, resting upon fixed standards, amounts to an automatic foreclosure of free and hence full inquiry and critical reflection. It is a mortgage against the future.

There is no sense in examining, investigating, observing—perceptual or ideational (reflective thinking)—unless these activities result in a *more* adequate grasp of the "why" or "what" of the *res,* the affair, the subjectmatter observed, examined, investigated; unless it results in a *greater, keener* appreciation and foresight of the consequentiality of the consequences. In fine, the "why" or "what for" functions in regard to intelligent behavior—(including knowing) as a part of the "how" or procedural method that has proved to be effective because not subjected to pre-established, antecedent conditions regarded as "normative" and inherently regulative. That the principle of the autonomy of knowing as inquiry, investigation, examination, search (not just *re*-search) is the very life blood of all intellectual endeavor worthy of respect is demonstrable in terms both of history and theory.

In philosophy, hypostatization of functional relations "rules the roost." Philosophers have clung the more tightly to what is alleged to be "in and by" its own nature or essence, identifying the total *raison d'être* of philosophy with unique concern with what is such and such absolutely, and not such and such because of its mere, inferior, connection with things of "merely" spatial and temporal being. Nothing can be of greater import in this connection than the fact that the natural sciences—astronomy, physics, chemistry, biology, etc.—all began their careers with this assumption of the absolute necessity of treating their subjectmatters as thus and so by essential nature; and they have all advanced in scientific knowings-knowns in the exact measure in which this assumption was negated and consideration of the connections of events as spatial-temporal affairs was substituted therefor. By a curious kink, the actual result of this historical development in the natural sciences has not been to lead to the adoption of the same method of inquiry in the human-moral subjectmatters; rather has it led to the intensification of the alleged dualism between the "normative" and the "descriptive" and the resolute, systematic identification, on the part of the human-moral studies, with what could be termed "normative itself" and "normative in authority" because based upon alleged inherent fixities and absolutes.

So far nothing has been said which bears directly upon the phrase "In Social Inquiry" as that occurs in the caption of this article. Its relevance will appear when we recal before there occurred the revolution that is associated with Copernicus, Galileo and Newton, *all* "physical science" was taken to be the cosmological or "natural" branch of *ontological philosophy* and that the revolution by which "natural philosophy" passed into the sciences of astronomy and physics (and later of physiology) took place when inquiry became concerned with *how,* namely the spatial-temporal order of events instead of with *what* (formal cause and essence) and with what for—final cause and teleology. There is no reason to suppose the course and destination of inquiry in human or "social" subjects (including those traditionally called "*moral*") be any different.

The transition and transformation did not occur at once. In the Newtonian system, space and time were still taken as entities on their own account and hence as separate from one another and also from what was supposed to take place within their fixed framework—that is, they were not *seen* nor yet treated as the *how* of nature but as its essential *what*. The doctrine of *Relativity* however completes the tale. Space and time are names for orders of events which moreover are integrally connected with each other. *How* things go on at last as far at least as scientific inquiry is concerned, has won the victory over *What* and What For. The victory will be achieved however only when inquiry into social whats and what fors is systematically viewed and treated as an included subordinate factor in determining *how* the subject-matter proceeds; thereby attaining scientific status. That is to say, the spatial-temporal order specifically involved constituting the resolution of a given problematic indeterminate situation.

Essays

The Field of "Value"

    In the present state of the subject of value, the decisive issue is methodological:—From what standpoint shall the subjectmatter of valuings and evaluations be approached? What postulates shall determine selection and treatment of this subjectmatter? The reference made above to "the present state of the subject" is important. It is not meant that the methodological question can be separated from that of subjectmatter, nor that the former should remain paramount indefinitely. On the contrary, if and when it is cleared up, we shall be able to go ahead and use it, testing and developing it as we proceed, without need for special discussion of it. But a glance at the controverted present state of inquiry shows that no question is more pertinent or more penetrating than the one asked by Mr. Pepper: "How guarantee that different writers on 'value' are discussing the same subject?"[1] And I find the phrase (in his previous sentence) "subject or field of value" equally significant. For the confused controversial state of the subject seems to arise from the fact that there is no agreement about the *field* in which events having value-qualifications are located. Till this field is reasonably settled, discussion is a good deal like firing birdshot in the dark at something believed to exist somewhere, the "where" being of the vaguest sort. In such a state of affairs, it would be pretentious to do more than put the methodological issue first or do other than offer an hypothesis.

---

1. Contained in the questions and comments preliminary to the present cooperative inquiry.

[First published in *Value: A Cooperative Inquiry,* ed. Ray Lepley (New York: Columbia University Press, 1949), pp. 64–77.]

I

I begin then by saying the hypothesis that gives direction to the following pages is that the field in which value-facts belong is *behavioral* so that the facts must be treated in and by methods appropriate to behavioral subjectmatter. The words "behavior and behavioral" are, however, far from self-explanatory. A few preliminary remarks are called for. As here employed, the words refer exclusively to events of the nature of *life-processes* in general and animal life-processes in particular. Objections and criticisms that are made from the standpoint of the assumption that the words apply only to what is stated in *physical* terms—those of strictly physical knowledge—are, accordingly, aside from the point. Life-processes have a physical aspect, and no account of them is adequate that does not draw from available physical knowledge. But this is a radically different matter from *reduction* to physical terms. Furthermore, while *human* behavior has, without doubt, an animal, as well as a physical, aspect, it has such distinctive features and properties that it cannot be reduced to exclusively physiological terms. It suffices here to cite the fact of *language*, that cannot occur without physical conditions nor without physiological processes, but that cannot be reduced to them without making nonsense of all its characteristic traits.

Reference to life-processes takes us only a little way in locating the field of value-events. The qualifications to be added are (1) limitation of life-processes to those of selection-rejection, and (2) specification of the fact that such processes serve, from the amoeba to the highest form of primate, to maintain all life-processes as a going-concern. That is, all have an *end*, not in the metaphysical or quasi-metaphysical (often called "mental") sense of that word, but in the sense in which *end* is equivalent to result, outcome, consequence:—in short, is a strictly *descriptive* term.

These qualifications, in connection with the primary statement about life-processes, indicate that the field in which value-facts are located is *behavioral* in a way that renders the facts open to observation and test in the usual sense of those words. Since the tendency of life-processes of selection-and-rejection is to sustain and continue life-processes in general (not merely those then and there engaged in), the word "field" is particularly applicable whenever the names *valuings* and *values* are used. For the hypothesis stated rules out any view that treats them as independent and self-contained and as momentary or short-span "acts." It rules out any view that assigns them to some peculiar agency or agent. The selections in question not only themselves extend over a considerable stretch of space and time but they cover, in their results or outcomes, the whole course of life, including, through the processes that effect reproduction, the life of the species.[2] Processes of rejection take in long-term functions of elimination, of protective defense, and of aggression directed against destructive elements.

There is no implication that the facts mentioned do more than locate the field in which value-events are located; it is not implied that they cover, without further qualification, these events. But even without further qualifications, certain *methodological* conclusions directly follow.

(1) Since the field is one of observable space-time facts, appeal to *introspection* when that word is used to designate observation of events that by definition are wholly *private* is ruled out. While the exclusion follows from the hypothesis presented, it is not arbitrary. On the ground of *any* theory, appeal to mere introspection is wholly inadmissable in *discussion*. That which is wholly private has to be left where it occurs and belongs—in private seclusion. Appeal to it in arguments directed to others is one of the Irish bulls of philosophy. The idea that the introspection of another person can be assumed to note the *same* fact repeats the bull; it doesn't escape it.

(2) It follows that since selection-rejection as life-processes always take in something—some *thing*—which is selected or rejected, the answer to the preliminary question raised by Dr. Lee "Is there any such thing as value which is not the value of some particular thing, event or situation?" is definitely negative.[3]

(3) Another methodological conclusion, given the hypothesis, is that there is no peculiar class of things (much less of "entities")

2. It is not meant that observations extending over much narrower fields are not legitimate in certain inquiries, but that observation of life-processes of selection *in respect to the issue in hand* must take into account their full reach.

3. The word "thing," as in the words *anything* (as in the phrase "any such thing" above), *something,* is to be taken idiomatically, not as denoting a substance, physical or mental. It covers events, situations, persons, groups, causes, movements, occupations, pursuits of all kinds.

to which value-qualifications can or should be attributed. The previous point indicates that "value" is an *adjectival* word, naming that which is a trait, property, qualification of some thing—in the broad sense of *thing* mentioned. It is like, say, the words good, fine, excellent. What is now added is, in effect, that when *value* is used to designate any special class or category of things, it is used as an abstract noun. If language had provided us with a special abstract noun (such as *goodness* in connection with *good*), say *valuity* or valueness, a good deal of ambiguous discussion resulting in incoherent conclusions might have been avoided. Anything under the sun may come into possession of what is named by "value" as its adjective. And cultural anthropology would seem to indicate that at some time and some place almost everything has in fact been assigned that qualification.[4]

(4) It is almost a restatement of the point just made to say that "intrinsic" as applied to "value" is so ambivalent as to be more than question-begging. It so effectually conceals the genuine question as to close discussion in advance. For, in one sense, the word is innocent; it only means that the trait in question *actually* belongs to a specified something *at the time and place:*—as snow is "intrinsically" white *if and when it is* white. But as a plus question-begging epithet, it is used to take the thing and its property out of all space-time connections, rendering them absolute. In this usage it is a belated survival of that "essence" which once was used in all branches of "science" to account for properties of things, making the latter *what* they "really" are. In every progressive branch of knowledge "essences" have long since given way to consideration of space-time connections. Progress of inquiry in the value-field waits upon a similar methodological change.

II

Discussion now arrives at consideration of the specific qualifications that accrue to life-processes of selection-rejection when they come into possession of value-qualifications proper. Introduction of the term "caring-for" to designate a particular

---

4. It is this fact that renders the preliminary question raised by Mr. Jessup especially searching:—the question, namely, as to the relation between occurrent values and standard values.

kind of selections-rejections may suggest the point to be made. *Carings-for* occur in the case of some sub-human animals, and are not of themselves equivalents of valuing. But they point in the direction of the latter. Caring-for mates and young is characteristic of the behavior of some animals. A robin, for example, manifests care in sitting upon eggs till they hatch; feeding and otherwise nurturing the young; keeping them warm, protecting them from enemies, helping them learn to fly, etc.

If one additional condition were added, we should be obliged, I believe, to identify these carings-for with valuings. But as far as we can tell, these carings-for, although systematized and extending across particular places and times, do not include express recognition of their result as the ground or reason for their being engaged in. *If* the animals in question have an anticipation or foresight of the outcome and if they perform the caring-for behaviors so that they are colored and directed by the foresight, *then,* on the basis of the hypothesis advanced, they fall within the value-field proper. In an illustration used by James, eggs in the case of a broody hen are "never-too-much-to-be-sat-upon." If the hen observed the outcome on account of which they are to be sat-upon, we should be obliged, I believe, to say that she "values" the sitting, and the eggs, and the chicks, as integral in and to the sitting.

The above is hypothetically stated. In the case of humans we know that the condition of foresight and use of what is foreseen as ground or reason is fulfilled. Since many varieties of things furnish grounds for various kinds of carings-for, we find, as might be expected, that carings-for, valuings, take many forms. In consequence, the word breaks up into a set of words including such behaviors as "Prizing, holding-dear, cherishing, esteeming, admiring, honoring, approving, reverencing, supporting, standing-up-for and/or by; being faithful, loyal, devoted to; concerned, occupied, with." And the phrase "interested in" has to be used, if at all, in the specifically behavioral sense in which a partner has an "interest in" a business, or as in cases in which an "interest" is subject to legal determination. Idiomatically, the word is still generally used, I believe, in this sense; but subjectivistic psychology has colored the word in its own direction and the result has so seeped over into discussions nominally philosophical that use of it is hardly safe.

Whichever one of the above words is used, it is evident that the *facts* involved extend widely across times, places, "objects," and agents-patients. There is a systematized interconnection of various special acts and "things" such as are given, in the case of digestion and circulation, the name of *function*. Whether this word is used or not in the case of prizings, esteemings, cherishings, etc., the observed facts emphasize a point previously made:— "Valuing" is *not* a special isolated type of act performed by a peculiar or unique agent, under conditions so unique that valuings and values can be understood in isolation from orders of fact not themselves of the "value" kind.

Accordingly, this is as appropriate a place as any to call attention to the ambiguity of the phrase "relational theory" as applied to theories about valuing. The hypothesis here advanced is "relational" as opposed to the "absolutistic" nature of some presentations of the "intrinsic" theory. But this highly general consideration leaves the nature of the "relation" in question open to a variety of interpretations. The idea that *value* is a relation between "mind," "consciousness," a "subject" and an "object"; or between an organism and an "object"; or between some special act variously named liking, enjoying, desiring, being interested-in (viewed as "mentalistic processes") are some of the current types of "relational" theory. All are radically different from the hypothesis here advanced. Indeed, I believe the attitude of taking valuing (when the absolutistic version is repudiated) as some kind or other of unique direct relation between two separate things accounts for more of the confused state of the subject than does any other one thing. Only if the "relation" in question is understood to be plural (since involving a variety of space-time connections of different things), not singular, and it is also definitely observed that the connections in question are *across* spaces, times, things, and persons, will "relational" theory lead to any commonly agreed upon conclusions.[5] In that case the "relations" will be seen to be the connections constituting a *transaction*, and "transactional" will displace "relational."

5. More specifically, until "liking," "desiring," "enjoying," etc., are identified in terms of some inclusive behavioral transaction, as long as they are taken to name separate acts, mental or organic, complete, ready-made in themselves, I doubt if there is much point in introducing reference to them. When they are identified as aspects of a behavioral transaction, the case is, of course, quite different.

III

So-called relational theories often retain an attenuated relic of absolutistic theories in the use of the term "intrinsic." This retention is manifested when "intrinsic" is placed in opposition to "extrinsic" and the latter is identified with a "value" belonging to things as mere means ("means-in-themselves"), and the former with the "value" belonging to things as "ends-in-themselves." In fact, the necessity of employing the phrase "in-themselves" shows that the absolutistic retention in question is *more* than attenuated. "In-themselves" is always a sure sign of denial of *connections,* and hence is proof of an affirmation of an absolute. As long as this continues, discussion of valuings-values will remain in its present backward state, as compared with the subjects in which "scientific" advance has taken place only because inquiry has abandoned search for anything "in itself," and has devoted itself instead to search for observable connections.

If observation, not conceptual (actually verbal) abstractions, be resorted to in this matter of "instrumental" and "final" values, it will be noted that things used as means (whether material or procedural means) are in fact prized, cherished, made subjectmatters of loving care and devotion, in every art and pursuit that has attained any desirable development. The notion that *value* is "instrumental" because "instruments-means" are what are prized hardly attains the dignity of a pun. Is there a special type of value, deserving a name of its own, in the case, say, of dogs or jewels being prized? If values are of an instrumental type when things as *means* are cherished, why not a *type* of dog-value or diamond-value in these other instances?

The idea that things as ends can be valued, cherished, held dear apart from equally serious valuing of the things that are the means of attaining them is more than a fallacy in theory.[6] The man who says he deeply or intensely values some "end" and then shows himself indifferent to, neglectful of, the things upon which the "end" depends is either a liar intent upon deceiving others or

6. Repetition of the phrase "*things* as means-ends" may seem finicky. But in the present state of discussion I do not believe too much care can be taken to obtain protection against the notion that there are such matters as means and ends in themselves; a notion of the same nature as that *value* is a "concrete" noun in and of itself.

is badly self-deceived. In spite of the currency of *theory* as to the difference, with respect to "intrinsic" value, between things that are means and things that are ends, the conduct of decent and competent people is better than their professed theoretical beliefs. They manifest their devotion to "ends" by the patient and constant care given to "means."

The practical consequences of theories which separate means and ends with respect to the value they possess are two-edged. On one side, their import is to render so-called "ends," in the degree of their ultimacy, "ideal" in the most utopian, sentimental, empty and impotent sense of that word. They are not only so "ultimate" as to be unattainable, but they lack directive power. I have yet to see an answer even proposed to the question: "Of what good is a 'final' value unless it *also* has 'instrumental' value?" The other edge concerns the implication that things which are means have no value of their own; no "intrinsic" value, in the intelligible sense of that word. This implication is best shown when we take an extreme case. *Fanaticism* is the legitimate practical outcome of sharp separation of means and ends as to value. When it is assumed as matter of course that certain "ends" are ends in and of themselves (and hence are ultimate), and therefore are not themselves capable of being subjected to inquiry and to measure of worth, attention properly (on the ground, that is, of the assumption) goes wholly to the means for attaining them. All the evils that result from acceptance of the theory that the "end justifies the means" are the outcome. Since whatever is set up as end is fixed and unquestionable, being such in and of itself, there is no need for examination of the *consequences* that in fact result from the use of certain things as means. Sadistic cruelties, brutal persecutions, only *seem* to be such. In reality, according to the logic, theoretical and practical, of the view, they are means of attaining values of such supreme worth that those who use means which seem to be inhuman, are in "reality" humble servants of ultimate overruling good. Escape from utopian unattainable "ideals" consists in fanatical devotion to whatever is arbitrarily set up as means. The latter view is the complementary aspect of the former. Any view which in the name of inherent difference in "type" between final and instrumental values sets up values *per se*, no matter what consequences or "ends" they *are* "instrumental" to, tends in practical logic to promote fanaticism.

IV

Some of the material found in the questions and comments preliminary to the present study gives evidence of a misapprehension that distorts the meaning of caring-for (valuing) in the sense of behavior which maintains in existence the things prized or cherished, the things in question being said to have existence prior to the prizing in virtue of which value-qualification accrues to them. No one, I suppose, would question that a pearl, say, takes on color-qualification when it comes into specified connections with light, optical apparatus, etc., and I hope it may also be assumed by this time that such connections as these, not a "relation" to mind, consciousness or whatever, is what counts. The hypothesis here offered is that a pearl takes on value-qualification under conditions of the same type—though not circumstantially the same. The following passage is, then, worth quoting because correction of the misapprehension it evinces should bring the position held into clearer relief.

> It seems to me that in some experiences ordinarily held to be valuable we are concerned with preserving the existence of an independently existing object that we prize, in other cases we are not so concerned. In the esthetic field, the former is the attitude of the curator of a museum, the latter the attitude of the visitor who merely wants to look at the pictures and who leaves their maintenance to the museum staff. Each type of prizing is legitimate and may be valuable, and they are distinct. So a complete theory of value must allow for both attitudes, and each must be assigned its distinctive kind of value.[7]

While I have difficulty in seeing how a reader of my original text could understand the relevant passage in such a way as to make this criticism seem pertinent, I welcome it, now that it has taken place, since it affords an occasion for fuller statement.

(1) There is a shift, occurring twice in the passage quoted, from that which is prized as that which is valuable over to the "experience" of prizing as that which is valuable. Presumably, the shift occurred because the latter expression states the view held by the author. But it is not mine nor relevant to mine. Aside

7. Statement by Mr. Rice in the preliminary questions and comments.

from the ambiguity of the word "experience" (since it is often given "mentalistic" meaning but may be used as a generalized equivalent of behavior), it is definitely implied that prizing is what is prized, and hence that which has "value." I do not doubt that *after* acts of prizing have taken place they are often submitted to judgment to see whether *they* should be prized, and hence "maintained" in future conduct. But such reflective inquiry and its judgmental conclusion is assuredly no part of an original prizing "experience." If I dwell upon this aspect of the passage, it is because it seems to me to afford a fine illustration of the vagueness in which the subject of value-field is at present wrapped.

(2) The words "maintenance in existence" are given, as in the curator illustration, an exclusively *physical* import. It is possible that there are some curators whose care does not extend beyond that point. How much care can be said to be in the "*esthetic* field" escapes me. If the acts of caring-for or prizing that are involved *are* esthetic (as I hope is the case with curators), then care for the physical preservation of a painting is surely but one aspect of a much more inclusive prizing.

(3) The "looking" of a visitor is a *behavioral* act on the hypothesis I have advanced. If the behavior in question is in the esthetic field, it is anything but a manifestation of "merely" wanting to look at pictures. The behavioral act of looking does not become esthetic merely because paintings are the *things* looked at. "Looking" may be a casual glance; it may be intended to identify the painter, or the probable commercial value of the picture, or to identify the scene represented, etc., etc.

(4) If the act of looking *is* in the esthetic field, then (i) a non-esthetic seeing or looking comes first, and in that sense has prior and independent "existence," and (ii) the act *becomes* esthetic in qualification when the seeing is cherished or prized as something worth sustaining and developing. No looking that is momentary is esthetic; the maintaining in question is explorative across spatial parts of the picture, and it takes time to be genuinely esthetic. A measure of esthetic worth is whether "seeing" is soon exhausted or one finds something new to appreciate at each seeing. The visitor who goes into raptures the very moment his eyes light on the painting is indulging in gush, not in esthetic envisagement. Esthetic perceptions are *trans*-actional more emphatically perhaps than any other kind of observation.

The present also seems a fit occasion to say something about so-called different types of value. I do not doubt that after the ground work has been laid in a general theory of valuings-values and of critical judgments (evaluations), it is needful in discussing problems of genuine importance to discriminate various aspects of value-qualification. Some specifiable aspects and phases are proper to esthetic theory; others to ethical theory; others to economic theory; others still to logical theory as methodology. But I believe (i) that reification of aspects into separate types is a weighty factor in producing the lack of agreement that now marks discussion in these subjects; and (ii) that until a ground work has been laid in a tenable general theory of valuings-values, forays into these subjects are so far from being helpful as to add to the present state of confusion in any attempt to arrive at a sound theory of "value."

V

I now come to consideration of *judgments* about valuings-values; namely to the topic of e-valuations. In the first place, with due respect to those holding the opposite opinion, I would say that there *are* such events as e-valuating inquiries terminating in judgments; and that, like judgments in all other fields, the latter are more or less well-grounded at given times. In short, propositions about values may be genuine propositions and not *mere* reports that a given thing is or has been valued. It seems to be generally admitted that genuine inquiry, resulting in genuine judgments, is possible and desirable in the case of so-called instrumental values. But it is often held that in the case of so-called final or ultimate values all that is possible is communication of a particular item of information, namely, that they are or have been valued, plus strangely enough, in some cases, the assertion that they *ought* to be universally valued, although no reason can be given beyond the assertion that they are "ends in themselves." As against this view, which is bound to play "logically" and practically into the hands of external "authorities," formulation of a comprehensive theory of the connection of evaluations with *de facto* occurrent valuings is indispensable.

Discussion begins with the fact that carings-for, cherishings, as *de facto* valuings have what in psychological language is called a *motor* aspect. Observation of the fact that animal selections-rejections are attended frequently with rage, fear, sexual affection and attachment, shows they also have an *emotive* aspect. The question of whether there is also an "intellectual" aspect determines the answer to be given the question whether direct prizings, etc., as valuings have genuine or "intrinsic" connection with evaluative judgments (and the latter with the former), or whether they constitute two separate kinds of events. The hypothesis presented answers this question in the sense of the first of these alternatives. Anticipation, foresight of the outcome, of a caring-for as *ground* for a behavioral caring-for, supplies the link of intrinsic connection.

For ground *when it is itself inquired into* is identical with *reason*. Given carings-for may have conditions of the kind often called "causal." If they are investigated to find out whether they are *sufficient* to warrant the particular outcome whose anticipation is the ground of a given valuing, then prizing enters explicitly into the class of events that are judgmental. There is no normal human being who does not have at times to raise the question whether some prizing he has more or less habitually indulged in should or should not be itself maintained in existence. If he more or less habitually raises that sort of question, he becomes aware that the "causal" conditions of some valuings are irrelevant and even perverting in respect to the result or consequence that has been prized. It is seen that class-membership, irrational prejudice, dicta proceeding for those in possession of special prestige and/or superior power, etc., etc., have operated to determine a given valuing (which as transactional includes that which is valued). From the inquiry and its conclusion (judgment) a changed prizing and thing prized necessarily proceeds. Judgment of values, in short, is the deliberate development of an aspectual constituent of the more direct prizings and cherishings that human beings as living creatures must and do continually engage in, and under such conditions that *at first* they are relatively "thoughtless." [8]

8. The answer to the question I raised in my original list of "Questions" as to whether the distinction between direct valuings and evaluations as judgments is one of separate kinds or one of emphasis is, accordingly, answered in the latter sense. I am the more bound to make this statement because in some still earlier writings I tended to go too far in the direction of separation. I still

As far as *de facto* prizings rest upon current mores, plus the manipulations of those in positions of superior economic, political, and/or ecclesiastical power, they are so perverting in effect as to provide whatever color of plausibility is possessed by the view that rational valuations are impossible. It is doubtful whether, at least for a long time to come, their operation can be wholly eliminated from the most reasonable evaluative judgments that can now be framed. But that is no reason for shutting out the attempt in advance and thereby maintaining the evils to which attention is called. Moreover, it is most decidedly to be noted that not many centuries ago conclusions in astronomy and physics were vitiated by the predominant influence of conditions of the kind mentioned; that less than a century ago biological inquiries were subjected to great distortion from the same source. The liberating movement that has taken place in these other fields of inquiry is sufficient ground for the attempt to emancipate valuings and evaluations from similar influences. The notion that there are such affairs as exclusively "final" values is now the chief obstacle to making the trial. It is hardly less than a moral tragedy to find those who profess "liberal" tenets actively aiding and abetting dogmatic absolutists.

Since my hypothesis is that the methods of inquiry in observation, formation and test of theories that have proved effective and fertile in other fields, be employed in the value-field, there is no reason for going into detail here as to the inquiries that will progressively yield sound judgments in the field of "value." It should, however, be pointed out that such inquiry will be systematically directed (i) to the *conditions* that at a given time determine the valuings that take place, and (ii) to the consequences that actually follow from valuings determined by that sort of conditions. In inquiries of this sort the "valuings" may be temporarily left out of account and attention go to the consequences produced by the uncriticized customs, prejudices, class-interests, and exercise of superior power (including particular claim to the power to settle penalties and rewards, temporal and "eter-

think the reason that actuated me is sound. In current discussion, traits distinctive of valuing are frequently indiscriminately transferred to valuation. But the resulting confusion can be escaped by noting the distinction to be one of phase in development. [See *Later Works* 15 : 101–8.]

nal") that determine the valuings. The idea that judgments about valuings-values must themselves be made in terms of values is on a par with such views as that judgments of color must be settled in terms of colors, not of conditions set by vibratory processes or corpuscular shocks. It is exactly the kind of methodological view that kept all the "sciences," or knowledge generally, in a retarded state for uncounted millions of years.

The question has been raised whether all value-judgments do not have the function, and implicitly the intent, to which the name "persuasion" can and should be given; and whether this fact does not confer upon them a property so peculiar as to mark them off from all other kinds of judgment. Upon the ground of the hypothesis here proposed, the answer to the first part of this compound question is affirmative (under a qualification to be mentioned), while the answer to the second part is negative. That the office of *moral* evaluations is to influence the behavior of others through forming in them an intellectual disposition favoring a certain kind of conduct does not seem to me open to question. The view is not so easily applicable to esthetic judgments. But I believe that adequate discussion would show that it holds. For the present occasion,[9] I limit myself to saying that wherever *standard* values figure in any way, the function of *should* or *ought* comes in, so that the office and intent of influencing, directing subsequent behavior, is clearly in evidence. The qualification mentioned above is that "persuasion" be limited to the *intent and office* of evaluative judgments, and not be treated as one constituent along with factual evidential constituents in the *subjectmatter* of the judgment.

That the use or "function" in question does not render evaluative judgments in any way unique in kind may be clearly seen by examining the case of judgments recognized to be of the "scientific" kind. Competent judgments (conclusions) in the field of astronomical, physical, physiological subjectmatters are, by the very definition of "scientific," the outcome of scrupulous and systematic care in selection of genuinely evidential material, with equal care in rejection of all subjectmatter whose presence can be

9. For more detailed discussion of this point, I refer to my article, "Ethical Subject-Matter and Language," the *Journal of Philosophy*, XLII (1945), 701–712 [*Later Works* 15 : 127–40]. "Persuasion" takes effect in selecting and ordering factual subjectmatter but is not itself any part of that subjectmatter.

traced to bias, prior commitment to a particular theory, professional prestige, popular repute, etc., etc. Both the morale and the technique of effective valuing are more highly developed at present in "scientific" subjects than in those conventionally allotted to the field of "value." The function of persuasion and of producing conviction is so far from being peculiar to judgments conventionally recognized to be in the value-field that it is now better exemplified in "scientific" inquiry and the propositions that result from it.

It follows from what has been said that there is nothing whatever that methodologically (*qua* judgment) marks off "value-judgments" from conclusions reached in astronomical, chemical, or biological inquiries. Specifically, it follows that the problem of "the relation of value to fact" is wholly factitious, since it rests upon and proceeds from assumptions that have no factual foundation. The connection of value-*facts* with other facts forms a problem that is legitimate-plus. It is indispensable. Evaluative judgments cannot be arrived at so as to be warranted without going outside the "value field" into matters physical, physiological, anthropological, historical, socio-psychological, and so on. Only by taking facts ascertained in these subjects into account can we determine the conditions and consequences of given valuings, and without such determination "judgment" occurs only as pure myth. I can hardly better conclude this statement of the theory I hold as to valuings and evaluations than by expressing my agreement with words of Dr. Stevenson when he said that moral evaluations should "draw from the whole of a man's knowledge"—extending the statement to apply to evaluations anywhere and everywhere.[10]

10. For the Criticisms which relate especially to this paper see *Value: A Cooperative Inquiry*, pp. 312–318.

Has Philosophy a Future?

I

There is one point in which all systems of philosophy agree with one another in spite of many conflicts in other respects. They all hold that what marks philosophical inquiry off from other intellectual undertakings is the inclusiveness of its subjectmatter. Their divergencies from one another do not spring from any difference on this matter; it arises from what is supposed by different systems to constitute that which is inclusive. On this point it suffices to cite one familiar case. Philosophies that hold that Spirit or Mind is all embracing are countered by systems asserting the same thing of Matter. The agreement about Inclusiveness does not furnish a secure point of departure for further work in philosophy.

Nevertheless, this fact is not brought forward in order to cast doubt upon the view that concern for what is inclusive, is after all the sign and seal of philosophical topics. The aim is to suggest that it has been looked for in the wrong direction so that it is worth while to try the experiment of turning around and about the direction in which what is comprehensive is to be looked for. The meaning of "The other way around and about" is obviously vague until the way with which it contrasts has been specified. The traditional direction of search is fortunately not hard to identify. That which has been taken to be the all-embracing has been given such names as Being, Reality, The Universe, Nature at Large, and so forth. These names have been supposed to designate that which is inherently marked off from everything else as

[First published in *Proceedings of the Tenth International Congress of Philosophy*, ed. E. W. Beth, H. J. Pos, and J. H. A. Hollak (Amsterdam: North-Holland Publishing Co., 1949), pp. 108–16, from paper read for Dewey by Sidney Hook at Amsterdam on 14 August 1948.]

partial. Hence, the bearing of the phrase "The other way around and about" is not hard to discover. Search that is specifically philosophical should be directed to what is most comprehensive *within* human affairs and occupations, not towards that which is completely independent of concerns and occupations that are distinctively human.

This change of direction is not, however, as hostile in respect to historical systems as it seems to be at first sight. For examination of these systems shows that in effect though not in profession they have always been human in the ends they served; indeed, they have frequently been only too human in the ways in which they have promoted their chosen ends. In any case, the view that underlies the present paper is that such words as Being, Reality, and Universe at Large have only been covers or cloaks for what in fact has been relative to the human. Instead, however, of arguing on behalf of this view, I simply place it in opposition to the traditional position which is no less an assumption than the one here taken. It may be also mentioned that every treatise dealing with the history of philosophy is compelled to recognize the human relativity of the systems dealt with for it classifies their material according to periods of time and according to the country in which the systems have made their appearance. The most important consideration, however, is that only the open recognition that philosophical issues and problems are related to circumstances of time and place can avoid the gulf which now exists between philosophy and science. Our "other way around and about" is contented to leave the eternal and the immutable alone in their solitude so as to be in accord with what is genuinely scientific, since the latter always deals with what is located in time and place.

That philosophy has not existed at all times nor in all countries is a commonplace. This fact, however, implies something that is not commonplace, namely that philosophy has made its appearance only when specific cultural conditions are present. The first of these conditions is the existence of a general state of uneasiness due to the danger of disintegration within the established order. Another requisite condition is that there be loyalty to the values that are found in the established order provided that the loyalty is intellectual instead of merely a matter of custom and habit. The times in which philosophy has flourished have, in short, been either times of great stress and strain in human affairs, or else, as in the case of Scholasticism, of an attempt to create an intellectual synthesis of a vast and highly diversified type of previous accomplishments.

II

The foregoing statement is not made, however, on its own account. What we are here concerned with is the kind of philosophy which will have to be developed in order to be relevant in the present crisis of human affairs. That this crisis is now inclusive in its extent is evident in its literally world-wide occurrence. The expression "One World" has to do with a world which is one only in the sense that it is unsettled and disturbed throughout all its parts and in the relation of these parts to one another. Moreover, the crisis is as intensive as it is extensive. Disturbances in family life, in the relation of the sexes, in industry and commerce, in politics, domestic and international, penetrate so deeply that the ground could not be covered without occupying about as many pages or even volumes as lines can be given on this occasion to the topic. I can only invite those who are interested to observe the facts of widespread uncertainty and strife for themselves. The results of any such observation may be confidently trusted to show that the present human situation is one of unsettlement, confusion, frustration, insecurity, and concealed if not open warfare.

I select here for special attention only one aspect of the disturbance. Not more than a single generation ago there was a general belief that democratic government was developing so surely and at such a rapid pace that its complete and speedy victory all over the world was assured. Today the revolt against democracy is so serious that political regimes which deny the rights of free assembly, free speech and free press, free choice of religion and political party, unblushingly assert that in this denial they represent a climax of democratic principles. In addition, they find devoted adherents to their cause even in countries having historic democratic background. The same state of tension is manifested in those tendencies which on one hand lead to formation of the "United Nations," and on the other side produce conditions which distort and indeed almost inhibit the realization of any co-operative unity.

In short, what we find everywhere is that immense increase occurring in a comparatively short time in the means which are at our disposal is attended with an equally great loss of assurance and of agreement with respect to the Ends in whose behalf the means are used. This inclusiveness of tension, uncertainty, and strife meets one aspect of subjectmatter that is specifically philosophical. Something else is required however to render the picture complete. Here again, because of the limitation of time at my disposal, I can only invite your own attention to facts that indicate the incapacity of present philosophy to deal with the present order of human unsettlement. The philosophies now at our command took shape when institutions existed that provided life with some kind of working guidance. Those institutions have broken down, hence they fail to provide the guidance which is now needed more urgently than at any previous time in human history. The breakdown has taken place so rapidly and so unexpectedly that no new integration of human relationships has had a chance to develop. On its negative side, this human situation presents a supreme challenge to philosophy in its existing state. The very features that once rendered past philosophies humanely useful are the very ones that unfit them for service in a radically changed human situation. On the positive side, however, this situation opens a supreme opportunity for the development of a philosophy which shall be relevant to the present.

The remoteness of the systems inherited from the past to the present human scene exhibits itself in a variety of forms. The case in which distance from the present scene is most obvious is the one in which those professionally occupied with philosophy devote themselves almost exclusively to the study of past systems. As a matter of scholarship the outcome is often admirable, but since the study is not conducted in order to discover the light these past systems shed upon what philosophy should now engage in, its outcome is a matter of history rather than of philosophy. Another movement active and even assertive within its own chosen but narrow limits, identifies philosophy exclusively with search for forms simply as forms; it engages in an attempt to discover forms that are comprehensive only because they are so abstract as to have no connection with any specific subject whatever, human or otherwise. This movement, in spite of or rather because of its devotion to acquisition of merely technical skill, results in forms that are useful only in producing more forms of the same empty type. This retreat from the present scene is, I believe, an expression of a growing sense that past systems are irrelevant to the present human state combined with a defeatism that has not the courage to search out a philosophy that shall be relevant.

In the third place, there is now an aggressive philosophical movement, which, on the basis of its own claims, is as relevant to our present human estate as the two movements just mentioned are aloof from it. This type of movement is one which in both intention and actual effect is devoted to the interest of a particular institutional organization, thereby subordinating the authority of intelligent inquiry to the authority of a particular social institution. Two varieties of this movement exist; one of them is new and is as far to the extreme Left as the other and older one is to the extreme Right. In spite of the gulf between them, the two together furnish an all but perfect illustration of the saying that extremes meet. The old form appeals to a supernatural spiritual authority; the new one bases itself upon economic affairs as strictly materialistic. Extremes meet, however, in that each type of philosophy is employed to support the claim of a particular institution to regulate the conduct of human life. Each one claims an authority which is so final and absolute as to confer upon the institution it represents not merely the right but the duty of enforcing by means of oppression and suppression, a special way of life for all mankind. The ecclesiastical mode of recourse to authoritarianism openly demands return to the institutional conditions as well as to the doctrines that flourished in the medieval age. Since this age was pre-scientific, pre-industrial, and pre-democratic, its irrelevance to the conditions which now prevail speaks for itself. In fact, the official representatives of this movement expressly claim that practically everything which is specifically modern and new is a heretical sinful departure from supernaturally established truth. The philosophy of the dogma at the extreme Left claims that it is the very climax and completion of all that is genuinely modern and scientific. As a matter of fact, its doctrine and its practices are such as to undermine this claim.

On the side of intellectual doctrine this philosophy involves an absolutism which is compelled to revert to what is now scientifically outgrown. It does not go as far back as to the middle ages, but it does revert to conditions in which the astronomy and physics of Newton took shape. This reversion is openly admitted or rather asserted. It is exhibited in express repudiation of scientific doctrines whenever they run counter to dogmas as interpreted by a shifting party line, e.g. the relational theories of space and time in physics, and modern theories of genetics. The convergence of these two scientific theories introduces a radically new cosmological background. Processes of change now hold the place in the constitution of nature which once was supposed to be held by what is immutable and eternal. Further evidence that the philosophical basis of the dogmas of the Left is derived from a scientifically outworn system is seen in the fact that in spite of its proclaimed emphasis upon the course of history, it finds itself compelled to pen the course of historical change within fixed limits. Its assumption that its own economic-political system embodies the culmination of historic processes amounts to an assertion that history has revealed its complete meaning and taught its final human lesson in the middle of the twentieth century. This denial of the occurrence of the novel, the unforeseen, the unexpected in history, would be comic were it not tragic in its consequences. Only an absence of imagination which is the product of a dogmatic attitude can fail to see that unless human beings destroy themselves, the time in which Man has already existed on earth constitutes a short episode in comparison with ages still to come. The whole scheme is monolithic. It holds that unity, whole-ness, is necessarily structural and static. Recent science has plainly disclosed that unity is a matter of the indefinitely ongoing process of inter-actions of things which by themselves are plural. Again extremes meet. The assumption that history is marked by movement toward a final goal is equally that of the Church on the one hand and of Totalitarian Bolshevism on the other. The difference between them concerns only that which is assumed to be the final goal. The historic emergence of a particular economic-political institution occupies in the modern system the same place that the historic appearance of Christianity occupies in the other and older system.

III

The foregoing discussion of the present state of philosophy is not engaged in for its own sake. Consideration of it is a necessary preliminary of a philosophy which shall be relevant to the problems and issues of our present life. The step to be first taken by a philosophy aware of its responsibilities is to search for and observe the conditions which have brought about such a vast disturbance of the old order in such a short time. My thesis on this point is that a return wave of processes and materials which originate in the laboratories where scientific work is carried on has entered into the common affairs, occupations, and interests of everyday life to such an extent as to be the occasion and source of the immense change which has taken place in the last few centuries. The detailed evidence for this proposition would show that the change in question began when natural science entered on its present course a short three centuries ago; it would show that the change has extended and deepened exactly as the new ways of scientific inquiries moved from the astronomy of the heavens into things closer and more intimate in the conduct of human life. It would show that this advance of scientific inquiry introduced orders of change where the older "science" had assumed an order of fixity and immutability. It is no paradox that the operations and materials which have so changed life have their source in observatories and laboratories remote from the affairs of daily life. This remoteness of the intellectual work of science from the customary and established occupations and concerns is precisely what renders the outcome of inquiry carried on for its own intellectual sake effective in bringing about change. Apart from the external leverage thus afforded, the rule of habit would have continued to be the rule; invention of new resources and discovery of new ends and purposes would have been the exception.

The fact that this return passage of what originated in an *intellectual* pursuit has gone far in producing the state of insecurity, fear, and strife is proof that up to the present time it has been double-faced or ambivalent in its consequences. Some of the results of the entry of science into daily life have been more helpful than harmful; productive on the whole of good rather than of evil. The reverse is true about either of its consequences. It is extremely doubtful, however, whether a single case can be found in which the predominatingly good does not have an offset of evil, and *vice versa* with respect to what is prevailingly evil. Now it is worthy of note that for a long time the presence of this return wave of science into our common everyday ways of living was the source of optimism. The incoming of science was hailed as the initial stage of an era of rational illumination; its conclusions were welcomed as ushering in an era of prosperity and of mutual understanding which would terminate finally in a state of universal peace among the peoples of the earth.

This period of indiscriminate laudation of science with respect to human consequences has lately given way to a time of equally indiscriminate pessimism and condemnation. It has become almost a daily occupation to point to harmful consequences of the passage of science into daily life. Articles and even books are constantly attacking science as the chief cause of the evils that now afflict mankind. The case of the bomb as the product of physical science and its highly destructive use is very much in point.

The purpose of dwelling upon the double-faced consequences of the invasion of our common everyday life by what originates in activities that are carried on for the sake of knowing, not of doing, is to fix attention upon that which at the present time is so absorbing, so far reaching, that it constitutes the subjectmatter of any philosophical inquiry which shall be relevant to existing conditions. To begin with, this matter is the first step in our other way around and about in the direction of philosophy. However, this turn-*about* is, after all but a *re*-turn to the view of philosophy put forward of old by Socrates. It constitutes search for the wisdom that shall be a guide of life. It marks a return to the original view of philosophy as a *moral* undertaking in the sense in which the moral and the deeply and widely human are identical. It diverges from the road which Socrates and subsequent philosophers pursued in their search. It diverges from their search for wisdom that will pilot Man over treacherous shoals and through panic-laden storms. The new science has in any case only existed a few short hundred years. And only in the last decades of this time has scientific inquiry placed at the disposal of man a natural world whose order is that of interconnected processes of change instead of one of the immobilities and fixities, which scientific inquiries had inherited from the older cosmological philosophy. The emancipation thus effected gives the final blow to the barriers which during the earlier phase of the new science separated nature and man from one another. Thereby it puts the resources of physics and physiology in the hands of man to be used in behalf of the life of man.

Our heritage from an earlier state of culture caused us to look upon science as if it were an isolated and independent entity complete in and of itself. To be in accord with the present practice of scientific inquiry, it must be seen and placed as one mode of human concern and occupation connected both in source and in outcome, with all other human interests and undertakings. It must be seen as the convergence to a focus of human activities that bear the names of art, politics, law, economics and even of such things as are sport and recreation. To take the needed step forward demands an additional, an almost revolutionary, change in psychological and philosophical doctrines formulated in a pre-scientific age. One typical illustration is afforded by the fact that "science" has been treated as the product of a special mental and internal faculty that was usually given the name of "reason." For only some such view would warrant the theory that science is a peculiar entity in and of itself instead of being a manifestation of a large number of convergent human activities in each of which material, moreover, is involved of that kind that traditional philosophy calls "external."

I have said that change in the direction of philosophy will be a return to the earlier view that the business of philosophy is intrinsically moral in its broadest human sense. As yet, however, one finds few philosophic outgivings which are intended to apply to the present situation that are not moralistic rather than moral. Subordination of the "spiritual" to the "materialistic" is freely bewailed. Men are fervently exhorted to reverse the beliefs and ways of action which have led to this subordination. But when the "spiritual" in question is examined, it is found to consist of the theological beliefs and institutions of a pre-scientific age; while the "materialistic" is found to consist of a lumping together of everything contained in the secularization going on since the medieval period. The complaint and the exhortation are moralistic rather than moral because they give no indication of the concrete means to be employed in dealing with what is bewailed and condemned. More precisely, such means as are recommended are strictly "internal"; they are so separated from conditions which actually ("externally") exist that the spiritual ends set up are empty and impotent. They operate actually only as reinforcements of the claims of belated institutions which survive from a bygone age.

The simple fact of the case is that up till the present the only subjectmatters that have been treated in a scientific way are physical and, of recent years, physiological. In consequence the outcome of science with respect to the conduct of human affairs is technical rather than human in moral sense. Were we to substitute the word "technical" for the word "materialistic," and the word "humanistic" for the word "spiritual," we should be in possession of a reasonably accurate description of the double-faced result of the return into daily life of what has originated in science. With respect to the required change in direction of philosophy, the primary step for a philosophy that turns around and about is then recognition, without reservation, that present conditions are disturbed and out of balance because of the partial and incomplete character of the science that enters into them. The inadequacy of existing philosophy to deal with present conditions is due to the fact that this philosophy is a deposit of a mixture of the old and the new pointing in opposite directions. Uncertainty and strife are the inevitable outcome.

The needed reconstruction of current views about the origin, the purpose, and the special business of philosophy cannot be undertaken for its own self or as a move which is complete in itself. At the very best, this reconstruction can only be one aspect of the larger enterprise of a reconstruction of institutions that will have to go on for an indefinitely long time. At best and at most, philosophy can have only a share in the work of reconstruction that has to be carried on. The actual change in human estate can be brought about only by the cooperative practical efforts of men of good will in all occupations and professions, not by philosophy itself. Nevertheless philosophy has its own place in the reconstruction, and its own intellectual contribution to make. It is only too common a practice to dismiss the suggestion that the human situation sets the problems for philosophy and determines the work that it is to do as romantic and even fantastic. In fact it embodies an attitude and a policy that are the height of sober prudence in comparison with the defeatism that would have philosophy operate in a human vacuum. It is also the height of sober prudence in comparison with the defeatism that proceeds as if human history already reached its climax and said its last word. In sober fact we are living in a stage in history which relatively speaking is so immature that, as has already been said, our science is technical rather than widely and deeply human. In sober fact, the future which is before man is so extensive that in comparison its past is but a brief and transitory episode in infancy. To view philosophy in the context of our present urgent needs and the resources which the further development of science will put at our command, is the measure of sanity and sober wisdom. The philosophers of the 17th, 18th, and 19th centuries did an important work in promoting conditions which removed obstacles to the progress of physical and physiological science. There is now a supreme challenge, a supreme opportunity. If Galileo and his successors could look in upon this gathering here today they would say "It is for you to do for the very life of man what we did for the physical and physiological conditions of that life. Discovery of these conditions was for us the immediate task that determined the end of our search. You possess the results of this search. It is for you to use them as means to carry forward the establishing of a more human order of freedom, equity and nobility. We accomplished the simpler and more technical part of the work. It is for you, possessors of a torch lit by our toil and sacrifice to undertake, with patient and courageous intelligence, a work which will hand on to *your* successors a torch that will illuminate a truly human world."

Philosophy's Future in Our Scientific Age
Never Was Its Role More Crucial

Few persons today would deny that philosophy has greatly declined in esteem and influence since the time when it was held to be the Science of Sciences and the Art of Arts. That its loss in repute and prestige has coincided with the transition from the medieval into the modern age would also be generally admitted. The decline of classic philosophy as *science* has kept even pace with the rise of the natural sciences of astronomy, physics, and physiology, which supplanted the metaphysical cosmology that prevailed before their rise and that provided the content of what was earlier taken to be science.

The falling off of philosophy as science does not compare, however, with its falling off as art. In the latter capacity it was once so supreme as to be in complete control of all the institutions of the Western world: not only the Church but politics and industry were subordinate to control by what, in effect, were sacred arts, consisting of regulations and prescriptions as to what was proper and right, proceeding, as they did, from those who claimed to speak with authority from on high. Following the scientific revolution came the industrial revolution, which in turn brought with it a large number of new arts which were profane as well as secular from the older standpoint.

The fine arts, as well as those of political and economic life, had indeed been so completely subordinated to religious-ecclesiastical arts that they seemed to be a part of the very order of nature. The new arts continually encroached on the old system until they crowded the authority of the sacred arts into a narrow place, where they became specialized and technical. The various divisions thereby created occasioned the dualisms that hold so prominent a place in modern philosophy. As matters of practical

[First published in *Commentary* 8 (October 1949): 388–94.]

living, the divisions then created are now manifested in the present state of worldwide moral confusion and uncertainty.

The industrial overturn coincided with the series of events that constitute the political revolution of the past few centuries. We do not have the phrase "separation of industry and church" to parallel the expression "separation of church and state." But for all practical purposes, the facts are identical in both cases. The word *landlord,* for example, was once full of the significance of the existing political order. Today it is rarely heard save in connection with keepers of hostels and owners of apartment houses. Moreover, replacement of the feudal overlord by the captain of industry speaks eloquently of the transition from the feudal age to the modern. Usury was once a sin; it now consists of those vast mechanisms for supplying credit without which the system of present industry and commerce would collapse into utter chaos.

The change that has taken place in the arts of living has had an immensely greater impact upon the life of the masses than has the change in science. This latter change is, indeed, highly important *as science.* It transformed matter and motion, and, along with them, the quantitative measurement of change in space and time, into the foundations of natural science. Quite probably, this change is the greatest single *intellectual* alteration that has taken place since man appeared on earth. It represents a total inversion of standards previously employed in all matters of natural science. The subjectmatter of the science of Greece and of the Middle Ages was saturated with human and moral values. In substance, it was an organization of the materials of the commonsense world—a world impregnated throughout with aesthetic and moral values. The new physical sciences introduced a gulf between the "natural" and the human or "moral." As an example, take the status of *matter.* In ancient science, matter was wholly passive; in the new scientific scheme it is positive and active, even, so to speak, aggressive.

In the classic system, change was of itself sure proof of lack of the immutability that belongs to things that "really" *are.* The central place of motion in the new science of Galileo and Newton displays the revolution that took place. In ancient science, nothing was less important than quantity. As a mere variation between more or less of something or other, it was a mark of the inherent vicissitude and infirmity of Being. Where would natural science be today without systematic use of measurement, direct and indirect?—But why continue? The corner-stones of classic Aristotelian "science" are precisely the things rejected by the constructors and developers of what has scientific standing today.

Nevertheless, while the intellectual revolution was extraordinarily vast, it was *intellectual,* and of prime concern only to members of the intellectual class; in contrast, the change in the arts of living came home to the mass of human beings right where they lived every day of their existence. The industrial revolution that followed the revolution in natural science altered the conditions under which human beings associate together. The change thus brought about was a change in the very *order* of institutions. The family, the home as centre of moral education and industry, the school, the legislative hall, the relation of country and city, of people to people in both war and peace, underwent changes that were radical.

With respect to the future of philosophy, it is important to note the changes that have occurred from time to time in the esteem attending the new science. In the earliest period, the "conflict of science and religion" marked the low rank given to science. The opposition of the representatives of the Church to science gave way later to a kind of truce. The practical advantages deriving from inventions, which translated scientific discoveries into instruments of everyday living, resulted in a kind of tacit division of fields. The regulation of all *spiritual*—of moral and ideal concerns—was assigned to the *old* institutions and beliefs. Control of affairs regarded as *material* was assigned—or at least permitted—to the *new* science. In philosophy, the net result was the creation of dualisms that are the intellectual manifestations of the divisions in life between that which is judged low and that which is regarded as supreme in value. Even today this insulation prevails between the subjectmatter of economic theory and the subjectmatter of moral theory. It prevails in spite of the fact that most moral problems are now what they are because of the conditions and problems of our economic life.

A much higher rating was given to the natural sciences in the time known as the "Enlightenment." It was an age in which science was hailed as the dawn of a new age in which reason would take charge of human affairs, and which, superseding the age of darkness, would be an epoch of freedom, harmony, and peace. In the 19th century the revolutionary temper of the 18th changed into an evolutionary approach. Towards the close of the 19th century, however, the increase of power in the hands of industrial and financial interests and arts attached the taint of materialism to natural science. The growth of class, national, and racial struggles tended to attach to it the threat of the revolutionary and the radical as well. The net outcome of the historical changes here summarized was to accentuate a sense of inherent difference between moral knowledge and that which is merely "natural."

II

A striking statement of this change of attitude at the end of the 19th century is found in the following passage, which is quoted from a writer who ranks as one of the most distinguished sociologists of the last century. Max Weber wrote: "What did science mean to the men who stood at the threshold of modern times? To artistic experimenters of the type of Leonardo and the musical innovators, science meant passage to *true* art and that meant for them the path to true *nature*. . . . And today? Science as the way to nature would sound like blasphemy to youth. To-day youth proclaims the opposite: redemption from the intellectualism of science in order to return to one's own nature and thereby to nature in general."

The author then goes on to speak of the time when it was believed that science would and should replace even theology as the only dependable source of knowledge "regarding the ways of God," substituting a genuine revelation for one that had been found to be spurious. He then continued: "Who—aside from big children found in the natural sciences—still believes that the findings of astronomy, biology, physics, or chemistry would teach us anything about the *meaning* of the world?" He pressed home the point with a quotation from Tolstoy, which the latter, he said, affirmed to be the "clearest answer" yet given to the question of the bearing of science on the meaning of life: "Science is meaningless because it gives no answer to *our* question, the only question important for us: what shall we do and how shall we live?"[1]

The wording of the first sentences of the above passage suggests the German romanticism; but the fact that the remarks about science came from those who had no interest in attacking science from a theological point of view renders it the more impressive. The passage stands as an expression of the transformation of the earlier optimism about science into fear and pessimism; and of late the mere disillusionment with science has passed into bitter hostility toward it. Science seems now to be held accountable for almost all the serious ills that afflict mankind. The earlier view that science was to replace theology as guide for human life has been changed into the view that the only way out of the present turmoil is return to the theological control of life embodied in the institutions of the Middle Ages. It is even held that, if evil is to be averted, natural science must be subjected to the authority of theology.

It would be an easy matter to mention facts which show that the attacks now made upon science are exaggerated and one-sided. Nevertheless, the point at issue cannot be disposed of by drawing up a balance sheet of items that are to the credit of science and those that belong on the debit side. Two facts of importance would still remain unsettled. One of them is that the methods developed and the conclusions reached in natural science constitute the most decisive factor in life as it is now lived all over the world. The other is that the consequences of the entrance of science into life are thoroughly ambiguous and double-faced. There is probably no case in which the good achieved by the intervention of science has not been offset by some evil; while, on the other side, it may be doubted if even the worst of these evils does not have an attendant benefit. Even if this statement of the two-facedness of the effects of science on life is extreme, it is still demonstrably correct that the consequences for good and evil that are wrought are complexly *inter*-wrought. A policy of either wholesale praise or blame is futile. And what is much more

1. Cited from Max Weber's *Essays in Sociology,* pp. 142–43, translated and edited by Gerth and Mills. New York, 1946.

serious, the one question worth asking is evaded: how does this doubleness, this ambivalence, in human consequences come about, and what, if anything, can be done about it?

A convincing answer to the first part of this question was recently given in an address on the occasion of an event that not long ago would have been one of unmixed congratulation. The occasion was the installation of the most powerful instrument now in existence for the exploration of secrets of the stellar universe. Yet the speaker, a man who himself has been connected with an organization for the extension of science, spoke the following words: "Knowledge and destruction have joined in a grand alliance. There is no way of telling what particular kind of knowledge is divertible to destruction; no classifying of knowledge into safe and unsafe . . . all knowledge is power; there is no segment of knowledge that cannot ultimately be employed to the detriment of mankind if that is what we elect to do with it."

It would be hard to find a more definite or a more sobering statement of what I called the ambiguity, the two-facedness, of science with respect to good and evil in human life. It would seem, however, as if the speaker might have been expected to go on to point out that since science now plays the decisive part in life, the only way to reduce its destructive consequences, and to further the advantageous ones, would be to bend every effort to obtain the kind of knowledge still lacking. It would seem as if the one thing needful would be to arrive at a knowledge that would enable us to foresee to some reasonable degree what will come to pass when we put our now internally shaken and confused store of knowledge to actual use.

For one would suppose it to be a mere commonplace that without ability to foresee the consequences of our acts, we are unable to direct and guide the activities we perform. What possibility is there of making wise choices and conducting ourselves intelligently, instead of blindly, unless we can anticipate the results of what we do?

We can hardly pick up a serious magazine today without finding a complaint that our technical knowledge has far outrun our human knowledge. Nevertheless, there are in existence two established institutions that claim to be in possession of the kind of knowledge needed, and they are more than willing to put this knowledge into effect when given the opportunity. Representatives of the Bolshevist Left claim that natural science of a kind so "natural" as to be materialistic needs only to be put systematically into effect, and that the source of existing evils is the existence of institutions that hold another faith. Representatives of the Catholic Right claim that *they* possess the *supra*-natural knowledge that is needed, and that the trouble is the evil will of human beings who refuse to submit to the guidance of that institutionally embodied knowledge.

It is to be expected that the representatives of these institutions should take the stand they do. But it is surprising that those who call themselves "liberals" should fail to see that *the absence of a knowledge genuinely humane* is a great source of our remediable troubles, and that its active presence is needed in order to translate the articles of their faith into works.

III

The bearing upon philosophy and its future of what has been said is not difficult to perceive. A hiatus exists within scientific inquiry, and it is intimately connected with our present disturbed and unsettled state. It is for the philosophers today to encourage and further methods of inquiry into human and moral subjects similar to those their predecessors in their day encouraged and furthered in the physical and physiological sciences: in short, to bring into existence a kind of knowledge which, by being thoroughly humane, is entitled to the name *moral*. Its absence seems to explain the prevailing worldwide state of uncertainty, suspense, discontent, and strife. It would also seem to indicate with startling clearness that the one thing of prime importance today is development of methods of scientific inquiry to supply us with the humane or moral knowledge now conspicuously lacking. The work needs to be done. It is not of urgent importance that it be done by philosophers, or by any other special group of intellectuals. It is, however, in harmony with the claim of philosophers to deal with what is comprehensive and fundamental that they take a hand, perhaps a leading one, in promoting *methods* that will result in the understanding that is now absent. This type of activity at least seems to be the only way to halt the decline of philosophy in influence and in public esteem and bring about something like restoration.

The problem is certainly not that of putting scientific inquiry under the control of some external institution, whether it be that of the Right or Left. The first step is to recognize that scientific inquiry is still so recent as to be immature and inchoate. It is to recognize that to arrest the development of scientific inquiry at the present stage is, in effect, to guarantee that insecurity, confusion, and strife will perpetuate themselves. What has been accomplished in the development of *methods* of inquiry in physiological and physical science now cries out for extension into humane and moral subjects.

Some twenty-five hundred years ago the forerunner and martyr of European philosophy declared that artisans had knowledge of the material processes and the ends of the activities they carried on. In consequence of this knowledge they were enabled to act intelligently within a very limited sphere. A shoemaker, for example, possessed the knowledge which enabled him to tell whether what was offered as a shoe was a real shoe or one only in appearance. He knew this because he knew the purpose for which shoes were made, and, in addition, knew the materials, the tools, and the processes by which leather or any other material could be made to serve the end in view. In short, in his one limited field he knew what was good and what was bad. The larger and more comprehensive knowledge required by man for the conduct of his more important affairs was not provided by a limited type of knowledge. The existing knowledge served a man as a cobbler but not a man as a member of a community of free men.

Search for the kind of understanding that was lacking in Athens, Socrates termed philosophy, the love of wisdom. It was to be the Science of Sciences, because the knowledge sought for was so comprehensive that it would enable specialized and technical ways of knowing to be put to use in behalf of a common and shared good.

The similarity of our present situation to that in which Socrates propounded the need for philosophy as a search for a knowledge that was lacking should, it seems to me, be reasonably obvious. The difference between the situations in width and depth is great and obvious. The present world is rather a group of external associations than a community; nevertheless, it repeats on a vast scale the human conditions from which the Socrates of old derived his plea for a devoted search for a knowledge out of which would issue an art that would do for man as man what the lesser arts did for man in minor, because technical, ways. Those philosophers who are now subjected to criticism from their fellow-professionals on the ground that concern with the needs, troubles, and problems of man is not "philosophical," may, if they feel it necessary, draw support and courage from the fact that they are following, however imperfectly, in the path initiated by the man to whom is due the very term *philosophy*.

IV

At all events, and in short, we are here presented with the conditions for finding an answer to the question, "Has philosophy a future?" We are supplied with the conditions, but not with the answer itself. The advance made by science in a comparatively short time is tremendous, but it is partial and out of balance. Its ambivalence with respect to good and evil, to construction and destruction, follows directly from its partial and one-sided estate. I have referred to the complaints now common which are made about the scantiness of our present knowledge about human beings and human affairs in comparison with what is known about distant galaxies of stars and about the equally remote constitution of atoms. What is held in view by the complainants is clear. But there is something in the use of the word "backwardness" that may account for the futility of these complaints. For they seem to suggest that all that is needed is to travel further on the road that natural science has already taken; while others claim that all that is necessary is to subject the uses we make of the scientific knowledge now in our possession to control by the "moral" knowledge we already possess.

The assumption that this latter knowledge is adequate *now and here* to the present strains man labors under is reflected in the appeal to "anchor science to morals" found in the address quoted. If our present store of moral knowledge does not enable us to foresee the consequences for good and evil that will issue from what, after all, is the most widely and deeply determining of all factors now operative in human life, the anchorage it can provide for science (the very science, by the way, that accounts for the *need* of anchorage) seems to be a shoal of sifting sands.

For how can the best moral will in the world provide secure anchorage for its good intentions if those intentions can be put into effect only through the medium of conditions, means, and instrumentalities which *may*—and which, it is admitted, in many cases actually *do*—pervert them from constructive to destructive purposes?

The situation at the very least offers to those who profess love of wisdom a reminder that in matters technical, physical, and now physiological, knowledge gives guidance that can be depended upon in forming policies of action in limited areas. This reminder may well be forcible enough to remind them also that their predecessors did a definite, a needed work, positively—and negatively against entrenched institutional opposition—and that without this work physiological inquiry could not have been brought to its present prosperous technical estate.

If this reminder does not suggest that they, *as philosophers,* have a certain responsibility under the present conditions, it should at least notify them that scientific inquiry is still only partial, one-sided, immature in its development, and that a highly important work in science remains to be done.

In its detail, the work they must do will be harder and slower than that already done. But the obstacles to be met in *initiating* the task are not as entrenched as were those met and conquered by their predecessors. The obstacles now to be met are mainly sluggishness, inertia, discouragement, exhaustion: a statement that applies both without and within philosophy. For while the opposition from institutional sources is vigorous and, temporarily at least, aggressive, its efficacy is not intrinsic, but is derived rather from the absence of organized active opposition on the part of those who might be engaged in the endeavor to rectify the existing enormous imbalance between that understanding which gives direction in technical matters and that which is absent just where it is vitally needed.

It is barely conceivable that the existing store of knowledge will undergo throughout the whole world the fate of slavish subjection to external power that it is already undergoing in countries under Bolshevist control. It is not conceivable that the course of physical and physiological knowing will be turned backward in any other way than by some such institutional distortion. What is most to be feared is a continuation of the policy of indifference to the extension, to the development of *methods* of inquiry into *human* conditions—*methods*[2] so basic that their results (and only these) merit the name *moral*. The fact that the professed and professional guardians of morals continue to assert the adequacy of moral standards and points of view that were framed in a society upon which competent understanding of the physical and physiological conditions of human life had not dawned, is one of the obstacles in the way of what needs to be done.

The force of a movement that in its own day and place had a claim to regard itself as "liberal" and as humanly progressive is also obstructive to what needs to be done. For it asserted that all that was necessary was to permit "Nature" to do its own beneficent work. It worked to get rid of some institutional customs and laws that had become humanly oppressive. But it was also a policy of systematic abnegation of the intelligence as a regulative factor in human affairs.

The obvious bad consequences of the policy of drift that ensued resulted in what the unthinking regard as revolutionary: a renewed strengthening of political power to offset the inhuman results of leaving to nature the work of man as man. For the one dependable factor in any policy is an intelligent grasp of the factors involved—an end not to be attained without systematic effort to complete the present one-sided, unbalanced state of "science."

V

The obstacles are great; but as the two matters just cited indicate, they are those of inertia rather than of vitality; and in

---

2. The word "methods" is italicized as a precaution against a possible misunderstanding which would be contrary to what is intended. What is needed is not the carrying over of procedures that have approved themselves in physical science, but *new* methods as adapted to *human* issues and problems, as methods already in scientific use have shown themselves to be in physical subjectmatter.

any case philosophers are not called upon to conduct that specific work of scientific inquiry upon which depends the ability of human beings to conduct human affairs with foresight and intelligence. Their predecessors did not execute the inquiries in physics that built up knowledge in that area to the point where that knowledge became its own adequate impetus. Their predecessors *did* however take the lead in attacking traditional factors that blocked the way. They contributed positively in no mean measure to development of standpoints and attitudes that passed, in the course of use, into more or less standardized instrumentalities of inquiry. Above all, their communications to the public furthered an intellectual climate which was unfavorable to old traditions and which welcomed with increasing eagerness the new scientific enterprise. Without such a cultural climate even the most important undertakings are born out of due season; they fade and die.

To mankind in general it makes little difference what group does the needed work; and, in any case, the work itself is much too large to be restricted to the members of any one calling. To *philosophers,* however, it is a vital matter that they have an active share in developing points of view and outlooks which will further recognition of what is humanly at stake and of how the necessary work may be initiated. What is called a climate of belief designates conditions so widely extended that they are no longer matters of book knowledge or the exclusive property of an intellectual class. The history of physical science demonstrates the large part that has to be played by cultural conditions which transfer what is *called* "knowledge" from a theoretical or intellectual possession into habitual, taken-for-granted, working attitudes of everyday use. There has of course to be willingness to hear and absorb, but that willingness is of a radically different sort from a conscious act of "will." Campaigns of persuasion and education carried on by those of ardent faith are intrinsic parts of the effective initiation of any new movement.

The philosophers who promoted the new movement in physical inquiry did not find it necessary to disown or conceal their ardent belief that the success of that movement was of high human importance. I do not know why their successors are called upon to behave differently in a matter that directly, not in a roundabout way, concerns on one side the future of human welfare and, on the other, the continuance of misery, uncertainty, instability, and strife. When knowledge possesses men instead of being something held in possession by them, its passage into activity is a matter of course. And knowledge does not possess men until it is heavily charged with that emotive faith in its value which impels action. Generous imagination and wide and liberal sympathies are needed to carry on the required activities. But what are these attributes save those which the adventurous thinkers of the past have claimed to belong to philosophy as a supremely liberal pursuit?

There is rife a peculiar notion that to suggest that philosophers have a specifically human office to perform is to propose that they be detached from the intellectual activity appropriate to them and converted into social reformers. The notion is so peculiar that it looks as if those who put it forth are moved by a covert defense-reaction in behalf of the human remoteness of the sort of philosophical discussion in which they are personally engaged. For the work that needs to be done *is* at the present juncture primarily *intellectual;* while the subjectmatter involved is of such supreme importance that it—and, I submit, it *alone*—satisfies that claim to universality or comprehensiveness of scope which was made when philosophy was a vital factor in life. This subjectmatter is not something factitiously added by the zeal of those occupied with it; it is that which is important to man as man. The fact of its crucial human importance does not detract from its status as *intellectual;* it does add to its power to move to action, once it is appreciated for what it is.

Even were there space for a consideration of what philosophy will specifically consist of in the future, it would contradict what has been said to attempt even to list its articles of doctrine. What has been said is not said in the interest of any existing variety or brand of philosophical doctrine—though it is likely that some among contemporary forms of thought are further on the way and therefore more promising than others. What is at stake is a definite change in the *direction* of philosophical inquiry; and it is in the interest of the *future* of philosophy that the present discussion is conducted. What is said is said in behalf of a future for philosophy as broad and as penetrating as that claimed by metaphysical and theological systems in their days of utmost vigor; but a philosophy that is to be fully relevant to a new age in which issues flow from natural science, and not from a supra-natural world or from a philosophy purporting to deal with what is super-mundane and super-human.

The position here taken is not hostile to systems of the past in so far as they were humanly relevant in their own days; it is hostile to them in so far as it is now attempted, in the interest of some particular institution, to blow their dying embers into a transient glow. For the sparks thereby emitted will give neither light by which to see nor heat by which to convert what is seen into conduct that refers to the well-being of man.

Can philosophers hope for a more arduous task or for a more inspiring cause to which to devote their intellectual efforts than the intellectual struggle lying ahead?

Experience and Existence: A Comment [1]

Mr. Kahn concludes his article by asking: "Does his [my] metaphysics include any existence *beyond* experience?" My answer is that my *philosophical* view, or theory, of experience does not include any existence beyond *the reach* of experience. The reader will see that in my answer I have made two changes in the wording of Mr. Kahn's question. The substance of the article that follows gives the reason for making these changes; in brief, it is that the question is so phrased as to repeat the ambiguities that will be shown to exist in his discussion;—ambiguities summed up in the wording of the question. For everything depends upon the view, or theory, of experience set forth in my book in its relation to the view, or theory, that is *attributed* to me concerning experience and existence.

I

In the course of his article Mr. Kahn makes statements about my view of experience which appear, upon the study I have given them, to be incompatible with each other. One of them is correct, or at least can be understood in a way that renders it substantially correct. The other one is false; or, it would probably be better to say, meaningless, because totally irrelevant. The view to which no exception is taken is the one presented first in the course of his article. He quotes from me as say-

1. The comment is upon an article, in the December 1948 issue of this journal, by Mr. S. J. Kahn, entitled "Experience and Existence in Dewey's Naturalistic Metaphysics," pp. 316–321.

[First published in *Philosophy and Phenomenological Research* 9 (June 1949): 709–13. For Sholom J. Kahn's article to which this is a reply, see this volume, Appendix 4.]

ing that on my view "experience is the foreground *of* nature."
This is as good a summary of my actual position as could be
stated in a few words; to safeguard its condensation from misunderstanding, note that the italicized "of" means that experience
is itself "natural" and as such is nature's *own* foreground. It thus
denies that "experience" is something superadded from outside,
whether by a *supra*-natural Being, or by an *extra*-natural Ego,
Subject, Self, Mind, Consciousness, or whatever. Unless this
point is steadily borne in mind, all the difficulties Mr. Kahn finds
in my philosophical discussion of experience in relation to existence will be justified. Just how and why he finds these ambiguities is not, however, an easy matter to determine. For in addition
to recognizing that "experience as foreground *of* nature" disposes of Santayana's criticism according to which "experience is
identical with immediacy," he goes on to say that my "full" account of experience includes "analysis of all its elements in their
complexities; the biological matrix of the organism, the social
matrix of other organisms and the environing world of nature."[2]
On this "full" view of experience, the answer *No* I have given
to the question quoted is "analytic," not an inference, nor an
interpretation.

Imagine, then, my surprise when, in the very next paragraph, I
find the following: "If Dewey does not reduce all experience to
immediacy and foreground, is it not true he *does* tend to reduce
all existence to experience, thereby failing to provide us with a
completely adequate picture of existence?"

How in the world the use of experience as providing philosophy with a method for arriving at statements about existence, a
use recognized to include the fullness of references that Mr. Kahn
correctly acknowledges, can suddenly be reduced to a condition
in which he adopts the statement of Santayana, "Naturalism
could not be more romantic; nature here is not a world but a
story," adding, moreover, that it commits me to a romanticism
consisting of "exaggeration of the ego," is all very confusing. But
it is not for me to try to explain why a view of experience so
"full" as to include "the environing world" is suddenly changed
into something termed an exaggeration of the ego. Nor is the
perplexity lessened by the fact that Mr. Kahn offers not a single

2. Passages quoted, *op. cit.*, p. 317 [this volume, p. 457].

bit of evidence, drawn either directly or indirectly from my writings, as the ground for his intimation that I reduce the natural world to a romantic tale. In the case of Santayana that conclusion follows logically from his view (which he then alternates to me) that experience is sheer immediacy. But Mr. Kahn has expressly repudiated that view; nevertheless, as I have said, he offers no shred of evidence for any *other* ground on which to base his notion that my view of experience reduces nature to a romantic story.

II

In another section of his paper, Mr. Kahn deals with specific statements in my writings. He finds a position set forth in my *Logic* which "from the standpoint of metaphysics at least" is "curiously ambiguous"; a statement that is connected with his previous statement that "the concept of existence (or its equivalent) must surely be included in any metaphysics naturalistic or otherwise." The passages just cited contain that misapprehension of what I explicitly say about "*metaphysical*" when the word appears in *Experience and Nature* that led me to substitute *philosophy* for *metaphysics* at the outset of this paper. Here as there the word *metaphysical* must be changed to *philosophical* if his question is to make sense in terms of my position. However, I shall postpone consideration of this point till after I have considered the "possible split between logic" and my theory of the relation of experience and nature which Mr. Kahn finds in certain passages of my *Logic*. He quotes from that book the statement that "constructive development of science has taken place through treating the material of the perceived world . . . in terms of properties that are logical rather than directly ontological."[3] Mr. Kahn is surely aware that the subtitle of my *Logic* is *The Theory of Inquiry*. How in the world he converts a statement of mine that *scientific* inquiry has found it necessary to introduce terms whose "properties" are connected with operations of that inquiry which is scientific rather than *directly* connected with existence into a putative denial that experience is of natural exis-

3. *Op. cit.,* p. 319 [this volume, p. 460].

tence is too much for me. The very sentence he cites from me speaks of inquiry dealing with "the *existential* material of the *perceived* world." I did not originate the problem constituted by the remarkable difference existing between the subjectmatter of physical science and the subjectmatter of the world as it is *perceived*; it has of course been almost the outstanding problem of all modern epistemological philosophy. I offered an hypothesis by which to account for the extraordinary difference existing between them: Namely, that inquiry which is specifically scientific (as distinct from common sense inquiries dealing with the directly perceived world) has found it of constructive use in *doing its own special work* to introduce terms that advance its own operation *as* scientific inquiry. Even if that hypothesis be completely wrong, nothing contained in it nor in my discussion of it will bear the interpretation put upon it by Mr. Kahn. As I have already mentioned, the very passage cited from me contains the words "treating the *material of the perceived world*" in a way that would seem to stare one in the face.

I always wonder on what ground those who reject the generalized view of "experience," such as is presented for example in *Experience and Nature,* justify their own acceptance of the findings of, say, astronomers and/or physicists working in the field of infra-atomic events. I am confident they do not believe these men draw on telepathy or consult spiritualistic mediums; and it is difficult to suppose that they believe it *all* comes about through *a priori* deliverances of Pure Reason. Were they to examine what the word "experience" stands for and names, including both *what* is experienced and the various *ways* in which it is experienced, with the gradual selection of those manners of experiencing that constitute the methods of scientific inquiry now in use (itself a matter of the continuity of "experience"), I think they might refrain from adverse criticism of a generalized view of experience upon which their own criticisms must rest for validity; or they would doubtless still find ground for adverse criticism of specific interpretations I have made on its basis. I certainly have never claimed infallibility for any particular experience, not even those which rest upon what *today* is taken to be warranted by the way of experiencing called scientific method. If my critics confined their criticisms to matters of specific interpretation, or if they pointed out that historically so many different interpretations have been put on the word by philosophers that it is now too late to rescue it from ambiguity, I might well be inclined to agree with them—especially as with respect to the latter point, I have moved myself progressively in the direction of using such terms as *Life-behavior* or *Life-activities,* with the understanding of course that, in the case of philosophy, the behavior and/or activities involved are those of *human* beings and hence are *culturally* affected throughout.

Mr. Kahn also cites a passage from my *Logic,* dealing with mathematical subjectmatter, in which it is stated that the account given of such subjectmatter in my *Logic* "renders unnecessary" the theory that this subjectmatter refers to a special ontological realm.[4] I should have supposed that it was a familiar fact that some theorists hold that mathematics *is* concerned with an ontological realm of Being superior to the realm of space-time existences with which *physical* science is concerned. I do not know how or why Mr. Kahn transforms the statement that the account I give renders unnecessary such a view into a possible (or seemingly probable) view that I am here denying my basic philosophical theory regarding experience as the natural foreground of the world. In any case, the view that terms distinctively *mathematical* are not *descriptive* of space-time existence did not originate with me; it is a commonplace with many if not with all mathematicians.

III

I come now to what, as far as I can judge, is the root of all the difficulties, ambiguities, inconsistencies that Mr. Kahn finds in my view of the relation of experience and existence. In a few pages in the last chapter of *Experience and Nature* I use the word "*metaphysical.*"[5] Mr. Kahn's whole treatment rests, as far as I can judge, upon the assumption that I regard philosophical and metaphysical as synonyms; or, at least, treat metaphysics as a name for that part of philosophy that is concerned with the relation of experience to existence, and, furthermore, that I use the

4. *Op. cit.,* p. 320 [this volume, p. 461].
5. See from bottom of p. 412 to the top of p. 416 [*Later Works* 1:308–10].

word *metaphysical* in the sense it bears in the classic tradition based on Aristotle. Nothing could be farther from the facts of the case. A few pages in the last chapter of *Experience and Nature* attempted to state a view upon which the words *metaphysics* and *metaphysical* would make sense on *experiential* grounds, instead of upon the ground of ultimate Being behind experience serving as its under-pinning.

I now realize that it was exceedingly naive of me to suppose that it was possible to rescue the word from its deeply engrained traditional use. I derive what consolation may be possible from promising myself never to use the words again in connection with any aspect of any part of my own position. Nevertheless, the text of my book makes it clear that I was proposing a use of the words so different from the traditional one as to be incompatible with it. And while I think the *words* used were most unfortunate I still believe that that which they were used to name is genuine and important.

This genuine subjectmatter is the fact that the natural world has *generic* as well as specific traits, and that in the one case as in the other experience is such as to enable us to arrive at their identification. And this is only the beginning of the matter. What is said of that which is named is said moreover in a discussion of the relation of *existence and value;* for concern for values as they eventuate in the course of life-experience is taken to be the concern that marks *philosophy* off from other intellectual undertakings. The three pages in which generic traits are discussed are *explicitly* devoted to the place occupied by values and the office they may render in the wise conduct of the affairs of life. Discussion of generic traits is opened by saying that a statement of them *seems* to have nothing to do with criticism and choice of values; that is, with "effective love of wisdom," this latter being the theme under discussion. The remainder of the discussion of them is devoted to showing that this specious conclusion (the one held in the traditional view) is reached because detecting and registering general traits is taken to be self-sufficient, the end of the matter. Against this view it is held that their detection and noting is in the interest of providing "a ground-map of the province of criticism"; criticism, that is, of values as concrete events. For example, "Barely to note and register that contingency is a [general] trait of natural events has nothing to do with wisdom." But to note contingency in its connection with a concrete *situation of life,* is that "fear of the Lord which is at least the beginning of wisdom." The entire discussion, while short, is given to showing that the sense and point of recognition of generic traits lies in their application in the conduct of life: that is, in their *moral* bearing provided *moral* be taken in its basic broad human sense.

The foregoing is not an apology for my use of the word "metaphysical." It is evoked by the misreading of my use of that word, which probably is not confined to Mr. Kahn. But what it names and stands for is here emphasized because in my treatment philosophy is *love of wisdom;* wisdom being not knowledge but knowledge-plus; knowledge turned to account in the instruction and guidance it may convey in piloting life through the storms and the shoals that beset life-experience as well as into such havens of consummatory experience as enrich our human life from time to time.

Contribution to "Religion and the Intellectuals"

The present loss of faith in science among intellectuals, and the accompanying reversion to moral attitudes and beliefs which intellectuals as a class had abandoned, is an outstanding event rendering the inquiry initiated by the editors of *Partisan Review* as timely as the issue is important. No one having an interest in the progressions and retrogressions of cultural life can fail to be interested in the question of its "cause" or conditioning source. When I say that to me the latter appears as obvious and as outstanding as is the event to be explained, I shall doubtless seem to be indulging in gross oversimplification. Even so, its statement may serve to illustrate the *point-of-view* from which the following discussion is undertaken.

In any case there is coincidence *in time* between the loss of intellectual nerve and the attendant reversion to a position not long ago discarded, and recent developments in human affairs. Accordingly, I shall indicate the grounds upon which I believe that much more than just coincidence is involved. The period during which loss of confidence and faith have increasingly taken place is also the exact period in which the relationship between nations, races, and groups or classes within each have been disturbed to the point of disorganization. The disturbance is worldwide in scope or range while internally it pervades every institution of life, political, economic, and cultural.

No one, I take it, can deny that the present all but universally pervasive shock followed hard upon the totalitarian revolutions in Italy and Germany. The two World Wars that have since occurred render it unnecessary to argue that the belief, previously current among all intellectuals of the liberal type, that we were

[First published in "Religion and the Intellectuals: A Symposium," *Partisan Review* 17 (February 1950): 129–33.]

entering upon an epoch in which there would be steady, even if slow, advance toward a peaceful world order, has undergone a tragic shock. Nor was belief in inevitable progress toward a happier and more equitable human order confined to the matter of peace among the peoples of the earth. It was joined with and supported by belief in the equally assured advance of democratic political regimes which would be marked by sure even if gradual advance in personal freedom, and which would include movement in the direction of equality in economic opportunity. These desirable ends were held to be a necessary outcome of common understanding that was sure to follow the continued advance of science.

For while the intellectuals of the nineteenth century abandoned that part of the eighteenth century Enlightenment which believed in a speedy because revolutionary establishment of a new and better order, it did so by accepting belief in a slower, longer, more gradual, but surer, *evolutionary* process. What might be lost in the time taken to reach the goal was to be more than made up by absence of the destructive violence of the revolutionary process.

It goes without saying that the foregoing is so summary that qualifications have to be introduced. But in the main the statement fairly reflects the Victorian optimism entertained by intellectuals of the liberal type. Moreover, the absence of qualifications which are needed is more than compensated for by an event to which no reference has been made. The close of the military alliance in which the Fascist and Nazi states were defeated by the union of the U.S.S.R. with political democracies has resulted in transforming the previous state of disorganization into downright cleavage. Even if the disruption should continue for a long time to be a Cold War, the chill is already so severe as to bury previous warm hopes and ardent confidence as in a glacial avalanche.

It seems incredible that such a widespread and pervasively penetrating collective overturn could take place without an equally serious shift in the attitudes of those involved in the institutional arrangements upset. While intellectuals are those most sensitive to disturbance and most reflectively aware of it, they are far from being the only ones affected. In a practical, less reflective, way loss of nerve and upset of equilibrium affect the mass of human beings. Indirect confirmation on this point is found in the position of those intellectuals who remained faithful to the old attitudes permeated with supernaturalism. In effect they are now saying in chorus: "We have long been telling you what would be sure to happen if you cut loose from the anchorage of supernatural authority. Now that it has taken place you can see for yourselves that your only hope of security lies in return to the supreme authority of religions claiming supernatural origin and support." Just as I write, this assertion is emphatically punctuated by the appeal, echoing around the whole globe, that all who have strayed from Rome, should now return to it in humble obedience; physically if possible during this present mid-century year, spiritually in any case.

Just as the issue about the intellectual class has to be placed in a larger socio-cultural context, so does the one about religion and for much the same reason. That the state and fortunes of religion cannot be separated from the estate of other large human affairs is recognized in effect—but only partially—when we are invited to consider: "Does the present trend imply that the scientific attitude of mind is being forsaken?" The acknowledgment is partial since "science" is the only other large human interest mentioned as needing to be taken into account. But what about the status of science itself? If it is being forsaken, and as far as it is, its desertion as well as the accompanying return to religion supernaturally viewed must have *its* particular "causal" conditioning. Is it not reasonable to suppose that as far as science is possessed and enjoyed by a relatively small group of "intellectuals" (even when those engaged in scientific pursuits are included as they must be), it is exposed to the ebb as well as to the flow of activities and interests which are neither religious nor scientific?

It is a well-known fact that the high tide of general esteem of science was in the period usually called Victorian: a period that may roughly be dated as that preceding the First World War; while the ebb of its lauded position began with the Second World War, and has become acute (and seemingly chronic as well) since the defeat of Germany and its allies has demonstrated that the alliance between the older democracies and the U.S.S.R. was external, superficial, formal. The cleavage of our one physical world is into two opposed worlds. Between them even the communication that is a condition of understanding and agreement is practically impossible.

In view of the uses to which "science" has been put in propaganda and in vastly increased destructiveness in war, it seems a matter of course that prior optimism about science be replaced by pessimism. When, as in the question asked, scientific attitude is referred to as one "of mind," it has to be recognized that the *mind* here in question is not the private intellect of this and that person or even of the group or class called *intellectual*. It stands for a pervasively extended and deeply permeating disposition in which collective disesteem, grounded in fear and nourished by organized distrust, is substituted for prior favorable public regard.

The fundamental consideration, then, with respect to the forsaking of the "scientific attitude of mind" would seem to be that the great mass of human beings has not deserted it for the simple reason that the mass never shared that attitude. The mass certainly experienced its *consequences,* however. Technological applications of science have for a long time, with continued acceleration, been the chief sources of human experiences on an ever-widening geographical scale and with ever-increasing intensity. As long as consequences were, on the whole, enjoyed "science" rated high. Now that war and threat of war are a conspicuous effect in the contact of nations and races, and now that depressions bring unemployment and insecurity, there does not appear to be any mystery in the desertions and recessions that take place. That the loss in esteem is not even greater than it is may well be due to the rise of physical chemistry and of biology which has provided "science" with a new and positive ground for popular favor.

We are thus brought to the further question: "Is some readjustment necessary by which the scientific attitude will be given a new place?" What is said below will explain, I hope, the omission in the passage quoted of the following words in the sentence cited: "in the intellectual hierarchy." For the position indicated by what has already been said is that a readjustment giving science a "new place" is a need of the very first order. The scientific attitude has had little place in the concerns and interests of highest importance to the mass of men. In consequence the attitude is inevitably contained and restrained in the class that is specifically intellectual.

Little or nothing has been explicitly said in the foregoing in response to the questions about religion we are invited to consider. I now add that, in my best judgment, what has been said about the isolation of "science," because of its virtual erection into something existing on its own account instead of an expression of all kinds of socio-cultural interests and activities, holds in equal, probably greater, measure of religion. I shall confine what I have to say on this point to the final question: "Assuming that in the past religions nourished certain vital human values, can these values now be maintained without a widespread belief in the supernatural?"

In view of the fact that religions in the degree in which they have depended upon the supernatural have been, as history demonstrates, the source of violent conflict, and destructive of basic human values, and in view of the fact that even now differences of religion divide the peoples of the earth, one summary answer to this question is that values will be sustained—effectively supported by a religion that is free from dependence upon the supernatural.

Not that anti-supernaturalism suffices, but that freedom from it will provide an opportunity for a religious experience to develop that is deeply and pervasively human and humane. Accordingly, when it is asked: "Will not the religious tradition of any civilization have to be essentially pluralistic?" my reply is that just as mankind may become all the richer when there is an assured ability on the part of each people to develop in its own preferred way, so it is with religious pluralisms among the peoples of the earth, provided there is freedom of inter-communication.

Aesthetic Experience as a Primary Phase
and as an Artistic Development

In a recent number of the *Journal of Aesthetics and Art Criticism*, Dr. Romanell finds that in my *Art as Experience* I speak of two forms or sorts of aesthetic experience.[1] I certainly do; Dr. Romanell has decided, however, that there must be some inconsistency in my so doing. However, I cannot find that he offers any evidence that my recognition of two forms renders them so incompatible with each other that my aesthetic is broken in two, unless it is that I speak both of "aesthetic" experience and of "the aesthetic phase of experience." Since the backbone and indeed the life-blood of my aesthetic theory (such as it is) is that *every* normally complete experience, every one that runs its own full course, is aesthetic in its consummatory phase; and since my theory holds also that the arts and their aesthetic experience are intentionally cultivated developments of this primary aesthetic phase, it demands presentation of evidence to accuse the main, the indispensable, intention of the theory with internal inconsistency. Since, as far as I have been able to ascertain, no evidence whatever is offered save use, on the purpose of two different expressions to mark the distinction between the primary form and the intentionally developed one of aesthetic experience, and since there is not the remotest reference to the part played in my aesthetic theory by the fact of development of the artistic out of the primary phase, I do not find anything to lay hold of with respect to making a reply.

To give evidence that this matter of development of the artistic way or form out of a primary aesthetic phase is the "heart, soul,

1. Vol. VIII (1949), No. 2, pp. 125–28.

[First published in *Journal of Aesthetics and Art Criticism* 9 (September 1950): 56–58. For Patrick Romanell's article to which this is a reply, see this volume, Appendix 5.]

and mind" (intention) of the entire book would be to write a synopsis of the whole book. Since the book is there for anyone to read, such a course seems to be as unnecessary as it is impossible to carry out in a periodical article. Hence I content myself here with calling attention, with respect to the primary phase of the aesthetic, to the first and third chapters. Their titles, "The Live Creature" and "Having an Experience" (with emphasis upon "an"), would seem fairly conclusive, without the need of much reference to the content of the chapters; hence, I merely mention here that most of the rest of the book is devoted to discussion of the arts as outgrowths of primary aesthetic aspects. I add, also, that considerable space is given to showing that "works of art" which are not developed out of a phase of primary experiences are *artificial* rather than *artistic:* a fact which of itself seems to prove not incompatibility in my view but the irrelevance of Dr. Romanell's criticism to that view.

There is, however, one statement in his article which, while not calling for a reply, affords me an opportunity, for which I am grateful, to say something concerning the general philosophy of experience of which the treatment of the aesthetic is one variety. The sentence in question is that in which Dr. Romanell asserts that development, each on its own account of what I have said in the case of aesthetic experience would "eventuate in two incompatible philosophies of experience." Since there is considerable evidence that others beside Dr. Romanell have failed to grasp fully or accurately this *general* theory, I welcome an opportunity to say something on that theme.

It amounts to the following: the case of aesthetic experience with its cultivated development of the artistic variety out of what is natural and spontaneous in primary experience provides what, in all probability, is the simplest and most direct way in which to lay hold of what is fundamental in all the forms of experience that are traditionally (but fallaciously) regarded as so many different, separate, isolated, independent divisions of subjectmatter. The traditional and still current habit of separating from each other subjectmatters that are respectively political, economic, moral, religious, educational, cognitive (under the name of epistemological) and cosmological, thereby treating them as being self-constituted, inherently different, is an illustration of what I reject in the case of the aesthetic.

Anthropologists have shown how communities that are relatively "primitive" do all they can possibly manage to do so as to clothe the useful activities that are necessary to maintain group life with the garb of the immediately, the aesthetically enjoyable—even at the expense of not adequately cultivating the "useful" but prosaic on its own account. Such facts provide, I repeat, the easiest way in which to lay hold of and understand what has taken place in the case of all the subjectmatters which non-experiential and anti-experiential philosophies have erected into so many isolated, independent, tightly self-enclosed compartments, dignified, however, with such names as domains, realms, spheres, of Being. It is difficult to find anything mysterious in the arts of the dance, song, drama, story-telling, which prolong and perpetuate the immediately satisfying phase of primary experiences. Painting, sculpturing, architectural constructions, accomplish the same type of development, only in more indirect and complex, and hence more disguised ways.

The bearing of these facts upon a philosophy that is resolved to do what it can to be faithful in its theoretical views to the facts concerning the origin and development of different forms of experienced subjectmatters is not too complicated to be grasped in its own terms. What stands in the way, what is obstructive, arresting, and distorting, proceeds from philosophies in which *functional* developments out of the satisfying phase of primary experiences are hardened, frozen, reified into so many inherent aboriginal divisive kinds of Being and of Knowledge.

I do not, accordingly, see how I can better terminate this brief paper than by quoting from a writing composed and published independently of and some years prior to *Art as Experience*. The passage not only sets forth the correct version of my view of two modes of the aesthetic, the primary and the artistic, but also states the principle of development that holds so universally in my theory of a variety of phases of experience such as morals, politics, religion, science, philosophy itself, as well as the fine arts, so as to dispose in advance of criticisms that convert the distinction of the primary and the artfully developed aspects of subjectmatter into two incompatible matters.

The passage reads:

There are substantially but two alternatives. Either art is a continuation, by means of intelligent selection and arrangement, of natural tendencies of natural events, or art is a pecu-

ESSAYS

liar *addition* to nature, springing from something dwelling
within the breast of man, whatever name be given to the
latter. In the former case, delightfully *enhanced* perception is
of the same nature as enjoyment of any object that is consummatory. It is the outcome of a skilled and intelligent art
of dealing with natural things for the sake of intensifying,
purifying, prolonging, and deepening the satisfactions they
(the things of everyday primary experiences) spontaneously
afford.[2]

It hardly seems necessary to say that, whatever be the merits
or demerits of such a theory, there is a radical difference between
continuity of development and original and inherent incompatibility; particularly when the nature of the difference applies
fundamentally to each and every variety of subjects treated from
the standpoint of a general and comprehensive philosophy of
experience.

---

2. *Experience and Nature*, p. 389 [*Later Works* 1:291].

Contribution to *Democracy in a World of Tensions*

In everyday speech "reaching an understanding" is the same as "arriving at an agreement"; in the words of the dictionary, it is the same as "coming to be of one mind." Moreover, in origin the expressions *agreement* and *disagreement* had the meaning of *agreeable* and *disagreeable*, indicating that being of one mind is a good deal more than a coldly intellectual affair.

I

The foregoing reference to familiar ways of speech is introduced because of its relevancy to the work of UNESCO. Such expressions as *arriving at, coming to, reaching,* imply a previous state of difference and discord. No argument is required to convince an observer that the peoples of the world are now in such a state of division as merits the name "Cold War": a division which is historically unprecedented in both extent and pervasiveness. It is also to the point that many nations have been so stirred by discords now constituting international anarchy, with all the threat to civilized life that anarchy brings with it, that they have joined in a concerted move to discover what organized intellectual attack can do to arrive at a common understanding—as a prelude to reach agreement in practice. For nothing less than this is the meaning of UNESCO. It may even be said that its existence stands as an acknowledgment of the place and office of recourse to the method of intelligence in a matter of utmost human concern. For the entire activity of UNESCO is centered in promotion of inquiry, discussion, and conference.

[First published as chapter 5 in *Democracy in a World of Tensions: A Symposium prepared by UNESCO,* ed. Richard McKeon and Stein Rokkan (Chicago: University of Chicago Press, 1951), pp. 62–68.]

Breakdown of traditional ways of dealing with conflict between nations is without doubt a large factor in bringing UNESCO into being. For long historic periods recourse to armed conflict was successful in at least keeping the peace for a time, though it did not do away with the division of interests that generate war. Now the price paid even by the victor in war tends to bankrupt civilization; destruction is as total as is the enlistment of all the elements of nature, land, sea, and air, in the work of destruction. With respect to diplomacy as a means of settlement, others than cynics would now agree with the saying that diplomacy is the means of maintaining, in the absence of open warfare, the clash of interests that is overt in war time. Yet when it was first said, it was taken to be a manifestation of the harsh spirit of an exceedingly bellicose nation.

To say that the formation and the work of UNESCO are an effort to substitute the method of intelligence for that of force in arriving at agreement among national states would be an indulgence in inflated optimism. But there is no exaggeration in saying that it offers the peoples of the world a symbol of what is now desirable, and of what may become an actuality in the future. That which serves as a symbol must possess some standing on its own account; mere air bubbles are evanescent as symbols as well as in fact. UNESCO has met this condition. Proof is found in the two cooperative intellectual explorations already made. The first of the inquiries dealt with Human Rights; the second with Democracy. No one would deny that differences, ideological and overtly practical, with respect to these matters underlie much of the present discord; they also loom large as threats of open warfare. Differences disclosed in the discussion of human rights centered about the relation of human beings as individuals to the society of which they are members. Roughly speaking, differences were found to turn on the fact that representatives of some states emphasized the *rights* of persons as individuals as against demands put forward on behalf of the state; representatives of other peoples that are organized into national states emphasized the *duties* that individuals owe to the state, and the supreme right of the latter to compel all its members as individuals to submit unquestioningly to its authority. Since the same issue is also found to be a source of division with respect to democracy, no harm can result if further discussion of the work of UNESCO is centered on the latter theme.

One of the most significant findings of the discussion of democracy is its conclusion that every nation now claims to be a democracy. Such a claim is peculiarly important when it is placed in contrast with the division that separated nations during the interval between the two World Wars. For at that time the outstanding feature of international disagreement was the violent attack of some nations upon the very idea of democracy and upon all democratic institutions with respect to their actual practices. Some nations went so far at that time as to hold that all serious evils and troubles of mankind, internal and external, have their root in attempting to maintain the institutions that came into being after the revolutions of the eighteenth century had overthrown survivals of the feudal order. This work, according to the critics, was wholly negative. It only substituted economic feudalism for the old feudalism of status. The first World War ended in a victory for the nations that continued to assert the sufficiency of democratic institutions. Subsequent events have proved, however, that the military victory was far from settling the issue. For the U.S.S.R. continued exactly the same kind of violent attack upon the older and traditional type of democracy that had marked the Fascist and Nazi states.

Evidence on this matter is conclusive. The "democracies" of the communist type pour forth a constant stream of assertions that political democracies of the older traditional type are a delusion, snare, and willful fraudulent pretense. The assertion is accompanied by an equally persistent effort to create revolutions which will overthrow the type of democracy found in the states which like Great Britain and the United States claim to represent the democratic principle. In its origin the doctrine that political institutions resulting from the eighteenth-century revolutions have now themselves to be overthrown by another revolution was hardly more than an exercise in dialectics that illustrated the union of opposites. But now that the U.S.S.R. is one of the most powerful national states of the whole world, the doctrine has become the central factor in the present world-wide cleavage.

II

UNESCO may initiate and may give direction to inquiries and discussions which will tend to locate the sources of existing disagreement and conflict. This location may serve in turn to indicate what needs to be done to resolve existing discords. But by its very constitution UNESCO cannot by itself alone carry the work of resolution of differences through to practical conclusion. That work can be done only by the peoples who are involved in the present world-wide division.

We cannot refrain accordingly from asking about the chances that the needed work will be undertaken. In particular, what are the obstacles that stand in the way; and what if any are the resources that are available in carrying out adequate development of intellectual approach to reaching an agreement? With respect to the matter of obstacles, recent events clearly point to the fact that adequate recognition of its responsibility on the part of the people of the United States is badly hindered by attacks made upon this country by the communist nations claiming to be democratic. For these attacks have produced an atmosphere in which the mere suggestion of the need for a critical examination of democracy in reference to the standing of one's own nation is widely taken as proof that those suggesting it are infected with communist virus.

Yet the place occupied in the organic law of the United States by guaranty of Civil Rights: rights of free speech, free press, free assembly, and freedom of belief and worship in religious matters, is fundamental and central. Taken collectively they constitute nothing less than an express recognition in the fundamental law of the land of the indispensable place held in a democracy by freedom of discussion and publicity. Philosophers had previously written about the importance of leaving mind free; but in the absence of explicit legal recognition of the right to free *public communication,* freedom "of mind" hardly amounted to more than a pious wish—of concern doubtless to writers on political philosophy and jurisprudence, but of slight importance in the actual conduct of organized social life.

There is now a disposition on the part of some persons to discount the importance of the Bill of Civil Rights on the ground that it represented a fear of government and a desire to limit its activities which are now outmoded. Historically speaking there can be no doubt that dread of governments as tending to extend their range of power until their power became so oppressive of the activities of the populace as to reduce the latter to the status of subjects rather than of citizens inspired the demand for many rights. With the exception of Great Britain, Holland, and some Scandinavian countries, dread of governmental activity was justified by the record of history. There was every reason why the Founding Fathers should have wished to render the citizens of the new Republic immune from the danger of having their freedom impaired by governmental activities. For the historic record upon the whole is that of governments using their power to subordinate the welfare of the mass of the population to the interests of a privileged class. To prevent its happening in its case was an outstanding aim of those who instituted and presided over the destiny of the new Republic.

That the occasion of the presence of guaranteed freedom of speech and free expression was fear of government loses its importance (save as a comment on despotic states) now that the existence and exercise of democratic rights tend to eliminate the conditions that generated the fear. What is now of account is that the Founding Fathers in accepting the theory of Natural and *Prepolitical* Rights selected the specific rights of freedom of discussion and public communication as the rights that are so basic and so intrinsic that *political* activity must not be allowed to infringe upon them. This fact is the more significant because the Constitution in its original state contained no guaranty of the primary *political* right—that of taking part, through the exercise of suffrage, in selection of the officials that constitute the governing body. The originally highly restricted right of suffrage has been progressively extended because of the particular liberties that were guaranteed—those of free public discussion of matters that concern the welfare of the people.

No mistake could be more unfortunate than to look upon the civil rights that were selected as prior and basic to political rights as a limitation of democratic political action. For it was a determination of the conditions under which and of the way in which genuinely democratic activity might best be assured. It would also be a mistake to regard the rights in question as simply a privilege to be enjoyed. It *is* a privilege and in ample measure. But at the present juncture, the outstanding fact is that these rights impose a responsibility. Given the present state of affairs both at home and in connection with other states, the way and degree in which we use or fail to use freedom of inquiry and public communication may well be the criterion by which in the end the genuineness of our democracy will be decided in all issues.

In the degree in which we fail to employ guaranteed freedom in the present critical and free discussion, without fear or favor, of the full meaning of democracy, and the relation to it of customs and institutions which now prevail, in that degree we fail to respond to the opportunity and the challenge presented in UNESCO. We reduce its work in effect to that of a debating club. The danger of failure on the part of political democracies in general and the United States in particular extends, moreover, beyond UNESCO itself to the cause of which it is a symbolic embodiment.

III

The danger to which we are exposed is not vague and general but specific and concrete. Communist national states have taken the relation between economic conditions in prevailing industrial and financial conditions and the welfare of the mass of the population as the exclusive criterion for passing judgment upon the reality that is behind a profession of democracy. In the abstract, temptation is strong to respond by pointing out the repressive and oppressive activity of the states behind the Iron Curtain with respect to other freedoms, and by pointing out how meagre is their actual attainment of economic welfare states. But in the concrete, concentration of energy, intellectual and practical, upon this *tu quoque* method of response is an evasion, whether so intended or not, of our own primary responsibility. Moreover, it plays into the hands of communist states. For their methods of suppression are so highly effective that our critical retorts do not reach their peoples, while our practice of freedom of communication is such that their assaults upon our democracy permeate; they make a positive appeal to those elements in our population that feel that our type of democracy is definitely unfavorable to *their* economic security and wellbeing.

The more important point, however, is that the issue of the relation of economic factors to other factors in the everyday life of a people constitutes a problem which would exist even if communist states had never come into being. The problem weighs, moreover, the more heavily the more a country is industrialized; hence it is most acute and most urgent in the United States as the most thoroughly industrialized of all nations. Free and critical discussion of the problem is of course in accord with the constitutional guaranty of the right of inquiry and of public expression. But the issue extends far beyond that point. Extensive critical examination of our own practices provides the only way in which the adequacy of our claim to be genuinely democratic may be tested in the concrete; it is also the only way in which measures for correction of defects can be discovered and put into effect.

Conditions that give rise to the problem of the relation between democracy in political and economic life are intrinsic. They do not depend upon the existence of communist states that are engaged in attacking our democracy. Life in every country of the globe, even in those least affected by the rise of machine and power industry, is undergoing transformation. Technologies which exist only because of the recent and rapid development of scientific knowledge are here to stay. In the United States, transition from a predominantly agrarian and rural economy to an industrial and urban one has gone on at a rate and with a pervasive thoroughness that would have seemed incredible even two short generations ago. The swiftness, the intensity, and extensity of the change left little time for foresight and next to no time for preparation. The rise of communist states may be an occasion for our giving serious attention to the issue. But the issue is with us anyway. It is in the interest of our own democracy to make it and the difficult problems it brings with it a subject of serious and systematic critical concern with a view to action. Superficially, discussion may seem to have got away from the theme of UNESCO. Not so in fact. The troubles that now plague the world are exhibited on the largest scale in tensions due to the splitting of the peoples of one globe into two *human* worlds. But they are far from being exhausted in the evils and dangers that attend this cleavage. The troubles *come home* to the peoples of every country in their own domestic affairs. As far as the work of UNESCO stands as a symbol of approach by the method of intelligence to the problems of international relationships, it also holds and sets forth the method that each several people needs to deal with problems and issues which are not exclusively its own but which it bears the primary responsibility for meeting. Responsibility for dealing with the sources of internal troubles that are due to rapid industrialization now rests most directly upon democracies of the older political type; they are the peoples with the longest experience of industrialization. Among the political democracies it rests with particular weight upon the people of the United States. For they are not only the most thoroughly industrialized among political democracies, but they are organically committed to a type of democracy in which political activity is determined by freedoms of discussion, conference, and communication in which all citizens have the right and the duty to participate.

Modern Philosophy

I

The expression "Modern Philosophy" has two senses. "Modern" stands for a period of time; it also stands for what marks off the systems of the last few centuries from Greco-Roman and medieval systems. This negative demarcation is more accurate than one which is positive. For in the scene presented to us little community can be found in the conclusions that have been reached. There is rather an exhibit of diverse and competing views. Such unity as exists is in the type of *problems* dealt with in their sharply marked difference from those of ancient and medieval times. Concern with issues that are formulated as dualisms is a report of extensive oppositions in life itself. This report is the distinguishing stamp of the accomplishments of modern philosophical discussion. It is notable that the modern system most ambitiously aiming at unity found its way to final complete unification on a road that was surveyed and laid out by the movement of contrarieties.

The postulates of the pages that follow are that (1) the dualisms which are the staple of modern philosophy are, in the first place, reflections, mirrorings, of clashes, cleavages in the cultural life of the West; and that (2) these splits and divisions are manifestations of the impact of new movements in science, industry, the arts generally, in religion and political organization upon institutions having deep roots in the past. The new movements gave a profound shock to established institutions, but they did not overthrow them. The vision of a new world was opened liter-

[First published as chapter 2 in *The Cleavage in Our Culture: Studies in Scientific Humanism in Honor of Max Otto,* ed. Frederick Burkhardt (Boston: Beacon Press, 1952), pp. 15–29.]

ally through exploration, discovery and migration, and symbolically in the new astronomy and physics. But in respect to concerns and values that were fundamental the vision that was congenial to the old world persisted. It had been generated and shaped in the customs and usages of untold centuries. This vision of two unlike worlds is the distinctive mark of philosophy that is modern in other than a chronological sense. Its specific expression is the dualisms with which philosophy has wrestled.

In the first phase of the modern movement, the deviation from the old assumed the guise of return; of restoration of what was even more ancient. This phase is recorded in the names by which they are called:—Renaissance, Revival of Learning, Reformation. But because of the intensity of the shock to old institutions by the new tendencies, the Reformation became the Protestant Revolt; the Revival of Learning passed into the Scientific Revolution; then came the Industrial and Political Revolutions. The fact that modern philosophies are the report of these changes does not signify that all of them were committed to the new. It means that everywhere philosophic inquiry was so sensitive to the breaks and cleavages that were introduced as to undertake reconciliations, adjustments, accommodations, compromises. But whatever mode was resorted to and wherever emphasis fell, the issues were of divisions formulated as dualisms.

The latter are so conspicuous that they come readily to mind: The material and spiritual, the physical and the mental or psychical; body and mind; experience and reason; sense and intellect, appetitive desire and will; subjective and objective, individual and social; inner and outer; this last division underlying in a way all the others. For the old presented itself to the adherents of the new movements as something external to what was vital and intimate; the inner was expressed in and supported by personal conscience, by private consciousness, by intuition—things set over against institutional pressures coming from without. Seen in retrospect, however, all of the above terms are reflections of an underlying institutional collective event, which may be roughly summed up as an invasion of the sacred by the secular.

In comprehensive retrospect, it also looks as if the great mass, the "common people," viewed the new not as in conflict with the old, but as its enlargement, as an added source of enjoyment. In effect, put in words, its attitude was: "Let us make the best of both worlds, this and the next." Members of the intellectual class were, however, compelled to take sides. Some of them fought for the right of the new science to a recognized place; others felt an obligation to defend the old from the encroaching impact of the new. The most overt and obvious clash bears the name "The Warfare of Science and Religion." Its details are now chiefly of historic interest. But it probably better expresses the core of the problems that lie back of the dualisms which philosophers formulated than does any other clash.

To those engaged in defense of the old, the very heart of the conflict was within science itself. For a passing glance at the old science, which had been pervasively absorbed into medieval theology as its intellectual structure, discloses how destructive was the new incoming natural science. The old "science" was in fact a Cosmology, in which the word Cosmos is to be understood literally:—that is, as a name for a harmoniously ordered, well-proportioned, and immutably defined (or finite) systematic whole, whose natural, or proper, culmination was Reason as Logos, *Ratio*. Changes occurred and produced excess and deficit in measure. But they were kept within fixed bonds by an immanent Logos. Science, as human knowing, was itself the realized manifestation of the immutable order of Nature. Because of the adoption of this system into the structural scheme of Christian faith, this "science" had become its backbone. While Nature had been deeply marred and corrupted by the Sin of Man, it remained the solid substance of the true knowing of "science," and supernatural agencies promised its ultimate restoration by means of divine intervention.

The effect of the new astronomy and physics was definitely disruptive; it was more than a shock in science. It profoundly disturbed the moral-religious convictions and institutions that had saturated for generations the imagination and emotions of man in the Western world. The crisis in which modern philosophy developed was in short broadly and deeply cultural, not technical. It is not necessary to do more than mention the total incompatibility of the new science with the old long accepted and deeply embedded cosmology. The measure of things that had been fixed by proportions of an artistic nature gave way to the measure of quantities, which in the earlier scheme had been matters of excess and deficiency occasioned by "accidents," which entered in but did not disturb the order of the whole. Motions took the place occupied earlier by control of movements by the Immutable. The "material" causation that had occupied a subordinate place in the old science was replaced by the all-important "efficient causation." "Final Causes," the Ends, which controlled changes tending by their own nature to fulfill purposes, were relegated to theology. What had been accident, contingency, in the earlier scheme became the necessary mechanistic structure of the natural world.

When one views the completeness of the intellectual disruption involved in the new physics one may be surprised that its consequences were not more catastrophic than was actually the case. But the logic of accommodation in the "practical" affairs of life is stronger than the logic of theoretical consistency. Events actually moved in the direction that was taken (as has been previously stated) by the mass of men, who were more concerned with immediate practical matters than with theories which to them were far away. That is to say, events moved intellectually as well as practically toward a division of fields and a division of jurisdiction between authorities placed in control of the two fields. Conflict was prevented because, by common consent, the two "domains" touched but did not overlap. The higher was spiritual, ideal; it was supreme provided it did not intrude too inconveniently on ordinary, everyday secular affairs. The lower was the range of week-day occupations and concerns that were permitted to go their own way provided they rendered due obeisance to the purely ideal supremacy of the spiritual.

Just as political revolutions are never as total and final in their immediate occurrence as they seem to both adherents and opponents, so in the case of the scientific, industrial, and political "revolutions" arising from the impact of the new upon the old. At every point the newer movements were deflected and more or less arrested by injection of elements that represent the actively operating presence of the old. In consequence, the dualism which is probably the most fundamental of all the dualisms with which modern philosophy deals is one that is rarely mentioned. It is the split between philosophy and science. In the Greek and medieval periods, philosophy *was* Science in the complete and ultimate sense of Knowledge. It was at once the apex, the culmination, of all other sciences, and their sure and unchangeable basis and guarantee. In the basic dualism of scientific and philosophic subjectmatters, philosophy became the owner, guardian, and defender of the interests, activities, and values that had been violently expelled from science. Baser "material" activities and concerns were assigned to natural science. And as the prestige of the supernatural declined philosophy took over the office of rational justification of those higher values that were no longer taken care of by science, and whose guarantee by revelation from on high was becoming precarious.

II

There are signs that we have now reached a state where conditions demand a marked change in both the subjectmatter and the office that have been assigned to philosophy, and which, in pointing the way to the kind of change that is needed, also supply the means, the instrumentalities by which it is to be carried into effect. It is perhaps too extreme to say that philosophy today is in a state of doldrums—in the dictionary sense in which doldrums "are the state in which a ship makes no headway because of calm or contrary winds." But only optimists, who at best are not numerous, would say that philosophy is making great headway at present.

Discussions of such issues as Empiricism versus Rationalism, Realism versus Idealism were warm and eager hardly more than a generation ago. They have now almost disappeared from the scene. Consideration of the other classic dualisms is in a state of quiescence. The place they once held is now filled, as far as not empty, by refining and polishing tools to be used, as far as appears, only in refining more tools of precisely the same kind. For these investigations avowedly are concerned with questions said to be those of form and of form only; that is, not forms of *any* subjectmatter. This course leads to philosophy's becoming a form of Busy-work for a few professionals. Otherwise, discussions seem to go into refinements of the history of bygone issues.

Meanwhile there *are* issues of utmost importance. They are indeed so urgent that their importance may be one source of taking refuge in formal issues as an escape. But in any case they are issues marked by that inclusive and underlying character that answers the claim made by traditional philosophy for depth and comprehensiveness as its distinctive mark. The problems concerned with the present state of man in the world are certainly inclusive in range. They are no longer local; they are of man throughout the whole wide world; north, south, east, west. This fact is too obvious to need more than mention. Their temporal range may need more specific attention. The present troubles of man and the resources available for dealing with them lie far back in the abyss of time. Both our means of intercommunication and the barriers that obstruct free exchange of ideas as well as of goods come from pre-human geological ages. More recent but still very ancient is man's animal ancestry. The organism's brain and nerves as well as stomach and muscles are the means through which all transactions with nature and with fellow men are carried on. They are also of pre-human origin. The animal is so deep in man *as* man that it is the occasion of many of the abiding troubles of human life.

Yet till recently there has been no basis for placing these troubles in a factual context. Hence there has been no basis for their scientific analysis and statement. Theological Ethics has attributed them to the corruption of man in consequence of original sin, demanding therefore the kind of remedy that only a supernatural agency can supply. The prevalent view among moralists not openly accepting the supernatural account attributes the ills in question to the inherent opposition and conflict in human nature between impulse and appetite on one side and reason and will on the other side: all being treated as entitative "faculties," and hence to be dealt with by means that, to say the least, are *extra*-scientific. Of late, psychiatry has developed treatments which come closer than any other devices to being scientific. But it operates in terms which are quasi-mystical. Unconsciousness is set up as an entity, a direct heritage from the earlier attitude that treated "Consciousness" as an entity. Recognition that the troubles in question proceed from conflicts between primitive animal elements and the elements that have been shaped by acculturation (i.e., transformed by "social" institutions) renders scientific resources available for specific factual analyses and reports. Their treatment can now be brought into line with the transformation already made in medical treatment of ills by means of use of the methods and conclusions of physical and physiological inquiry.

The foregoing has a certain importance on its own account. It is here mentioned, however, as an illustration. The fact exemplified is, negatively, that the earlier period of modern natural inquiry was such as to evoke and justify the dualisms that were the staples of philosophical discussion; positively, it stands for the fact that natural science in its own advance to maturity now renders these dualisms as unnecessary as they have proved to be futile. The substitution of continuities in the place of breaks and isolations has broken down the separation and opposition of philosophy to natural science; a separation which was inevitable as long as the state of scientific inquiry was definitely adverse to specifically human activities and values. The substitution of extensive continuities for sharp divisions and isolations has for its foundation the systematic thoroughgoing abandonment of the frame of reference, the standpoint and outlook, that was the necessary result of the assumption that knowing and knowledge were assured and secure only as they dealt with what is inherently fixed, immutable. When *process* is seen to be the "universal" in nature and in life, continuity, extensive spatially and temporally, becomes *the* regulative principle of *all* inquiry that claims to be scientific.

The change is so recent that it is still generally regarded as technical and confined. It is out of the question to do more here than mention some of the outstanding aspects of that change in the frame of reference of natural inquiry which is anything but technical—which in fact is so extensive as now to render scientific conclusions directly available in and for philosophical inquiry.

Replacement of fixity and the separations consequent upon it by process and continuity was first achieved in the knowing of plant and animal life. For a time, it was incomplete with respect to this subjectmatter. The category of fixation which was abandoned with respect to "species" was retained in search for immutables in the process of "evolution." More important, of course, was resistance from vested institutional interests, since life, especially human life, was to them the last ditch of entrenched external authority. The persistence of this resistance is now an important, probably *the* most important, factor in maintaining "social" and moral subjects in their notably backward estate.

The objection is made that the inclusion of man and his concerns and values within the scope of continuous process involves degradation of man to the level of the brutes. It comes with particularly poor grace from those who insist upon man's total corruption because of original sin. But it also involves *denial* of continuity of process. For continuity involves variation and differentiation of a cumulative sort, while the doctrine of reductive degradation treats continuity of development as if it were bare repetition. Employment of motion as a basic principle in physics was also partial in its earlier phase. For it was accompanied by the belief that motions occur within a fixed empty shell of space and time, and that they centre in and are conducted by immutable atomic particles. Now that the Newtonian framework is replaced by that of Relativity (from the standpoint of popular understanding not a very happy name), the old separations of space and time from each other, and of both of them from the events taking place within them, have lost all shadow of standing. Space and time, instead of being nouns or names of "entities," are now qualifications of events, more accurately represented by adverbial form than even by adjectival phrases. "Matter" is represented by a mathematical expression which, like all such symbols, is transformable at need into symbols applicable to other aspects of the indefinitely extensive process which is nature. The "mechanistic" in its earlier sense is now inapplicable save to selected segments and sections which are usable as mechanisms of chosen operations. In the advance alike of physical and physiological inquiry, the fixed separations set up between man and nature make way for specifically determined continuities. The methods and findings of natural science in consequence become available resources for systematic use by philosophic inquiry, provided the latter is willing to make a renunciation that is a sacrifice only for those having vested institutional interests in perpetuating the eternal and immutable as the proper and only assured marks of "Reality" at large as *the* "Object" of science.

In spite of attendant handicaps, the earlier phase of "modern" philosophy made notable contributions to the advancement of the new astronomy and physics. It accomplished this work both negatively and positively. It brought critical attacks to bear upon institutional obstacles that stood in the way—thereby forwarding, whether it was so intended or not, "liberal" movements in the broader human field. They opened up large and generous vis-

tas of the natural world, and projection of these views contributed largely to formation of the specific working instruments
that were needed by the new natural science. The heaviest handi-
cap under which philosophy labored in doing this work of liberation was that, instead of doing its work openly, it operated
under cover of that which it continued to view as Ultimate Being
or Reality at large. Because its work was done under cover, those
who engaged in development of the "modern" philosophy of that
period mostly failed to note that the service which was genuinely
rendered was that of liberation in *human* affairs. In respect to
Reality only futile contention resulted. And the service actually
rendered was distorted by the assumption that the human in
question was isolated from the world with which physical science dealt. The persistent hold of the assumption is best shown
in the fact that it was maintained in full force at the very time
natural inquiry was actually transforming human relations.

III

Philosophy that is thoroughgoing in acknowledgment
that human activities, affairs, successes and failures, trials and
tribulations, resources and liabilities, values positive and negative, are its proper subjectmatter is now able to employ the methods and conclusions of natural inquiry as its systematic ally in
performance of its own office: That of furthering observations of
the problems that are deeply and widely involved in the contemporary state of man, and that of contributing to formation of a
frame of reference in which pertinent hypotheses for dealing
with the problems can be projected.

The postulate underlying the validity of this position is, of
course, that inquiries in the human field, in the so-called "social"
sciences, are now in as backward a state as was physical inquiry
a few centuries ago—only "more so." To me this is a fact so obvious that no argument for it is needed. But a few outstanding
considerations will be set forth. At present we are not even aware
of what the *problems* are in and of the human field. On the overt,
so-called "practical" side, the ever-accelerating rate at which the
troubles and evils, as the raw materials of problems, are piling up
and spreading offers a convincing demonstration of backward-

ness. Further evidence is furnished by two significant features of the attitude taken toward them. One is the current revival of the policy of despair embodied in the doctrine that man's sinful nature is the source of these troubles so that recourse to the supernatural is indicated; the former optimistic assumption that exhortation and idealistic preaching will suffice being now pretty effectively discounted.

The other feature is the policy of despair represented in the current clamor of accusations that natural science is itself a chief source of a large number of present evils, and that arresting its further development (instead of use in constructive advancement of competent human inquiry) is the remedy to be employed. Evidence of backwardness on what is usually called the "theoretical" side (as if it were not itself supremely practical) is equally convincing. It is not excessive to say that at present social maladjustments and ills are taken "as is," in the raw, as if they were of themselves problems in the scientific sense. This is precisely as if in physics the destruction of houses by lightning, or the harmful deterioration of metal by rusting, were taken not as the occasion of search for the conditions that constitute the problem, but as itself the problem; or as if in physiology the occurrence of malaria and of cancer were taken in their brute occurrence to be scientific problems. In the case of "lightning" it is clear that no scientific progress was made until it was at least determined where the problem was located; namely in the field of electrical events, and that further progress in specific determination of the problem occurred as physics progressed in understanding of electrical phenomena. Until malaria was located in the general field of infection by parasites of insect origin attempts to deal with it were purely "empirical" in the disparaging sense of that word. The case of cancer is even more significant. In short, the saying that problems well-stated are already half-solved errs only in not going far enough. Problem-stating and problem-solving are two aspects of one and the same operation. It is because of this fact that the present state of "problems" in the subjectmatter of human inquiry is so deplorably significant.

Further evidence as to the backward state of inquiry in this field is the assumption that now possesses pretty complete control of inquiry into human subjectmatter. This assumption is that the various important aspects of organized human behavior are so isolated from one another as to constitute separate and independent subjects, and hence are to be treated each one by methods peculiar to it in its severalty. The subjectmatter is chopped up and parceled out into, say, jurisprudence, politics, economics, the fine arts, religion and morals. "Sociology" in its origin was presented as a means of overcoming this splitting up; it seems to have developed into another subject with its own special subjectmatter—which it has been largely occupied with attempting to determine. In this connection, it is profitable to note that physical inquiry in its earlier phase was also divided into separate subjects; and that its progress is marked by inquiries that have to be designated by introducing hyphens and adjectival phrases. The distinction among them is fast becoming one of phase or emphasis in the direction of inquiry, not one of barriers due to the subjectmatters.

What has been said will be misunderstood if it is taken to signify that philosophy can or should offer solutions for human problems or even determine on its own account what the problems *specifically* are. But there is a preliminary work urgently in need of doing. It is similar to that done in the seventeenth, eighteenth, and a large part of the nineteenth centuries in getting physical inquiry free from the burdens that were imposed by cultural conditions of earlier periods; and, positively, in building up a sense of the frame of reference, the kind of standpoint and of outlook, in which human problems are to be specified and hypotheses for their resolution projected and tested. It is worth while to note again that human subjectmatter now has spatially and temporally the comprehensive scope that philosophic reflection has claimed as its own distinguishing mark. The breakdown of the barriers between man and nature now extends so far and wide that the futile problem of the dualism of mind-and-body may be exchanged for specific problems as to how transactions of organism and environment as they take place retard and assist human endeavors for humane ends. The question of "natural resources" is much less confined than is usually supposed; it needs broadening to take in the way in which natural conditions enter into every phase of human concern, whether as resource or as liability.

What was just said about the inclusive and penetrating state of human activities and concerns indicates that one of the prime problems today is to show that human material in its full scope is now the proper subjectmatter of philosophy. The case of assaults upon "science" as if it were an entity by itself, having its own independent career, is a case in point—as is equally the indiscriminate laudations sometimes lavished upon it. What is called science, like knowing in every form, is one aspect of organized human behavior; it is so far from being isolated and independent that it is engaged in and shaped by continual transactions of give-and-take with every other form of organized human behavior. There is an open field awaiting students of the historical aspects of philosophy in showing how the course of natural science has been affected by the cultural concerns in religious rites and dogmas, in economics, politics, law, and the arts, whether "fine" or "useful." What is wanted is not a "synthesis," a formal unification imposed from without, but specific studies of intercommunication, and of the blocks and arrests that have unduly exaggerated one phase of human behavior and minimized other phases; as, for one example, the historic cultural conditions which rendered physical inquiry so one-sidedly specialized as to give it its present predominatingly technical temper. Systematic pursuit of this line of inquiry will remove Morals from the narrow isolated field in which it has been progressively confined by disclosing the demonstrable fact that it is the culmination and focus of what is distinctively humane in all values and disvalues of all the modes and aspects of collective, organized behavior.

The way ahead is hard and difficult for philosophy as for every other phase of human endeavor; for, after all, the change demanded in philosophy is but one aspect of the reconstructions now possible and urgently required in every phase of human life. Philosophy can hardly take the lead in introducing that new epoch in human history which is now the alternative to ever-increasing catastrophe. But it can, if it has enduring courage and patience, engage cooperatively in the prolonged struggle to discover and utilize the positive ways and means by which the cause of human freedom and justice may be advanced in spite of the uncertainties, confusions, and active conflicts that now imperil civilization itself. The opportunity for engaging in cooperative work is open. The initial step in philosophical endeavor is systematic constructive use of the resources that the different phases of natural inquiry have now put in our hands. Utilization *in fact* of these resources must of course extend far beyond the particular activities called by the names of either science or philosophy. But those engaged in philosophical pursuits can, if they will, have a share in the undertaking, thereby regaining for the subject to which they have pledged themselves significance and vitality which are generous, liberal, humane.

It may well be that the isolation of "science" from other organized human pursuits, occupations, and values was originally a measure of protection. Perhaps if it had not disclaimed responsibility for connection with and bearing upon other aspects of collective activity and concern, the institutional obstacles to its survival would have been more than grave; they might have been insuperable. But none the less, systematic acceptance of the doctine of its aloofness left its course to be one-sidedly determined by and connected with but one particular type of human interest and behavior:—that termed Economic which in turn was identified with the "material." This identification and the isolations that followed in consequence have conferred undue strength upon institutional operations that have tended to enhance the profit and power of class-sections and nationalistic segments at the expense of our common humanity. This state of human life inevitably recoils to produce insecurity and conflict. A choice of immense human import will be made in the coming days. We shall either perpetuate and intensify the evils that tragically afflict us by continuing petulant and futile complaints directed at natural inquiry or we shall begin to utilize the physical, intellectual and moral resources provided by scientific understanding to promote conditions of freedom, equity, and wellbeing in which all human beings share. The choice reaches so deep and wide that the career and destiny of philosophy is but one factor among many. But for philosophy its part is not minor. It now has the opportunity and challenge to take part by showing how systematic use of the resources provided by the methods and conclusions of natural inquiry can serve the interests of our common humanity. Philosophy that assumes a responsible even if humble share in this work will drink of living springs from which to draw renewed vitality.

Appendixes

Appendix 1
A Letter to Mr. Dewey concerning John Dewey's Doctrine of Possibility

University of Virginia,
February 10, 1949

Dear Mr. Dewey:

Recently I was reading, with a small group of students, portions of John Dewey's *Logic.* I observed with interest that their difficulties centered about the treatment of *possibility.* June arriving, the students departed to actualize possibilities they had secretly entertained throughout the semester. As for the perplexities, they left them as a parting gift to me.

It seems prudent to bespeak your assistance, for I have in mind that you are related to the author of the *Logic,* one John Dewey, somewhat as René Descartes is related to the author of the *Meditations.* My purpose is to seek a better understanding of John Dewey's doctrine, rather than to offer criticism, and still less to propose ideas of my own. From moment to moment I state conjectures as to John Dewey's meaning. I trust that any distortion introduced by an earlier will be corrected by a later conjecture.

Having sat at John Dewey's feet many, many years ago, I dare to make a general introductory observation concerning my understanding of the position of that Socrates. To John Dewey, dualisms are abhorrent. Initial dualisms will insure terminal collapse. Modern philosophical thought has failed because dualisms, implicitly or explicitly espoused, controlled the course of speculation. There are, of course, genuine distinctions to be made. Such distinctions emerge within the existential matrix of inquiry. Analysis should disclose how and why the distinctions arise. Thus, retrospectively, they may be related to tensions, to

[First published in *Journal of Philosophy* 46 (26 May 1949): 313–29. For Dewey's reply to Albert G. A. Balz, see this volume, pp. 280–94.]

stresses and strains, in the life-process matrix of all inquiry. The distinctions—say, between "knower" and "known," "mental" and "physical," or whatever—are functional in the process of inquiry. In the *theory* of inquiry, such distinctions must be understood *prospectively,* as factors conditioning the accomplishment of inquiry. The distinctions, however, must not be petrified, either with respect to their generating conditions or with respect to their functional conditioning of the inquiry process, for such petrification means that the philosophical enterprise fails before it is begun. This, in brief and inadequately, is my understanding of John Dewey's general position. It is my hope that my conjectures, terminologically and otherwise, will be in accord with that position. Should I fail in this, dear Mr. Dewey, and should you kindly help me as of yore, please point out quite freely where I have erred in representing John Dewey's teaching.

My conjectures will relate primarily to the distinctions between *potentiality* and *possibility,* the *existential* and *non-existential,* and related distinctions.

The author of the *Logic* makes a firm distinction between *potentialities* and abstract *possibilities* (p. 289 [*Later Works* 12: 288–89*]: the terms are italicized in the text). The former are said to be "existential 'powers' that are actualized under given conditions of existential interaction." Possibility is said to be "a matter of an operation as such—it is operability."

I pause here to offer a preliminary conjecture as to John Dewey's meaning and to give a first indication of the question to which my conjectures are intended to lead. Potentialities are existential and are actualized under given conditions of existential interaction. Are possibilities a special group of potentialities, existential and actualized under given conditions of existential interaction, but distinguished from other potentialities because of their special operative function within the process of inquiry? The *Logic* of John Dewey is the theory of inquiry. Inquiry is a living process, a going-on within the wider living-process-matrix. (It is difficult for me to think of this matrix without considering it as itself within a far more comprehensive context, including the motions of double stars, the breaking of waves upon a reef, and the il-

---

* Bracketed numbers following citations of Dewey's *Logic* refer to corresponding pages in *Later Works* 12.

limitable flight of events. But this may be inacceptable to John Dewey, or, perhaps, irrelevant to the theory of inquiry.) Potentialities, presumably, are to be understood in terms of this living-process-matrix. Potentialities are many and varied—of birds for flying, of tulip bulbs for blossoming, of hounds for pursuing the fox. Since inquiry is a living process, and it is conceded that it does go on, I assume that it implies the actualization of potentialities under appropriate conditions of existential interaction. It seems not inappropriate to designate these potentialities as inquiry-potentialities. In so far as the theory of inquiry succeeds and we know to what inquiry leads, we know, or at least know better, what is meant by inquiry-potentialities and what is meant by calling them *inquiry*-potentialities. (Of course, these as well as other potentialities can be objects of inquiry on the part of the several sciences. But a confession of my own prejudices may be needed. There seems to me to be a danger in the philosopher's relying too seriously on the particular findings or bodies of findings proclaimed by scientists. Give scientists an inch and they are tempted to take, not ells, but parsecs, and claim squatters' rights over what the philosopher fondly takes to be his domain.) In the existential living-process matrix of inquiry, and in the inquiry process, it seems necessary to acknowledge a distinction between the inquiring thing and everything else that may be implicated in one or another inquiry. The distinction may be stated in the terms, the "organism" and the "environment." This distinction, of course, must not be taken as a dualistic petrification. Moreover, as I understand John Dewey, the "environment" is a term of extraordinarily rich and comprehensive meaning, especially when the term is used in the theory of inquiry. There is a sense, I conjecture, in which inquiry-potentialities could be said to be resident in both the inquiring-organism and in the environing-conditions-of-inquiry. In another sense, they are peculiarly resident within the organism. The inquiry-process involves the co-functioning, the co-actualization, of potentialities. Assuming the accord of this with the teaching of John Dewey, quite tentatively I conjecture that "possibilities" are comprised with the group of "inquiry-potentialities" and the latter within potentialities that are actualized under given conditions of existential interaction. (Whether inquiry-potentialities should mean a special set of potentialities, occurring in man, say, but not in butterflies, or potentialities actualizable in a special manner in the inquiry-process but also actualizable under different conditions in a different manner, and related questions, I leave to one side. Candidly, I must say that I find John Dewey's doctrine extraordinarily difficult to state, if one is to avoid mis-representation on the one hand, and on the other hand to avoid sentences so replete with clauses of stipulation and qualification that even a Hegel would be envious! In reading John Dewey, if I may reflect my experience, one goes astray unless one realizes the incredible concreteness of meaning that every word implies. I could wish—it is impertinent for me to say this, dear Mr. Dewey,—not that John Dewey would learn from the biologists, but that the biologists could learn from John Dewey the burden of meanings that the terms "organism" and "environment" must carry!)

The present conjecture, then, is that in some sense possibilities may be a sub-class of potentialities or even of inquiry-potentialities. For the purpose of throwing further light on this conjecture, other texts may be considered. "The organic responses that enter into the production of the state of affairs that is temporally later and sequential are just as existential as are environing conditions" (p. 107 [110]). "Organic interaction becomes inquiry when existential consequences are anticipated; when environing conditions are examined with reference to their *potentialities;* and when responsive activities are selected and ordered with reference to actualization of some of the potentialities, rather than others, in a final existential situation" (p. 107 [111], italics mine). On page 129 [132] an object is said to be "a set of qualities treated as *potentialities* for specified existential consequences." Declarative propositions are said to state potentialities (p. 162 [164]; on pp. 388–389 [386] an important passage urges that the categories of potentiality and actuality must not be confused). Organic responses are existential. In the inquiry-process— this would seem to be in accord with what precedes—there is the co-functioning of many potentialities. Perhaps it might be more accurate to state that in the inquiry process, at each and every stage, there is the intricate co-functioning of potentialities in various stages of actualization. A distinction as to sources seems to be requisite. Although co-functioning, "organism" is distinguishable from "environment"; better, perhaps, intra-organic potentialities from extra-organic. That is to say: given environing conditions, but no organism, inquiry-process could not arise and go on; again, given the organism, but no environing conditions, the inquiry-process could not arise and go on. Of course, in fact, there is always an-organism-in-environing-conditions and environing-conditions-for-an-organism. Retrospectively viewed, the inquiry process seems to emerge from a matrix so intensely concrete that there is artifice even in a hard-and-fast distinction between the "organism" and the "environment" as potentiality-sources. Would John Dewey accept this as a means of representing this concreteness?—in the living process, the "environment" is the environment-for-this-organism, and the "organism" is the organism-for-and-in-this-environment. As it were, the organism evokes and defines the environment-for-it; the environing conditions are brought into focus for inquiry by *this* organism in its total present condition; reciprocally, the environmental conditions operate to attune the organism to them, contributing to a certain focussing of intra-organic conditions. Given these safeguards, it does not seem unreasonable to distinguish two sets of potentialities compresent at every moment in the inquiring process, summarily represented by "organism" and "environment." For the sake of brevity, I use the symbols, o- and e-potentialities.

I would now return to page 289 [289]. John Dewey, having distinguished *potentialities* from abstract *possibilities,* and having defined the former as existential "powers" actualized under given conditions of existential interaction, makes additional statements concerning possibilities. Possibility—operability—"is existentially actualized *only* when the operation is performed not with or upon symbols but upon existences." (The *only* is *not* italicized in the original.) Possibilities are existentially actualized provided the operation is performed upon existence. Is it fair or not to represent John Dewey's view by this? There are o-potentialities. Some of these, at least, in view of the inquiry-process, may be called inquiry-potentialities. (It is understood, of course, that the inquiry-process always involves co-functionings and co-actualizations as previously indicated.) Inquiry-(i)-potentialities, or at least some of them, should be called *possibilities,* because as operations they *can* be performed with or upon symbols, and *when* so performed are possibilities. Such operations, I assume, since they happen, are in themselves actualizations or stages in a process of actualization. Viewed retrospectively, they are emergent from o-potentialities present in the wider context of potentialities and actualizations of the concrete inquiry process. What o-potentialities, what i-potentialities, become operations with and upon symbols is a question that need not be considered. A symbol-operation, once going on, must be understood in terms of what eventuates in the inquiry-process. It is functional as anticipatory of what *may* happen in the further course of the process. In this manner its status as a possibility is defined. Quite tentatively, then, I conjecture that a symbol-operation may be viewed in two ways: retrospectively, as a stage of actualization of (some) potentialities; prospectively, as functionally anticipatory, as a possibility.

I further assume, dear Mr. Dewey, that symbols, at least in their materiality, are "existential" or existents. (It is understood that John Dewey, on page 51 [57], makes a distinction between signs and symbols, employing the former for so-called natural signs, the smoke that pours from a chimney, and the latter for artificial signs, such as "smoke.") It then seems fair to state that there are operations with or upon symbols and other operations not directly concerned with symbols. Both, so it appears to me, could be called existential operations, operations with or upon symbol-existents and operations with other existents. All activities within the living-process matrix of inquiry are existential and may be viewed as moments in the actualization of co-functioning o- and e-potentialities. A stage of actualization dependent upon symbol-existents, the making and using of symbols, where the focussing of potentialities is primarily intraorganic, may be exceptional or involve an organism of exceptional endowment (*cf.* p. 43 [49]). Please believe, dear Mr. Dewey, that I do not wish to be captious. I seek only clarification as to John Dewey's doctrine. That doctrine would be clearer to me were I permitted to state it in this manner:—Every actualization occurs under given conditions of existential interaction. There are processes of the actualization of potentialities which could not lead to the fruits to which in fact they do lead were symbol-existents not available and not used. They are thus actualizations under special conditions of existential interaction. These fruits, in view of their function in the further on-going inquiry-process are possibilities and they may receive, or define the conditions of, a further actualization-of-potentialities when the operation is not directly performed with or upon symbols but upon existents other than symbols. The theatre of the processes for which symbol-existents are indispensable is primarily intra-organic, although remotely, here and elsewhere, the co-functioning of the intra- and extra-organic is implied. When a particular inquiry-process has reached its end-in-view in a situation marked by the resolution of the tension pertaining to that particular inquiry-process, then an entertained possibility may receive its functional actualization under conditions of interaction which could be described as the consummation of an intricate co-functioning of the organism and environment. This consummation is, of course, an actualization with respect to which possibilities were functionally anticipatory (pp. 107–109 [111–13]).

As a further preliminary step, I would like now to consider the meaning of "idea" and of "non-existential." The paragraph on page 289 [289] continues:

> A strictly *possible* operation constitutes an idea or conception. Execution of the operation upon symbolized ideational material does not produce the consequences constituting resolution of tension. It produces them . . . only by operationally introducing conditions that institute a determinate kind of interaction.

An idea is "an anticipation of something that may happen; it marks a *possibility*" (p. 109 [113]). "Without some kind of symbol no idea; a meaning that is completely disembodied can not be entertained or used" (p. 110 [114]). On page 113 [117] the phrase occurs: "an idea that stands for a possible solution." On pages 112–113 [116] John Dewey writes:

> It was stated that the observed facts of the case and the ideational contents expressed in ideas are related to each other, as, respectively, a clarification of the problem involved and the proposal of some possible solution; that they are, accordingly, functional divisions in the work of inquiry. Observed facts in their office of locating and describing the problem are existential; ideational subject-matter is non-existential. How, then, do they cooperate with each other in the resolution of an existential situation? The problem is insoluble save as it is recognized that both observed facts and entertained ideas are

operational. Ideas are operational in that they instigate and direct further operations of observation; they are proposals and plans for acting upon existing conditions to bring new facts to light and to organize all the selected facts into a coherent whole.

In sum: an idea or conception is a possible operation. It is a possibility or marks a possibility. It is an anticipation. It can not be without a symbol.

If previous conjectural re-statements of John Dewey's doctrine are acceptable, the meaning of the expression, "non-existential," I assume, must be somewhat as follows. The idea, the ideational subject-matter, the anticipatory possibility, as a happening, as a moment in a going-on, is, of course, existential. I have dared call it a momentary stage of actualization of potentialities. But functionally the idea is anticipatory of what is not yet going on. In the developing situation in which the idea or possibility is now a factor, it points to a situation that may come about if certain changes are instituted, a situation wherein resolution of tension shall have been effected. The idea, then, is existential-in-reference, since it points to a situation in which the inquiry process may eventuate. But the idea or possibility is non-existential in the sense that it anticipates what does not yet exist and what will not exist unless appropriate activities are undertaken by the organism under the co-functioning of intra- and extra-organic conditions. Indeed, if these activities are undertaken, the process may be viewed retrospectively to reveal the sense in which the ideational factors were non-existential. This functional non-existentiality of process factors, or rather, this functioning of factors, depends upon the use of symbol-existents—(and, should one add, the use of natural sign materials?). Intra-organic resources, if materials for signs and symbols were not available and were not used, could not achieve the entertaining of possible operations in the transactional inquiry process. It appears to be the case that the coming-into-being of the possible is at the same time the accrual of a functional inquiry status to an existent or existential "stuff" and so the latter becomes symbol. So to speak: the idea makes the stuff into a symbol at the moment when the stuff makes possible the emergence of the idea.

I do hope, dear Mr. Dewey, that the preceding has not seriously distorted John Dewey's general position. It is intended to be preparatory for examination of the treatment of *possibility*. On page 280 [279] we read that "it is the very nature of ordered discourse to deal with possibilities in abstraction from existential material." Now John Dewey regards the case of mathematics as crucial. "The ability of any logical theory to account for the distinguishing logical characteristics of mathematical conceptions and relations is a stringent test of its claims" (p. 394 [391]). His logical theory must show that mathematical subject-matter is an outcome of intrinsic development within the comprehensive pattern of inquiry. The theory must account for "the form of discourse which is intrinsically free from the *necessity* of existential reference while at the same time it provides the *possibility* of indefinitely extensive existential reference" (p. 394 [391]). "Ordered discourse is *itself* a series of transformations conducted according to rules of rigorous (or necessary) and fruitful substitution of meanings" (p. 395 [392]). John Dewey states that in preceding chapters what was in view is discourse conducted in reference to some final existential applicability. Mathematical discourse is then described:

> When . . . discourse is conducted exclusively with reference to satisfaction of its *own* logical conditions, or, as we say, for its own sake, the subject-matter is not only non-existential in immediate reference but is itself formed on the ground of freedom from existential reference of even the most indirect, delayed and ulterior kind. It is then mathematical. (P. 396 [393].)

"The contents of a mathematical proposition are freed from the necessity of any privileged interpretation" (p. 398 [395]). Transformations of meanings involve operations that may themselves be abstracted. Transformation becomes transform*ability* in the abstract (p. 399 [396]). Transformation, as I understand it, may take place in two ways. It is, in either case, I assume, an operation, a process, and existential in this (perhaps unimportant) sense. Operations may have in view the *enactment* of what are to be regarded as *possibilities* in relation to that anticipated enactment. In the other case, the operations proceed without regard to eventual enactment. At this level the operations are controlled by demands springing from the nature of transformability in the abstract. Here the operations concern ideas, i.e., possibles. The "subject-matter or *content* of discourse consists of *possibilities*.

Hence the contents are non-existential even when instituted and ordered with reference to existential application" (p. 395 [392]). Moreover, "as possibilities, they require formulation in symbols. Symbolization . . . is of the very essence of discourse as concerned with possibilities" (p. 395 [392]). In one sense, as I understand it, the operations are on, with, or by means of symbols. But while a symbol is a bit of existential stuff, it is not a *symbol* without an idea. In another sense, then, the operations are on, with, or by means of ideas. Yet, again, since there is no idea without a symbol, the operations are concerned with symbols. The ideas are possibles, existential in that they are operations or factors in operations in the inquiry-process, non-existential in that they are in discourse freed from the necessity of existential reference, and again non-existential in that, if referred to existence, the reference is to a terminal situation which may or may not come to be.

John Dewey's doctrine on the possibles should be considered, one would think, in relation to the tradition which would assign an ontological status to them. On pages 131–132 [134–35], he refers to the earlier classic ontology, and to a more recent tendency to regard "the conceptual subject-matter as constituting a realm of abstract possibility also taken as complete in itself, not as indicating possibilities of operations to be performed. While the resulting metaphysical status assigned is very different from that of classic ontology, there is nevertheless the same hypostatization of a logical function into a supra-empirical entity" (cf. p. 399 [396], pp. 389–390 [387]). The operational theory of possibility is set over against an ontological theory (p. 399 [396]; on page 271 [269–70] we read that, by means of formulation, practical actual ways of acting become representative of possible ways of acting; and on page 302 [301–2], that universal propositions are formulations of possible operations). Again: "The position here taken does hold . . . that the operations of transformability which determine mathematical subject-matter are, or constitute, the Realm of Possibilities in the only meaning logically assignable to that phrase" (p. 401 [398]).

On page 404 [401], however, there occurs a passage that is striking.

> While it is not claimed that this operational-functional interpretation of isomorphic patterns of relationships *disproves* the interpretation of mathematics that refers it to an onto-

logical ground, it is claimed that it renders that interpretation unnecessary for *logical* theory, leaving it in the position of any metaphysical theory that must be argued for or against on *metaphysical* grounds.

This passage, more than any other, tempts me to conjecture.

Let me call the interpretation of mathematics, or of possibility generally, which refers it to an ontological ground, the "ontological doctrine," with the understanding that this could take many forms. Let me further suppose that a student of John Dewey's *Logic* were to say: The *Logic* is a magnificently convincing analysis of what does go on in the process of inquiry. The passage above suggests several questions. Is there an interpretation of the Deweyan theory which would render an ontological doctrine, not merely *unnecessary* for *logical* theory, but *unnecessary?* unnecessary for metaphysics in the sense that a metaphysics complementary to and in harmony with the operational theory would contain no doctrine concerning an ontological ground of possibility, of mathematics? If so, just what is this interpretation? On the other hand, if the operational theory be accepted, but be regarded as *permitting* (not requiring) supplementation by a metaphysics which may successfully argue for an ontological doctrine, what interpretation of the operational theory makes this permissive? what factors in it leave room for such a possible metaphysical supplementation? Again, one may imagine the student confronting a different question. Is it conceivable that the operational theory, while making an ontological doctrine *un*necessary for this superb analysis of the process of inquiry, nevertheless *requires* for the satisfaction of philosophic interests a metaphysical supplementation and a supplementation involving an ontological ground for the possibles? If so, what factors in the operational account point to this requirement?

It seems possible to discern one line of conjectural interpretation that would render any problem of arguing for an ontological ground unnecessary in the sense that the question would be defined as illusory by the operational theory. Everything here would pivot upon construing possibilities as a sub-class of potentialities. If ideas, possibles, are operations, they are events in the flight of events. They are existential in that they are moments in the intricate co-functioning of intra- and extra-organic conditions. They are moments in a living process. It is granted that ideas, possibles, ideational subject-matter, are, with respect to their anticipatory function, in relation to what may but may not come to be, non-existential. But in themselves, as events, as discriminable factors in a developing process, they are as brutally existential as the upthrusting of the foliage of my daffodils. If, then, we are to employ the ancient distinction of potentiality and actualization, and allied terms, it seems consistent to look upon ideas, possibles, as actualizations of potentialities, or as stages, moments, products, incidents in such actualization. In virtue of their office in the inquiry process, in virtue of all that is so splendidly disclosed in the *Logic,* they, or the potentialities without which they would not eventuate, might well deserve a special name. They are potentialities that, in the inquiry process, lead to possibilities, to activities anticipatory in significance. Now the sub-class might well define problems of exceptional interest for several sciences. I mean this in the innocuous sense that stones, daffodils, and butterflies do not engage in inquiry processes and men sometimes do, and science might be interested in the facts and what they imply. But vitally important as the distinction between possibility and potentiality may be for the analysis of the inquiry process, on the conjecture now being pursued I am unable to perceive why "possibility," "ideas," "possibles," could occasion a special metaphysical problem. John Dewey's student, on this conjecture, could say: Metaphysics may well need to employ such distinctions as that between potentiality and actualization. In the total field of our acquaintance with the flight of events, the stately procession of the stars should be noticed, but no less (and no more?) the darting of the dragonfly and the efforts of the gardener depressed by the stunted foliage of his iris, while entertaining the anticipatory interpretation that his garden may be infested with mice. Assuredly the metaphysician would exclaim over the richly qualified tissue of events. Potentiality and actualization would designate aspects of the realm of facts requiring scientific and metaphysical reckoning. Given the conjectural interpretation, however, the sympathetic student of John Dewey's theory could declare that no *special* metaphysical issue would be occasioned by the fact that within this realm inquiry does go on and that like other processes the distinction between potentiality and actualization is pertinent to it. Even mathematics, however notable it is within and for the analysis of inquiry, would not demand a metaphysical discussion as to whether mathematics must be referred to an ontological ground.

I do not wish, dear Mr. Dewey, to over-emphasize a single isolated text, which may have meant little more than a gesture on the part of John Dewey. Since my objective, however, is not so much criticism as opportunity for clarification, I beg leave to continue my suppositions. Suppose the sympathetic student were to wonder concerning a metaphysical supplementation to the operational theory, and ask: what features of the operational theory should be taken as points of departure for the metaphysical discussion? Everything here, I conjecture, would depend upon the interpretation of "possibility," "possibles," "idea," and "operation." Ideas are operational. They direct further operations of observation. They mark possibilities. They are functionally anticipatory. Is it possible, the student might ask, without distorting John Dewey's analysis of the process of inquiry, to say that these terms may be construed in two ways? In one way we are primarily if not exclusively concerned with their function in the process of inquiry. Construed in another way, at least the possibility of a metaphysical discussion is indicated. The inquiry activity is a complex one, going on amid and dependent upon varying and cumulative intra- and extra-organic conditions. With respect to the end in view, the process could be considered as a single operation. With respect to its complexity, it may be regarded as consisting of many operations. Some of these operations are ideas. They are possibilities, operabilities, that point to something which may come about. Because idea-operations can not exist without symbols, they may be called symbol-operations. Idea-operations perform a special function in the total complex inquiry-operation. In the inquiry-process, then, the idea is an operation defining further possible operations. For the purpose of analyzing the process of inquiry, it may be urged, nothing more need be said concerning "idea" or "possibles." They may be interpreted under the over-all distinction between potentiality and actualization, as previously indicated, without prejudice to their office in the inquiry-process.

Is it permissible, however, to view "idea" and "possibles" in another way, without conflict with the analysis of the inquiry process? The question, however it may be answered, is *suggested* by some of John Dewey's phrases. Ideas are proposals or plans for acting; ideas mark possibilities; ideas stand for a possible solution. Could this be said?—ideas, possibles, define or determine operations; the anticipated operation is, in part at least, determined in its nature by the nature of the idea or possible; the inquirer perceives possibilities of operation, and distinguishes one from another, by means of ideas, by noting what they are. Suppose the hypothesis be entertained that the observational data concerning planets be made intelligible, as to their orbital paths, by means of some geometrical conception—circle, ellipse, or whatever. Circle or ellipse appear to be factors defining possibilities of interpretation looking toward resolution of tension. The geometric conception seems to enter as if, in view of its intrinsic nature, it exerted control over the formulation of possibilities entertained and over activities in accord with the several possibilities. Thus indeed they mark possibilities. Purely as an expedient to make these conjectures clear, may I revert to an historical philosophy? Ideas, says Descartes in effect, in so far as they are modes of thought (of think*ing*) all proceed from me in the same manner. On the other hand, the term may signify essences, natures, possessing their several intrinsic characters. Now I assuredly do not wish to impose upon John Dewey a Cartesian interpretation. Is it possible, however, that a faintly similar distinction could be used, without distortion of John Dewey's analysis of inquiry, to indicate the possibility of construing the terms in more than one way? In the inquiry process there are operations which involve the apprehension of an idea or possible in its intrinsic constitution and thereby introduce certain characters into the process, with the consequence that an anticipatory symbol-operation or symbol-operations mark a stage of the process. However, according to the conjecture now being pursued, ideas or possibles can be regarded objectively, as it were, as essences (to use an old-fashioned term) or natures for which symbols, such as "circle," "ellipse," stand. Ideas or possibles are then that which is discoursed about when discourse takes the form of being free from the necessity of existential reference while providing the possibility of indefinitely extensive existential reference. Symbols, whatever their existential materiality, are symbols because they stand for ideas. The inquiry process may be adequately analyzed as if there were no more to be said concerning ideas or possibles than is said in terms of the operational analysis of the inquiry process, and for the purpose of that analysis nothing more *need* be said. It would be complementary to that analysis, not substitutional for it, were anything more to be said.

· In terms of this conjecture, it seems to me, the occasion for metaphysical interest leading to possible complementation of the analysis would be the real or seeming independence of the possible, of that which is represented by the symbol. In some curious fashion, the possible or essence seems to insist on the manifestation of its own nature. (In view of my incompetence with respect to logic and mathematics, dear Mr. Dewey, I really should not venture into these deep waters!) It appears to exercise dominion over the processes of inquiry—at least to the ignorant this seems to be a formidable characteristic of what mathematics talks about: The observational data seem to exert pressure upon the astronomer. Nothing can be done about them—they must be accepted as they are at a given stage of the inquiry process. His construction of possibilities, of anticipatory interpretations, must conform to them. Of course, more or revised observational data may alter their demands, but their brute factuality demands conformity. But, on the other hand, nothing can be done about the possibles. If the circle be envisaged in the idea-symbol-operation, then the circle, as it were, asserts its sovereign dominion. The data may or may not accord with the nature of the circle, but the circle, the essence, is inflexible in its demands. If the ellipse, then the ellipse. This (real or apparent) dominion awakens, and rightly, it seems to me, metaphysical curiosity. Whether speculation would lead to the necessity for an ontological ground for the possibles, and what form an ontological doctrine would take, I prudently decline to consider. I am content to say that, so far as I can see, the conjecture indicates what might awaken metaphysical speculation. In some such manner a metaphysics, complementary to John Dewey's analysis of inquiry, might arise, and, it may well be, leave that analysis of the living process unaffected.

I have suggested, however, that the sympathetic student might think of still another possibility. It is that John Dewey's analysis does not only permit supplementation by some doctrine giving some form of ontological status to the possibles, but really needs a metaphysical doctrine for its further support. (I am entering even deeper and stormier waters!) Of the import of this conjecture and of its clarificatory value I am quite uncertain. It appears to collide with John Dewey's position. Perhaps the collision is not as calamitous as it might seem. It may mean only this, that for a complete and rounded *system*, for thorough satisfaction of theoretical systematic philosophic and speculative interest, a metaphysical doctrine reckoning with the objectivity of the essences would be necessary. On the other hand, the conjecture might mean that the operational theory needs metaphysical support, that it needs to be sustained on one side, that it lacks full convincingness without the buttressing of some type of ontological grounding of the possibles. Suppose the sympathetic student were venturesomely to entertain this conjecture, even were he to anticipate the discovery that John Dewey's doctrine requires no buttressing, with what could he begin? What points would he adduce? What in the operational theory suggests that metaphysical speculation might add to its stature? What would the metaphysician argue for? What needs further recognition in order that John Dewey's *Logic* may be wholly convincing?

Prudence would suggest that I now close this letter. My pursuit of the conjecture can produce no definitive results. Its pursuit, however, may lead me to a better understanding of the profound significance of John Dewey's doctrine. Accordingly, I venture to say that again the seeming independence of the possible, what I have called its exercise of dominion, comes to mind. I suspect that it is this feature—real or apparent—that has led to doctrines concerning an ontological ground. It is assumed, for purposes of discussion, that some inquiry processes happen as if they were governed, were given determinate character, by the nature of the possible as such. The idea-operation is in some aspect what it is in virtue of the nature of the essence, whatever the mystery that may reside here. But there is no idea without a symbol. For the purposes of our conjectural pursuit, let us take this to mean, or also to mean, that there is no idea-operation without a symbol, that an idea-operation and a symbol-operation are one and the same operatively, in their anticipatory function. Now the symbol too has a fixity, a fixity of meaning. The symbol in its materiality is conventional. But

> the meaning which a conventional symbol has is not itself
> conventional. For the meaning is established by agreements

of different persons in existential activities having reference
to existential consequences. . . . But, *in so far* as it [i.e., "the
particular existential sound or mark"] is a medium of communication, its meaning is common, because it is constituted
by existential conditions. (P. 47 [53].) Any word or phrase
has the meaning which it has only as a member of a constellation of related meanings. Words as representatives are
part of an inclusive code. The code may be public or private.
A public code is illustrated in any language that is current in
a given cultural group. (P. 49 [55].)

Let me assume now for exploratory purposes the following: (1)
The possible as such, of seemingly independent nature, however
metaphysical reflection may interpret this. To avoid terminological confusion, it may be called an idea or essence. What is intended may be indicated by saying it is the kind of entity that the
geometer talks about when one asks him what is the nature,
what the properties, or intrinsic characters, of the triangle or
circle. (2) Possibilities, anticipatory in function: these may be in
part constituted in virtue of the fact that some possible and its
properties—an essence—has been noted. Thus the possibility is
entertained that planetary orbits have an elliptical nature. (3)
Symbol-operations: perhaps these could be called idea-usings,
idea-operations, activities involving the operational influence of
ideas; but as there are no ideas without symbols, ambiguity (on
my part) may be avoided by using only the expression, symbol-
operations. (4) Symbols, whose meanings are not conventional
and are established as stated. The fixity of the symbol is the fixity
of its meaning. Presumably it is carried over into the symbol-
operation. In terms of the present conjectural standpoint, the
student's curiosity is aroused concerning the establishment of
the symbol's meaning in relation to the (seeming) objectivity of
the idea or essence. The meaning is established by agreements in
existential activities—that is to say, in activities—having reference to existential consequences. The establishment, one surmises, determines *that* the symbol shall mean, that it shall be a
symbol, and also *what* it shall mean. Is it valid to distinguish
at this point the idea or essence from the symbol or symbol-
meaning, in order to ask: is the symbol-meaning, so established,
the essence, the idea, the possible? does the establishment of the

symbol-meaning, so to speak, create the idea? Is it the idea in the only sense in which this term and its synonyms should be used? Alternatively, could it be said that *what* the symbol shall mean depends upon noting the idea or essence in its seemingly independent being? Crudely expressed—does the meaning established for t-r-i-a-n-g-l-e depend upon the nature of the triangle, where what is intended by "nature" is suggested when it is said that it is of the nature of the triangle that the sum of its interior angles equals 180°? Is there in the living process of symbol-meaning establishment a discovery of the nature of the triangle? or is the nature of the triangle, so to speak, invented in process of inventing the symbol and the establishment of what it shall mean? Is it invented in the sense repudiated by Descartes when he declares that he has not invented the determinate form, nature, or essence, "triangle"? Such a symbol has meaning only in a constellation of meanings. Does the social investiture of the material with symbol-function occur, so to speak, in view of the recognition, of some activity of apprehension, of a constellation of ideas (essences), so that the constellation of symbol-meanings accords with the former?

I am not sure, dear Mr. Dewey, of the import of these questions with respect to John Dewey's analysis of the inquiry process. This is all the more true because I am neither a mathematician nor a logician. I can imagine, however, that a competent person could say: the operational account of mathematical discourse, of its nature and conditions as discourse, is definitive; it, however, is not defective, but deficient in that it does not sufficiently reckon with what mathematical discourse is *about*, with the "objects" of such discourse. Such an one might conclude that a metaphysical foundation for the operational view is needed. A somewhat different line of speculation might be pursued. Without symbols, no ideas. But let us understand this to mean: without symbols and their fixities, there are no operations of such a nature as common sense would describe as having an idea; and this means that, without a symbol, an idea, essence, or possible can not be worked upon or with, can not be taken advantage of, can not contribute to the determination of a possibility or anticipatory interpretation. When an operation is instituted and its specific character determined by means of a symbol whose representative function is due to social investiture, the operation must proceed in harmony with the symbolic fixities. This is what occurs in the process of inquiry and nothing more is required in order to make the process of inquiry in so far intelligible. Inquiry-processes, however, go on in a far wider context of changes. If metaphysics should interest itself in the conditions of all these changes, inquiry-processes are especially notable. John Dewey has told us what these processes are. That such processes do go on it is a task of metaphysical reflection to make intelligible. It must consider at least the possibility that a distinction between the idea, essence, the possible as such, and the symbol with its social investiture of representational function can be entertained. The distinction may be unnecessary for the analysis of what does go on in the living process of inquiry. Functionally, so to speak, the possible is replaced by the symbol of the possible, or, more accurately, by an operation governed by the fixity of the symbol. Thus inquiry goes on as if the control of the operation were immediately vested in the symbol itself, and is indeed functionally so vested. Whatever may be involved from a metaphysical standpoint in these remarkable life-processes, the making and using of symbols does go on. Hence operations with symbols go on as if the symbol, however instituted in its representative function, were the source of its seeming authority. Only an operational theory can possibly account for what does go on in the existential process of inquiry, whatever grounds for the operational process itself need be assigned in order to make intelligible how such very remarkable living processes of actualization of potentialities can occur.

I must bring these conjectures, not to a conclusion, but to an end. I am inclined to agree, dear Mr. Dewey, that John Dewey's analysis of inquiry does not disprove the possibility of a metaphysics seeking for an ontological ground of the possibles. It may well be unnecessary for logical theory. Perhaps his doctrine permits complementation in such a manner or perhaps it requires it. I remain in a state of uncertainty. However, I feel that I can in some measure comprehend how a thinker, deeply convinced by John Dewey's analysis of inquiry, may nevertheless feel that it at once needs inclosure within a body of metaphysical speculation and also indicates directions in which such speculation should go.

I send this to you with misgivings, for I may have distorted

John Dewey's doctrines and manifested my unworthiness as John Dewey's pupil. I hope that you are now enjoying the sunshine of Florida. And I also hope that this letter concerning John Dewey's Doctrine of the Possibles may have the good fortune of giving you some amusement during an idle hour. On your journey northward in April, will you kindly pause for a day with me? Then Socrates and the slave-boy may verify, ten thousand times over, and without benefit of science, our exciting anticipation that from daffodil bulbs will come daffodil blossoms.

With abiding gratitude and affection, believe me,

Faithfully yours,

ALBERT G. A. BALZ

Appendix 2
An Aid to Puzzled Critics[1]
By Arthur F. Bentley

Church and Smullyan undertake their reports[2] from a specialized point of view: namely, that logic and psychology offer radically different inquiries into radically different subjectmatters. They treat this point of view as if it were commonly known and everywhere accepted, but nevertheless as a fact which Dewey and Bentley overlook (Smullyan), or as one which by its very neglect permits these writers to regard themselves as investigating logic though actually working in different territory (Church). They thus allege a manifest deficiency in the constructions they review. Church's attitude is that "these papers take us outside the field of pure logic and into those of biology and sociology." Smullyan holds that there is "no evidence . . . that Dewey and Bentley have a clearer conception of the distinction between logic and the behavioral theory of inquiry than" has a certain psychologist he names, to whose work, he fancies, the writers give their "manifest approval"; and he adds that "it is only by confusing the two subjectmatters that they could have been led to affirm that 'modern logic' is undependable without a developed theory of behavior." Under this approach both reviews seem to us to

1. The following is a communication prepared in 1948, revised in 1949, given approval by Dewey in April, 1949, and sent to the editor of the *Journal of Symbolic Logic* in September, 1949. It was originally intended to be offered for publication as a reply to criticisms by Church and Smullyan. We held it out, however, until shortly before the *Knowing and the Known* (Boston, 1949) book appeared, and then sent the communication to the editor as a memorandum, not for publication, but for the information of any reviewer of that book. The *Journal* did not put it to use in that way.
2. Alonzo Church, review of four papers by John Dewey and Arthur F. Bentley, the *Journal of Symbolic Logic*, Vol. X (1945), pp. 132–33. Arthur Francis Smullyan, review of a paper, "'Definition,'" by John Dewey and Arthur F. Bentley, *ibid.*, Vol. XII (1947), p. 99.

[First published as chapter 17 in Bentley's *Inquiry into Inquiries: Essays in Social Theory*, ed. Sidney Ratner (Boston: Beacon Press, 1954), pp. 320–24.]

make defective reports upon the positions we occupy. In addition, neither review so much as mentions any of the half-dozen leading characteristics of our construction. We recognize fully that reports on scattered papers cannot be as accurate as those on organized books, and it is not at all by way of complaint, but rather as precaution for the future, that we desire to reply. We shall not take space to develop, nor to discuss in any way, the merits of the main issues; nor shall we take space to examine specific charges of error against us, since debatable postulatory oppositions are involved in nearly all such cases. We aim to limit ourselves to the correction of statements about our position which seem to us to be misapprehensions.

There can be no possible objection—rather only strong endorsement—when Church and Smullyan employ the postulatory positions they occupy as the basis for their criticisms. For them, however, to treat the failure of other men to employ these positions as evidence that those other men have overlooked them, or are perhaps unaware of them altogether, is something different. Before all of us alike is the distinction between logic and psychology. We regard this distinction as primarily academic, or perhaps even in a more special sense as pedagogical. Church and Smullyan put a much higher valuation on it than this, however, when they take it to represent a basic differentiation of fact. As pedagogical it has been thoroughly well known both to Dewey and to Bentley since their college days. As a positive presentation of fact it has long since been opened up to persistent inquiry. Dewey's first publication in book form on this subject was forty-five years ago (1903) [*Studies in Logical Theory*], and this was followed by his treatises of 1916 and 1938 [*Essays in Experimental Logic* and *Logic: The Theory of Inquiry*]. Bentley has approached the subject in books from the linguistic side in 1932 and 1935 [*Linguistic Analysis of Mathematics* and *Behavior, Knowledge, Fact*], and in sundry papers since then. If psychology is taken as inquiry into the psychological facts of human living, then beyond it one still finds human living involved when one turns to logic taken as dealing with logical facts. No matter how "pure" one makes his logic, it is still by and of men on earth; or, if it is not, then its isolation therefrom should be explicitly set down and described, and not merely taken for granted as adequate basis for construction at one time and for criticism at another. On our side, for us to assert such a common behavioral setting for both logic and psychology is not to attempt to absorb one into the other any more than it is to fail to notice the academic distinction involved. Instead—and this is a quite different matter—it is to endeavor to bring together into observation and inquiry much that today commonly enters as severed, and to seek to develop in human union certain phases of the system of human living in which both occur. It is just this that the recent joint studies of Dewey and Bentley have undertaken: to carry forward further research into the logical and the psychological as alike human. In it they no more seek to reduce logic to psychology than they seek to reduce psychology to logic. They face the split as they find it, in its various aspects. On the one side is logic, employing basically a terminology of a traditionally psychological character which involves or implies a "division" of men's "faculties" in a form which psychologists have today almost wholly abandoned; and demanding rigid fixations both of the elements out of which to build, and of the operations to be used in building. On the other side is psychology, which has lost its old confidence in the terms which it still uses as basic for its more comprehensive dealings with the main phases of the environed living of organisms: terms such as stimulus, action, reaction, and response. Here lies a region in which research is much needed, one that has no more bias on the psychological side than on the logical, one with no bent whatever for the reduction of the latter into the former. In such a situation an allegation of deficient acquaintances fails to do justice to the facts. Such an allegation, indeed, comes much as if one should object to biophysical research on the ground that the would-be biophysicist is ignoring the distinction between living and non-living matter, and should know better.

Closely akin to the above failure to give adequate statement is another comment in the Church review. This is to the effect that if one seeks firm names (such a search being the specified primary objective of the papers under review) then "the objective of exactness . . . ultimately requires that firm names be embedded in a firm language," while any language, to be firm, must rest upon "explicit listing of the primitive words or symbols, and explicit statement of the formation rules and rules of inference." This comment does not at all meet the distinction presented in our work. In one of the earlier of the papers under review, we forecast the position further developed later on: namely, that accuracy and exactness should be theoretically differentiated on the basis of a differentiation of name from symbol. We used "firm" with respect to naming in the sense of accuracy of naming. The "primitive" in the reviewer's sense lies in our region of exactness. We accept his "primitive," not as a hoped-for absolute control over naming, but as one of the verbal instruments for the technical formulation of a special theory of exactness. For our reviewer to say that firm naming cannot be achieved without initial foundation in "primitives" is adequate expression of his own position. For him to use this statement, however, as a criticism of our work is for him to leave our work itself wholly out of the situation. Here is no question of right or wrong between two procedures, but a preliminary question of correctness or incorrectness in setting down what one of the procedures is. The development of the use of primitives as the initial step in the fixation of namings is one program (theirs). The differentiation of symbols from names in such a way that a full symbolic system can be applied to a naming system to guide and aid it under a wide presentation of both symbols and namings as the activity of human beings is a contrasted program (namely, ours).

A further comparable misapprehension in the first review is assuredly its inference from a condensed phrasing in an early paper, taken apart from further development, that our position (or perhaps more narrowly directed, Bentley's position) "seems to be intended as a verdict against the step of abstraction . . . in pure semantics . . . hence presumably likewise against that involved in treating pure geometry in abstraction. . . ." Abstracting, however, is a process which we regard as characteristic in one way or another of all behavior, and not merely of the logical, so that its rejection thumbs down by what the reviewer calls a "bare dictum" would seem inconceivable to us as an attitude or expression of our own. We trust the constructive element may, in further readings, be found in recent work. It certainly is present in Dewey's treatment of proposition as proposal, and in his discussions of generals and abstracts of various kinds in his *Logic: The Theory of Inquiry*.

The second of the two reviews, except for the point mentioned in the opening paragraph above, seems to have nothing to do with any phase of our work, and certainly little or nothing to do with the subjectmatter of the paper on "definition." We dropped the word "definition" provisionally in our own work with regret, but it was not the word "definition," as Smullyan writes, but instead "the jumble of references" attached to the word in present logics, which we believed, and said, could not be brought into order without "a fair construction of human behavior across the field." This reviewer's attention is almost wholly given to the psychologist he mentions, intead of to us, and while we did, indeed, offer a citation from the psychologist with "manifest approval," we did it, not for his theoretical construction, of which little has yet been published or become known to us, but for his lively attention to facts as compared with some other workers, and for a certain remark he made from the psychological point of view, which we were pleased to find closely paralleling a remark of Ernest Nagel's from the logical point of view. Our position on the relation of logic and psychology would seem to us to be unmistakably set down in such passages as that at the end of a paper on "'Definition'" which Smullyan reviews, in footnote No. 13 of a paper on "Logicians' Underlying Postulations" in *Philosophy of Science,* 1946, and in repeated comments on the applications of the words "behavior" and "nature" throughout all the series of papers.

We appreciate the close analysis and counter-criticism given by Church to some of our criticisms of the often incoherent use of terminology in many current logical discussions. We expect to find faults in our own examination comparable to those in the texts we examined, and we believe also that somewhat comparable faults can be pointed out in Church's further treatment. We are not interested in particular defects, but in the status of our common linguistic background which permits so many confusions in the procedures of keen workers in the field. Better knowledge in this respect should, we feel, greatly benefit us all.

Appendix 3
How, What, and *What For* in Social Inquiry
Edited by Joseph Ratner

Ratner's cover note: This article was left unfinished in content and form; the import of the argument for "social inquiry," for example, is barely indicated.

The basic postulation in the following discussion is that the heart and life blood of *intelligent* behavior consists of continued and deliberate attention to the relation of things which are viewed and treated as means to those which are viewed and treated as consequences, the connection between them being thoroughly reciprocal. Consequences have to be determined on the ground of what is selected and handled as means in exactly the same sense in which the converse holds. This demands constant attention if activities are to be intelligently conducted; otherwise behavior is either routine or spasmodic.

The word "postulation" is used instead of "postulate" in order to emphasize that postulation is itself a case of behavioral activity and hence is an integral component of the entire behavioral process; "postulate" is often, perhaps usually, employed in another sense, namely, that of a principle laid down in advance and consequently one exercising some authoritative control over the behavior that ensues.

I do not argue the case here because this entire article is an exposition of the position just set forth. But it is fitting to point out that the distinction just made is of basic, not merely casual import. For what is at stake is nothing less than the status and function of behavior; whether it is basic and hence controlling and authoritative within the whole scope of intelligent activities

[From unpublished 1964 typescript in the John Dewey Papers, Box 59, folder 12, Special Collections, Morris Library, Southern Illinois University at Carbondale, 12 pp. For Dewey's article, see this volume, pp. 333–40.]

(the only kind which are specifically human) or whether the category of behavior is superficial and negligible, the properties that render activities intelligent being derived from some source extraneous and superior to behavioral explanation—whether this superior source is called *soul, mind, subject, intellect,* or *brain,* makes little difference. It makes little difference because instead of taking *soul, mind,* etc., as names of properties that intrinsically belong to behavior, they are taken non-behaviorally.

The bearing of the position just stated is probably most immediate and direct in application to that centrally important way of intelligent behavior which is designated *knowing.* The outcome of knowing is institution of the subject matters that are said to be the knowns, be they of everyday "practical" behavior, or of that theoretical way of behavior termed "science."

Postponing for the present further consideration of the import of this position upon what is designated *knowns,* I continue with the bearing of my view upon the processes and operations constituting *knowing* when it is systematically inquired into as a mode of behavior. Probably the most obvious consequence is *negative:* there is no need whatever to resort either to ontological or epistemological terms, or that mixture of both which has flourished so abundantly in the post-medieval systems commonly called "modern" but which in fact are mainly antique, loaded as they are with Greek-medieval ideas of which *Being* as synonymous with the immutable or unchanging is uncritically taken as the all-determining authoritative "fact." In support of the statement just made I call attention to the place occupied and the office performed in "modern" philosophy (so-called) by matters designated by the names *subject, object, mind-world,* however mind be viewed, as sense, or as "rational" intellect *nous.*

In anticipation of later discussion, I note at this point that it was theoretically possible ("conceivable") at the outset of the modern era to view the *subject, object,* etc. as discriminated from and connected with one another on the basis of their functions respectively and reciprocally performed, the service rendered by each in the effective promotion of cognitive, intellectual behavior—that is, *knowing.* But what took place actually and historically is that the inherited bias in favor of the *immutable* transformed the distinction and the relation of the *subject* and *object, mind* and *world,* into opposite immutable ontological kinds. There are few systems and/or doctrines of the post-fifteenth century (no matter whether sensationalistically empirical or rationally noetic, whether idealistic, "spiritualistic" or "materialistic-mechanistic") that can be understood without steady attention to the fact that they are operating in terms of the mental and the material, the psychical and the physical, or more generally the inherently subjective and inherently objective, as two independently given immutable kinds of existence. The fact that as existences they were endowed with spatial-temporal qualities was of immense technical importance, when compared with the prior *supra*-temporal-spatial value accorded to "Being." However the technical advance was rendered negligible because of the ingrained habit of treating "knowing" as an action-reaction taking place between two independent and opposed kinds of entitative existences. Here again I call attention to the fatal heritage of Greek-medieval ontology which perverted a theory of knowing professing to be independently "epistemological," by introducing into every aspect and phase of the theory the ancient identification of true Being with the unchanging—the "essentially" and "by nature" immutable.

II

I come now to the specific subjects constituting the title of this article, the mode of treatment consisting, as already indicated, in regarding the *how*, the *what* (or subjectmatter), and the *why* or *what for* as interconnected transactional distinctions which are essential to understanding conduct of all intelligent behavior and especially the way of behaving that is knowing.

It is hardly necessary to engage in elaborate argument in behalf of the proposition that there is no intelligent human behavior which does not depend on *foresight of consequences* that are likely to ensue from the course of behavior entered upon. Without going into the matter in detail it is pertinent to refer here to a previous article of mine on "Common Sense and Science,"[1] in which the distinction between them, inclusively and exclusively,

1. "Common Sense and Science: Their Respective Frames of Reference," *Journal of Philosophy*, 8 Apr. 1948, XLV, 197–208 [see this volume, pp. 242–56].

is shown to be the *range of consequences* intentionally or de-signedly involved. A man crossing a street has to note, observe, heed what is going on with respect to the consequences of the *particular* act in which he is engaged. A system of red and green lights to direct the course of traffic *generally* is a technological device that could not exist without the extensive inquiry which constitutes the way or form of scientific knowing.

Anticipated, foreseen consequences constitute, or are, the *what* of that which is done, of the behavior enacted. Foresight of con-sequences (as the what of a given behavior) serviceably operates by directing deliberate search for the specific conditions which will produce the consequences that are foreseen. The compre-hensive, the inclusive, foresight that distinguishes the *scientific* way of knowing is the means for attaining consequences in the most economical and effectual way. Since the more generic the foresight the less likely is the kind of action which will be obstruc-tive and troublesome in forming and executing future plans, sci-entific knowing is better than common sense. Both satisfy, the one broadly, the other narrowly, the conditions to be met in such conduct as is intelligent, in contrast to merely routine behavior and/or behavior casually and hastily improvised.

The most general and important *theoretical* implication of what has just been said is that any doctrine which finds a sepa-ration or conflict within *intelligent* behavior between its *what* and its *how* distorts the basic facts. In knowing, foreseen con-sequences which form its *what* are an integral component of the *how*, that is, the procedure, or method, of knowing. If this were not the case, if foresight did not accomplish a distinctive use, service, office, function of this sort, there would be no differ-ence between foresight and the idle daydreaming in which con-sequences are anticipated on the ground of their immediate agreeableness. In intelligent activity separation of the *what* of the activity from its *how*, results inevitably in those absurdities which bear respectively the names of *ends-in-themselves* and *means-in-themselves*—a striking instance of giving way to the ever-present philosophical fallacy of reifying, hypostatizing that which in fact is functional. A volume could be written upon the harm that has resulted in moral-political theory by treating things, *res*, subjectmatters which function as means and consequences, as if they were such "by nature" or in their "essential" being; the inevitable outcome, logically, of setting up some things as ends-in-themselves and other things as inherently, necessarily, means-in-themselves.

As a specific example, look at the sharp division that is currently accepted as gospel truth between *moral* subjectmatters and *economic* subjectmatters. The separation is now so thoroughly established as to be regarded as virtually "self-evident." In consequence inquiry, knowing, in both cases is tied down in advance. It is *pre*-committed to reaching certain conclusions instead of conclusions which result from following freely the leads of inquiry. If certain matters are in and of themselves means and only means, and other things are of necessity, by nature or essence, ends and only ends, all that "inquiry" can be is a dialectical development of things and relations already asserted to be so fixedly given "by nature" or in essence as to be completely immune to significant investigation. They are in effect if not in name sacred, protected by a tabu that is not to be brought into question under any circumstances. At the very time when moral (i.e., the human) consequences of industrial and financial institutions are most in need of systematic critical scrutiny the latter are brought under the cover of being necessary because of the demands of nature and the former—the prevailing moral principles and standards which were relevant to situations radically different from ours—are given a thoroughly factitious, artificial authoritative prestige.

As previously emphasized, in Greek-medieval science, immutability being the inherent necessary property of any and all subjectmatters which are "scientific" was carried over and projected into the physical and the psychological objective-subjective domains of existence. The "revolution" actually effected in "modern" science consisted in the substitution of two immutables for the one ontological, rational, immutability of Greek-medieval science. In consequence, the significance of the scientific revolution for the theory of knowings-knowns is still the central issue in contemporary philosophical thought.

III

I now take up the *what for* or *why* in its connection with the means-consequence function. It is possible, though not of course certain, that the presence of "what" in any expression has a certain "what for" import not to be found in the expression "why." At all events, it is present in some expressions, and this fact may be used to suggest that what *for* in its reference and bearings is a refined amplification of the *what* as foreseen consequences and that the *what* is not consequential or of moment with respect to behavior unless it is a matter of affection, in the sense of care, concern, deliberate consideration of the "why," the purpose.

Determination of *why* is required to complete apprehension of the *function* served by the *what*. Like the *what*, the *why* is subject to reification; and all so-called "normative" theory is the result of treating the "what" or "why" as something absolute, or as "in itself," instead of in the use to which it is actually put. Whatever may be said about certain subjectmatters as subjects of mere description as over against those which are said to be normative, when one fastens attention upon *method* it is clear that accurate and comprehensive knowledge—that kind of knowledge termed "scientific"—has coincided with elimination of concern with essences, inherent natures, and the substitution of deliberate respect for the body of spatial-temporal factualities that are involved. Until the "normative" subjects take to heart the lesson of the history of scientific inquiry, there is no hope of making any assured advance. It would be difficult to hit upon a fact for investigation that would prove more fertile or more rewarding for the theory of knowings-knowns than study of the role played in the history of astronomy, physics, physiology, geology, by fixed standards, principles, as determinative and hence as authoritative.

Every procedure resting upon fixed standards amounts to an automatic foreclosure of free and hence full inquiry and critical reflection. It is a mortgage against the future. There is no sense in examining, investigating, observing—perceptual or ideational—unless these activities result in *more* adequate grasp of the "why" or "what" of the *res*, the affair, the subjectmatter observed, examined, investigated, unless they result in *greater, keener* appreciation and foresight of the consequentiality of consequences. In fine, the "why" or "what for" functions in regard to intelligent behavior (including knowing) as a part of the "how" or procedural method that has proved to be effective because not subjected to pre-established, antecedent conditions regarded as "normative" and inherently regulative. That the principle of the autonomy of knowing as inquiry, investigation, examination, search (not just *re*-search) is the very life blood of all intellectual endeavor worthy of respect is demonstrable in terms both of history and theory.

So far nothing has been said which bears directly upon the phrase "In Social Inquiry" as that occurs in the caption of this article. Its relevance will appear when we recall that all physical science—before there occurred the revolution that is associated with Copernicus, Galileo and Newton, was taken to be the cosmological or "natural" branch of "ontological philosophy." The revolution by which "natural philosophy" passed into the sciences of astronomy, physics and later of physiology, took place when inquiry became concerned with *how* (namely the spatial-temporal order of events), instead of with *what* (formal cause and essence) and with *what for* (final cause and teleology). There is no reason to suppose the course and destination of inquiry in human or "social" subjects (including those traditionally called "moral") must be any different.

The transition and transformation did not occur at once. In the Newtonian system, space and time were still taken as entities on their own account and were separate from one another, and also from what was supposed to take place within their fixed framework—that is, they were not seen nor treated as the *how* of nature, but as its essential *what*. The doctrine of Relativity completes the tale. Space and time are names for orders of events which moreover are integrally connected with each other. *How* things go on at least as far as scientific inquiry is concerned has won the victory over *what* and *what for,* and has broken down the status of space and time as entities fixed in themselves and having independence of whatever is taken to occur within their confining boundaries. The supposed scientific basis for separating space and time as major "*whats*" from minor "whats" which take place within them is abolished once and for all. But the full significance of Relativity Theory for scientific inquiry will be achieved only when inquiry into social *whats* and *what fors* is systematically viewed and treated as an included subordinate factor in determining *how* the subjectmatter proceeds. For thereby scientific status is attained, the spatial-temporal order specifically involved constituting the resolution of a given problematic indeterminate situation.

In philosophy, hypostatization of functional relations "rules the roost." Philosophers have clung the more tightly to what is alleged to be "in and by" its own nature or essence, identifying the total *raison d'être* of philosophy with unique concern with what is such and such absolutely, and not such and such because of its mere, inferior, connection with things of "merely" spatial and temporal being. Nothing can be of greater import in this connection than the fact that the natural sciences—astronomy, physics, chemistry, biology, etc.—all began their careers with this assumption of the absolute necessity of treating their subjectmatters as thus and so by essential nature; and they have all advanced in scientific knowings-knowns in the exact measure in which this assumption was negated and inquiry into the connections of events as spatial-temporal affairs was substituted therefor. Unfortunately the actual result of this historical development in the natural sciences has not been to lead to the adoption of the same method of inquiry in the human-moral subjectmatters; rather has it led to the intensification of the alleged dualism between the "normative" and the "descriptive" and the resolute, systematic identification of the human-moral studies with what may be termed "normative itself" and "normative in authority" because based upon alleged inherent fixities and absolutes.

JOHN DEWEY

HONOLULU, HAWAII 1951

Appendix 4
Experience and Existence in Dewey's Naturalistic Metaphysics
By Sholom J. Kahn

I

Students of Dewey's works, especially of the classic statement of his metaphysical position in *Experience and Nature,* are
familiar with his definition of experience as "the interaction of
an organism with its environment." In a sense, all of Dewey's
philosophic enterprise, with its persistent attacks upon "dualism,
discontinuity, and passivity,"[1] has consisted of a varied application of this definition. It is a master-conception whose uses are
almost infinite; however, it involves an initial difficulty which
this discussion will attempt to formulate.

For Dewey, of course, experience occurs within the framework
of "nature," which is a realm of "existence" composed of "events"
("Every existence is an event."[2]), but the universe he pictures
is one in which "experience" bulks large: the most distinctive
feature of his writings lies in its acute analysis of the modes of
interaction in experience. By Dewey's own familiar statement,
however, "metaphysics is cognizance of the generic traits of *existence.*"[3] Thus, the distinctively metaphysical problem persists:
What is the relationship between experience and existence in
Dewey's naturalistic universe? Is his analysis of experience an
adequate summary of the "traits of existence"?

In attempting to clarify this question, it will be helpful to begin
with a consideration of George Santayana's oft-quoted criticism
of Dewey's metaphysics (in a review of *Experience and Nature*)

1. Morton G. White, *The Origin of Dewey's Instrumentalism* (Columbia,
1943), p. 32.
2. *Experience and Nature* (Open Court, 1926), p. 71 [*Later Works* 1:63].
3. *Ibid.,* p. 51 [*Later Works* 1:50], italics ours.

[First published in *Philosophy and Phenomenological Research* 9 (December
1948): 316–21. For Dewey's reply, see this volume, pp. 383–89.]

to the effect that he dwells only on "immediate experience" and thus makes experience all "foreground."[4] Robert D. Mack has done a useful job of analyzing this issue, pointing out chiefly the extent to which Dewey's reference to experience is part of his application of the denotative method used in the sciences. Dr. Mack distinguishes three points in the process of inquiry or discovery at which "immediate experience" enters: (1) the problematic situation *out of which* knowledge arises; (2) the materials *appealed to* for the analysis and testing of hypotheses; and (3) the new or fresh consummatory experience *to which* knowledge leads.[5]

Dewey, in his own reply to Santayana's charge that (because of Dewey's emphasis on the "foreground") his naturalism is "half-hearted," replied with a counter-charge that Santayana's naturalism is "broken-backed," because it presupposes a "break between nature and man." Without denying the importance of the foreground, Dewey stressed that "it is the foreground *of* nature," thus at once denying any possibility of solipsism and re-emphasizing the importance for his philosophy of the concept of continuity.[6] Dewey's philosophy is remarkable above all for its recognition that a full conception of experience must include an analysis of all its elements in their complexities: the biological matrix of the organism; the social matrix of other organisms and the environing world of nature; and the immediate foreground of consciousness, which provides us with the data for knowledge both of ourselves and of the world. To accuse Dewey of any such "reductionist" position as that "nothing but the immediate is real" is to display a perverse sort of blindness, indeed, and to indulge in what Dewey has rightly condemned as mere "dialectical manipulation of the idea of 'immediacy.'"[7]

However, there was another sort of criticism included in Santayana's essay which may perhaps contain a fuller element of truth. He wrote: "Naturalism could not be more romantic: na-

4. "Dewey's Naturalistic Metaphysics," *Journal of Philosophy,* Vol. XXII (1925), pp. 673–688 [*Later Works* 3:367–84].
5. *The Appeal to Immediate Experience* (King's Crown Press, 1945), especially pp. 60–67.
6. "'Half-Hearted Naturalism,'" *Journal of Philosophy,* Vol. XXIV (1927), pp. 57–64 [*Later Works* 3:73–81].
7. *The Philosophy of John Dewey,* Paul A. Schilpp, ed. (Northwestern University, 1939), p. 555 [*Later Works* 14:40].

ture here is not a world but a story."[8] If Dewey does not reduce all experience to immediacy and foreground, is it not true that he *does* tend to reduce all existence to experience, thereby failing to provide us with a completely adequate picture of existence? If this were true, Dewey would simply be committing the romantic fallacy ("the exaggeration of the ego," as in Fichte's philosophy) in a twentieth-century idiom. A strong historical argument for this criticism could be made by tracing Dewey's considerable indebtedness to the romantic tradition in philosophy, esthetics, and social and educational theory.

II

This problem, of the relation between the realms of experience and existence, might conceivably be solved in three different ways:

1) Experience and existence might be treated as identical.

2) They might be treated as two distinct realms, with separate types of descriptions, though one would include the other, as in classic philosophy.

3) They might be treated as somehow related, describable in the same terms, with one including the other, perhaps as the potential includes the actual.

The first two of these possibilities can, I think, be eliminated immediately: Dewey is neither a Berkeleian idealist, nor is he unaware of the Kantian critical tradition. We may, therefore, safely go on to consider the third possibility and the issue which it presents. In a sense, Dewey often seems to avoid (not to evade) this issue; in *Experience and Nature,* for example, he insisted that he was using experience as "method, not distinctive subject-matter."[9] On the whole, he seems unalterably opposed to any type of separate realm which may be pictured as standing beyond or behind experience in such a way as to determine it completely. Thus, in a recent article, written in collaboration with Arthur F. Bentley, we find:

8. "Dewey's Naturalistic Metaphysics," *op. cit.,* p. 680 [*Later Works* 3:375].
9. *Op. cit.,* p. 10 [*Later Works* 1:371], and Chapter I generally.

We tolerate no "entities" or "realities" of any kind, intruding as if from behind or beyond the knowing-known events, with power to interfere, whether to distort or to correct. . . . To sum up: Since we are concerned with what is inquired into and is in process of knowing as cosmic event, we have no interest in any form of hypostatized underpinning. Any statement that is or can be made about a knower, self, mind, or subject—or about a known thing, an object, or a cosmos—must, so far as we are concerned, be made on the basis, and in terms, of aspects of events which inquiry, as itself a cosmic event, finds taking place.[10]

Nevertheless, the fact remains (and Dewey sometimes seems to recognize it) that some such relation as we have pictured is necessary to complete a naturalistic metaphysics. The expansion of our realm of experience would not be possible without a larger realm of events *into which* it could expand. The two "realms" need not differ in any essential, since they are both composed of events ("inert" matter, too, translated into the energy components of its atoms, is made up of events). Is not the "sum total of events" a concept necessary for a naturalistic metaphysics and one which Dewey might very well accept? Totality must surely be one of the "generic traits" of "existence."

What exactly is the relationship of existence to experience in this picture? Without pretending to exhaust the subject here, we may perhaps list a few of the alternatives which suggest themselves. Existence can be treated as a very-well-established hypothesis concerning "the unknown" which makes the search for further knowledge and experience seem reasonable and motivated. It can be seen as a kind of ideal limit towards which experience is striving, somewhat as in Peirce's familiar definition of truth as "that concordance of an abstract statement with the ideal limit toward which endless investigation would tend to bring scientific belief." It can be seen as a realm of possibility which experience makes actual for us: all the events of existence would thus constitute a huge (perhaps infinite) universe waiting to be discovered thru experience.

10. "Transactions as Known and Named," *Journal of Philosophy,* Vol. XLIII (1946), pp. 534–535 [this volume, pp. 111–12].

III

Whether considered as hypothesis, ideal limit, potentiality, or in any other way, the concept of existence (or its equivalent) must surely be included in any metaphysics, naturalistic or otherwise. In his most recent extended work, *Logic: The Theory of Inquiry*,[11] Dewey touches on this issue in the context of an operational logic, but, from the viewpoint of metaphysics at least, the result remains curiously ambiguous.

Especially in the last part of his book ("The Logic of Scientific Method"), Dewey is very emphatic on the point that his logic does not involve any necessary ontological reference. Thus, with reference to the subject-matter of science, he says:

> Existential interactions must have *potentialities* such that they are capable of formulation in terms of motions defined by application of the conceptions, M, T and L.[12]

Admitting the *descriptive* value of "the classic formulation in terms of qualitative changes," he insists that

> Constructive development of science has taken place through treating the material of the perceived world . . . in terms of properties that are logical, rather than directly ontological.[13]

Similarly, he argues for a non-ontological view of causation.[14]

In his discussion of mathematics, when Dewey treats "The Category of Possibility," he develops it in strictly operational terms and argues against any "Realm of Possibility" (capital letters in the middle of a sentence would in themselves spell condemnation to anyone familiar with Dewey's style!) conceived as having an ontological status. Using the illustration of a map and surveying, he develops the point of view that:

> The reference of mathematical subject-matter that is given at any time is not ontological to a Realm of Possibilities, but to further operations of transformation.[15]

11. Henry Holt & Co., 1938. Since the writing of this article, a further volume on logic, by John Dewey and Arthur F. Bentley, *Knowings and Knowns,* has been announced by the Beacon Press.
12. *Ibid.,* p. 482 [*Later Works* 12:476].
13. *Ibid.*
14. *Ibid.,* Chapter XXII, *passim,* and "Conclusion."
15. *Ibid.,* p. 402 [*Later Works* 12:399].

The conclusion of that same section, however, leaves the question of a "Realm of Possibility" open for metaphysics:

> While it is not claimed that this operational-functional interpretation of isomorphic patterns of relationships *disproves* the interpretation of mathematics that refers it to an ontological ground, it is claimed that it renders that interpretation unnecessary for *logical* theory, leaving it in the position of any metaphysical theory that must be argued for or against on *metaphysical* grounds.[16]

Does not this open the way for a possible split in Dewey's thought between logic and metaphysics?

Elsewhere in the *Logic*, Dewey makes occasional use of the categories of potentiality and actuality (usually translated into operational terms). He uses the familiar example of food as "edible" in his discussion of form and matter.[17] In his "General Theory of Propositions," he introduces the section on "Existential Propositions" with the following remarks:

> The subject-matter or content of the first main division of propositions consists of observed data or facts. They are termed *material* means. As such they are potentialities which, in interaction with other existential conditions produce, under the influence of an experimental operation, the ordered set of conditions which constitute a resolved situation. *Objective interaction* is the overt means by which the actualized situation is brought into existence. What was potential at a given time may be actualized at some later time *by sheer change of circumstantial conditions,* without intervention of any operation which has logical or intellectual intent as, when water freezes because of a specified change in temperature.[18]

Does not this admit a "realm of possibility" independent of experience?

The closest Dewey comes in the *Logic* to an answer to the metaphysical question is in the chapters on "The Existential Matrix of

---

16. *Ibid.,* p. 404 [*Later Works* 12:401].
17. *Ibid.,* pp. 388–389 [*Later Works* 12:386].
18. *Ibid.,* p. 288 [*Later Works* 12:288]. Last two italics ours.

Inquiry" (Chapters II and III). There we find such statements as the following:

> There are things in the world that are indifferent to the life-activities of an organism. But they are not parts of *its* environment, save potentially.[19]

> There is, of course, a natural world that exists independently of the organism, but this world is *environment* only as it enters directly, and indirectly into life-functions.[20]

Statements like these admit that "existence exists" (a tautology, of course, but one that sometimes seems necessary!), but do not tell us much about its "generic traits" or the precise nature of its relations to experience. And they seem to contradict statements like the one previously quoted to the effect that "we have no interest in any form of hypostatized underpinning."[21]

To conclude: the questions we should like to ask Dewey might be summarized as follows: (1) Does his metaphysics include any existence *beyond* experience? (2) If it does, as some of the passages cited above indicate, what are its "generic traits"? (If existence is merely "potential" experience, what precisely is the *status* of the potential?) From a pragmatic viewpoint, of course, such questions might possibly be dismissed as unanswerable—or *relatively* unimportant. In any case, Professor Dewey would certainly oblige many of his grateful students if he were to attempt a further clarification of this major metaphysical problem.

19. *Ibid.*, p. 25 [*Later Works* 12:32].
20. *Ibid.*, p. 33 [*Later Works* 12:40].
21. See Note 10.

Appendix 5
A Comment on Croce's and Dewey's Aesthetics
By Patrick Romanell

The *Journal of Aesthetics*[1] recently featured a brief but very stimulating discussion on aesthetic theory between two of the most distinguished philosophers of today, Benedetto Croce of Italy and our own John Dewey. Commenting upon the former's criticisms of his position, Dewey asserts that he finds no "common ground" at all between both parties. He then proceeds to state why there is none. The reason given for the absence of common ground is that his critic's avowed attempt "to establish the place of art in the system of mind" and his own proposal to understand the place of art in the life of man are at odds in purpose. Consequently, Croce fits art into "a preconceived system of philosophy," the "idealistic" one in this case, but Dewey analyzes it "in its own language."

Granting that Dewey is perfectly justified in his claim that no common ground exists between Croce and himself as far as their *aim* in theorizing about art is concerned, nevertheless both thinkers agree on at least one crucial point. No matter to what extent they differ with respect to the specific nature of aesthetic experience, they share the basal assumption that the proper *subject-matter* of a philosophy of art is "aesthetic experience" itself. The fact that Croce believes in the "cognitive character" of such experience and Dewey does not, makes no difference to the general point at issue. For their difference in the *species* of the subject-matter of aesthetics does not imply their difference in its *genus*.

Moreover, strange as it may sound to both parties and to others, Croce and Dewey not only hold in common the above as-

1. Vol. VI, No. 3, March 1948, pp. 203–209 [*Later Works* 15:97–100, 438–44].

[First published in *Journal of Aesthetics and Art Criticism* 8 (December 1949): 125–28. For Dewey's reply, see this volume, pp. 395–98.]

sumption as to what the field of aesthetics comprises, but they suffer together from a common confusion because they share at the same time another conception of aesthetic subject-matter without being aware of the fact that the two assumptions are incompatible in character. This second conception appears in Dewey's reply to Croce as "the aesthetic phase of life-experience." The latter, being a neo-Hegelian rather than a neo-naturalist, is fond of calling it "the artistic moment of the spirit" in his *Estetica*.

Although Dewey's two phrases "aesthetic experience" and "the aesthetic phase of life-experience" may sound on first hearing as if they denote the same subject-matter, they really mean different things on closer examination. The development of each of these *whats* of aesthetics would eventuate in two opposite philosophies of experience. The first leads to a *pluralistic* conception of experience, where "aesthetic experience" is viewed as a special kind marked off from other kinds with which it is loosely connected. In contrast, the second phrase leads to a *monistic* view of experience, in which the aesthetic is one of its aspects interacting with the rest. On the first hypothesis, the aesthetic is *in* experience; on the second, it is a phase *of* experience. The difference is, respectively, one between a substantival and an adjectival analysis of art. In a substantival analysis the distinctions made are, to use geometrical terms, "perpendicular." For example, art is cut off from science and thus the two of them are conceived as separate kinds of things. On the other hand, in an adjectival analysis distinctions are "transversal," by which we mean, correspondingly, that the aesthetic and the scientific cut across each other and thus are mutually complementary. In short, distinctions in the substantival sense refer to different *things in experience*, but distinctions from the adjectival point of view refer to different *qualities of experience*.

Since I have already reported elsewhere[2] the fact that the late Giovanni Gentile, to my mind the most thoroughgoing Hegelian in the history of philosophy, showed successfully how Croce's "logic of distincts" is incompatible with his "idealistic" aesthetics, I need not on this occasion go into that side of the polemic. I should like, however, to submit the argument that Dewey's un-

2. P. Romanell, *The Philosophy of Giovanni Gentile*, Vanni, New York, 1938; *Croce Versus Gentile*, Vanni, New York, 1946.

resolved mixture of his two implicit, if not completely explicit, definitions of aesthetic subject-matter, (1) aesthetic experience (2) aesthetic phase of experience, is inconsistent with the fundamental direction of what he himself called with approval "empirical pragmatic aesthetics."[3]

I shall try to prove my point by means of an apparent detour. Ironically enough, the germ of my proof is to be found in another of Dewey's works, A Common Faith,[4] published in the same year (1934) as his Art as Experience.[5] The first chapter of the former volume skilfully develops the "difference between religion, a religion, and the religious" for the express purpose of denying the existence of "religious experience" as "a separate kind of thing" which is "marked off from experience as aesthetic, scientific, moral, political." It should be noted in passing that the implication here is that, while there is no such thing as religious experience, there definitely exists a kind of experience which is itself aesthetic, etc. At any rate, he defends "the religious" as a "quality of experience" which may "belong to all these experiences" and thus proposes an adjectival analysis of the field under consideration in order to dispose of religion "in the substantive sense." So much so that he insists with impeccable logic that there is a "gulf" between those who make "something specific" out of "religious experience" and his own position which develops another conception of the nature of "the religious phase of experience." Note the adjectival method of approach to religion embodied in the last quoted phrase from his pen, "the religious phase of experience," as over against the alternative way of approaching the subject-matter of religious philosophy in terms of "religious experience." To sum up, his philosophy of religion in A Common Faith is beautifully clear and consistent (whether it is adequate or true is another question of course), because he sticks to his adjectival analysis of the field he is theorizing about and does not shift to the other type of analysis. There Dewey is a functionalist throughout and thus is faithful to his empirical method of philosophizing in general.

Having completed our short detour, it is pertinent at this junc-

3. *The Philosophy of John Dewey*, ed. P. A. Schilpp, Northwestern University, Evanston, 1939, p. 554 [*Later Works* 14:38].
4. Yale University Press, New Haven, 1934. Ch. I especially [*Later Works* 9].
5. Minton, Balch, New York, 1934. Ch. I especially [*Later Works* 10].

ture to wonder why Dewey does not stick to his guns in his philosophy of the aesthetic. Is it because he believes that "aesthetic
experience" is a fact but "religious experience" is not? Surely he
can't believe *that* as a good empiricist! For, given his pragmatic
"postulate" of knowledge, from which he admits *Art as Experience* is treated, what is sauce for the goose of philosophy of religion is sauce for the gander of philosophy of art. If there is no
such thing as "religious experience," then by the same logic there
is no such thing as "aesthetic experience." Or putting it in positive terms, if a sound theory of religion is only possible on the
condition that its subject-matter be conceived adjectivally, that
is, as "the religious phase of experience," then by the same token
an adequate theory of art should be restricted to "the aesthetic
phase of life-experience." In brief, as goes the "religious quality"
of experience, so should go its "aesthetic quality." A thoroughgoing adjectival analysis, like the Petrine God, who is "no respecter of persons," is no respecter of phases.

Had Dewey stuck to his functional logic, he would have begun
his *Art as Experience* with the same avenue of approach as is carried through his book on religion, *A Common Faith*. Just as the
first chapter of the latter is actually "Religion versus the Religious," so the first chapter of the former could and should have
been called "Art versus the Artistic." He would have then developed the difference between art, *an* art, and the artistic in correspondence with his "difference between religion, *a* religion, and
the religious." The distinction between the noun "art" and the
adjective "artistic" would have led him to the same type of analysis, namely, the adjectival one, as his distinction between "religion" and "the religious." My point, however, is *not* that he does
not analyze art *as the artistic*, but rather that unfortunately he
combines this adjectival way of interpreting the aesthetic subjectmatter with the substantival analysis of art *as aesthetic experience*. The very title of his *Art as Experience* carries the ambiguity in approach to which I am referring, notwithstanding that
the author himself claims to be following only one "mode of
approach."

I take it that the peculiar task of an "empirical pragmatic aesthetics" is to do justice to those insights which remove the chasm
between art and experience, a chasm inherent in "the compart-
mental conception of fine art," which erroneously and snob-

bishly sets it upon "a far-off pedestal." Everybody knows that Dewey is a great reformer by nature and nurture. Personally, I do not doubt the far-reaching significance, both theoretical and practical, of his emancipation proclamation announced in *Art as Experience*. If, however, such a social message is to be made intelligible by aesthetic philosophy, then the author must defend clearly and distinctly an adjectival analysis of art *alone,* because the substantival way of analyzing art as "aesthetic experience" leads inevitably to the misconception of art as a "separate realm," a consequence contrary to the chief moral of his book. For, since *the how* and *the what* of any analysis go together, the idea of a "separate realm" follows logically from a substantival method of approach. Now, despite the fact that Dewey rightly "protests against the museum conception of art" and even makes reference to "the fallacy from which that conception springs," his dual position, however, on the nature of the subject-matter of the aesthetic field commits the same fallacy in its more sophisticated form of "aesthetic experience," which, notwithstanding its alleged "continuity" with "ordinary experience," turns out to be perforce a specifiable entity denoting a distinct kind of thing that can exist all by itself. Even a cursory comparison of Dewey's philosophy of art with his philosophy of religion would immediately reveal that he is more anti-church than he is anti-museum, all of which, to be sure, is psychologically and socially intelligible but not logically so.

To bring my comment on Dewey's aesthetics to a close, an "empirical pragmatic aesthetics" cannot logically become what it claims to be unless it gets rid of the inconsistency between its polar opposites: the idea of art as a special *type* of experience and the idea of art as a special *phase* of it. Either view perhaps can be developed coherently but not both together. It is precisely the eclectic attempt at fusion of the two that spells utter confusion.

Notes

The following notes, keyed to the page and line number of the present edition, explain references to matters not found in standard sources. In quotations from Dewey's letters, clearly mechanical typewriting errors ("chpater," for example) have been silently corrected.

21n.2   Bühler] See chap. 21, "Die Undverbindungen," in Karl Bühler's *Sprachtheorie* (Jena: G. Fischer, 1934).

51n.14–16   James's . . . eighteen-eighties] For James's essays, see "On Some Hegelisms," *Mind* 7 (April 1882): 186–208; "On Some Omissions of Introspective Psychology," ibid. 9 (January 1884): 1–26; "What is an Emotion?" ibid. 9 (April 1884): 188–205; and "On the Function of Cognition," ibid. 10 (January 1885): 27–44.

99.15   *Matter and Motion* . . . lucidity] On 22 January 1946 Dewey wrote to Bentley, "Years ago I had a copy of Maxwell's little book—I think when I was at Ann Arbor; I remember thinking it was the only thing on physical science principles I could understand" (Bentley Collection). While reading proof for *Knowing and the Known,* Dewey wrote to Bentley, "By all means insert passage quoted from Clerk-Maxwell—As to place whether galley 16 or 32 I leave it all to you" (13 April 1948, Arthur F. Bentley Collection, Manuscripts Department, Lilly Library, Indiana University, Bloomington). For the passage, see this volume, extract at 278.8–13.

122n.2–10   Compare J. R. Firth . . . thoughts."] In his 31 August 1945 letter to Bentley (Bentley Collection), Dewey enclosed two pages of quotations from Firth's *The Tongues of Men,* including those that appear in this passage.

130n.1–3   "The Aim . . . written,] Dewey called Bentley's attention to Kantor's newly published article (4 April 1946, Bentley

Collection). Although too late to incorporate a discussion of it in their *Journal of Philosophy* article, Bentley added this footnote reference.

151.28–29   *Solvitur ambulando*] The question is resolved by action.

173.10–11   Nagel, . . . Sciences,"] On 15 November 1945, Dewey informed Bentley: "I have just read Nagel's article in the last Jn. It has so many good things in it that I wish he would get firm hold [on] the framework in which they belong. His special field of knowledge could be dam useful if he would venture into their setting. I keep having the feeling that there ought to be some way of approach that would lead him to observe where he belongs. . . . When you get time read Nagel's piece as sympathetically as possible with a view to telling what he needs to get the pattern" (Bentley Collection).

185n.1–4   In his . . . p. 830.] Dewey supplied this quotation. On 9 October 1945 Dewey wrote to Bentley, "Russell has just published a book on the History of Philosophy. The last chapter is on Philosophy of Logical Analysis—I havent looked at any other chs. I wanted to see if there was anything that would throw light on your statement of R's postulations." Dewey then quoted from Russell: "From Frege's work it followed that arith and pure math generally is nothing but a prolongation of deductive logic p 830" (Bentley Collection). Bentley replied, "I am putting a footnote at bottom of page 1-A of the mss as follows, which I would be very glad if you would verify precisely, as I will get no opportunity to see the book" (n.d., Bentley Collection). Dewey added commas after "arithmetic" and "generally" and marked Bentley's retyped quotation "OK."

187n.1   Otto Neurath] On 30 July 1945 Dewey suggested to Bentley for this footnote: "I think a brief listing of the points where Neurath has broken with the remark that as yet they have not been developed in system (or something of that sort) would be a good idea" (Bentley Collection).

239n.6–7   Dewey's comment . . . interpreter.] See Dewey to Bentley, 14 July 1944, Bentley Collection.

241.8   an associate] Ruth Herschberger.

276.7   One reviewer] See C. West Churchman and T. A. Cowan, "A Discussion of Dewey and Bentley's 'Postulations,'" *Journal of Philosophy* 43 (11 April 1946): 217–19.

281.3–8   "As . . . perfunctory."] The quotation is from "Beliefs and Existences." This essay was originally published as "Beliefs and Realities," *Philosophical Review* 15 (March 1906): 113–29, from Dewey's 28 December 1905 presidential address to the American Philosophical Association, Cambridge, Mass. Dewey revised it for inclusion in his 1910 collection, *The Influence of Darwin on Philosophy and Other Essays in Contemporary Thought* (New York: Henry Holt and Co., 1910), pp. 169–97. For the quotation, see p. 196 [*Middle Works* 3:99].

300.37–301.2   "Word . . . Thought."[5]] Although the triangular scheme is discussed on p. 11 of *The Meaning of Meaning*, this quotation does not appear in any edition of the book.

345.30   preliminary question raised by Dr. Lee] In *Value: A Co-operative Inquiry*, Harold N. Lee states, "Thus it is evident that I would answer my own question in the same way that Dewey answers it: no, there is no such thing as value that is not the value of some particular thing, event or situation" (p. 154).

351.18–28   It . . . value.] For Philip Blair Rice's objection to Dewey's "altogether gratuitous" interpretation of this passage, see Rice, "Science, Humanism, and the Good," *Value: A Co-operative Inquiry*, pp. 270n–71n.

357.26–28   Dr. Stevenson . . . knowledge"] Dewey quotes from Charles L. Stevenson's *Ethics and Language*, about which he wrote to Horace S. Fries, "In some respects it is better than most writing on ethical method—but its 'psychological' socalled—foundations are terrible" (18 September 1945, Horace S. Fries Papers, State Historical Society of Wisconsin, Madison).

369.1–2   Philosophy's . . . Crucial] *Commentary* appended the following note to Dewey's essay:

This month national homage is being paid to John Dewey on the occasion of his ninetieth birthday; and it is with a sense of

privilege that Commentary presents here the distinguished
philosopher's challenging vision of the role that philosophy—
the science of sciences—must play in the years ahead if it is
to fulfill its responsibilities to its high mission and to our
common human need. This essay embodies, in revised and
expanded form, the message sent by Professor Dewey to the
International Congress of Philosophy which met in Amsterdam in the summer of 1948 [see this volume, pp. 358–68].

374.9   the speaker,] For the address of Raymond B. Fosdick, president of the Rockefeller Foundation, at the dedication of the
Hale Telescope on 3 June 1948, see "Largest Telescope Dedicated to Man's Service at Palomar," *New York Times,* 4 June
1948, pp. 1, 15.

376.15   artisans] For Socrates on artisans, see Plato, *Apology*
22–23; *Theaetetus* 146–47.

390.1–2   Contribution . . . Intellectuals"] *Partisan Review* 17 (February 1950): 103–5, prefaced "Religion and the Intellectuals:
A Symposium" with an editorial statement beginning: "One
of the most significant tendencies of our time, especially in
this decade, has been the new turn toward religion among
intellectuals and the growing disfavor with which secular attitudes and perspectives are now regarded in not a few circles
that lay claim to the leadership of culture." The statement
suggested five "major aspects of this complex subject, with
the hope that the contributors will touch upon all or several
of these aspects by way of discursive comment": the causes of
the religious revival, the credibility of religion for intellectuals, religion's relationship to culture, religion's relationship
to literature, and the relationship of religious consciousness
to religious beliefs.

400.25   Human Rights;] This essay is published in the second
UNESCO inquiry. For the first UNESCO inquiry, see *Human Rights: Comments and Interpretations,* A Symposium
edited by UNESCO, with an introduction by Jacques Maritain (New York: Columbia University Press, 1949).

Note on "What Is It to Be a Linguistic Sign or Name?"

On 23 June 1945 Dewey sent an original, three-page type-script to Arthur F. Bentley "not for publication but as evidence of good faith" (letter and typescript in Bentley Collection, Manuscripts Department, Lilly Library, Indiana University, Bloomington). Bentley typed on p. 1: "Following is new start for Sign paper sent 5–25." Dewey's "paper sent 5–25"—"What Is It to Be a Linguistic Sign or Name?"—is published in this volume for the first time. Dewey's "new start" for this paper (with mechanical typewriting errors corrected) appears below:

Animal behavior in certain extremely familiar cases displays or exhibits transaction such that certain constituents in them *act, operate* or *work*,[1] as preparatory of transactions to take place later. Such familiar cases are the clucks of a mother hen to its young when food is seen or its warning cries and bustling behavior when an enemy is descried; such are the amatory prancings and struttings of cocks in presence of a female of their species.

1 It does not take elaborate analysis of such cases to observe that the behaviors in question are the earlier portions of a behavior-sequence enduring in time and of spatial spread wider in and extension in space. In ordinary language this fact is stated by calling the behaviors in question "preparatory" to behavior to follow, that which follows being their completion or fulfillment—provided once more the words preparatory, completion and fulfilment are taken in strictly matter of fact way, free from the influence of doctrinal interpretations;—that is, strictly as a statement of a space-time event.

---

1. Emphasis upon these verbal forms is intended only to indicate that such is the case as observable fact no matter how the fact is to be explained or described in detail or whether or not any reasonable explanation can be given at the present time. The statement if of a fact that is "brute," that is, prior to a fact and the datum for a reasoned account.

2   Nor does it require elaborate analysis to observe that the behaviors in question are strictly *transactional*. That is to say, while they have been set forth in the previous paragraph from the standpoint of a mother-bird and a male, there is taken for granted as active participants or partners the presence of the young and of a female; so that the statement could just as properly be made through mention of the latter with the place of the other partner taken for granted—and hence not explicitly stated.

The illustrative material just mentioned is taken from the behavior of animals fairly well "up" in the physiological scale. But these particular cases were selected simply in the interest of obviousness for illustrative purposes. Behavior of the amoeba is equally illustrative if once the point is grasped—Describe.

II

If we formulate what happens in the above cases as typical of any physiological subjectmatter, we reach the conclusion that in such behavior as transactional what takes place can be described only if and when a *sign* or *representational* aspect is taken into the account:—in that certain conditions which are directly and "sensibly" there can be correctly described only as concerned with or taking account of conditions as yet future in time and distant in space—where "distant" stands for all events which are not those of direct contact. The warning and calling behavior of the mother hen extends directly across space in the direction of and to the place of the young; it also covers the changes in direction and place that will occur as there follow gatherings about food or being brooded. Temporally, the transactions extend and over future behaviors of eating, being protected or copulation—as the case may be. When we introduce an *observer* of the transaction (as we are bound to do when we describe, take account of, or "know"), we say and are bound to say that the earlier phase of the whole transaction is a sign or or is representative of the later phase. All physiological subjectmatter is such that no observation or account (description) is possible that fails to take emphatic notice of this fact and of what follows from it: Or stated in the terms of circularity previously stressed, physiological subjectmatter *as known* is known only in terms that acknowledge the sign—or representative—qualifications or properties.

(B   You wont like these last words and they can easily go out   But Oxford Dict; "To qualify—"to describe or designate in a particular way." Qualification: "that which fits for a certain office or function.")

What is said in no way involves a statement that nothing of the sort described as sign-behavior is found in physical subject-matter. That is a matter of the result of specific factual inquiries. What is emphatically involved is that the subjectmatter of behavioral inquiry, even of the simplest sort, (such as that of the amoeba) is such that inquiry—or knowing—procedures and techniques must never lose sight of their signatory or representative phase.

III

Now signs as signals (something about stimulus & response?) Then Signs as Designatory, Specification.

Textual Apparatus

Index

Textual Notes

The following notes, keyed to the page and line number of the present edition, discuss problematical readings adopted in the critical text.

61.20–21 *Knowing . . . together.*] This sentence, revised from the *Journal of Philosophy* (JP), appeared in roman type on *Knowing and the Known* (KK) galley 20. Dewey underscored it and wrote in the margin, "I would even suggest italicizing this sentence to arrest attention"; Arthur F. Bentley then wrote "italic" in the margin ("Galleys carrying Dewey revisions," envelope 67, KK files, Bentley Collection, Manuscripts Department, Lilly Library, Indiana University, Bloomington). The italicization, not made for KK, has been made in the present edition as a Works emendation.

79.17 cannot] Dewey instructed Lucille M. Myers, Beacon Press, that "cannot" should be "uniformly one word" (4 September [1948], Beacon Press Papers, Boston, Mass.). All instances of "can not" in KK, therefore, have been regularized in this edition.

152.13; 153.2 subjectmatter] Dewey had written as early as 19 March 1942 to Bentley, "I had noticed . . . a rather marked tendency on my own part to use the word 'subjectmatter'" (Bentley Collection). While reading proof for KK, Dewey wrote to Myers about the word, which had been housestyled in JP articles as "subject-matter": "I prefer 'subjectmatter' without hyphen" (4 September [1948], Beacon Press Papers). On 2 October he wrote again to Myers, "My personal preference is for subjectmatter—one word no hyphen" (ibid.). In accordance with Dewey's clear preference, unless used in quoted material, the hyphenated form has been emended to "subjectmatter" in this volume.

155.32–33   Moreover, what is striking here] In JP and on KK galley
50 this sentence began "What is striking here, moreover,"; on
the galley Dewey circled "moreover" and indicated a transposition, adding "tr" in the margin. Bentley then marked the
sentence to begin "Moreover, what is striking here" ("Galleys carrying Dewey revisions," envelope 67, KK files, Bentley
Collection). The transposition, not made for KK, has been
made for the present edition as a Works emendation.

183.1, 12, n.1, n.3   him.[51] . . . 52. We] The JP article had 51 footnotes, the last at 183.12. While reading KK galleys, Dewey
wrote to Bentley, "I added in footnotes a reference to my
Logic pp 125–7 where I discuss *demonstration as* pointing"
(11 November 1948, Bentley Collection). Dewey's superscript
"52" was inserted at 183.1, and footnote 52 text added *following* footnote 51 text. The necessary corrections have been
made in this edition: superscript numbers in the text at 183.1
and 183.12 have been transposed, and footnotes 51 and 52
have been transposed.

244.29   as well as a field of application.] JP read at this point "and of
a field of significant application." To Bentley's query Dewey
replied: "My phrasing is awkward. I would suggest as a possibility either a comma or dropping the 'and' and inserting
'as well as a field of application.' . . . (I doubt if the word
'significant' is particularly 'significant' here. Cut it out)"
(Bentley to Dewey, 12 May 1948; Dewey to Bentley, 14 May
1948, Bentley Collection). No change was made for KK; for
this edition, however, the copy-text has been emended as
Dewey intended.

252.21–22   concern or care . . . with respect to] Dewey wrote to
Bentley about revising this passage from JP for KK: "The
sense will be clearer if the words 'Concern or care' are
changed to the plural and 'that is' to 'that are,' and below put
in the word 'respectively' after 'scientific concern' making a
verbal change in the phrase 'with respect to,' to avoid repitition" (14 May 1948, Bentley Collection). No changes were
made for KK.

252.39   from; and is *of* in the sense] JP read at this point "from and
is *of.*" Dewey wrote to Bentley about an omission: "It looks
as if at the end of that line the clause after 'is *of*' 'in the sense

in which *of* is *off* has dropped out" (14 May 1948, Bentley Collection). The omitted words—"in the sense"—were supplied in KK, but "and" at 252.39 was changed to "which" The "and" has been restored for this edition.

256n.2   1705–1774] These are Abraham Tucker's birth and death dates. The *Oxford English Dictionary,* from which Dewey quotes, gives the dates "1768–74," the publication dates of the multi-volume *The Light of Nature Pursued,* the source of Tucker's quotation s.v. "organism." No emendation has been made in this instance.
    This footnote was a last-minute addition to KK. Dewey wrote to Bentley enthusiastically on 9 November 1948 about discovering the Tucker quotation in the *Oxford:* "If I had found it in time, I'd been in favor of quoting it in a footnote" (Bentley Collection). Two days later, Dewey informed Bentley that he had, indeed, added the material as a footnote to his chapter (11 November 1948, Bentley Collection).

280.12; 284.9; 287.20–21; 288.10–11   cannot] See textual note for 79.17.

287.13   dear A——,] All references to "Albert Balz" or "Mr. Balz" in Dewey's letter in JP were changed for KK. This one, however, incorrectly changed from "Mr. Balz" to "Mr. A——," has been emended to "dear A——." See similar change from "dear Mr. Balz" to "dear A——" at 291.35.

320.1   intended] Dewey had originally typed "while it is intended" and then x'd-out "it." On the assumption that he also meant to x-out "is", both words have been deleted.

320.6   which while] Dewey had originally typed "which which while". In correcting his error, he inadvertently x'd-out "while" instead of "which".

325.25   are such as to provide] In two variant carbon copies (DTS and BTS), Dewey's typist, Alma Fogarty, left space after "as to" for a five-letter word she could not decipher. Dewey later revised original pages matching DTS and BTS. This emendation has been adopted from Dewey's revision of this passage on the original page matching BTS (variant carbon copies in John Dewey Papers, Box 58, folder 9, Special Collections,

Morris Library, Southern Illinois University at Carbondale, 23 pp., and in Bentley Collection, 23 pp.; extant original typescript pages, Dewey Papers, Box 58, folder 16, 31 pp.). For all revisions, see this volume, Dewey's Revisions in "Importance, Significance, and Meaning."

325.32–33   We . . . life behavior] On DTS and BTS Fogarty made a notation about a missing page in Dewey's manuscript that she was retyping. The page has never been located. Dewey later remedied this problem in two ways (see Dewey's Revisions in "Importance, Significance, and Meaning"). His revision on the original page matching DTS has been adopted as an emendation.

326.12–13   wholly . . . lodged in] In DTS and BTS Fogarty left space after "entity" for a nine-letter word she could not decipher. On DTS Dewey underlined "entity" and drew two vertical lines in the margin. He later revised the passage on the original page matching BTS; this revision has been adopted as an emendation.

329.16   by means of] The words "by means of" do not appear in DTS or BTS; Fogarty left thirteen spaces for undecipherable text. Either "through" or "by means of" could be inserted; "by means of" is preferable because it matches better the space Fogarty allowed and, more importantly, Dewey preferred it in a similar context during this period of time. See this volume, 289.38, where Dewey changed "through" in the JP article to "by means of" for the appendix of KK.

332.1   are [###] to] In DTS and BTS Fogarty allowed at this point almost an entire line for undecipherable text.

340.25   For. The victory will be] A discarded page was apparently inadvertently given to the typist, who incorporated the text in the typescript. The text has been deleted in this edition. For complete explanation, see Textual Commentary, pp. 540–42.

343.3–4, 5–6, 8; 344.5; 349.20–21; 356.27–28, 33, 36, n.4   subjectmatter(s)] For Dewey's spelling of the word during this period, see textual note for 152.13.

343n.1–2   1. Contained . . . inquiry.] Editor Ray Lepley informed Dewey that he was adding this footnote and making other revisions in printer's copy because of "the omission of material from the introduction" to the volume (Lepley to Symposium Colleague, 16 February 1948, Dewey Papers).

349.12　As . . . discussion] Lepley interlined the introductory phrase in printer's copy.

350.2　difference,] After Lepley deleted this comma in printer's copy, either he or Dewey restored it in proof.

350.10–11　utopian, sentimental,] To the typescript's "utopian or sentimental" Columbia University Press added a comma in printer's copy and queried "ok?" in the margin. In proof the phrase was further changed when either Dewey or Lepley deleted "or" and added another comma after "utopian".

350.20　matter] Columbia University Press's addition of "a" in printer's copy to Dewey's typical phrase "as matter of course" has been rejected as an editorial sophistication.

351.18–27　experiences . . . its distinctive kind] Lepley made several changes in printer's copy to correct Dewey's quotation from Philip Blair Rice.

354.23　sort of] In printer's copy Columbia University Press changed the typescript "or" in "sort or" to "of" and queried "OK?" in the margin.

355.3–5　as to provide . . . impossible.] In printer's copy Lepley made two changes in the typescript version of this sentence: "that they provide *the view [ab. del. 'those who hold'] that rational valuations are impossible whatever color of plausibility it [ab. del. 'their view'] possesses." Columbia University Press then further revised the sentence and transposed the clauses; since Dewey read proof and apparently approved, the Columbia University Press changes have been accepted as emendations.

356n.3　"Persuasion"] After Lepley changed the typescript "The office" to "The use" in printer's copy, either he or Dewey changed the two words to "'Persuasion'" in proof.

356.29　use or] In printer's copy Lepley changed the typescript "office of 'function'" to "use or 'function.'"

357.5–7 The . . . now] Lepley revised this sentence in printer's copy. In the Dewey Papers (Box 58, folder 6) are carbon copies of the last two pages, pp. 23 and 24, of the typescript for this essay. Dewey's ink alterations, all in the sentence at 357.5–9 ("The . . . it."), appear below within brackets:

> So far as concerns [*intrl. w. caret*] the function of persuasion [*bef. del. comma*] and of producing convictions which direct subsequent behavior, *instead of being [*intrl. w. caret*] peculiar to judgments conventionally recognized to be in the value-field, that work [*w. caret ab. del.* 'function'] is now best exemplified in "scientific" inquiry and the propositions resulting [*alt. fr.* 'result' *aft. del.* 'that'] from it.

> Because Dewey read proof, the published version has been accepted as his final intention.

358.7; 361.8; 365.23; 367.7   subjectmatter(s)] See textual note for 152.13.

361.25–26; 364.6   a philosophy] For Dewey's use of "a philosophy" elsewhere in this essay in discussing a specific philosophical system, see 364.4 and 367.16.

366.23   which material, moreover,] The misplacement of a comma is similar to that at 359.32 ("fact, however, implies"). In this case, to make sense contextually, the comma after "which" has been moved to follow "material" and a comma added after "moreover".

367.30   a share] For a similar construction, see the following essay at 380.20–21, where Dewey uses "have an active share in". The "a" omitted before "share" at 367.30 has been restored in this edition.

370.26; 371.34, 35; 379n.5; 381.19, 23   subjectmatter] See textual note for 152.13.

383.13   me] At 383.2 ("asking:"), the typescript reads "asking two questions of me. The first one reads:". In the process of revising, Dewey added "by them" after "me" at 383.13, apparently referring to Kahn's two questions. However, when Dewey deleted the typescript passage concerning the two questions, he neglected to delete the corresponding "by them", which has therefore been deleted for this edition.

384.1   on my view] *Philosophy and Phenomenological Research*'s
        change of Dewey's characteristic expression "on my view" to
        "in my view" has been judged an editorial refinement and
        therefore rejected for this edition.

387.18 view] Dewey apparently wrote both "Mr. Kahn transforms"
        at 387.17 and "gets transformed" after "view" at 387.18
        with the intention of deleting one phrase. Since neither phrase
        was deleted in the published version, however, "gets trans-
        formed" has been deleted here.

387.21 the view] There is a blank space at this point in the clean
        typescript, indicating that the typist probably could not de-
        cipher Dewey's writing or alteration.

391.26 has been] Dewey's only alteration in the clean, retyped copy-
        text document (Bentley Collection, 8 pp.) occurs at this
        point. Dewey deleted in ink the words "has been" and wrote
        above them the word "was." Dewey may have restored "has
        been" in proof, however, because elsewhere in this sym-
        posium contribution (393.34, 40; 394.1), he uses "has been"
        in identical contexts.

396.6   first and third chapters.] The first three chapters of *Art as
        Experience* are "The Live Creature," "The Live Creature and
        'Ethereal Things,'" and "Having an Experience."

396.34, 36; 397.7, 20, 35–36   subjectmatter(s)] See textual note for
        152.13.

408.13 shock to] The typescript reads at this point "shock given to".
        Dewey apparently deleted the word "given"; however, "to"
        was misprinted as "of".

411.2, 12, 31; 413.32; 415.21; 416.35, 39; 417.3, 7–8, 27;
        418.2   subjectmatter(s)] The typescript for this essay was
        not typed by Dewey. For Dewey's spelling of "subjectmatter"
        during this period, see textual note for 152.13.

413.13 divisions] Omission of the final "s" in "divisions" was
        probably a printer's error. The plural of the typescript has
        been restored here since it is unlikely Dewey would have
        made "divisions" singular without changing "isolations" as
        well ("isolations" is similarly used at 419.17).

419.13–14   systematic acceptance of the doctrine of its aloof-
ness] Dewey typed "acceptance of the doctrine of its" as an
interline on p. 21 of the typescript (TS²) and, apparently after
sending off the original to Horace S. Fries for publication,
inserted on the carbon copy a caret in ink after "systematic".
The ambiguous interlineation, misplaced before "systematic",
has been repositioned in this edition.

419.15   but] Dewey interlined "but" in ink with a caret on the carbon copy of TS² p. 21, apparently after sending off the original. The word did not appear in the published version.

Textual Commentary

Volume 16 of *The Later Works of John Dewey, 1925–1953*, spanning 1949 to 1952, contains all Dewey's writing published during those years except for miscellaneous pieces that will appear in *Later Works* 17. *Later Works* 16 includes eight essays and *Knowing and the Known*, Dewey's collaborative work with Arthur F. Bentley, published in 1949 and based on articles published between 1945 and 1949. *Later Works* 16 also includes four typescripts not published during Dewey's lifetime. These writings deal with philosophy in its technical aspects and in its relationship to the world, while political and social affairs appear as a secondary theme in those essays directed toward a wide audience. Several writings offer a choice of copy-text;[1] discussion will follow the order of the volume contents.

The typescripts included here are largely an outgrowth of Dewey's lengthy association with Bentley. "What Is It to Be a Linguistic Sign or Name?" and "Values, Valuations, and Social Facts," both written in 1945, appear here for the first time. "Importance, Significance, and Meaning" and "*How, What,* and *What For* in Social Inquiry" were written between 1949 and 1951; both have been published in a variant form.[2] Additional material for three of these typescripts is included in this volume: in the apparatus Dewey's further thoughts appear in a section entitled Note on "What Is It to Be a Linguistic Sign or Name?" and in a section entitled Dewey's Revisions in "Importance, Signifi-

1. Textual decisions for this volume are based on Fredson Bowers, "Textual Principles and Procedures," *The Later Works of John Dewey, 1925–1953,* ed. Jo Ann Boydston (Carbondale and Edwardsville: Southern Illinois University Press, 1984), 2:407–18.
2. See *John Dewey and Arthur F. Bentley: A Philosophical Correspondence, 1932–1951,* ed. Sidney Ratner and Jules Altman (New Brunswick, N.J.: Rutgers University Press, 1964), pp. 647–68.

cance, and Meaning"; "*How, What,* and *What For* in Social Inquiry" as edited by Joseph Ratner is included in the text as Appendix 3.

Three of the eight essays—"The Field of 'Value'" (a contribution to a symposium on value), "Religion and the Intellectuals"
(a contribution to a *Partisan Review* symposium), and "Experience and Existence: A Comment"—have underlying typescripts;
the first two essays mentioned were published more than once
in Dewey's lifetime. "Experience and Existence" is a reply to
Sholom J. Kahn, and "Aesthetic Experience as a Primary Phase
and as an Artistic Development" is a reply to Patrick Romanell.
Dewey surveys the social and political scene in "Modern Philosophy," a contribution to the Max C. Otto commemorative volume, *The Cleavage in Our Culture;* in "Religion and the Intellectuals"; and in his contribution to *Democracy in a World of
Tensions,* a symposium conducted and published by the United
Nations Educational, Scientific, and Cultural Organization. Effects of the Cold War are perceptible in "Has Philosophy a Future?" Dewey's address delivered by Sidney Hook to the Tenth
International Congress of Philosophy in Amsterdam in the summer of 1948, and in "Philosophy's Future in Our Scientific Age,"
published in *Commentary* and intended as a popular version of
Dewey's new introduction to *Reconstruction in Philosophy.*[3]

Tributes, activities, and interviews[4] commemorated Dewey's
ninetieth birthday, 20 October 1949. The *New York Times* reported that Dewey was "disturbed at all the 'fuss and bother'
being made about his birthday," which he had hoped to spend
quietly with his wife, Roberta, and his two adopted children,
John and Adrienne. "But that is not to be."[5] Among the ceremonies honoring Dewey was a three-day series of meetings in
New York City focusing on problems of democracy in education:

3. Boston: Beacon Press, 1948, pp. v–xli [*The Middle Works of John Dewey,
1899–1924,* ed. Jo Ann Boydston (Carbondale and Edwardsville: Southern
Illinois University Press, 1982), 12:256–77].
4. For interviews of Dewey, see, for example, "John Dewey, at 90, Finds Tension of World May Result in Good," *New York Herald Tribune,* 15 October 1949, p. 7 (Lester Grant); "John Dewey, at 90, Reiterates His Belief
that Good Schools Are Essential in a Democracy," *New York Times,* 16 October 1949, sec. 4, p. 9 (Benjamin Fine); and "America's Philosopher Attains an Alert 90," ibid., magazine sec., pp. 17, 74, 75 (Irwin Edman).
5. Ibid., 19 October 1949, p. 31.

a birthday dinner on 20 October at the Commodore Hotel followed by all-day sessions at the Society for Ethical Culture and Columbia Teachers College. Dewey spoke briefly at the dinner: "If we are ridden by fear we lose faith in our fellow beings, and that is the unforgivable sin. . . . If we lose faith in human beings and human nature our outlook is sad indeed." [6]

A few months before Dewey's death on 1 June 1952, Bentley described Dewey as having "kept at work, not merely with circular process, but with increments of advance much longer than most others of his age." [7] Dewey's correspondence during these last years attests to his remarkable mental and physical resilience. In one of his last letters to Bentley, Dewey wrote from Tucson, Arizona, where he was recovering from surgery: "If I ever get the needed strength I want to write on *knowing* as the way of *behaving* in which . . ." [8]

Knowing and the Known, with Arthur Fisher Bentley

Eleven years younger than Dewey, Bentley studied briefly in Germany and received his Ph.D. degree in economics from the Johns Hopkins University. In 1895–96, as lecturer in sociology at the University of Chicago, he attended Dewey's seminar on the theory of logic. Leaving academic life, he worked as a journalist in Chicago for several years, published *The Process of Government,* [9] and spent most of his life in Paoli, Indiana, where he operated an apple orchard and continued to publish books and articles on a broad range of topics. The Dewey-Bentley association

6. Ibid., 21 October 1949, pp. 1, 28. At ceremonies honoring Dewey at the New School for Social Research on 19 October, Alvin Johnson credited Dewey with helping "liberate man from fear" (ibid., p. 1).
7. Bentley to Joseph Ratner, 28 February 1952, Joseph Ratner/John Dewey Papers, Special Collections, Morris Library, Southern Illinois University at Carbondale. In quotations from all typed letters, clearly mechanical typewriting errors ("chpater," for example) have been silently corrected.
8. Dewey to Bentley, 9 April 1951, Arthur F. Bentley Collection, Manuscripts Department, Lilly Library, Indiana University, Bloomington.
9. (Chicago: University of Chicago Press, 1908); see pp. 254–57 on Dewey's "Interpretation of Savage Mind." After publication of this book, Bentley wrote later to Joseph Ratner, "there was a 'break-down'" (7 September 1948, Ratner/Dewey Papers).

began when Bentley sent Dewey a copy of *Linguistic Analysis of Mathematics* in November 1932 and Dewey acknowledged it in May 1935.[10] During that summer Dewey read proof for Bentley's *Behavior, Knowledge, Fact*. Bentley in the preface to that book expressed his obligation to Dewey, and Dewey reciprocated a few years later in his preface to *Logic*.[11]

Bentley later described their relationship to Joseph Ratner, who was collecting material for a Dewey biography: "I doubt if I ever spoke to Dewey in Chicago. . . . But when we finally got together it was apparent we had been developing collaterally—he in his form of expression, and I in mine."[12] Dewey's seminar "was a big one and I made no personal contact. I must have felt strong influence while writing Process Govt, for he was one of four assorted heroes to whom inscription was made on first draft (only to be dropped as too nutty-looking later on). . . . I sent him copy of Linguistic Analysis. He apparently barely glanced at it till [Ernest] Nagel called his attention to it. . . . He wrote me a note. We exchanged a few. He surprised me in Preface to Logic by mentioning me." "We understood each other—what each was after, that we could contribute something to each other."[13] "He kept me in balance and enabled me to try what otherwise I would not have tried."[14]

In 1945 Dewey also described their relationship: Bentley "never had academic recognition in spite of his books. . . . Sociology is his main concern; he got off into psychology and the theory of knowledge because of problems that met him in writings on so-

10. Bentley to Dewey, 15 November 1932; Dewey to Bentley, 22 May 1935, Bentley Collection. *Linguistic Analysis of Mathematics* (Bloomington, Ind.: Principia Press, 1932). Bentley wrote in this book about "the importance of Dewey's work in advancing our understanding" of "problems of logic and language" (p. 43).

11. "In view of the specific criticisms I have felt compelled to direct against John Dewey's characterization of psychology as science, it is proper for me here to give strong expression to my affiliation with him in broader issues of inquiry and method. My obligation to him is great and of long standing—far greater than I have anywhere in the text found opportunity to display" (*Behavior, Knowledge, Fact* [Bloomington, Ind.: Principia Press, 1935], p. ix). "Since it happens that there is no reference in the text to the writings of A. F. Bentley, I wish to record here how much I owe to them" (*Logic: The Theory of Inquiry* [New York: Henry Holt and Co., 1938], pp. iv–v; *Later Works* 12:5).

12. Bentley to Ratner, 4 June 1948, Ratner/Dewey Papers.

13. Bentley to Ratner, 3 August 1948, ibid.

14. Bentley to Ratner, 7 September 1948, ibid.

ciety. Before I met him I thought perhaps, from his style, that he might be soured by lack of academic recognition. Then when I did meet him I found him to be one of the most genial men Ive ever known. . . . While I had been moving steadily in the direction taken by Bentley I had some difficulty in grasping the force of his position when I first became acquainted with his writings." [15] "Largely due to him, Ive finally got the nerve inside of me to do what I should have done years ago." [16]

Dewey and Bentley began exchanging letters focusing increasingly on language. Many of their letters are in the John Dewey Papers, Special Collections, Morris Library, Southern Illinois University at Carbondale. Bentley, however, carefully preserved nearly all their voluminous correspondence, now housed in the Bentley Collection, Manuscripts Department, Lilly Library, Indiana University, Bloomington. A selected version is available in *John Dewey and Arthur F. Bentley: A Philosophical Correspondence, 1932–1951,* ed. Sidney Ratner and Jules Altman (New Brunswick, N.J.: Rutgers University Press, 1964). In addition to his discussion in the introduction to that work, Sidney Ratner emphasized in a letter the symbiotic partnership portrayed in the correspondence:

> The Dewey-Bentley correspondence shows that *K&K* is an *authentic joint* production—a demonstration of the importance of the actual intellectual *transactions* Dewey and Bentley participated in—each contributing ideas, criticizing and reformulating the other's position on different issues and arriving through a *reasoned consensus* on a final formulation that satisfied *both* authors. This is as much a Dewey book as the Dewey-Tufts *Ethics!* [17]

Dewey wrote to Bentley on 12 June 1942, "I dont know whether there is a difference between us, save that you are more scrupulous in use of words than I am—to my own loss." The next day he added, "Ive often thought that the fact that our backgrounds and our immediate problems were so unlike made your

---

15. Dewey to Edward Octavius Sisson, 9 August and 14 September 1945, copy, ibid.
16. Dewey to Grace A. De Laguna, 25 October 1945, copy, ibid.
17. Ratner to Harriet F. Simon, 17 May 1987, Center for Dewey Studies, Southern Illinois University at Carbondale.

work helpful to me in a way that agreement from one with the same general background and set of problems could not possibly effect."[18] Several months later, Dewey wrote:

> I realized in later years that in many places my terminology was still too much of the old type. . . . Ive been trying to write something fairly extensive to clear up some points and be sufficiently definite so that I wouldnt be badly misunderstood. Its been a hard job and Im not thru yet—I have had to keep starting over again. When I get it in better shape Ill inflict it on you. . . . Negatively, in avoiding the use of certain words, Ive made an improvement that should help keep "lice" off, but on the positive side there just dont seem to be the right words available.[19]

In June 1943, rereading Bentley's letter commenting that they needed the "beginnings of a firm terminology," Dewey wrote: "You never said a truer word than that I write atmospherically with absence of hard and fast words. . . . Perhaps the time has come to do something in trying to fix a set of leading words. I dont seem to be able to write continuously, but may be I could collaborate on words if you gave a start."[20] With this their project was launched. Dewey was eighty-three years old, Bentley seventy-two.

After book publication six and one-half years later, while assembling the accumulated drafts and correspondence, Bentley prepared a "Sketch of the Development of the Book Knowings and the Known" in which he explained: "The reason why pains is taken to store all this material away is that it can be much better regarded as a flowing together of streams of scientific and linguistic development than as the operations of some form of personality or mentality."[21] This document is referred to in the

18. Dewey to Bentley, 12 and 13 June 1942, Bentley Collection. In 1941–42, as visiting lecturer in Columbia's philosophy department, Bentley gave talks on a "Program of Research into Language" (Sidney Ratner, *Philosophical Correspondence*, p. 43).
19. Dewey to Bentley, 3 November 1942, Bentley Collection.
20. Bentley to Dewey, 2 April 1943; Dewey to Bentley, 25 June 1943, ibid.
21. Bentley, "Sketch of the Development of the Book Knowings and the Known," 5 December 1949, ibid., *Knowing and the Known* files (hereafter, KK), folder 84.

following discussion, which presents a cross-section of a complex process and outlines Dewey's role as contributor, editor, adviser, and consultant in drafting, writing, revising, publishing, and proofreading.

Some of the numerous drafts Bentley prepared (Bentley Collection) bear Dewey's hand; these are referred to in the following discussion. Of equal if not greater textual significance is the massive Dewey-Bentley correspondence, of which it is possible to cite only a sampling. Proceeding chronologically, the discussion treats the journal articles, the book publication, and then presents a textual analysis of *Knowing and the Known* with a detailed examination of Dewey's major contributions—the preface, chapter 10, and the appendix. A publication summary of *Knowing and the Known,* listing author(s) and underlying texts (journal articles and Dewey typescripts) for each chapter, follows.

JOURNAL ARTICLES

Bentley first prepared and sent to Dewey several general drafts; Dewey replied with comments and sketches of his own. Once the field of endeavor was delineated, discrete units emerged to be developed as articles. "Drafts I–X were made between July and October 1943. . . . Dewey was hospitalized in November of that year and Drafts XI–XV were in the nature of personal memoranda of my own to hold the position. Drafts XVI–XXVI began late in November and continued through December" ("Sketch of the Development"). While recovering from his operation for kidney stones, Dewey wrote revealingly about his attitude and the significance of their correspondence. Reassuring Bentley that "there is really no big question as to whether what you say . . . squares with my Logic or not," Dewey wrote:

> I want to say this as strong as I can make it. I am not stuck on anything in the Logic—certainly not on its vocabulary— My own development was slow & tentative. I can claim only that I never permitted pride in what I had written in the past to slow it up. In fact I rarely look at what Ive written in the past. When I do, its for some special reason & when I find

Publication Summary

John Dewey and Arthur F. Bentley, *Knowing and the Known* (Boston: Beacon Press, 20 September 1949)

Chapter	Author	Published Articles and Dewey Typescripts
Preface	JD/AFB	2 typescripts[a]
Introduction: A Search for Firm Names	JD/AFB	"A Search for Firm Names," *Journal of Philosophy* [JP] 42 (4 January 1945): 5–6
1. Vagueness in Logic	AFB	"On a Certain Vagueness in Logic," JP 42 (4 and 18 January 1945): 6–27, 39–51
2. The Terminological Problem	JD/AFB	"A Terminology for Knowings and Knowns," JP 42 (26 April 1945): 225–47
3. Postulations	JD/AFB	"Postulations," JP 42 (22 November 1945): 645–62
4. Interaction and Transaction	JD/AFB	"Interaction and Transaction," JP 43 (12 September 1946): 505–17
5. Transactions as Known and Named	JD/AFB	"Transactions as Known and Named," JP 43 (26 September 1946): 533–51, 560
6. Specification	JD/AFB	"Specification," JP 43 (21 November 1946): 645–63
7. The Case of Definition	JD/AFB	"Definition," JP 44 (22 May 1947): 281–306
8. Logic in an Age of Science	AFB	"Logicians' Underlying Postulations," *Philosophy of Science* 13 (January 1946): 3–19
9. A Confused "Semiotic"	AFB	"The New 'Semiotic,'" *Philosophy and Phenomenological Research* 8 (September 1947): 107–31
10. Common Sense and Science	JD	"Common Sense and Science: Their Respective Frames of Reference," JP 45 (8 April 1948): 197–208, and typescript[b]
11. A Trial Group of Names	JD/AFB	"Concerning a Vocabulary for Inquiry into Knowledge," JP 44 (31 July 1947): 421–34
12. Summary of Progress Made	JD/AFB	[no documents]
Appendix: Dewey's Reply to Albert G. A. Balz	JD	Reply to "A Letter to Mr. Dewey," JP 46 (26 May 1949): 329–42, and JP transcription of Dewey's letter[c]

a. Typescript typed by Dewey, enclosed in Dewey to Bentley, 3 September 1947, Bentley Collection, Manuscripts Department, Lilly Library, Indiana University, Bloomington, 2 pp.; typescript not typed by Dewey, dated 15 September 1947, Joseph Ratner/John Dewey Papers, Box 45, folder 9, Special Collections, Morris Library, Southern Illinois University at Carbondale, 3 pp.

b. Typescript not typed by Dewey, "Common Sense and Science: Their Respective Frames of Reference," Ratner/Dewey Papers, Box 44, folder 2, 22 pp.

c. Sent by Herbert W. Schneider to Balz, 4 May 1949, Balz Papers, Manuscripts Department, Alderman Library, University of Virginia, Charlottesville, 19 pp.

something that I still like & hold to, Im tickled stiff. . . . So this correspondence with you has been the first conscious serious effort I ever made to get a firm terminology. . . . I'll be glad to make a fresh start whenever it helps.[22]

Bentley's "Sketch of the Development" continues: "The drafts now began to sketch the entire field." Further drafts "ran from XXVII to XXXV from January to April 1944 and were followed by still more extensive work in XXXVI and XXXVII." Dewey's revisions of early material may be seen, for instance, in draft XXXII, entitled "Naturalistic Specifications for Knowings and Knowns."[23] In an exchange typical of their working method, Dewey sent Bentley a three-page sketch on terminology prefaced by the disclaimer "I have no confidence in my ability re terminology." Bentley replied that it would be "simpler and easier" if he first finished the draft he was working on "as clean as I can" and sent it to Dewey. He would then take Dewey's sketch "along the same lines," "work that out in detail" against his own, and "report on any variations."[24]

Frequently during their correspondence Dewey explained his motivation for writing. Commenting on Bentley's drafts, for example, Dewey wrote:

> What you write stimulates me to go over my previous position and try to bring it up nearer to date, so that much of what I write is more pertinent to revision of my own previous views than it is to the work in hand. I only hope some of it will be useful as background—but for heavens sake dont pay attention to it when it doesnt fit in fairly directly.[25] . . . As you doubtless understand I didnt write the stuff in these letters with a view to incorporation.[26]

Bentley used Dewey's material in various ways, incorporating some directly, using much in the course of further development.

22. Dewey to Bentley, 27 December 1943, Bentley Collection. Bentley had written to Dewey on 21 December 1943 about usage of the word "fact" (ibid.).
23. Dated 28 March 1944, ibid., KK, folder 6.
24. Dewey to Bentley, 29 December 1943, Bentley Collection; Bentley to Dewey, [ca. 5 January 1944], Dewey Papers.
25. Dewey to Bentley, 1 February 1944, Bentley Collection.
26. Dewey to Bentley, 21 July 1944, ibid.; transcription, Dewey Papers.

Dewey's contributions during this period include, for instance, a two-page sketch on the general nature of "our inquiry to attain knowledge of kn" "evoked" by Bentley's previous sketch; a three-page outline of the inquiry; and a six-page sketch on "usable specifications for knowings and known as aids to naturalistic knowledge about or of knowledge."[27]

Dewey and Bentley, "A Search for Firm Names," *Journal of Philosophy* 42 (4 January 1945): 5–6, and Bentley, "On a Certain Vagueness in Logic," ibid. 42 (4 and 18 January 1945): 6–27, 39–51

Bentley's "Sketch of the Development" calls attention to letters exchanged at the end of May 1944 "for development at critical points." Dewey's 26 May letter, engaging "in a general survey," broaches what is apparently a disagreement. "I am inclined to think that our purpose and position would be clearer if in this set of papers we confined ourselves to a positive statement," "cutting out practically *all* reference to the position of others."[28]

"The paper was now dividing into two sections, the title 'Fact, Event, Designation' appeared and attention began to be given to deficiencies in prevailing Logics. Further specialization in organization now showed itself. . . . LXX–LXXVII. These drafts worked up 'Vagueness in Logic'" ("Sketch of the Development"). Bentley sent drafts to Dewey for his reaction and comments; Dewey wrote apologetically in July, "Im sorry to be of so little use on the Logic paper"; "sorry not to have done more on the vagueness paper, but shall have to hold it a little longer."[29] Dewey made, however, many "suggestions of verbal changes."[30]

Dewey had earlier sent Bentley a sketch for an introductory paper; by late August Bentley sent a draft to Dewey, who, re-

27. Dewey to Bentley, 26 March [1944], 7 and 12 June 1944, Bentley Collection (transcription of 7 June 1944 letter, Dewey Papers).
28. Dewey to Bentley, 26 May 1944, Bentley Collection; transcription, Dewey Papers. See also Bentley's reply, 31 May 1944, Bentley Collection. Dewey pressed his point, writing to Bentley on 6 June 1944 that he favored "minimum use of special quotations from given writers—the latter change constantly and can be piled up almost indefinitely, and run the danger of getting the reader to thinking about *their* positions rather than about ours" (ibid.; transcription, Dewey Papers).
29. Dewey to Bentley, 12 and 31 July 1944, Bentley Collection.
30. See, for instance, Dewey to Bentley, 21 August 1944, ibid.

sponding with a few suggestions, wrote, "I like the idea of a preface to the whole series."[31] During September the paper evolved and Dewey wrote, "The idea of Program (or Plan) of Inquiry instead of prefatory note is all to the good."[32] What originally was incorporated as a "Prefatory Note" to "On a Certain Vagueness in Logic" became, with revisions, a separate introductory paper.[33]

They began to discuss the problem of signatures. Dewey was reluctant to sign the logic paper. Writing to persuade him, Bentley cited as arguments Dewey's contribution—greater than he realized—to the paper, the significance of Dewey's contribution to the project through letters and sketches, and, most important, the value of Dewey's name.[34] Dewey replied on 23 August that the reason for signing is "desire to be associated all the way thru; the reason for not signing is that it assumes work on my part I havent done." Dewey had no "unwillingness to sign" because of Bentley's "approach, either in substance or form."[35] After considering several ways to handle the problem, they agreed that both would sign the introductory paper, which would state "that the series as a whole is joint, while the responsibility in some is primarily that of one of us, that of the present paper" being Bentley's.[36]

When they had earlier discussed publication, Dewey wrote that he thought the *Journal of Philosophy* offered "the most promising outlet" but was not "set on it." "The fact it comes out fortnightly is an advantage other things equal."[37] In September both the introductory paper and Bentley's logic paper were ready. Dewey wrote to Bentley, "Any thing I find I can enter on the second carbon you are sending, and then the job can go to the Journal," adding a few days later that Bentley should send the material off "without waiting for or expecting any further

---

31. Dewey to Bentley, 23 August 1944, ibid. Dewey's 7 June 1944 sketch begins: "First Paper Introductory Statement of aim and desire; of standpoint; of connection of work with that of others; those included, those left out" (ibid.; transcription, Dewey Papers).
32. Dewey to Bentley, 20 September 1944, Bentley Collection.
33. See draft LXXVI, ibid., KK, folder 11.
34. Bentley to Dewey, 19 August 1944, Bentley Collection.
35. Dewey to Bentley, 23 August 1944, ibid.
36. Dewey to Bentley, 29 August 1944, ibid.
37. Dewey to Bentley, 10 March 1944, ibid.

comments from me on the carbon you send me. Then we can get at the next issue." [38]

Dewey and Bentley, "A Terminology for Knowings and Knowns," *Journal of Philosophy* 42 (26 April 1945): 225–47
"LX–LXIXB. Here a differentiation entered that became the Terminology paper" ("Sketch of the Development"). In mid-December 1944 Dewey sent Bentley a nine-page draft entitled "A Terminology for Knowings and Knowns" that became the basis for sections I and II of the article (this volume, pp. 47–56). Defining a crucial aspect of his contribution, his role as editor, Dewey wrote:

> The enclosed is something I did with your paper of 9/8/44—LXII. I did the job partly to get a feeling that I was earning my keep as partner. But more to see if I was getting things straight myself. If I am making headway in that direction there may be some advantage in my re-editing. Having had to work myself to get it, and yet being much nearer you at the start than the average reader, I may be able to judge where the sticking points in understanding are likely to be. On the whole I have tried only to expand what is in your paper. [39]

By late January 1945 Dewey thought the paper "ready for press." [40] He read proof and expressed misgivings about the name order. [41]

Dewey and Bentley, "Postulations," *Journal of Philosophy* 42 (22 November 1945): 645–62
"LXXX–LXXXIX. Under titles 'Knowings, Knowledge, and the Known,' and 'Naturalistic Postulation,' these became the paper on 'Postulation.' . . . Look up Dewey's sketch of June 12 [1944]" ("Sketch of the Development"). Bentley used Dewey's six-page sketch for his draft LXXXI, entitled "Knowing, Knowl-

---

38. Dewey to Bentley, 2 and 8 September 1944, ibid.
39. Dewey to Bentley, 15 December 1944, ibid.
40. Dewey to Bentley, 28 January 1945, ibid.
41. Dewey to Bentley, 19 and 20 April 1945, ibid.

edge, and the Known."[42] Dewey thought this paper "should be
as sharp as possible" and should appear "next as summing up
what has gone before and making transition to following."[43]
Prefaced by the disparaging "My hesitation in sending this on is
the fear you will take it more seriously than I do. For once Ive
condensed instead of expanding," Dewey sent Bentley another
sketch in May 1945 that became the basis for section I of the article (this volume, pp. 74–77), referring to it the next day as "my
two page introduction."[44] On a later draft for this paper Dewey
added an "s" to the title, "Postulation," and wrote below, "How
about Plural?"[45] In late June Dewey reported that he was "sending mss" to the *Journal*; publication was delayed, however, until
the fall because of the "unusual amount of contributions, and the
difficulty of fitting in a long article."[46] Dewey read proof and sent
it to Bentley with only "a few slight queries."[47] During this period salutations changed from "Dear Dewey" and "Dear Bentley"
to "Dear John" and "Dear Arthur."

C. West Churchman and T. A. Cowan reviewed "Postulations"; Dewey drafted a reply and sent a copy to Bentley, writing
"When I get your comments I'll fix up the letter if you think it is
a good idea—It doesn't foreclose public statement later. Maybe
if they had waited till we had published the other articles, they
wouldn't have written as they have." Dewey's reply, intended as
"a note" rather than "a public comment," stated: "I welcome the
partial degree of approval that seems to be expressed. But there
are other matters that puzzle me."[48] It appears that Dewey did
not send the reply.

Bentley, "Logicians' Underlying Postulations," *Philosophy of
Science* 13 (January 1946): 3–19
    Bentley sent drafts of his article to Dewey, who responded

---

42. Dated 20 June 1944, ibid., KK, folder 20.
43. Dewey to Bentley, 21 February 1945, Bentley Collection.
44. Dewey to Bentley, 8 and 9 May 1945, ibid.
45. Draft P-ix-F, 20 May 1945, ibid., KK, folder 23.
46. Dewey to Bentley, 21 June and 8 October 1945, Bentley Collection.
47. Dewey to Bentley, 10 November 1945, ibid.
48. Dewey to Bentley, 24 April 1946, enclosing reply, ibid. The reply is a revi-
    sion of reply Dewey sent to Bentley 23 April (ibid.). For Churchman-Cowan
    review, see *Journal of Philosophy* 43 (11 April 1946): 217–19.

with comments and suggestions for "verbal changes," not all of which Bentley accepted. For instance, Dewey suggested italicizing "all" in the phrase "all their behaviors" (193n.14–15).[49] During July and August 1945 they exchanged letters discussing content; by early September Dewey had "gone over the last versions" of Bentley's paper.[50]

Dewey and Bentley, "Interaction and Transaction"; "Transactions as Known and Named"; and "Specification," *Journal of Philosophy* 43 (12 and 26 September, 21 November 1946): 505–17; 533–51, 560; 645–63

> Apparently a year or more, probably from summer 1945 to summer 1946 was devoted to disentangling and development of Interaction, Transaction, and Specification. Fourteen drafts were prepared in 1945 and nineteen drafts, starting the numbering afresh as I–XIX [in 1946]. The earlier titles had the form "Specification and Transaction." In September 1945 this changed most generally to the "Specification of Transaction." . . . Attention is called to the difficulty of disentangling the three aspects of the material and to the extensive re-writings involved. ("Sketch of the Development")

Dewey later informed Adelbert Ames, Jr., that Bentley "wrote most of the two transaction articles."[51] Dewey, however, advised Bentley about organization, writing, for example, "I wonder whether . . . it may not prove better to make Specification a separate article," and suggesting at one point the wording "This matter is merely mentioned here; it is considered at length in our next paper, on Specification" (see 111.11–13, "Transaction . . . next.").[52] After reading Bentley's draft on "self-actional treatment of behaviors" (123.23), Dewey sent Bentley "one of the historical reminiscences (of philosophical doctrines) that the text

49. Dewey to Bentley, 30 July [1945], Bentley Collection. See also Dewey to Bentley, 15 August [1945], ibid.
50. Dewey to Bentley, 2 September 1945, ibid.
51. Dewey to Ames, 27 June 1949, Dartmouth Eye Institute Papers, Dartmouth College Library, Hanover, N.H. Dewey wrote frequently to Ames during this period. Much of their correspondence is published in *The Morning Notes of Adelbert Ames, Jr.*, ed. Hadley Cantril (New Brunswick, N.J.: Rutgers University Press, 1960).
52. Dewey to Bentley, 9 and 25 March [1946], Bentley Collection.

suggests to me."[53] Two days later Dewey suggested several additions that Bentley adopted: the sentences "The . . . ignored." (120.25–31), "The . . . treated." (122.27–123.2), and "In . . . impossible." (123n.11–13); as well as the clause "womb . . . isolation." (121.12–13).[54] In April Dewey informed the *Journal of Philosophy* that both transaction articles "would be along fairly soon" and he hoped "reasonably prompt publication" could now be arranged.[55]

Dewey's material for "Specification" includes an outline, notes, and suggestions sent in late 1945, as well as material sent in early 1946.[56] In January, for example, Dewey prepared a six-page draft based on a Bentley draft and wrote that he was continuing the "certain amount of transcribing" that had been successful before; he cautioned Bentley against taking what he wrote too seriously lest it prevent his "writing freely enough to be of any use in the future." He described his two kinds of changes, one in the sentence order "to procure what seemed to me an easier flow for the reader" and the other "crossing the ts and dotting the is of what you have."[57] The next month, Dewey informed Bentley that he had received "some pp. revisions or additions" but would wait until he had completed the entire draft before writing since "comments Ive made page by page before reading what came after havent always turned out very well." Although it was "ok and more with me" that Bentley incorporate "some of the things Ive written to you," such things were "not to be taken as belonging to the paper unless they are offered as such or as emendations of your text."[58] In March Dewey sent a large amount of material

53. Dewey to Bentley, 23 March 1946, ibid.
54. Dewey to Bentley, 25 March [1946], ibid.
55. Dewey to Bentley, 15 April 1946, ibid. On 4 April Dewey had written to Bentley, "Send me the Journal copy and Ill go over it and forward it. Ill guarantee Ill make no change in sense without your authorization first" (ibid.). On 17 April Dewey wrote to Bentley, "It isnt needful, unless you have some special points, to submit your final revisions to me; they can go direct." "But if you prefer to send them to me, I'll go over them and get them in promptly to the JOURNAL" (ibid.). On 25 April Dewey wrote to Bentley, "Ill hold it of course till Ive heard from you, and then send it" (ibid.).
56. See, for example, Dewey's outline of 17 September 1945 and notes, suggestions, and comments of 20 September, 30 November, and 3, 4, and 8 December 1945, ibid.
57. Dewey to Bentley, 13 January 1946, ibid.
58. Dewey to Bentley, 25 February 1946, ibid.

based on Bentley's Specification drafts, including a five-page draft; a two-page draft for "Designation" (closely corresponding to text at 140–43); and a rewritten passage (matching 146.10–28, "Alien . . . transaction.").[59] In April, commenting on the "feel of some repitition in moving back and forth," Dewey raised the question of whether the article "wouldnt profit by some consolidation."[60] Ill for two months, Dewey wrote in June: "I think my mind is beginning to show some faint signs of beginning to work again" and, a week later, "Yes, I think I am [in] shape to tackle the Specification paper now; send it on, and I'll go over it."[61]

Dewey and Bentley, "'Definition,'" *Journal of Philosophy* 44 (22 May 1947): 281–306

"Paper 'Definition' was written the last half of 1946 with drafts numbered I–XVIII" ("Sketch of the Development"). On draft XVIII Dewey wrote above the title, "I think 'quotes' makes this the right title." On this draft Dewey also inserted "in connection with" (172.26), changed "deems necessary" to "proposes" (173.7), and changed "shelves, and not" to "shelves instead of" (175.24).[62] Dewey's notes accepted by Bentley include a criticism that "the last paragraph probably goes unnecessarily into detail about mathematics"; a discussion of the "historical reference" to Aristotle, incorporated in the first two paragraphs of section II (157–58); a comment on the distinction between syntactics and semantics (159.27–160.13); a suggestion to sharpen the point about John Stuart Mill (158.23–29); and a sketch for a footnote (footnote 9).[63] In November 1946 Dewey praised the finished article, thinking it "one of the best things yet"; it "ties things together in a way that will be a decided help to all readers." Although "a devastating criticism as a whole, the tone is good."[64] In May 1947 Dewey and Bentley corresponded about

59. Dewey to Bentley, 12 and 21 March 1946, ibid. See also Dewey material sent 22 and 23 March 1946, ibid.
60. Dewey to Bentley, 10 April 1946, ibid.
61. Dewey to Bentley, 13 and 21 June 1946, ibid. Dewey had written to Bentley on 30 April about a sinus attack and on 25 May about "a flu infection that brought on a urinary infection" (ibid.).
62. Ibid., KK, folder 42.
63. Dewey to Bentley, 11 and 25 October 1946, Bentley Collection.
64. Dewey to Bentley, 8 November 1946, ibid.

reading proof for this article and sending off the manuscript for the next.[65]

Dewey and Bentley, "Concerning a Vocabulary for Inquiry into Knowledge," *Journal of Philosophy* 44 (31 July 1947): 421–34
   In early September 1946 Dewey had begun work on the vocabulary paper, writing:

> I sat down to make out a list of vocabulary words; the immediate result is enclosed. I dont think much of it. The fact is I seem confused about what we should try to do—and fall between two stools. One is to set forth a kind of key-list to central terms in our positive construction; the other is more critical, putting emphasis on weaknesses and confusions in current usages.[66]

In this letter Dewey reported the "two different significations" for "inter" in the *Oxford English Dictionary;* for Bentley's incorporation in the text, see 264.33–35. The wording of the "Epistemological" entry (262) reflects Dewey's suggestion in March 1947 that as far as this word "is related directly or by implication to assumption of a separate knower & known (including the to-be-known) all epistemological words are ruled out by our basic thesis." [67] Dewey's revisions in drafts include the insertion of "with . . . implications," (263.35–36) and the italicization of "*physiological*" (269.1).[68] When Dewey read proof in July, he suggested several changes including, for example, the wording "and, . . . behaviorally." (262.27) and the expansion "Might . . . inquiry.'" (271.7–10). Dewey, in turn, approved changes Bentley made in proof.[69]

Bentley, "The New 'Semiotic,'" *Philosophy and Phenomenological Research* 8 (September 1947): 107–31
   Dewey consoled Bentley about rejection by one journal and

65. See, for example, Dewey to Bentley, 1 and 9 May 1947; Bentley to Dewey, 3, 6, 7 May 1947, ibid.
66. Dewey to Bentley, 4 September 1946, ibid.
67. Dewey to Bentley, 24 March 1947, ibid.
68. Draft VII, dated 19 March 1947, ibid., KK, folder 58; draft VIII, dated 2 April 1947, ibid., folder 59.
69. Dewey to Bentley, 12 and 19 July 1947, Bentley Collection.

Bentley's second journal choice: "I cant see that Philosophy of Science amounts to a great deal"; "I should imagine" that *Philosophy and Phenomenological Research* "would jump at the chance to publish your piece."[70] Referring to Bentley's article as "the Morris paper," Dewey and Bentley apparently considered it separate from the overall project. Dewey read Bentley's drafts, writing in July 1946, "Hope to get your Morris paper back to you soon"; in October he offered "one suggestion" about the word "need" that "might be worth a brief footnote" to which Bentley replied that he was using Dewey's point "as well as I could get it in."[71]

BOOK PUBLICATION

In 1946 Dewey had refused an offer to publish their articles in book form.[72] By the spring of 1947, although not all the projected papers had been prepared, Dewey and Bentley began seriously considering book publication. Other participants in the ongoing dialogue urged publication: Felix Kaufmann, philosophy professor at the New School for Social Research, his student Jules Altman, and Joseph Ratner, who, long associated with Dewey, established a relationship with Bentley during this period.

In May Bentley informed Dewey that Kaufmann and Altman, regarding the vocabulary paper as a strong conclusion to the series, recommended early publication. Dewey replied that, although previously of "two minds," he now favored publication "if we can get good publishers." "It would be mighty convenient for *us* to have the articles together" and "we will probably get more attention" from a book. In deciding what should be in-

---

70. Dewey to Bentley, 2 November 1945, ibid.
71. Dewey to Bentley, 25 July and 7 October 1946; Bentley to Dewey, 14 October 1946, ibid.
72. On 9 March 1945, informing Bentley about letters recently received from the Philosophical Library, Dewey suggested, "If we wanted to put this series when finished into a book, maybe they would take it" (ibid.). On 4 February 1946 Dewey reported to Bentley that the firm had made an offer to publish the essays and had sent an advance of $500, which Dewey had returned (ibid.). On 25 April 1946 Dewey reported to Bentley that Philosophical Library had sent him copies of a book contract, but Dewey had replied "that the series wasnt completed and it was too early to discuss the matter" (ibid.).

cluded in addition to the jointly signed articles, Dewey approved inclusion of Bentley's two individually signed articles, the Morris article unless Bentley thought it "too technically controversial," and, possibly, a paper Dewey was planning to write on Signs. However, Dewey wrote ten days later that publication should not be delayed for this paper and, in addition, he "concluded on thinking it over it is better to hold the publication in book form down to the articles strictly pertinent to that one subject."[73] They decided to exclude additional papers, limiting the book to eleven articles. Bentley drew up an outline for a book tentatively entitled "Towards a Natural Theory of Knowings and Knowns." He and Dewey discussed the title, Dewey supposing "the briefer the title the better, like Knowings and Knowns." The plural form, however, being awkward, "may be 'Knowing and the Known' would serve—but that is only a casual suggestion."[74]

Bentley, with Joseph Ratner's help, set out to find a publisher, reporting to Dewey that both Oxford University Press and Henry Holt and Co. agreed to publish the book, "but neither can promise earlier than the spring of 1949."[75] Bentley reopened negotiations with Beacon Press, whose director, Melvin Arnold, had earlier expressed interest. Arnold had written to Bentley that their series of papers "has been most impressive." If they had not yet arranged book publication, "we should be glad to consider putting them into a small book on a standard royalty basis." Bentley had replied that he preferred to "postpone the question of publication" for a year or two and suggested that, if Arnold was "still interested" at that time, he "take the question up" with Dewey.[76] Now Bentley wrote to Arnold that he and Dewey had decided not to delay any longer.[77]

A nonprofit organization established in 1854 by the American Unitarian Association to print, distribute, and sell religious books, Beacon Press in the early twentieth century broadened

73. Dewey to Bentley, 15 and 25 May 1947, ibid.; Bentley to Dewey, 5, 8, and 14 May 1947, ibid. For Dewey's earlier, unpublished sign paper, see this volume, pp. 297–309.
74. Dewey to Bentley, 11 June 1947, Bentley Collection.
75. Bentley to Dewey, 22 June 1947, ibid.
76. Arnold to Bentley, 19 February 1947; Bentley to Arnold, 28 February 1947, ibid.
77. Bentley to Arnold, 15 June 1947, ibid.

its program to include ethical, sociological, and philanthropic works. In the mid-1940s the Boston firm underwent another expansion that resulted in its being regarded as a "university press" specializing in scholarly publications. In 1948 Beacon published a reprint of Dewey's 1920 *Reconstruction in Philosophy* with his new introduction and, in 1949, *The Wit and Wisdom of John Dewey* as well as *Knowing and the Known*.

Arnold replied to Bentley's letter that Beacon was "most definitely . . . interested in publishing your manuscript. We are moving into the philosophical field on a major scale." Beacon would process the book "in about the normal time in the publishing industry—about six months after receipt."[78] After Bentley arranged for Dewey to make the agreement, Dewey sent a binding letter on 30 July 1947 to Arnold: "I am glad to join Mr A F Bentley in giving my full approval. If it will shorten the time of publication you may regard this letter as committing me to the contract."[79]

Bentley informed Arnold that reprints of the vocabulary paper would be available soon and that the Morris paper was scheduled for publication in the near future. Replying to Arnold's query about their selection of a book title, Bentley sent a list of eleven chapters at the top of which appeared "Knowing and the Known," writing, "We considered a dozen or more titles, and this one got all the approvals."[80] The chapter order followed the order of article publication except for two shifts, the last three chapters to be Bentley's "Logicians' Underlying Postulations," Bentley's Morris paper, and the joint vocabulary paper.

As Bentley had played the major role in writing, so he continued to play the major role in publication. At this point it seemed necessary only to make revisions, decide how to handle acknowledgments and matters of format, verify quotations and citations, and, possibly, add preface and conclusion. Because of a series of mishaps and unexplained delays, however, what was expected to be a fairly straightforward six-month operation took

78. Arnold to Bentley, 18 July 1947, ibid.
79. Dewey to Arnold, 30 July 1947, carbon copy sent to Bentley ca. 30 July 1947, ibid.
80. Bentley to Arnold, 5 and 9 August 1947; Arnold to Bentley, 5 August 1947, ibid.

two years, allowing for the late addition of two articles written by Dewey.

Dewey and Bentley, Preface. When Bentley had proposed earlier that Dewey write a preface for the series in the event of publication, Dewey had replied, "The only thing I see appropriate to a preface would be that you had done most of the work!"[81] Now Bentley broached the topic again, writing to Joseph Ratner, "If I could get JD to write it, that would be fine. But how?" A week later, Bentley wrote to Ratner, "Your suggestion that I put the preface up to Dewey was profitable. I did. He came right back with a preface."[82] Bentley revised Dewey's preface; Dewey approved changes and sent the revised document to Beacon in mid-September. For textual discussion of preface, see below, pp. 522–23.

The book was to be set from article reprints revised by Bentley in cooperation with Dewey. Bentley had at the outset made a request of Arnold that he later came to regret: "I would like to have some competent person employed to examine the maintenance of free running reference from subjects to predicates, and especially the case of the unruly 'it.'" Offering to pay for this service, Bentley continued, "There is very little one can do to make such matter readable, but I believe a competent person free from philosophical or logical specialization might be able to improve the structure materially in this respect." Arnold was "happy to have a competent copy editor go through the manuscript for the small points you discussed in your letter" but would "not think" of having Bentley bear the cost.[83] As Bentley started sending material, Arnold reported that they had already begun the "editorial sandpapering" Bentley suggested.[84]

Bentley informed Dewey about his revisions and Dewey usually approved or offered advice about handling problems. For ex-

81. Bentley to Dewey, 26 May 1947; Dewey to Bentley, 27 May 1947, ibid.
82. Bentley to Ratner, 1 and 9 September 1947, Ratner/Dewey Papers. See also Bentley to Ratner, 10 and 21 August 1947, ibid.; Bentley to Dewey, 9 August 1947, Bentley Collection.
83. Bentley to Arnold, 20 July 1947; Arnold to Bentley, 25 July 1947, ibid.
84. Arnold to Bentley, 5 August 1947, ibid.

ample, Dewey wrote about Bentley's word change (64.1–2): "Technological ok instead of technical"; and suggested for the revision of the last sentence in the "Specification" chapter (153.3–5): "I should imagine dropping the last sentence and inserting one to the effect that there here involved a problem for future work and that it was hoped that what has been said suggested the direction that would be taken—not proper wording but something to intimate that the further treatment wouldnt break away but carry further."[85] Bentley also sent Beacon separate lists of changes to be made. Bentley discussed with Ratner and Dewey the possibility of including a list of revisions in the book, perhaps in the form of an appendix.[86]

The suggestion of Beacon copyeditor Elizabeth Best to use the first chapter, "A Search for Firm Names," as an introduction was "OK" with Dewey; Bentley planned to add a short concluding chapter; and Altman would prepare the index.[87] Dewey proposed to Arnold that Bentley's name appear first on the title page. After being informed by Arnold of this change, Bentley thanked Dewey, writing that although he had "handled certain machinery that you would not have handled," he could not have done it "without the sweeping surveys you had made in the past, nor without your attention to what was going on."[88] However, Beacon later informed Bentley that this would not be the case, referring to the "unavoidable, if unwritten law that the name of the senior" collaborator "appears first as deference to his advanced age and longer scholarly career." "This particular protocol seems never to have been violated."[89]

Publication, originally scheduled for spring of 1948, was suddenly moved up to December 1947. "Horrified" by the shift, Best wrote to Bentley: "My earnest prayer is that by having had the manuscript revised carefully we can save some delay over the galley proofs. Even so, I hope you can send us your revisions fairly soon so that we can get started on the copyediting."[90] By early

85. Dewey to Bentley, 11 September 1947, ibid.
86. Bentley to Ratner, 8, 22, and 23 December 1947, Ratner/Dewey Papers.
87. Dewey to Bentley, 2 October 1947, Bentley Collection; Bentley to Ratner, 18 October and 13 December 1947, Ratner/Dewey Papers.
88. Arnold to Bentley, 3 December 1947; Bentley to Dewey, 8 December 1947, Bentley Collection.
89. Quoted in Bentley to Dewey, 18 March 1949, ibid.
90. Best to Bentley, 21 October 1947, ibid.

November Bentley had sent all the copy to Beacon.[91] To Joseph Ratner he sent a revised contents page containing an introduction, ten chapters, and "perhaps also a two or three page conclusion."[92]

After delays Beacon informed Bentley to expect galley proof in January, possibly in time to meet the original spring 1948 publication date. Hospitalized twice during this period for a kidney and bladder infection and planning for the contingency that he might need help, Bentley arranged for additional sets of proof to be sent to Dewey, Ratner, and Altman.[93] He sent Ratner a "memo of the changes made in text, apart from purely technical ones of citation and reference" and later promised an acknowledgment for his assistance (5).[94]

By February, when Bentley received the first galleys, he had recovered sufficiently to return to work. Problems immediately appeared. Bentley found that he had no record for some corrections he had made. He realized that when he had sent Ratner correction sheets in December, he also sent the set of reprints he had "pawed over and mauled" in the process of making revisions. Also, Beacon had not returned the copy Bentley had furnished, which included typewritten sheets of changes.[95] Bentley wrote to Dewey, "This is a HELL of a mess. Some of my emendations sent the Press were overlooked by it; and I can find no carbons."[96]

Bentley sent Arnold a series of angry letters complaining about Beacon's reediting of their text. On 12 March 1948, for example, insisting that Dewey's words be restored, Bentley wrote to Arnold: "The amount of work I have to do is at least three times what it would have been if you had let the language alone, except

91. Bentley wrote to Ratner on 27 October 1947 that he had sent Best "finished up to III" (Ratner/Dewey Papers); on 7 November 1947 he wrote to Dewey, "I have now all the copy sent off to Beacon" (Bentley Collection); and he wrote to Best on the same date that he had sent everything (ibid.).
92. The contents page, dated 7 November 1947, includes a tentative eleventh chapter, "The Case of Fact" (enclosed in Bentley to Ratner, 8 November 1947, Ratner/Dewey Papers).
93. Bentley to Ratner, 23 December 1947, ibid.; Bentley to Best, 6 March 1948, Bentley Collection.
94. Bentley to Ratner, 13 December 1947 and 9 February 1948, Ratner/Dewey Papers.
95. Bentley to Ratner, 8 February 1948, ibid.; Bentley to Dewey, 11 February 1948, Bentley Collection.
96. Bentley to Dewey, 12 February 1948, ibid.

where manifest flaws existed." He listed "samples" where Beacon's meddling "destroyed my whole statement" and made sentences "unintelligible"; he cited changes that were "not only clumsy in expression but made the sense almost undiscoverable." In some cases Bentley restored the text, in others he revised further.[97] Dewey, after several sympathetic letters to Bentley, wrote to Arnold:

> I should have written you before to say how seriously troubled I have been about the handling in your printing office of Bentley's and mine copy—and this in spite of the fact that your proofreader must have had copy already in type. The material was technical and philosophical. If the proofreader had any doubts I should suppose it would have been his or her duty to ask questions of the authors. Instead he or she made changes wholesale, many of which went much beyond the bounds of verbal and grammatical matters, not only changing the intended meaning but distorting it, in many cases making the text say the contrary of what was written. It happens that Mr Bentley who has had to bear the brunt of the work is unusually careful in his use of words especially when the point to be conveyed is one that is not that which is most usually read. In fact his exactitude in use of language is almost of the mathematical order.

Arnold replied apologetically to Dewey, "We thought we were carrying out his original request to us for copyediting, but it is apparent that we have been quite clumsy."[98]

Dewey and Bentley considered forgoing the revisions and reversing course. Dewey suggested in his letter to Arnold that Beacon prepare a new set of proofs from unrevised reprints and telegraphed Bentley, "I SUGGEST YOU WIRE ARNOLD THAT WE HAVE ORIGINAL ARTICLES REPRINTED IMPOSSIBLE TO MAKE CORRECTIONS ON PRESENT PAPER."[99] However, months earlier, Bentley had written significantly to Joseph Ratner, "Even if I wished

97. Bentley to Arnold, 12 March 1948, ibid.
98. Dewey to Arnold, 18 March 1948; Arnold to Dewey, 26 March 1948, Beacon Press Papers, Boston, Mass.
99. Dewey to Bentley, 22 March 1948, Bentley Collection.

to restore to old form, it might now be too late to be practicable." Bentley realized that any action on restoration "would have to be taken right away—if still practicable." [100] Dewey, also recognizing they had passed the point of no return, wrote to Bentley that he would advise letting Beacon "start all over, unless it would now make more work than the other way." [101] Their decision was not to reverse course after all but to continue with revisions for book publication.

Ratner may have identified part of the difficulty. When Dewey wrote to him expressing displeasure with the "unbelievable" job Beacon was doing, "and they had printed copies with few corrections to work from," Ratner agreed that it was "pretty shocking" but offered "one extenuating possibility": "Bentley sent me a copy of the Jrnls of Phil. he sent to Beacon and if he marked them up the way he marked up the set he sent me, the problem any typesetter would face would be pretty difficult." [102]

In May an additional chapter was inserted and a summary added.

Dewey, "Common Sense and Science: Their Respective Frames of Reference," *Journal of Philosophy* 45 (8 April 1948): 197–208

On 6 May Bentley wrote to Dewey, "Would there be any possibility of your being willing to put this paper in the book?" to which Dewey replied that he would be "proud" to include it "if you think it belongs." [103] The new article was revised and inserted as chapter 10, between Bentley's Morris paper and the vocabulary paper. Dewey, truly proud of this piece, had written to Sidney Hook in April, "I feel as if for the first time in my life I had got to the point I had been working towards, in sections and by fits and starts for fifty years or so. The article in the last Journ is its firstfruits." Several months later, he wrote to Herbert W. Schneider that "the greatest discovery on philosophy Ive ever

100. Bentley to Ratner, 13 December 1947, Ratner/Dewey Papers.
101. Dewey to Bentley, 7 April 1948, Bentley Collection.
102. Dewey to Ratner, 25 March [1948]; Ratner to Dewey, 31 March 1948, Ratner/Dewey Papers.
103. Bentley to Dewey, 6 May 1948; Dewey to Bentley, 8 May 1948, Bentley Collection. On 12 May 1948 Bentley suggested to Arnold that Dewey's article be added; Arnold wrote to Bentley on 17 May approving the addition (ibid.).

made is that between common sense and science as reported in" this article.[104] For textual discussion of chapter 10, see below, pp. 523–24.

Dewey and Bentley, Chapter 12. Summary of Progress Made. Bentley sent Dewey drafts of an appended comment, which, in the early stages of discussion, was apparently planned as the introduction to the volume. It was decided that acknowledgments, which had earlier appeared in the preface and then as a separate note, would best be incorporated here (p. 279). When the material was ready for Beacon in mid-May as chapter 12, Dewey wrote, "I dont believe I want to write anything," and commented on Bentley's suggestion of "Postscript" for a title that he would be "inclined to include a colon:—and then Some Results to Date."[105] They eventually agreed upon "Summary of Progress Made" as the chapter 12 title. Dewey later suggested changes and Bentley sent revision sheets to Beacon.

For several months in 1948 Bentley and, to a lesser extent, Dewey read and revised several sets of galleys, material circulating between the press in Boston; Bentley in Paoli; and Dewey in New York City, Nova Scotia, and Key West or Miami Beach, Florida. Following his initial dismay, Bentley was encouraged as he read revised galleys.[106] Dewey revised galleys "mostly with reference to clarity of expression"; he instructed Bentley, "Any changes

104. Dewey to Hook, 25 April 1948, Sidney Hook/John Dewey Collection, Special Collections, Morris Library, Southern Illinois University at Carbondale; Dewey to Schneider, 13 February 1949, Herbert W. Schneider Papers, Special Collections, Morris Library, Southern Illinois University at Carbondale. Dewey also wrote to Ames about his article; see Dewey to Ames, 6, 12, and 16 November 1947, and Ames to Dewey, 25 November 1947 and 26 May 1948, Dartmouth Eye Institute Papers. Ratner wrote to Dewey suggesting possible uses for the article (23 May 1948, Ratner/Dewey Papers).
105. Dewey to Bentley, 14 May 1948, Bentley Collection. On 23 May Bentley sent revisions to Beacon (ibid.).
106. Bentley wrote to Ratner on 5 April 1948, "I cannot really *read* it at all till the mutilations are removed. It is incredible. . . . One does not see such things in first reading. It is a job to root them all out" (Ratner/Dewey Papers). On 13 June 1948, however, he wrote to Dewey, "The more I muddle the proof around, the better it seems to come—defects I find, i.e. are minor, and curable" (Bentley Collection). First working galley, second working galley, and final galley, ibid., KK, envelopes 72–74.

you make all right—not necessary to get my approval." [107] Bentley asked Mary Clemens Mahew Smith, Beacon's new copyeditor, to send revised galleys to his brother-in-law, Judge Bayard Henry Paine, Nebraska Supreme Court.[108] In addition, Ratner read galleys; Altman used galleys to prepare the index; Kaufmann read galleys that Paine read; and Ratner, because of Bentley's eye problems, used galleys to verify quotations and references.[109] Dewey and Bentley received galleys for chapters 10 and 12 in August, returned final galleys in November, and decided to place notes at the end of each chapter.[110] They expected page proof by year's end.

In late December, however, Lucille M. Myers, Beacon's new copyeditor, informed Bentley that printers could not take galleys for a few weeks; in February 1949, hearing nothing from Beacon, Bentley complained to Arnold of the delays and gave instructions that separate page proof not be sent direct to Dewey.[111] Arnold informed Dewey that page proof was expected by early March, bound books by late spring.[112] Bentley received page proof when expected and in mid-March returned the completed index and revised page proof to Beacon. He had found "several cases in which what was correct in the galleys changed to error on the pages" and noticed "minor defects" in the copy "never detected till now." He acknowledged that while he had "spent the greater part of a year on this proof, part of the work has had value in improved expression."[113] Bentley hoped the book would be out

107. Dewey to Bentley, 12 and 15 February 1948, Bentley Collection.
108. Bentley to Smith, 31 May 1948, ibid.
109. On 29 May 1948 Bentley wrote to Ratner offering him the task of verifying quotations (Ratner/Dewey Papers); during the next months Bentley and Ratner corresponded about verification (ibid.). Bentley instructed Beacon about citation corrections, for instance, writing to Beacon copyeditor Lucille M. Myers on 1 August 1948 about a reference to William James (Bentley Collection). Galleys used by others, ibid., KK, envelopes 68–71.
110. Dewey wrote to Bentley on 2 November 1948, "Personally I would like to see the notes at the end of the chapter but should prefer to have the decision come from you." "The new galleys seem to me pretty accurately looked out for, but I havent given them close check by the original articles" (Bentley Collection).
111. Myers to Bentley, 20 December 1948 and 24 February 1949; Bentley to Arnold, 3 February 1949, ibid. Dewey spent much of this period in Jamaica.
112. Arnold to Dewey, 21 February 1949, Beacon Press Papers.
113. Bentley to Dewey, 18 March 1949, Bentley Collection. Page proof, ibid., KK, envelope 75.

soon; in the spring, however, Dewey and Bentley added an appendix, and *Knowing and the Known* was finally published in the fall.

Dewey, Reply to "A Letter to Mr. Dewey," *Journal of Philosophy* 46 (26 May 1949): 329–42

In early 1949, while in Montego Bay and Discovery Bay, Jamaica, Dewey prepared a reply to Albert G. A. Balz to appear in the *Journal of Philosophy* with Balz's letter. In January Dewey wrote to Bentley about "one sad experience lately," a letter "from a man who took his Ph D at Col when I was still teaching: a criticism of a point in my Logic"; Dewey had written to Balz but doubted that Balz would "change his mind about publishing his piece."[114] Balz did not change his mind, sending Dewey in February a revised open letter.[115] When Dewey finished his reply, he sent Bentley a copy of it, writing, "Ive spent more time on the enclosed than Balz's piece was worth but if I ever undertake writing a simple direct statement of the Logic it will have been worth while."[116] Dewey described to others the value this piece had for him. To Joseph Ratner Dewey wrote that he "got some needed experience in simplification out of it"; to Ames he wrote later, "I grudged the time & effort at the time, but it led me to go over a lot of things & try to put them together, & I think it paid me."[117] Responding to Bentley's suggestion, Dewey wrote, "Nothing would please me more than to have my Balz screed in the book." Dewey thought he might need to "fix it up" a little "but it would delay publication still longer. Maybe we can start another book."[118] With a few revisions, Dewey's reply was inserted as an

114. Dewey to Bentley, 18 January 1949, Bentley Collection. On 23 November 1948 Dewey had sent Balz a postcard acknowledging receipt of Balz's letter; on 16 January 1949 Dewey replied to Balz (Albert G. A. Balz Papers, Manuscripts Department, Alderman Library, University of Virginia, Charlottesville). For Balz's published letter, see this vol., Appendix 1.
115. Balz to Dewey, 20 February 1949, ibid. Dewey replied on 7 March that he would prepare a reply soon (ibid.).
116. Dewey to Bentley, 4 April 1949, Bentley Collection. Calling Dewey's reply "a corker," Bentley sent it to Kaufmann to look over. "I think he will like it very much" (Bentley to Dewey, 14 and 26 April 1949, ibid.).
117. Dewey to Ratner, 8 April 1949, Ratner/Dewey Papers; Dewey to Ames, 27 May 1949, Dartmouth Eye Institute Papers.
118. Dewey to Bentley, 26 April 1949, Bentley Collection.

appendix. For textual discussion of the appendix, see below, pp. 524–26.

In July Dewey returned page proof for the appendix and index, adding to the latter a reference under "abstract" and inserting "problem" as an entry with a reference to the appendix.[119] In mid-September Dewey informed Bentley that he had seen in the *New York Times* "a statement that our book was to come out on my birthday—also that it was a contribution to the 'science of meaning.'"[120] He also wrote to Sidney Hook about the notice, adding that the press has had the book "for a long time and the postponement has been rather irritating."[121] Later that month he and Bentley had books in hand.[122]

Reception

Published in September 1949, *Knowing and the Known* was well received.[123] Solomon Weinstock assessed the writers' aptitudes and achievement: "Dewey brings to this task his unparal-

119. Dewey to Bentley, 2 July 1949, ibid.
120. Dewey to Bentley, 17 September 1949, ibid. For notice, see "Books—Authors," *New York Times,* 12 September 1949, p. 19.
121. Dewey to Hook, 18 September 1949, Hook/Dewey Collection.
122. Dewey to Bentley, 26 September 1949; Bentley to Dewey, 6 October 1949, Bentley Collection.
123. The following list includes earlier reviews of articles as well as reviews of *Knowing and the Known: American Journal of Sociology* 57 (September 1951): 200 (Anselm Strauss); *Annals of the American Academy of Political and Social Science* 268 (March 1950): 224 (Charles W. Morris); *Christian Leader* 132 (January 1950): 20–21 (Llewellyn Jones); *Crozer Quarterly* 27 (April 1950): 182 (William K. Wright); *Humanist* 10 (January–February 1950): 30 (Harold A. Larrabee); *Journal of Philosophy* 43 (11 April 1946): 217–19 (C. West Churchman and T. A. Cowan, review of "Postulations"); ibid. 47 (12 October 1950): 608–10 (Harry Todd Costello); *Journal of Symbolic Logic* 10 (December 1945): 132–33 (Alonzo Church, review of "A Search for Firm Names," "On a Certain Vagueness in Logic," "A Terminology for Knowings and Knowns," and "Postulations"); ibid. 12 (September 1947): 99 (Arthur Francis Smullyan, review of "'Definition'"); ibid. 15 (June 1950): 156 (Paul Ziff); *Modern Schoolman* 27 (May 1950): 322–26 (James Collins); *New Scholasticism* 25 (April 1951): 230–32 (Rudolf Harvey); *New Yorker* 25 (29 October 1949): 115; *Philosophic Abstracts* 11 (Winter 1949): 106; *Philosophical Review* 59 (April 1950): 269–70 (Max Black); *Philosophy* (London) 27 (July 1952): 263–65 (W. Mays); *Saturday Review of Literature* 32 (22 October 1949): 15, 44 (Harold A. Larrabee); *School and Society* 70 (19 November 1949): 336; *Scientific Monthly* 72 (Feb-

leled range of philosophical appraisal, Bentley his long concentration on straight wordings and adequate postulations for
behavioral inquiry"; they do "not pretend that the work therein
reported attains full scientific status" but rather "is a start in that
direction."[124] Llewellyn Jones explained Dewey's motivation:
since "much that Dewey had found to report has been misunderstood" because of language difficulties, "mostly verbal hang-
overs from earlier and more 'abstract'" systems, "a determined
effort is made to clear all this old language off the boards." "The
job is so complete that the very word 'knowledge' itself takes a
beating."[125] Harold Larrabee placed the book within the Dewey
canon as an outgrowth of his 1938 *Logic* and his 1896 "The Reflex Arc Concept in Psychology," which "foreshadowed" the
"'transactional' point of view set forth."[126] Fitting the book into
a philosophic context, Sidney Ratner called it "a notable exposition and extension" of "the naturalistic approach to human intelligence, which Darwin began and which James, Peirce, and
Dewey fostered in different ways"; and Anselm Strauss wrote,
"As a reminder of the bankruptcies of dualistic thinking, Dewey
is without peer."[127]

Most reviewers discussed the chapters of criticism, Larrabee,
for instance, describing Dewey and Bentley as "appalled and
scandalized by the 'linguistic chaos' in the works of eminent logicians."[128] W. Mays, however, after admitting that criticisms are
"often to the point," questioned whether the "large amount of
confusion and inconsistency" Dewey and Bentley found might
not "reflect a failure on their own part to understand these
authors."[129]

Reviewers found much to praise. Some singled out areas for
special mention and gauged the book's audience: Strauss thought
its index "useful," its footnotes "voluminous and interesting,"

ruary 1951): 135–36 (Solomon Weinstock); *Social Research* 17 (June 1950):
248–50 (Sidney Ratner); *U.S. Quarterly Book List* 6 (March 1950): 29.
124. Weinstock, *Scientific Monthly*, p. 135.
125. Jones, *Christian Leader*, p. 20.
126. Larrabee, *Saturday Review*, p. 16.
127. Ratner, *Social Research*, p. 248; Strauss, *American Journal of Sociology*,
p. 200.
128. Larrabee, *Saturday Review*, p. 16.
129. Mays, *Philosophy*, pp. 263–65.

and recommended it to social psychologists; *Philosophic Abstracts* called Dewey's reply to Balz "perhaps the high light of the work"; and to Sidney Ratner the book was "a rich feast" awaiting "semanticists and those interested in the history of ideas." [130] Many acknowledged that the work was technical and difficult but worth the struggle. The *New Yorker* called the writing "remarkably bright and metaphoric," and Weinstock found the book to be "tightly written, making little compromise with conventional expression." [131] Sidney Ratner observed the "verve and sprightliness of the analysis"; Larrabee stated that the book consisted "not of warmed-over conclusions, but of close, technical spadework on the frontiers of logic"; and the *United States Quarterly Book List* review included such adjectives as "biting," "enlightening," "contentious," and "provocative." [132]

On the other hand, *Knowing and the Known* encountered criticism from expected quarters. Charles W. Morris wondered whether "the proposed terminology is yet sufficiently developed to permit" descriptions of the "actual processes of knowing." [133] Granting that "on its positive side it is primarily a variety of old-fashioned pragmatism of the best American vintage," Mays found that "Dewey's view of logic as an instrumental form of enquiry dominates the scene and with it a refusal to draw any factual distinction between psychology and logic." [134] Rudolf Harvey and James Collins criticized Dewey and Bentley for ignoring metaphysics, Collins, however, cautioning, "Theists should be wary about occupying the breastworks which Dewey has thrown up and which he has invited them to defend at their own risk. For to some extent they must agree with Dewey's own line of thought." [135]

In 1945 and 1947 the *Journal of Symbolic Logic* had published reviews by Alonzo Church and Arthur Francis Smullyan of "'Definition'" and several preceding articles (see footnote 123).

130. Strauss, *American Journal of Sociology*, p. 200; *Philosophic Abstracts*, p. 106; Ratner, *Social Research*, p. 249.
131. *New Yorker*, p. 115; Weinstock, *Scientific Monthly*, p. 135.
132. Ratner, *Social Research*, p. 248; Larrabee, *Saturday Review*, p. 44; *U.S. Quarterly Book List*, p. 29.
133. Morris, *Annals of the American Academy of Political and Social Science*, p. 224.
134. Mays, *Philosophy*, pp. 263, 264–65.
135. Harvey, *New Scholasticism*, p. 232; Collins, *Modern Schoolman*, p. 323.

Bentley wrote a reply but did nothing with it. In early 1949, preparing for book publication, he wrote to Dewey about the reply he had "fixed up" almost "a year ago" and sent another copy. "My recollection is you thought well of sending it." He asked Dewey whether he had any suggestions, approved sending it, or objected to joint signatures.[136] Dewey thought the reply "should be published and I wouldnt want the absence of my name to give the impression I didnt agree a hundred percent. But there should be some limit to my getting credit for work you do. What would you say to a footnote saying it was written by you but that I had read it and was in complete agreement? Seems to me that would cover the ground." [137] Bentley replied that he would not send in the reply "for publication" but instead would "send it to the editors as a memorandum to give any reviewer they may find for the book." [138] Bentley's reply, entitled "An Aid to Puzzled Critics," did not appear in the *Journal of Symbolic Logic* but was later published as chapter 17 in Bentley's *Inquiry into Inquiries: Essays in Social Theory,* ed. Sidney Ratner (Boston: Beacon Press, 1954), pp. 320–24. It is included in the present edition as Appendix 2.

Following Dewey's 30 July 1947 binding letter to Arnold, Beacon sent Dewey and Bentley advance royalty checks of $250 each. Apparently nothing more was said about a formal contract until 13 April 1950, when Arnold sent contracts (also dated 13 April 1950) to Dewey for him to sign and send on to Bentley. The contract, two copies of which Dewey returned to Arnold, stipulated a 10% royalty on sales up to 7,500, 12 1/2% on sales between 7,500 and 12,500, and 15% on sales above 12,500.[139]

Beacon's September 1949 impression is the only edition published during Dewey's lifetime. In 1960 Beacon issued a paperback reprint, which was out of print by 1967. On 26 July 1972 rights reverted to Altman and the estate of John Dewey. In August Altman gave permission to reprint *Knowing and the Known* as a section in *Useful Procedures of Inquiry,* by Rollo Handy and E. C. Harwood (Great Barrington, Mass.: Behavioral Re-

136. Bentley to Dewey, 1 February 1949, Bentley Collection.
137. Dewey to Bentley, 13 February 1949, ibid.
138. Bentley to Dewey, 18 March 1949, ibid.
139. Arnold to Dewey, 13 April 1950, and Dewey to Arnold, 6 June 1950, Beacon Press Papers; contract, 13 April 1950, ibid.

search Council, 1973), pp. 87–190. By 1975, *Knowing and the Known* was again out of print and, with the permission of Altman and the Center for Dewey Studies, Greenwood Press, Westport, Conn., issued a reprint.

In 1963 La Nuova Italia Editrice initiated plans for an Italian translation, which was published in 1973.

Beacon's total book sales never reached 7,500 and royalty did not rise above 10%. Sales increased markedly when the paperback was first issued, rising to 1,768 for 1 May to 31 October 1960, and then leveling out to an annual average of 435. The Behavioral Research Council, however, expected to sell 9,000 of its 10,000 copies; as of September 1988 it had sold or distributed over 8,500 copies.

TEXTUAL ANALYSIS

Knowing and the Known (KK) was registered for copyright on 10 October 1949 in the name of Beacon Press, under A 36800, following publication 20 September 1949. Of the fifteen pieces constituting KK, only the preface and chapter 12 were not previously published. All Dewey's previously published contributions appeared in the *Journal of Philosophy* (JP).

Copy-text

Except for the preface and chapter 12 (both set from typescripts), setting copy for KK was the revised reprint of the journal articles supplemented by additional revisions. Comparing KK with JP reveals citation expansion and correction attributable to Joseph Ratner. Comparison also reveals substantial revision in both body and footnotes of articles; material was frequently added and occasionally deleted, and substantives and accidentals changed. Though it is not possible to trace every revision in the complex procedure, it is clear that, particularly while proofreading, Dewey played an active role in revising accidentals as well as substantives, changing punctuation and word forms. Returning final galleys to Beacon in November 1948, Dewey informed Bentley that he "made a few changes in punctuation, such as putting commas at both ends of dependent clauses; inserting a few semicolons in long sentences when it seemed to me they made reading easier," and made a few transpositions "when a slight

change in order of words seemed to make reading easier." [140] The
following explanation shows that Dewey's extensive and deliberate revision of accidentals eliminates JP as a possible choice for
copy-text.

When Dewey read the first set of KK galleys, he returned to
Bentley those on which he wrote.[141] Dewey's markings and queries suggesting accidentals revisions (many of which Bentley
adopted) indicate his attention to punctuation and emphasis on
clarity: At 11.15–16 ("employ, . . . tests,"), there was no comma
after "employ" on galley 3; Dewey inserted the comma and
wrote in the margin, "or else dele comma after tests." At 11.28
("come:"), a dash followed "come" on galley 3; Dewey inserted
the colon, deleted the dash, and queried the change in the margin. At 18.29 ("safe"), Dewey queried the comma that appeared
after "safe" on galley 6 and Bentley deleted it. At 45.21 ("problem,"), Dewey added the comma on galley 15. At 45.29 ("Logic,
we believe,"), Dewey added both commas on galley 15. At 58.8
("part;"), there was no punctuation after "part" on galley 19
and Dewey added a comma. At 60.25 ("it"), Dewey inserted a
comma after "it" on galley 20. At 65.11–12 ("(though . . . namings)"), this passage was punctuated differently in JP and galley
21: no parenthesis preceded "though"; no commas followed
"heavily" or "from" at 65.11; and a comma followed "namings"
at 65.12. On the galley Dewey bracketed "though . . . namings,"; wrote in the margin "not grammatically clear"; and added
the two commas. At 81.10 ("events,"), Dewey queried deleting
this comma on galley 26. At 83n.18 ("is,"), although the comma
has been added here as a Works Source emendation, it is interesting to note that Dewey wanted to make this addition on galley
27. At 103.23 ("*ad lib.:*"), Dewey added a dash after the colon
on galley 33, but either he or Bentley deleted it. At 152.19
("hazes."), Dewey added the quotation marks on galley 49. At
159n.7 ("movements, . . . liquids,"), Dewey inserted both commas on galley 51. At 163n.1–2 ("appraisers"), JP and galley 52
read "appraisors"; Dewey corrected the spelling on the galley.

In addition to altering punctuation in the revising process,
Dewey also restored words to the form he preferred. For example, JP, which had an identifiable housestyle, had consistently

140. Dewey to Bentley, 11 November 1948, Bentley Collection.
141. Ibid., KK, "Galleys carrying Dewey revisions," envelope 67.

hyphenated "subjectmatter." Dewey had written as early as 1942 to Bentley, "I had noticed . . . a rather marked tendency on my own part to use the word 'subjectmatter.'"[142] On 4 September 1948, reading chapter 10 galleys, Dewey wrote to Myers, "I prefer 'subjectmatter' without hyphen"; Myers noted on Dewey's letter "no hyphen in subject matter preferred" and assured Dewey that she was "taking the hyphen out wherever it occurs."[143] Because Myers had misinterpreted Dewey's handwriting, confusion arose and Dewey wrote a month later to Bentley, "Ill write her at once to print as one word unless you object. I cant recal every preferring the hyphenated form. In my previous books, especially the Logic Im reasonably sure I used the one word form." He wrote to Myers the same day, "My personal preference is for subjectmatter—one word no hyphen—just as is Bentley's."[144] Myers replied that final revised galleys for the book had just arrived; "as far as I have been able to check the printer seems to have carried out the proper printing of 'subjectmatter', but if you should find a place missed either by him or by me, I shall be most grateful if you will indicate it."[145] When the appendix was inserted later, JP hyphenated "subjectmatters" were changed. Myers wrote to Dewey in late June 1949, "As you will note the printer copies subject-matter from the Journal letter, but I have corrected this in all the instances I think."[146] In accordance with Dewey's and Bentley's strong preference during this period, variant forms missed by Beacon have been editorially emended for this edition.

Another word Dewey restored to the form he preferred is "cannot," housestyled by JP to "can not." When Dewey wrote to Myers about "subjectmatter" on 4 September 1948, he also instructed: "'cannot' uniformly one word." Myers noted on his letter, "cannot—1 word." Beacon changed the word throughout the volume; overlooked instances have been regularized for this edition.

142. Dewey to Bentley, 19 March 1942, Bentley Collection.
143. Dewey to Myers, 4 September [1948]; Myers to Dewey, 13 September 1948, Beacon Press Papers.
144. Dewey to Bentley, 2 October 1948, Bentley Collection; Dewey to Myers, 2 October 1948, Beacon Press Papers. Bentley also corresponded with Myers in September and October 1948 about this word (Bentley Collection).
145. Myers to Dewey, 18 October 1948, Beacon Press Papers.
146. Myers to Dewey, 29 June 1949, ibid.

In summary, because JP imposed its own housestyling on accidentals, and because Dewey revised and restored accidentals, JP could not serve as copy-text for the present edition. Copy-text for KK is the first impression, September 1949, which has been sight collated against the copyright deposit copy and found to be invariant. A few necessary corrections have been accepted from JP as emendations of copy-text; see Emendations List for typographical corrections at 62.6 and 92n.8, for example, and punctuation corrections at 47n.1 and 259.10.

Dewey's Substantive Revisions

Because the material was first published in JP, all substantive variants between KK and JP for Dewey's single and joint contributions are listed in this volume in Substantive Variants in *Knowing and the Known*. Some substantive variants resulted from Dewey's correspondence about galleys. For instance, at 259.34–260.2 ("offering . . . Trans-actor."), Dewey suggested revised wording for the *"Actor"* entry that "might be helpful"; Bentley replied, "Your suggestions excellent. I am attempting to incorporate them directly." At 265.17 (*"that, what,* and *how."*), Bentley revised the phrase for KK in response to Dewey's suggestion that the *"Knowledge"* entry "could be strengthened if the wording were treated as a kind of summary. Thus 'He knows *that, what* and *how.'*" At 272.1–5 ("It . . . object."), Dewey suggested this expansion of the *"Term"* entry.[147] Dewey's comments also resulted in substantive revisions at 134.26 ("much more") and at 135.12–16 ("cultural— . . . history."). Dewey suggested additions incorporated by Bentley at 133.31–34 (", with . . . them"), at 135.4–6 ("If . . . other."), at 136.32 ("(including the purposive)"), and at 133n.2–5 ("Progress . . . literature.").[148] At 276.14–15, Bentley italicized two words in accordance with Dewey's advice: "Underscore academical and pedagogical to contrast with *factual* 3 lines below."[149]

Other substantive variants between KK and JP derive from Dewey's markings and queries on galleys he returned to Bentley

147. All in Dewey to Bentley, [25 February 1948]; Bentley to Dewey, 27 February 1948, Bentley Collection.
148. All in Dewey to Bentley, 1 March [1948], ibid.
149. Dewey to Bentley, 20 May 1948, ibid.

("Galleys carrying Dewey revisions"). As the following listing shows, Bentley either adopted, discarded, or used Dewey's suggestions to revise differently. Dewey's revisions on chapter 1 galleys include the following: At 9.20–23 ("a change . . . refer."), galley 2 read "which sometimes does, and sometimes does not, mean the same." Dewey bracketed the passage and wrote in the margin, "not quite clear as to reference of 'which' and 'the same.'" Bentley subsequently revised the passage. At 12.10–11 ("the propositions in question are facts,"), galley 3 read "the proffered propositions are facts,". Dewey deleted "proffered", added quotation marks to "propositions", and inserted "in question"; Bentley rewrote "in question" more clearly in the margin. At 14.16 ("while"), Dewey inserted "and," before "while" on galley 4 and wrote in the margin, "I had difficulty in getting the sense here till I inserted 'and,'"; Bentley, however, made no change. At 20n.8 ("which, nevertheless,"), galley 6 read "that still"; Dewey deleted these two words and wrote "which nevertheless" in the left margin, and Bentley rewrote "which nevertheless" in the right margin. At 44.27 ("apart from"), galley 15 read "without"; Dewey drew an arrow from the word to the margin and wrote "(apart from (?))." At 44.31 ("is manifest."), galley 15 read "is manifest, not only on the side of credulous acceptance,"; Dewey underscored this line of print with an arrow to both margins. He wrote at the right, "not very clear" and, at the left, wrote about substance. Bentley subsequently heavily revised this paragraph.[150]

Dewey's revisions on galleys for chapters 2–7 are listed in the section entitled Notes on Substantive Variants in *Knowing and the Known*. See also emendations and textual notes for Dewey's revisions at 61.20–21, "*Knowing . . . together.*" and 155.32–33, "Moreover, . . . here."

Dewey's typescripts exist for the preface, chapter 10, and the appendix. Substantive variants between KK and these typescripts

150. On 22 February 1948 Dewey wrote to Bentley about chapter 1 galleys. He commented about the quotation from Tarski at 33.21–22 ("a sentence . . . otherwise"), "I wish you *had* said something as to 'satisfaction'"; and criticized the passage at 35.3–11 ("Designation . . . thing.") for being "so condensed as to require so much knowledge of Tarski as not to be very readily grasped" (ibid.).

indicate the evolution of text and are also listed in Substantive Variants in *Knowing and the Known*.

Preface

In early August 1947 Bentley sent both Dewey and Joseph Ratner two sketches for a prefatory note; Bentley asked Dewey in his accompanying letter, "What do you suggest? You may have a wholly different idea."[151] When Dewey did not respond, Bentley wrote to him in early September that the preface "ought to be written by you, and be personally characteristic." On 3 September Dewey sent a draft to Bentley, writing that though "not at all proud of the enclosed," he thought it would be "better to get something on paper fairly promptly." He had followed "what seemed to me the moving principles of your sketch."[152] Commenting that Dewey's preface was "first class for our purpose," Bentley sent Dewey a retyped version with "slight tentative changes," one additional sentence (at 4.11–13) "to bring in a direct hitch-up with your Logic, as Inquiry," and a summary of the articles' previous publication.[153] Dewey approved Bentley's changes on 11 September, writing that the additional sentence "can certainly go in without notification." Bentley then retyped the revised preface and sent Dewey two copies, one "the original to go to the Beacon Press. If it is satisfactory to you, will you please send it direct." On 17 September Dewey informed Bentley that he had sent Beacon the preface.[154]

The two-page typescript (TS), entitled "Preface," enclosed with Dewey's 3 September 1947 letter to Bentley (Bentley Collec-

151. Bentley to Dewey, 9 August 1947, ibid. On 10 August [1947] Bentley wrote to Ratner, "You have given us so much good advice, that anything you suggest about a preface will be welcomed. I enclose two sketches I am mailing now to J.D." (Ratner/Dewey Papers, enclosing Bentley's two prefatory notes).

152. Bentley to Dewey, 1 September 1947; Dewey to Bentley, 3 September 1947, Bentley Collection. Bentley wrote that he was enclosing another draft using Dewey's earlier suggestions; this draft is not attached to the letter but may be the same one Bentley sent to Ratner a week earlier. On 21 August [1947] Bentley had written to Ratner enclosing a draft containing Ratner's "stuff" (Ratner/Dewey Papers, enclosing draft dated 21 August 1947).

153. Bentley to Dewey, 8 September 1947, Bentley Collection. Bentley's typed copy of Dewey's preface, both with and without Bentley's alterations, ibid., KK, folder 63.

154. Dewey to Bentley, 11 and 17 September 1947; Bentley to Dewey, 14 September 1947, Bentley Collection. On 20 September 1947 Bentley informed Beacon Press (ibid.) and Ratner (Ratner/Dewey Papers) that Dewey had forwarded the preface.

tion) is the basis for the version printed in KK. The retyped three-page typescript (TS[1]), dated 15 September 1947, that Dewey later approved and sent to Beacon is in the Joseph Ratner/John Dewey Papers, Box 45, folder 9, Special Collections, Southern Illinois University at Carbondale. Substantive variants between KK, TS, and TS[1] are listed in Substantive Variants in *Knowing and the Known,* and Dewey's TS alterations appear in Alterations in Manuscripts. TS is credited as the source of two emendations.

Chapter 10. Common Sense and Science
In May 1948, when Dewey and Bentley agreed to add the JP article to KK, they discussed substantive revisions to be made on the 8 April reprint. At 242.15 ("to be"), Bentley wrote that perhaps "as" would "be better—though there will be better than that for phrasing, no doubt." Dewey approved changing "to be" to "as," but no change was made for KK, perhaps because neither Dewey nor Bentley was enthusiastic about it. At 251.8–24 ("Just . . . man."), Dewey expanded this discussion in response to Bentley's suggestion.[155] At 252.28 ("sharply"), Bentley twice queried Dewey's use of "radically" at this point in JP. Dewey instructed Bentley to delete the word, adding later, "Though the dictionary gives 'extremely' and I have a fondness for using the word in that sense if it gives rise to misapprehension Ill change it."[156] At 253.1–3 ("H_2O . . . water."), Bentley queried the JP version, and Dewey replied that if it "isnt clear the sentence should certainly be rewritten."[157] At 255.32 ("indicated."), Dewey advised Bentley to delete material from the JP paragraph "or if you think it better for the purpose of the volume . . . cut out the whole paragraph."[158] The paragraph was deleted. At 256.2 ("*facta* and *facienda*"), Dewey explained to Bentley his change of "facts" to "facta" for KK: "I think I wrote facta . . . to go with the 'facienda.'" "But a and s being next each other I often hit one when I intend the other." Bentley replied that "'facta'

155. Both revisions from Bentley to Dewey, 12 May 1948; Dewey to Bentley, 14 May 1948, Bentley Collection. Bentley wrote about "a turn of phrasing" that "might fit in somewhere with your discussion of labor-atories," to which Dewey replied, "The text should certainly be changed to bring that in."
156. Bentley to Dewey, 6 and 12 May 1948; Dewey to Bentley, 8 and 14 May 1948, ibid. The word is also discussed in Bentley to Dewey, 17 May 1948, and Dewey to Bentley, 21 May 1948, ibid.
157. Bentley to Dewey, 12 May 1948; Dewey to Bentley, 14 May 1948, ibid.
158. Dewey to Bentley, 14 May 1948, ibid.

had better be restored—and probably italics for both words";
Dewey wrote, "Facta I restored."[159] At 248n.3–10 ("As . . .
available."), Dewey informed Bentley about his revision of this
footnote and a few days later sent a typed passage to Arnold to
replace the revision sent earlier.[160]

Dewey wrote to Arnold on 20 May that he was sending the
reprint "with a few revisions." He informed Bentley on the same
day that he had gotten a "couple more copies of my Jn article"
and was "fixing them up as best I can" to send to Beacon. "They
will of course send a copy of proof to you, and you make any
further changes you find advisable."[161] Later, while reading chapter 10 galleys, Bentley queried Dewey about his use of "them" in
two ways in the first paragraph;[162] the first "them" was changed
to "these ways" at 242.8–9. As discussed above, Dewey while
reading galleys instructed Beacon about his preferred word forms
and, in September, returned revised galleys to Myers.[163]

In addition to the JP article, a clean, twenty-two page typescript (TS), not typed by Dewey, entitled "Common Sense and
Science: Their Respective Frames of Reference" (Ratner/Dewey
Papers, Box 44, folder 2), has also been collated against chapter
10 and substantive variants included in Substantive Variants in
Knowing and the Known. TS and JP are credited as the source of
seven emendations.

Appendix: Dewey's Reply to Albert G. A. Balz

On 4 April 1949 Dewey sent Bentley a copy of his reply to
Balz, writing from Jamaica: "Ive had the devil of a time getting
typing done, and am myself the world's worst typist as you have
reason to know."[164] JP prepared a transcription of Dewey's letter
to be used for the 26 May publication. On 4 May Herbert W.
Schneider, editor of JP, sent Balz a carbon copy of the JP tran-

159. Dewey to Bentley, 14 and 21 May 1948; Bentley to Dewey, 17 May 1948,
    ibid.
160. Dewey to Bentley, 21 May 1948, ibid.; Dewey to Arnold, 24 May 1948,
    Beacon Press Papers.
161. Dewey to Arnold, 20 May 1948, ibid.; Dewey to Bentley, 20 May 1948,
    Bentley Collection.
162. Bentley to Dewey, 28 August 1948, ibid.
163. Dewey to Myers, 6 and 11 September 1948, Beacon Press Papers.
164. Dewey to Bentley, 4 April 1949, Bentley Collection. This copy of Dewey's
    reply to Balz has not been located in the Bentley Collection.

scription, writing, "It took us considerable time and patience to decipher some of his writing."[165] JP proof was ready the following week.

In the meantime, Bentley and Ratner revised Dewey's letter and prepared a new document to be used for the KK appendix. On 7 May Bentley sent this document to Dewey along with the carbon of Dewey's letter. On 10 May Bentley wrote to Dewey explaining that Ratner would revise further if Dewey wished and retype if necessary. Ratner apparently sent the document to Beacon on 10 May.[166] However, on 8 May Dewey wrote to Bentley that he was writing JP "to send proof Balz article direct to you—I'll do what I can but Im going thru one of my sudden collapses at a very unfortunate time."[167] On 11 May Bentley reported to Dewey that he would send the JP proof to Beacon and had "wired the Press that it would be in substitution for the manuscript Ratner sent yesterday."[168] Bentley later informed Ratner, "As you know the Ratner-Bentley-midnight-oil version of the reply to Balz went down the flume, and the J. Phil version was substituted."[169]

In this letter to Ratner, Bentley also discussed revisions made in the article: "Beacon Press with its usual skill sent in the J. Phil copy to printers 'as is,' with the result that all 'dear Albert Balz's' went into type, and so Dewey has had to order them to take them out, and leave only 'Dear A.' Also at least 50—and possibly many more—instances of subject-matter (style of the Journal) have to be changed to subjectmatter (style of the book)." When she sent KK page proof, Myers asked Dewey about the salutation change;[170] the single instance missed, at 287.13, has been emended editorially with a textual note. After reading page proof, Dewey informed Bentley on 12 July about a correction at 289.38, which he hoped he had sent in time. "It may be the passage is still open to misconstruction but should have had to rewrite the entire 8 lines to make reasonably sure it would not be. . . . The best I

165. Schneider to Balz, 4 May 1949, enclosing transcription, Balz Papers.
166. Bentley to Dewey, 7 and 10 May 1949, Bentley Collection. The Ratner-Bentley version, ibid., KK, folder 78, 26 pp.
167. Dewey to Bentley, 8 May 1949, Bentley Collection.
168. Bentley to Dewey, 11 May 1949, ibid.
169. Bentley to Ratner, 7 July 1949, Ratner/Dewey Papers.
170. Myers to Dewey, 29 June 1949, Beacon Press Papers.

could do was to change 'through' into 'by means of.'" Dewey
wrote to Beacon the same day, "Change 'through' to 'by means
of.'" [171]

Neither the original typed reply Dewey sent to JP nor the carbon copy sent to Bentley is extant. The closest thing to that document is the JP transcription (JPTR) that Schneider sent to Balz.
Substantive variants from JP and JPTR are listed in Substantive
Variants in *Knowing and the Known,* and JPTR is credited as the
source of accidentals emendations. The Ratner-Bentley version
has no authority.

Dewey's reply to Balz is also published as chapter 6, "In De-
fense of the Theory of Inquiry," in *On Experience, Nature and
Freedom,* ed. Richard J. Bernstein (Indianapolis, Ind.: Bobbs-
Merrill Co., 1960), pp. 133–49.

In the present edition, the subhead "Dewey's Reply to Albert
G. A. Balz" replaces the KK "A Letter from John Dewey" on the
contents page and has been added to the appendix title as an
emendation. KK endnotes appear as footnotes in the present edition. The index prepared by Altman and Bentley and revised by
Dewey has been incorporated in the index to the present edition.
Emendations of copy-text appear in the Emendations List identified by source, either the journal publication or Works emendations made here for the first time.

TYPESCRIPTS

What Is It to Be a Linguistic Sign or Name?

The preface to *Knowing and the Known* [this volume,
pp. 4–5] states: "As continuance of our present work we hope
the future will see the completion of papers on the . . . significance of the wide range of employment, both philosophically
and in practical life, of the word 'sign' in recent generations."
The subject of signs had periodically interested Dewey. See, for
example, "Peirce's Theory of Linguistic Signs, Thought, and

---

171. Dewey to Bentley, 12 July 1949, Bentley Collection; Dewey to Beacon Press,
12 July 1949, Beacon Press Papers.

Meaning," *Journal of Philosophy* 43 (14 February 1946): 85–95 [*Later Works* 15 : 141–52].

In July 1944 Dewey sent Bentley a typescript entitled "Concerning Signs," on which Bentley afterward noted: "7–31–44 See also later draft 5–25–45."[1] This "later draft" is "What Is It to Be a Linguistic Sign or Name?" In December Dewey wrote to Bentley, "I never did anything with the paper on signs I started last summer." Attaching two pages of notes, Dewey explained, "The enclosed is an attempt to remedy that defect."[2] Dewey wrote to Bentley the following spring, "I looked over my old paper on 'signs' and started rewriting it." Dewey discussed his "emphasis in the revision" and explained that he had "made some progress because of our correspondence."[3]

Stealing time from the articles he was collaborating on with Bentley, Dewey completed and sent the revised, eighteen-page typescript "What Is It to Be a Linguistic Sign or Name?" to Bentley on 25 May 1945. In his letter of the same date he wrote:

I feel ashamed about the enclosed; I had no business switching off for even two days from the job immediately afoot. I can only say there was a kind of inward pressure that made me feel I had to do it—a sort of getting a memorandum of my development since writing the Logic. It was rather dashed off; I havent even stopped to make typographical corrections and needs no attention till the Journal articles are finished. When they are done Ill consider rewriting with view to publication, perhaps Philosophy of Science.[4]

Bentley dated the typescript "5–25–45" and, referring to "Concerning Signs," wrote at the top of the first page, "See first Draft with Letter 7–31–44."[5]

Dewey continued work on the subject; he wrote to Bentley one month later, "Instigated by what you said about my sign paper

1. "Concerning Signs," carbon copy, Bentley Collection, 13 pp. A photocopy of this document is in the Ratner/Dewey Papers, Box 44, folder 4.
2. Dewey to Bentley, 19 December 1944, Bentley Collection.
3. Dewey to Bentley, 12 May 1945, ibid. On 21 December 1944 Bentley had written to Dewey about "a way of broadening the procedure" (ibid.).
4. Dewey to Bentley, 25 May 1945, ibid.
5. "What Is It to Be a Linguistic Sign or Name?" ibid., 18 pp. A photocopy of this document is in the Ratner/Dewey Papers, Box 46, folder 4.

and the specification article [see this volume, pp. 131–53] I sat down and write the enclosed—not for publication but as evidence of good faith."[6] For this typescript,[7] see this volume, Note on "What Is It to Be a Linguistic Sign or Name?"

Although Dewey planned to return to the subject, he apparently never did. He wrote to Bentley in late 1945, "I am not doing anything now with my sign paper; your comments and my further reflections showed me it needed development."[8] In 1947, considering an article on the subject for inclusion in *Knowing and the Known,* Dewey wrote, "You may remember I once wrote a paper on Signs, or 'Representation' and Signs. It didnt come off, or rather I got off the track in one or two places I might like to try again."[9] Bentley replied that Dewey's previous paper had been "collateral to what we have been doing," but that his "proposed new try at it might perhaps produce just what is needed." He asked if Dewey could "perhaps make such a paper deliberately into a concluding chapter."[10] A year later, however, as publication of *Knowing and the Known* drew nearer, Dewey adopted a tone of resignation: "Ive always meant to do another" paper on Signs "and do it nearer right, but Ive had too many other things. And I cant do it now or in time to get it in."[11]

Although not the ultimate formulation Dewey had hoped for, "What Is It to Be a Linguistic Sign or Name?" represents his final statement on the subject and merits inclusion among his collected works. It is published here for the first time. Copy-text for this paper is the unpublished typescript in the Arthur F. Bentley Collection, Manuscripts Department, Lilly Library, Indiana University, Bloomington, 18 pp. Pp. 4, 12, 13, and 14 are ribbon copies; the rest are carbon copies. See Alterations in Manuscripts for Dewey's changes. Except for the silent correction of clearly mechanical typewriting errors, such as "ficitious" for "fictitious"

6. Dewey to Bentley, 23 June 1945, Bentley Collection. See Bentley to Dewey, 19 June 1945, ibid.
7. Original, ibid., 3 pp. Bentley typed on p. 1: "Following is new start for Sign paper sent 5–25 see comments his letter 6–23–45." Although Dewey wrote on p. 1 "I have carbon," no carbon has been located. A photocopy of this "new start" is in the Ratner/Dewey Papers, Box 46, folder 4, 3 pp.
8. Dewey to Bentley, 8 December 1945, Bentley Collection.
9. Dewey to Bentley, 15 May 1947, ibid.
10. Bentley to Dewey, 20 May 1947, ibid.
11. Dewey to Bentley, 8 May 1948, ibid.

at 299n.3, emendations made for this edition are listed in the Emendations List.

Values, Valuations, and Social Facts

This is a reply Dewey wrote in response to Emile Benoit-Smullyan's "Value Judgments and the Social Sciences," *Journal of Philosophy* 42 (13 April 1945): 197–210. On 22 May 1945 Dewey informed George R. Geiger that he had "written a reply" which he hoped "to get in shape to send in soon."[12] On 20 June he sent this reply to Bentley, writing:

> First about that value article in Jn. It was such a terrible mix-up and I have written on that very topic before[13] was so stirred up I sat down and dashed off something. I never did anything with what I wrote, just got it off my chest and thought I could use of it in a systematic article later on the whole subject—that is the subject of Values, Valuations and sociological subjectmatter; I started collecting material on the topic quite a while ago. But as you have look at the Jn article I send you a copy, uncorrected, of what I wrote.[14]

Bentley noted on the signed, nine-page typescript at the upper right-hand corner, p. 1: "By John Dewey 1945 see his letter 6–20–45." Attached are Bentley's typed notes, 1 p.[15]

Dewey mentioned this article almost three years later: "I wrote a reply but never sent it in—[Benoit-Smullyan] didnt seem worth it."[16] In early 1949 Dewey wrote to Bentley, "I wrote and still have in mss a reply to something he wrote years ago on Value published in the Journal Phil. He was terribly and yet rather instructively mixed up—I mean by the latter word he showed up the current state of the subject."[17]

Dewey wrote in the above 1949 letter that he still had the reply in manuscript; when he sent Bentley the typescript in 1945, he

12. Dewey to Geiger, 22 May 1945, copy, in Ratner/Dewey Papers.
13. For Dewey's article one year earlier, see "Some Questions about Value," *Journal of Philosophy* 41 (17 August 1944): 449–55 [*Later Works* 15:101–8].
14. Dewey to Bentley, 20 June 1945, Bentley Collection.
15. "Values, Valuations, and Social Facts," ibid., 9 pp., with Bentley's notes, 1 p.
16. Dewey to Bentley, 13 April 1948, ibid.
17. Dewey to Bentley, 13 February 1949, ibid.

had written, "I have a carbon so dont bother to return it." [18] In the John Dewey Papers, Box 55, folder 1, Special Collections, Morris Library, Southern Illinois University at Carbondale, is an earlier, incomplete (pp. 3–10), original typescript that does not correspond to the complete document in the Bentley Collection.

Never submitted to the *Journal of Philosophy*, this reply is published here for the first time. Copy-text is the signed, ribbon-copy typescript in the Arthur F. Bentley Collection, Manuscripts Department, Lilly Library, Indiana University, Bloomington, 9 pp. Dewey's alterations in the document are listed in Alterations in Manuscripts. Except for the silent correction of clearly mechanical typewriting errors, such as "consewuence" for "consequence" at 313.2, emendations made for this edition appear in the Emendations List.

Importance, Significance, and Meaning

Dewey's correspondence reveals that he considered this essay important and that he planned to publish it. Although he obviously worked on it long and hard, for a number of reasons— illness, age, possibly the demanding subjectmatter—he never succeeded in completing it to his satisfaction.

On 24 January 1950 Dewey wrote to Bentley from New York City, "I have just been writing something for the Journal which was going to you as soon as properly typed. . . . The nominal title is Importance, Significance, Meaning." [19] Three weeks later Dewey wrote from Key West, Florida: "Ive spent a lot more time on the article I referred to—an attempt to make a condensed restatement of the K & K point of view from the standpoint of everyday material, than I expected. I still have to get a revised copy properly retyped, but I hope it will get to you within the next fortnight." [20]

Dewey wrote to others about this paper: to Sidney Hook, "Ive been at work on an article for the Jn to restate the theory of knowing"; and to John D. Graves, "For a month Ive been stead-

18. Dewey to Bentley, 20 June 1945, ibid.
19. Dewey to Bentley, 24 January 1950, ibid.
20. Dewey to Bentley, 17 February 1950, ibid.

ily at work writing and rewriting an article for a journal of philosophy try to outline a theory of how we know and what we know on the basis of facts that can be observed." [21]

On March 10 Dewey wrote to Bentley: "I suppose Ive dribbled and dripped well over a hundred pages in the article I spoke [of]; its now down to 18 type-written pages, largely lines double spaced." He expected "to get my mss off tomorrow for retyping." [22] Ten days later he reported to Bentley, "I got off my Journal article today. . . . The idea is not new; but Ive introduced a new angle." [23] On the same day, Dewey informed Adelbert Ames, Jr., that he had asked the typist "to send you a carbon. My mss is in such shape she may not be able to get it all in proper shape but that is my fault not hers, and I hoped the sense would be gettatable even if there are still typing errors." [24]

Dewey was referring here to having sent his typescript to Alma Fogarty, New York City, whom he asked to retype it with several copies and send one directly to Bentley. Early in April Dewey wrote to Bentley about the copy Fogarty sent to him: "Im ashamed I let the carbons go out in such terrible shape; I had left out one page entirely, and my typing was illegible in a number of places and the typist had to guess on material she isnt particularly familiar with at best." [25]

A few days later Dewey wrote to Bentley about publication: "I am of two minds about the idea of sending the article where it might reach a scientific public; I dont think 'Science' would take it; the Scientific Monthly might." [26] He described to Hook his hopes for the article: "I think if I can only get it stated it is the most accurate and the most comprehensive statement of what Ive been driving at that Ive ever made." [27] Dewey wrote to Ames about "another attempt" and promised him a copy. [28]

21. Dewey to Hook, 25 February 1950, Hook/Dewey Collection; Dewey to Graves, 10 March 1950, Dewey Papers.
22. Dewey to Bentley, 10 March 1950, Bentley Collection.
23. Dewey to Bentley, 20 March 1950, ibid.
24. Dewey to Ames, 20 March 1950, Dartmouth Eye Institute Papers.
25. Dewey to Bentley, 5 April 1950, Bentley Collection. Dewey also apologized to Ames (12 April 1950, Dartmouth Eye Institute Papers).
26. Dewey to Bentley, 10 April 1950, Bentley Collection.
27. Dewey to Hook, 11 April 1950, Hook/Dewey Collection.
28. Dewey to Ames, 12 April 1950, Dartmouth Eye Institute Papers.

Still recovering from a virus attack, Dewey returned to work; he wrote to Bentley on 19 April, "I am at least out of bed and have done a little typing re-writing the importance piece," which, however, was "going to have the disadvantage I fear of being too long to come out in one issue." [29]

In late May Dewey described to Bentley his "three attempts" to start over again: "the first two went into the [wastebasket] after two or three pages; the last one is still under consideration." [30] Dewey succeeded in preparing a new section, writing to Bentley on 4 June: "Well Ive finally made a stab at rewriting the importance article. The enclosed as prefatory may [be] off the beam. But from my point of view it is reasonably accurate." [31] Interestingly, this time around, Dewey typed a serial comma in the title after "Significance." Bentley commented on this section, "I have read several times the prefatory pages for your Importance paper. I do not find a thing that I would suggest to change or to add." [32]

Although Dewey wrote to Bentley about plans to revise, [33] he did not submit the article for publication. He later explained to Ames:

Nothing has been done about the Importance article. For some unknown reason one page was missing from the sheets I sent to have properly retyped; by the time I got around to attending to the gap, I was down with a rather severe virus attack, and the after effects, in connection with other deficiencies proper at my age prevented my doing any intellectual work at all for about six months. [34]

To Bentley's query about the article's publication Dewey replied, "I never tried to do anything with it." [35] Several months later Bentley described to Joseph Ratner his "urging" Dewey to publish this essay, which not only he but "several other" of Dewey's

29. Dewey to Bentley, 19 April 1950, Bentley Collection.
30. Dewey to Bentley, 21 May 1950, ibid.
31. Dewey to Bentley, 4 June 1950, ibid.
32. Bentley to Dewey, 8 June 1950, Dewey Papers and Bentley Collection.
33. Dewey to Bentley, 19 June 1950, Bentley Collection and Dewey Papers.
34. Dewey to Ames, 9 November 1950, Dartmouth Eye Institute Papers.
35. Bentley to Dewey, 14 February 1951, Dewey Papers and Bentley Collection; Dewey to Bentley, 21 February 1951, Bentley Collection.

"friends had examined." However, "nothing came of it, so far as I know, and I was afraid I had pushed it too hard. It seemed to all of us to need a little more high-pressurizing, and that was all. But if he was not feeling up to it, then, of course, it should not be done."[36]

Two authoritative typescripts have been located for this essay: a carbon copy, on onionskin, in the John Dewey Papers (DTS), Box 58, folder 9, Special Collections, Morris Library, Southern Illinois University at Carbondale, 23 pp.; and a carbon copy, on light-weight bond, in the Arthur F. Bentley Collection (BTS), Manuscripts Department, Lilly Library, Indiana University, Bloomington, 23 pp. At the top of p. 1 on the copy Fogarty sent to Dewey is written, not in Dewey's hand: "Rec'd 3/30/50 from Mrs. A. Fogarty, 1305 / Amsterdam Ave / NY 27" (DTS). At the top of p. 1 on the copy sent to him, Bentley noted: "Received from Mrs A Fogarty / 1305 Amsterdam Ave NY — / 3–31–50" (BTS).

Fogarty made at least four additional copies of the typescript for Ames, Graves, Ratner (all sent directly to them),[37] and probably one for publication. Since she could not make that many copies in a single sitting, she had to type the essay twice, with two sets of carbon copies; DTS and BTS represent these two sittings. Similar (both carbon copies, both twenty-three pages) but clearly not identical, they differ in minor ways, such as Fogarty's corrections of errors and pagination, as well as a few substantives. Since both typescripts obviously stem from the same missing basic document, they have equal authority.[38]

36. Bentley to Ratner, 6 December 1951, Ratner/Dewey Papers.
37. Ames wrote to Dewey on 7 April 1950, "I got your manuscript 'Importance, Significance and Meaning' a few days ago" (Dartmouth Eye Institute Papers). Graves wrote to Dewey on 2 April 1950, "Friday I received from Mrs. Fogarty a copy of your article entitled 'Importance, Significance and Meaning'" (Dewey Papers). On 24 March 1950 Ratner wrote to Dewey, "I haven't heard from Miss Fogerty. I'm looking forward to the article" (Ratner/Dewey Papers). On 30 March 1950 Ratner wrote, "I've just rec'd and read the article on Importance" (Dewey Papers). The typescript Fogarty sent to Ratner (Ratner/Dewey Papers, Box 45, folder 3, 23 pp.) is a carbon copy identical to DTS, but on light-weight bond instead of onionskin.
38. See Fredson Bowers, "Multiple Authority: New Problems and Concepts of Copy-Text," *Essays in Bibliography, Text, and Editing* (Charlottesville: University Press of Virginia, 1975), pp. 447–87.

As Dewey's rewritten "prefatory" section, sent to Bentley on 4 June 1950, represents his later intentions for this section, it appears for the first time in the present edition at 318.1–320.14. Writing to Dewey early in 1951 about manuscripts Dewey had let him "see during the past year," Bentley listed "Importance, Significance and Meaning Draft with a page 9 of the earlier copy missing in this copy Sent 3–31–50 New Introduction to this paper, about 3 pp, sent sometime later."[39] Referring to this new section, Bentley noted at the top of p. 1 in Fogarty's typescript: "See a 3-page later substitute for Note 1" (BTS).

Copy-text for the introductory section at 318.1–320.14, therefore, is the unpublished, original typescript in the Arthur F. Bentley Collection, Manuscripts Department, Lilly Library, Indiana University, Bloomington, 3 pp. (a photocopy of this document is in the Joseph Ratner/John Dewey Papers, Box 45, folder 3, Special Collections, Morris Library, Southern Illinois University at Carbondale). Dewey's alterations are listed in Alterations in Manuscripts.

Copy-text for the remainder of the essay is a conflation of the carbon copy of the typescript, typed by Fogarty, in the Dewey Papers, and the carbon copy of the typescript, also typed by Fogarty, in the Bentley Collection. Substantive variants between the two documents have been recorded in the Emendations List. Emendations have been accepted from the essay's publication in *John Dewey and Arthur F. Bentley: A Philosophical Correspondence, 1932–1951*, ed. Sidney Ratner and Jules Altman (New Brunswick, N.J.: Rutgers University Press, 1964), pp. 658–68. For Dewey's superseded introductory section, see *Philosophical Correspondence*, pp. 657–58.

Dewey made several markings on DTS in blue-green ink; underlinings and some marginal marks appear at 321.6–7 ("inquiry . . . ways,"), 323.4–5 ("determination of subjectmatters"), 328.7 ("magic"), 328.16 ("theory."), and 330.9–10 ("historical absentmindedness"). Additional, more generalized marginal vertical strokes, possibly indicating a need for further revision, appear at 326.3–9 ("Another . . . operates"), 326.17–19 ("On . . . function."), 326.24–30 ("those . . . inquiries."[2]), 327.1–8

39. Bentley to Dewey, 14 February 1951, Dewey Papers and Bentley Collection.

("use . . . concern."), 327.11–14 ("There . . . food."), 327.23–24 ("To . . . civilization."), 327.25–29 ("but . . . theory."), 327.33–38 ("—and . . . estate."), 328.34–38 ("*De facto* . . . existence."), 329.22–330.6 ("Even . . . intention."), 330.24–32 ("It . . . respect."), 331.3–8 ("knowing . . . incurred."), and 332.16–24 ("Only . . . important.").

In the Dewey Papers (Box 58, folders 15 and 17; Box 59, folders 1 and 2) are early draft pages for this essay; the missing page that both Dewey and the typist mentioned (see emendation at 325.32–33) is not among them.

Also in the Dewey Papers (Box 58, folder 16) are pages showing the revision attempts Dewey described in the April to November 1950 correspondence cited above. In addition to the carbon from one set of typing (DTS), Fogarty sent Dewey the ribbon copy from both sets of typing (DTS and BTS), which differ slightly in pagination, lineation, and a few substantives. Dewey then revised these two ribbon copies.

There are extant thirty-one assorted pages from these two sets, twenty-five of which have Dewey's typed and holographic revisions (in blue ink, black ink, and pencil). In several instances Dewey revised the same page from each set; these dual revisions vary considerably in medium, extent, and substance, with few changes in common. Therefore, Dewey apparently made at least two independent revision attempts without trying to incorporate earlier changes into the later revision. The chronology cannot be satisfactorily determined from either the media used or the pagination sequence (a possible exception being the few pages designated "A," which may represent a later revision). Since Dewey's final intent cannot be established, it is not possible to construct a complete viable revised text. In several instances, however, emendations have been adopted from Dewey's revisions as corrections of copy-text: see, for example, emendations at 325.25 and 326.12–13. The original pages matching DTS are designated TS[1], those matching BTS designated TS[2].

Conflicting, incomplete, frequently illegible and ambiguous, the revisions on TS[1] and TS[2] attest to the effects of age and illness that Dewey described. At the same time, however, they reveal Dewey's remarkable continuing intellectual activity at the age of ninety-one. All are listed in Dewey's Revisions in "Importance, Significance, and Meaning."

How, What, and *What For* in Social Inquiry

Recovering from a long, weakening illness (what he referred to as a "virus attack"), Dewey began work on what was probably—aside from a few, brief miscellaneous items—the last paper he wrote for publication. He dated his manuscript 15 and 16 December 1950, entitled it "Means and Consequences—*How, What,* and *what for,*" and apparently asked Joseph Ratner (who had worked closely with him on many pieces, including his revised introduction to *Experience and Nature*) to prepare it for the typist and edit where necessary. Ratner, in turn, clearly wrote out illegible words, deleted and rewrote two passages (adding the instruction "see over" for one), made a few changes, and typed three pages.[40]

Within two weeks Dewey received copies of the professionally prepared, thirteen-page typescript, two carbons of which went to Ratner.[41] From New York City on 2 January 1951 Dewey sent a carbon to Bentley, writing: "We are leaving for Honolulu in a few days; I am hoping the change in climate will do me some good. . . . I wrote the enclosed pages on Means-Consequences while in bed. Its a first draft and unfinished. I may feel like working on it on the boat or in Honolulu."[42]

Bentley received the typescript on 5 January and replied two days later:

You certainly have put your long illness to admirable use. You have distilled out of the many possible words a direct

40. Ratner/Dewey Papers, Box 45, folder 7, 20 pp.: pp. 1–17 handwritten by Dewey with Ratner's clarifications; pp. 18–20 typed by Ratner, probably from Dewey's undecipherable material. Dewey numbered holograph pages 1A–17A at the upper left-hand corner; Ratner wrote and encircled page numbers 1–20 at the upper right-hand corner. Holograph pages beyond 17A are no longer extant. This document is considered precopy-text for Dewey's paper.
41. "Means and Consequences—*How, What,* and *What For,*" ibid., 2 carbon copies, 13 pp. each.
42. Dewey to Bentley, 2 January 1951, Bentley Collection.

straight presentation which, if grasped as it ought to be grasped by the people concerned, would quadruple-power investigation all along the line. I especially liked the paper because, every page, probably without exception, gave some new inspection of the situation—the simple direct kinds that count.[43]

In this letter Bentley went on to discuss Dewey's word choices and readership. Noticing that Dewey spoke of "this Journal," meaning *Journal of Philosophy,* Bentley wondered whether he had "given up the idea of the wider audience of inquirers." If Dewey did want to go "further afield," Bentley suggested as "a quick and easy solution" that he expand his subtitle to read "*How, What,* and *What For* in the Social Sciences."

During his month in Honolulu, Hawaii, Dewey stayed at the Halekulani Hotel on Waikiki Beach. Dewey wrote to Bentley from Honolulu on 18 January: "Got here this AM & found your letter—My memory still suffers from the virus blackout & I cant recal the piece you speak of & don't know whether I have a copy—if so Ill see the changes you suggest are made."[44] However, three days later Dewey wrote, "I find I have a copy with me of the How, What & What For article, and am making the changes indicated in your note. I am referring to previous article ["Common Sense and Science"] with mention of where it was published but *not* to 'this Journal'—However I dont know where to send it instead."[45]

One week later Bentley wrote, "I don't want to go too far in making suggestions about your How, what and what for paper," but thought that with some revisions "it would be fine for Scientific Monthly."[46] Dewey wrote in early February from Honolulu, "The sunshine has been grateful but I can't report any great improvement in my medical condition." He hoped, however, "to

43. Bentley to Dewey, 7 January 1951, Dewey Papers and Bentley Collection. Bentley noted on the typescript: "Received 1–5–51 from JD" (carbon copy, Bentley Collection, 13 pp.). For Bentley's consecutive notes after first, second, third, and fourth readings, see "Dewey Mns / Means and Consequences," 5 and 8 January, 14 February 1951, 4 pp., filed with Dewey's typescript.
44. Dewey to Bentley, 18 January 1951, ibid.
45. Dewey to Bentley, 21 January 1951, ibid.
46. Bentley to Dewey, 28 January 1951, ibid.

get my paper off . . . before long" to Howard A. Meyerhoff, *Scientific Monthly* editor, and was "changing the title in accord" with Bentley's suggestion.[47]

On 19 February Dewey wrote two similar letters to Bentley from Honolulu, the second of which reads:

> I succeeded in getting a clean copy typed of the "How" article, & have a carbon to send you but as we are leaving here soon may wait till we are in NY City to mail.
>
> In adopting the addition "In Social Inquiry" I have extended the introductory material. . . .[48]

When Dewey left Honolulu in late February, he did not return to New York City but went to Los Angeles, California, and Tucson, Arizona, for medical tests, blood transfusions, and surgery. In April he wrote to Bentley from Tucson that he seemed to be "reaching a stage of recuperation from my hernia operation" in which he could return to considering publication of his "How, What & What For paper." He agreed with Bentley in preferring a journal specializing in scientific rather than philosophic inquiries.[49]

On 21 April Bentley replied: "Fighting a hernia after all the physical struggles you have had is no desirable 'dessert.'" Although "hopeful to see" Dewey's paper "in print," Bentley did

47. Dewey to Bentley, 7 February 1951, ibid. Bentley replied on 14 February making additional suggestions (Dewey Papers and Bentley Collection). For Dewey's changes in response to Bentley's suggestions, see alterations at 333.1–2, 334.1–2, and 336.2–3 in Alterations in Manuscripts. The alteration at 333.1–2 indicates that Dewey began to add "In the Social Sciences," as Bentley had suggested, but changed his mind and wrote "Social" over "the." At 334.1–2 ("basic instead of derived"), Dewey replaced "autonomous" in response to Bentley's suggestion. On 7 January 1951 Bentley had written to Dewey: "There is one word in your paper, and only one, which some way I do not like—and never did like—My trouble is all with the 'feel' of the word, not with your use. This is 'autonomy.' There is too much 'auto' in it, and too much 'nomy.' I know where you began to use it and why. Nevertheless I am happier when I don't see it" (Dewey Papers, Bentley Collection). Dewey replied, "I shall use a paraphrase instead of the word 'autonomy'" (7 February 1951, Bentley Collection).
48. Dewey to Bentley, 19 February 1951, ibid., enclosed in Dewey to Bentley, 21 February 1951. Dewey's first letter: "I have just had a clean copy typed of How What & What For in the Social Sciences expanded somewhat in that the introductory part points out . . ." (ibid.).
49. Dewey to Bentley, 16 April 1951, ibid.

not want to "let it be a burden" for him. "Any paper would have to be fixed up a bit to suit" *Scientific Monthly*. "Last time you wrote," Bentley continued, "you had the manuscript revised— that was before you left Honolulu, and you were planning to send it in to the magazine and I think to send me the revised text after you reached New York." He had shown Dewey's "previous draft" to three people, who were "all anxious to see the paper published."[50] The next day Bentley sent a postcard explaining that he would soon send the address Dewey had requested.[51] A week later he sent Dewey the address of Gladys M. Keener, executive editor, *Scientific Monthly*.[52]

Dewey may have sent his paper to *Scientific Monthly* or may have continued working on it; in any case, the revision prepared in Honolulu was never published. The earlier version, "Means and Consequences—*How, What,* and *What For,*" is published, from the carbon in the Bentley Collection, in *John Dewey and Arthur F. Bentley: A Philosophical Correspondence, 1932–1951,* ed. Sidney Ratner and Jules Altman (New Brunswick, N.J.: Rutgers University Press, 1964), pp. 647–54.

The ribbon copy prepared in Honolulu—possibly submitted for publication or lost as Dewey traveled from place to place—is no longer extant. The Bentley Collection does not contain a carbon of this typescript, indicating that Dewey never sent one to Bentley. If he had, Bentley would surely have written to Dewey about it, made notations about it, and, as with all Dewey's correspondence and typescripts, meticulously catalogued it.

However, in the John Dewey Papers, Box 59, folders 11–13, Special Collections, Morris Library, Southern Illinois University at Carbondale, is a carbon of this typescript, the revision upon which it is based, and other related documents, all of which will be discussed.

Dewey took with him to Honolulu the first, thirteen-page typescript (TS[1]) prepared in New York (carbons of which had been sent to Bentley and Ratner), made changes on pp. 1, 2, 3,

50. Bentley to Dewey, 21 April 1951, ibid. Bentley was sure that Horace Fries, one of the three who had read Dewey's paper, "would be glad" to assist if Dewey wished. For Fries's comments, see "Fries on Dewey paper," 25 February 1951, ibid., 4 pp., filed with Dewey's "Means and Consequences."
51. Bentley to Dewey, [22 April 1951], Dewey Papers.
52. Bentley to Dewey, 30 April 1951, ibid.

and 5, and "extended" it. Dewey used pencil for a few alterations, blue ink for most. In pencil he deleted "Means and Consequences" from the title and added "In Social Inquiry." In blue
ink he added "Page One" at the upper right-hand corner of p. 1
and deleted "M & C" at the upper right-hand corner of pp. 2–13.
In blue ink he began his extension at the foot of p. 13 (340.1–
3, "So . . . recal") and continued it in blue ink (340.3–20, "before . . . situation.") on hotel stationery. When he finished revising, someone at the Halekulani typed a "clean copy" that
incorporated his changes and the text of six sheets of six-by-
seven-inch notepaper imprinted "Halekulani / Honolulu 15, Hawaii." In blue ink at the upper right-hand corner Dewey numbered these sheets pp. 14, 15, 16, 17, 17, 18; entitled pp. 16–18
"How, What & What For"; and signed p. 18. In blue, black, and
green ink he made changes in the holograph addition. The altered thirteen-page TS¹ with Dewey's six-page holograph addition (TS¹⁻ᴴ) is, therefore, assumed to be what was given to the
typist in Honolulu; TS¹⁻ᴴ, clearly authorial, has served as copy-
text for Dewey's paper. The original document is in the Dewey
Papers, Box 59, folder 13. All Dewey's alterations are listed in
Alterations in Manuscripts.

The "clean copy" prepared in Honolulu is, then, the second
typescript (TS²). The TS² carbon in the Dewey Papers (also Box
59, folder 13) is typed on the verso of ten sheets of letter paper
bearing a 1 5/8-by-1 3/4-inch vignette in the upper left-hand corner and imprinted "Halekulani / Honolulu 15, Hawaii." A few
necessary emendations have been accepted from TS², but because the typist was unfamiliar with Dewey's hand, most readings are from the TS¹⁻ᴴ copy-text. All changes in copy-text are
listed in the Emendations List.

Dewey's correspondence reveals that, as was to be expected at
ninety-one, he often felt the effects of age and illness, a condition
causing two problems concerning the relationship of TS¹⁻ᴴ to
TS²: the position of Dewey's holograph addition and the existence of two p. 17s.

It is not clear whether Dewey intended his holograph text
as an insertion or addition. To Bentley he wrote about "extending" and "expanding" the "introductory part" without defining "introductory." In black ink he repaginated pp. 7–12 of the
thirteen-page TS¹⁻ᴴ as pp. 5–10, resulting in the pagination se-

quence 1–6, 5–10, 13. The top of the first renumbered page—
p. 7, renumbered as p. 5—is torn away, either accidentally or to
facilitate an insertion.[53] Dewey did not indicate, however, by any
alteration—mark, line, caret—precisely *where* he wanted to
place the text. Confronted by unclear pagination and instructions, the TS[2] typist merely added on the holograph material.
Since Dewey's intent cannot be determined, TS[2] has not been
emended.

The problem of two p. 17s (17a and 17b) is not a simple case of
mispagination. Based on its linkage in content to other pages and
the significance of Dewey's alterations, 17b seems to be a discarded page inadvertently given to the typist.

17a, beginning "but as" (340.20), flows directly from p. 16,
ending "as the *how* of nature," (340.19–20). On the other hand,
17b (beginning "has broken down") does not flow from p. 16 but
from what is apparently a superseded p. 16 (ending "The Theory
of Relativity").[54] Although 17b does not flow smoothly from 17a,
ending "For." (340.25), the typist managed to include it there by
overlooking the period and inserting "and" before "has broken
down."

P. 18, signed by Dewey, is clearly intended as the final page.
17b (ending with the sentence "But the full significance of Relativity Theory for scientific inquiry will be") flows into the un-
altered p. 18, beginning "achieved" (340.25). 17a, however, flows
into the altered p. 18. 17a ends with the sentence (340.23–25)
"*How* things go on . . . has won the victory over *What* and
What For." In black ink Dewey made three alterations in this
sentence and—directly linking 17a to p. 18—inserted "The victory will be" at the top of p. 18, above the title. The typist, however, unable to include this phrase following 17b, deleted it in
TS[2]. Because 17b flows smoothly neither from the preceding

53. The few lines missing from the TS[1-H] document must have been present
in TS[1-H] as given to the typist because they are present in TS[2] (336.24–29,
"way . . . improvised"; identical text in Bentley and Ratner TS[1] carbons).
54. P. 16, Dewey Papers, Box 59, folder 11. Before he gave his completed revision
to the typist, Dewey had apparently discarded some pages obviously written
at the same time on Halekulani notepaper in blue ink, and entitled "How,
What & What For." Two superseded pages, p. 14 [?] and p. 16, are in folder
11. This folder also contains other drafts written on Halekulani letter paper,
in blue ink but untitled: pp. 2–4 and pp. 8–10, dated 27 January; pp. 4–7,
dated 7 February.

page nor into the succeeding page, Dewey's final intent seems to have been to discard it. In this edition the text of 17b has been deleted and Dewey's inserted phrase restored (see emendations at 340.25). Dewey's alterations on 17b ("hence . . . for") are listed in Alterations in Manuscripts at 340.25.

On TS² are a few revisions, clearly in Joseph Ratner's hand, indicating that Dewey probably gave or sent this TS² carbon to Ratner after returning to New York City. Since it is not known if Dewey ever acknowledged these few changes, they have not been accepted for this edition.

The documents remaining to be discussed concern Ratner's work on the paper after Dewey's death. Dewey gave Ratner not one but two TS² carbons. Ratner made a few changes on one TS² carbon and, as explained above, returned it to Dewey. Probably in 1964, possibly planning to edit Dewey's unpublished writings, Ratner extensively revised the second TS² carbon.[55] He made the footnote on pp. 337–38 part of the text, repositioned after "theory." at 339.17 Dewey's ambiguous "extension," and left unchanged the TS² inclusion of 17a and 17b. After Dewey's reference at 336.3 to "Common Sense and Science" (published in April 1948), Ratner inserted an asterisk, the footnote " *Thomas p 147," and instructed the typist, possibly Alice Davis: "Alice: at this point line clear across page; entire item mentioned in Thomas, p. 147 exactly—another line—Then proceed with text." An edition of Milton Halsey Thomas's bibliography of Dewey was published in 1929 and 1939 by Columbia University Press; in 1962 the University of Chicago Press published Thomas's *A Centennial Bibliography*. Ratner of necessity is referring to the 1962 edition.

The typist prepared a typescript incorporating Ratner's revisions.[56] She and Ratner then made some adjustments to create

55. Ibid., Box 59, folder 13, 10 pp. Slightly darker than the first carbon, the second TS² carbon is typed on identical Halekulani letter paper and bears Ratner's holograph revisions on every page and the verso of p. 1.

56. Ibid., 11 pp. Also extant are the first two pages from another typescript incorporating Ratner's revisions, apparently prepared by Robert Clopton; on the verso of p. 2 is the handwritten note: "Joe: I didn't have time to proofread beyond p. 7. When you mail my copy to me, please, if you will, enclose 'my' copy of the draft from which we worked. Thanks again Bob 12/21/64" (ibid., Box 59, folder 12, 2 pp.). Although the details of this partial typescript are unknown, the 1964 date is significant.

Ratner's final document: corrected a few errors by hand, inserted p. 9 restoring two inadvertently omitted sentences, and attached this typed cover note:

> This article was left unfinished in content and form; the import of the argument for "social inquiry," for example, is barely indicated. The Mss. has been edited by Joseph Ratner.[57]

Because Ratner worked always with Dewey's authorization, and because his revisions create a markedly different document, Dewey's paper edited by Ratner has been included in this volume as Appendix 3.

ESSAYS

The Field of "Value"

Dewey wrote "The Field of 'Value'" for *Value: A Cooperative Inquiry*, edited by Ray Lepley (New York: Columbia University Press, 1949). In his introduction, p. 3, Lepley explains that the "immediate stimulus" to the volume was Dewey's 1944 article "Some Questions about Value,"[1] which challenged others to present their views. "When by the autumn of 1945 no one had responded to this challenge, it was suggested to Dewey that a cooperative study, or symposium, on value might be organized and might take his article as a starting point." As planned by Lepley, participants were to submit questions and comments, which were to be mimeographed and circulated; prepare a draft; exchange papers for criticism; and revise for publication. Participants' further criticisms and rejoinders would be included in the volume.

Completing his essay before a planned trip to China in the spring of 1946, Dewey wrote to Sidney Hook from Key West, Florida: "I was busy writing my piece for the value symposium of Lepleys; have finished it and sent it off to get carbons etc

---

57. Final document, with Ratner's note, ibid., 12 pp.
  1. *Journal of Philosophy* 41 (17 August 1944): 449–55 [*Later Works* 15 : 101–8]. "Some Questions about Value" is reprinted in the introduction to *Value*, pp. 4–12.

made. Its earlier I guess than the date set, but if I should go to China, Ill have no chance to work on it later. So instead of making a draft I tried to do the whole business independently of comments supposed to be made on the draft. . . . If I get carbon in time Ill send you one."[2]

He informed Hook two weeks later that he had "an extra carbon or so of my Value piece, which Ive called The Field of Value" and might mail him one; "I got off the set of four to Lepley not long ago."[3] Apparently Dewey did not mail a carbon to Hook, since he wrote to him in April: "I suppose Lepley would circulate the 4 copies I sent him from K. W. right away so you would have had one before this. I've just learned he had been holding them till the date officially set for all papers. I have an extra copy. Could you come in sometime Sat?"[4]

Dewey also discussed his essay with Joseph Ratner, writing to him in March about one thing he "forgot to put in" along the line of Ratner's query about Dewey's position on ethical theory.[5]

Writing to Hook about drafts he received, Dewey evaluated papers by Henry David Aiken, Philip Blair Rice, A. Campbell Garnett, and Stephen C. Pepper in March; in June he commented that DeWitt H. Parker's was "hopelessly subjective I should say from a hasty reading."[6] Dewey, however, contributed no criticisms to the volume and no rejoinder to Garnett's criticism of his essay. Remaining contributors were C. E. Ayres, George R. Geiger, Lewis E. Hahn, Bertram E. Jessup, Harold N. Lee, E. T. Mitchell, and Charles Morris.

In February 1948 Lepley wrote to contributors about publication of the volume then entitled *Symposium on Value*, which he hoped to have ready for use as a text by the following autumn.[7] After comparing proposals by Harvard University Press and Columbia University Press, he wrote that he was selecting Columbia. Lepley reported that most contributors had rejected the proposal to economize by omitting criticisms and rejoinders from the volume. He suggested omitting the planned bibliography on

2. Dewey to Hook, 8 March [1946], Hook/Dewey Collection.
3. Dewey to Hook, 22 March 1946, ibid.
4. Dewey to Hook, 10 April [1946], ibid.
5. Dewey to Ratner, 25 March 1946, Ratner/Dewey Papers.
6. Dewey to Hook, 22 March 1946 and 27 June [1946], Hook/Dewey Collection.
7. Lepley to Symposium Colleague, 16 February 1948, Dewey Papers.

value; contributors apparently approved, since the volume includes no bibliography.

In this letter Lepley described his minimal editorial alterations "to make the manuscript more uniform," involving, for instance, deletion of titles and regularization of footnotes. He added the following note to Dewey explaining revisions necessitated by the omission of material from the introduction:

> In order to adjust to the omission of the preliminary "questions and comments," I have in your paper inserted this footnote [343n.1−2] after the question you quote page 1 from Pepper: "Contained in the preliminary questions and comments submitted to this symposium." On page 5 line 1 [345.30], I have inserted the word "preliminary" before the word "question," and deleted the first sentence from the footnote which follows [see emendation at 345n.4]. The footnote on page 6 I have changed by adding "preliminary" before the word "question"; by substituting "especially" for "particularly"; and by deleting the sentence which was enclosed in parentheses [346n.1−2; see emendation at 346n.3]. On page 13 [351.2−4], I revised the first sentence of section IV to read: "Some of the material found in the questions and comments submitted at the beginning of this symposium give evidence . . . etc." And the footnote on page 14 [351n.1] I changed to: "Statement by Rice in the preliminary questions and comments."

Dewey finally received proof in January 1949; he commented to Boyd H. Bode that "It must [be] three years now" since he had written this article. Lepley had "spent the intervening time trying to get a publisher. I got the proof last week & that after indemnity money had been put up."[8]

Reviews of the symposium volume, published by Columbia University Press in 1949, were generally favorable.[9] Two reviewers suggested that the plan of including criticisms and rejoinders be

8. Dewey to Bode, 22 January 1949, private collection of Eleanor Bode Browne.
9. *Value: A Cooperative Inquiry* was reviewed in *Hibbert Journal* (London) 48 (July 1950): 396 (F. H. Heinemann); *Journal of Philosophy* 48 (25 October 1951): 705−6 (Charles A. Baylis); *Library Journal* 74 (15 December 1949): 1902−3; *Mind* 60 (July 1951): 430−33 (R. M. Hare); *Philosophical Review* 60 (1951): 99−101 (William K. Frankena); *Review of Metaphysics* 4 (Sep-

used for other symposia.[10] According to Iredell Jenkins, the study "explored in all its detail" the "complexity of the value-act."[11]

William K. Frankena found Dewey's essay "interesting but not surprising or clarifying" and Dewey's views "the main storm center of the discussion."[12]

Reviewers disagreed about Dewey's influence: the *Times Literary Supplement* found most contributors to this "lively" exchange of views "docile to Professor Dewey's pragmatic and humanistic approach."[13] Charles A. Baylis, however, thought that many paid Dewey's queries "only a polite bow" and developed their own "special theses."[14] Frankena, Jenkins, and James L. Jarrett observed that not all schools of thought were represented; R. M. Hare noted contributors' "common presuppositions."[15]

Baylis, calling the collective effect "scattering," preferred "fewer essays, longer and better integrated"; Jarrett, however, judged the "closely reasoned" essays complementary.[16] The *United States Quarterly Book List* said that, "considering the chaotic state of value theory today," the study was "too minute and controversial" for the general reader but "a windfall" for students of the subject.[17]

After publishing the book, Columbia University Press returned printer's copy typescript to editor Ray Lepley, whose widow, Maud A. Lepley, graciously gave that document to the Center for Dewey Studies in December 1987. It is now housed at Southern Illinois University at Carbondale (Dewey VFM 87, Special Collections, Morris Library).

tember 1950): 96–104 (Iredell Jenkins); *Saturday Review of Literature* 33 (6 May 1950): 60 (Robert Bierstedt); *School and Society* 70 (17 December 1949): 416; *Times* (London) *Literary Supplement*, 23 June 1950, p. 393; *U.S. Quarterly Book List* 6 (March 1950): 31; and *Western Humanities Review* 5 (Spring 1951): 207–8 (James L. Jarrett).
10. Robert Bierstedt, *Saturday Review of Literature*, p. 60; James L. Jarrett, *Western Humanities Review*, p. 207.
11. Jenkins, *Review of Metaphysics*, p. 99.
12. Frankena, *Philosophical Review*, p. 99.
13. *Times Literary Supplement*, p. 393.
14. Baylis, *Journal of Philosophy*, p. 705.
15. Frankena, *Philosophical Review*, p. 99; Jenkins, *Review of Metaphysics*, p. 96; Jarrett, *Western Humanities Review*, p. 207; Hare, *Mind*, p. 430.
16. Baylis, *Journal of Philosophy*, p. 705; Jarrett, *Western Humanities Review*, p. 208.
17. *U.S. Quarterly Book List*, p. 31.

The ribbon copy twenty-four-page typescript (TS), not typed by Dewey, that was used for printer's copy is copy-text for this essay. On printer's copy (PC) are various markings not made by Dewey: those by Lepley in ink and those by Columbia University Press (CUP) in pencil and colored pencil.

Since Dewey wrote to Bode in January 1949 that he "got the proof last week," he was aware of changes made both by Lepley and CUP in PC. For the present edition, PC substantive changes have been accepted as authoritative.

The required revisions Lepley had described appear in PC and have been accepted. Other substantive changes made by Lepley and accepted as approved by Dewey include, for instance, those in the quotation at 351.18–28 and in the sentence at 357.5–7 (see textual notes for these and other revisions by Lepley). Lepley's editorial, stylistic changes, however, such as deleting titles, have not been accepted; the TS "Mr." and "Dr." have been restored throughout.

Markings made by CUP in PC include, in addition to printing specifications (in lead pencil and blue, green, and purple pencil), changes in substantives and accidentals (in red pencil). Most substantive changes have been accepted (see, for instance, textual notes for 354.23 and 355.4–5). However, accidentals and stylistic changes (several of which CUP queried "OK?" in the margin) have been rejected in favor of the TS spelling and punctuation idiosyncrasies: for instance, "etc." instead of the PC "and so on" throughout, double punctuation (both colon and dash after "methodological" at 343.3), and word forms ("ground work" instead of the PC "groundwork" at 353.22–23 and "class-membership" instead of the PC "class membership" at 354.26). The TS designation of subheads, a formal matter, has been silently maintained (for instance, "(1)" instead of the PC "1." at 345.17 and "(i)" instead of the PC "(a)" at 352.28).

Collation of TS and PC against the published version in *Value: A Cooperative Inquiry*, ed. Ray Lepley (New York: Columbia University Press, 1949), pp. 64–77 (V), reveals that Dewey made further revisions in proof. Lepley undoubtedly read proof also and made some revisions, such as those at 343n.1–2 and 351.2–3 necessitated by the change of volume title from *Symposium in Value*. Substantive changes in V have been considered authoritative and accepted as emendations. In the cases of V errors, the

TS/PC substantive has been restored (for example, "become" instead of "became" at 352.24). Accidentals changes in V, however (including the change of the TS/PC "esthetic" to "aesthetic," undoubtedly made by Lepley for uniformity in the volume), have not been accepted.

The Emendations List for this essay, recording all variants between TS, PC, and V, serves as a historical collation.

Collation of V against a second printing in 1951 revealed no changes in Dewey's essay.

In the John Dewey Papers, Box 58, folder 6, Special Collections, Morris Library, Southern Illinois University at Carbondale, are the last two pages of a carbon copy of the typescript used as printer's copy. For Dewey's ink alterations in one sentence, see textual note for 357.5–7. Since Dewey read and revised proof, the published version has been accepted as his final intention.

Has Philosophy a Future?

Dewey wrote this paper to be read by Sidney Hook at the Tenth International Congress of Philosophy, held in Amsterdam from 11 to 18 August 1948. He wrote to Hook on 9 June that he hoped "to have paper ready" soon "if I can only stop rewriting."[18] In early July, recovering from a tonsillectomy, Dewey wrote to Hook, "I hope I can get something to you before Aug 1." His title, he thought, would be "Is there a Possibility for Philosophy? or to that effect."[19]

In late July from Hubbards, Nova Scotia, Dewey mailed his completed paper directly to Amsterdam, writing to Hook:

It has taken some days longer than I expected to do the Amsterdam paper. I am [now] in the state where I am doubtful whether I did not try something too ambitious—perhaps pretentious would be the better name. A more immediate trouble is that it is probably too long, though I dont know what the time limit is. If, as I fear, it is too long (and I have left a lot out which could and should be said) and the time

18. Dewey to Hook, 9 June 1948, Hook/Dewey Collection.
19. Dewey to Hook, 11 July 1948, ibid.

rule is held to rather strictly, I dont see but Ill have to impose upon you making the necessary excisions. If I could have finished it a week earlier I could have sent it to a typist in N Y to make a clean typescript. As it is I am afraid the best you can receive will be a fairly legible mss. . . .

As you will note, I have not given the paper a title. "Has Philosophy a Future?" is about the best Ive been able to think of. But I thought you after reading it might hit something better. The challenge-opportunity theme is supposed to run thru the paper but I havent seen any way to employ it in the title that isnt awkward.[20]

World War II had interrupted the philosophy congresses (the Ninth International Congress of Philosophy had been held in 1937 in Paris), and the Cold War affected the Tenth Congress.[21] The congress was structured so that plenary sessions were held in the morning, concurrent sessions in the afternoon. The United Nations Educational, Scientific, and Cultural Organization (UNESCO) sponsored three afternoon sessions for the discussion of international problems; Hook read Dewey's paper at the second session, "La liberté et son fondement," on 14 August, 2:00 P.M. The first and third UNESCO sessions, 13 and 16 August, were entitled "Les fondements philosophiques de l'Humanisme" and "Les différentes conceptions de la démocratie et leurs fondements philosophiques."

Dewey's paper was published in *Proceedings of the Tenth International Congress of Philosophy* (Amsterdam, 11–18 August 1948), ed. E. W. Beth, H. J. Pos, and J. H. A. Hollak (Amsterdam: North-Holland Publishing Co., 1949), pp. 108–16, in the section "Entretiens de l'Unesco," pp. 99–150, which follows the inaugural and plenary sessions.

Hook recalled in a telephone conversation[22] that, after delivering Dewey's paper, he gave it to a clerk at the congress. Since

20. Dewey to Hook, 29 July 1948, ibid.
21. For reports of the congress, including descriptions of the East-West conflict, see Sidney Hook, *Out of Step* (New York: Harper and Row, 1987), pp. 405–19; Herbert W. Schneider, "International Congresses and the International Federation of Philosophical Societies," *Journal of Philosophy* 45 (4 November 1948): 636–43; and Morris Weitz, "Congress of Philosophers," *Standard* 35 (December 1948): 102–8.
22. 19 November 1987, with Simon, Center for Dewey Studies.

Hook did not have a copy and no other copy has been located, copy-text for this paper is its only publication, in *Proceedings*. What appear to be scattered pages of early, rough drafts are in the John Dewey Papers, Box 58, folder 4, Special Collections, Morris Library, Southern Illinois University at Carbondale.

In the conversation cited above, Hook recalled that he just polished up Dewey's paper but did not need to make the "excisions" Dewey mentioned. Because Dewey's paper was not retyped and may have been difficult to decipher, and also because of inadequate proofreading (Hook recalled that he did not read proof), the numerous typographical errors in copy-text have required more than the usual amount of emendation.

Philosophy's Future in Our Scientific Age

In late January 1949 Dewey wrote from Key West, Florida, to Joseph Ratner about the derivation and destination of his latest "article—not yet revised—about philosophy along the line of two previously written—one for the Amsterdam Congress," the other his new introduction to *Reconstruction in Philosophy*. "This one I have Commentary in mind for and have tried to make it less technical."[23] A few days later Dewey wrote to Max C. Otto, "I am at work on a more popular version" of the 1948 introduction to *Reconstruction in Philosophy;* "I think the people in the *social* subjects are the ones now to aim at trying to reach."[24] At the end of January Dewey informed Ratner that he was sending his article to Alma Fogarty, New York City, to be retyped and was asking her "to send you a carb[on.] My mss is in such shape that tho she is good there will be some lacunae but not I fancy to interfere with understanding." Expecting to leave Key West soon, Dewey had instructed Fogarty to send the typescript to Jamaica.[25]

23. Dewey to Ratner, 23 January 1949, Ratner/Dewey Papers. For the Amsterdam Congress, see preceding essay; for the introduction to the reprint of *Reconstruction in Philosophy* (Boston: Beacon Press, 1948), pp. v–vli, see *Middle Works* 12:256–77.
24. Dewey to Otto, 26 January 1949, Max C. Otto Papers, State Historical Society of Wisconsin, Madison.
25. Dewey to Ratner, 31 January 1949, Ratner/Dewey Papers.

Dewey wrote to Ratner on 10 February from Montego Bay, Jamaica, British West Indies, that he had not yet "heard anything" from Fogarty—"due probably to mail system." Dewey's next sentence revealed that he was justifiably worried: "As I didnt have a carbon its probably lucky I told her to send a carbon to you." [26]

Ratner replied on 16 February that he had received his copy of the article the previous week. Fogarty's "accompanying note said she was sending it on to you and that some passages were her 'interpretations' of yr typescript. She must be pretty good because in only a few places did the Mss. seem a little out of joint in language." [27]

By 25 February Dewey had not yet heard from Fogarty and wrote to Ratner about his lack of "confidence in the mail system here. It was a relief to me to know you had [a copy.]" Now "I know at least it isnt lost for good and at the same time I am fearful to ask you to trust it to the mails here with airmail postage. If as you say the typist did a good job, maybe you could send it to the Commentary office with a brief statement explaining the state of things." [28] Hours after mailing this letter, however, Dewey dashed off a note informing Ratner that Fogarty's typescript had "safely arrived." [29]

In early March Dewey wrote to thank Ratner for "sending your copy—The typing was very well done but some of the sentences were very awkward and Ive had to correct my own verbal constructions in a no. of places. I see things much better after the original production has got cold." [30]

In early April Dewey reported to Ratner that after he had made changes in the typescript and other typists had worked on it, "between me & them the whole thing got into awful shape." Dewey had returned it to Fogarty on 7 April, asking "her to make a carbon for you & that I would write you to get it & keep the other for my return" to New York City. [31]

"Philosophy's Future in Our Scientific Age" was published in

26. Dewey to Ratner, 10 February 1949, ibid.
27. Ratner to Dewey, 16 February 1949, ibid.
28. Dewey to Ratner (typed), 25 February 1949, ibid.
29. Dewey to Ratner (handwritten), 25 February 1949, ibid.
30. Dewey to Ratner, 3 March [1949], ibid.
31. Dewey to Ratner, 8 April 1949, ibid.

Commentary 8 (October 1949): 388–94, in "The Study of Man" series. This series ran from November 1945 to July 1963, with an article in each monthly issue until 1959, when it became an occasional feature. Other contributors included Daniel Bell, Bruno Bettelheim, Nathan Glazer, Oscar Handlin, and Sidney Hook. Dewey's earlier article in the series, in October 1947, was "Liberating the Social Scientist" [*Later Works* 15:224–38].

In November Rubin Gotesky wrote to Dewey: "*Commentary* sent me a copy of your recent article on the 'Future of Philosophy' and asked me to comment on it. I hope in the near future to develop some of the ideas which were awakened in me as a result of a careful perusal of your article. I'll send you my comments before sending them to the editor of *Commentary* for your criticism." [32] Gotesky's comments, however, never appeared in *Commentary*.

In the John Dewey Papers, Box 58, folder 4, Special Collections, Morris Library, Southern Illinois University at Carbondale, are a few pages, numbered 14–19, that appear to be part of an early draft of this article. As the correspondence quoted above indicates, Dewey frequently did not keep carbons. Because of this, and also possibly because he worked on the article in several cities, the typescript Fogarty prepared is not extant. Therefore, copy-text for this article is its only publication, in *Commentary*.

Experience and Existence: A Comment

Sholom J. Kahn, a student of John Herman Randall, Jr., published "Experience and Existence in Dewey's Naturalistic Metaphysics" in *Philosophy and Phenomenological Research* 9 (December 1948): 316–21 (PPR). Dewey immediately drafted a comment, had it retyped with at least one carbon, revised it for PPR, and sent an unrevised carbon to Joseph Ratner. Six months later, Dewey's "Experience and Existence: A Comment" appeared in PPR 9 (June 1949): 709–13.

On 7 January 1949 Dewey wrote to Ratner: "You may remember the article in Dec Phenom Research—Ive written a Comment & got a clear typed copy—Ive made a few verbal corrections in

---

32. Gotesky to Dewey, 3 November 1949, Dewey Papers. A philosopher, educator, and author, Gotesky wrote about politics and philosophy.

the script Im sending to the Jn but havent in the carbon [I] enclose."[33] In this letter Dewey described Kahn's article as an "amalgam" of references mentioned in footnotes and references "picked up in Col. classes   Net Result Hash." Dewey suggested that Ratner "might drop Lyle Eddy a card . . . saying you have it if he wants to call for it."

Lyle K. Eddy and Dewey had met the previous summer, when Eddy enrolled as a doctoral student in philosophy at Columbia University. They frequently discussed criticism and misunderstandings of Dewey's ideas, and Dewey knew Eddy would be interested in reading his comment. Eddy, who met Ratner through Dewey, recalled that he received Dewey's comment one week later: "I made a typed note (at the time of receipt) that I had received it through Ratner on January 15, 1949."[34]

Eddy wrote to Ratner a few weeks later that he had "neglected to return" Dewey's article and was enclosing "it in this letter. Thanks for the use."[35] This nine-page typescript (TS), not typed by Dewey, in the Joseph Ratner/John Dewey Papers, Box 46, folder 12, has been chosen as copy-text for Dewey's comment.[36]

Comparison of PPR with TS reveals more than one level of revision. Dewey (as he explained to Ratner) "made a few verbal corrections in the script" he sent to PPR; undoubtedly, many changes in PPR (such as the addition of a clarifying "either" before "directly" at 385.1 and the required substitution of "are" for "is" at 388.26) represent Dewey's "corrections." In addition to these revisions, the long paragraph at 386.19–387.8 dealing with critics (which probably resulted from Dewey's subsequent discussions with Eddy or Ratner) is not present in TS. Since Dewey submitted his comment in early January and it was published in June, he had sufficient time to make such an insertion.

With a few exceptions (see textual notes for emendations at

33. Dewey to Ratner, 7 January 1949, Ratner/Dewey Papers.
34. Eddy to Simon, 27 September 1987, Center for Dewey Studies. Eddy explained in this letter that his relationship with Dewey began when he sent Dewey a copy of his University of Chicago master's thesis, "The Challenge of Dewey's Philosophy to Its Critics." Dewey's "prompt and very positive" response (2 August 1948, copy in Ratner/Dewey Papers) influenced him to complete his graduate work at Columbia.
35. Eddy to Ratner, 7 February 1949, Ratner/Dewey Papers.
36. Another typescript, retyped by Eddy, is in the John L. Childs Papers, folder 24, Special Collections, Morris Library, Southern Illinois University at Carbondale.

383.13 and 384.1), substantive revisions in PPR, clearly authorial, have been accepted as emendations for this edition. Accidentals not involved with substantive revisions and without substantive implications have been retained from TS.

Kahn's article is included in this volume as Appendix 4; for his
rejoinder, see "The Status of the Potential: A Reply to Professor
Dewey," PPR 9 (June 1949): 714–16.

Contribution to "Religion and the Intellectuals"

In 1950 *Partisan Review* (PR) published "Religion and
the Intellectuals: A Symposium" in four installments, February
through May. Dewey's contribution appeared in the February
issue along with essays by James Agee, Hannah Arendt, Newton
Arvin, W. H. Auden, Robert Graves, Marianne Moore, and I. A.
Richards. In March contributors were A. J. Ayer, R. P. Blackmur,
Sidney Hook, Alfred Kazin, Philip Rahv, Isaac Rosenfeld, Allen
Tate, and Paul Tillich; in April, Robert Gorham Davis, Allan
Dowling, James T. Farrell, Jacques Maritain, Henry Bamford
Parkes, and Meyer Schapiro; and in May, William Barrett, George
Boas, Clement Greenberg, Irving Howe, Paul Kecskemeti, Dwight
Macdonald, and William Phillips. In September PR reprinted the
entire symposium as a monograph, with the same title, as "PR
Series Number Three," 139 pp.

PR prefaced each journal installment, as well as the book-
length reprint, with an editorial statement setting forth the
theme and the questions that contributors addressed (see note
for 390.1–2).

Despite Dewey's participation, he was not impressed by the
symposium; he wrote to Boyd H. Bode in April: "The Partisan
review has been publishing a series on the intellectuals return to
religion—I dont [think] much of the series, a lot of different authors—the March no had a good one by Sidney Hook and a
darn good one by some one named Paul [Isaac] Rosenfeld whom
I cant place." [37]

On 18 December 1949 Dewey had sent a three-page draft of
his article to fellow contributor Sidney Hook, writing in his accompanying letter: "I enclose a carbon of my Partisan Review
piece. I probably can count on more understanding & sympathy

37. Dewey to Bode, 1 April 1950, Eleanor Bode Browne.

from you than from many of the editors. You will recognize the 'Amsterdam' note."[38] Dewey noted on the draft, "Havent made typing corrections. I assume you have the P R 'Questionaire.'" Although it serves to indicate the development of Dewey's thought, this draft corresponds too loosely with the published version to be considered copy-text.

Dewey apparently revised his draft, had it retyped, and sent a carbon to Arthur F. Bentley; in the Bentley Collection, Manuscripts Department, Lilly Library, Indiana University, Bloomington, is an eight-page typescript (TS) for Dewey's contribution (entitled in Bentley's hand "Faith and Science"). This clean version, not typed by Dewey, is copy-text for this article. For Dewey's single alteration, see textual note for 391.26. An identical untitled eight-page carbon, without this alteration, is in the Joseph Ratner/John Dewey Papers, Box 46, folder 13, Special Collections, Morris Library, Southern Illinois University at Carbondale.

Conforming to his practice, Dewey probably further revised the typescript he sent to PR and, in addition, made corrections in proof. Substantive emendations, undoubtedly authorial, have been accepted from publication of TS in PR 17 (February 1950): 129–33. TS accidentals have been changed only when associated with substantive revisions. The reprinting in *Religion and the Intellectuals,* PR Series No. 3 (New York: Partisan Review, 1950), pp. 53–57, was found to be identical to the journal publication.

Aesthetic Experience as a Primary Phase and as an Artistic Development

This reply represents Dewey's last published statement of his esthetics theory, his most complete being *Art as Experience.*[39] An exchange between Benedetto Croce and Dewey had appeared in March 1948 in the *Journal of Aesthetics and Art Criticism* 6, pp. 203–9 (JAAC) [*Later Works* 15:97–100, 438–44].

38. Dewey to Hook, 18 December 1949, enclosing draft, Hook/Dewey Collection, Box 3, folder 14. "The 'Amsterdam' note" is a reference to "Has Philosophy a Future?" which Hook had read for Dewey in Amsterdam at the Tenth International Congress of Philosophy, 11–18 August 1948 (this volume, pp. 358–68).
39. *Later Works* 10. For Dewey's other writings on esthetics, see ibid., pp. 375n–76n.

Patrick Romanell's "A Comment on Croce's and Dewey's Aesthetics" appeared in JAAC 8 (December 1949): 125–28 [this volume, Appendix 5], and "Aesthetic Experience as a Primary Phase and as an Artistic Development," Dewey's reply, in JAAC 9 (September 1950): 56–58. In the absence of other documents for this item, the published JAAC version is copy-text for Dewey's reply.

Contribution to *Democracy in a World of Tensions*

Richard P. McKeon asked Dewey in late 1949 to write the introduction to a symposium on democracy being prepared by the United Nations Educational, Scientific, and Cultural Organization (UNESCO). Founded in 1945, UNESCO became in 1946 a specialized agency of the UN, with headquarters in Paris. McKeon, a philosophy professor at the University of Chicago, had been Dewey's student and, later, colleague at Columbia University in the 1920s and 1930s. Active in UNESCO, McKeon had been selected as editor of this symposium. In December 1949 Dewey informed Sidney Hook: "To my surprise McKeon not only asked me to write a preface to the booklet on democracy UNESCO is getting out but said his interest in social-moral matters had brought him much nearer to my position."[40]

Acknowledging receipt of Dewey's introduction, with which he was "delighted," McKeon wrote to Dewey in late January 1950: "Your presentation of the responsibilities of the Western democracies, and particularly the United States, within the framework set up by such international organizations as UNESCO provides a very forceful introduction."[41]

The very nature of Dewey's introduction conflicted with the political situation, however, and McKeon wrote to Dewey two months later requesting two changes: a different placement of his essay and the deletion of two sentences. UNESCO officers, McKeon explained, feared that using Dewey's essay as the foreword to a volume that included contributors from beyond the Iron Curtain "might brand the volume as anti-Communistic in

40. Dewey to Hook, 18 December 1949, Hook/Dewey Collection.
41. McKeon to Dewey, 23 January 1950, personal collection of Mrs. Richard P. McKeon, Chicago, Ill.

the eyes of the Soviet Union and endanger the personal safety of contributors from Poland, Czechoslovakia and Hungary." McKeon suggested that "difficulties would be removed if we printed your essay as a contribution to the symposium rather than as the foreword."

McKeon also asked permission to omit from the "opening paragraph" of section II [pp. 401–2] the following two sentences, "which ascribe major responsibility for the work of UNESCO to the United States":

> Since the Iron Curtain prevents cooperation with communist states in carrying out the task to be executed, the responsibility for following up the work of UNESCO rests for the time being exclusively upon the peoples of states having the traditional political type of democracy. Since the United States is at the present time the most powerful of all such nations, the weight of responsibility falls most heavily upon the people of that country.[42]

Dewey graciously replied on 24 March: "The reaction of the Secretariat is a natural one and perhaps I should have anticipated it, especially as I was quite aware of writing from a Western and American point of view; in fact in a way that was the raison d'etre of the whole essay; of course it will be all right to make the change to a contribution and also to strike out the offending" material.[43] Dewey's essay was published the following year, with the deletion, as chapter 5 in *Democracy in a World of Tensions: A Symposium prepared by UNESCO*, ed. Richard McKeon and Stein Rokkan (Chicago: University of Chicago Press, 1951), pp. 62–68. This publication is copy-text for the essay.

Democracy in a World of Tensions includes McKeon's description of the symposium's origin and procedure (pp. v–xi), "The UNESCO Questionnaire on Ideological Conflicts concerning Democracy," and an "Analytical Survey of Agreements and Disagreements" based on responses to the questionnaire (pp. 447–512). In the selected bibliography, Dewey is represented by *The Public and Its Problems* and *Freedom and Culture*. The volume's

42. McKeon to Dewey, 20 March 1950, Dewey Papers.
43. Dewey to McKeon, 24 March 1950, Mrs. Richard P. McKeon. Although these two sentences were deleted, Dewey expresses the same idea, with similar wording, at the end of the essay, 406.1–11.

thirty-three essays, selected from responses to the questionnaire, are designated not by titles but by roman numerals and contributors' names; Dewey is listed in the topical index under the headings "Western versus Eastern Democracy," "Political Problem," "Crucial Differences," "Toleration of Dissentient Opinions," and "Nature of the Disagreement."

Reviews of *Democracy in a World of Tensions,* the second UNESCO symposium, were mixed.[44] Joseph S. Roucek thought the volume "merely another useless addition" to "compendia of semantic jiu-jitsu," and Louis Martin Sears declared himself "surfeited" by "some of the most abstractly tedious writing in the entire field of political science."[45] On the other hand, Marshall Knappen, while acknowledging that such a book must inevitably be "repetitious and disjointed," still recommended it "for those who profess to speak of democracy and its true meaning"; John A. Irving thought the contributors "carried out a difficult assignment with precision and objectivity"; and S. G. Rich, Jr., finding the writing "stimulating," "provoking," even at times "humorous," thought the volume would prove to be of "considerable value as supplementary reading" in college courses.[46] Reviewers mentioned Dewey as a contributor but did not comment on his essay.

Modern Philosophy

In 1947 Max C. Otto, Dewey's longtime friend, retired from the University of Wisconsin philosophy department. At Otto's retirement banquet on 6 May in Madison, the following

44. UNESCO's first inquiry, *Human Rights: Comments and Interpretations,* was published by Columbia University Press in 1949. *Democracy in a World of Tensions* was reviewed in *American Sociological Review* 16 (June 1951): 425–26 (Joseph S. Roucek); *Annals of the American Academy of Political and Social Science* 275 (May 1951): 164–65 (Louis Martin Sears); *Antioch Review* 11 (June 1951): 253 (Paul Bixler); *Canadian Forum* 31 (October 1951): 162 (Frank H. Underhill); *Christian Century* 68 (7 March 1951): 305–6 (Marshall Knappen); *Current History* 20 (March 1951): 172; *Foreign Affairs* 29 (July 1951): 666; *New Leader* 34 (15 October 1951): 20–21 (Sidney Hook); *Queen's Quarterly* (Kingston, Canada) 58 (Winter 1951–52): 598–600 (John A. Irving); and *Western Humanities Review* 5 (Autumn 1951): 411–12 (S. G. Rich, Jr.).
45. Roucek, *American Sociological Review,* p. 425; Sears, *Annals,* pp. 165, 164.
46. Knappen, *Christian Century,* p. 306; Irving, *Queen's Quarterly,* p. 599; Rich, *Western Humanities Review,* pp. 411, 412.

message from Dewey was read: "Wherever he is, he will continue to speak for freedom and human justice, a freedom and justice based on understanding the things that are most worth while."[47] Dewey wrote to Otto that summer, "I was glad, but not surprised, to hear from [Horace S.] Fries what a friendly occasion the dinner was; only sorry I couldnt have been there."[48]

Several months before the banquet, Otto's colleagues, Fries and Frederick H. Burkhardt (who had delivered an address at the banquet), and Boyd H. Bode, a former colleague, had begun planning a volume in Otto's honor. Dewey's correspondence discussing the project, particularly with Fries, shows clearly that Dewey was not only a contributor but was also instrumental in shaping the volume.

In January 1947 Fries wrote to request Dewey's "advice and help" on this book, which, its planners hoped, "will really amount to something. None of us want to agree merely on 'another set of essays.'" Fries described "two different ideas as possible themes," one a "so-called 'definitive' statement of Scientific Humanism," the other, proposed by Bode and having more appeal, "the pervasive and disruptive 'dualism' which pervades modern life." Fries asked Dewey:

1. Will you write the general introductory essay?
2. If so, will you send us a brief of it in advance that we can use in an effort to clarify the theme for the other contributors?
If you can say yes to No. 2, choose any promising theme you care to, including either of the above themes.[49]

A week later Dewey wrote to Fries from Key West, Florida, that he was "very much interested," "heartily in sympathy," and would "be glad to do whatever I can do." Dewey found himself "rather inclined to Bode's suggestion," which had "the advan-

---

47. *The Max C. Otto Jubilee: Dinner Addresses* (Madison, Wis.: Otto Jubilee Committee, 1947), p. 20; a copy of this pamphlet is in the Max C. Otto Papers, Box 13, folder 2, State Historical Society of Wisconsin, Madison. On 27 March 1947 Dewey had sent this note to Horace S. Fries "to read if the com in charge thinks best" (Horace S. Fries Papers, State Historical Society of Wisconsin, Madison).
48. Dewey to Otto, 14 July 1947, Otto Papers. On 8 July 1947 Fries had reported the banquet's success to Dewey (Fries Papers).
49. Fries to Dewey, 17 January 1947, ibid.

tage of locating the root of the problems, the evils, that would
have to be dealt with in the other topics. It gives so to say something definite to chew on that should keep the treatment out of
the glittering generalities that seem to haunt professional liberals." Dewey felt that Bode could write the introductory essay
"better than I or than anyone else I know."

Dewey then discussed his own contribution: "What I could do
best would be along the line of developments in science" and
what those developments "have done in outlawing traditional
dualism—as of man and nature, individual and social etc." [50]

Early in February Fries wrote to thank Dewey for his "good
suggestions and co-operation." He and Burkhardt proposed that
Bode "do the introductory chapter on dualisms" and that Dewey
"do a chapter (or two, if you can use them) on natural and social
science." [51]

A few days later Dewey replied to Fries that he had exchanged
letters with Bode, who "urged me to do the Introductory chapter; after getting yours I wrote him again why I thought he
should do it." "A non technical chapter as the opening would be
an excellent" way to increase the audience:

> Most of these memorial volume[s] do not circulate I think
> outside a rather narrow circle. With Bodes analysis of our
> present state and the other non-philosophically technical ar-
> ticles, maybe this volume could receive a wider hearing. I
> should be in favor of aiming at that anyway—for the theme
> is of wide human application and *should* receive wide atten-
> tion if the volume is reasonably "popular"—i.e., human in
> style. And Otto above the rest of us deserves it. [52]

Continuing the discussion of theme, Dewey wrote to Fries in
early March: "I am sure that neither Bode & I want to impose
our view on you—But I have always been struck with Bode's
keen feeling for the cleavages in our culture & their effect in edu-

50. Dewey to Fries, 24 January 1947, ibid. Perhaps indicating the priority he assigned to this chapter, Dewey wrote to Sidney Hook that he was "precom-
mitted" to "the proposed volume for Otto (who is retiring)" (23 January
[1947], Hook/Dewey Collection).
51. Fries to Dewey, 9 February [1947], Fries Papers.
52. Dewey to Fries, 13 February 1947, ibid.

cation, philosophy, religion &c." Dewey wanted, as did Bode, "to suggest that subject while of course the final decision is with you who began the project." In this letter Dewey discussed chapter topics and contributors.[53] Several weeks later Dewey wrote to Fries "to say that articles suggesting remedial measures instead of just diagnoses are more than all to the good."[54]

In April Dewey wrote to Sidney Hook about ideas for his chapter and hinted that there might be a problem: "The topic suggested for me in the Otto volume if one comes off is the cleavage between social and physical inquiry." While working on an article for *Commentary,* Dewey explained, he had "got off too far into general philosophy" and had to rewrite the article. However, Dewey thought that "from the point of view of philosophy there were some good things" in his first draft, some of which he might use for the Otto volume.[55]

Later in April Fries wrote to Dewey, "If your chapter or a summary of it will help direct the other contributors, we shall send out copies of it, when you have it."[56] In May Dewey described to Fries the unexpected turn his chapter had taken:

What Ive written so far instead of being an exposition of dualisms turns out to be rather a rather condensed and somewhat dogmatic, because condensed, statement of why and how the historic dualisms are what is the matter, or the cause of what is the matter, with present philosophy, with some suggestions as to how to get out and get on.

In other words, I seem to have taken philosophy as one of the fields of subjectmatter to be discussed in the volume. So I thought I better report that fact to you for the sake of its possible bearing on other subjects and contributors.

53. Dewey to Fries, 3 March [1947], ibid.
54. Dewey to Fries, 14 April [1947], ibid.
55. Dewey to Hook, 1 April 1947, Hook/Dewey Collection. For Dewey's *Commentary* article, see "Liberating the Social Scientist: A Plea to Unshackle the Study of Man," *Commentary* 4 (October 1947): 378–85 [*Later Works* 15:224–38]. Dewey had mentioned the same article in his 24 January and 3 March 1947 letters to Fries (Fries Papers) and, in the first letter, also linked the theme with his earlier "The Crisis in Human History: The Danger of the Retreat to Individualism," *Commentary* 1 (March 1946): 1–9 [*Later Works* 15:210–23].
56. Fries to Dewey, 23 April [1947], Fries Papers.

Dewey wrote that he might be able to send Fries a "carbon of the rough draft," but was rather afraid "that the present effort doesnt tie into Bodes as well as I expected to have it do." [57]

In early July Dewey completed his chapter and sent it to Fries, commenting, "It took me longer to finish the enclosed than I expected. It is heavier than I wish it were." [58] Fries replied three days later, "We probably could have done little or nothing with the Otto volume had your chapter come earlier. But now I believe we can settle down to writing a definite but tentative outline to submit to possible contributors for their suggestions." [59]

Later in July Fries informed Dewey that "some carbon copies of your chapter have been made" and sent to Burkhardt, Bode, George R. Geiger, and Eduard C. Lindeman. "After another run of copies I'll be glad to send you one." They hoped "to have the volume fully under way by fall." [60] In September Dewey informed Fries that there was "no need to send copy of paper as I kept one." [61]

In October Dewey sent a single page to Fries, writing: "I rewrote the last page of my piece some time ago & have kept forgetting to send it to you. Hope its legible." [62]

Although Dewey completed his chapter on schedule, the volume, beset by difficulties, was not published for five years. In December Fries informed Dewey that they had agreed upon a tentative outline and "decisions about the contributors and chapters represent pretty well the consensus of opinion of Dewey, Bode, Geiger, Burkhardt, Fries." [63] Burkhardt, who left Wisconsin during this period to become president of Bennington College in Vermont, took on the job of editor, with Fries and Geiger substituting as necessary.

Problems of obtaining the original essays apparently arose. In January 1949 Dewey wrote to Bode, "Do you ever hear anything about the Otto volume? I dont—And if, when and as the articles are all in there is still getting a publisher and the firms are darn

57. Dewey to Fries, 20 May 1947, ibid.
58. Dewey to Fries, 5 July 1947, ibid.
59. Fries to Dewey, 8 July 1947, ibid.
60. Fries to Dewey, 20 July 1947, ibid. Fries declined Dewey's offer to help with the expense of having carbons made (Dewey to Fries, 16 August 1947; Fries to Dewey, 29 August 1947, ibid.).
61. Dewey to Fries, [8 September 1947], ibid.
62. Dewey to Fries, 11 October 1947, ibid.
63. Fries to Dewey, 7 December 1947, ibid.

shy now especially of those with a philosophical slant."[64] A few weeks later, in a postscript to a letter to Bode, Dewey added, "I don't hear anything about the Max volume—Do you?"[65]

After the volume was assembled, Burkhardt approached Boston's Beacon Press. In June 1950 Fries informed Dewey that Burkhardt had a letter from Beacon indicating "an interest in the Otto volume but which put off any decision for about six months on the ground that if the Press is going well then, they will publish it. In the meantime Burkhardt plans to find out how much of a subsidy Harper would need."[66]

Naturally, Dewey was impatient. He complimented Fries on his "piece for Max's volume (if it can only get bodily existence)"; to Bode he wrote, "I wish by the way our volume could come out—Its the more needed every day that passes."[67]

In October Fries wrote to Dewey, "I gather there will soon be a decision from the Beacon Press."[68] In January 1951 Fries informed Dewey that he had written to Melvin Arnold of Beacon, "who has the manuscripts for the Otto volume, but have not heard as yet."[69] In March Fries wrote to Dewey about problems and thanked Dewey for his "generous offer of financial help." Fries had appealed to contributors, but

> the replies which have come in are discouraging in the sense that they make me very dubious as to the desirability of going through with the venture, because I believe there will be fewer injured feelings if we drop it than if we continue. If this belief is correct, there is no doubt but that the venture should be dropped. However, I shall try to get another offer from the Press on the basis of their selling and distributing "our share" of the copies. Then, I shall again circulate the contributors and try to gain a decent consensus.

Fries wanted to avoid "any sign of 'pressuring' any one, yet a few are very anxious to publish." "Burkhardt and I," Fries wrote,

64. Dewey to Bode, 22 January 1949, Eleanor Bode Browne.
65. Dewey to Bode, 2 March 1949, ibid.
66. Fries to Dewey, 27 June 1950, Dewey Papers. Fries later reported to Dewey that there was "no news as yet on a publisher," but "Burkhardt and I (and I believe some others) are making soundings" ([September] 1950, ibid.).
67. Dewey to Fries, 30 August 1950, Fries Papers; Dewey to Bode, 16 September 1950, Eleanor Bode Browne.
68. Fries to Dewey, 7 October 1950, Dewey Papers and Fries Papers.
69. Fries to Dewey, 6 January 1951, Fries Papers.

"probably should have recommended dropping the project the minute it began to call for financial help. At that point we were both very dubious about the outcome."[70]

In April Fries informed Dewey that there was "no word as yet" from Beacon about his proposal, adding as a postscript, "Word received which is not definitive. More later."[71] Three weeks later Fries reported to Dewey: "It finally looks as though an agreement can be reached about publication of the Otto volume."[72]

On 22 September 1952, after Dewey's death in June, Beacon Press published *The Cleavage in Our Culture: Studies in Scientific Humanism in Honor of Max Otto*, edited by Frederick Burkhardt. Although Fries had discussed the possibility of eighteen to twenty chapters,[73] the final count was twelve; in addition to Dewey, Bode, Fries, Geiger, and Lindeman, the authors were Horace M. Kallen, Arnold Dresden, Norman Cameron, A. Eustace Haydon, Harold Taylor, C. E. Ayres, and G. C. Sellery.

Reviewers[74] praised the writing: Keith McGary called the "brilliant set" of studies, which had "a freshness and unity of purpose," a "proper tribute" to Otto.[75] G. Watts Cunningham considered the essays to be "well written"; *United States Quarterly Book Review* commented on their "sustained excellence."[76]

Dewey's chapter was described as "clear and searching" and "one of its best."[77] J. W. Cohen thought the volume "pervaded" by Dewey's philosophy, which elevated "American experience, its buoyant pluralism and its democratic experimentalism, to the status of a potential world philosophy for the future."[78]

However, reviewers also criticized the book's content. Cohen thought that, though "lively and pertinent," the essays did not

70. Fries to Dewey, 19 March 1951, ibid. Dewey pledged $250.
71. Fries to Dewey, 6 April 1951, Dewey Papers (with postscript) and Fries Papers.
72. Fries to Dewey, 27 April 1951, Fries Papers.
73. Fries to Dewey, 2 November 1947, ibid.
74. *The Cleavage in Our Culture* was reviewed in *Antioch Review* 13 (September 1953): 411–14 (Keith McGary); *Booklist* 49 (15 November 1952): 97; *Ethics* 64 (October 1953): 65–67 (G. Watts Cunningham); *Hibbert Journal* (London) 53 (October 1954): 95–97 (Virginia Black); *U.S. Quarterly Book Review* 9 (March 1953): 48; and *Western Humanities Review* 7 (Spring 1953): 170–73 (J. W. Cohen).
75. McGary, *Antioch Review*, pp. 414, 413.
76. Cunningham, *Ethics*, p. 66; *U.S. Quarterly Book Review*, p. 48.
77. McGary, *Antioch Review*, p. 412; J. W. Cohen, *Western Humanities Review*, p. 170.
78. Cohen, *Western Humanities Review*, pp. 170, 171.

come to grips with "the major practical and theoretical issue of our tortured epoch."[79] It seemed to Virginia Black "that the votaries of scientific humanism in propounding a philosophy of experiential unity unwittingly speak for dogma despite their hatred of it."[80] Cunningham perhaps best expressed reaction to the volume when he wrote that despite criticisms, it was "a substantial contribution to social theory"; echoing Dewey's conviction that the volume was "more needed every day," and that the theme had "wide human application and *should* receive wide attention," Cunningham continued:

> It deserves to be read and pondered by all who are concerned with the present sorry state of the world. Whatever may be said about the volume's systemic foundations, what I take to be its main message remains and is sound in principle: the essential negation of our sundry little absolutes in all fields, and especially in those of ethics and religion. If taken seriously in practice, this message could redeem us from much silly talk and more tragic behavior.[81]

Dewey had written to Fries on 20 May 1947 that he might be able to send him a "carbon of the rough draft" of his chapter; whether he did so or not, this draft is not extant.

Dewey apparently had the draft professionally retyped with at least three carbon copies and, on 5 July, probably after making some changes in it, sent the original to Fries. On 5 September Dewey informed Fries that there was "no need to send copy of paper as I kept one."

Three typescripts for Dewey's chapter have been found: one in the John Dewey Papers, Box 52, folder 10, Special Collections, Morris Library, Southern Illinois University at Carbondale (TS¹); and two in the Joseph Ratner/John Dewey Papers, Box 46, folder 6, Special Collections, Morris Library, Southern Illinois University at Carbondale (TS¹ and TS²). All three are untitled, twenty-one-page carbon copies. The first twenty pages of the three documents—a clean, retyped typescript, not typed by Dewey—are identical in every respect.

However, the last page of TS², also a carbon copy, differs from

79. Ibid., p. 172.
80. Black, *Hibbert Journal,* p. 96.
81. Cunningham, *Ethics,* p. 67.

the last page of TS[1]; it is typed by Dewey, with his alterations. Dewey wrote to Fries on 11 October 1947 that he "rewrote the last page" of his piece "some time ago & have kept forgetting to send it to you." How the rewritten page came to rest in the Ratner/Dewey Papers is not clear. Dewey may have given it to Ratner to add to his collection of materials for the Dewey biography he was working on at that time.

Because TS[2] p. 21 is clearly Dewey's rewritten, final version of that material, and because TS[2] is identical to TS[1] otherwise, the complete TS[2] has served as copy-text for the present edition.[82]

Substantive changes in Dewey's chapter, undoubtedly authorial, have been accepted from its publication as "Modern Philosophy" in *The Cleavage in Our Culture,* ed. Frederick Burkhardt (Boston: Beacon Press, 1952), pp. 15–29, and recorded in the Emendations List with the symbol CC. Dewey probably made most of these changes before sending the chapter to Fries.

For Dewey's alterations on TS[2] p. 21, see Alterations in Manuscripts. Dewey apparently made some of his ink alterations on the carbon of this page after sending the ribbon copy to Fries. The following revisions, not incorporated in the published version, have been made for this edition: addition of a comma after

---

82. Following is the superseded TS[1] p. 21 that was replaced at 419.5–37 by "vitality . . . vitality." (Dewey Papers, Box 52, folder 10, and Ratner/Dewey Papers, Box 46, folder 6):

vitality that are genuinely liberal and humane.
    It may well be that the isolation of "science" which rendered it technical, and aloof from human applications, thereby leaving human affairs to be determined by institutional interests in competitive industry and in competitive national politics that are *not* determined by intelligent or competent knowing, but by agencies actually alien to such determination, was a measure of protection. Perhaps if it had not disclaimed all intrinsic bearing on human affairs, the institutional obstacles to its advance would have been more than grace; they might have been insuperable. But we are now paying a high price for its perpetuation. It has given institutional operations that tend to the power and profit of a class-section or a nationalistic section of mankind an undue advantage, which in its present recoil oppresses the freedom and distorts the welfare of our common humanity, and which also threatens the destruction of all, including its own security of wellbeing. Petulant attack may further divert the uses to which our resources of knowing are put; but it will not arrest the onward course of science. The alternative is systematic use of scientific resources in the widest and most generous manner possible. Philosophy that assumes a responsible, however humble share, in this work will drink of the living springs from which it will draw renewed life.

"none the less" at 419.13, placement of a phrase at 419.13–14, and the addition of "but" at 419.15. See Textual Notes for the last two.

The accidentals of TS^2, even though not typed by Dewey, are more characteristic than are those of CC, which added and regularized punctuation. Unless involved with substantive changes or possessing substantive implications, copy-text accidentals have been followed.

H. F. S.

Emendations List

All emendations in both substantives and accidentals introduced into the copy-text are recorded in the list that follows, with the exception of the changes in formal matters described below. The copy-text and source of emendations for each item are identified in the head note for that item; abbreviations are supplied if used in the list of emendations for that item. The page-line number at the left is from the present edition; all lines of print except running heads are counted. The reading to the left of the square bracket is from the present edition; the bracket is followed by an abbreviation for the source of that reading's first appearance. The order of sigla following the bracket indicates the chronological order from the first to last appearance of the lemma. A semicolon follows the last of the sigla for sources. Rejected readings following the semicolon are listed in reverse chronological order, with the earliest version, usually copy-text, appearing last.

W means Works—the present edition—and is used for emendations made here for the first time. The symbol WS (Works Source) is used to indicate emendations made within Dewey's quoted material that restore the spelling, capitalization, and some required substantives of his source (see headnote to Substantive Variants in Dewey's Quotations).

For emendations restricted to punctuation, the curved dash ~ means the same word(s) as before the bracket; the inferior caret ∧ indicates the absence of a punctuation mark. The abbreviation [*om.*] means the reading before the bracket was omitted in the editions and impressions identified; [*not present*] is used where appropriate to signal material not appearing in the identified sources. The abbreviation [*rom.*] means roman type and is used to signal the omission of italics; [*ital.*] means italic type and is used to signal the omission of roman type. *Stet* used with an edition or impression abbreviation indicates a substantive reading retained from an edition or impression subsequently revised; the rejected variant follows the semicolon. An asterisk before an emendation page-line number indicates that the reading is discussed in the Textual Notes.

A number of formal, or mechanical, changes have been made throughout:

1. *Knowing and the Known* chapter headings ("Chapter One") have been deleted and arabic numbers placed before chapter titles; chapter endnotes in *Knowing and the Known* appear as footnotes in the present edition.

2. Matters of style in *Knowing and the Known* footnote citations have been corrected where necessary; capitalization and punctuation in references to Dewey's *Logic: The Theory of Inquiry* have been made uniform.

3. Superior numbers have been assigned consecutively to footnotes throughout an essay or chapter.

4. Book and periodical titles are in italic type; "the" appearing before periodical titles is in lowercase roman type; articles and sections of books are in quotation marks.

5. Periods and commas have been brought within quotation marks.

6. With the exception of *Knowing and the Known,* single quotation marks have been changed to double when not inside quoted material; however, opening or closing quotation marks have been supplied where necessary and recorded. Opening and closing quotation marks around extracts have been omitted.

The following spellings have been editorially regularized to the known Dewey usage appearing before the brackets:

cannot] can not 79.17, 126.9, 127.30, 138.35, 142.24, 142.26, 164.12, 168.11, 169.12, 183.9, 263.28, 264.7
centre(s)] center 91.16, 101n.29–30, 107.20–21, 118.14, 122.27, 371.15, 414.10
cooperate (all forms)] co-operate 48.19, 56.21, 77.16–17, 116n.8, 257.4, 400.24
coordination] co-ordination 116n.7–8
meagre] meager 404.23

Knowing and the Known

Copy-text for *Knowing and the Known* (KK) is the copyright deposit copy (A 36800) of the first impression (Boston: Beacon Press, 1949). The source of emendations, except those made for the first time in the present edition, is given for each chapter.

Preface

Emendations have been accepted from the typescript typed by Dewey, enclosed in Dewey to Arthur F. Bentley, 3 September 1947, Bentley Collection, Manuscripts Department, Lilly Library, Indiana University, Bloomington, 2 pp. (TS); and from the typescript not typed by Dewey, dated 15 September 1947, Joseph Ratner/John Dewey Papers, Box 45, folder 9, Special Collections, Morris Library, Southern Illinois University at Carbondale, 3 pp. (TS¹).

4.6, 21   cooperative] TS, TS¹; co-operative KK

1. Vagueness in Logic

Emendations have been accepted from "On a Certain Vagueness in Logic," *Journal of Philosophy* 42 (4 and 18 January 1945): 6–27, 39–51 (JP).

8n.6	A Reply."] W; a Reply." KK, JP
9.9	Richards'] W; Richard's KK, JP
10n.6	Subject-Matter] WS; Subjectmatter KK; [*not present*] JP
16n.4	nineteen-twenties] JP; ~∧~ KK
19n.5	cooperative] W; co-operative KK; coöperative JP
24n.12	compare note] W; Compare Note KK; [*not present*] JP
24n.26; 32n.1	*Formalization*] stet JP; *The Formalization* KK
30.37	*Formalization*] W; *The Formalization* KK; [*not present*] JP
31.20	distinction] JP; disinction KK
33n.6	Our] W; our KK, JP
37.23	cannot] W; can not KK, JP
38.15	"difficult] JP; ∧~ KK
38.28	common-sense] WS; ~∧~ KK, JP
39.10	worth while] WS; worth-while KK; worthwhile JP
40n.5	pp. xvii–xviii] W; p. xvii KK, JP
41.21	p. 360,] W; p. 361, KK, JP
41n.2	p. 370, n. 4)] W; p. 370) KK, JP

2. The Terminological Problem

Emendations have been accepted from "A Terminology for Knowings and Knowns," *Journal of Philosophy* 42 (26 April 1945): 225–47 (JP).

47n.1   "loose,"] JP; ∧~," KK
*61.20–21   *Knowing . . . together.*] W; Knowing and the known,
         event and designation—the full knowledge—go forward
         together. KK; The full knowledge—knowing and the
         known—event and designation—go forward together. JP
61n.3; 68n.7   subject-matter] JP; subjectmatter KK
61n.5   sentences] JP; sentence KK
62.6   explicitly] JP; explicit KK

3. Postulations

Emendations have been accepted from "Postulations," *Journal of Philosophy* 42 (22 November 1945): 645–62 (JP).

79n.8   Wood] *stet* JP; Woods KK
83n.18   is,] WS; ~∧ KK, JP
83n.19   under "the] W; "~ ∧~ KK, JP
85n.1   Is] W; is KK, JP
85n.1   Be] W; be KK, JP
86n.24   space-time] JP; spacetime KK
88n.8   380;] W; ~: KK; [*not present*] JP
88n.12   *Malade*] W; *malade* KK, JP
90.11   "stimulus,"] JP; "~∧" KK
92.16   behavioral] JP; behaviorial KK
92n.8   knowledge,] JP; knowlege, KK

4. Interaction and Transaction

Emendations have been accepted from "Interaction and Transaction," *Journal of Philosophy* 43 (12 September 1946): 505–17 (JP).

99.28   generalised] WS; generalized KK, JP
103n.13   #4.)] W; #4). KK; pp. 239–240.) JP
106n.6   Insofar] JP; In so far KK
107.38   setup] WS; set-up KK, JP
107.39   cannot] WS; can not KK, JP
109n.4   Be] W; be KK, JP

5. Transactions as Known and Named

Emendations have been accepted from "Transactions as Known and Named," *Journal of Philosophy* 43 (26 September 1946):533–51, 560 (JP).

117n.2   Uexküll,] W; Uexkull, KK, JP
117n.13   p. v,] W; p. xi, KK, JP
117n.16   VI] W; V KK; [*not present*] JP
119.7   neighbours] WS; neighbors KK, JP
119.13–14   pp. 48–49] W; p. 48 KK; p. 56 JP
119.16,17   rose-comb] JP; ∼∧∼ KK
119.19–20   unanalysed] WS; unanalyzed KK, JP
119n.12   *Reviews*] JP; *Review* KK
121n.11   "Psychologists'] W; "Psychologists's KK; [*not present*] JP
121n.13   pp. 266–291.] W; pp. 226–291. KK; [*not present*] JP
123n.1   Section IV, #4] W; Section #4 KK; [*not present*] JP
124.8   desiccated] W; dessicated KK, JP
124n.4,7   Müller] W; Mueller KK, JP
124n.5,9   Müller] WS; Mueller KK, JP
124n.5   to-day,] WS; today, KK, JP
125n.7–8   life space] WS; ∼-∼ KK, JP
128.23   Khan] W; Kahn KK, JP

6. Specification

Emendations have been accepted from "Specification," *Journal of Philosophy* 43 (21 November 1946):645–63 (JP).

132n.9   in] JP; ∼- KK
136.39–40   important.] JP; ∼, KK
139.5–6   inadequate] JP; inaedequate KK
143n.1   "term"] *stet* JP; "terms" KK
145n.3   *Self*] W; ∼, KK, JP
*152.13; 153.2   subjectmatter] W; subject-matter KK, JP

7. The Case of Definition

Emendations have been accepted from "'Definition,'" *Journal of Philosophy* 44 (22 May 1947):281–306 (JP).

*155.32–33   Moreover, . . . here] W; What is striking here, moreover, KK, JP

157n.12   1944]).] W; ~]∧. KK; ~∧). JP
158n.1   I,] W; I, i, KK, JP
159n.5   essence,] JP; ~∧ KK
163n.3   p. 20,] W; pp. 19–20, KK, JP
163n.4   text-books] WS; textbooks KK, JP
163n.5   recognised,] WS; recognized, KK, JP
165n.21   p. 345,] JP; 345, KK
166n.6   "Analysis and the] W; "The KK, JP
166n.13   p. 478.] W; p. 479. KK, JP
166n.14   Part I,] W; Vol. I, KK, JP
166n.14   pp. 93–94.] W; p. 93. KK, JP
166n.17   Was] W; was KK, JP
167.13   key term] WS; ~-~ KK, JP
167.18   Its] W; its KK, JP
169.2   Are] W; are KK, JP
170.7   definition,] WS; Definition, KK, JP
174.16   ascribe meanings] WS; ascribe meaning KK, JP
179.4   "verification"] JP; ∧~" KK
180.24   artificially] JP; artifically KK
181n.8   Section 2.] W; Section 1. KK, JP
*183.1   him.[51]] W; ~.[52] KK; ~.∧ JP
*183.12   secured.[52]] W; ~.[51] KK, JP
*183n.1   51. Cf.] W; [52]Cf. KK; [*not present*] JP
*183n.3   52. We] W; [51]We KK, JP

8. Logic in an Age of Science

Emendations have been accepted from "Logicians' Underlying Postulations," *Philosophy of Science* 13 (January 1946):3–19 (PS).

186.13; 197.33   cannot] W; can not KK, PS
186n.22   72] W; 70 KK, PS
187.16   *Studies in*] W; *Studies of* KK, PS
187.16   1903, the] W; 1903. The KK, PS
187n.8; 188.12   subject-matter] WS; subjectmatter KK; subject
          matter PS
188.18   autonomous; . . .] W; ~; ∧∧∧ KK, PS
190.30   operations";] W; ~;" KK, PS
190.31   those] WS; these KK, PS
191.1   subject matter] WS; subjectmatter KK; subject-matter PS
191.5   coordinate] PS; co-ordinate KK
191.8   system building] PS; ~-~ KK

192n.3–4   to attempt to separate 'Nature'] WS; to separate 'nature'
        KK, PS
192n.12   578–80.] W; ~). KK; ~.) PS
193n.26   World-Order] W; ~ₐ~ KK, PS
193n.33   p. 472.)] W; ~.ₐ KK, PS
196n.28   sense data] WS; ~-~ KK, PS
199n.6   29] W; 28–29 KK; [not present] PS
199n.7; 199n.7–200n.1   Nature] WS; nature KK; [not present] PS
201n.10   'particulars.'" The] W; 'particularsₐ'" An KK, PS
203n.7   An] W; an KK, PS
204n.6   follows.] PS; ~: KK
204n.8   Defence] W; Defense KK, PS
204n.10   My] W; my KK, PS
204n.13   pp. 273–300.] W; pp. 273–299. KK; pp. 25–30. PS
205.11   Analysis.] W; ~." KK, PS
205.14   664).] W; 666). KK, PS
205.18   employed).] W; ~.) KK, PS
205n.1   'sense-datum'] PS; "~' KK
206.5   CS,] WS; CS, p. KK, PS
206.6   compare] W; Compare KK, PS
206.18   relation] WS; relations KK, PS
209n.6   Phenomenological] W; Phenomeological KK, PS

9. A Confused "Semiotic"

Emendations have been accepted from "The New 'Semiotic,'" *Philoso-phy and Phenomenological Research* 8 (September 1947):107–31 (PPR).

210.14   occur" (p. 2).] W; occur," (p. 2)ₐ KK; [not present] PPR
210n.5   "preparatory,"] W; "~ₐ" KK; [not present] PPR
213.37   signifies"] PPR; ~." KK
214.13   significata"] PPR; ~." KK
215.23   organization.[12]] W; ~.[13] KK; ~.ₐ PPR
215n.13   12. The] W; 13. The KK; [not present] PPR
216.13   signifying"] W; ~." KK; [not present] PPR
216.17   prescriptors"] W; ~." KK; [not present] PPR
216.20   time.[13]] W; ~.ₐ KK; ~.[11] PPR
216n.12   13. Elsewhere] W; [12]~ KK; [11]~ PPR
217.22   location] W; ~. KK; [not present] PPR
218n.1   "where,"] PPR; "~." KK
218n.4   I,] W; I, i, KK, PPR

220n.1,13 preparatory-stimulus] WS; ~∧~ KK, PPR
221n.13   on] W; [*not present*] KK, PPR
226.19   "The] W; "the KK, PPR
228.7   suspicion):] PPR; ~:) KK
228.7   The] W; the KK, PPR
229.22   subjectmatter] W; subject-matter KK; subject matter PPR
234.30   pp.] W; p. KK, PPR
238n.14   chapter,] PPR; ~∧ KK
239n.17   subject-matter] WS; subjectmatter KK; subject matter
          PPR
239n.25   *Language,*] W; ~∧ KK; [*not present*] PPR

10. Common Sense and Science

Emendations have been accepted from "Common Sense and Science:
Their Respective Frames of Reference," *Journal of Philosophy* 45 (8
April 1948):197–208 (JP); and the typescript, not typed by Dewey,
in the Joseph Ratner/John Dewey Papers, Box 44, folder 2, Special Collections, Morris Library, Southern Illinois University at Carbondale,
22 pp. (TS).

243.27   instance—,] TS; ~,— KK, JP
*244.29   as well . . . application.] W; and of a field of significant ap-
          plication. KK, JP; and also of bearings or significant appli-
          cation. TS
244.32   judgement] WS; judgment KK, JP, TS
245.9   every-day] WS; everyday KK, JP, TS
246.19   cooperate] TS; co-operate KK; coöperate JP
246.27   Since] TS, JP; ~, KK
247.2   sense or] *stet* TS, JP; sense of KK
247.6   *à faire*] WS; *faire* KK, JP, TS
247.8   "what] WS; "that KK, JP; anything "that TS
247.8   do] WS; do with KK, JP, TS
247.8   with";] W; ~;" KK, JP; ~," TS
247.21   cannot] TS; can not KK, JP
248.10   life-behavior] W; ~—~ KK; ~∧~ JP, TS
251.14   done, indeed] W; ~∧ ~, KK; [*not present*] JP, TS
*252.39   from; and is *of*] W; from; which is *of* KK; from∧ and is *of*
          JP; from:— TS
254.31   case] W; ~— KK; [*not present*] JP, TS
255.4   then,] TS, JP; ~∧ KK

11. A Trial Group of Names

Emendations have been accepted from "Concerning a Vocabulary for Inquiry into Knowledge," *Journal of Philosophy* 44 (31 July 1947): 421–34 (JP).

259.10   "Exact"] JP; "~," KK
266.9   *Perception-Manipulation.*] W; *Perception-manipulation.* KK, JP
266.13   characterizations.] W; ~." KK; [*not present*] JP
267.10   subject-matter] JP; subjectmatter KK
272.15   *Space-Time.*] W; *Space-time.* KK, JP
272.36   *Vague:*] W; ~. KK; [*not present*] JP

12. Summary of Progress Made

276n.1   four] W; three KK
277n.1   1891] W; 1894 KK

Appendix: Dewey's Reply to Albert G. A. Balz

Emendations have been accepted from the *Journal of Philosophy* transcription of Dewey's letter (JPTR) sent by Herbert W. Schneider, editor of JP, to Balz on 4 May 1949 (Balz Papers, Manuscripts Department, Alderman Library, University of Virginia, Charlottesville, 19 pp.); Dewey's letter appeared in *Journal of Philosophy* 46 (26 May 1949): 329–42 (JP).

280.2   Dewey's . . . Balz] W; [*not present*] KK, JP, JPTR
280.6   pp. 313–329.] W; pp. 329–342. KK; [*not present*] JP, JPTR
*280.12; 284.9; 287.20–21; 288.10–11   cannot] JPTR; can not KK, JP
*287.13   dear A——,] W; Mr. A——, KK; Mr. Balz, JP, JPTR
287.21   role] JPTR; rôle KK, JP
287.25   ever-going] JPTR; evergoing KK; ever-/going JP
289.24–25   organism] *stet* JPTR; organisms, KK, JP
292.20   psychological: note] JPTR; psychological! Note, KK, JP

What Is It to Be a Linguistic Sign or Name?

Copy-text for this paper is the unpublished typescript, typed by Dewey, in the Arthur F. Bentley Collection, Manuscripts Department, Lilly Library, Indiana University, Bloomington, 18 pp., dated 25 May 1945. Emendations at 300.6 and 305.26 have been adopted from Bentley's corrections on the typescript (B).

297.15   deputies,] W; ~∧
297.15   a] W; A
297n.4   given] W; given in
297n.6   p. 464.)] W; p. 404.∧
298.8   around.] W; ~∧
298.8   and] W; [*not present*]
298.17   anything new,] W; ~, ~∧
298.17   of] W; of of
298.18   function] W; function capacity
298.19–20 more ready] W; ready
298.20   enter] W; it enters
298.22   than] W; that
298.32   perversion.] W; ~∧
298.34   prevent] W; prevents
299.7   vitreous,] WS; vitreuous,
299.8–9   an unluminous] WS; a unlumnous
299.9–10 [the material . . . tests],] W; ∧~∧ ,
299.11   "The] W; ∧~
299.21   continually] W; conually
299.24   were] W; [*not present*]
299.25   say] W; [*not present*]
299.30   is to tell] W; to tell
299n.3   realm] W; [*not present*]
299n.4   effort] W; [*not present*]
299n.5   as characteristics] W; characteristics
299n.6   form,"] W; ~∧"
299n.9   original.)] W; ~).
299n.9   "represents,"] W; "~∧"
300.1   it is] W; it it
300.6   not know] B; now
300.6   the spoken] W; the the spoken
300.7   what the written] W; why the wrotten
300.10   instances] W; instance
300.11   usage,] W; ~∧
300.12   say,] W; ~∧

300.21   signness] W; signess
300.26   to take] W; [*not present*]
300.35   Ogden-Richards's] W; Ogden-Richards
300.35   "epistemological"] W; "~∧
301.2   Thought."⁵] W; ~."∧
301.4   2.] WS; 2∧
301.4   referent] WS; Referent
301.6   Symbolism] WS; symbolism
301.6   *How*] WS; *how*
301.7   *Related?"*] WS; *related*."
301.7   passage] W; passage is
301.9   as] W; as as
301.10   problem"] W; ~∧
301.13   out] W; how
301.14   that it] W; the it
301.16   inquiring] W; inquiry
301.29   they proffer] W; he proffers
301.29, 31, 37   their] W; his
301.30   they are] W; he is
301.34   "thought"] W; "~∧
301.35   kind] W; [*not present*]
301.36   they call] W; he calls
301.37   "external contexts,"] W; ∧~∧"
301n.1   11.] W; 11∧
301n.2   p.] W; p∧
302.2   or repeated] W; repeated
302.4   and (eventually] W; (and eventually marks (and eventually
302.5   become] W; becomes
302.9   takes] W; taken
302.10   thoughts] W; ~)
302.10   authors)] W; ~∧
302.11   hear] W; hears
302.19   in an] W; in an an
302.26   the triangle] W; the the triangle
302.29   that] W; that that
302n.3   p. 229 and p. 230] W; p. 228 and p. 234
302n.3   Bentley] W; Bentlay
302n.4   Knowns,] W; *Knowns.*
302n.4   26,] W; 26.
303.3   be] W; [*not present*]
303.11   reader's] W; readers
303.13   presentation of] W; presentation
303.15   one and] W; one and and

303.17   "referent"] W; "~∧
303.17   very] W; same very
303.21   "referent."] W; "~∧"
303.24–25   distinction] W; about *Meaning* Signs are spoekn of as
          carrying meanings,—and words as sign-vehicles. distinction
303n.3   a commercial] W; a a commercial
304.1   us] W; [*not present*]
304.7   gross] W; grose
304.14   behaviors] W; behavior
304.17   utensils,] W; ~∧
304.23   casual] W; causal
304n.4   the existence] W; The existence
305.4   it] W; it it
305.6   à] W; a
305.7   customary] W; ~,
305.14   are transactions] W; are of transaction
305.15   is usually,] W; is is usually,
305.16   grass,] W; garsz,
305.18   say,] W; ~.
305.26   that] W; that that
305.26   more] B; [*not present*]
305.29   things in] W; the things in
305.32   be] W; [*not present*]
305.33   considerations] W; consideration
305.33–34   argument.] W; ~∧
305n.2   and] W; [*not present*]
306.2   previously] W; previous
306.3   times] W; times of
306.4   was, say,] W; ~∧ ~∧
306.8   and,] W; ~∧
306.9   no longer in] W; in no longer
306.10   they have been no more] W; have they been any more
306.11   through] W; though
306.22   that] W; such as
307.1   emphasis,] W; ~.
307.9   direction,] W; ~∧
307.11   etc., etc.] W; ~∧, ~.,
307.13   is,] W; ~∧
307n.1   repetition] W; repitition
307n.5   E.] W; E∧
307n.6   *Science*,] W; ~.
307n.6   4,] W; 4. (
307n.6   entitled] W; ~,

307n.7   Realism?"] W; ~,ₐ
307n.8   No.] W; ~ₐ
307n.9   subjectmatter] W; subject matter
308.10   aspects] W; aspect
308.13   that is,] W; this
308.15   the material] W; the the material
308.16   as] W; [*not present*]
308.20   separated] W; separted separated
308.20   subjectmatter] W; subjectmatter and are subjectmatter
308.22–23   "signi*fied*,"] W; "~,ₐ
308.24   "philosophic")] W; "~"ₐ
308.25   which imply] W; which openly asser to which imply
308.25   "Objects"] W; ₐ~"
308.26   else—] W; ~,
308.26–27   or speakers] W; ospeakers
308.27   whatever—] W; ~ₐ
308.28   (c)] W; (3)
308n.7   Knowns."] W; *Knowns.*ₐ
308n.9   *Inquiry.*] W; ~ₐ
308n.13   constitutes] W; constitute
308n.15   is] W; [*not present*]
308n.16   See, for example,] W; ~. ~.
309.3   being] W; being is
309.5–6   because] W; become
309.29   in] W; in in
309.36   to] W; to to
309.37   ever] W; every

Values, Valuations, and Social Facts

Copy-text for this reply is the unpublished typescript, typed by Dewey, in the Arthur F. Bentley Collection, Manuscripts Department, Lilly Library, Indiana University, Bloomington, 9 pp., dated 20 June 1945.

310.12   repetition.] W; repitition.
310.13   Benoit-Smullyan's] W; Benoit's-Smullyan's
310.17   represented] W; represent
310.17–18   Lévy-Bruhl] W; Levy-Bruhl
310.24–25   occasions:] W; occassions:
310n.1   XLII,] W; ~,,
311.15   acts] W; facts

311.33   commonplace] W; common place
312.8   component. . . .] W; ~ . . .
312.19   say,] W; ~ᴧ
312.34   by] W; by by
313.9   obligation," etc.] W; ~ᴧᴧ ~."
313.38   say, of] W; ~ᴧ ~,
313.39   science, the] W; science, and the
313.40   incredibility.] W; ~/
314.3   Benoit-Smullyan] W; benoit-smullyan
314.5   prizings,] W; ~ᴧ
314.13   kind.] W; ~ᴧ
314.16   become] W; becomes
314.19   consideration.⁴] W; ~.ᴧ
314.20   difference] W; differences
314.21   derived,] W; ~;
314.23   specified,] W; ~ᴧ
314n.13   "components"] W; "~ᴧ
314n.13   that] W; that that
314n.13–14   preventing] W; prevents
314n.15   their] W; them
315.12   dealing with] W; dealing with dealing with
315.12   signifies] W; signified
315.22   Benoit-Smullyan] W; Benoit-Smullan
315.29–30   *scientist.*"⁵] W; ~".ᴧ
315.30   "neutrality"] W; "~ᴧ
315.32   deep-seated] WS; deepseated
315n.1   cit.,] W; Cit.,
316.1   into] W; in to
316.2   subjectmatter,] W; ~ᴧ
316.4   article.] W; ~ᴧ
316.7   "evaluations."] W; "~ᴧ"
316.11   overrides] W; overides
316.15   valuings] W; valuinga
316.24   a case] W; case
316.27   3.] W; (3)
316.28   subjects] W; subject
316.36–37   this and that] W; that and that
316.40   may say,] W; may,
316.40   be] W; be be
317.6   There are] W; There

Importance, Significance, and Meaning

Copy-text for the introductory section, 318.1–320.14, is the unpublished typescript, typed by Dewey, in the Arthur F. Bentley Collection, Manuscripts Department, Lilly Library, Indiana University, Bloomington, 3 pp., sent to Bentley 4 June 1950.

Copy-text for the remainder of the essay is a conflation of the typescript carbon copy dated 30 March 1950, not typed by Dewey, in the John Dewey Papers, Box 58, folder 9, Special Collections, Morris Library, Southern Illinois University at Carbondale, 23 pp. (DTS), and the typescript carbon copy dated 31 March 1950, not typed by Dewey, in the Bentley Collection, 23 pp. (BTS). Emendations have been accepted from the BTS publication in *John Dewey and Arthur F. Bentley: A Philosophical Correspondence, 1932–1951* (PC), ed. Sidney Ratner and Jules Altman (New Brunswick, N.J.: Rutgers University Press, 1964), pp. 658–68. Emendations have also been adopted from Dewey's revisions on extant ribbon-copy pages of the two typescripts (Dewey Papers, Box 58, folder 16, 31 pp.). Original pages matching DTS are designated TS¹, those matching BTS are designed TS². For all revisions, see Dewey's Revisions in "Importance, Significance, and Meaning."

318.7	prepared] W; preparws
318.9	Bentley] W; bentley
318.10	1949);] W; $\sim_\wedge$;
318.11	*Behavior,*] W; Behavior.
318.11	*Fact*] W; fact
318.12	*Think*] W; Think,
318.14	(1938).] W; (1939).
318.20	number] W; niumber
318n.1	(1949).] W; (1948).
319.5	contemporary] W; contempare
319.12–13	relationships] W; a relationships
319.15	the issues,] W; the the issues,
319.16	the chief] W; the the chief
319.21	they were] W; they they were
319.29	formation of] W; formation
319.31	directed] W; and direct
319.34	relationships] W; trelationship
319.34	age;] W; $\sim_{,,}$;
319.39	guidance of] W; guidance of of
*320.1	intended] W; is intended

320.3   undertaken] W; under taken
*320.6   which while] W; which which
320.11   as naming] W; as as naming
321.2–3   degrading a] TS^1; a degrading DTS, BTS
321.25   (from] TS^2; $_\wedge\sim$ DTS, BTS
321.25   and *view*] TS^2; *of view* DTS, BTS
321.26   article)] TS^2; $\sim_\wedge$ DTS, BTS
322.19   inquiry,] DTS; $\sim_\wedge$ BTS
322.19   *using*] BTS; [*rom.*] DTS
322.28   function or] PC; function of DTS, BTS
322.36   had] PC; has DTS, BTS
323.4   constituted by] TS^1; constituted not by DTS, BTS
323.12–13 he regards as unimportant] DTS; are not regarded as
           important BTS
323.15   for] DTS; of BTS
323.17   like] DTS; like some of BTS
324.21   the inquiry] DTS; inquiry BTS
325.20   proceeds,] TS^2; $\sim_\wedge$ DTS, BTS
*325.25   are such as to provide] TS^2; are such as to   means in
           a use that provides DTS, BTS
*325.32–33 We . . . life behavior] TS^1; (Page 9 missing in the ms.)
           DTS, BTS
325.35   phases] DTS; phrases BTS
325.39   whether dog or man,] TS^2; dog or man$_\wedge$ DTS, BTS
326.6   sensory] PC; asensory DTS, BTS
*326.12–13 wholly . . . lodged in] TS^2; extraneous
           entity   been so lodged with DTS, BTS
326.19   unity] TS^1, TS^2; entity DTS, BTS
328.4   seems] PC; seem DTS, BTS
328.14   suffices] TS^2; suffice DTS, BTS
328.18   means-to-consequences] TS^2; means in consequences
           DTS, BTS
328.38   place,] PC; $\sim_\wedge$ DTS, BTS
*329.16   by means of] W; [*not present*] DTS, BTS
329.25   put] PC; out DTS, BTS
330.34–35 with respect] DTS; in respect BTS
331.2   distinctively human activity] TS^1; human intelligently con-
           ducted activity DTS, BTS
331.9   meaning] TS^2; meanings DTS, BTS
331.10   with] TS^1, TS^2; [*not present*] DTS, BTS
331.23   and as such is] TS^1; as such it is DTS, BTS
331.25   into,] DTS; $\sim$; BTS

332.14   a "domain"] PC; "domain" DTS, BTS
332.19   "meaning"] W; "meanings" DTS, BTS
332.21   intend,] PC; ~‸ DTS, BTS

How, What, and *What For* in Social Inquiry

Copy-text for this paper is the revised January 1951 typescript, not typed by Dewey, 13 pp., with signed, holograph addition, pp. 14–18 (TS[1-H]). Emendations have been accepted from the second typescript (TS [2]), prepared in Honolulu January–February 1951, not typed by Dewey, 10 pp. Both documents are in the John Dewey Papers, Box 59, folder 13, Special Collections, Morris Library, Southern Illinois University at Carbondale.

334.2   and hence] TS[2]; and hence and hence TS[1-H]
334.2   as authoritative] *stet* TS[1-H]; authoritative TS[2]
334.3   entire] *stet* TS[1-H]; whole TS[2]
334.5   from] TS[2]; from from TS[1-H]
334.9   belong intrinsically in and to] *stet* TS[1-H]; belong and to in-trinsic TS[2]
334.36   , nous).] W; ‸~.) TS[2]; ‸~.). TS[1-H]
334.40   *performed*] TS[1-H]; [*rom.*] TS[2]
334.40   *service*] TS[1-H]; [*rom.*] TS[2]
335.7   and/or] *stet* TS[1-H]; and/of TS[2]
336.3   "Common Sense and Science"] W; ‸Common-Sense and Scientific Knowing‸ TS[2], TS[1-H]
336.8   observe,] TS[2]; orbserve, TS[1-H]
337.30   the moral] *stet* TS[1-H]; moral TS[2]
338.20   clear] W; unclear TS[2], TS[1-H]
338.29   than] *stet* TS[1-H]; that TS[2]
339.15   not] W; nor TS[2], TS[1-H]
339.21   *raison d'être*] W; *raison d'etre* TS[2], TS[1-H]
340.2   "In Social Inquiry"] W; "In the Social Sciences" TS[2]; "*In the Social Sciences*" TS[1-H]
340.4   is] *stet* TS[1-H]; it TS[2]
340.5   *all*] TS[1-H]; [*rom.*] TS[2]
340.7   revolution] *stet* TS[1-H]; revelation TS[2]
340.8   astronomy and] *stet* TS[1-H]; astronomy, TS[2]
340.9   *how,*] TS[1-H]; [*rom.*] TS[2]
340.11   teleology.] TS[2]; ~). TS[1-H]
340.14   "*moral*")] W; "moral"‸ TS[2]; "*moral*"‸ TS[1-H]

340.17 hence as] *stet* TS[1-H]; were TS[2]
340.19 *seen*] TS[1-H]; [*rom.*] TS[2]
340.19 yet] *stet* TS[1-H]; [*om.*] TS[2]
340.21 however] *stet* TS[1-H]; [*om.*] TS[2]
340.23 at last] *stet* TS[1-H]; [*om.*] TS[2]
340.23 as far at least] *stet* TS[1-H]; at least as far TS[2]
*340.25 For.] W; *for,* [For. TS[1-H]] and [*not present* TS[1-H]] has broken down the status of space and time [Space and Time TS[1-H]] as entities fixed in themselves and having independence [hence independent TS[1-H]] of whatever is taken to occur within their confining boundaries. The supposed scientific basis for separating space and time [Space and Time TS[1-H]] as major "*whats*" [*rom.* TS[1-H]] from [from the TS[1-H]] minor "*whats*" [ʌwhatsʌ TS[1-H]] which take place within them is abolished once and [*not present* TS[1-H]] for all. But the full significance of Relativity Theory for scientific inquiry will be TS[2], TS[1-H]
*340.25 The victory will be] *stet* TS[1-H]; [*om.*] TS[2]
340.25 however] *stet* TS[1-H]; [*om.*] TS[2]
340.27 *how*] TS[1-H]; [*rom.*] TS[2]
340.27–28 subjectmatter] TS[2]; subject/matter TS[1-H]

The Field of "Value"

Copy-text for this essay is the typescript (TS), not typed by Dewey, that was used as printer's copy (Dewey VFM 87, Special Collections, Morris Library, Southern Illinois University at Carbondale, 24 pp., courtesy of Maud A. Lepley). Substantive changes made in printer's copy (PC) and in *Value: A Cooperative Inquiry,* ed. Ray Lepley (New York: Columbia University Press, 1949), pp. 64–77 (V), have been accepted as emendations. The following list, recording all variants between TS, PC, and V, serves as a historical collation.

343.3 methodological:—] TS; ~:ʌ V, PC
*343.3–4, 5–6, 8; 344.5; 349.20–21; 356.27–28, 33, 36, n.4 subjectmatter(s)] W; subject matter V, PC, TS
343.10 up,] TS, PC; ~ʌ V
343.14 Mr.] TS; [*om.*] V, PC
343.16 Subject?"[1]] PC, V; ~?"ʌ TS
343.16 his] V; the PC, TS
343.24 or] V; nor PC, TS

*343n.1–2   1. Contained . . . inquiry.] V; ¹Contained in the ques-
            tions and comments preliminary to this symposium.
            PC; [not present] TS
344.4   behavioral] TS; ~, V, PC
344.20, 21 that] V; which PC, TS
344.25   qualifications] V; first qualifications PC, TS
344.25   added] V; noted PC, TS
344.29   going-concern.] TS; ~ₐ~. V, PC
344.29   all have] V; they have PC, TS
344.32   consequence:—] TS; ~ₐ— V, PC
344.32   is a] V; as a PC, TS
344.35   behavioral] V; [rom.] PC, TS
345.1   whenever] V; to whatever PC, TS
345.1   are used.] V; apply. PC, TS
345.5   themselves] V; may PC, TS
345.10   defense, and of] V; defenseₐ and even PC, TS
345.19   that] V; which PC, TS
345.21   any] PC, V; [rom.] TS
345.21   mere] V; such PC, TS
345.22   inadmissable] TS; inadmissible V, PC
345.30; 346n.1 preliminary] PC, V; [not present] TS
345.30   Dr.] TS; [om.] V, PC
345.33   given] PC, V; given in TS
345n.4   The] PC, V; See No.   of the questions in the document
            submitted. The TS
345n.7   pursuits] TS, PC; ~, V
346.4–5   like, say, the words] V; likeₐ the words, say, PC, TS
346.12   its] V; an PC, TS
346n.1   that] V; which PC, TS
346n.1   Mr.] TS; [om.] V, PC
346n.1–2   especially] PC, V; particularly TS
346n.2   searching:—] TS; ~ₐ— V, PC
346n.3   values.] PC, V; values. (See Nos. 7 and 22 of the list.)
            TS
347.8   etc.] TS; and so on. V, PC
347.21   sat-upon,] TS, PC; ~ₐ~, V
347.22   the eggs,] V; also the eggs, PC, TS
347.22   chicks,] V; ~ₐ PC, TS
347.33   has to be] V; would be PC, TS
347.33–34   if at all,] V; if it were taken PC, TS
347.35   as in cases] V; in the cases PC, TS
347.39–40   use of it] V; its use PC, TS
348.1   facts] V; [rom.] PC, TS

348.6   etc.,] TS; and so on, V, PC
348.6   made:—] TS; ~:$_\wedge$ V, PC
348.8   conditions] V; conditions which are PC, TS
348.9   understood in isolation from] V; understood without refer-
         ence to many PC, TS
348.15   highly] V; very PC, TS
348.21   (viewed] V; (all viewed PC, TS
348.21   current] V; [*not present*] PC, TS
348.22   All] V; But they PC, TS
348.24   valuing] V; Valuing PC, TS
348.26   confused] V; present confused PC, TS
348.27   does] V; [*not present*] PC, TS
348.29   things),] TS, PC; ~)$_\wedge$ V
348.29   singular, and] V; singular, while PC; singular; while TS
348.32   agreed upon] TS; ~-~ V, PC
348.34   displace] V; then displace PC, TS
348n.1   etc.,] TS; and so forth V, PC
348n.5   case is, of course,] PC, V; case, of course, is TS
349.11   an affirmation] V; affirmation PC, TS
*349.12 As . . . discussion] PC, V; Discussion TS
349.13   state,] TS, PC; ~$_\wedge$ V
349.14   place only] V; place, PC; place TS
349.17   abstractions,] TS, PC; ~$_\wedge$ V
349.25–26 of dogs] V; that dogs PC, TS
349.26   being] V; are PC, TS
*350.2   difference,] TS, V; ~$_\wedge$ PC
350.6   given] V; they give PC, TS
350.10   "ideal"] PC, V; as "ideal" TS
*350.10–11 utopian, sentimental,] V; utopian or sentimental,
         PC; utopian or sentimental$_\wedge$ TS
350.14   *also*] V; [*rom.*] PC, TS
350.17   value,] TS, PC; ~$_\wedge$ V
*350.20 matter] *stet* TS; a matter V, PC
350.23   to measure] V; measure PC, TS
350.24–25 means for] V; means of PC, TS
350.26   outcome.] V; consequence. PC, TS
350.27   being] V; since it is PC, TS
350.30   only] PC, V; these only TS
350.31   logic,] PC, V; ~$_\wedge$ TS
350.31   practical,] PC, V; ~$_\wedge$ TS
350.33   inhuman,] TS; ~$_\wedge$ V, PC
350.35   consists] V; is found PC, TS
350.39   *per se,*] TS; [*rom.*] V, PC

350.40   they *are*] V; *they* are PC, TS
351.2–3   questions . . . study] V; questions and comments preliminary to this symposium PC; documents submitted by Dr.
Lepley TS
351.4   the meaning] V; the import of the meaning PC, TS
351.4–5   in the sense of] V; as involving PC, TS
351.5   which] V; that PC, TS
351.5–6   in existence . . . cherished,] V; the things prized or cherished in existence, PC, TS
351.7   prizing] PC, V; ~, TS
351.10   etc.,] TS; and so on, V, PC
351.14–15   circumstantially] V; circumstancially PC, TS
351.18   It] TS; [*no* ¶] ~ V, PC
*351.18   experiences] PC, V; cases experiences TS
*351.20   independently] PC, V; independent TS
351.21; 352.15, 17, 21–22, 24, 28, 28–29, 30, 34, 35, 38, 39;
353.7 esthetic] TS, PC; aesthetic V
*351.24   Each] PC, V; Either TS
*351.26   So a] PC, V; A TS
*351.27   attitudes,] PC, V; types, TS
*351.27   its distinctive kind] PC, V; a distinct type TS
351.32   fuller] V; a fuller PC, TS
351.37   it] PC, V; [*not present*] TS
351.37   mine.] PC, V; mind. TS
351n.1   by Mr. Rice] W; by Rice V, PC; of Mr. Rice, TS
351n.1   in . . . comments.] PC, V; No. 9. TS
352.3   is definitely] PC, V; definitely TS
352.11   value-field] V; the value-field PC, TS
352.24   become] *stet* TS, PC; became V
352.27   etc., etc.] TS; and so on and so on. V, PC
352.32–33   that . . . esthetic;] W; that is momentary is aesthetic;
V; is esthetic that is momentary; PC, TS
352.37   goes] PC, V; does TS
353.3, 11–12   ground work] TS; groundwork V, PC
353.9   I believe (i)] W; I believe (1) PC, V; (i) I believe TS
353.14   any attempt] V; the attempt PC, TS
353.30   plus] TS, PC; ~, V
354.6   question] V; question as to PC, TS
354.6–7   prizings, etc.,] TS; prizings (and so on) V, PC
354.8   former),] V; ~)ᴧ PC, TS
354.11   foresight] W; ~, V, PC, TS
354.11   outcome,] V; ~ᴧ PC, TS
354.12   caring-for,] V; ~ᴧ PC, TS

354.12–13   the link] V; a link PC, TS
354.14   *into*] PC, V; [*rom.*] TS
354.15   may] V; [*not present*] PC, TS
354.17   outcome] TS, PC; ~, V
*354.23   sort of] PC, V; sort or TS
354.26, 33   that] V; which PC, TS
354.26   class-membership,] TS; ~∧~, V, PC
354.27   dicta] V; dictas PC; dictates TS
354.28   etc., etc.,] TS; and the like, V, PC
354.35   *at first*] V; [*rom.*] PC, TS
355.3   ecclesiastical] PC, V; eccelesiastical TS
*355.3–4   as to provide] PC, V; that they provide TS
*355.4–5   whatever . . . impossible.] PC, V; those who hold that rational valuations are impossible whatever color of plausibility their view possesses. TS
355.18   exclusively] V; merely PC, TS
355.23   theories that] V; theories, which PC, TS
355.28   *conditions* that] V; *conditions* which PC, TS
355.29   place,] TS, PC; ~; V
355.30   determined] PC, V; that are determined TS
355.33   class-interests,] TS; ~∧~, V, PC
355n.2   valuing] V; one PC, TS
355n.2   valuation.] V; the other. PC, TS
355n.4   in] V; of PC, TS
356.19   esthetic] TS; aesthetic V, PC
356.21   occasion,⁹] V; ~,∧ PC, TS
356.23   directing] TS; ~, V, PC
356.24   behavior,] TS; ~∧ V, PC
356.28   judgment.] V; ~.⁹ PC, TS
*356.29   use or] PC, V; office of TS
356n.1–2   article, . . . XLII] PC, V; article, in THE JOURNAL OF PHILOSOPHY, Vol. XLII, pp. TS
356n.2–3   701–712.] TS, V; 701–12. PC
*356n.3   "Persuasion"] V; The use PC; The office TS
356n.4   factual subjectmatter] W; factual subject matter, V, PC; subject matter TS
357.2   etc., etc.] TS; and so on. V, PC
*357.5–7   The . . . now] PC, V; So far as the function of persuasion, and of producing convictions which direct subsequent behavior, peculiar to judgments conventionally recognized to be in the value-field, that function is now TS
357.7   better] V; best PC, TS
357.13   or biological] PC, V; biological, etc., TS

357.29   everywhere.[10]] PC, V; ~.∧ TS
357n.1   10. For . . . see] PC, V; [not present] TS
357n.1–2   Value . . . pp. 312–318.] W; pp. 312–318, below.
            V; pp. 000–000, below. PC; [not present] TS

Has Philosophy a Future?

Copy-text for this paper is its publication in *Proceedings of the Tenth
International Congress of Philosophy* (Amsterdam, 11–18 August 1948),
ed. E. W. Beth, H. J. Pos, and J. H. A. Hollak (Amsterdam: North-
Holland Publishing Co., 1949), pp. 108–16.

*358.7   subjectmatter] W; subject-matter
 359.32   fact, however, implies] W; ~∧ ~, ~,
 359.33   commonplace,] W; ~∧
 359.35   existence] W; existance
 360.15   life] W; live
*361.8; 365.23; 367.7   subjectmatter(s)] W; subject matter
 361.19   relationships] W; relationship
 361.21   challenge] W; challange
*361.25–26; 364.6   a philosophy] W; philosophy
 361.40–362.1   whatever,] W; ~∧
 362.10   claims] W; clams
 362.12   of movement] W; of movements
 362.33   representatives] W; representative
 362.37   Left] W; left
 363.31   ongoing] W; on going
 364.12   everyday] W; every day
 365.1   doubtful,] W; ~∧
*366.23   which material, moreover,] W; ~, ~∧ ~∧
 366.28   intended] W; intented
 367.9   with respect] W; with the respect
 367.19   into] W; into to
*367.30   a share] W; share
 368.15   challenge,] W; ~∧
 368.16   successors] W; success

Philosophy's Future in Our Scientific Age

Copy-text for this essay is its publication in *Commentary* 8 (October
1949): 388–94.

*370.26; 371.34, 35; 379n.5; 381.19, 23   subjectmatter] W; subject
       matter
373n.1   pp. 142–43,] W; pp. 141–42,
373n.2   1946.] W; 1944.
374.13   divertible] WS; divertable

Experience and Existence: A Comment

Copy-text for this reply is the typescript (TS), not typed by Dewey, in
the Joseph Ratner/John Dewey Papers, Box 46, folder 12, Special Collections, Morris Library, Southern Illinois University at Carbondale,
9 pp. Emendations have been accepted from its publication in *Philosophy and Phenomenological Research* 9 (June 1949): 709–13 (PPR).

383.2   asking:] PPR; asking two questions of me. The first one
        reads:
383.3   *beyond*] PPR; [*rom.*]
383.10, 13; 385.19   that] PPR; which
*383.13   me] *stet* TS; me by them PPR
383n.3   Metaphysics,"] PPR; *Metaphysics*$_\wedge$
383n.3   pp. 316–321.] PPR; (~).
*384.1   on my view] *stet* TS; in my view PPR
384.19   I have] PPR; [*not present*]
384.27   the use] PPR; a use
385.1   either] PPR; [*not present*]
385.2   as the ground] PPR; to serve as ground
385.2   his intimation] PPR; the suggestion
385.3–4   that conclusion] PPR; it
385.4   view] PPR; view that to me
385.4–5   (which . . . me)] PPR; (as to him)
385.5   that experience] PPR; experience
385.6   view; nevertheless,] PPR; view, and yet,
385.6   he] PPR; [*not present*]
385.8   his] PPR; the
385.33   that] PPR; the
385.34   connected] PPR; [*not present*]
386.13   be] PPR; were
386.19–387.8   I . . . throughout.] PPR; [*not present*]
386.27   names,] W; name, PPR; [*not present*] TS
*387.18   view] W; view gets transformed PPR, TS
387.19   here] PPR; in this case
387.21   world.] PPR; existential world.

*387.21 the view] PPR; [*not present*]
387.21 terms] PPR; terms which are
387.22 not] PPR; [*not present*]
387.22 space-time] PPR; [*not present*]
387n.2 See . . . p. 416.] PPR; *Experience and Nature,* from bottom
          of P. 412 to top of P. 415.
388.4   words] *stet* TS; worlds PPR
388.6   serving] PPR; [*not present*]
388.7   under-pinning.] PPR; ~.[6]
388.20–21 their identification.] PPR; identification of them.
388.22 that which is named] PPR; what they name
388.22 moreover] PPR; [*not present*]
388.26 are] PPR; is
388.27 values] PPR; them
388.30 criticism] PPR; cricitism
388.33 this specious] PPR; [*not present*]
388.34 reached] PPR; [*not present*]
388.35 general traits] PPR; them
388.38 ; criticism, that is,] PPR; [*not present*]
388.38 events.] PPR; events; that is to say, of warranted judgment.
388.38–39 For example,] PPR; [*not present*]
388.39–40 [general]] PPR; [*not present*]
389.1   its] PPR; [*not present*]
389.2   "fear] PPR; ∧~
389.4   and point] PPR; [*not present*]
389.5   application in] PPR; application to and in
389.5   that is,] PPR; [*not present*]

Contribution to "Religion and the Intellectuals"

Copy-text for this symposium contribution is the typescript, not typed by Dewey, in the Arthur F. Bentley Collection, Manuscripts Department, Lilly Library, Indiana University, Bloomington, 8 pp. Emendations have been accepted from its publication in *Partisan Review* 17 (February 1950):129–33 (PR).

390.3   loss . . . intellectuals,] PR; loss among intellectuals of faith
          in science∧
390.5   which] PR; which hardly more than a generation ago were
          supposed by
390.5   class had abandoned,] PR; class to have been outlawed
          scientifically,

390.5   is] PR; is such
390.6   rendering] PR; as to render
390.6   editors of] PR; editors of the
390.10   latter] PR; latter point
390.12   seem] PR; seem to many
390.12   gross] PR; a gross
390.14   the following] PR; this particular
390.15   In . . . is] PR; There is in any case
390.16   the attendant] PR; its attendant
390.17   , and . . . affairs] PR; [not present]
390.18   shall] PR; shall proceed to
390.23   disorganization.] PR; disorganization, actual and
          threatened.
390.25   cultural.] PR; even cultural.
391.6   belief] PR; beliefs
391.7   be] PR; also be
391.8   which] PR; [not present]
391.9   These] PR; In addition, these
391.10   desirable] PR; desirable and widely desired
391.11   understanding . . . follow] PR; understanding due to
391.13   For] PR; [no ¶] For
391.16   by accepting belief in] PR; by means of
391.20   process.] PR; method.
391.22–23 the statement] PR; it
391.24   the absence of] PR; introduction of all
*391.26   has been] PR; was
391.29   downright] PR; a downright
391.32   confidence] PR; confidences
391.33   such] PR; [not present]
391.34   overturn] PR; overturn of this sort
391.35   shift] PR; upset
391.35   those involved in] PR; those who, taken severally, are com-
          ponents of
391.36   arrangements upset.] PR; arrangements, domestic and
          international, which are its gross and obvious features.
391.36   those] PR; those who are
391.37   and] PR; and are
391.40–392.1 position] PR; attitude
392.1   remained] PR; remain
392.1–2   old attitudes] PR; older intellectual and moral attitudes
          that are
392.6   return to] PR; return to acceptance of
392.8   support."] PR; support for themselves."

392.8   Just as I] PR; At the time I
392.8   this] PR; the importance of this
392.13   about] PR; concerning
392.21   needing] PR; having
392.28   is] PR; will be
392.29; 393.27   which] PR; that
392.38   is] PR; [*not present*]
392.39   worlds. Between them] PR; worlds between which
392.39   the] PR; [*not present*]
392.39–40 communication that] PR; communication, which
392.40   agreement] PR; ∼,
393.1   In view] PR; In such a state of affairs, particularly in view
393.1–2   propaganda] PR; propaganda to upset intellectual
           equilibrium,
393.2   vastly] PR; the vastly
393.2   in war,] PR; of war,
393.2   seems] PR; is rather
393.3   prior] PR; the prior
393.4   pessimism.] PR; a pessimism that marks the lowest ebb
           ever reached by anything bearing the name "science."
393.5   as] PR; [*not present*]
393.7–8   It stands for] PR; For it is
393.8–9   disposition in which] PR; disposition of a public substitu-
           tion of
393.10–11 distrust, . . . regard.] PR; distrust, which even if it con-
           tinue to be but a Cold War chills to its marrow warm hopes
           and expectations which only a short time ago were ardently
           burning.
393.14   has] PR; have
393.15   the mass] PR; they
393.15   shared that attitude.] PR; possessed it.
393.15   The mass] PR; They most
393.23   insecurity,] PR; insecurity, with fear of their return rife,
393.29   We are] PR; The discussion is
393.35   very] PR; [*not present*]
393.35–39 The . . . intellectual.] PR; What has been lacking,
           however, is a place for the scientific attitude in the manage-
           ment and conduct of all the significant concerns and atti-
           tudes of mankind, not a place in any "hierarchy" even if it
           be that of an intellectual class. For the latter attitude is inev-
           itably contained and restrained. In view of what has already
           been said, I shall not expatiate upon a point that is funda-
           mental to all that has been said.

393.40   Little] PR; [*no* ¶] Since, however, little
393.40   in the foregoing] PR; [*not present*]
393.41   are] PR; were
393.41–394.1   consider.] PR; answer,
394.3   account] PR; account, originating presumably in intellect
394.3–4   an expression of] PR; in and from the movement of
394.4   kinds] PR; varieties
394.5   religion.] PR; what is named *religion.*
394.12   conflict, and] PR; conflicts,
394.13   in . . . fact] PR; [*not present*]
394.13–14   differences . . . earth,] PR; differences with respect to
         what may be called the proper techniques of the operation
         of the supernatural are conspicuously divisive,
394.15   values] PR; more values
394.15   sustained—] PR; sustained, and will be more
394.16   supported] PR; ~,
394.18   Not] PR; [*no* ¶] Not
394.23   an] PR; [*not present*]
394.24   on the part] PR; [*not present*]
394.24–25   preferred] PR; referred
394.25   it is] PR; [*not present*]
394.25   pluralisms] PR; pluralism
394.26   provided] PR; provided always
394.26   inter-communication.] PR; inter-communication and of
         trans-communication.

Aesthetic Experience as a Primary Phase and as an Artistic Development

Copy-text for this reply is its publication in *Journal of Aesthetics and Art Criticism* 9 (September 1950): 56–58.

395.10, 11   aesthetic] WS; esthetic
395.20   on the] W; on
395n.1   Vol. VIII] W; Vol. VII
395n.1   No. 2,] W; No. 21,
*396.6   first and third chapters.] W; first two chapters.
396.21   in which] W; of which
*396.34, 36; 397.7, 20, 35–36   subjectmatter(s)] W; subject matter
397.38   There] WS; [*no* ¶] ~

Contribution to *Democracy in a World of Tensions*

Copy-text for this essay is its publication as chap. 5 in *Democracy in a World of Tensions: A Symposium prepared by UNESCO,* ed. Richard McKeon and Stein Rokkan (Chicago: University of Chicago Press, 1951), pp. 62–68. No emendations have been made.

Modern Philosophy

Copy-text for this essay is the second copy of the untitled typescript (TS²) in the Joseph Ratner/John Dewey Papers, Box 46, folder 6, Special Collections, Morris Library, Southern Illinois University at Carbondale, 21 pp., in which only the last page is typed by Dewey. Emendations have been accepted from its publication as "Modern Philosophy" in *The Cleavage in Our Culture: Studies in Scientific Humanism in Honor of Max Otto,* ed. Frederick Burkhardt (Boston: Beacon Press, 1952), pp. 15–29 (CC).

407.1	Modern Philosophy] CC; [*not present*]
407.6	medieval] CC; Medieval
407.11	those of] CC; those
407.13	is a report] CC; are reports
407.19	(1)] CC; [*not present*]
407.22	that (2)] CC; that, in the second place,
407.27	The vision] CC; Vision
407.27	was] CC; has
408.2	respect to] CC; [*not present*]
408.3	the vision] CC; a vision
408.9	the deviation] CC; deviation
408.13	But because] CC; Because
*408.13	shock to] W; shock of CC; shock given to TS²
408.22	wherever] CC; whatever
408.23	were] CC; remained those
408.24	that] CC; [*not present*]
408.31	conscience, by] CC; conscience;
408.32	consciousness,] CC; ~;
408.32	intuition—things] CC; intuition; they were
408.34	an underlying] CC; a underlying
408.37	great] CC; [*not present*]
408.39	source] CC; opportunity and source
408.40	put . . . was:] CC; its attitude put in words would be:
409.1	worlds,] CC; ~∧

409.5–6   The . . . Religion] CC; [*ital.*]
409.7   better] CC; [*not present*]
409.8   formulated] CC; formulated and wrestled with
409.18   whose natural,] CC; the natural,
409.18   culmination] CC; culmination of which
409.19   Logos,] CC; *Logos* and
409.23   the adoption] CC; adoption
409.26   the true] CC; true
409.26   "science," and] CC; "Science"; while
409.30   science. It] CC; science; it
409.31   that] CC; which
409.40   "accidents," which] CC; "accidents∧" that
410.1   but] CC; but that
410.2   control] CC; the control
410.2–3   Immutable. The] CC; immutable. In consequence, the
410.4   by the] CC; by
410.6   tending . . . to] CC; that by their own nature tended to
410.8   necessary] CC; necessary and
410.12   actually] CC; [*not present*]
410.16   men,] CC; ~∧
410.18   far] CC; very far
410.19–20   jurisdiction between] CC; jurisdictions between the
410.20–21   fields. Conflict] CC; fields, which were supposed not to conflict
410.21   was prevented] CC; [*not present*]
410.21–22   the two "domains"] CC; they
410.29   occurrence] CC; occurrent
410.29   seem] CC; seem to be
410.31   arising from] CC; that manifested
410.32   were] CC; have been
410.34   old.] CC; old at their core.
410.39   Knowledge.] CC; knowing.
*411.2, 12, 31; 413.32; 415.21; 416.35, 39; 417.3, 7–8, 27;
    418.2   subjectmatter(s)] W; subject matter CC, TS²
411.3   that had been] CC; which were
411.4   Baser] CC; "~
411.7   that] CC; which
411.25   Consideration] CC; One finds consideration
411.25   is] CC; [*not present*]
411.30   only; that is,] CC; only, that is∧ those that are
411.30   *any*] CC; any substance or
411.31   philosophy's] CC; philosophy
411.35   taking] CC; the tendency to take

411.36   formal] CC; merely formal
411.37   issues] CC; [*not present*]
412.1   made by traditional philosophy] CC; that traditional phi-
          losophy has made
412.2   mark.] CC; marks.
412.2   problems] CC; issues and problems
412.4   range.] CC; the range.
412.4   local; they] CC; local, but
412.10   barriers] CC; barrier
412.12   organism's] CC; organisms'
412.14   fellow men] CC; fellow man
412.16   many of] CC; man of many of
412.18   recently] CC; very recently
412.23–24   not openly accepting] CC; who do not openly accept
412.24   attributes] CC; usually attributes
412.28   that, . . . are] CC; which are, to say the least,
412.31   quasi-mystical. Unconsciousness] CC; quasi-mystic. The
          Unconscious
412.38   line] CC; lines
412.39   made] CC; making
412.39–40   by means of] CC; through
413.3   that] CC; that in
413.3   modern] CC; the modern
413.4   such] CC; in such a state
413.9   has] CC; has now
*413.13   divisions] *stet* TS²; division CC
413.15   that] CC; which
413.18   When] CC; Only when
413.19   life,] CC; life could
413.20   becomes] CC; become
413.23   to do more here] CC; here to do more
413.24   that change] CC; the change
413.25   inquiry] CC; inquiry that involves a width and depth of
          scope
413.25   which] CC; that
413.26   technical—] CC; ~,
413.26   which in fact] CC; that, in fact,
413.26   now] CC; [*not present*]
413.26–27   scientific conclusions] CC; it
413.27   and for philosophical] CC; carrying out the distinctive
          office of philosophical
413.30   in the knowing of] CC; in connection with
413.32   which] CC; that

413.33–34   immutables] CC; the immutables
413.36–37   external] CC; [*not present*]
413.38   the] CC; [*rom.*]
413.40   is made] CC; [*not present*]
413.40   the inclusion] CC; inclusion
413.40–41   his concerns] CC; of human concerns
413.41   continuous] CC; continuity of
414.1   brutes. It] CC; brutes
414.3   But it] CC; It
414.3   *denial*] CC; a denial
414.5   sort, while] CC; while while
414.5   doctrine] CC; concept
414.7   Employment] CC; In its earlier phase, employment
414.8   partial . . . phase.] CC; partial.
414.16   Space and time, instead] CC; Instead
414.17   are] CC; space and time are
414.21   the indefinitely] CC; an indefinitely
414.22   which is nature] CC; [*not present*]
414.23   save] CC; same
414.24–25   alike . . . inquiry,] CC; of physical and physiological inquiry alike‿
414.25   separations] CC; separation
414.26   make] CC; now makes
414.29   the latter] CC; it
414.31   perpetuating] CC; perpetuation of
414.32   only] CC; [*not present*]
414.32   *the* "Object"] CC; the object
414.37   upon] CC; upon the
415.1   the natural] CC; a different sort of natural
415.2   the] CC; [*not present*]
415.10   *human*] CC; [*rom.*]
415.10   affairs. In respect to] CC; affairs, not of
415.11   Reality] CC; Reality in general, where
415.11   futile] CC; [*not present*]
415.11–12   the service actually rendered] CC; this service
415.12   the assumption that] CC; taking it for granted that
415.14–16   dealt. The . . . relations.] CC; dealt, in spite of the overwhelming change in human affairs actually taking place.
415.18   Philosophy] CC; [¶] Natural science in its own growth toward maturity has now done away with the grounds which were taken as the foundation of those errancies. Philosophy
415.21   able] CC; avle
415.25   that of] CC; [*not present*]

415.34   and of] CC; [*not present*]
415.37–416.1   of backwardness] CC; [*not present*]
416.4   so that] CC; and that
416.6   will] CC; would
416.8   feature] CC; one
416.8   represented in] CC; now represented by
416.10   and that] CC; so that
416.11   use in] CC; [*not present*]
416.14   practical)] CC; practical as the advance of physical theory
    has amply demonstrated)
416.17   of themselves] CC; [*not present*]
416.32   not] CC; now
417.1   constitute] CC; be
417.2   are] CC; [*not present*]
417.6   it] CC; but it
417.15   due to the] CC; in
417.15   subjectmatters.] W; subject matters. CC; subject matter.
    TS²
417.21   centuries] CC; century
417.22   physical inquiry . . . imposed] CC; free from burdens of
    physical inquiry imposed
417.25   human] CC; [*not present*]
417.25   are to be] CC; may be
417.26   projected] CC; be projected
417.26   It] CC; In this connection, it
417.27   again] CC; [*not present*]
417.29   mark.] CC; mark. That the human situation is now
    worldwide in extent is obvious without argument. The
    source of both our resources and of barriers lies far back in
    the abyss of time. Now only pre-human animal life is in-
    volved in the structure and in the sufferings and doings of
    man today, but also conditions formed in geological ages.
417.30   so] CC; [*not present*]
417.31   wide that the] CC; wide. The
417.32   be exchanged] CC; now be profitably exchanged
417.32   transactions] CC; the transactions
417.37   or] CC; of
418.1   problems today is to show] CC; problems of philosophy
418.1–2   scope . . . philosophy.] CC; range as the frame of refer-
    ence in which problems are to be located is to indicate in
    some detail that such is the fact.
418.3   if] CC; [*not present*]
418.6   aspect] CC; manner

418.7   behavior; it is so] CC; behavior so
418.8   and shaped by] CC; [*not present*]
418.9   give-and-take] CC; Give-and-take
418.10   is] CC; is, for example,
418.10   students of] CC; those concerned with
418.10   historical] CC; historic
418.12   in religious rites] CC; called religious doctrine
418.13   dogmas, in] CC; dogma,
418.14   "synthesis," a] CC; "synthesis∧" or
418.16   and of] CC; and
418.20   present] CC; [*not present*]
418.25   the modes] CC; modes
418.30   that] CC; the
418.31   which] CC; that
418.40   *in fact*] CC; [*rom.*]
419.6   liberal,] CC; liberal and
*419.13   systematic acceptance] *stet* TS²; acceptance CC
*419.14   aloofness] *stet* TS²; systematic aloofness CC
*419.15   but] *stet* TS²; [*not present*] CC
419.16–17 identified] CC; commonly identified
419.17   isolations] CC; isolation
419.18   in consequence] CC; as its consequence
419.18   conferred] CC; operated to confer
419.19   that] CC; that that
419.28   wellbeing] W; well-being CC; wellbing TS²
419.28   which] CC; all which
419.29   share.] CC; have a share.
419.29   so] CC; so so
419.33   resources] CC; resourced
419.35   humble] CC; a humable

Substantive Variants in
Knowing and the Known

This section records substantive variants between the *Knowing and the Known* copy-text (Boston: Beacon Press, 1949) and two precopy-text forms: publication in the *Journal of Philosophy* and Dewey's typescripts. Chapters 1, 8, and 9, written by Arthur F. Bentley, are not included here. Wording changes necessitated by book publication, such as references to "chapters" rather than "papers," are not listed. Corrections and substantive revisions of footnotes are listed, but formal citation changes, such as addition of place of publication, are not.

Variant sources are identified for each chapter and abbreviations supplied if necessary. The reading before the bracket is from the present edition; variants follow the bracket. A curved dash ~ means the same word(s) as before the bracket; a caret ∧ means the absence of a punctuation mark or footnote. A grid # before the entry indicates that the text has been emended and the reading appears in the Emendations List. An asterisk * before the entry indicates that there is a note on the variant; these notes appear in the following section, Notes on Substantive Variants in *Knowing and the Known*.

Preface (Dewey and Bentley)

Listed below are the substantive variants between the *Knowing and the Known* copy-text (KK), pp. v–vii [this volume, pp. 3–5], and two typescripts. The earlier typescript (TS), typed by Dewey, is enclosed in Dewey to Arthur F. Bentley, 3 September 1947 (Bentley Collection, Manuscripts Department, Lilly Library, Indiana University, Bloomington, 2 pp.); the revised typescript, not typed by Dewey (TS¹), is dated 15 September 1947 (Joseph Ratner/John Dewey Papers, Box 45, folder 9, Special Collections, Morris Library, Southern Illinois University at Carbondale, 3 pp.).

   3.6–7   upon . . . made] TS¹, KK; reported upon TS
   3.7   conviction] TS¹, KK; belief TS

3.10   essential.] TS^1, KK; much needed. TS
3.10   This conviction] TS^1, KK; The belief TS
3.11   We hold] TS^1, KK; It rests upon the belief TS
3.13–14 subjectmatters] TS^1, KK; the subjects that are TS
3.14   The scientific method] TS^1, KK; That method TS
3.18   imposition.] KK; imposition to wish to use them. TS^1, TS
3.18–19 research,] TS^1, KK; knowing, TS
3.22   with one another] TS^1, KK; [*not present*] TS
3.22   their] TS^1, KK; [*not present*] TS
3.22–23 join . . . difficulties] TS^1, KK; pursue this method, differences TS
3.23   turn out] KK; turn out in the end TS^1, TS
3.25   one of] TS^1, KK; one in TS
3.26   method;] TS^1, KK; method of procedure; TS
3.28   this] TS^1, KK; that TS
3.29   Our] TS^1, KK; We find that TS
3.29   future] TS^1, KK; [*not present*] TS
3.29   knowledge about knowings] TS^1, KK; knowing of knowledge TS
3.30   requires] TS^1, KK; is integrally connected with advance in TS
3.30   is] TS^1, KK; to be TS
3.30   integrally] TS^1, KK; intimately TS
3.31   reference] TS, KK; reference which TS^1
3.31–32 we employ] TS^1, KK; [*not present*] TS
4.1   proceeded.] TS^1, KK; developed. TS
4.1   development] TS^1, KK; studies TS
4.2   grasped most readily] KK; most readily grasped TS^1, TS
4.2   distinction of] TS^1, KK; differences between TS
4.3   from . . . self-actional] TS^1, KK; and the self-active and the inter-actional TS
4.3   points of view] TS^1, KK; procedures TS
4.3   is] KK; are TS^1, TS
4.4   that] TS^1, KK; the TS
4.7   It] TS^1, KK; For it TS
4.9   It] TS^1, KK; This method TS
4.9   assertions] TS^1, KK; assertion TS
4.10   attempts] TS^1, KK; an attempt TS
4.11   them.] TS^1, KK; it. TS
4.11–12 It . . . or] TS^1, KK; [*not present*] TS
4.12–13 beyond inquiry.] KK; beyond. TS^1; [*not present*] TS
4.13   the tests . . . flexibility] TS^1, KK; this this test TS
4.14   our] TS^1, KK; our own TS
4.14   any attempts] TS^1, KK; the attempt TS

4.14   would be] TS¹, KK; is TS
4.15   —a rupture—] TS¹, KK; [*not present*] TS
4.15   employ.] TS¹, KK; are employing. TS
4.15–16   Our . . . nevertheless,] TS¹, KK; This statement TS
4.16–17   mean . . . reject] KK; mean that we disregard or reject
          TS¹; even rule out TS
4.17   criticisms] TS¹, KK; criticisms made TS
4.18   however, require] TS¹, KK; require however TS
4.18   of such criticisms] TS¹, KK; [*not present*] TS
4.20   that] KK; which TS¹, TS
4.20   presented.] TS¹, KK; presented about knowledge. TS
4.21   trust] TS¹, KK; believe TS
4.22   the outcome] TS¹, KK; there TS
4.22   progress] TS¹, KK; advance TS
4.22   firmness] KK; that firmness TS¹, TS
4.24   progress . . . fact.] TS¹, KK; advance. TS
4.25–37   The . . . footnote.] KK; [*not present*] TS¹, TS
4.38–5.4 As . . . generations.] TS¹, KK; [*not present*] TS
5.5–12   The . . . 1948] KK; Of the eleven papers presented, that of
          Chapter IX was published in *Philosophy of Science,* and
          that of Chapter X in *Philosophy and Phenomenological Re-
          search.* The remainder have appeared in *The Journal of
          Philosophy.* TS¹; [*not present*] TS

Introduction: A Search for Firm Names (Dewey and Bentley)

Listed below are the substantive variants between the *Knowing and
the Known* copy-text, pp. xi–xiii [this volume, pp. 6–7], and "A
Search for Firm Names," *Journal of Philosophy* 42 (4 January 1945):
5–6.

6.10   to be] so that it could be
6.13   manner] manners
6.14   such agreement on] agreement such as this as to
6.19   are to be] will be
6.19   a series of] perhaps half a dozen
6.20   some over] and some over
6.20   names,¹] ~,∧
6.21   set up] [*not present*]
6.22   undertaken] have
6.22   consolidated] combined

6.29   opening chapter] paper now offered, the first of the group,
6n.1–5   1. Of . . . comment.] [*not present*]
7.2   they yielded] them to be yielding
7.6–7   that there is a need for] of the need of
7.8   it is done] [*not present*]
7.12   to cure it.] for its cure. The single signature attached, is, as
          was indicated above, little more than a mark of the division
          of labor.
7.13–21   One . . . dominance.²] [*not present*]
7.23–24   designed primarily for] primarily for the purpose of
7.25–26   great variety of the confusions that] confusions and in-
          consistencies which
7.27–28   that influence the writers'] which influence their
7.29   hope] hope that
7.31–32   concerned . . . personalities.³] directed solely to that end.ₐ
7n.1–2   2. In . . . Specifications.] [*not present*]
7n.3–7   3. As . . . 205.] [*not present*]

2. The Terminological Problem (Dewey and Bentley)

Listed below are the substantive variants between the *Knowing and the
Known* copy-text, pp. 47–78 [this volume, pp. 46–73], and "A Terminology for Knowings and Knowns," *Journal of Philosophy* 42 (26 April
1945):225–47.

46.10   Theories of knowledge] [*ital.*]
46.14   have asserted] believe
46.16   hold] believe
46.16   undertaking should be placed] should be undertaken
46.18   a form of "factual" inquiry,] "factual inquiry,"
46.20   on] upon
46.28   shall] we shall
46.32   assume] assume that
47.2   to which] which
47.2   attention] attention to
47.2   add] add to
47.4   has] has as yet
47.4   undertaken as yet,] undertaken
47.13–14 respect to] [*not present*]
47.16   that the sort of namings] which namings such as
47.18   such observations] observations such
47.19–20 excludes, as being] treats as

47.23   are] is
47.26   that] which
47.28   and naming] [*not present*]
47n.6   to be introduced later,] later to be introduced,
48.1–2   will advance and improve.] advances to similar use under
          similar aim.
48.2   that are] which are
48.3   that claim] which claim
48.6   test in work, where] test, in work in which
48.7   through] solely through
48.8   research solely,] research, and
48.9   *ipse dixit.*] *ipse dixit* assertion.
48.12   which,] [*not present*]
48.13   by us here and now] [*not present*]
48.25–26 that are now] which now are
48.28   that] which
*48.32   knowings as themselves facts.] knowledge as itself fact.
48.34   exactly the same sense] the same sense exactly
48.35   that] which
49.3   we pointed out instances,] instances were pointed out
49.3–4   in the works of] among
49.12   likewise] likewise also
49.16   that] which
49.21   separation] separation which
49.24   the "spiritual"] a "spiritual"
49.24   essence] soul
49.24   from the] from a
49.25–26   , often . . . activities] [*not present*]
49.27–50   Sometimes . . . deployed.] [*not present*]
49n.1   vague word.] of our vague words.
49n.1   standing, however,] standing and useful
49n.1   where] where vague
49n.2   is intended] is all that is intended
49n.2–6   and it . . . definiteness.] and where no stress of the types
          suggested by "object," "entity," or "phenomenon" enters.
          In such situations only should it be used.
50.20–21 To see language,] The seeing of language∧
50.21   all] all of
50.25   made] [*not present*]
50.29   being] [*not present*]
50n.1–4   4. Alfred . . . *et al.*] [*not present*]
51.1   far] [*not present*]
51.5   something] [*not present*]

51.5   *in*] *by*
51.12   it was] was
51n.7   Our] our
51n.13   6.610;] 6.610, 2.661;
51n.14   For William James's] [6]For James's
51n.16   *The*] the
51n.22   reprinted] (all reprinted
51n.26–27   Is Mind to Be] is Mind to be
52.14   research.] ∼.[6]
52.16   earlier] previously
52.17   as to] about
52.17   influence of materials introduced] introduction of material
52.17–18   inadequate sources.] an incompetent source.
52.26   basis] basis that
52.28   conclusions] the conclusions
52.29–30   *knowings* are] *knowing* is
52.30   inseparable from *the knowns*—] the inseparable correlate
          of *the known*—
52n.1   three] also three
52n.7   [1943],] (1942),
53.4   facts,] Facts,
53.7–8   *about* "in fact"] about
53.8   we apply . . . Fact.] we use the word as something which is
          definitely identifiable in the range of observation and firm
          naming.
53.17   what is known.] that which is known.
53.24   position] position which
53n.2–3   in Chapter 1, Section IX.] in our preceding paper,
          pp. 48–49. Use of quotation marks to indicate that "a
          name" is under consideration rather than "the named" is
          common, and some logicians have attempted to make a pil-
          lar of construction out of it. We have exhibited the unrelia-
          bility of this in the preceding articles. Solely as a matter of
          passing convenience we shall follow the custom at times, and
          also at times capitalize a word to indicate that "the named"
          and not the "name" is intended. The procedure is both
          vague and linguistic, and so may be classified along with
          the "vague words" one must ever keep a sharp eye upon.
54.8–37   In . . . inquiry.] [*not present*]
55.8   that] which
55.9   differentiated] as differentiated
55.14   This, again,] And this∧ again∧
55.15   we shall inquire into] we have to do with

55.19   assert] assert that
55.21   that] which
55.22−23   An . . . affirmative] The fact that attempted affirmative
           answers
55.23   results in regarding] result in construing
55.24   —and this] [*not present*]
55.25   Likewise,] And
55.26   considered] [*not present*]
55.27−28   is equally absurd] has comparable absurdity
55n.2   dominance] currency
56.16   name] names
56.16−17   clear also] also clear
56.26   to other names] to one another
56.27   one another.] each other.
56n.8   , we hope,] [*not present*]
56n.9−11   The . . . recalled.] [*not present*]
57.14, 15 that] which
*57.20   hope we shall] hope that we will
57.26   said] said that
57.27−28   Throughout . . . a] "Knowledge" will remain through-
           out our entire treatment a
57.30   Even] But even
57.39   means] means that
58.1   primarily] [*not present*]
58.1−2   specifically] in some other sense
58.3   except . . . other] [*not present*]
58.5   knowing, nor] knowing; neither
58.6   pretense of being a] pretenses as
58.6   thus] and thus
58.7   maintaining] maintain
58.8   part; but] part. But
58.8   the exhibits] what
58.8   secured] found
58.8−9   the preceding . . . the logics] the logics
58.10   should] would
*58.11   offers] offered
58.14   action.] action. [¶] In general we shall postpone discussion
           of many intricately inter-related problems that suggest
           themselves as we go along. To the more important of these
           we shall devote special short papers when opportunity
           offers. This seems the only course practicable if we are not
           to wander so widely at times that objectives will be lost to

view. Above all we assert and continue to assert—and it
might be well if we could repeat it on every page—that our
procedure is solely by hypothesis.

58.27–28   establish] name
58.28   as] [*not present*]
58.28   and name it "fact"] [*not present*]
58.28–29   knowings and its knowns] aspects—all its knowings and
all its knowns—
58.33   in] upon
58.34–35   *factual aspects*] [*rom.*]
59.1–6   Fact, . . . place.] [*not present*]
59.6   note] shall note
59.7   extensions,] extension,
59.9   Fact] Fact that
59.13   or] nor
59.17   by] through
59.18   used here] here used
59.20–21   are required] is required,
59.30   entire activity—] action, the activity,
59.37   replacement] replacement is
60.1   adopt] now adopt
60.1–2   both . . . would] then, as the case stands at this stage, both
words would
60.14   inserting gratuitously] gratuitous insertion of
60.15   we] what we
60.16   taking] taking is
60.17   one—] one, and
60.19   we are considering.] of our consideration.
60.20   In] To
60.21   to be] as
*60.23–24   in system] [*not present*]
60.24   proposed.] required.
60.26   *namings*,] [*rom.*]
60.27   on] and, on
60.38–39   events are designational.] designational, *are*
Designations.
60.39–40   The . . . designation.] [*not present*]
61.2   difficult.[12]] ~.ₐ
61.7   that,] which,
61.11   research at] research, at the
61.11–12   rose . . . absolutes.] rose in the shelter of its glorified absolutes to credal strength.

61.13   Clerk Maxwell] ~-~,
61.15   thus gained] gained thus
61.18   change. Any] change; any
#61.20–21   Knowing . . . go] The full knowledge—knowing and the
             known—event and designation—go
61.22   not] and not
61n.1–2   12. This . . . follows:] [*not present*]
61n.2–20   "Similarly . . . up."] ∧~.∧ [*text present in Journal of Phi-
             losophy at 62.14, after* 'Events.']
#61n.5   sentence] sentences
61n.6   within] within[13] . . . [13]A vague word, be it observed.
62.1   a sound] sound
62.13   circularity] circularity which
62.24   To] But
62.24   , though,] [*not present*]
62.24   about] as to
62.36   among] of
62.37   in terms of] with respect to
63.23   are to] have to
63.32   being] [*not present*]
63.32   not] and not as
63.32–33   unless] unless, indeed,
64.1   strictly] solely
64.1–2   technological] technical
64.13   to stress most strongly] most strongly to stress
64.17   *direct*] nevertheless direct
64.20   heredity,] heredity, let the genes prove all they may;
64.27   hope] hope that
64n.7–8   We . . . however,] It rightfully belongs, however, we
             believe,
64n.10   for the] to supply the
64n.11   to the adoption of] for
64n.11   our] [*not present*]
64n.13   than] than are
65.1   , as currently used,] [*not present*]
65.2   exact] precise
65.4   that] which
65.7   secured.[16]] ~.∧
65.18   shall assign] assign
65.20–21   such . . . naming] accuracy in naming such
65.27   However, the] The
65.28   probably] probably, however,

65n.1–7   16. The . . . Chapter 11.] [*not present*]
66.8   definition"¹⁷ involves] definition"_∧ involved
66.11   logical program.] *Logic,* as inquiry.
66.11–12   defects . . . were] defects we exhibited in the traditional
           logics¹⁷ were
66.12   connected with] due to
66.13   the accurate] [*not present*]
66.13–14   of their own subjectmatters] [*not present*]
66.15   consistency] issues of consistency
66.15–18   in . . . behavior] [*not present*]
66.21   that are] [*not present*]
66.22   not] and not
66.24   Selection] But selection
66.24–25   , however,] [*not present*]
66.27   follow] follow later
66.28   central issue in] issue central to
66.36–37   took form] gained organization
66n.1   17. See . . . I.] ¹⁷"On a Certain Vagueness in Logic," this
           JOURNAL, Vol. XLII (1945), pp. 5–27; 39–51. The Peirce
           citation is used on p. 8.
67.1   motion"—that] motion," namely, that
67.3   Before] But before
67.4–5   observation . . . made] a different type of observation was
           made
67.5–6   in a manner essentially] that was basic to it, and that we
           may call
67.6   enters] may be seen
67.24   should be] [*not present*]
67.24   provided.] provided for them.
67.24–29   procedure . . . work. In] procedure, not as more real or
           more generally valid than any other, but as the one that at
           this stage is needed in the field in which we work, is the
           transactional, in which is asserted the right to see together,
           extensionally and durationally, much that conventionally is
           talked of as if composed of irreconcilable separates. In
67n.4   Bewegung"] Bewegungen,"
67n.8   However, it] For the present, however, it is impracticable. It
68.3   not] and not
68.7   with] where commonly
68.8   named uncertainly] are uncertainly named
68.8   hand] side
68.9   with] [*not present*]

68.9   named] are named
68.12(2)   what] that which
68.13   "*a*] [*rom.*]
68.19   should] [*not present*]
68.19   of] to
68n.1   "Field"] It
68n.5–6   See . . . 17.] [*not present*]
69.1   that] which
69.4–5   Occurrence and] Occurrence,
69.12   of] as to
69.16   When we turn] Turning
69.20   among] as one among a series of
69.23   a behavioral] as behavioral
69.41   to be discussed fully] fully to be discussed
70.2   the] the "cognitive" or
70.3   processes] aspects
70.9   alone;] alone, but
70.9–10   , they name the] [*not present*]
70.10   occurs] occurs as
70.23   laid out,] sketched,
70.27   *Event:*[22] ~:$_\wedge$
70.31–32 conformity with] conform to
70n.1–2   22. The . . . Chapter 11.] [*not present*]
71.7   *Definition:*[23] ~:$_\wedge$
71.9–10   durational transition.] temporal change.
71.17   *Transaction:*[24] ~:$_\wedge$
71.22   *Behavior-Agent:*] *Behavior-Agency:*
71.23   agent] agency
71.32   *Occurrence:*[25] ~:$_\wedge$
71n.1–2   23. The . . . goes.] [*not present*]
71n.3–6   24. For . . . *event.*] [*not present*]
71n.7–8   25. The . . . Chapter 11.] [*not present*]
72.6   *Sign:*] *Signs:*
72.9   as process] [*not present*]
72.9   (not in] (and not as
72.10   specialization] specialty
72.21–25 The . . . made.] [*not present*]
72.27   that] which
72.37   as *inquiry*] [*not present*]
*72.38   science offers sound guidance.] it is our best knowledge.
72.38   Scientific specification] Specification
72.39   why, then, should not] why$_\wedge$ should not then$_\wedge$
72.40   knowings] the knowings

72.40   known?] knowns themselves?
73n.1   one is at times] which at times one is
73n.4   even] and even

3. Postulations (Dewey and Bentley)

Listed below are the substantive variants in the *Knowing and the Known* copy-text, pp. 79–102 [this volume, pp. 74–95], and "Postulations," *Journal of Philosophy* 42 (22 November 1945): 645–62.

74.4   knowns,] knowns, upon which we have made preliminary
         reports in preceding papers,
74.10   fiat] [*ital.*]
75.5   that] which
75.14   say observation] say that observation
75.19   proclaim] boast
75.19   that] that since nature is known,
75.21   that which] what
75.24   being] [*not present*]
75.24   instead] [*not present*]
75.25   be secured.] come.
*75.26   then] [*not present*]
75.26   the postulations] them
75.26   efficiency] the efficiency
75.27   never] but never
*75.27   of circularity] [*not present*]
75.29   that] which
75n.1–2 Heretofore . . . have.] We have avoided it heretofore, or
         hope we have, altogether.
75n.5   discussions] papers
76.4   type.⁴] ~.∧
76.10   that] the inquiry
76.11   they most emphatically] that most emphatically they
76.15   subjectmatter] subject-matters
76.17   It is very frequently] One frequently hears
76.18   himself] oneself
76.21   attitude] attitudes
76.25   by] for
76n.1–6 4. Max . . . facts."] [*not present*]
77.3–5   If . . . others.] [*not present*]
77.9   need for] need of
77.15   interest] interest that

77.16   hope] hope that
77n.4   authors] joint authors
77n.4   volume] paper
77n.9   distinction] distinction which is
77n.13   hold] holds
78.4   programs for] programs of
78.11–12 expression. It] expression—it
78.12   is because of] being for
78.12   latter characteristic] reason
79.3–4   Physiologic-psychologic Straitjackets] A Physiologic-psy-
          chologic Straitjacket
79.17   that] which
79.18   observation] observation which
79.20   works hopefully] hopefully is working
79.20   that] which
79.25   descriptions] descriptions which
79n.1   'em; And] 'em . . . and
79n.5   an identification] [*not present*]
79n.5   that] which
79n.6   view] view which
79n.11   issue . . . between] issue between
79n.12   offer] tender
79n.13   examination.] examination could hardly be more neatly
          drawn.
80.2   this latter] that
80.23   vicious] so vicious is
80.24   this] the
80.26–27 the locus] locus
80.28–29 expansive . . . in.] *obiter dicta* which scientists in their
          arm chairs so happily enjoy.
81.1–2   *except . . . knowns.*] [*rom.*]
81.2–3   differs . . . locus] is commonly taken with stress on the or-
          ganism as the locus
81.4   proceeding] presumptively proceeding
81.4   detachment] a high degree of detachment
81.5   as a phase of] with stress on
81.8   here held to be] [*not present*]
81.8   required] essential
81.9   achieved.] obtained.
81.18   as if we set] much as with
81.18–19 left somewhat] left, or
81.21   we find] which we find
81.24   cannot . . . more] can no more help it
81.27   that] which

81.27–28   sufficed, until that time,] sufficed thitherto
81.30   the components] complements
82.1–2   ("event" . . . "existence")] [*not present*]
82.2   Similar] Frequent similar
82.2   appear frequently;] appear—
82.20–21   nor . . . own] [*not present*]
*82.22   then and there] [*not present*]
82n.4   for future workers.] in the future.
82n.7   having] having for the particular case
82n.8   value . . . case.] value.
82n.13   *Logic*,] Dewey's *Logic*,
82n.16, 17   in] as in
83.10   whether] either
83.16   behind or] [*not present*]
83.17   the name.] it.
83n.4   Although] These, although
83n.5   these attitudes] [*not present*]
83n.6   that] which
83n.12   to work thoroughly] thoroughly to work
83n.14   Dewey,] the citation being from Dewey,
83n.15–16   the statement by] [*not present*]
83n.22   One] A man
*83n.22   with] [*not present*]
83n.22   or] nor
83n.23   on.] upon.
83n.24   this word] it
84.23   been elsewhere] elsewhere been
84.24   approach] approximation
84.25   about knowledge] about knowledges,
84n.3   even some that] and some even which
84n.8   in] through
84n.13   in] in exactly
84n.13   are] [*not present*]
84n.13   subjectmatters.] matters.
85.6   are to] must
85.12   backward] backwards
85.21   emphatic—] emphatic, as
85.21–22   denial everywhere prevalent—] everywhere prevalent
        denial,
85.25   needed.] that is needed.
85n.4   *knowings* are] *knowing* is
85n.5   inseparable from] the inseparable correlate of
85n.5   *knowns*] *known*
85n.9   approach] approach which

86.11, 14   that] which
86n.2   as follows] [*not present*]
86n.5–6   to . . . properly.] properly to represent our approach.
86n.7   In] Names, in
86n.7   postulation names] postulation,
86n.9   as being] as
86n.11   postulation] postulate
86n.13   plaint] plaints
86n.19   plans. They] plans, and
86n.27   dominate] dominance
86n.27   the . . . apply.] their pertinence.
87.9   inquiry—for] inquiry. For
87.12   *transaction*] [*rom.*]
87n.1   of this] [*not present*]
87n.3   out] [*not present*]
87n.5   this] and this
87n.8   that] which
87n.10   Again,] Or again:
88.4–5   presumed . . . beyond.] behind.
88.12–13   specifications] specification
88n.7–9   (*A* . . . 170.)] [*not present*]
88n.14   Its words] The medical Latin readable by any high-school
        student, assuming that he reads at all,
*89.25   the more complete] a richer
89.25   frame] [*not present*]
89.25   for] with respect to
89.26   and in] and
90.2   developed elsewhere.] offered in due course.
90.8   protozoa] protozoa, through "the wisdom of the body,"
90.20   logic] a logic
92.17   *E* and] *E,*
92n.14–15   discussions] discussion
93.3   , if taken as] [*not present*]
93.10   Still . . . development] What is still missing from the pre-
        ceding development (although repeatedly mentioned)
93.10   until] until after
93.11   gained] given
93.11   knowledge] account
93.11–12   an efficient] the full
93.19   may be] is done
94.22   properly] most properly
94.25   even] even those
94.25   peculiarly) those] peculiarly those)

4. Interaction and Transaction (Dewey and Bentley)

Listed below are the substantive variants between the *Knowing and the Known* copy-text, pp. 103–18 [this volume, pp. 96–109], and "Interaction and Transaction," *Journal of Philosophy* 43 (12 September 1946): 505–17.

96.3	Our . . . a] In recent papers looking towards a
96.4	placed special stress] special stress was placed
96.20	interactions. The] interactions, but the
96.20–21	, however,] [*not present*]
96.24	which] that
97.21	is] was
*97.23	just] complete
*97.25	observed—and as it is] observed, and
97.32–33	these stages today,] stages in this form today∧
98.2	the animistic personifications] animistic personifying
98.3	personalizations of] personalizing statements about
98.12	By . . . trace] We may, by way of introduction, sketch
98.19	firmly established] established firmly
98n.2	his "metaphysics"] that
98n.5	had,] had managed to have,
99.8	which] that
99.16	that] which
99.29	their] the
100.1	for] of
100.15	Reaction on] Reaction of
100.31	however,] however, of course,
100.34	Transaction.] Transaction, using capitalization and hyphenization as a convenience of the moment when some form of stress upon the words is desired.
100.34; 101.1	all] all of them
100n.1–2	The . . . us.] [*not present*]
101.2–9	We . . . used.[7]] They are as follows:
101.10	things] ~[8]
101n.1–9	7. Our . . . eyesight.] [*not present*]
101n.9	The] [8]We use the
101n.9–10	as . . . is] [*not present*]
101n.10	deliberately chosen] deliberately,
101n.10	retains] has retained
101n.11	uses,] status∧
101n.11	almost wholly] comparatively
101n.11–12	the . . . philosophers'] theorists'

101n.12–13   which . . . "entity"] [*not present*]
101n.13   our future use,] [*not present*]
101n.13   where a] the
*101n.13   *outcome*] [*rom.*]
101n.13–14   inquiry . . . involved,] inquiry, we employ
101n.14   will be employed] [*not present*]
101n.29   1924] 1923
101n.32   more] most
102n.8   described to him] reported on
102n.8–9   her office] the office
102n.9   devoted] gave her
102n.9   to her] [*not present*]
102n.10   1945] 1946
102n.10–11   it "was . . . he] "it fails to do justice to the structural meaning of the parts." He
103.23   *ad lib.*:] *ad lib.*:[12] . . . [12]A striking example of mixed inter-actional and self-actional procedures will be found in the recent work of Charles Morris, *Signs, Language and Behavior* (1946). Professor Morris introduces the sign as a form of stimulus "caused" by the "properties" of "objects," and does this without any preliminary inquiry into or ex- position of the pertinence of either "property," "object," or "causation" for such a specialized development. He defines behavior as exclusively the "purposive action" of muscles and glands, but leaves uninvestigated the status of "pur- posiveness" in such a location. He then brings stimuli and behaviors together, so far as sign-process is concerned, through the insertion between them of "dispositions" which may be spoken of physiologically as habits if one wishes, but which are in effect uninvestigated surrogates for the an- cient "mental" states. Dispositions transform into interpre- tants; interpretants require interpreters. Superimposed upon them, whether separately or together, are the terms "denotata" and "significata" taken over from the older log- ics and epistemologies but nowhere factually investigated in connection with signs and behaviors. The result is a me- chanical organization of vocabularies purporting to be a new science called Semiotic and providing a basis for the solution of the most troublesome modern problems of logic and knowledge.
103n.5   that which] what
103n.15   that] which

104.25   which] that
105.1   essential to] characteristic of
105.8–9   feature] feature of it
105.9   hatred] hatred for him
105.16   acceleration] the acceleration
105.28   development] development next
105.28   Moreover,] Nevertheless,
105.28   the new view] it
105.29   transactional] transactional within and
106.15–16 failure . . . was] "unalterable" particle, with respect to
          its unalterability, was
107.8–9   with which] which
107.9   deal.] deal with.
107.24   more and more] ever more
108.5   clear] it plain
108.33   activity in scientific enterprise.] activity, *intellectually*
          described.
108.33   His position is] Thus he declares
109.1   appears to have] achieves
109.2   freer] more modernized
109.2–4   a world . . . it.] the characteristics of these transforma-
          tions within scientific construction.
109.4   In . . . the] With reference to the
109.5   of] as to
109.5   wave] the wave
109.5–11 and his . . . they] [*not present*]
109.11   held] had held
109.12–13 further] that
109.13–15 they . . . or] [*not present*]
109.17   In reply] [*not present*]
109.28   men.] men. We have previously indicated the type of con-
          struction we shall use for this problem, and at a later time
          will give it extended treatment.

5. Transactions as Known and Named
(Dewey and Bentley)

Listed below are the substantive variants between the *Knowing and the Known* copy-text, pp. 119–43 [this volume, pp. 110–30], and "Transactions as Known and Named," *Journal of Philosophy* 43 (26 September 1946): 533–51, 560.

110.3   the preceding chapter] a preceding paper
110.6   On] Upon
*110.12   knowing] knowledge
110.25–111.2   In . . . application.] [*not present*]
110n.4–5   For . . . Chapter 11.] [*not present*]
111.6–7   form of . . . Specification,] form of event-specification, i.e.,
           of the named Object,
111.11   knowing-known] knowings-known
111.12   chapter and] paper,
111.13   next.] paper next to follow, and then, at a still later time,
           the manner of organization we find existing between Defini-
           tion,[5] Specification, and Transaction, will be examined.
111.24   confront] stand over against
111.37; 112.1   that] which
111n.3   dictators.] dictators. / [5]"Definition," in our use, is based on
           Symbol, where "symbol" stands for a highly refined devel-
           opment of language, characteristic primarily of mathemat-
           ics. Symbol in no case indicates Name or other form of sign
           except the symbolic in definition.
112.21   It was said] The preliminary characterization
112.21   that] was that
112.21   represents] represented
112n.4–9   The . . . implication."] [*not present*]
113.5   into] in
113.9   *Transaction*] *Trans-action*[8] . . . [8]We shall permit ourselves
           to continue the free use of capitalization and hyphenation
           for purposes of emphasis as the contexts may suggest.
113.21, 28, 33, 38; 114.8, 19   *Transaction*] *Trans-action*
*113.29   fact] "a fact"
113.29   other] the other
115.3   *Transactional*] *Trans-actional*
115n.11   such] all such
115n.11   those] [*not present*]
116.3   when it is] where
116n.3–4   usually taking place] taking place mostly
117.17   discoveries,] discoveries about it,
117n.7   Child,] Childs,
117n.10   it is a "mutual] "~~~∧~
117n.13–18   To . . . environment.] [*not present*]
118.32   steadily gaining] gaining steadily
#119.7   (p. 48);] (p. 56);
119.22   a clear] clear
119.24   nor] [*not present*]

119n.1   Such an entitative] Incidentally this
119n.3   things-named)] $\sim_\wedge$
#119n.12   *Review,*] *Reviews,*
119n.13–16   T. . . . environments."] [*not present*]
120.5   asexual] a sexual
121.8   still] nevertheless still
121.11   expect merely] merely expect
121.20   important.[17]] $\sim._\wedge$
121n.7–13   17. For . . . pp. 226–291.] [*not present*]
122.1, 2   everything] all of the
122.2   in] among
122.7   skin, following] skin and then follow
122.7   further] [*not present*]
122.10   subjectmatter] subject-matters
122.11   involves] involve
123.9   technological] technical
123n.4   the traditional exaggeration] traditional exaggeration; and
          it is
124.17–18   roused . . . "soul."] made some sense because of the
          "immortal," not because of the "soul."
124.18   Its] But its
124.18   wholly] [*not present*]
124.20–21   double-talk; and] just double-talk. And
124.28–29   *behavioral*] [*rom.*]
124n.3   Edwin G.] [*not present*]
125.3   transactional] trans-actional
125.22   soon see] begin to see
125.28   an] [*not present*]
125n.12   a series] series
126.12   occurrence.] event.
126.20   process.] process. You can have a physical interpretation of
          sounds on the moon, but no linguistic interpretation there
          unless there is *language* to interpret. And language requires
          praticipants.
126.21–22   , assuming . . . waves,] [*not present*]
126n.1   apply] apply as a group
126n.1   to the attitudes] to some
127.37   naming in such separation] naming, such
127.37–38   it can be used] we can use it
127.40   named] nameds
128.5–6   such envisionment is then] then such envisionment is
129.40   long. Would] long; would
130.18   which] that

6. Specification (Dewey and Bentley)

Listed below are the substantive variants between the *Knowing and the Known* copy-text, pp. 144–69 [this volume, pp. 131–53], and "Specification," *Journal of Philosophy* 43 (21 November 1946):645–63.

131.1	Specification] Specification[1] . . . [1]We wish to express thanks to Jules Altman for various examinations of materials he has made for us, and equally for his helpful comments.
131.3	Having] In two recent papers we have
131.3	at . . . those] [*not present*]
131.4	and named] [*not present*]
131.4	which we have styled] as
131.4–5	"transactions," we] ∧transactions.∧ We
131.5	proceed] wish
131.5	examine] consider
131.5	linguistic activity] process of linguistic determination freed from certain of the presumptions of symbolic definition,
131.6	through] by means of
131.6	Transaction] transaction
131.6	established:] identified:
131.6	namely, Specification.[1]] the process, namely, of Specification.[3]
131.8	Designation,] designation,
131.8	behavioral] [*not present*]
131.9	which comprises] (forming
131.10	activities, and] process)
131.10	, in . . . evolution,] [*not present*]
131.11	earlier] early
131.11	activities] processes
131.12	and more intricately] more highly
131.12	specialized] specialized and more intricately involved
*131.12	activities] processes
131.15	the "that"] "that"
131.16	"fact"] "fact" was made
131.16–17	"knowledge," was made] "knowledge,"
131.23	perhaps] about
131.24	having] which has
131.26	details.[2]] ∼.∧
131n.1	1. We] [3]∼
131n.4–5	We . . . emphasis.] [*not present*]
131n.6–7	2. For . . . 11.] [*not present*]

132.10–13   The . . . made.] [*not present*]
132.18   its most] the most
132.18   advanced stage.] the most advanced.
132.22   reserved] reserved for another place and
132.23–27   In . . . Definition.] [*not present*]
132n.1–8   Of . . . inquiry.] [*not present*]
133.31–34   , with . . . them] [*not present*]
133n.2–5   Progress . . . literature.] [*not present*]
134.20   distinct] separate
134.26   older forms] an older form
134.26   much more] just as
134n.6–7   For . . . 11.] [*not present*]
135.4–6   If . . . other.] [*not present*]
135.7–8   spoken names are.] are spoken.
135.12–13   cultural— . . . existence."] cultural.
135.13–15   "Sea-serpents" . . . today.] It may be extinct as a name
    today.
135.15–16   Trilobites . . . history.] So are the trilobites, but they are
    none the less animal for that.
136.32   (including the purposive)] [*not present*]
136.35   Developing behaviors] Behaviors
136.35   indirections] a type of indirection
136.35   of action] in their process
136.35–36   of types] [*not present*]
136.36   are] is
137n.14   in his *Die*] (*Die*
138.3   directly.] directly. (When we come to the differentiation of
    Symbol from Name, and the establishment of Symbol as
    itself sign-process, further exposition will be needed, but
    this task is postponed for the present.)
138.25–26   environment, . . . processes,] environment∧ and the in-
    tervening region∧
138.29   can,] can readily,
139.22   Symbol] Symbol[9] . . . [9]Symbol as the third level of behav-
    ioral sign, and Definition as a symbolic process severed
    from the designatory process of specification, are not dis-
    cussed in the present paper. They are non-naming proce-
    dures. Present discussion would take much space, and the
    added complication would increase the difficulties of pre-
    sentation for our immediate purpose. We here merely call
    attention to the fact that place must be reserved for their
    consideration later.
139.28   Signal thus] Signal, this is to say,

139.34   catches] catch
139.34   starts] start
139.36   for] to
140.3   here.⁹] ~.∧
140.6   to those of] is found in
140.20   an isolate,] isolate∧
140.27   develops from] differentiates upon
140.28   Signaling is] The signaling is
140n.1–8 9. Allowing . . . arise."] [*not present*]
141.5   detachment] detachments
141.18   late] later,
141.23   metaphysical] [*not present*]
141.24   "things"] sorts of "things"
141.24   taken] supposed
142.5   designation-event] ~∧/~
142.23   necessary] necessary so
142.23   cases so] cases
142.39   preliminary] particular
143.11–12 comes into being there,] there comes into being,
143.13   among] as among
143.26   The illustrations] Illustrations
143.32   appear as] appear in
#143n.1   "terms"] "term"
143n.4   implication.] implication. Later attention to the word will
          be necessary.
144.18–19 *a . . . situation.*] [*rom.*]
144.28   sketch] preliminary sketch
144.36   recent studies,] important recent studies∧
145.7   daily] everyday
145.8   evolving] loose
145.8   which answers well] most of the time well
145.9–10 is limited . . . makes,] that is about all; and the more
          pretentiously it is used,
145.20–21 pronoun, which] pronoun (which
145.22   grammar.] grammar where the pronoun is said to be a sub-
          stitute for the noun). The common noun comes to succeed
          the proper noun.
145.26   communicative] contextual
145.29   this] these
145.35   In] It is in
145.35   the view] that the view
146.17   operative] contextual
146.27   had provided] should provide
146.27   statement] the statement

146n.2   this statement.] the statement made in the text.
146n.3   examined] touched on by one of the writers of the present
          paper
147.8   far more] more
147.8   forth] forth by far
147.8   Take] Get
147.34–38 Our . . . discarded.] [*not present*]
147n.1   William Beebe, editor,] [*not present*]
147n.1   1944),] 1945),
148.5   that] which
148n.8–10 For . . . name.] [*not present*]
149.13   naming] naming generally,
150.6–24 The . . . oscillate.] [*not present*]
150.34   characterizations] characteristics
151.4   John Dewey] One of the writers of the present paper
151.12   should] would
151.24   leans heavily towards] is heavily on
151.24   side,] side of the issue,
152.19   "hazes."] ∧~·∧
*152.20   defect] defects
152.26   those] workers
152.27   qualifications,] qualification,
153.2   transaction] transmission
153.3–5   These . . . followed.] To these subjects we shall return in a
          later paper.

7. The Case of Definition (Dewey and Bentley)

Listed below are the substantive variants between the *Knowing and the Known* copy-text, pp. 170–204 [this volume, pp. 154–83], and "'Definition,'" *Journal of Philosophy* 44 (22 May 1947): 281–306.

154.3–7   It . . . mathematics] In our preceding papers the word
          "definition" was accepted for the procedures of
          mathematics
154.7–8   but by rejecting it] but was rejected
154.8   the procedures of] [*not present*]
154.17   discussion] paper
154.19   us] us, for the moment,
*154.21   we ourselves stood] ourselves
154.22   employment] endorsement
154.22   specialized] highly specialized
155.1   as a specification] as usable

155.2   now] now itself
155.2   be itself] be
155.3   characterization.] "characterization," i.e., to that of a crude
          and loose preliminary form of naming.
155.22   more] better
155.26   the presence of] [*not present*]
155.26   "actor"] ∧~∧
155.26   implied)] understood)
155n.1   Chapter 6, Section IV.] *ibid.*, Vol. XLIII (1946),
          pp. 645–663. The word "definition," i.e., today is pretense,
          not precision. Instead of having distinctive superiority over
          "specification," its current rating is the inferiority of
          "characterization."
156.8   similar] similar that
156.14   *Webster* (revision 1947)] Webster's (1934 copyright)
156.17   such as "dictionary] "~~∧~
157.20   should] would
157n.2   under . . . formulations,] [*not present*]
157n.8   level. It] level; it
*157n.8   science;] knowledge,
*158.1–2 process of] tool for
*158.5   thus held] held thus
*158.5   which] that
158.14   an] and
159.3   the recognition of] recognizing
*159.5   as the] the
159.21   "things,"] "thing,"
159n.14   as if directly incorporated] [*not present*]
159n.15   at . . . text] as a part of our text at this point
160.7   such treatments] this treatment
160.10   exhibits] echoings
*160.10   conventional] old artificial
*160.30   science] knowledge
160.30–36 Act . . . action.] [*not present*]
161.11   things that] things which
161.25   further] other
161n.5   historical] historic
163.5   (1901),] (1911),
164.11   logistic] logical
*164.17   as are] as
*164.18   definitions,] definitions are,
165n.11   up on] upon
165n.13   p. 12,] p. 11,

165n.16 Carnap, R.,] [*not present*]

165n.24 The] [*not present*]

166.17 uncertain as to what] uncertain, beginning, middle, and end, what

167.23–26 Throwing . . . sciences.] Apart from the "dictionary" kind, all definition is set down as "scientific definition," logic and mathematics being consolidated with "science" as branches of it.

168.7 inevitable] "~"

168.15 pertinent to logic] [*not present*]

170.2 deliberation] deliberations

170.4 On the list of questions] Among the questions

170.5 offered] set up

170.5 by . . . Association] [*not present*]

170.6 especial] [*not present*]

170n.5 his old query] a query

170n.6–171n.1 other . . . that] others followed him so strongly in its discussion that

171.1 firm] solid

171.6 tautology.] wholly unnecessary tautology.

171.30–31 published . . . 1946,] all published in the past year, and all in this JOURNAL,

171.32 are] are papers

172.9 but] but in the present paper

173n.1 pp. 617–630.] pp. 607–630.

174.5 described] elsewhere described

175.12 Against] Over against

175.27 *his*] [*rom.*]

176.24 added] added to them

177.26–27 towards the obliteration] in obliteration

177.29–178.2 effectiveness . . . tests] desirability of his organization of his procedure, as if it had to undergo a set of tests

177n.5 into] in to

177n.11 the word] [*not present*]

178.14 only equated] only

178.28 varied] variant

178n.1 *Ibid.,* pp. 27 ff.] *Loc. cit.,* p. 31.

179.5 In] [*no* ¶] In

179.5–6 the report . . . that] [*not present*]

179.15 by acute] in the writings of acute

179.16 engaged] engaged as a group

180.25 organize] recognize

181.25 absurdities] difficulties,

181n.8 *Op. cit.* Book I,] *A System of Logic,* I, 1,
182.2 developed] pursued
182.3 using] presenting
182.4 instead of being undertaken] rather than
182.6–9 Ostensive . . . organization.] [*not present*]
182.10 If . . . may] We may, if we try,
182.21 which] that
182.22 the finger in] the finger-nail in
182.36 first] his first
#183.1 him.[52]] ~.∧
#183n.1–2 52. Cf. . . . pp. 125–127.] [*not present*]

10. Common Sense and Science (Dewey)

Listed below are the substantive variants between the *Knowing and the Known* copy-text (KK), pp. 270–86 [this volume, pp. 242–56], and two precopy-texts: "Common Sense and Science: Their Respective Frames of Reference," *Journal of Philosophy* 45 (8 April 1948):197–208 (JP); and "Common Sense and Science: Their Respective Frames of Reference," typescript (TS) (Joseph Ratner/John Dewey Papers, Box 44, folder 2, Special Collections, Morris Library, Southern Illinois University at Carbondale, 22 pp.).

242.7 self-enclosed;] JP, KK; self-enclosed in itself; TS
242.8–9 these ways] KK; them JP, TS
242.10 way] KK; [*not present*] JP, TS
242.12 be knowable] KK; exist JP, TS
242.14 being] JP, KK; [*not present*] TS
242.14 which] JP, KK; that TS
242.15 a trade,] JP, KK; A trade, TS
242.16 This transaction] JP, KK; This transaction is one that TS
242.17 No one] JP, KK; Nothing and no one TS
242.19 each is] JP, KK; both are TS
242.21 things] JP, KK; such things TS
242.21 only are] JP, KK; are not TS
242.22 in] JP, KK; save in TS
242.24 change;] JP, KK; a change, TS
242.25 very] JP, KK; [*not present*] TS
242.25 of *locus*] JP, KK; in locus TS
242.26 previously] JP, KK; they previously TS
243.5 by means of] JP, KK; through TS
243.6 rules and] JP, KK; them as rules or TS

243.6   that proceed] JP, KK; proceeding TS
243.7   other transactions] JP, KK; the former TS
243.8–9   trade . . . transaction] JP, KK; trade as a transaction is
          cited TS
243.9   in order] JP, KK; [*not present*] TS
243.9   found] JP, KK; looked for and found TS
243.12   together] JP, KK; along TS
243.13–15 milieu . . . could] JP, KK; milieu:—with one another
          and without which (in the case of both human and
          non-human partakers) human beings could TS
243.15   stay alive,] JP, KK; exist₍ TS
243.15   accomplishing] JP, KK; accomplishing or doing TS
243.16   *Party,* so that] JP, KK; *Party;* while TS
243.17   suffered] JP, KK; suffered by one TS
243.17   possibly] JP, KK; [*not present*] TS
243.18   it is] JP, KK; [*not present*] TS
243.20   which he modifies,] JP, KK; may modify, TS
243.20   in virtue of] JP, KK; through TS
243.23   upon] JP, KK; upon individuals TS
243.26   in which] JP, KK; along with TS
243.26   conditions partake—] JP, KK; conditions— TS
243.27   language] JP, KK; the case of language TS
243.29   (as in] JP, KK; (as TS
243.30–31 view that] JP, KK; [*not present*] TS
243.31   are] JP, KK; as being TS
243.31   entities),] JP, KK; beings), TS
243.32   what] JP, KK; everything which TS
243.32   that process] JP, KK; every process TS
243.33   gets] JP, KK; is TS
243.33–34 attention . . . familiarity.] JP, KK; notice. TS
243.34   As] JP, KK; Just as TS
243.34   air] JP, KK; presence of the air TS
243n.3   individualism)] JP, KK; Individualism) TS
243n.4   that] JP, KK; that have TS
243n.4   "individuals"] JP, KK; ₍Individuals₍ TS
244.1   take part] JP, KK; are parties TS
244.2   and think,] JP, KK; think₍ TS
244.2   dreams.] JP, KK; dream: although the disorder commonly
          found in the latter is due to the absence of the control
          which is exerted when we are awake by the participation of
          immediate present factors. TS
244.7   *medium,* or] JP, KK; *medium*₍ the TS
244.8   execution or] TS, KK; execution of JP

244.8   of human] KK; all human JP; and *on* of every human TS
244.9   activities, . . . being] JP, KK; action; it is TS
244.11   impoverishment in] JP, KK; impoverishment of TS
244.13   in which the medium] JP, KK; of the cases where there is
           an enriching and refining of the medium TS
244.13–14 on . . . enriched.] KK; on is one in which human life is
           enriched. JP; on. TS
244.17   theme] JP, KK; themes TS
244.18   Only] JP, KK; It is TS
244.18   active] JP, KK; and actual TS
244.19   does anyone become] KK; does any one become JP; that
           one becomes TS
244.20   which] JP, KK; that TS
244.20   world.] JP, KK; world. And it is *only* by such direct partak-
           ings that knowledge of the acquaintance kind comes about.
           TS
244.22   demarcates] JP, KK; delimits (and in that sense "defines")
           TS
244.23   by identifying it with] JP, KK; as that of TS
244.24   on as it is] JP, KK; on, and TS
244.24   suffered.] JP, KK; suffered, by human beings. TS
244.24   I] JP, KK; Bearing this fact in mind, I TS
244.24   then] JP, KK; [*not present*] TS
244.27   while] JP, KK; and TS
244.28   apart from them] JP, KK; [*not present*] TS
244.28   then] JP, KK; [*not present*] TS
#244.29   of a field of] JP, KK; also of bearings or TS
244.35   "mankind," or] JP, KK; "mankind‸" or even TS
244.36   exigent] JP, KK; exigent in fact TS
245.1   need] JP, KK; the need TS
245.1   means] JP, KK; the means TS
245.3   common customs and] JP, KK; certain customary TS
245.8   the following:] JP, KK; a usage described as follows: TS
245.10   that] JP, KK; which TS
245.12   The] JP, KK; What but the TS
245.13   only] JP, KK; what but TS
245.16–17 "intelligence . . . action."] JP, KK; [*ital.*] TS
245.17   This] JP, KK; And while this TS
245.17   of sense] JP, KK; [*not present*] TS
245.19–21 psychology . . . activity.] JP, KK; psychology, it seems
           to tell how they actually function as they occur in life, if
           not in books. TS
245.21   may] JP, KK; may then TS

245.24   should] JP, KK; should we describe TS
245.25   H$_2$O] JP, KK; H$_2$O$_4$ TS
245.25   be described save] JP, KK; save TS
245.33–34   are without place and] KK; have neither place nor JP, TS
245.34   uses] JP, KK; a set of uses TS
245.35–246.1   it is . . . sense.] JP, KK; it is in terms of the latter that water or anything else that is a *thing* for common sense is known. TS
245n.2   dates . . . cited] JP, KK; dates, in the illustrative passage cited, from TS
245n.2–3   earlier than] JP, KK; from TS
245n.3   limited] JP, KK; limited and TS
246.2   case] JP, KK; one TS
246.4   things,—] JP, KK; things, namely— TS
246.6–7   a particular "*so-and-so*"] JP, KK; the particular so-and-so TS
246.7   "*that,*" and a] JP, KK; "that$_\wedge$" and the TS
246.12   repay] JP, KK; will repay TS
246.17   most definitely] JP, KK; with utmost definiteness TS
246.22   philosophers] JP, KK; philosophies TS
246.25   "inner"] JP, KK; so-called "inner" TS
246.25–26   component] JP, KK; member TS
246.29–30   "*object of consideration.*"] JP, KK; an "*object* of consideration." TS
246n.3   in living.] JP, KK; of life. TS
#247.1–2   sense of] KK; sense or JP, TS
247.4   and] JP, KK; [*not present*] TS
247.4   over] JP, KK; [*not present*] TS
247.8   into] JP, KK; into anything TS
247.9   has changed] JP, KK; passed TS
247.12   under*takings*] JP, KK; under*taking* TS
247.16   philosophy that is] JP, KK; philosophy, or TS
247.20   so] JP, KK; [*not present*] TS
247.20   activity that] JP, KK; activity, where TS
247.21   matters here] JP, KK; matters TS
247.21   I] JP, KK; Although I TS
247.21   refrain, however,] JP, KK; refrain TS
247.22   idiomatic] JP, KK; the idiomatic TS
247.25   emphasis on] JP, KK; [*not present*] TS
247.30   fuse] JP, KK; so fuse TS
247.32   moreover] KK; the JP, TS
247.33   named. Apart] JP, KK; named) that apart TS

247.34   and when a] JP, KK; when the TS
247.34–35   it is always] JP, KK; there is only TS
247.35–36   supremacy of] JP, KK; primacy and supremacy of the TS
247.36   distinctions] JP, KK; the distinctions TS
247.36–37   usually] KK; [*not present*] JP, TS
247.37   denied] JP, KK; doubted TS
248.5   artificial] JP, KK; wholly artificial TS
248.6   needs to be] JP, KK; should be TS
248.7–8   occur . . . served] JP, KK; are *distinguished* and about the function or use served TS
248.8   distinctions.] JP, KK; distinction. TS
248.12   lies in cases] JP, KK; is that TS
248.14   of the] JP, KK; or the TS
248.15   a cognitive] JP, KK; the cognitive or "intellectual" TS
248.17   (suspend) immediate activity] KK; (suspend) immediate activity, JP; (suspend immediate activity) TS
248.17   so that what] KK; and what JP; so that which TS
248.18   *overt*] TS, KK; [*rom.*] JP
248.18   an *examination*] KK; that *examination* JP; an activity of *examination* TS
248.20   organs . . . etc.,] KK; a sense-organ, JP, TS
248.20   the factors] JP, KK; factors TS
248.21   obstacles] KK; blocking obstacles JP, TS
248.21   from] JP, KK; and TS
248.21   that] KK; which JP, TS
248.22   For when] JP, KK; As TS
248.23   the one] JP, KK; one TS
248.23   a factor] JP, KK; doer or factor TS
248.24   other hand, to] JP, KK; other, to the TS
248.26   *with respect to*] JP, KK; with respect *to this case and other* TS
248.26   *this*] JP, KK; *the* TS
248.26   finds a] JP, KK; takes its TS
248.27   "the state and course" of life-concerns.] JP, KK; ∧the state and course∧ of the concerns of life. TS
248.27   Petrifaction] JP, KK; The petrifaction TS
248.28   kind, that are] KK; kind∧ which are JP; kind, TS
248.30   the "vicious"] JP, KK; a "vicious" TS
248n.3–10   As . . . available.] KK; Under certain conditions it includes "problem, question," and such phrases as "in regard, reference, respect to." JP, TS
249.6–8   place . . . natural] JP, KK; place, since the scientific revo-

lution of a few centuries ago, in philosophies which have
assumed that this revolution made natural TS

249.8–9   itself necessarily set] JP, KK; itself; thereby setting TS

249.12   separations. Thereby,] JP, KK; separations, thereby rendering, TS

249.12–13   irony, it renders] JP, KK; irony, TS

249.19   of responsibility] JP, KK; responsibility TS

249.21   has to] JP, KK; can TS

249.22   in] JP, KK; only in TS

249.24   ultimate] JP, KK; only TS

249.26   matter] JP, KK; cause TS

249.28   of concern.] KK; of philosophic concern. JP; for philosophic concern. TS

249.28   The] JP, KK; For this reason the TS

249.29   accordingly] JP, KK; [*not present*] TS

249.31   life; that is,] JP, KK; life, and TS

249.36   the outcome] JP, KK; [*not present*] TS

249.38   which render its problems] JP, KK; that its problems are TS

250.1   are they] JP, KK; is their discussion TS

250.3   a chart] KK; chart JP; the chart TS

250.3   away.] JP, KK; away, while in addition the respect of the public is on the wane. TS

250.7   that of] KK; that of the framework of JP, TS

250.7   the questions] JP, KK; questions TS

250.8   difference.] JP, KK; difference:—Namely, that of the source and the consequence of the difference between two frames of reference. TS

250.8   stands,] JP, KK; stands otherwise, TS

250.9   *not*] JP, KK; [*rom.*] TS

250.12   care that] KK; care which JP, TS

250.12   marks off scientific activity] JP, KK; marks scientific activity off TS

250.17–18   , as already remarked,] JP, KK; [*not present*] TS

250.18   is often] JP, KK; has often been TS

250.19   central] JP, KK; very important TS

250.20   epistemology] JP, KK; theories of knowledge (epistemologies) TS

250.20   in setting the themes] JP, KK; as central themes TS

250.21   philosophy.] JP, KK; philosophic thought. TS

250.24   that] JP, KK; which TS

250.25   *work*] JP, KK; work, TS

250.26   constituting] JP, KK; who constitute TS

250.28   although its] JP, KK; its TS

250.28   is becoming] JP, KK; becoming in fact TS
250.29   physicians] JP, KK; physicians (at one time the chief class practicing, as distinct from literary physicists and phys- iologists) TS
251.8   distinctive] JP, KK; especial TS
251.8–24   Just . . . man.] KK; [*not present*] JP, TS
251.25   The] JP, KK; [*no* ¶] ~ TS
251.27   one] JP, KK; [*not present*] TS
251.34–35   work . . . sense] JP, KK; work of the organs of sense TS
251.35–36   was refined and extended] JP, KK; were refined and in- definitely extended TS
251.36   by adoption] JP, KK; by means TS
252.2   distinctive] JP, KK; [*not present*] TS
252.3   a concern and occupation] JP, KK; an affair TS
252.3   those] JP, KK; the concerns TS
252.4   that grow] JP, KK; growing TS
252.4–5   In . . . simple.] JP, KK; The answer is simple in principle. TS
252.5–36   Doing . . . with.] KK; Knowing and doing are terms, in the sense of delimiting conditions, of both common-sense and scientific concerns. What differentiates them from each other is the relative *position* occupied by the two factors that are indispensable in both. In the affairs of common sense, knowing is for the sake of agenda, of things that have to be done and done in certain ways in the course of human life; in which both the *what* and the *how* of doings and ados is a matter to be studied and learned, directly and by transmission of whatever other human beings have found out and communicated. In science as a concern, doing is extensive and highly technological—*vide* any laboratory— but it is for the sake of advancing the system of knowings- knowns. The *position* of the terms of common-sense con- cern is reversed, though *as* doing and knowing they remain of the same order.

   That science is *about* the subject matters of common-sense concern can only be illustrated here as it is exemplified in a single case:—that of H_2O_4 as *about* water. That this case is representative or typical is somewhat concealed from view by the fact that "science" now has attained an extensive body of subject matter as the result of prior scientific indus- try. But I believe slight reflection will show that unless this material when traced back be rooted in common-sense materials and hence indirectly, even if remotely, *about* them, there would be *nothing* for it to be about. TS

252.13   there is] KK; is there, JP

252.25   H$_2$O] KK; H$_2$O$_4$ JP

252.28   of] KK; [*ital.*] JP

252.28   sharply] KK; radically JP

252.35   common sense concerns] KK; common-sense concern JP

#252.39   from; which is *of*] KK; from$_\wedge$ and is *of* JP; from:— TS

252.39   in the sense] KK; [*not present*] JP, TS

252.39   in which . . . from:—] KK, JP; [*not present*] TS

253.1   off] JP, KK; away TS

253.1–3   H$_2$O . . . water.] KK; H$_2$O$_4$ [, TS] where not one single property of use and enjoyment belonging to the former is to be found in the latter. JP, TS

253.4   that] KK; which JP, TS

253.5   activity is the] KK; activity is that JP; activity, is the TS

253.6   which] JP, KK; that TS

253.8–9   affairs; together with an] JP, KK; affairs, and the TS

253.9   judgment] JP, KK; the judgment TS

253.10   of the] JP, KK; the TS

253.10–11   preferences, . . . beings.] JP, KK; preferences$_\wedge$ and aversions, of those engaged in the latter. TS

253.12   "practical,"] JP, KK; "radical;" TS

253.13   "theoretical."] JP, KK; $_\wedge$theoretical,$_\wedge$ in the sense of extension, promotion, of the methods of knowing and the conclusions known. TS

253.16   transformation] JP, KK; transformations TS

253.20   any] JP, KK; every TS

253.20   that] JP, KK; which TS

253.22   which] KK; that JP, TS

253.26   since it demanded] JP, KK; since there was TS

253.29–31   exemption . . . hypostatization.] JP, KK; this exemption from extraneous concerns is somehow inherent in the essence or "nature" of knowing is shee hypostization. TS

253.31–38   The exemption . . . terminus.] KK; The ground for the effort (and it *is* a struggle) to keep science "pure" from subjection to other concerns than that of knowing is itself *practical* in that it is *moral* in the sense of being in the best interests of the concerns and care of *human living* in general, as well as of the scientific occupation in particular, that it be conducted in behalf of its own advancement. TS

253.35   "pure," that is free,] KK; "pure" JP
253.37   the conduct] KK; conduct JP
253.38–254.8   This end . . . customs.] KK; This end may be called
the *ideal* of scientific knowing in the moral sense of the
word "ideal." But like other ideals for proper direction of
conduct it is not yet completely realized any more than its
present degree of purity has been achieved without a hard
struggle. Concerns due to war and to industry conducted
for pecuniary profit have obviously acted to influence the
problems selected (chosen) for investigation, even though
they no longer determine the conclusions reached as extraneous interests—those of "religious" institutions, for example—once determined the picture of the cosmos that was
accepted as "scientific." JP; And this is a regulative that is
sometimes called an *ideal*, an end which is rarely completely realized. The needs of war and to some extent those
of business conducted for pecuniary profit are not in control of the conduct of inquiry, but they certainly affect the
selection of problems to be inquired into. The result is a
certain one-sidedness in the conduct of inquiry due to its
overweighting in a given direction. TS
254.8–9   harmful as well as stupid] JP, KK; foolish as well as
harmful TS
254.9–11   "purity" . . . noting that] KK; [*not present*] JP, TS
254.14   cares] JP, KK; care TS
254.17   the human] JP, KK; human TS
254.17   dominant] JP, KK; [*not present*] TS
254.17–18   concern . . . the matters] JP, KK; concern, whatever
they may be at a given time and place, which determine the
matters TS
254.19–255.3   The . . . account.] KK; [*not present*] JP, TS
255.4   of high importance] KK; that is of philosophical concern
JP; which may be regarded as philosophical TS
255.5   relation] JP, KK; connection TS
255.5   concerns] JP, KK; affairs TS
255.5–6   science . . . other.] KK; common sense and of science
with each other. JP; common sense and of science. TS
255.6   It] KK; But it JP, TS
255.8   While] JP, KK; And while TS
255.9   which] JP, KK; that TS
255.10–11   inquiry, contributes to clear vision] JP, KK; inquiry∧
can contribute to a statement TS

255.12   itself] JP, KK; of itself TS
255.12–13   problem of concern] KK; problem as one of philosophical concern JP, TS
255.13–14   pointing out that a reference] JP, KK; saying the references that have been made TS
255.14   *return*] JP, KK; [*rom.*] TS
255.15   is] JP, KK; are TS
255.16   or] JP, KK; and TS
255.16   There] TS, KK; For there JP
255.18   now] JP, KK; [*not present*] TS
255.18   in] KK; in an JP, TS
255.20   *problem,*] JP, KK; [*rom.*] TS
255.20–21   concerns] JP, KK; is TS
255.22   evil] JP, KK; the evil TS
255.22   good] JP, KK; the good TS
255.23   to find . . . is] JP, KK; that of how it is TS
255.25   that] JP, KK; one TS
255.26   *here*] JP, KK; *there* TS
255.27   And] JP, KK; And at all events TS
255.28   vital.] JP, KK; vital in importance. TS
255.28   concern] JP, KK; its concern TS
255.31   an attempt] JP, KK; the attempt TS
255.32   indicated.] KK; indicated. [¶] This issue is not one to be
discussed at the tail-end of an article. I hope to return to
some aspects of it in a later paper; [in one dealing with TS]
especially the *aspect presented in [question of TS] the
historical-cultural conditions that switched philosophy off
from the human [*not present* TS] issues of the [relation between the TS] concerns and subject-matters [subject∧
matters TS] of science and common sense into the question
of how to reconcile them [regarded TS] as rival *knowings
about [accounts of TS] ultimate reality [Reality TS]. JP, TS
255.32   is in] JP, KK; is fairly in TS
255.34–36   the isolations, . . . the concerns,] KK; the dualisms in
which philosophy has been bogged down is to recur to [*not
present* TS] the concerns, JP, TS
255.37   they are] JP, KK; they express and maintain TS
255.37–38   indissoluble active union] JP, KK; active and intimate
participation TS
255.38   human] JP, KK; human beings TS
255.38   factors;] KK; factors, and JP; materials and processes; TS
255.39   traits . . . so] JP, KK; the *emotional* and *intellectual* so TS

256.1 independent . . . from] JP, KK; separated from TS
256.1 practical concerns,] JP, KK; [*not present*] TS
256.2 done,] JP, KK; done$_\wedge$ and from *ados* that are forced upon us in the process of living that they are aspects of living as the affair most inclusively and intensively practical of all affairs. Were this course tried, it is possible that philosophers would contribute to the introduction of an "age of the *common* man." TS
256.2 *facta* and *facienda*,] KK; facts and facienda, JP; [*not present*] TS
256.2–4 that . . . body of] JP, KK; [*not present*] TS
256.4 transactions.[8]] KK; ~.$_\wedge$ JP; [*not present*] TS
256n.1–10 8. In . . . transaction.] KK; [*not present*] JP, TS

11. A Trial Group of Names (Dewey and Bentley)

Listed below are the substantive variants between the *Knowing and the Known* copy-text, pp. 287–306 [this volume, pp. 257–74], and "Concerning a Vocabulary for Inquiry into Knowledge," *Journal of Philosophy* 44 (31 July 1947):421–34.

257.2 Undertaking] Undertaking (45.5)[1] . . . [1]We shall refer to preceding papers in this JOURNAL by use of the figure 45 for Vol. XLII (1945), and by the figures 46 and 47 for the two succeeding volumes, in each case following the year number by the page number after a decimal point. The papers have appeared in Volume XLII (1945), pp. 5, 39, 225, and 645; Volume XLIII (1946), pp. 505, 533, and 645; Volume XLIV (1947), p. 281. See also "Logicians' Underlying Postulations" in *Philosophy of Science,* Vol. 12 (1945), p. 3, and "The New 'Semiotic'" to appear in the September, 1947, issue of *Philosophy and Phenomenological Research.*
257.7 procedure.[1]] procedure (46.645).
257.11–12 thus rejecting] rejecting thus
257.17 in itself] to itself
257.19–20 deliberate effort] effort deliberately
257.23–25 a sound . . . postulation.] sound, and we postulate accordingly.
257n.1 See Chapter 3.] [*not present*]
258.6 decision] the decision
258.7 dicta taken to be] evidence taken as
258.21 study for all inquiry into] inquiry for the theory of

258n.5   (q.v.),] (which see),
259.6   preliminary assignment,] more general assignment,
259.8   characterization.] characterization (47.281).
259.18   that if] and that if
259.21–25   ; and . . . applications] [*not present*]
259.27   adjectives are desirable] adjectives
259.28   separate ranges.] separate processes are desirable.
259.34–260.2   offering . . . Trans-actor.] should never be used without the most careful specification under explicit postulation.
260.17–23   Transactionally . . . human."] [*not present*]
260.24   level of biological inquiry] [*not present*]
260.26   physical or] [*not present*]
260.32–33   ; covers . . . inquiry] [*not present*]
260.36   following;] following (46.657);
260.39   Its appearance is regarded] Regarded
260.40   epistemological inquiries that] procedures which
261.2   system.] system (45.238).
261.12   elsewhere.] anywhere else.
261.13–14   *Connection: . . . Relation.*] [*moved from aft.* 'Circularity' *entry*]
261.31   Fact] fact
261.34   signal.] signal (46.657).
261.40   chaos.] chaos (47.281).
262.7   use.⁴] ~.ₐ
262.8   fact.] fact (45.237; 46.653).
262.9–10   (q.v.) as a naming] (as a naming) (q.v.)
262.13   Cues organizing characterizations;] [*not present*]
262.13–14   characterizations . . . Not] Developed characterization building towards specification (46.659); accordingly, not
262.14   narrowed] unduly narrowed
262.14   brought] it is brought
262.16–18   A name . . . naming.] [*not present*]
262.23   that,] which,
262.35   employed] employed (as 45.245)
262.35   Existence.)] existence.)
262n.1   4. Chapter . . . Section I.] [*not present*]
263.2   behavioral] [*not present*]
263.2–3   (q.v.) . . . use] in its own specific uses (q.v.)
263.6–8   Hence . . . era.] [*not present*]
263.10   supporting] underlying
263.27   *Existence*] *existence*
263.40–264.3   Whether . . . Section IV.] [*not present*]

264.24–25   in individualized phrasing] in terms of the individual
265.17   *that, what,* and *how.*] *that* and he knows *what.*
265.17   should require] requires
265.19–20   accounts] account
265.34   namings-knowings] naming-knowings
266.4   word-meanings,] meanings,
266.12–14   In . . . "cues."] [*not present*]
266.15   naming] linguistic
266.19   (Try] (Try substituting,
266.20   speaking in terms of] [*not present*]
266.20   or] or using
266.31   , at times,] [*not present*]
266.37–38   assumed . . . free] considered free
266.38   conventional distortions.] probable hearers' distortions.
267.24–25   Always . . . but] [*not present*]
267.25   never as] Never to be treated as
267.25   substantively stressed "act,"] an act at a spot,
267.26–29   Always . . . knowing.] [*not present*]
267.33–34   The . . . it.] [*not present*]
267.39–268.2   *Percept:* . . . "existing."] [*not present*]
268.16   not through] not
268.31   logics.] logics.⁵ . . . ⁵For some illustrations see Bentley,
        "Logicians' Underlying Postulations," *Philosophy of Science,* Vol. 13 (1946), pp. 3–19.
269.1–2   *Reaction:* . . . (q.v.).] [*moved from aft.* 'Reality' *entry*]
269.3   not as] not
269.18, n.1–2   (q.v.).⁶ . . . 6. See . . . presentation.] (q.v.). See
        Dewey, *Logic: the Theory of Inquiry,* p. 55, for such a presentation.
269.28   Used] Used (46.509)
269n.4–5   , namely the "self,"] [*not present*]
271.1–4   The . . . be.] [*not present*]
271.18–21   A non-naming . . . *Symboling, Symbolization:*] [*not present*]
271.37   concept.] concept (45.15; 45.24).
272.1–5   It . . . object.] [*not present*]
272.7   generality . . . its] generality makes it a much safer word to
        use in epistemological discussion than its more
272.7–8   substitutes, Entity and Substance,] substitutes. See *Object, Entity, Substance.*
272.8–14   and more . . . Section II.] [*not present*]
272.16   , in older usage,] [*not present*]

272.27   *Transactor:* See *Actor.*] [*not present*]
272.29   in that] such that
272.36–39   *Vague:* . . . implied.] [*not present*]
273.7–8   words . . . representative] words, as we have said, are
          representatives
273.8   the postulation we have adopted.] our postulation,
273.8–14   The remainder . . . discussion.] while others are recom-
          mended more generally as aids to clarification. Contrasted
          with these are other words, shown to be confusedly used,
          among them some so debased that their ejection from all
          technical discourse is unqualifiedly urged. Such a variety of
          treatments is probably the best than can be expected in ex-
          amining vocabularies as ambiguous as those that have been
          under attention. We are *seeking* the firm (q.v.), not trying
          to decree it.
273.15   With] Finally with
273.15   central] [*not present*]
273.15–16   knowings-knowns] knowing-knowns
273.17–18   namings, . . . existential] namings are basic existential
273.18–19   renew . . . caution.] repeat what has been said often
          enough before:
273.19   all aware] as well aware as any opponent can be
273.19   knowings, as behaviors,] naming-knowings
273.20   , or among,] [*not present*]
273.20   ranges of behaviors.] fields of behaviors variously—whether
          analogically or otherwise—styled knowings.
273.20–274.5   We . . . it.] The critical issue concerns existence-
          knowing (fact-knowing) taken as presumptively prior to or
          apart from naming-knowing. When so taken, what is the
          organization between, or the system of, the two ranges?
          Much more of an answer is needed than is given by cue-
          guidance or loose characterization. Specification becomes
          essential, and for this, in the complex case, explicit postula-
          tion is the need.

Appendix: Dewey's Reply to Albert G. A. Balz

Listed below are the substantive variants between the *Knowing and the Known* copy-text (KK), pp. 313–29 [this volume, pp. 280–94], and two precopy-texts: Reply to "A Letter to Mr. Dewey," *Journal of Philosophy* 46 (26 May 1949):329–42 (JP); and the JP transcription of

Dewey's letter (JPTR) sent by Herbert W. Schneider, editor of JP, to Balz on 4 May 1949 (Balz Papers, Manuscripts Department, Alderman Library, University of Virginia, Charlottesville, 19 pp.).

280.9–10   Discovery Bay, Jamaica] JP, KK; [*not present*] JPTR
280.11   A——:] KK; Albert Balz JP; Alfred Balz JPTR
280.18   On the] JP, KK; On JPTR
281.10   should] JP, KK; [*not present*] JPTR
281.13–14   a development] JP, KK; development JPTR
281.28   A——,] KK; Albert Balz, JP; Alfred Balz, JPTR
281.29   in coming to] JP, KK; coming at JPTR
282.16   blocks—in] JP, KK; blocks. In JPTR
282.18   that] JP, KK; [*not present*] JPTR
282.38–39   subjectmatters] KK; subject-matters JP; subject matter JPTR
283.3   the one] JP, KK; one JPTR
283.6   equally] JP, KK; usually JPTR
283.14   as names] JP, KK; [*not present*] JPTR
283.14   disparate] JP, KK; separate JPTR
283.21   full] JP, KK; its full JPTR
283.27   A——,] KK; Albert Balz, JP; Alfred Balz, JPTR
283.29–30   taken . . . knowledge.] JP, KK; [*ital.*] JPTR
283.36   have] JP, KK; had JPTR
284.1–3   belonging . . . context.] JP, KK; [*ital.*] JPTR
285.16   instigating] JP, KK; the instigating JPTR
285.17   the use . . . further] JP, KK; their use JPTR
285.27   so far] JP, KK; as far JPTR
285.29   A——,] KK; Albert Balz, JP; Alfred Balz, JPTR
285.32   being made] JP, KK; making JPTR
285.38–39   *scientific*] JP, KK; the scientific JPTR
285.40   adhesions.] JP, KK; adhesion. JPTR
286.2   it] JP, KK; [*not present*] JPTR
286.7   a maximum] JP, KK; the maximum JPTR
286.7   uses.] JP, KK; use. JPTR
286.14   case] JP, KK; [*ital.*] JPTR
286.21   away] JP, KK; away from JPTR
286.25   rendered] JP, KK; [*not present*] JPTR
286.25–26   as . . . inquiry.] JP, KK; [*ital.*] JPTR
286.27   its] JP, KK; [*not present*] JPTR
286.28   space and time] JP, KK; space-time JPTR
286.29   themselves] JP, KK; themselves to JPTR
286.32   A——,] KK; Mr. Balz, JP, JPTR

286.40   its] JP, KK; [*not present*] JPTR
287.3   last] JP, KK; recent JPTR
287.9   geometry. While] JP, KK; geometry∧ while JPTR
#287.13 Mr. A——,] KK; Mr. Balz, JP, JPTR
287.18   *as*] JP, KK; [*rom.*] JPTR
287.20   "essences."] JP, KK; "essence". JPTR
287.23   the *ontological*,] JP, KK; *ontological*, JPTR
288.1   of something] JP, KK; something JPTR
288.1–2 occurring, that is,] KK; occuring, that is, JP; [*not present*] JPTR
288.4   subjectmatters] KK; subject-matters JP; subject matter JPTR
288.7   other with] JP, KK; other. With JPTR
288.8   knowledge. Controversy] JP, KK; knowledge∧ controversy JPTR
288.17–18 placing . . . inquiry] JP, KK; taking JPTR
288.19   controversy.] JP, KK; controversy in the context of Inquiry. JPTR
288.20–21 a mass] JP, KK; mass JPTR
288.25   setting into] JP, KK; setting, JPTR
288.28   from their own] JP, KK; *from their* JPTR
288.38   *between*] JP, KK; [*rom.*] JPTR
289.2   to say separation] JP, KK; [*ital.*] JPTR
289.15   "environment,"] JP, KK; ∧environments∧∧ JPTR
289.18   (in] JP, KK; (all JPTR
#289.24–25 organisms,] JP, KK; organism∧ JPTR
289.28   unified functionings.] JP, KK; certified functions. JPTR
289.29   distinctions] JP, KK; distinction JPTR
289.29   are] JP, KK; it is JPTR
289.31   *as*] JP, KK; [*rom.*] JPTR
289.38   by means of] KK; through JP, JPTR
290.1   to slough] JP, KK; been able to slough JPTR
290.6–7 the subjectmatter] KK; the subject-matter JP; subjectmatter JPTR
290.11   as an] JP, KK; as the JPTR
290.20   *Inquiry,* transfers] JP, KK; *Inquiry.* It transfers JPTR
290.26   pursued] JP, KK; used JPTR
290.32   life. To] JP, KK; life; while to JPTR
290.34   when used . . . affairs] JP, KK; [*not present*] JPTR
291.11   related] JP, KK; relative JPTR
291.15   which] JP, KK; [*not present*] JPTR
291.35   A——,] KK; Mr. Balz, JP, JPTR

292.1   *on . . . interpretation*] JP, KK; [*rom.*] JPTR
292.6   new] JP, KK; a JPTR
292.8   subjectmatters] KK; subject-matters JP; subjectmatter JPTR
292.16   in which] JP, KK; where JPTR
292.18   *scientific*] JP, KK; [*rom.*] JPTR
292.25   matter] JP, KK; a matter JPTR
293.1   *under*] JP, KK; *under* the JPTR
293.16   was] JP, KK; as JPTR
293.33   has] JP, KK; had JPTR
293.38   restatement,] JP, KK; a restatement, JPTR
294.9   which] KK; that JP, JPTR

Notes on Substantive Variants in *Knowing and the Known*

Some substantive variants between *Knowing and the Known* and the *Journal of Philosophy* (JP) derive from Dewey's markings and queries on book galleys ("Galleys carrying Dewey revisions," envelope 67, *Knowing and the Known* files, Arthur F. Bentley Collection, Manuscripts Department, Lilly Library, Indiana University, Bloomington). Dewey read the first set of book galleys and returned to Bentley those he revised. Bentley either adopted, discarded, or used Dewey's suggestions to revise differently. This section records Dewey's substantive galley revisions and Bentley's notations.

The reading before the bracket is from the present edition. A description of Dewey's revision or query follows the bracket. A dagger † before the entry indicates that no revision was made for *Knowing and the Known* and therefore no entry appears in the Substantive Variants section.

48.32   knowings as themselves facts.] JP and galley 16 read "knowledge as itself fact." On the galley Dewey bracketed "knowledge" and queried it in the margin, and Bentley wrote "knowing" in the margin.

†48.39   this] On galley 16 Dewey underscored "this" and wrote "that (?)" in the margin.

†57.17–18   misapprehensions] Dewey changed the plural to singular on galley 19.

57.20   hope we shall] Galley 19 read "hope we will" [changed from "hope that we will" in JP]. Dewey deleted "will" and wrote "shall" in the margin.

58.11   offers] Dewey changed "offered" to "offers" on galley 19.

60.23–24   in system] Dewey inserted these two words with a question mark on galley 20.

72.38   science offers sound guidance.] Galley 24 read "science
          [changed from "it" in JP] is our best knowledge." Dewey
          added quotation marks to "knowledge" and wrote re-
          vealingly to Bentley about his change: "I do not see how
          any 'knowledge' could be better than the best" ([20 Febru-
          ary 1948], Bentley Collection).

75.26   then] Dewey inserted "then" on galley 25.

75.27   of circularity] Dewey added these two words with a ques-
          tion mark on galley 25.

82.22   then and there] Dewey added these three words with a
          question mark on galley 27.

†82n.10   aspectual] On galley 27 Dewey underscored "aspectual"
          and wrote "contextual (?)" in the margin.

83n.22   with] Dewey added this word with a question mark on gal-
          ley 28.

†84.24   to knowledge] On galley 28 Dewey deleted "knowledge"
          and wrote "knowings (?)" in the margin.

89.25   the more complete] JP and galley 29 read "a richer"; on the
          galley Dewey inserted a caret after "richer" and wrote "and
          freer (?)" in the margin.

97.23   just] JP and galley 31 read "complete"; on the galley Dewey
          circled the word and wrote in the margin, "'complete' (as it
          stands alone) may be misunderstood because of failure to
          see the force of concluding phrase." Bentley deleted "com-
          plete" and wrote "just" in the margin.

97.25   observed—and as it is affected] JP and galley 31 read "ob-
          served, and affected"; on the galley Dewey inserted the
          dash and wrote, "Insert 'as' between 'and' 'affected' (?)" in
          the margin. Bentley wrote "as it is" in the margin.

101n.13   outcome] On galley 33 Dewey underscored "outcome" and
          wrote "ital (?)" in the margin.

110.12   knowing] Dewey changed "knowledge" to "knowing" on
          galley 35.

†110.19   Event.] On galley 35 Dewey marked a caret below "Event."
           and drew a guideline to the margin, where he wrote "or
           Existence (?)."

†112.18   event] On galley 36 Dewey inserted a caret after "event"
           and wrote "s (?)" in the margin; Bentley deleted the query.

 113.29   fact] On galley 36 Dewey deleted the "a" in "'a fact'" and
           queried the deletion in the margin.

†130.7   still] On galley 42 Dewey deleted "still" and wrote "even"
           in the margin.

 131.12   activities] JP and galley 42 read "processes"; on the galley
           Dewey circled the word and wrote in the margin, "For
           some reason, I dont know just why, 'operations' seems
           more specific name here. An operation is process, but *pro-
           cess fitted* in system."

 152.20   defect] JP and galley 49 read "defects"; on the galley
           Dewey deleted the "s" and wrote "or else vaguenesses (plu-
           ral)" in the margin.

†152.21   this] On galley 49 Dewey deleted "this" and wrote "the" in
           the margin.

 154.21   we ourselves stood] JP and galley 49 read "ourselves"; on
           the galley Dewey inserted a caret after "ourselves" and
           wrote "were" in the margin.

†156.24   things other] On galley 50 Dewey inserted "as" between
           these two words and wrote to Bentley, "I suggest inserting
           'as' because after all words are a kind of things themselves"
           ([21 February 1948], Bentley Collection).

†156.25   along . . . make.] On galley 50 Dewey marked the trans-
           position "is easy to make along conventional lines." and
           wrote "tr" in the margin.

 157n.8   science;] On galley 50 Dewey changed "knowledge" to
           "science" and wrote, "(In its own terms, it *was* 'Knowl-
           edge'—but Kn. of things which by their own 'nature' were
           only probable or contingent—*sometimes* so but not al-
           ways)" in the margin.

158.1–2   process of] JP and galley 50 read "the tool for"; on the galley Dewey circled "tool" and wrote "process" in the right margin, and "Proce[ss] means agency" in the left margin. Bentley then deleted "the tool" and wrote "process for" in the margin.

158.5   thus held] Dewey marked the transposition from "held thus" on galley 51, adding "tr" in the margin.

158.5   which] Dewey changed "that" to "which" on galley 51.

159.5   as the] Dewey inserted "as" on galley 51.

160.10   conventional] JP and galley 51 read "old artificial"; on the galley Dewey bracketed "old artificial isolations of form from content" and wrote to Bentley that the phrase "is a little ambiguous. . . . It would be ok to change 'the old' to 'current' or 'habitual' or something of that kind" ([21 February 1948], Bentley Collection).

160.30   science] JP and galley 51 read "knowledge"; on the galley Dewey circled the word and wrote "science (?)" in the margin.

164.17–18   as are . . . definitions,] JP and galley 53 read "as syntactical and semantical definitions are,"; Dewey marked the transposition on the galley and wrote "tr" in the margin.

Dewey's Revisions in "Importance, Significance, and Meaning"

Listed below are Dewey's revisions in two typescripts for "Importance, Significance, and Meaning." Copy-text for this essay is a conflation of two slightly variant typescripts, one in the John Dewey Papers and the other in the Arthur F. Bentley Collection.[1] Dewey's typist prepared two sets of "Importance, Significance, and Meaning" and sent a carbon from one set to Dewey and a carbon from the other set to Bentley.

Dewey did not revise his carbon but did later revise assorted ribbon-copy pages from both sets.[2] Twenty-five of these thirty-one extant pages bear Dewey's typed and holographic revisions. In the list that follows, ribbon copies matching the Dewey Papers carbon are designated by the symbol TS[1]; ribbon copies matching the Bentley Collection carbon, by the symbol TS[2]. Where Dewey revised the same text in TS[1] and TS[2], these dual revisions have been listed. However, in those cases where Dewey revised a passage in several ways on a single typescript, only what seems to be Dewey's latest revision is listed.

Thirty-one of forty-six ribbon-copy pages were preserved. Only TS[1] text is extant for revisions at 320.30 and 330.37–331.1, and only TS[2] text for revisions at 321.18–29, 323.39–325.2, and 327.39–329.5. Both TS[1] and TS[2] texts are extant for Dewey's revisions at 320.35–321.16, 322.29–323.32, 325.4–327.37, 329.5–16, and 331.2–332.24. Bracketed notations for the extant texts appear in the list of variants.

Because the revisions are ambiguous, editorial judgment has necessarily been used to interpret them to reflect, as nearly as can be determined, Dewey's intent. For instance, as Dewey often did not indicate in any way where he meant to place insertions, they have been positioned where they seem logically to fit, whether in relation to a given word,

---

1. Typescripts, carbon copies, in Dewey Papers, Box 58, folder 9, Special Collections, Morris Library, Southern Illinois University at Carbondale, 23 pp.; and Bentley Collection, Manuscripts Department, Lilly Library, Indiana University, Bloomington, 23 pp.
2. Dewey Papers, Box 58, folder 16, 31 pp.

sentence, or paragraph. Undecipherable words are rendered as [*illeg. word(s)*]; likely transcriptions appear with a bracketed italic question mark [?]. Dewey's few mechanical typewriting errors have been corrected. Words Dewey omitted in the course of revision are indicated by [*om.*]; words he clearly intended to delete but did not are omitted from this list. Underlined words are indicated by [*ital.*]. A caret ∧ indicates Dewey's deletion or omission of a punctuation mark. Missing letters, words, or punctuation necessary to the sense of the revision are shown in brackets.

The reading before the bracket is from the present edition; Dewey's revision follows the bracket. A grid # indicates that the text has been emended and the reading appears in the Emendations List.

320.30   life-behavior] particular life-behavior previously TS[1] [*TS[1] only*]

[320.35–321.16   *TS[1] and TS[2]*]

320.35   specific way of] [*om.*] TS[1]

#321.2–3   a degrading] degrading a TS[1]

321.10   as to] with respect to TS[1]

321.11   They . . . danger;] In the presence of danger they are watchful, wary; TS[2]

321.12–13   themselves . . . unawares.] themselves, and also in so conducting themselves as to catch their prey unawares. TS[1]; themselves and in obtaining, perhaps agressively their prey unawares, in the ordinary course of events[.] TS[2]

321.13–14   Be it remembered that] [*om.*] TS[2]

321.14–15   what is . . . some] What is in here said is taken as it is intended, namely as concerned with *observable behavior,* not with some TS[2]

321.16   and] [*om.*] TS[2]

[321.18–29   *TS[2] only*]

321.18   present] visibly, practically [*illeg. word*] present TS[2]

321.18–19   case of wild] [*om.*] TS[2]

321.19   with . . . familiar] [*om.*] TS[2]

321.21   them in] them and that the examination is concerned with TS[2]

321.21   do:] do:— TS[2]

321.22   *how*] upon *how* TS[2]

321.22   behavior.] behavior of a more directly or conclusive sort. TS[2]

321.23   made] put forth TS[2]

321.24   reader, but to] reader; they are meant to TS[2]

#321.25   from] (from TS[2]

#321.25   *of view*] and *view* TS[2]

#321.26   article] article) TS[2]

321.27–28   knowing. . . theories.] knowing treated as inquiry. TS[2]

321.29   II] [*om.*] TS[2]

[322.29–323.32   *TS[1] and TS[2]*]

322.29–30   end-in-*view*, . . . entertained;] end-in-*view*; TS[1]

322.30   a need to be] the need of being TS[1]

322.30–31   its meeting . . . fulfill] meeting, or failing to fulfill, TS[1]

322.32   in consequence,] [*om.*] TS[1]

322.33   observation, namely, the] observation. For the TS[1]

322.33–34   actually occurring] that actually occur later, TS[1]

322.34   view.] view have to be themselves noted in order to test the validity of the observation of something *as sign.* TS[1]

322.40   affect it] affect its use as *pattern* of inquiry TS[1]

323.1   III] II [*in left margin of first paragraph is written "rewrite"*] TS[2]

323.2   Before . . . said] Accordingly before concluding from the case cited TS[1]; Accordingly before we conclude TS[2]

323.3   human] all human TS[2]

323.3   is that inquiry] are inquiries which, TS[2]

323.3–4   an intermediate and] intermediate or TS[2]

#323.4   way . . . not by] way of behavior is constituted by TS[1]; ways of behavior, are concerned on one hand with TS[2]

323.5–6   subjectmatters . . . consequences,] subjectmatters on one hand as *means to consequences,* TS[1]; *subjectmatters* taken as means to consequences, TS[2]

323.6–7   and . . . of means] and, on the other hand, of things as *consequences of means* TS[1]; and on the other hand with determination of *consequences* of means TS[2]

323.7   would] would plainly TS[2]

323.7   if] should TS[2]

323.7–8   constantly] [*ital.*] TS[2]

323.8   look-out so as] look-out in order TS[1]; look-out TS[2]

323.8   results] [*ital.*] TS[2]

323.9   direction),] direction as they bear on arriving at this[?] proposed goal), TS[2]

323.9   instance] case TS[2]

323.13   in signifying, telling] with respect to signifying, telling, TS[1]; *signifying,* (i.e., serving as *signs* or evidence), TS[2]

323.13   directive] [*om.*] TS[2]

323.14–15   But . . . he] But as a matter of the *theory* of inquiry he TS[1]; Yet in advance he TS[2]

323.17–18   are heeded] would usually be heeded TS[2]
323.18   his] his own TS[1]
323.20   reaching . . . window] [*om.*] TS[2]
323.20   has . . . case] has, in the given case, TS[1]; has in the then & there given case TS[2]
323.21   the way . . . patient.] the way of treatment that is to be tried. TS[1]; what is to be done in respect to the patient. TS[2]
323.22   But what is] What is however TS[2]
323.22   this case] any case TS[2]
323.22   (1) that] (1) that (i) TS[2]
323.22   observations] observations are TS[2]
323.23   or] [*om.*] TS[2]
323.24   "hitch"] "hitch" or threatened one TS[2]
323.24   with] with, TS[1]; with, and (ii) that they TS[2]
323.25   varied and continuous] more varied, and temporally more inter-connected TS[2]
323.27   study the board] continue [to] study the sign-board TS[2]
323.27–32   hours, . . . had to come] hours, and had to use various instruments to make out just what the board said, or was a sign of, with respect to how to proceed; and at that, as if he had to call upon a store of facts previously learned and also to consult a store of facts *to be* learned by reading more books, periodicals, etc., to find out what the seen fact indicated or told as a sign, and also had to come TS[1]; a long time[,] coming TS[2]
[323.39–325.2   *TS[2] only*]
323.39   not have] *not* need TS[2]
323.39   investigate] investigate with respect to TS[2]
323.39   that is settled] where to go has in his case been settled TS[2]
323.39–324.1   advance, and his] advance. His TS[2]
324.1–2   asserted] assumed TS[2]
324.3   his goal] that his goal TS[2]
324.4–5   the assumption] assumption TS[2]
324.7   every patient;] *every* patient. TS[2]
324.7   accordingly it provides] It provides accordingly TS[2]
324.8–10   As . . . other,] [*om.*] TS[2]
324.10–16   it does . . . case.] In its vague generality it is taken for granted. This fact is more important for the theory of inquiry (& hence of knowing than appears on the surface. It shows, quite conclusively that in & for inquiry, its specific *what* or subject is the *how* or way, method and the [2 *illeg. words*]. No word used in phil is more *ambivalent—End*

as *both terminator* [2 *illeg. words*] that is, sheer limit
when TS²

324.19–22   *Practically* speaking . . . find] *Practically* speaking
when reached inquiry in it is over with. The end of inquiry
as long as it exists is with a view to finding TS²

324.22–23   it . . . inquiry] it so as to reach the end in the sense of
the close of inquiry TS²

324.24   absurdity. It] absurdity; it TS²

324.25   done.] done. Nevertheless it is often indulged in in the
sense that the all[?] important dis[tinction] between the two
is overlooked in the statement of them. TS²

324.26–27   under given conditions,] [*om.*] TS²

324.31   matter.] matter. For example, temporal spatial[?] condi-
[tions?] are of primary importance in in[quiry?] [*illeg.
word*] they are conditions of determination of what subjects
are evidential—are signs to be heeded. TS²

325.1   which is] [*om.*] TS²

325.1   exceedingly] exceedingly difficult and TS²

325.2   first . . . observations] involving making and continually
revising observations made, TS²

[325.4–327.37   *TS¹ and TS²*]

325.4   ends-in-view] [*ital.*] TS¹

325.4   are also used as means] serve as necessary conjoint means
TS¹; are means TS²

325.5   Consequences] Foreseen consequences like most[?] ends-in
view TS¹; Consequences as ends held *in view* TS²

325.5–6   *in process* . . . changing] *in process* of development
TS¹; *in process,* changing TS²

325.6   continues, . . . as proper] continues, provided it has or
gave[?] direction[?], change being as proper TS¹; continues: for change is as necessary TS²

325.7   and settled] or settled TS²

325.7   an end as a destination] end as destination TS¹; end as a
destination TS²

325.8   Observation] For observation TS²

325.10   proceeds] proceeds, TS²

325.11   function of] function, as TS¹; function, that of TS²

325.11   This] ¶ This TS²

325.12   will not] need not TS²

325.13   upon . . . It] upon in that case. ¶ It TS¹; upon. It TS²

325.13–15   acknowledged . . . bearing.] acknowledged as of fundamental importance with respect to the *theory of knowing*

as inquiry as knowing[?]. TS[1]; acknowledged to be involved as an indispensable function of observed facts when
we are concerned with the *theory* of knowing. TS[2]

325.15–19   For . . . behavior.] For [*illeg. word*] determination
through an[?] observation of existing conditions [*illeg.
word*] manifestation[?] & office as means to[?] useful[?]
consequences [*illeg. word*] corresp[onding?] determination[?] through reflection (or *reasoning*) of ends in view as
consequences[?] of[?] means to [*illeg. word*] the life[?] &
the [*illeg. word*] use[?] traditional language[?]. *The* category of knowing seen[?] as inquiry [*illeg. word*] that of
means-consequence where the hyphen stands not for
disjunction[?] but for nece[ssary?] con-junction. It remains
to add that neither means nor consequences nor their
connection with one another can *be understood* on *the*
grounds[?] of *the* theory here set forth save in terms of life-
behavior. TS[1]; For they prove that treating things as means
to consequences and also treating proposed ends-in-view as
means to a final consequence is the life-blood of intelligent
behavior in general and of inquiry as a particular phase of
intelligent behavior. TS[2]

#325.19–26   As . . . operate.] In theory[?] even during observation
and [*illeg. words*] of space time[?] conditions as means &
reflective propositions[?] of consequences[?] as ends in view
there is as matter of observable fact constant *imaginative* reference to the way of action, of doing-making, by
which[?] they are believed[?] testable, and wherever *knowing* runs its full course the overt *behavior* that ensues is &
is treated as the deepest experimental test. TS[1]; As a matter
of record rather than as an additional matter, it is here
noted that as long as inquiry proceeds, both the conditions
observed as signs of the matter to be dealt with and ends-
in-view that are entertained as means of directing activity
are tentative, on trial; while the measure of the competence
of inquiries engaged [in] is the degree in which observations
made are such as to provide *improved* means with which to
operate. TS[2]

#325.27–34   dogmas, . . . as they] dogmas, with respect to *inquiry,*
to knowing *in process,* they are fatal. To be *bound* in advance to a given conclusion is the exact contrary of being
required to inquire so as to find out the means of reaching a
conclusion as a decision that warrants resumption of decisive behavior. [¶] We thus return to the thesis of knowing

as intermediate & mediate in life behavior and, in the case
of dog chasing rabbit, as they TS¹; dogmas, may be converted into a positive resource[.] [¶] That it is intermediate
between a trouble, a "hitch" and the resumption of straight
away, and in such a way as to mediate, or furnish for the
means of, resumption is the fact that is common to the
motorist pausing in his journey to look so that he may the
more securing resume his travelling to an intended destination; to the case of the physical who devotes time and energy to diagnosis of the case he is called upon to treat as the
means of arriving at a suitable course of remedial treatment, and also in the case of an animal who by his organic
constitution pauses to listen and to look as a conditioning
factor in his subsequent activities. [¶] Consider, for example dog chasing a rabbit and the behavior of the rabbit
in being chased, as they TS²

325.35   air as successive] air, as successive but TS²
#325.35   phrases] aspects TS²
325.37   one of them] of them, TS²
325.39   so manifest] also manifest TS²
#325.39   dog or man] whether dog or man, TS²
325.40–326.1   behavior it is easier] behavior, it is easier in their
          case TS²
326.3   life-activity in their case.] life-activity. TS²
326.4   the latter] the case of prehuman animal behavior TS²
326.8   particular] [*om.*] TS²
326.9   operates.] functions. TS²
326.9   sensation,] "sensation," TS²
326.11   does not seem] hardly seems TS²
326.11   that they] they TS²
#326.12–13   extraneous entity   been] wholly extraneous
          non-natural factor have got TS²
#326.13   lodged with] lodged in TS²
326.14   human activities and affairs] *human* activities TS²
326.14   blind vision.] blind vision to recognition of what takes
          place in other living creatures. TS²
326.18–19   the differences] differences arise and function TS¹
#326.19   within the entity of] within the unity of TS¹, TS²
326.19   pattern arise and function.] pattern. TS¹
326.20–21   is . . . fortunate] is also at stake in a large variety of
          other highly complicated controversial issues. It is fortunate
          accordingly TS²
326.21–22   intention . . . understanding] main intention of this

paper is to obtain understanding TS¹; intention of this
paper is to obtain *understanding* TS²
326.23 view . . . acceptance.] view. TS¹; view rather than to ensure its acceptance. TS²
326.23 The latter would] For understand[ing] is prerequisite[?] to
intelligent denial of the point[?] while its acceptance would
TS¹
326.27 other side . . . say] other side, resort to reduction, *via*, say,
TS²
326.28 terms that] conditions which TS²
326n.1–2 To . . . "spiritualistic"] "Spiritualistic" TS²
326n.3 explanations] explanations in philosophy TS²
327.17 artefacts.] artefacts than are say their skills in climbing and
hanging. TS²
327.18 called] called (the existence of arts and artefacts) TS²
327.22 human] of human TS²
327.23–24 lies at the other pole.] is quite another matter. TS²
327.26 if . . . even] even if there were set forth TS²
327.27 only] say only TS²
327.29 readers . . . considering] to force readers into consideration
of TS²
327.29 cited] [*om.*] TS²
327.36 both skills] skills TS²
327.37 *environing* and organic] the *environing* and the organic
TS²
[327.39–329.5 TS² *only*]
327.39 natural] "natural" TS²
327.41 and would] or would TS²
328.1 instruments of action,] instrumentalities, TS²
328.2 on paper by human beings] by human beings on paper TS²
328.3 transformation] a transformation by means of which they
are converted TS²
328.3 which stand] to stand TS²
328.4 two] two matters TS²
328.5 intimately] and intimately TS²
328.6 act] act, TS²
328.6–7 attempt . . . imagination.] attempt even in imagination to
view them in separation. TS²
328.8–9 as themselves were] have themselves been TS²
328.10 conditions . . . material] conditions, when material environmental TS²
328.11 consequences.] consequences were lacking. TS²
328.12 accumulating] an accumulation of TS²

328.12   as evidence] in evidence TS²
#328.14   suffice] suffices TS²
328.16   how that is so,] *how,* TS²
328.16   theory.] theory, such is the fact. TS²
328.17   hoe] hoe, TS²
328.17–18 rudest gardener who] gardener who however rude TS²
#328.18   means in consequences] means-to-consequences TS²
328.20   put, the end it serves,] put; of the purpose it serves; TS²
328.21–22 means to consequent events,] means-to-consequent-
           events, TS²
328.23–24 without . . . played] without any sense of the part they
           played TS²
328.26   presents to view,] presents, TS²
328.27   mere] a mere TS²
328.28   human behavior has] *human* behavior has then TS²
328.29   It] This event TS²
328.30   indifferent . . . heeding,] indifferent, but that observation as
           heeding∧ TS²
328.31   *in-view.* Its being itself] *in-view.* Futurity ceases to be
           merely *de-facto. Being* TS²
328.33   the latter] the future event TS²
328.33–34 directive in subsequent proceedings.] present directive.
           TS²
328.35   as *de facto*] when *de facto* TS²
328.36   view.] present view. TS²
328.37   still] [*om.* ?] TS²
328.39   existence.] actual existence. TS²
328.41   tells] says and tells TS²
329.1   information;] information, or TS²
329.1–2   advice; . . . human] advice, and a warning, as if a human
           being TS²
329.2   threatening] a threatening TS²
329.3   makes possible a vast] creates a cultural environment in
           which takes place a vast TS²
329.4–5   this extension, . . . traditions] the *linguistic* extension,
           say in the customs & traditional cherished folklore TS²
[329.5–28 *TS¹ and TS²*]
329.5–16   of remote . . . Wisdom] of a community in some early
           stage of culture could not have occurred had there not first
           taken place the physical use of a hoe as a means of attaining
           an end-*in-view* so that the latter becomes an end in factual
           existence. Nor could the enduring embodiment in cultural
           tradition by means of language have occurred unless when

the intended consequence had been existentially attained,
the resulting existence be viewed as a consequence of something that happened in the past and hence no longer exposed to sensory perception.

Given these conditions of foresight and hindsight, there is
present the possibility, no matter how slowly or in what
roundabout ways, of planning far ahead and of reaching,
by means of words as names, far back into the past for
means by which to carry plans into execution: the farther
the look-backwards the longer the scope of the forward
look—and *vice versa, re*-organization of past events being
the *end-in-view.* ¶ Wisdom TS²

329.18   care for . . . store] care for, while the present store thus
           becomes TS²
329.19   present and future.] the future. TS²
329.20   means] the storing from the past that constitutes means
           TS²
329.23–24   terrifically powerful new] potent TS²
329.24   new mechanical] mechanical TS²
329.25   the events] events TS²
329.27   *con*sequential;] *con*sequential. Hence they are TS²
329.28   but . . . them.] but cannot be said to use them. TS²
330.37–331.1   to be . . . distinguishing] to learn that the position
           taken holds that the distinguishing TS¹ [*TS¹ only*]
#331.2   human intelligently] distinctively human TS¹ [*TS¹ only*]
[331.2–332.24   *TS¹ and TS²*]
#331.2   conducted activity] activity TS¹; conducted human ac-
           tivity, TS²
331.3–8   varieties, . . . incurred.] varieties∧ with respect to its mea-
           sure as *intelligent,* is consideration, weighing, passing upon,
           judging the *importance* of what ever is presented, or in any
           way entertained in the inquiries, the knowing, that take
           place when difficulties and obstacles are incurred. TS¹; va-
           rieties∧ knowing included, is the demand made in it and
           upon it, with respect to its measure *as* intelligent, to weigh,
           estimate, judge or pass upon the *importance* of what is pre-
           sented, or is in any way entertained. TS²
#331.8–9   term; . . . ways] term, while significance and meanings
           are names for the two specific ways TS¹; term, while sig-
           nificance and meaning are specific ways TS²
#331.9–10   the issue . . . dealt;] importance needs to be dealt with.
           TS¹; the issue of importance presents itself and has to be
           dealt with. TS²

331.10–11   there being . . . behavior] For since all behavior
        TS¹; Because all life behavior TS²
331.11–12   transactional . . . has] transactional involving both
        organic and environing conditions, importance has
        TS¹; *trans*actional importance has TS²
331.12–14   to both . . . behavior.] to each of the components of in-
        quiry or knowing. TS¹
331.15   Both] Each TS¹
331.15   have] has TS¹
331.16   they *bear*] for each of them bears TS¹
331.16–17   activity . . . subsequent.] way any given activity is per-
        formed and hence upon [what] results or follows as its out-
        come. TS¹
331.17–18   import the following activity;] import or bring the ac-
        tivity that follows or is subsequ[ent;] TS²
331.23   consequence] *con*sequent TS¹
#331.23   reached, as such it] reached, and as such TS¹
332.24   important.] important. [*written on verso of p. 22 is* "last
        pp Imp"] TS²

Alterations in Manuscripts

In the lists that follow appear Dewey's changes both at the typewriter and by hand. The medium for each item is described in the headnote to that item. All Dewey's alterations made in the course of writing and revision appear here except for strengthened letters to clarify a word, irrelevant typed letters attached to a word, false starts for a word, transposition of letters in a legible word, and mendings over illegible letters. Dewey's corrections of typographical errors, whether by typing over or marking over by hand, are also not recorded as alterations, except when the possibility exists that the error might have been another word or the start of another word rather than a simple typographical mistake.

The word(s) before the bracket refers to the original manuscript. If the manuscript has been emended or the spelling regularized, a grid # before the entry means the reading of the present edition is in the Emendations List, or, for Preface to *Knowing and the Known,* in Substantive Variants in *Knowing and the Known.* When reference is made to one of two or more identical words in the same line of the present edition, some preceding or following word or punctuation mark is added for identification.

For Dewey's alterations, which appear to the right of the bracket, the abbreviation *del.* (deleted) is used to show material marked out by hand; *added* also refers to alterations by hand. *Intrl.* may mean either typewritten (*t.*) or handwritten interlineations; the description in each headnote makes this clear. All carets are made by hand; when carets are used with handwritten alterations, they are in the same medium as the alteration. For material deleted at the typewriter, *x'd-out* is used. The abbreviation *alt. fr.* (altered from) refers to words altered in some way from a variant form. The abbreviation *undrl.* applies to underlining by hand, and *quots.* signifies quotation marks.

With respect to position, when an addition is a simple interlineation, the formula is *intrl.* or *intrl. w. caret.* When a deletion positions the interlineation, *intrl.* is dropped and *ab.* (above) is used; the formula then reads *ab. del.* 'xyz', *w. caret ab. del.* 'xyz', or *ab. x'd-out* 'xyz.' *Bel.*

(below) means interlined below without a caret unless mentioned. *Ov.* (over) means inscribed over the original letters, not interlined. The abbreviations *bef.* (before) and *aft.* (after) signal a change made on the same line, whether the original line or interline. The abbreviation *insrtd.* (inserted) refers to additions that cannot be called interlineations but are of the same nature.

When an alteration incorporates a prior revision, that revision is described between brackets immediately following the single word to which it refers, or an asterisk * is placed before the first word to which the description in brackets applies.

Alterations in Preface to *Knowing and the Known*

The document is a ribbon-copy typescript enclosed in Dewey to Arthur F. Bentley, 3 September 1947, Bentley-Dewey Correspondence, Bentley Collection, Manuscripts Department, Lilly Library, Indiana University, Bloomington, 2 pp. Unless designated *t.*, alterations are in ink. A grid # before an entry in this item means the reading of the present edition is in the Substantive Variants in *Knowing and the Known*.

3.5	acute] *bef. del.* 'in that field'
3.5	controversy,] *comma added*
3.7	in] *t. intrl. w. caret*
3.8	degree of] *t. intrl. w. caret*
3.8–9	understanding,] *comma added*
3.9	advantage,] *comma added*
#3.13–14	subjects] *aft. x'd-out* 'devel'
3.14	developed.] *aft. x'd-out* 'advanced'
3.15	implies] *t. alt. fr.* 'impises'
3.18	methods] *aft. del.* 'those'
3.18	of imposition] *intrl. w. caret*
#3.18–19	knowing,] *comma added*
#3.22–23	this] *alt. fr.* 'the' *bef. del.* 'same'
#3.22–23	method,] *aft. x'd-out* 'th'
3.25	Accordingly] *aft. insrtd.* '¶'
3.26	it is placed] 'placed' *intrl. w. caret*
3.29	belief] *aft. del.* 'the'
#3.29	knowing] *aft. x'd-out* 'the'
3.30	dependability] *t. ab. x'd-out* 'in integrity'
#3.30	to be] *w. caret ab. del.* 'is'
#4.3	procedures] *intrl. w. caret*

4.3–4	systematically]	*intrl. w. caret*
4.4	is]	*intrl. w. caret*
4.4	fact]	*bef. del.* 'is'
4.5	which]	*t. ab. x'd-out* 'that adts'
4.6	cooperative]	*aft. x'd-out* 'a'
4.6	as such]	*intrl. w. caret*
4.8	as]	*t. ab. x'd-out* 'in terms of'
4.8	events]	*bef. x'd-out* 'as'
4.8	terms]	*aft. x'd-out* 'durational in time'
#4.10	an]	*ov.* 'the'
4.10	openness and]	'and' *intrl. w. caret*
#4.13	this]	*aft. x'd-out* 'tead'
#4.14	the]	*ov.* 'an'
4.15	very]	*intrl. w. caret*
#4.15	employing]	*alt. fr.* 'employ' *aft. del.* 'trying to'
#4.16–17	even]	*bef. x'd-out* 'impose'
4.17	absolute]	*aft. del.* 'an'
4.17	points]	*alt. fr.* 'point'
4.18	however]	*intrl. w. caret*
4.18	that]	*bef. del.* 'that'
4.19	be]	*intrl. w. caret*
4.19	itself]	*bef. del.* 'be'
4.21	initiate]	*ab. del.* '* serve to further' [*aft. x'd-out* 'accomplish']
4.22	sort,]	*comma added*
4.22	firmness]	*aft. del.* 'mutual'
4.23	an]	*aft. x'd-out* 'the'

Alterations in "What Is It to Be a Linguistic Sign or Name?"

The document is a typescript in the Arthur F. Bentley Collection, Manuscripts Department, Lilly Library, Indiana University, Bloomington, 18 pp., dated "5–25–45" by Bentley. Pp. 4, 12, 13, and 14 are ribbon copies; the rest are carbon copies. Page numbers are typed at the upper left-hand corner; p. 9 is marked "9–10." Unless designated *penc.* or *ink*, alterations are typed. "*Added*" in this list means added at the typewriter. Mechanical typewriting errors at 300.36, 301.8, 301.10, and 308n.10 have been corrected in the text.

297.1	Linguistic]	*aft. x'd-out* 'Sign?'
297.5	is appearing]	*aft. x'd-out* 'has appeared'
297.6	not]	*aft. x'd-out* 'be'

297.7   much] *aft. x'd-out* 'the'
297.10   a different] *aft. x'd-out* 'getting'
297.11   directly] *intrl.*
297.12   while . . . case of] *intrl. w. ink caret*
297.15   representatives:—] *dash intrl.*
297.18   treated . . . as] *ellipsis intrl.*
297.20   defined,] *aft. x'd-out* 'described'
297.22   or] *ov.* 'of'
297.23   person-things,] 'person' *alt. fr.* 'personal'; *ab. x'd-out*
           'mind'
297.24   all but] *intrl.*
297n.4   being] *aft. x'd-out* 'my [*ab. x'd-out* 'the'] text'
297n.6   Vol.] *aft. x'd-out* 's.v.,'
298.2   As] *aft. x'd-out and penc. del.* 'They are'
298.2   human] *aft. x'd-out* 'as'
298.4   range,] *aft. x'd-out* 'either'; *comma added*
298.4   particularity,] *aft. x'd-out* 'an' [*aft. x'd-out* 'or']
298.4−5   and flexibility] *intrl.*
298.7   Peirce's] *ab. x'd-out* 'the'
298.7   statement] *bef. x'd-out* 'of'
298.8   around] *bef. x'd-out comma*
298.8−9   being able to employ] *ab. x'd-out* 'and employing'
298.9   the] *alt. fr.* 'their'
298.9−10   or representatives] *ab. x'd-out* 'as'
298.11   specified] *intrl.*
298.14   the indefinitely] *intrl.*
298.18   function] *intrl.*
298.22   application of] *intrl.*
298.29   these] *aft. x'd-out* 'they are'
298.30   significance of] 'of' *bef. x'd-out* 'having'
298.36   passage] *aft. x'd-out* 'original'
298.37   and] *aft. x'd-out opening paren.*
298.37   sign] *bef. x'd-out* 'as a case of'
298.37   (linguistic)] *intrl.*
298.38   case,] *comma aft. x'd-out closing paren.*
298.38   strictly] *intrl.*
298.39   only] *ab. x'd-out* 'cont'
298.39   a behavioral] *ab. x'd-out* 'this'
298.40   as] *aft. x'd-out* 'that'
299.2   passage] *aft. x'd-out* 'whole'
299.3   viz.] 'v' *ov.* 'V'
299.4   in fact,] *intrl.*
299.6   after] *aft. x'd-out* 'he says'

299.7   grey] *aft. x'd-out* 'white or'
299.8   which] *aft. x'd-out* 'that is'
#299.8–9   unlumnous] 'un' *intrl.*
299.9   flame] *bef. x'd-out comma*
299.12   a] *alt. fr.* 'any'
299.15   It] *aft. del.* 'Aside from persiste'
299.17   perversion] *aft. x'd-out* 'the'
299.19   reading] *aft. x'd-out* 'the'
299.22   Discussion] *aft. x'd-out* 'The matter of the T'
299.23   they] *bef. x'd-out* 'were the'
299.24   words] *bef. x'd-out comma*
299.30   entirely] *aft. x'd-out* 'not to'
299.31   at] *aft. x'd-out* 'is'
299n.1   current] *aft. x'd-out* 'many of the'
299n.2   the discussion . . . misty] *ab. x'd-out* 'into a fictitious realm'
299n.3   just] *aft. x'd-out* 'exactly this'
299n.3   this] *intrl.*
299n.4   view] *ab. x'd-out* 'make certain'
299n.4–5   fundamental] *intrl.*
299n.5   things] *aft. x'd-out* 'certain things'
299n.6   "pure] *intrl.*
299n.6   form"] *aft. x'd-out opening quots.*
300.2–3   (socially)] *aft. x'd-out* 'and well'
300.8   for.] *period ov. comma*
#300.10–11 instance . . . understood] *ab. x'd-out* 'established cases of social usage'
300.11   still] *intrl.*
300.16   iron,] *aft. x'd-out* 'dog'
300.21   reference,] *bef. x'd-out* 'of the'
300.22   (i)] *ab. x'd-out* 'is the'
300.24   serves] *alt. fr.* 'serve'
300.24   *direction*] *alt. fr.* '*directions*'
300.31   previously] *aft. x'd-out* 'reference'
300.32   the charge] *aft. x'd-out* 'cha'
300.33   largely.] *bef. x'd-out superscript* '5'
300.33   It] *aft. x'd-out superscript* '5'
300.33   still] *intrl.*
300.34   because . . . influence,] *intrl.*
300.36   explcitly] *intrl.*
300.37   quoting,] *aft. x'd-out* 'Word'
301.5   sentence] *aft. x'd-out* 'passage'
301.6   *theoretical problem*] *undrl.*

301.7   *three*] *intrl.*
301.8   consituents] *ab. x'd-out* 'terms'
301.9   as if] *aft. x'd-out* 'alre'
301.10   so] *aft. x'd-out* 'while the'
301.10   rheoretical] *aft. x'd-out* 'remaining'
301.11   then] *intrl.*
301.12   the issue] 'the' *intrl.;* 'issue' *alt. fr.* 'issues'
301.15   controversies] *aft. x'd-out* 'endless'
301.15   possibly] *aft. x'd-out* 'be'
301.16   thing] *alt. fr.* 'things'
301.17   social] *aft. x'd-out* 'it'
301.18   how] *aft. x'd-out* 'who'
301.25   to] *aft. x'd-out* 'or'
301.27   especially] *alt. fr.* 'specially'
301.29   the] *ab. x'd-out* 'his'
301.29   of] *bef. x'd-out* 'his own p'
301.30   what] *aft. x'd-out* 'he is'
301.31   common] *intrl.*
301.32   three things, namely] *intrl.*
301.33   a sign] 'a' *intrl.*
302.2   repeated] *aft. x'd-out* 'or [*ab. x'd-out* ', and'] continued
          repitition,'
302.6   that] *aft. x'd-out* 'That the "solution given takes for
          granted the exi'
302.13–14   "mental processes"] *quots. added*
302.14   their] *aft. x'd-out* 'the medium of'
302.19   as an . . . in an] *ab. x'd-out* 'as why one sound stands for a
          given thing, *say bread, [*intrl.*] in Enlish and another sound
          for the same'
302.20   a certain] *aft. x'd-out* 'and another sound'
302.20   for,] *comma added*
302.23   apparatus] *bef. x'd-out* 'by which it is reached.'
302.32   or the] *ab. x'd-out comma*
302.32   who *uses* signs,] *ab. x'd-out* ', user of signs—'
303.1   authors] *aft. x'd-out* 'writers' [*aft. x'd-out* 'the writers']
303.2   this] *aft. x'd-out* 'it'
303.5   general] *intrl.*
303.6   controversies] *aft. x'd-out* 'dis'
303.11   I] *aft. x'd-out* 'I turn now to some'
303.12–13   to pass . . . said] *intrl.*
303.13   and turn to presentation] *ab. x'd-out* 'to present some'
303.14–15   or underlying postulate] *ab. x'd-out* 'consideration'
303.15   behavioral] *aft. x'd-out* 'operations'

303.17   is] *intrl.*
303.18   sign and] 'sign' *bef. x'd-out comma*
303.20   establish the] 'the' *ab. x'd-out* 'a'
303.20   specifically] *alt. fr.* 'specified'
303.20–21   named or designated] *ab. x'd-out* 'or named thing'
303.21   which] *aft. x'd-out* 'as its "referent."'
303.22   especially] *ab. x'd-out* 'particurly'
303.23   unless] *aft. x'd-out* 'without being'
#303.24–25   Signs are] *ov.* 'and meanings,'
303.26   names] *aft. x'd-out* 'scientific'
303.27   reference] *aft. x'd-out* 'sign-'
303.28   those] *aft. x'd-out* 'scientific'
303.30   scientific] *aft. x'd-out* 'in'
303.31   on . . . level,] *intrl.*
303.31   in the] *aft. x'd-out* 'in the early,'
303.32   distinctive] *ab. x'd-out* 'different'
303n.2   one undivided and] *intrl.*
303n.2   *Referent*] *alt. fr.* '*Reference*'
303n.2   its inseparable] *ab. x'd-out* 'its'
303n.3   constituents of a] *ab. x'd-out* 'me constitu factors in'
303n.4   of] *ov.* 'or'
304.1   in] *intrl.*
304.1   concerns] *aft. x'd-out* 'no'
304.5   type] *ab. x'd-out* 'kind'
304.6   relatively] *aft. x'd-out* 'a tib' [*ab. x'd-out* 'releavtive']
304.7   nature] *aft. x'd-out* 'and'
304.7   are] *aft. x'd-out* 'they'
304.9   course of] *bef. x'd-out* 'life'
304.12   linguistic] *aft. x'd-out* 'use'
304.13   viewed] *aft. x'd-out* 'treated'
304.14   habits,] *comma ov. x'd-out* 'of'
304.14   customs,] *bef. x'd-out* 'of action'
304.14   which] *in penc. ab. penc. del.* 'that'
304.14–15   physiologically,] *alt. fr.* 'physiological,'
304.15   ear;] *semicolon alt. in ink fr. comma*
304.15   and] *bef. x'd-out comma*
304.16   materials] *aft. x'd-out* 'both'
304.18   the] *ab. x'd-out* 'a'
304.24   first,] *comma added*
304.24   specifiable] *intrl.*
304.25   operations,] *aft. x'd-out* 'acti'
304.25–26   which . . . beings,] *ab. x'd-out* ', to escape any technical or and quasi-mystical association'; 'involve' *alt. fr.* 'involving'; 'human' *aft. x'd-out* 'persons'

304.27   secondly,] *comma added*
304.29   subjectmatter] *aft. x'd-out* 'which'
304.30   "referent"] *opening quots. added*
304.31   conjointly,] *aft. x'd-out* 'in strict'
304.34   any] *intrl.*
304.34   drawn] *intrl.*
304n.2   knowings] *alt. fr.* 'knowing'
304n.2   knowns] *alt. fr.* 'known'
304n.3   claim] *aft. x'd-out* 'mer'
304n.3   "Science."] *aft. x'd-out* 'scienti'
305.1   or reflective] *ab. x'd-out* 'reflective'
305.4   postulates] *aft. x'd-out* 'instead'
305.4   and explicitly] *intrl.*
305.5   hence] *aft. x'd-out* 'ca'
305.5   related] *aft. x'd-out* 'connected'
305.7   the customary,] 'the' *intrl.*
305.9–10   gesturing] *aft. x'd-out* 'speech'
305.10   enter as] *in penc. ab. penc. del.* 'are'
305.12   "signs"] *aft. x'd-out* 'signs and'
305.12   referents."] *aft. x'd-out opening quots.*
305.13   and are] 'are' *intrl.*
305.14   using] *alt. fr.* 'use'
305.19   determined] *aft. x'd-out* 'evoke'
305.24   in conjunction] *intrl.*
305.26   that] *bef. penc. del.* 'are'
305.28   are] *aft. x'd-out* 'surro'
305.28   occasion] *alt. fr.* 'occasions'
305.31   discussion,] *aft. x'd-out* 'kn'
305.32   dealt] *aft. x'd-out* 'be briefly'
305.32   briefly.] *intrl.*
305.32   The] *aft. x'd-out* 'Any [*aft. x'd-out* 'The re'] scientific [*intrl.*] account of names [*ab. x'd-out* 'them'] in their differences from'
305.33   extensive] *aft. x'd-out* 'much'
305.34   (1)] *intrl.*
305.34   departure] *aft. x'd-out* 'starting point'
305.34   are] *aft. x'd-out* 'is'
305.34   the] *intrl.*
305.35   names] *aft. x'd-out* 'the'
305.35   popular] *aft. x'd-out* 'or' [*intrl.*]
305.35   usage:] *colon ov. period*
305.37   Scientific] *aft. x'd-out* 'Th'
305n.1   later] *aft. x'd-out* 'this' [*ab. x'd-out* 'the distinctive']
305n.1   as] *ab. x'd-out* 'is'

305n.1   total] *aft. x'd-out* 'subsequent' [*aft. x'd-out* 'later']
305n.2   which . . . involved in] *ab.* '*is of course involved in' [*ov.* 'taking place subsequently']
305n.2–3   the position] *aft. x'd-out* 'this poisiton'
306.1   things,] *aft. x'd-out* 'new'
306.2   and cases] *intrl.*
306.3   event] *ab. x'd-out* 'change' [*aft. x'd-out* 'thing']
306.3   times] *bef. x'd-out* 'reagrded as *of the pre-scientific—,' [*intrl.*]
#306.4   say the production] *intrl.*
306.5   is] *bef. x'd-out* 'that'
306.5   fact] *aft. x'd-out* 'processes'
306.6   physical] *intrl.*
306.6   by] *ab. x'd-out* 'in'
306.7   were] *aft. x'd-out* 'by'
306.8   and] *bef. x'd-out* 'have remained ever s'
306.14   refinement,] *bef. x'd-out* 'and'
306.15   elaboration] *bef. x'd-out* 'of'
306.16   sort.] *bef. x'd-out superscript* '12'
306.17   In] *aft. x'd-out superscript* '12'
306.18   such] *aft. x'd-out* 'th'
306.24   physicist] *bef. x'd-out* 'or chemist'
306.25   the] *aft. x'd-out* 'my'
306.26   primarily] *intrl.*
306.27   range] *aft. x'd-out* 'of'
306.29   popular] *aft. x'd-out* 'its *popular* sense'
306.29   *what*] *aft. x'd-out* 'H'
306.30   thing] *intrl.*
306.30–31   connections.] *bef. x'd-out superscript* '12'
306.31   This] *aft. x'd-out superscript* '12'
306.31   however,] *intrl.*
306.32   its own or] *intrl.*
306.34   &] *ab. x'd-out comma*
306.35   bodily organs of] *in ink ab. ink del.* 'eyes, tongue, throat and temperature organs'
306.36–37   one who is *a*-scientific,] *ab. x'd-out* 'a-scientific person'
306.37   the procedural] 'the' *ab. x'd-out* 'its'; 'procedural' *aft. x'd-out* 'method'
306.38   or] *aft. x'd-out* 'by'
306.39   immediate] *aft. x'd-out* 'its'
306.40   one] *aft. x'd-out* 'the one with'
307.2   indefinitely] *alt. fr.* 'indefinite'
307.4   running through] *ab. x'd-out* 'involved in'
307.5–6   operations[12]] *superscript* '12' *added*

307.6–7 "practical"] *aft. x'd-out* 'the'
307.8 psychology] *aft. x'd-out* 'one sided'
307.10 a] *intrl.*
307.10 operation-product] *intrl.*
307.12 what] *ab. x'd-out* 'that which'
307.13 the name] 'the' *ab. x'd-out* 'the'
307.16 spatial-range] *aft. x'd-out* 'space'
307.18 On] *alt. in penc. fr.* 'One'
307.19 Accomplishment] *alt. fr.* 'Accomplished' [*alt. fr.* 'Accomplishing']
307.19 of] *intrl.*
307.19 knowings-knowns] *alt. fr.* 'knowing-knowns'
307.20 that] *alt. fr.* 'the'
307.21 performance] *aft. x'd-out* 'accomplished' [*aft. x'd-out* 'perfi']
307.22 belongs.] *bef. x'd-out superscript* '12'
307n.3 its] *aft. x'd-out* 'the'
307n.3 because of] *insrtd. w. guideline in penc. for penc. del.* 'by'
307n.4 attention to] *in penc. aft. penc. del.* 'proper emphasis upon what'
307n.4 of—] *dash aft. x'd-out comma*
307n.4 as simply] 'as' *ab. x'd-out* 'just'
307n.5 call] *aft. x'd-out* 'would'
307n.5 the] *ab. x'd-out* 'two'
307n.5 article] *alt. fr.* 'articles'
307n.5 of] *bef. x'd-out* 'by'
307n.6 *Philosophy*] *aft. x'd-out* 'the'
307n.11 manipulative] *aft. x'd-out* 'the'
307n.13 presence] *bef. x'd-out* 'of'
307n.15 the latter.] 'the' *alt. fr.* 'them'
308.1 To] *aft. x'd-out* 'The'
308.2 the] *aft. x'd-out* 'a'
308.2 capacity] *aft. x'd-out* 'or'
308.2 of reference] *ab. x'd-out* 'to refer'
308.6 which] *aft. x'd-out* 'to'
308.9 taken,] *aft. x'd-out* 'capable'
308.9–10 distinguish] *aft. x'd-out* 'select'
308.11 The] *aft. x'd-out* 'The three in'
308.12 things] *intrl.*
308.12 as] *intrl.*
308.13 —apart,] *aft. x'd-out* '. and from'
308.14 many] *intrl.*
308.17 is] *ab. x'd-out* 'becomes'
308.17 becomes] *aft. x'd-out* 'is'

308.18   those] *aft. x'd-out* 'that'
308.18   volumes,] *aft. x'd-out* 'chapte'
308.19   logistics] *bef. x'd-out* 'or semantics'
308.19   *logical* considerations] *ab. x'd-out* 'form "syntax"'
308.19   are treated as] *ab. x'd-out* 'is treated as'
308.19–20   inherently separated] *ab. x'd-out* 'completed'
308.20   from] *bef. x'd-out* 'sense.'
308.20   subjectmatter] *aft. x'd-out* 'from those of'; *bef. x'd-out* 'or sense'
308.20   conclusions] *ov.* 'sense.'
308.22   It] *aft. x'd-out* 'The'
#308.25   Objects"] *aft. x'd-out* 'objects'
#308.26   something else,] *bef. x'd-out* 'whether'; *ab. x'd-out* 'signs and other and'
308.26   Processes] *aft. x'd-out* 'The'
308n.1   adjective] *ab. x'd-out* 'word'
308n.1   in italics,] *ab. x'd-out* 'with emphasis'
308n.2   They] 'T' *ov.* 't' *aft. x'd-out* 'On the contrary'
308n.3   signs of a] *intrl.*
308n.3   to] *intrl.*
308n.6   symbols] *aft. x'd-out* 'the'
308n.8   the word] *intrl.*
308n.8   suggested] *ab. x'd-out* 'a name' [*aft. x'd-out* 'emp']
308n.8   name] *aft. x'd-out* 'apply'
308n.8   the inclusive] 'the' *ab. x'd-out* 'this particular'
308n.9   *The Theory of Inquiry*] *intrl.*
308n.10   indiacted] *intrl.*
308n.10   is] *aft. x'd-out* ', however,'
308n.11   and] *aft. x'd-out* 'th'
308n.12   enact] *ab. x'd-out* 'devlop'
308n.13   referr*ing*] *alt. fr.* 'referring'
308n.13   in . . . function] *intrl.*
#308n.13   constitute] *alt. fr.* 'constitutes'
308n.14   in another] *aft. x'd-out* 'the subjectmatter of the refer*ent*'
308n.14   of . . . referent.] *intrl.*
308n.15   I] *aft. x'd-out* 'is'
308n.15   "object"] *alt. fr.* '"objects"'
308n.16   name.] *aft. x'd-out* 'a'
309.1–2   as legitimate outcome] *ab. x'd-out* 'a certain'; 'legitimate' *aft. x'd-out* 'the'
309.3   being] *aft. x'd-out* 'of which'
309.5   and often] *ab. x'd-out* 'but usually'
309.5   called *ontological*] *intrl.*
309.6   supreme] *aft. x'd-out* 'higher and surpeme'

309.6   nature] *bef. x'd-out* 'called *ontological*'
309.7   Being] 'B' *ov.* 'b'
309.7   (always in Capitals)] *intrl.*
309.8   capable] *aft. x'd-out* 'not,'
309.8   actuality] *ab. x'd-out* 'existence'
309.8   "Realm"] 'R' *ov.* 'r'
309.9   favored] *alt. fr.* 'favorite'
309.9   revelling] *alt. fr.* 'reveling'
309.10   Scientific] *aft. x'd-out* 'The'
309.11–13 narrowly . . . subjectmatter, of] *ab. x'd-out* ' * "tpe" of
          [*intrl.*] reference or application and to be are enacted by
          operations whose controlling puporse is the advancement of
          that kind of knowings-known which'; 'tending' *aft. x'd-out*
          'by'
309.14   duration] *aft. x'd-out* 'range and'
309.15   given] *aft. x'd-out* 'scientific'
309.17   developments] *aft. x'd-out* 'the'
309.18   centuries] *bef. x'd-out* '(refinfocred by useful technological
          developments) this quality is'
309.19   scientific] *aft. x'd-out* 'it'
309.20   this] *ab. x'd-out* 'the'
309.21   often] *intrl.*
309.22–23   , expressed . . . attitudes,] *intrl.*
309.26   isolationism,] *alt. fr.* 'isolation'
309.26   into] *aft. x'd-out* 'con'
309.28   great] *bef. x'd-out* 'change'
309.29   in] *bef. x'd-out* 'the'
309.33   physiological] *alt. fr.* 'physical'
309.33   marks] *aft. x'd-out* 'makes'
309.36   instead of being one of] *ab. x'd-out* 'is not one'
309.37   "lower"] *aft. x'd-out* 'narrow terms'
309.39   transactions] *aft. x'd-out* 'inter'
309.39   which] *aft. x'd-out* 'that'
309.40   working] *aft. x'd-out* 'a'

Alterations in "Values, Valuations, and Social Facts"

The document is a signed, ribbon-copy typescript in the Arthur F. Bentley Collection, Manuscripts Department, Lilly Library, Indiana University, Bloomington, 9 pp., dated "6–20–45" by Bentley. Page numbers are typed at the upper left-hand corner. Unless designated *t.* or *penc.*, alterations are in ink.

Bentley underlined two foreign phrases ("*Respice Finem*" at 312.1–2 and "*par excellence*" at 312.19–20). These markings have been accepted because Dewey italicized both phrases elsewhere: "*Respice Finem*" in an earlier draft for this reply (John Dewey Papers, Box 55, folder 1, Special Collections, Morris Library, Southern Illinois University at Carbondale); "*par excellence*" at 316.13.

310.1	Valuations,] *comma added*
310.2	paper,] *comma added bef. del.* 'on'
310.3	Mr. Benoit-Smullyan] *t. intrl. w. caret*
310.4	conclusions] *bef. del.* 'may'
310.4	now seems] 'seems' *w. caret ab. del.* 'are'
310.6	that sciences] 'that' *t. w. caret ab. x'd-out* 'of a'
310.6	may] *t. ab. x'd-out* 'will'
310.7	dealing] *aft. del.* 'future'
310.7	future] *intrl. w. caret*
310.9	be] *aft. del.* 'my'
310.9	discarded.] *period added bef. del.* 'as threshed out straw.'
310.11	cases] *bef. del.* 'of cases'
310.12	that] *ov.* 'such'
310.12	sort of] *intrl. w. caret*
310.12	to be] *w. caret ab. del.* 'of the nature of'
310.14	upon] *aft. x'd-out* 'for'
310.14	this] *alt. fr.* 'that'
310.15	article] *bef. x'd-out* 'leads me'
310.15	results] *aft. del.* 'ca'
310.16–17	strictures] *t. alt. fr.* 'structures'
310.18	by the] 'by' *intrl. w. caret*
310.18	"purists"] *closing quots. added*
310.18	side;] *semicolon alt. fr. comma*
310.22	defective.] *period added bef. del.* 'for reasons which I shall now attempt to state.' [*aft. x'd-out* 'speak']
310.24	said] *aft. del. illeg. word*
311.1	speech,] *comma added*
311.1	name] *bef. del.* 'both'
311.1	both] *intrl. w. caret*
311.4	order] *w. caret ab. x'd-out* 'nature'
311.4	judgments.] *period ov. comma*
311.4	For] *ab. del.* 'that is,'
311.4	they] *ov.* 'which'
311.6–7	the course of] *intrl. w. caret*
311.10	Valuations,] *comma added*
311.11	failure] *bef. x'd-out* 'to'
311.13	consequence,] *alt. fr.* 'consequences'; *comma added*

311.13–14   transferred] *aft. x'd-out* 'atti'
311.14–15   as appraisals and estimations] *t. intrl. w. caret and guideline aft. x'd-out* '*—or estimating' [*t. intrl.*]
#311.15   facts] *aft. x'd-out* 'acts in which'
311.16   habits] *aft. del.* 'agains'
311.16   so as] *w. caret ab. del.* 'to try'
311.17   respective] *intrl. w. caret*
311.17   claims,] *aft. del.* 'relative'; *comma t. ov. period; bef. del. superscript* '2'
311.18   given] *aft. x'd-out* 'a'
311.18   valuing.] *aft. x'd-out* 'vauion.'
311.19   confused] *aft. x'd-out* 'the confusion in'
311.20   prefix] *aft. del.* 'shall'
311.23   on to,] *t. alt. fr.* 'ont'; *comma added*
311.23–24   anything] *aft. del.* 'practically'
311.24   prized.] *period added*
311.24–25   Because] 'B' *ov.* 'b' *aft. del.* 'and'
311.25   it becomes] 'it' *intrl. w. caret;* 'becomes' *alt. fr.* 'become'
311.25   "value."] *quots. added*
311.25   values] *bef. del.* 'but persons and things'
311.26   then] *intrl. w. caret*
311.26   "valued."] *period added bef. del.* 'in this case.'
311.26   *judgment*] *bef. intrl. and del.* 'h'
311.27   however] *intrl. w. caret*
311.27   a] *intrl.*
311.27   value—] *dash added aft. x'd-out* 'which is subje'
311.28   its] *ov.* 'the'
311.30   Does] *t. ab. x'd-out* 'is' [*aft. x'd-out* 'I']
311.31   The . . . commonplace] 'T' *ov.* 't'; *moved w. caret and guideline fr. aft.* 'discussion.' [*period ov. comma*]
311.32   outside] 'o' *ov.* 'O'
311.33   also] *intrl.*
311.34   admonition] *alt. fr.* 'admonitions'
311n.1   made] *aft. x'd-out* 'in ques'
311n.1   above] *moved w. caret and guideline fr. aft.* 'text'
311n.2   aspect in] 'aspect' *ab. del.* 'element'
311n.3   prizing] *intrl. w. caret*
311n.3   behavior] *bef. del.* 'of the prizing sort'
311n.3   But] *w. caret ab. del.* 'What i said is that'
311n.3   aspect is] 'aspect' *ab. del.* 'element'
311n.3   concerned with investigation of] *w. carets ab. del.* 'directed at' [*aft. x'd-out and del.* 'to']
311n.4   "judgment,"] *alt. fr.* '"judgments,'; *closing quots. added*

311n.4   depends] *aft. del.* 'definitely'
311n.4–5   specifically] *intrl. w. caret*
311n.5   instance,] *comma added*
311n.5   or] *alt. fr.* 'of'
311n.5   some class] 'some' *intrl. w. caret*
311n.5   instances,] *comma added*
311n.6   become] *aft. x'd-out* 'come under questio'
311n.6   is felt it] *intrl. w. caret*
311n.6   in] *bef. del.* 'for the'
311n.7   until] *aft. x'd-out* 'without'
311n.7   inquiry.] *aft. del.* 'careful'
312.1   "reason."] *period ov. comma*
312.1   It is expressed in] *ab. del.* 'and in general of'
312.1–2   *Respice Finem*] *undrl. by Bentley*
312.2   consequences] *aft. x'd-out* 'the'
312.2   before acting] *added*
312.4   After] 'A' *ov.* 'a' *aft. del.* 'I come'
312.4   prefatory] *aft. x'd-out* 'these' [*t. alt. fr.* 'this']
312.4   I come] *intrl. w. caret*
312.13   such] *aft. x'd-out* 'a way'
312.15   dwell] *bef. del.* 'at any length'
312.15   likeness] *aft. del.* 'close'
312.15–16   imputed] *aft. x'd-out* 'su'
312.16   judgment] *bef. del.* ', in the case of judgment of values,'
312.16   and] *bef. x'd-out and del.* 'wha'
312.18   can] *aft. del.* 'one'
312.18–19   be found.] *ab. del.* 'find;'
312.19   It] 'I' *ov.* 'i'
312.19–20   *par excellence,*] *undrl. by Bentley*
312.20   awareness] *aft. del.* 'the'
312.20   the] *aft. del.* 'or'
312.22   that are] *w. caret ab. del.* 'and of'
312.22   to] *aft. del.* 'in'
312.22   specifiable] *intrl. w. caret*
312.23   action.] *bef. x'd-out* 'to be taken.'
312.25   judgments.] *period ov. comma*
312.25   In] 'I' *ov.* 'i' *aft. del.* 'and'
312.26   consequence,] *comma added*
312.26   it] *intrl.*
312.26   automatically,] *comma added*
312.26   difference] *aft. x'd-out* 'fii'
312.28   subjectmatters] *alt. fr.* 'subject matters' *aft. del.* 'scientific'
312.28   of science.] *added*

312.31   aspects and constituents of] *t. ab. x'd-out* 'in all'
312.31   over] *aft. x'd-out* 'and'
312.33   appears] *ab. del.* 'seems'
312.33   There] 'T' *ov.* 't' *aft. del.* 'It is mediated,'
312.34   that it is mediated by] *intrl. w. caret*
312.34   some change] *ab. del.* 'transfer' [*aft. x'd-out* 'a [*t. alt. fr.* 'an'] intermei']
312.35   because of judgment] *intrl. w. caret*
312.35–36   talking] *aft. del.* 'actually'
312.36   behavioral-prizings] *aft. x'd-out* 'prizing-'
313.1   proper,] *aft. del.* 'but'
313.2   (and "values")] *parens. ov. dashes*
313.2   results] *alt. fr.* 'result' *aft. del.* 'may'
313.2   as] *aft. del.* 'from'
313.2   having] *bef. x'd-out comma*
313.3   an attitude] *aft. x'd-out* 'a more intelligent'
313.3–4   understanding] *bef. x'd-out* 'towat'
313.6   overt] *t. intrl.*
313.6   shift] *aft. x'd-out* '*fact*'
313.14   well] *aft. x'd-out* 'be'
313.14   be] *aft. x'd-out* 'to'
313.23–24   something] *aft. x'd-out* 'existential'
313.26   save] *t. w. penc. guideline ab. x'd-out* 'else than'
313.28   fail to] *t. w. penc. guidelines ab. x'd-out* 'do not'
313.28   which] *aft. x'd-out* 'in'
313.28   have to be met] *t. intrl. w. penc. guideline;* 'have to be' *insrtd. for x'd-out* 'are'
313.29   scientific] *bef. x'd-out* 'inquiries [*t. alt. fr.* 'inquiry'] are met by cases of judgment.'
313.30   course] *aft. penc. del.* 'the'
313.30   logical] *t. intrl.*
313.31   denial,] *aft. x'd-out* 'the'; *bef. x'd-out* 'that'
313.32   are] *aft. x'd-out* 'and'
313.37   just] *aft. x'd-out* 'the'
314.3   other] *alt. fr.* 'others'
314.3–4   writers] *intrl. w. caret*
314.4   *judgment,*] *alt. fr.* 'judgments'; *undrl.; comma added*
314.4   the distinction] *aft. del.* '*as* jsudgments'
314.5–6   relatively indirect] *aft. del.* 'the'
314.6   these prizings] *w. caret ab. del.* 'they'
314.7   inspection.] *period ov. comma bef. del.* 'and see how matter stand when the substitution is made. In this case'
314.7   We] 'W' *ov.* 'w'

314.7   start] *aft. del.* 'should'
314.8   fact:—] *dash added*
314.9   engaged] *aft. x'd-out* 'coninually'
314.10   preferences,] *comma added*
314.10   also] *intrl. w. caret*
314.11   them.] *period added bef. del.* 'For [*intrl.*] every discussion
          of a policy to be adopted or rejected * is such a valuation,
          although many discussions fail to satisfy the conditions of a
          scientific conclusion.' [*ab. del.* 'being of that nature, even
          though they vary immensely with respect to success in satis-
          fying the logical conditions tha enable the conclusion of a
          discussed to the name of judgment.']
314.11   All] 'A' *ov.* 'a' *aft. del.* 'that'
314.11   all] *intrl.*
314.11–12   widespread] *aft. del.* 'any degree of'
314.12   concern are] *aft. del.* 'interest or'; *bef. del.* 'in some
          measure'
314.12   expressions] *aft. x'd-out* 'both'
314.12–13   direct] *intrl. w. caret*
314.13   Evaluations] 'E' *ov.* 'e' *aft. del.* 'just mentioned and that'
314.13   defend,] *comma added*
314.13–14   to support and buttress,] *t. intrl. w. caret*
314.14   question.] *period ov. comma bef. del.* 'would seem also
          [*aft. x'd-out* 'to be'] to be undeniable facts'
314.15   pressure] *aft. del.* 'the'
314.16   the] *alt. fr.* 'these'
314.17   group-values] *hyphen added*
314.18   subjected] *alt. fr.* 'subject'
314.22   specifically,] *aft. x'd-out* 'more,'
314.22   valuings] *aft. x'd-out* 'valuings in the sense alrready speci-
          fied and'
314.23   phase] *bef. x'd-out period*
314.27   in] *bef. x'd-out* 'the'
314.27   the more] *aft. del.* 'cash of'
314n.1   not] *t. intrl.*
314n.4   discussions] *aft. x'd-out* 'the'
314n.5   procedures] *aft. x'd-out* 'that which is sta'
314n.5   which are] 'which' *aft. x'd-out* 'in the case of'
314n.7   intensification] *aft. x'd-out* 'strengthening'
314n.12   "emotional-volitional"] *aft. x'd-out* 'things excluded'
314n.13   are] *aft. x'd-out* 'we'
314n.13   their] *t. alt. fr.* 'they'
314n.14   the effort] 'the' *t. alt. fr.* 'their'
315.1   cases.] *period ov. comma*

315.1   But the] 'B' *ov.* 'b'; 'the' *ov.* 'its'
315.1   *subjectmatter*] *undrl.*
315.1   of investigation] *intrl. w. caret*
315.3   concerned] *aft. del.* 'still'
315.5   nature of] *intrl. w. caret*
315.6   now] *alt. fr.* 'no'
315.6   out,] *comma added*
315.6   learning,] *comma added*
315.8   logical or theoretical] *t. intrl. w. caret*
315.10   cases of] *t. intrl.*
315.10   valuing] *t. alt. fr.* 'valuings'
315.10   differentiated] *aft. del.* 'intelligently'
315.11   any] *aft. x'd-out* 'other'
315.13   as] *aft. x'd-out* 'denial'
315.15   try] *aft. x'd-out* 'reduce'
315.15   prizings] *aft. x'd-out* 'the'
315.16   molecular] *alt. fr.* 'molecules as'
315.21   conclusion] *t. alt. fr.* 'conclusions' *bef. x'd-out* 'drawn'
315.23   our] *aft. x'd-out* 'Mr'
315.28   sciences,"] *comma t. alt. fr. period*
315.29–30   *scientist*] *t. alt. fr.* '*scientists*'
315n.2   of the] *bef. x'd-out* 'fact'
316.1   inquiries] *aft. x'd-out* 'social the'
316.9   than] *t. alt. fr.* 'that'
316.10   geographical] *t. intrl. w. caret*
316.15–16   behavior] *aft. x'd-out* 'the [*ab. x'd-out* 'a'] temporal'
316.21   events] *bef. x'd-out* 'have their'
316.21–22   characteristic] *bef. x'd-out* 'feat'
316.30   events of an] *t. intrl.;* 'an' *aft. x'd-out* 'the'
316.30   sort] *t. intrl.*
316.31–32   intimately & still] *t. ab. x'd-out* 'even'
316.32   preferences,] *t. intrl.*
316.34   which] *aft. x'd-out* 'that'
316.35   impartial] *aft. x'd-out* ', or"'
316.35   now] *t. intrl.*
316.36   astronomy] *aft. x'd-out* 'physica'
316.37   scientific] *t. alt. fr.* 'scientist'
316.38   had earlier] *t. intrl.*
317.1   investigation] *aft. x'd-out* 'the socio'
317.4   finding] *aft. x'd-out* 'taking'
317.7   problems] *aft. del.* 'are'
317.7   are all] 'are' *intrl. in penc.;* 'all' *bef. penc. del.* 'gather about'
317.7   aspects of] *intrl. in penc. w. caret*

317.7   associated] *moved w. penc. guideline fr. bef.* 'problems
          aplenty.'
317.8   behavioral] *t. intrl. w. caret*
317.8   called] *aft. x'd-out* 'a'

Alterations in "Importance, Significance, and Meaning"

The document for the introductory section to the essay, 318.1–320.14,
is the ribbon-copy typescript in the Arthur F. Bentley Collection, Manuscripts Department, Lilly Library, Indiana University, Bloomington,
3 pp., sent to Bentley 4 June 1950. Unless designated *ink*, alterations are
typed.

318.2   essay] *ab. x'd-out* 'article'
318.3   reasonably] *ab. x'd-out* 'fairly'
318.4   it] *ov.* 'is'
318.4   form] *alt. fr.* 'forms' *aft. x'd-out* 'has'
318.5   a] *ab. x'd-out* 'the'
318.5   articles] *ab. x'd-out* 'papers'
318.6   The] *aft.* 'no ¶' *insrtd. and circled in ink; marked in ink to
          run on*
318.8   periodical] *aft. x'd-out* 'reference to'
318.12   *How . . . by*] *intrl.*
318.16   independent] *alt. fr.* 'independently' *aft. x'd-out* 'maturing'
318.17   which] *aft. x'd-out* 'that'
318.17–18 not . . . the] *ab. x'd-out* 'neither the outcome of'
318.19   critical] *intrl.*
318.21   in conclusions] *ab. x'd-out* 'of conclusions'
318.22   inquiries] *aft. x'd-out* 'studies'
318.22   having] *ab. x'd-out* 'have'
318.23   is] *ab. x'd-out* 'was'
318.23   valid] *ab. x'd-out* 'valid source of'
318.24   community] *intrl.*
318.24   as] *aft. x'd-out* 'in'
319.1   (since . . . one] *ab. x'd-out* '(by one'; 'but' *aft. x'd-out*
          'one of'
319.2   authors] *aft. x'd-out* 'two'
319.3   interest] *alt. fr.* 'interests'
319.5   side] *aft. x'd-out* 'science of'
319.6   bear] *in ink ab. ink del.* 'bore'
319.7   scientific] *ab. x'd-out* ', that is scientific,'
319.7–8   and effective] *intrl. in ink*

319.8   method of] *bef. x'd-out* 'dealing with'
319.8   inquiry] *aft. ink del.* 'effective'
319.9   work] *ab. x'd-out* 'study'
319.9   involves] *alt. in ink fr.* 'involved'
319.9   study] *ab. x'd-out* 'revision'
319.10   theories] *alt. fr.* 'theory'
319.11   intellectual] *aft. x'd-out* 'the'
319.11   that] *aft. x'd-out* '*for the inquiries' [*aft. x'd-out* 'of the']
319.11–12 are competent] *aft. x'd-out* '*will be able' [*aft. x'd-out*
          'would provide a dependable']
319.12   initiate] *aft. x'd-out* 'deal with scientifically with'
319.12   the] *intrl.*
319.12   human] *bef. x'd-out* 'contacts'
319.13   that] *aft. x'd-out* 'as they'
319.13   or] *ab. x'd-out* 'and'
319.14   The] *aft. x'd-out* 'Dewey's'
319.16   reaching] *aft. x'd-out* 'lead'
319.18   direction] *aft. x'd-out* 'any'
319.18   a time] *aft. x'd-out* 'an a'
319.18–19 scientific,] *aft. x'd-out* 'physica'
319.19   and political] *aft. x'd-out* 'revolutions'
319.19   have] *ab. x'd-out* 'has'
319.23   philosophical] *aft. x'd-out* 'systems'
319.23   inefficacy] *ab. x'd-out* 'irrelevance'
319.23–24 life-activities] *aft. x'd-out* 'existing' [*ab. x'd-out*
          'present']
319.24   centre] *alt. fr.* 'centred'
319.25   method] *alt. fr.* 'methods'
319.25   of] *intrl.*
319.25   knowing] *bef. x'd-out* 'that'
319.26   in] *bef. x'd-out* 'a'
319.27   in a] *intrl.*
319.27   fruitful] *alt. fr.* 'fruitfully' *aft. x'd-out* 'invetig'
319.29   the] *ab. x'd-out* 'a'
319.29   formation] *aft. x'd-out* 'intelliget'
319.29–30 intelligent] *aft. x'd-out* 'and use of'
319.31–32 on . . . number)] *intrl.*
319.34   present] *bef. x'd-out* 'and the coming'
319.36–37 faithful . . . of wisdom] *ab. x'd-out* 'with his conviction
          that it is love of wisdom'
319.38   policies] *aft. x'd-out* 'the'
319.39   the] *intrl.*
319.39   of our common] *intrl.*

319.40   The] *aft. x'd-out* 'I hope this'
319.41   otherwise] *bel. x'd-out* 'essay is'
320.1   while] *bef. x'd-out* 'it'
320.2   with . . . method] *intrl.*
320.4   historical] *bef. x'd-out* 'philosophical' [*alt. fr.* 'philosophies'
         [*alt. fr.* 'philosophy']]
320.5   main] *aft. x'd-out* 'po'
320.5   *Knowing*] *aft. x'd-out* 'book'
320.5   the] 't' *ov.* 'T'
320.6   which] *bef. x'd-out* 'while'
#320.6–7   which with respect to language employed are] *intrl.*
320.9   issues.] *aft. x'd-out* 'subjec'
320.10   towards] *aft. x'd-out* 'after'
320.11   as] *bef. x'd-out* 'the'

Alterations in "*How, What,* and *What For* in Social Inquiry*"

Two documents are involved for this item, both in the John Dewey Papers, Box 59, folder 13, Special Collections, Morris Library, Southern Illinois University at Carbondale. Alterations from 333.1–340.3 are on the ribbon-copy typescript prepared in January 1951 on Esquire bond, not typed by Dewey, 13 pp.; alterations appear on pp. 1, 2, 3, 5, 13. In blue ink Dewey added "Page One" at the upper right-hand corner of p. 1 and deleted "M & C" [Means and Consequences] at the upper right-hand corner of pp. 2–13. In black ink he repaginated pp. 7–12 as pp. 5–10.

In blue ink Dewey added two paragraphs; he began this holograph addition at the foot of p. 13 (340.1–3, "So . . . recal") and finished it (340.3–30, "before . . . situation.") on hotel stationery. Beginning at 340.4, therefore, alterations are on six sheets of six-by-seven-inch notepaper imprinted "Halekulani / Honolulu 15, Hawaii," numbered 14–18, with two page 17s. Dewey paginated at the upper right-hand corner, entitled pp. 16–18 "How, What & What For," and signed p. 18.

All alterations are by hand and, unless *black ink, green ink,* or *penc.* is designated, in blue ink.

333.1–2   *How, . . .* Inquiry] *bel. penc. del.* 'MEANS AND CON-
           SEQUENCES—'; 'In Social [*ov.* 'the'] Inquiry' *added in
           penc.*
333.3   I] *added in penc. and blue ink*
333.14   The] *aft. blue ink del.* 'I' [*added in penc.*]

333.14–15   instead of "postulate"] *moved w. caret and guideline fr. aft.* '"postulation"'
333.15   emphasize] *w. caret ab. del.* 'make it as evident as possible'
333.19   some] *in penc. w. caret ab. del.* 'a certain degree of'
334.1   basic] *ab. del.* 'autonomous'
334.1–2   instead of] *ab. del.* 'and' [*intrl.*]
334.2   derived] *intrl.*
334.2   and hence as] *intrl. w. caret;* 'hence' *further intrl.*
334.2   as authoritative] 'as' *intrl.*
334.3   entire scope] *ab. del.* 'whole matter'
334.3   which,] *comma added bef. del.* 'in'
334.3–4   *intelligent,] comma added*
334.4–5   the properties that render it] *w. caret ab. del.* 'it being'; 'the' *ov.* 'as'
334.5   are] *w. caret ab. del.* 'is'
334.5   from] *intrl. w. caret bef. del.* 'without, of'
334.5   a] *ov.* 'some'
334.6   this outside factor is] *intrl.;* 'factor' *aft. del.* 'source'
334.7   *brain] bel. del.* 'it' [*intrl. w. caret*]
334.7   difference.] *period ov. comma*
334.7–8   It . . . since] *ab. del.* 'in as far as'
334.9   that belong] *intrl. w. caret;* 'belong' *ov.* 'wil'
334.9   intrinsically] *alt. fr.* 'intrinsic'
334.9   & to] *intrl.*
334.9–10   as far as the latter] *ab. del.* 'which'
334.15   *knowns] undrl. in penc. bef. del. comma*
334.16   termed] *in penc. w. caret ab. del.* 'named'
334.39   function] *in penc. w. caret ab. del.* 'service'; *bef. del.* 'performed'
334.40   performed (the *service*] *intrl. in penc. w. caret; paren. ov. comma*
334.40   rendered)] *paren. added in penc.*
336.2–3   a previous] *ab. del.* 'my'
336.3   of mine] *w. caret ab. del.* 'in this Journal'
340.1–2   So . . . phrase] *added*
#340.2   "*In the Social Sciences*"] *added; quots. added in penc. and blue ink*
340.2–3   as . . . recal] *added*
340.4   that is] *intrl. w. caret*
340.5   physical] *ab. del.* 'natural'
340.10   the] *ov.* 'a'
340.15   transition] *aft. del.* 'change'
340.15   In] *aft. del.* 'Eve'
340.16   still] *intrl. w. caret*

340.17   & hence] *added*
340.17   as separate] 'as' *intrl. w. caret*
340.18   also] *intrl. w. caret*
340.18   their] *alt. fr.* 'them'
340.18   fixed] *aft. del.* 'as a'
340.19   seen] *w. caret ab. del.* '*felt*'
340.19   yet] *added in black ink*
340.19   the] *ov.* 'an'
340.21   completes] *alt. fr.* 'completed'
340.22   moreover] *intrl. w. caret*
340.23   as far] *aft. black ink del.* 'wins,'
340.23   at least] *intrl. in black ink w. caret*
340.24   has won] *intrl. in black ink w. caret*
#340.25   & hence] *intrl. w. caret*
#340.25   is] *in black ink ov.* 'was'
#340.25   occur] *in black ink ab. undel.* 'exist'
#340.25   the minor] *intrl.*
#340.25   whats] *alt. fr.* 'what'
#340.25   which] *intrl. w. caret*
#340.25   take] *alt. fr.* 'takes'
#340.25   is] *aft. del.* 'as their framework'
#340.25   for] *aft. del.* 'and' [*insrtd.*]
340.25   The victory will be] *insrtd. in black ink w. guideline*
340.25   however] *intrl. in black ink w. caret*
340.27   subordinate] *alt. in black ink fr.* 'subordinated'
340.27   factor] *in black ink ab. del.* 'measure'
340.28   proceeds;] *semicolon in black ink ov. comma*
340.28   thereby] *aft. del.* 'and is'
340.28   attaining] *alt. fr.* 'attains'
340.28–30 That . . . problematic] *added in black ink*
340.30   indeterminate situation.] *added in green ink*

Alterations in "Modern Philosophy"

The document is a carbon copy of the last page, p. 21, of the second copy of the untitled typescript in the Joseph Ratner/John Dewey Papers, Box 46, folder 6, Special Collections, Morris Library, Southern Illinois University at Carbondale, 21 pp. It is the only page typed by Dewey. Unless designated *t.*, alterations are in ink.

419.6   generous,] *comma added*
419.7–8   organized] *t. intrl. w. caret*
419.8   pursuits,] *comma added*

419.8   occupations,] *comma added*
419.9   if] *alt. fr.* 'it'
419.11   institutional] *alt. fr.* 'institutions'
419.13   less,] *comma added*
419.13–14 acceptance . . . its] *t. intrl. w. caret; aft. x'd-out* 'it's'
419.15   but] *intrl. w. caret*
419.18   have] *t. alt. fr.* 'has'
419.19   operations] *aft. x'd-out* 'human'
419.19   have tended] *t. ab. x'd-out illeg. word*
419.19   enhance] *aft. x'd-out* 'the power'
419.20–21 at the expense] *t. intrl.*
419.22   A] *aft. x'd-out* 'There'
419.24   the evils] *aft. x'd-out* 'the conditions of'
419.25   by] *bef. x'd-out* 'petulant'
419.25   continuing petulant and futile] *t. intrl.*
419.25   directed] *aft. x'd-out* 'of [*aft. x'd-out* 'of'] the'
419.26   physical,] *t. intrl.*
419.26   intellectual] *bef. x'd-out comma*
419.27–28 promote] *aft. x'd-out* 'further'
419.28   conditions] *aft. x'd-out* 'the'
419.28   all] *t. intrl.*
419.29   reaches . . . wide] *t. ab. x'd-out* 'tends'; 'reaches' *t. alt. fr.*
          'reached'
419.30   of philosophy] *aft. x'd-out* 'is but one'
419.31   But] *bef. del.* 'neverthless'
419.31   for] *t. w. caret ab. x'd-out* 'of'
419.31   its] *aft. x'd-out* 'itself'
419.31   now] *t. w. caret ab. x'd-out* 'has'
419.32   opportunity] *bel. x'd-out* 'of' [*t. intrl.*]
419.32   challenge] *aft. x'd-out* 'the'
419.32   to] *aft. x'd-out* 'of'
419.32–33 systematic] *aft. del.* 'the'
419.35   responsible] *t. alt. fr.* 'responsibility'
419.36   from] *aft. x'd-out* 'that'

Line-End Hyphenation

I. Copy-text list.

The following are the editorially established forms of possible compounds that were hyphenated at the ends of lines in the copy-text:

3.25–26	cooperative	144.23	self-actional
4.3	inter-actional	146.18	transaction
19.7	metalanguage	150.13–14	Non-symbolically
58.20	spotlight	156.18	snapshot
59.12	three-fold	159.5	so-called
77n.13	subjectmatter	162.25	non-verbal
85.1	today	166.7	counter-instances
88n.10–11	non-observable	170.16	so-called
88n.29	transdermal	175.39	Old-timers
94.10	checkerboard	186n.19	non-natural
103.2	sub-classification	191.8	presupposed
109.12	counterpart	191.11	interbehave
111.6	Transaction	197.33	non-natural
113.19	reorganization	198.10	presupposed
114.14	self-action	198.19	ongoing
116n.5	non-simultaneous	214.21	pseudophysical
120.18–19	interactional	216n.5	nontechnical
121.1	interactional	232.6	low-life
121.2	self-actional	238.18	penthouse
122.10	subjectmatter	242.7	self-enclosed
125.19	sub-naming	243.35	transaction
125n.1	transactional	247.19	transactions
125n.13	pseudo-logical	251.4	*labor*-atories
129.7	commonplace	256n.10	transaction
138.12	transactionally	258.8	subjectmatters
139.33–34	transactional	258.26	touchstones
140.14	subjectmatter	260.30	subjectmatter
143.11	sub-human	263.11	subjectmatters

263.33	lifetime	325.35	ongoing
264.2	non-naming	327.12	pre-humans
264.8	transactional	332.8	pre-established
268.34	self-oriented	337.16–17	subjectmatters
270.5	Coterminous	348.2	interconnection
273.2	air-waves	357.20	socio-psychological
277.2–3	subjectmatters	360.20	widespread
282.30	subjectmatters	365.27	*re*-turn
284.37–38	subjectmatter	370.9	Today
285.13	day-dreaming	371.4	corner-stones
290.38	subjectmatters	396.39	self-constituted
291.2	subjectmatter	397.12	story-telling
303.25–26	pre-scientific	402.6	world-wide
305.25	socio-cultural	415.29	so-called
308.15	safeguarded	418.15–16	intercommunication
321.20	ongoing		

II. Critical-text list.

In transcriptions from the present edition, no line-end hyphens in am-
biguously broken possible compounds are to be retained except the
following:

6.8	well-founded	125.9	by-passes
58.4	non-corporeal	132.7	Inter-actions
59.2	proto-linguistic	135.14	"Sea-serpents"
66.5	"spectrum-like"	135.21	self-actional
76.10	re-examination	150.13	Non-symbolically
81.19	"double-fronted"	171n.3	time-wasting
88n.10	non-observable	173n.4	subject-matter
89.2	mind-matter	201.11	self-subsistent
93.23	non-extensionals	255.1	pre-determination
103.7	inter-actional	263.14	extra-behavioral
103.26	pseudo-interactional	301.19	de-signated
108.31	self-actional	303n.2	co-partners
112.24	inter-acting	303.25	pre-scientific
114.26	inter-actional	309.23	life-blood
115.22	self-actional	314n.2	psycho-analytic
118.17	self-actional	326.36	foot-gears
119.8	co-operating	327.30	pre-commitments
121.9	"non-natural"	330.25	pre-occupation
122.27	one-sided	337.18	"self-evident"

Substantive Variants
in Dewey's Quotations

Dewey's substantive variants in quotations have been considered important enough to warrant this special list. Dewey represented source material in varying ways, from memorial paraphrase to verbatim copy, in some places citing his source fully, in others mentioning only authors' names, and in others omitting documentation altogether. All material inside quotation marks, except that obviously being emphasized or restated, has been searched out; Dewey's citations have been verified and, when necessary, emended. Except for the kinds of emendations noted in the following paragraph and recorded in the Emendations List, all quotations have been retained as they appear in the copy-text.

Although Dewey, like other scholars of the period, was unconcerned about precision in matters of form, many of the changes in quotations may well have occurred in the printing process. For example, comparing Dewey's quotations with the originals reveals that some editors and compositors house-styled the quoted materials as well as Dewey's own. Therefore, in the present edition, the spelling and capitalization of the source have been restored; these changes are recorded in the Emendations List as Works Source (WS) emendations (Works—the present edition—emendations derived from Dewey's source). Similarly, in cases of possible compositorial or typographical errors, corrections either of substantives or accidentals that restore original readings are recorded as WS emendations. Moreover, Dewey frequently changed or omitted punctuation in quoted material. When such changes or omissions have substantive implications, the punctuation of the source has been restored; these corrections are also recorded in the Emendations List with the symbol WS.

Dewey often did not indicate that he had omitted material from his source. Omitted short phrases appear in this list; lengthy omissions are noted by a bracketed ellipsis [. . .]. Italics in source material have been treated as substantives; both Dewey's omitted and added italics are noted here. Minor differences between Dewey's quotations and the source attributable to the context in which the quotation appears, such as changes in number or tense, are not recorded.

Notations in this section follow the formula: page-line number from the present edition, followed by the lemma, then a bracket; after the bracket, the original form appears, followed by the author's surname, shortened source-title from the Checklist of References, and the page-line reference to the source, all in parentheses.

Knowing and the Known

50.7   abstract,] abstracts, (Quine, *Mathematical Logic*, 152.19)
51n.2   say] say, therefore, (Peirce, *Collected Papers*, 5:151.25)
88n.7   position like] position, just like (James, *Pluralistic Universe*, 380.26; *Essays in Radical Empiricism*, 170.37)
100.8   If] If, as in Article 2, (Maxwell, *Matter and Motion*, 26.27)
106.10   particles.] objects. (Einstein and Infeld, *Physics*, 58.2)
106n.6   Insofar] Insofar, however, (Swann, "Relation of Theory," 193.1.8–9)
107.32   'The path] 'path (Frank, *Physics*, 39.2.2)
107.39   describe] e.g., describe (Frank, *Physics*, 53.1.39)
108.1   The law] this law (Frank, *Physics*, 53.2.36)
108.25   electromagnetic] [*ital.*] (Einstein and Infeld, *Physics*, 151.14)
109.7   one] *we* (Einstein et al., "Quantum-Mechanical Description," 777.2.37)
109.8   certainty] *certainty (i.e., with probability equal to unity)* (Einstein et al., "Quantum-Mechanical Description," 777.2.37–38)
109.18–19   criteria of physical] criterion of (Bohr, "Quantum-Mechanical Description," 696.1.30)
109.21   a modification] the fundamental modification (Bohr, "Quantum-Mechanical Description," 702.2.6–7)
116n.9   directing power of heredity] [*ital.*] (Osborn, *Origin*, 16.25–26)
119.9   the gene] a gene (Huxley, *Evolution*, 65.17)
119n.15–16   organism] organisms (Dobzhansky and Montagu, "Natural Selection," 588.1.24)
120n.6   concepts] qualities (Mayr, *Systematics*, 113.31)
122n.4   as simply] merely as the (Firth, *Tongues of Men*, 19.26)
122n.5   just live] live just (Firth, *Tongues of Men*, 19.26–27)
122n.5   space which] what (Firth, *Tongues of Men*, 19.27)
122n.7   never] never really (Firth, *Tongues of Men*, 20.3)
122n.10   outer] outward (Firth, *Tongues of Men*, 19.22)
125n.6   ecological psychology] psychological ecology (Lewin, "Defining," 309.10)
140n.7   stimulus] stimuli (Bartley and Chute, *Fatigue*, 343.39)

150.10   application or specification] *application* or *specification*
          (Quine, *Mathematical Logic,* 171.35)
156.19   kinds] kind (*Webster's,* 688.2.32)
156.22   equivalences] equivalence (*Webster's,* 688.2.35)
163.15   indefinables.] indefinable. (Adamson, "Definition,"
          1:259.1.56–57)
165.15   thing:] thing (taking "thing" [. . .] mental states, &c.):
          (Davidson, *Definition,* 32.4–6)
168.18–19 cannot] cannot however (Dubs, "Definition," 573.13)
169.15   mental] psychological (Reid, "Definitions," 171.12)
169n.3–4 an . . . operation] a definitional operation (Reid, "Defini-
          tions," 170.24)
169n.4   These distinctions] the distinctions which I marked sym-
          bolically by such terms as definitional *relation, operation* and
          rule (Reid, "Definitions," 171.30–31)
172.3   specification of meaning] [*ital.*] (Kaplan, "Definition," 281.4)
173.27   generic meaning] [*ital.*] (Nagel, "Some Reflections," 624.39)
181.20   been] usually been (Mill, *Logic,* 92.11)
244.31   feeling,] feeling, or (*Oxford,* s.v. "common sense," 3.)
245.9   every-day affairs.] the every-day affairs of life. (*Oxford,* s.v.
          "common sense," 2.b.)
245.16–17 intelligence in its] intelligence, esp. as (*Oxford,* s.v.
          "sense," 11.)
246.5   *that*] [*rom.*] (*Oxford,* s.v. "thing," I.3.)
246.6   occupied, engaged, concerned, busied,] concerned (in action,
          speech, or thought) (*Oxford,* s.v. "thing," I.3.)
246.15   the Latin] L. (*Oxford,* s.v. "matter," IV.)
246.16   used] employed (*Oxford,* s.v. "matter," IV.)
246.19   circumstance,] circumstance, fact, question, (*Oxford,* s.v.
          "matter," IV.19.)
246.20   things] things, etc. (*Oxford,* s.v. "matter," IV.19.)
246.20   is the object] may be an object (*Oxford,* s.v. "matter,"
          IV.19.)
246.20–21 or of practical] or practical (*Oxford,* s.v. "matter,"
          IV.19.)
246.29–30 *object of consideration*] matter of thought, considera-
          tion (*Oxford,* s.v. "subject," III.13.)
247.10–11 that is forced on] forced upon (*Oxford,* s.v. "ado," 4.)
247.11   a difficulty, trouble.] labour, trouble, difficulty. (*Oxford,* s.v.
          "ado," 4.)
258n.5   (q.v.),] (which see), (Runes, *Dictionary,* 161.1.15)
281.3–4   disagreements with one another] disagreements (Dewey,
          "Beliefs and Existences," 196.18) [*Middle Works* 3:99.34]

281.4   in comparison] compared (Dewey, "Beliefs and Existences,"
         196.19) [*Middle Works* 3:99.35]
281.4–5 disagreements] disagreement (Dewey, "Beliefs and Exis-
         tences," 196.19–20) [*Middle Works* 3:99.35]
281.7   as to conclusions] in solutions (Dewey, "Beliefs and Exis-
         tences," 196.23) [*Middle Works* 3:99.38]

What Is It to Be a Linguistic Sign or Name?

297.17   relation] a relation (Peirce, *Collected Papers,* 2:155.13)
299.10   that material] the material of *that* (Peirce, *Collected Papers,*
         2:189.14–15)
299.11   *rather of this precept,*] rather this precept (Peirce, *Collected
         Papers,* 2:189.16)
299.11–12 more useful] that is more serviceable (Peirce, *Collected
         Papers,* 2:189.16)
299.13   *are to*] [*rom.*] (Peirce, *Collected Papers,* 2:189.18)
299.13   get] gain (Peirce, *Collected Papers,* 2:189.18)
299.14   that word.] the word. (Peirce, *Collected Papers,* 2:189.19)
301.4   3. The] 3. A (Ogden and Richards, *Meaning,* 243.21)
301.6   *problem*] [*rom.*] (Ogden and Richards, *Meaning,* 243.22)

Values, Valuations, and Social Facts

312.10   a choice,] choice, (Benoit-Smullyan, "Value Judgments,"
         202.31)
315.27   upon] on (Benoit-Smullyan, "Value Judgments," 204.33)
315.27   value judgments] all judgments with valuational components
         (Benoit-Smullyan, "Value Judgments," 204.37–38)
315.28   and must] and that they must (Benoit-Smullyan, "Value
         Judgments," 204.38)
315.30   contempt] a contempt (Benoit-Smullyan, "Value Judgments,"
         204.40)

The Field of "Value"

347.19   never-too-much-to-be-sat-upon] never-to-be-too-much-sat-
         upon (James *Psychology,* 2:387.21)
357.27   whole] [*ital.*] (Stevenson, *Ethics,* 336.4)

Philosophy's Future in Our Scientific Age

372.18   the men] these men (Weber, *Essays,* 142.4)
372.20   passage] the path (Weber, *Essays,* 142.6)
372.25   thereby] therewith (Weber, *Essays,* 142.14)
372.30–31   big children found] certain big children who are indeed
            found (Weber, *Essays,* 142.28)
372.32   would teach] could teach (Weber, *Essays,* 142.30)
372.35   clearest answer] simplest answer (Weber, *Essays,* 143.21)
373.1   *our*] [*rom.*] (Weber, *Essays,* 143.22)
374.12   alliance. There] alliance [. . .] there (Fosdick, "Telescope,"
            1.3.24–28)
374.12   telling] foretelling (Fosdick, "Telescope," 1.3.29)
374.13   destruction;] destructive ends. There is (Fosdick, "Telescope,"
            1.3.30–31)
374.13   no classifying of] no method of classifying (Fosdick, "Tele-
            scope," 1.3.31–32)
374.14   knowledge is] knowledge has become dangerous. Indeed,
            knowledge has always been dangerous, for knowledge means
            (Fosdick, "Telescope," 1.3.34–37)
374.14   power; there] power, [. . .] There (Fosdick, "Telescope,"
            1.3.37, 15.1.3–35)
374.15   knowledge that] knowledge [. . .] which (Fosdick, "Tele-
            scope," 15.1.36–39)
374.16   elect] deliberately elect (Fosdick, "Telescope," 15.1.42)
377.35   science to morals] our knowledge to moral foundations (Fos-
            dick, "Telescope," 15.1.119–20)

Experience and Existence: A Comment

384.24   true] true that (Kahn, "Experience and Existence," 317.24)
            [*Later Works* 16:458.2]

Contribution to "Religion and the Intellectuals"

392.18   the present trend] this new trend ("Editorial Statement,"
            104.36)

Aesthetic Experience as a Primary Phase and as an Artistic Development

395.11   experience] life-experience (Romanell, "Comment," 125.33) [*Later Works* 16:464.10]
396.33–34   incompatible] opposite (Romanell, "Comment," 125.35) [*Later Works* 16:464.13]
398.1   *addition*] [*rom.*] (Dewey, *Experience and Nature,* 389.13) [*Later Works* 1:291.8–9]
398.1   dwelling] dwelling exclusively (Dewey, *Experience and Nature,* 389.14) [*Later Works* 1:291.9]
398.2   given to] given (Dewey, *Experience and Nature,* 389.15) [*Later Works* 1:291.10]
398.3   *enhanced* perception] enhanced perception or esthctic appreciation (Dewey, *Experience and Nature,* 389.16) [*Later Works* 1:291.11–12]
398.7–8   they . . . spontaneously] which they spontaneously (Dewey, *Experience and Nature,* 389.21) [*Later Works* 1:291.15–16]

Modern Philosophy

411.18–19   are the . . . winds.] The condition of a ship in which, either from calms, or from baffling winds, she makes no headway; (*Oxford,* s.v. "doldrum," 2.b.)

Checklist of References

This section gives full publication information for each work cited by Dewey and Arthur F. Bentley. Books in Dewey's personal library (John Dewey Papers, Special Collections, Morris Library, Southern Illinois University at Carbondale) have been listed whenever possible and indicated by a degree symbol °. When page numbers were given for a reference, the edition has been identified by locating the citation; for other references, the edition listed here is the most likely source by reason of place or date of publication, general accessibility during the period, or evidence from correspondence and other materials.

Adamson, Robert. *A Short History of Logic.* Edinburgh and London: William Blackwood and Sons, 1911.

———. "Definition." In *Dictionary of Philosophy and Psychology,* edited by James Mark Baldwin, 1:259–60. New York: Macmillan Co., 1901.

Aldrich, Virgil C. Review of *Signs, Language, and Behavior,* by Charles W. Morris. *Journal of Philosophy* 44 (5 June 1947):324–29.

Ayer, Alfred J. *Language, Truth and Logic.* New York: Oxford University Press, 1936.

Baldwin, James Mark, ed. *Dictionary of Philosophy and Psychology.* New York: Macmillan Co., 1901.

Bartley, Samuel Howard, and Eloise Chute. *Fatigue and Impairment in Man.* New York: McGraw-Hill Book Co., 1947.

Baylis, Charles A. "Critical Comments on the 'Symposium of Meaning and Truth.'" *Philosophy and Phenomenological Research* 5 (September 1944):80–93.

Beebe, William, ed. *The Book of Naturalists.* New York: Alfred A. Knopf, 1944, 1945.

Benoit-Smullyan, Emile. "Value Judgments and the Social Sciences." *Journal of Philosophy* 42 (13 April 1945):197–210.

°Bentley, Arthur F. *Behavior, Knowledge, Fact.* Bloomington, Ind.: Principia Press, 1935.

°———. *Linguistic Analysis of Mathematics*. Bloomington, Ind.: Principia Press, 1932.

°———. *The Process of Government: A Study of Social Pressures*. Chicago: University of Chicago Press, 1908; 2d ed., Bloomington, Ind.: Principia Press, 1935; 3d ed., Principia Press, 1949.

°———. *Relativity in Man and Society*. New York: G. P. Putnam's Sons, 1926.

———. "The Behavioral Superfice." *Psychological Review* 48 (January 1941):39–59.

———. "The Factual Space and Time of Behavior." *Journal of Philosophy* 38 (28 August 1941):477–85.

———. "The Human Skin: Philosophy's Last Line of Defense." *Philosophy of Science* 8 (January 1941):1–19.

———. "The Jamesian Datum." *Journal of Psychology* 16 (1943):35–79.

———. "Observable Behaviors." *Psychological Review* 47 (May 1940):230–53.

———. "On a Certain Vagueness in Logic." *Journal of Philosophy* 42 (4 and 18 January 1945):6–27, 39–51. Revised as "Vagueness in Logic," chap. 1 in *Knowing and the Known*. Boston: Beacon Press, 1949. [*The Later Works of John Dewey, 1925–1953*, edited by Jo Ann Boydston, 16:8–45. Carbondale and Edwardsville: Southern Illinois University Press, 1989.]

———. "Postulation for Behavioral Inquiry." *Journal of Philosophy* 36 (20 July 1939):405–13.

———. "Sights-Seen as Materials of Knowledge." *Journal of Philosophy* 36 (30 March 1939):169–81.

———. "Situational Treatments of Behavior." *Journal of Philosophy* 36 (8 June 1939):309–23.

———. "Some Logical Considerations concerning Professor Lewis's 'Mind.'" *Journal of Philosophy* 38 (6 November 1941):634–35.

Bentley, Arthur F., and John Dewey. *Knowing and the Known*. Boston: Beacon Press, 1949. [*Later Works* 16:1–294.]

———. "A Terminology for Knowings and Knowns." *Journal of Philosophy* 42 (26 April 1945):225–47. Revised as "The Terminological Problem," chap. 2 in *Knowing and the Known*. Boston: Beacon Press, 1949. [*Later Works* 16:46–73.]

"A Biophysics Symposium." *Scientific Monthly* 64 (March 1947):213–31.

Black, Max. "The Limitations of a Behavioristic Semiotic." *Philosophical Review* 56 (May 1947):258–72.

———. "A New Method of Presentation of the Theory of the Syllogism." *Journal of Philosophy* 42 (16 August 1945):449–55.

Bohr, Nils. "Can Quantum-Mechanical Description of Physical Reality Be Considered Complete?" *Physical Review* 48 (15 October 1935): 696–702.

Boring, Edwin G. *A History of Experimental Psychology.* New York: Century Co., 1929.

———. "The Use of Operational Definitions in Science." *Psychological Review* 52 (September 1945): 243–45.

°Bridgman, P. W. *The Logic of Modern Physics.* New York: Macmillan Co., 1927.

———. "Some General Principles of Operational Analysis." *Psychological Review* 52 (September 1945): 246–49.

Bronstein, Daniel J. Review of *Signs, Language, and Behavior,* by Charles W. Morris. *Philosophy and Phenomenological Research* 7 (June 1947): 643–49.

Brunswik, Egon. "Organismic Achievement and Environmental Probability." *Psychological Review* 50 (May 1943): 255–72.

Brunswik, Egon, and Edward C. Tolman. "The Organism and the Causal Texture of the Environment." *Psychological Review* 42 (January 1935): 43–77.

°Buchler, Justus. Review of *An Introduction to Peirce's Philosophy,* by James Feibleman. *Journal of Philosophy* 44 (8 May 1947): 306–8.

Bühler, Karl. *Die Krise der Psychologie.* Jena: Gustav Fischer, 1927.

Burks, Arthur W. "Empiricism and Vagueness." *Journal of Philosophy* 43 (29 August 1946): 477–86.

Burr, H. S. "Field Theory in Biology." *Scientific Monthly* 64 (March 1947): 217–25.

Carnap, Rudolf. *Formalization of Logic.* Cambridge: Harvard University Press, 1943.

°———. *Foundations of Logic and Mathematics. International Encyclopedia of Unified Science,* edited by Otto Neurath, vol. 1, no. 3. Chicago: University of Chicago Press, May 1939.

———. *Introduction to Semantics.* Cambridge: Harvard University Press, 1942.

°———. "Logical Foundations of the Unity of Science." In *International Encyclopedia of Unified Science,* edited by Otto Neurath, vol. 1, no. 1, pp. 42–62. Chicago: University of Chicago Press, July 1938.

———. "Testability and Meaning." *Philosophy of Science* 3 (October 1936): 419–71; ibid. 4 (January 1937): 1–40.

The Century Dictionary and Cyclopedia. New York: Century Co., 1897. [s.vv. "definition"; "sign."]

Church, Alonzo. *Introduction to Mathematical Logic.* Part 1. Princeton, N.J.: Princeton University Press, 1944.

————. "Definition." In *The Dictionary of Philosophy,* edited by Dagobert D. Runes, pp. 74–75. New York: Philosophical Library, 1942.

————. Review of "A Search for Firm Names," "A Terminology for Knowings and Knowns," and "Postulations," by John Dewey and Arthur F. Bentley; and "On a Certain Vagueness in Logic," by Bentley. *Journal of Symbolic Logic* 10 (December 1945): 132–33.

Churchman, C. West, and T. A. Cowan. "A Challenge." *Philosophy of Science* 12 (July 1945): 219–20.

————. "A Discussion of Dewey and Bentley's 'Postulations.'" *Journal of Philosophy* 43 (11 April 1946): 217–19.

Chute, Eloise, and Samuel Howard Bartley. *Fatigue and Impairment in Man.* New York: McGraw-Hill Book Co., 1947.

Cohen, Morris R. *A Preface to Logic.* New York: Henry Holt and Co., 1944.

————. "The Faith of a Logician." In *Contemporary American Philosophy,* vol. 1, pp. 227–47. New York: Macmillan Co., 1930.

Cohen, Morris R., and Ernest Nagel. *An Introduction to Logic and Scientific Method.* New York: Harcourt, Brace and Co., 1934; 4th printing, 1937.

Commons, John R. *Legal Foundations of Capitalism.* New York: Macmillan Co., 1924.

Copilowish, Irving M., and Abraham Kaplan. "Must There Be Propositions?" *Mind* 48 (October 1939): 478–84.

Cowan, T. A., and C. West Churchman. "A Challenge." *Philosophy of Science* 12 (July 1945): 219–20.

————. "A Discussion of Dewey and Bentley's 'Postulations.'" *Journal of Philosophy* 43 (11 April 1946): 217–19.

Davidson, William L. *The Logic of Definition.* London: Longmans, Green, and Co., 1885.

Descartes, René. *La Dioptrique.* In *Oeuvres de Descartes,* edited by Charles Adam and Paul Tannery, 6: 79–228. Paris: L. Cerf, 1897–1910.

Dewey, John. *Art as Experience.* New York: Minton, Balch and Co., 1934. [*Later Works* 10.]

————. *Context and Thought.* University of California Publications in Philosophy, vol. 12, no. 3, pp. 203–24. Berkeley: University of California Press, 1931. [*Later Works* 6: 3–21.]

————. *Essays in Experimental Logic.* Chicago: University of Chicago Press, 1916.

°————. *Experience and Nature.* Chicago: Open Court Publishing Co., 1925. [*Later Works* 1.]

°————. *How We Think.* Boston: D. C. Heath and Co., 1910. [*The*

Middle Works of John Dewey, 1899–1924, edited by Jo Ann Boydston, 6:177–356. Carbondale and Edwardsville: Southern Illinois
University Press, 1978.]

———. *How We Think: A Restatement of the Relation of Reflective
Thinking to the Educative Process.* Boston: D. C. Heath and Co.,
1933. [*Later Works* 8:105–352.]

°———. *Logic: The Theory of Inquiry.* New York: Henry Holt and
Co., 1938. [*Later Works* 12.]

———. "Beliefs and Existences." In his *The Influence of Darwin
on Philosophy and Other Essays in Contemporary Thought,*
pp. 169–97. New York: Henry Holt and Co., 1910. [*Middle Works*
3:83–100.]

°———. "By Nature and by Art." *Journal of Philosophy* 41 (25 May
1944):281–92. [*Later Works* 15:84–96.]

°———. "Common Sense and Science: Their Respective Frames of
Reference." *Journal of Philosophy* 45 (8 April 1948):197–208. Revised as "Common Sense and Science," chap. 10 in *Knowing and
the Known.* Boston: Beacon Press, 1949. [*Later Works* 16:242–56.]

———. "Conduct and Experience." In *Psychologies of 1930,* edited by
Carl Murchison, pp. 409–22. Worcester, Mass.: Clark University
Press, 1930. Republished in *Philosophy and Civilization,* pp. 249–
70. New York: Minton, Balch and Co., 1931. [*Later Works* 5:
218–35.]

°———. "Ethical Subject-Matter and Language." *Journal of Philosophy* 42 (20 December 1945):701–12. [*Later Works* 15:127–40.]

°———. "How Is Mind to Be Known?" *Journal of Philosophy* 39 (15
January 1942):29–35. [*Later Works* 15:27–33.]

———. "The Naturalistic Theory of Perception by the Senses." *Journal of Philosophy* 22 (22 October 1925):596–605. Republished in
Philosophy and Civilization, pp. 188–201, with the title "A Naturalistic Theory of Sense Perception." New York: Minton, Balch and
Co., 1931. [*Later Works* 2:44–54.]

°———. "Peirce's Theory of Linguistic Signs, Thought, and Meaning."
Journal of Philosophy 43 (14 February 1946):85–95. [*Later Works*
15:141–52.]

°———. "The Reflex Arc Concept in Psychology." *Psychological Review* 3 (July 1896):357–70. Republished in *Philosophy and Civilization,* pp. 233–48, with the title "The Unit of Behavior." New
York: Minton, Balch and Co., 1931. [*The Early Works of John
Dewey, 1882–1898,* edited by Jo Ann Boydston, 5:96–109. Carbondale and Edwardsville: Southern Illinois University Press, 1972.]

———. Rejoinder to Charles W. Morris. *Journal of Philosophy* 43
(9 May 1946):280. [*Later Works* 15:331–32.]

°———. "Some Questions about Value." *Journal of Philosophy* 41 (17 August 1944):449–55. [*Later Works* 15:101–8.]

Dewey, John, and Arthur F. Bentley. *Knowing and the Known*. Boston: Beacon Press, 1949. [*Later Works* 16:1–294.]

———. "A Terminology for Knowings and Knowns." *Journal of Philosophy* 42 (26 April 1945):225–47. Revised as "The Terminological Problem," chap. 2 in *Knowing and the Known*. Boston: Beacon Press, 1949. [*Later Works* 16:46–73.]

Dewey, John, et al. *Studies in Logical Theory*. University of Chicago Decennial Publications, 2d ser., vol. 11. Chicago: University of Chicago Press, 1903. [*Middle Works* 2:293–375.]

The Dictionary of Philosophy. Edited by Dagobert D. Runes. New York: Philosophical Library, 1942. [s.vv. "definition"; "fact"; "knowledge."]

Dictionary of Philosophy and Psychology. Edited by James Mark Baldwin. New York: Macmillan Co., 1901. [s.vv. "definition"; "fact"; "represent."]

Dobzhansky, Th., and M. F. Ashley Montagu. "Natural Selection and the Mental Capacities of Mankind." *Science* 105 (6 June 1947):587–90.

Dubislav, Walter. *Die Definition*. 3d ed. Leipzig: F. Meiner, 1931.

Dubs, Homer H. "Definition and Its Problems." *Philosophical Review* 52 (November 1943):566–77.

Ducasse, C. J. "Is a Fact a True Proposition?—A Reply." *Journal of Philosophy* 39 (26 February 1942):132–36.

———. "Propositions, Truth, and the Ultimate Criterion of Truth." *Philosophy and Phenomenological Research* 4 (March 1944):317–40.

"Editorial Statement." In "Religion and the Intellectuals: A Symposium," *Partisan Review* 17 (February 1950):103–5.

Einstein, Albert, and Leopold Infeld. *The Evolution of Physics*. New York: Simon and Schuster, 1938.

Einstein, Albert, B. Podolsky, and N. Rosen. "Can Quantum-Mechanical Description of Physical Reality Be Considered Complete?" *Physical Review* 47 (15 May 1935):777–80.

Eisler, Rudolf, ed. *Wörterbuch der Philosophischen Begriffe*. 4th ed. 3 vols. Berlin: E. S. Mittler and Son, 1927–30.

Feigl, Herbert. "Operationism and Scientific Method." *Psychological Review* 52 (September 1945):250–59.

Firth, John Rupert. *The Tongues of Men*. London: Watts and Co., 1937.

Fosdick, Raymond B. Speech quoted in "Largest Telescope Dedicated to Man's Service at Palomar," by William L. Laurence, *New York Times*, 4 June 1948, pp. 1, 15.

Frank, Philipp. *Between Physics and Philosophy*. Cambridge: Harvard University Press, 1941.

———. *Foundations of Physics. International Encyclopedia of Unified Science*, edited by Otto Neurath, vol. 1, no. 7. Chicago: University of Chicago Press, 1946.

Gentry, George V. Review of *Signs, Language, and Behavior*, by Charles W. Morris. *Journal of Philosophy* 44 (5 June 1947): 318–24.

———. "Some Comments on Morris's 'Class' Conception of the Designatum." *Journal of Philosophy* 41 (6 July 1944): 376–84.

°Gödel, Kurt. "Russell's Mathematical Logic." In *The Philosophy of Bertrand Russell*, edited by Paul Arthur Schilpp, pp. 125–53. Evanston and Chicago: Northwestern University, 1944.

Goldschmidt, Richard. *Physiological Genetics*. New York: McGraw-Hill Book Co., 1938.

Goudge, Thomas A. "The Conflict of Naturalism and Transcendentalism in Peirce." *Journal of Philosophy* 44 (3 July 1947): 365–75.

Griffith, Coleman R. *Principles of Systematic Psychology*. Urbana: University of Illinois Press, 1943.

Hartshorne, Charles. "Ideal Knowledge Defines Reality: What Was True in 'Idealism.'" *Journal of Philosophy* 43 (10 October 1946): 573–82.

Hartung, Frank E. "Operationalism: Idealism or Realism?" *Philosophy of Science* 9 (October 1942): 350–55.

———. "Operationism as a Cultural Survival." *Philosophy of Science* 11 (October 1944): 227–32.

Henderson, Lawrence J. *The Fitness of the Environment*. New York: Macmillan Co., 1913.

Hull, Clark L. *Principles of Behavior*. New York: Appleton-Century-Crofts, 1943.

———. "The Problem of Intervening Variables in Molar Behavior Theory." *Psychological Review* 50 (May 1943): 273–91.

Huxley, Julian Sorell. *Evolution, the Modern Synthesis*. New York and London: Harper and Brothers, 1943.

———, ed. *The New Systematics*. Oxford: At the Clarendon Press, 1940.

Infeld, Leopold, and Albert Einstein. *The Evolution of Physics*. New York: Simon and Schuster, 1938.

International Encyclopedia of Unified Science. Edited by Otto Neurath, Rudolf Carnap, and Charles W. Morris. Vol. 1, nos. 1, 2, 3, 7; vol. 2, no. 1. Chicago: University of Chicago Press, 1938–46.

°James, William. *Essays in Radical Empiricism*. New York: Longmans, Green and Co., 1912.

°———. *A Pluralistic Universe*. New York: Longmans, Green, and Co., 1909.

°————. *The Principles of Psychology*. 2 vols. New York: Henry Holt and Co., 1893.

————. "Epilogue." In *Psychology*, American Science Series, Briefer Course, pp. 461–68. New York: Henry Holt and Co., 1893.

Jennings, H. S. *Behavior of the Lower Organisms*. New York: Columbia University Press, 1906.

°Johnson, William Ernest. *Logic*. Part 1. Cambridge: At the University Press, 1921.

°Joseph, Horace William Brindley. *An Introduction to Logic*. 2d ed., rev. Oxford: At the Clarendon Press, 1916.

Kahn, Sholom J. "Experience and Existence in Dewey's Naturalistic Metaphysics." *Philosophy and Phenomenological Research* 9 (December 1948): 316–21. [*Later Works* 16: 456–62.]

Kantor, J. R. *Psychology and Logic*. Vol. 1. Bloomington, Ind.: Principia Press, 1945.

————. "The Aim and Progress of Psychology." *American Scientist* 34 (April 1946): 251–63.

————. "An Interbehavioral Analysis of Propositions." *Psychological Record* 5 (December 1943): 309–39.

————. "The Operational Principle in the Physical and Psychological Sciences." *Psychological Record* 2 (January 1938): 3–32.

Kaplan, Abraham. "Definition and Specification of Meaning." *Journal of Philosophy* 43 (23 May 1946): 281–88.

Kaplan, Abraham, and Irving M. Copilowish. "Must There Be Propositions?" *Mind* 48 (October 1939): 478–84.

Kaufmann, Felix. *Methodology of the Social Sciences*. New York: Oxford University Press, 1944.

————. "Discussion of Mr. Nagel's Rejoinder." *Philosophy and Phenomenological Research* 5 (March 1945): 350–53.

————. "Scientific Procedure and Probability." *Philosophy and Phenomenological Research* 6 (September 1945): 47–66.

Keyser, Cassius Jackson. "A Glance at Some of the Ideas of Charles Sanders Peirce." *Scripta Mathematica* 3 (January 1935): 11–37.

Korzybski, Alfred. *Science and Sanity: An Introduction to Non-Aristotelian Systems and General Semantics*. New York: International Non-Aristotelian Library Publishing Co., 1933.

Lalande, André, ed. *Vocabulaire Technique et Critique de la Philosophie*. Paris: Librairie Félix Alcan, 1928.

Langford, Cooper Harold, and Clarence Irving Lewis. *Symbolic Logic*. New York: Century Co., 1932.

Lewin, Kurt. "Defining the 'Field at a Given Time.'" *Psychological Review* 50 (May 1943): 292–310.

°Lewis, Clarence Irving. *Mind and the World-Order: Outline of a Theory of Knowledge*. New York: Charles Scribner's Sons, 1929.

———. *The Pragmatic Element in Knowledge*. University of California Publications in Philosophy, vol. 6, no. 3, pp. 205–27. Berkeley: University of California Press, 1926.

———. *A Survey of Symbolic Logic*. Berkeley: University of California Press, 1918.

———. "In Reply to Mr. Baylis." *Philosophy and Phenomenological Research* 5 (September 1944):94–96.

———. "The Modes of Meaning." *Philosophy and Phenomenological Research* 4 (December 1943):236–49.

Lewis, Clarence Irving, and Cooper Harold Langford. *Symbolic Logic*. New York: Century Co., 1932.

London, Ivan D. "Psychologists' Misuse of the Auxiliary Concepts of Physics and Mathematics." *Psychological Review* 51 (September 1944):266–91.

McGill, V. J. "Subjective and Objective Methods in Philosophy." *Journal of Philosophy* 41 (3 August 1944):421–38.

Margenau, Henry. "On the Frequency Theory of Probability." *Philosophy and Phenomenological Research* 6 (September 1945):11–25.

———. "Particle and Field Concepts in Biology." *Scientific Monthly* 64 (March 1947):225–31.

Maxwell, James Clerk. *Matter and Motion*. Edited by Sir Joseph Larmor. London: Society for Promoting Christian Knowledge, 1891, 1920.

Mayr, Ernst. *Systematics and the Origin of Species*. New York: Columbia University Press, 1942.

°Mead, George Herbert. *Mind, Self and Society from the Standpoint of a Social Behaviorist*. Edited by Charles W. Morris. Chicago: University of Chicago Press, 1934.

Menger, Karl. "The New Logic." *Philosophy of Science* 4 (July 1937):299–336.

Mill, John Stuart. *A System of Logic, Ratiocinative and Inductive*. 8th ed. New York: Harper and Brothers, 1874.

Montagu, M. F. Ashley, and Th. Dobzhansky. "Natural Selection and the Mental Capacities of Mankind." *Science* 105 (6 June 1947):587–90.

°Moore, G. E. *The Philosophy of G. E. Moore*, edited by Paul Arthur Schilpp. Library of Living Philosophers, vol. 4. Evanston and Chicago: Northwestern University, 1942. ["An Autobiography," pp. 3–39; "A Reply to My Critics," pp. 535–677.]

———. Contribution to "Symposium: The Nature of Sensible Appearances." *Proceedings of the Aristotelian Society,* sup. vol. 6 (1926):179–89.

———. "A Defence of Common Sense." In *Contemporary British Phi-*

losophy, 2d ser., pp. 193–223. London: George Allen and Unwin; New York: Macmillan Co., 1925.

———. "Proof of an External World." *Proceedings of the British Academy* 25 (1939): 273–300.

°Morris, Charles W. *Foundations of the Theory of Signs. International Encyclopedia of Unified Science,* edited by Otto Neurath, vol. 1, no. 2. Chicago: University of Chicago Press, July 1938.

———. *Signs, Language, and Behavior.* New York: Prentice-Hall, 1946.

———. Comments on Abraham Kaplan's "Content Analysis and the Theory of Signs." *Philosophy of Science* 10 (October 1943): 247–49.

———. Rejoinder to Dewey. *Journal of Philosophy* 43 (20 June 1946): 363–64.

———. Reply to Dewey. *Journal of Philosophy* 43 (28 March 1946): 196. [*Later Works* 15 : 473.]

°———. "Scientific Empiricism." In *International Encyclopedia of Unified Science,* edited by Otto Neurath, vol. 1, no. 1, pp. 63–75. Chicago: University of Chicago Press, July 1938.

Nagel, Ernest. "Can Logic Be Divorced from Ontology?" *Journal of Philosophy* 26 (19 December 1929): 705–12.

°———. "Logic without Ontology." In *Naturalism and the Human Spirit,* edited by Yervant H. Krikorian, pp. 210–41. New York: Columbia University Press, 1944.

———. "Mr. Russell on Meaning and Truth." *Journal of Philosophy* 38 (8 May 1941): 253–70.

———. Review of *Introduction to Semantics,* by Rudolf Carnap. *Journal of Philosophy* 39 (13 August 1942): 468–73.

———. Review of *The Philosophy of G. E. Moore,* edited by Paul Arthur Schilpp. *Mind* 53 (January 1944): 60–75.

———. Review of *Psychology and Logic,* vol. 1, by J. R. Kantor. *Journal of Philosophy* 42 (11 October 1945): 578–80.

°———. "Russell's Philosophy of Science." In *The Philosophy of Bertrand Russell,* edited by Paul Arthur Schilpp, pp. 319–49. Evanston and Chicago: Northwestern University, 1944.

———. "Some Reflections on the Use of Language in the Natural Sciences." *Journal of Philosophy* 42 (8 November 1945): 617–30.

———. "Truth and Knowledge of the Truth." *Philosophy and Phenomenological Research* 5 (September 1944): 50–68.

Nagel, Ernest, and Morris R. Cohen. *An Introduction to Logic and Scientific Method.* New York: Harcourt, Brace and Co., 1934; 4th printing, 1937.

°Neurath, Otto. *Foundations of the Social Sciences. International Encyclopedia of Unified Science,* vol. 2, no. 1. Chicago: University of Chicago Press, October 1944.

The New Systematics. Edited by Julian Sorell Huxley. Oxford: At the Clarendon Press, 1940.

New York Times. "Largest Telescope Dedicated to Man's Service at Palomar," 4 June 1948, pp. 1, 15.

Notes and Queries (London) 4 (20 September 1851):203–4. ["Hyphenism, Hyphenic, Hyphenization."]

°Ogden, C. K., and I. A. Richards. *The Meaning of Meaning: A Study of the Influence of Language upon Thought and of the Science of Symbolism.* London: Kegan Paul, Trench, Trübner, 1923; New York: Harcourt, Brace and Co., 1923, 1938.

Osborn, Henry Fairfield. *The Origin and Evolution of Life.* London: G. Bell and Sons, 1917, 1918.

Oxford English Dictionary. Oxford: At the Clarendon Press, 1897, 1933. [s.vv. "ado"; "affair"; "common sense"; "definition"; "doldrum"; "inter"; "interaction"; "matter"; "organism"; "sense"; "sign"; "subject"; "thing"; "transaction."]

°Peirce, Charles S. *Collected Papers of Charles Sanders Peirce.* Edited by Charles Hartshorne and Paul Weiss. Vols. 1, 2, 3, 5, 6. Cambridge: Harvard University Press, 1931–35. ["Questions Concerning Certain Faculties Claimed for Man," 5:135–55; "How to Make Our Ideas Clear," 5:248–71.]

———. *A Syllabus of Certain Topics of Logic.* Boston: Alfred Mudge and Son, 1903.

Pepper, Stephen C. *The Basis of Criticism in the Arts.* Cambridge: Harvard University Press, 1945.

———. "The Descriptive Definition." *Journal of Philosophy* 43 (17 January 1946):29–36.

———. "Reply to Professor Hoekstra." *Journal of Philosophy* 42 (15 February 1945):101–8.

Quine, Willard Van Orman. *Mathematical Logic.* 2d printing. Cambridge: Harvard University Press, 1947.

———. "On Universals." *Journal of Symbolic Logic* 12 (September 1947):74–84.

Reid, John R. "What Are Definitions?" *Philosophy of Science* 13 (April 1946):170–75.

Richards, I. A., and C. K. Ogden. *The Meaning of Meaning: A Study of the Influence of Language upon Thought and of the Science of Symbolism.* London: Kegan Paul, Trench, Trübner, 1923; New York: Harcourt, Brace and Co., 1923, 1938.

Romanell, Patrick. "A Comment on Croce's and Dewey's Aesthetics." *Journal of Aesthetics and Art Criticism* 8 (December 1949):125–28. [*Later Works* 16:463–67.]

Runes, Dagobert D., ed. *The Dictionary of Philosophy.* New York: Philosophical Library, 1942.

Russell, Bertrand. *The Analysis of Mind.* New York: Macmillan Co., 1921.

°———. *A History of Western Philosophy.* New York: Simon and Schuster, 1945.

°———. *An Inquiry into Meaning and Truth.* New York: W. W. Norton and Co., 1940.

———. *Introduction to Mathematical Philosophy.* New York: Macmillan Co., 1919.

———. *Mysticism and Logic.* New York: Longmans, Green and Co., 1918.

———. *Principles of Mathematics.* Cambridge: At the University Press, 1903.

———. *The Problems of Philosophy.* New York: Henry Holt and Co., 1912.

———. *Sceptical Essays.* New York: W. W. Norton and Co., 1928.

———. "Knowledge by Acquaintance and Knowledge by Description." *Proceedings of the Aristotelian Society,* n.s. 11 (1910–11): 108–28.

———. "Logical Atomism." In *Contemporary British Philosophy,* 1st ser., pp. 359–83. London: George Allen and Unwin; New York: Macmillan Co., 1924.

———. "On the Nature of Acquaintance." *Monist* 24 (January, April, July 1914): 1–16, 161–87, 435–53.

———. "The Philosophy of Logical Atomism." *Monist* 28 (October 1918): 495–527; ibid. 29 (January, April, July 1919): 32–63, 190–222, 345–80.

°———. "Reply to Criticisms." In *The Philosophy of Bertrand Russell,* edited by Paul Arthur Schilpp, pp. 681–741. Library of Living Philosophers, vol. 5. Evanston and Chicago: Northwestern University, 1944.

Ryle, G. Contribution to "Symposium: Negation." *Proceedings of the Aristotelian Society,* sup. vol. 9 (1929): 80–96.

Sellars, Roy Wood. "Does Naturalism Need Ontology?" *Journal of Philosophy* 41 (7 December 1944): 686–94.

———. "The Meaning of True and False." *Philosophy and Phenomenological Research* 5 (September 1944): 98–103.

Simmel, Georg. *Soziologie: Untersuchungen über die Formen der Vergesellschaftung.* 2d ed. Leipzig: Duncker and Humblot, 1922; 3d ed., 1923.

Skinner, B. F. "The Operational Analysis of Psychological Terms." *Psychological Review* 52 (September 1945): 270–77.

Smullyan, Arthur Francis. Review of *Signs, Language, and Behavior,* by Charles W. Morris. *Journal of Symbolic Logic* 12 (June 1947): 49–51.

————. Review of "'Definition,'" by Dewey and Arthur F. Bentley. *Journal of Symbolic Logic* 12 (September 1947): 99.
A Standard Dictionary of the English Language. New York: Funk and Wagnalls Co., 1893. [s.v. "definition."]
Stevens, S. S. "On the Theory of Scales of Measurement." *Science* 103 (7 June 1946): 677–80.
Stevenson, Charles L. *Ethics and Language.* New Haven: Yale University Press, 1945.
Studies in the Nature of Facts. University of California Publications in Philosophy, vol. 14. Berkeley: University of California Press, 1932.
Swann, W. F. G. "The Relation of Theory to Experiment in Physics." *Reviews of Modern Physics* 13 (July 1941): 190–96.
"Symposium on Operationism." *Psychological Review* 52 (September 1945): 241–94.
Tarski, Alfred. *Introduction to Logic and to the Methodology of Deductive Sciences.* New York: Oxford University Press, 1941.
————. "The Semantic Conception of Truth and the Foundations of Semantics." *Philosophy and Phenomenological Research* 4 (March 1944): 341–76.
Tolman, Edward C., and Egon Brunswik. "The Organism and the Causal Texture of the Environment." *Psychological Review* 42 (January 1935): 43–77.
Tolman, Richard C. "Physical Science and Philosophy." *Scientific Monthly* 57 (August 1943): 166–74.
Ushenko, Andrew Paul. *The Problems of Logic.* Princeton, N.J.: Princeton University Press, 1941.
Vocabulaire Technique et Critique de la Philosophie. Edited by André Lalande. Paris: Librairie Félix Alcan, 1928. [s.vv. "définition"; "fact."]
°Watson, John B. *Behaviorism.* New York: W. W. Norton and Co., 1925.
Weber, Max. *From Max Weber: Essays in Sociology.* Translated and edited by H. H. Gerth and C. Wright Mills. New York: Oxford University Press, 1946. ["Science as a Vocation," pp. 129–56.]
Webster's New International Dictionary of the English Language. 2d ed. Springfield, Mass.: G. and C. Merriam Co., 1947. [s.v. "definition."]
°Weitz, Morris. "Analysis and the Unity of Russell's Philosophy." In *The Philosophy of Bertrand Russell,* edited by Paul Arthur Schilpp, pp. 57–121. Evanston and Chicago: Northwestern University, 1944.
Wertheimer, Max. *Productive Thinking.* New York: Harper and Brothers, 1945.
————. "Experimentelle Studien über das Sehen von Bewegung." *Zeitschrift für Psychologie* 61 (1912): 161–265.
————. "On Truth." *Social Research* 1 (May 1934): 135–46.

Weyl, Hermann. "Mathematics and Logic." *American Mathematical Monthly* 53 (January 1946):2–13.

°Whitehead, Alfred North. *Process and Reality: An Essay in Cosmology.* New York: Macmillan Co., 1929.

Wilson, Edmund B. *The Cell in Development and Heredity.* 3d ed. New York: Macmillan Co., 1928, 1937.

Woodger, J. H. *The Axiomatic Method in Biology.* Cambridge: At the University Press, 1937.

———. *Biological Principles: A Critical Study.* London: K. Paul, Trench, Trubner and Co., 1929.

Wörterbuch der Philosophischen Begriffe. 4th ed. 3 vols. Edited by Rudolf Eisler. Berlin: E. S. Mittler and Son, 1927–30. [s.vv. "definition"; "tatsache."]

Wright, Sewall. "The Physiology of the Gene." *Physiological Reviews* 21 (July 1941):487–527.

Zirkle, Raymond E. "The Particle Physics Approach to Biology." *Scientific Monthly* 64 (March 1947):213–17.

Index

Behavioral event, 69, 84–87
Behavioral sciences, 64 and *n*,
70, 122–26
Behaviorism, xv–xvi, xx, 79*n*
Behavior-object, 68, 71, 259
Behavior of the Lower Organisms (Jennings), 137*n*
Being, 371; conception of, 334–35,
358–59, 384, 397, 449–50; in
mathematics, 387; in physics, 104
Beliefs: assignment of, 371; attitude toward, 390; of Moore,
203; of pre-scientific age, 366
"Beliefs and Existences," 470
Benoit-Smullyan, Emile: Dewey's
reply to, xxxiii*n*, 310–17
Bentley, Arthur F., 302*n*; articles
reviewed, 276; collaboration
with Dewey, ix–xxxviii, 6*n*,
318–19, 443–47, 458; criticizes logics, 8–45, 184–209,
297*n*; development of, 51*n*–
52*n*; misunderstood, 275–76;
on Morris, 210–41; positions
of, 47*n*, 52, 90*n*, 101*n*, 270*n*,
299*n*, 308*n*
Bentley, Charles F., xii*n*
Bergson, Henri: organismal theory of, 117*n*
Berkeley, George: as idealist, 458;
vs. Newton, 292
Bernard, Claude, 88*n*
Bernays, Paul, 18, 38
Between Physics and Philosophy
(Frank), 149*n*
Bill of Civil Rights, 402
Biological: as name, 260
Biological Principles (Woodger),
117*n*
Biological sciences: as division,
63–65; relation to semiotic,
211–13; use of transaction in,
115–21

Biology: nature of, 148, 149, 357,
372, 443; rise of, 339, 355,
393, 455; study of behavior in,
135–39
"Biophysics Symposium, A,"
121*n*
Black, Max, 186*n*, 210*n*
Body: vs. mind, 417; vs. soul,
124*n*
Bohr, Niels Henrik David, 108–9
Bolshevism: claims of, 375; control by, 379; on history, 363
Bolzano, Bernard, 18
Boole, George, 185
Boring, Edwin G., 124*n*; on definition, 170
Bosanquet, Bernard: Carnap on,
20*n*, 24*n*
Bradley, Francis Herbert: objective idealism of, 115*n*
Bridgman, Percy W.: on definition, 170–71, 170*n*–71*n*;
"hazes" of, 152; on nature,
192*n*
Broglie, Louis Victor de, 107
Bronstein, Daniel J., 210*n*
Brunswik, Egon, 125*n*, 144, 232*n*
Buchler, Justus, 10*n*
Bühler, Karl, 21*n*, 137*n*, 232*n*,
468
Burks, Arthur W.: on definition,
166, 168, 181*n*
Burr, H. S., 121*n*
Burrow, Trigant, 117*n*

Caird, Edward: objective idealism
of, 115*n*
"Can Logic Be Divorced from
Ontology?" (Nagel), 16*n*
Capacities: in psychology, 136
Care, 247
Carings-for, 346–47, 351,
353–54

718   INDEX

Inquiry (*continued*)
  haviorial, 110, 322–26; of
  Dewey vs. Bentley, 318–19;
  efficiency of, 288–93; freedom
  of, 284, 337, 339, 340, 403,
  452, 455; into behavioral sciences, 122–26; into knowings,
  72–73, 86–89, 127; Kantor
  vs. Dewey on, 192; Kaufmann
  on, 195, 196*n*; knowing as, 4,
  320–21, 454; levels of, 100–
  104, 276–78; methods of, 91,
  96–97, 112–15, 146, 148, 152;
  model for, 98–100; nature of,
  112, 114–15, 258, 264, 267,
  268, 272, 285, 349; postulations for, 74–77, 80–82;
  problems in, 281–83; relation
  to value, 313, 355; results of,
  353; scientific, 253–55, 316–
  17; as subjectmatter of logic,
  187 and *n*, 188; terms of, 385–
  86; uses of, 82–84, 140, 144,
  286–87, 311*n*, 312, 399, 401
*Inquiry into Meaning and Truth,
  An* (Russell), 199*n*, 200–202
Insecurity, 393, 419
Institutions: authority of, 362,
  369, 376; breakdown of, 361,
  366, 371, 401, 407, 408; reconstruction of, 367; relation
  to democracy, 404
Instrumentalism: intention of,
  291–92
Instrumentality, 411
Instrumental values, 349, 350,
  353
Integration: in *Logic*, 101*n*
Intellect: as entity, 326, 334, 449
Intellectual: philosophy as, 381;
  relation to valuing, 311*n*, 312,
  354; science as, 364, 372; severance of, 249, 255

Intellectuals: attitudes of, 390–
  94, 409
Intelligence: for human affairs,
  245, 380; for international
  conflict, 399, 400, 405; as regulative factor, 379
Intelligent: distinctive feature of,
  333–35, 448, 450–51
Inter: as name, 258, 264–65
Interaction, 240; Balz on, 428–
  29; as name, xxxiii–xxxiv, 71,
  265 and *n*; nature of, 6, 132,
  135, 138, 192, 363; as procedure, 66–68; as stage of inquiry, 100–104, 127, 128, 130;
  vs. transaction, 4, 63, 96, 112*n*,
  113–15, 144; uses of, 98,
  105–6, 116–21, 124
Interest: involved in valuing, 347,
  348
International conflict: need for
  intelligence in, 399–406
*International Encyclopedia of
  Unified Science* (Neurath),
  187*n*
Interpretant: Morris on, 9, 34–
  35, 45, 222; relation to interpreter, 231; in semiotic, 234–
  35, 237–39
Interpretation: Carnap on, 31;
  Russell on, 160
Interpreter: Morris on, 9, 34–35,
  222; relation to interpretant,
  231; in semiotic, 232, 234
Intervenors. *See* Thirds
Intrinsic theory: applied to valu-
  ing, 346, 348–50
Introduction to Logic (Tarski),
  40*n*, 41*n*–42*n*
Introduction to Semantics (Car-
  nap), 17–32
Introspection, 345
Intuition, 186*n*; Kaufmann on,

126; field theory in, 121*n*, 264; impact of, 408, 409, 410; principles of, 165*n*, 316, 363, 414; rise of, 65–67, 289, 338, 339, 340, 355, 369, 453, 455; techniques of, 125, 148–49, 366, 372; uses transaction, xxxiv, 96–100, 104–9, 121, 139

Physiological: vs. behavioral, 136, 137, 270; as name, 268

Physiological activities, 288, 304

Physiological science: as region, 64, 70

Physiology: as discipline, 122–23, 221*n*, 344, 412; method in, 63, 126, 127, 326, 356–57, 366, 367, 378, 379; rise of, 289, 292, 338, 340, 368, 369, 375, 376, 414, 453; study of behavior in, 135–39; subjectmatter of, 88 and *n*, 271, 309; uses transaction and interaction, 110, 116–18, 138

Planck, Max, 99

Planning: in inquiry, 329–30, 336

Plato: on artisans, 471

Pluralism: in religion, 394

Podolsky, B., 109

Political science: Bentley's role in, xxv

Politics: dictation by, 243*n*, 255; movements in, 362–63, 375, 407; nature of, 360, 366, 369, 390–91, 396, 397, 417, 418; revolution in, 319, 370

Positive, 97–98

Positivism, 310; revolt against, xiv–xv, xxxiii*n*

Possibility: Balz on, 423–42; use of, 282–83

Postulates: arbitrary, 306–7, 333, 448; of Lewis, 193*n*; vs. postulations, 75–76, 78–80; for value, 343

Postulational method, 3, 4

"Postulation for Behavioral Inquiry" (Bentley), 47*n*

Postulations: as behavioral activity, 333, 448; for behavioral events, 80–82, 84–85; of Dewey and Bentley, 47*n*, 48, 58, 187–90, 257–58, 273–75; of Kantor, 190–92; in logic, 184–87; in mathematics, 287; for namings and named, 86–90; orientation for, 92–94; role in inquiry, 74–77, 82–84

Potentiality: vs. actualization, 434, 435; nature of, 427–28, 460, 461; relation to possibility, 424–26; use of, 282–83

Power: governmental, 402–3

Practice: in inquiry, 323–24; relation to logical theory, 92*n*, 134*n*, 190

Pragmatic, 183*n*; as name, 268

Pragmatism: in Dewey-Bentley collaboration, xxv, xxviii–xxix; of Morris, 33–35; of Peirce, 238, 239*n*; survival of, xxxvii–xxxviii

Pratt, Carroll C., 170*n*

Precedent. *See* Tradition

Precept: Peirce on, 66, 299

Preface to Logic, A (Cohen), 184*n*, 194

Premise: vs. observation, 48

Preparatory-stimulus, 233; Morris on, 210*n*, 211, 213, 220

Primitive: Bentley vs. Church on, 445–46; esthetic element in, 397

Principia Mathematica (Russell and Whitehead), xviii

Principles: authoritative, 338, 453

Principles of Behavior (Hull), 125*n*

Pagination Key to the First Edition of *Knowing and the Known*

The list below relates the pagination of the 1949 Beacon Press edition of *Knowing and the Known* to the pagination of the present edition. Before the colon appear the 1949 edition page numbers; after the colon are the pages with corresponding text from the present edition. Chapter endnotes in the 1949 edition appear as footnotes in the present edition.